Samurai

Samurai

An Encyclopedia of Japan's Cultured Warriors

Constantine Nomikos Vaporis

An Imprint of ABC-CLIO, LLC
Santa Barbara, California • Denver, Colorado

Library of Congress Cataloging-in-Publication Data

Names: Vaporis, Constantine Nomikos, 1957-
Title: Samurai : an encyclopedia of Japan's cultured warriors / Constantine Nomikos Vaporis.
Description: Santa Barbara, California : ABC-CLIO, 2019. | Includes bibliographical
    references and index.
Identifiers: LCCN 2018045146 (print) | LCCN 2018045584 (ebook) |
    ISBN 9781440842719 (ebook) | ISBN 9781440842702 (hard copy : alk. paper)
Subjects: LCSH: Samurai—Encyclopedias.
Classification: LCC DS827.S3 (ebook) | LCC DS827.S3 V36 2019 (print) |
    DDC 952/.025—dc23
LC record available at https://lccn.loc.gov/2018045146

ISBN: 978-1-4408-4270-2 (print)
       978-1-4408-4271-9 (ebook)

23 22 21 20 19   1 2 3 4 5

This book is also available as an eBook.

ABC-CLIO
An Imprint of ABC-CLIO, LLC

ABC-CLIO, LLC
147 Castilian Drive
Santa Barbara, California 93117
www.abc-clio.com

This book is printed on acid-free paper ∞

Manufactured in the United States of America

For Μαρία

Contents

Alphabetical List of Entries

Topical List of Entries

PEOPLE

Arai Hakuseki (1657–1725)

Foreign-Born Samurai

Fukuzawa Yûkichi (1835–1901)

Ii Naosuke (1815–1860)

Isoda Koryûsai (1735–1790)

Itô Hirobumi (1841–1909)

Kakizaki Hakyô (1764–1826)

Katsu Kaishû (1823–1899)

Kido Takayoshi (Kido Kôin) (1833–1877)

Kumazawa Banzan (1619–1691)

Miyamoto Musashi (c. 1584–1645)

Nonaka Kenzan (1615–1663)

Oda Nobunaga (1534–1582)

Ôshio Heihachirô (1793–1837)

Saigô Takamori (1828–1877)

Sakai Banshirô (1833–?)

Sakamoto Ryôma (1836–1867)

Sakuma Shôzan (1811–1864)

Takebe Ayatari (1719–1774)

Tani Tannai (or Mashio, 1729–1797)

Tokugawa Hidetada (1579–1632)

Tokugawa Iemitsu (1604–1651)

Tokugawa Ietsuna (1641–1680)

Tokugawa Ieyasu (1543–1616)

Tokugawa Yoshimune (1684–1751)

Tokugawa Yoshinobu (Keiki, 1837–1913)

Toyotomi Hideyoshi (1537–1598)

Watanabe Kazan (1793–1841)

Yamaga Sokô (1622–1685)

Yamauchi Katsutoyo (1545–1605)

Yoshida Shôin (1830–1859)

MATERIAL CULTURE AND SAMURAI PRACTICES

Armor

Books of Heraldry (*bukan*)

Clothing

Coming of Age (*genpuku*)

Disrespect Killing (*burei-uchi*)

Double-Guilt Doctrine (*ryôseibai*)

Falcony (*takagari*)

Family Crests (*kamon*)

Firearms

Hairstyle

Helmet (*kabuto*)

Horseback Riding Ceremony (*onorizome*)

Male-Male Love (*nanshoku*)

Martial Arts (*bugei*)

Names (Samurai)

Preface

My interest in the samurai began at a young age. It grew out of a general fascination with Japan and the Japanese language that developed during middle school. This was a direct result of going to watch numerous Japanese movies at film festivals that were held in Boston in the late 1960s and early 1970s with my father and brothers. Of particular interest to me were the samurai films—*chanbara*, the so-called Japanese "spaghetti Westerns"—and other more serious fare that are now considered classics, such as *Seven Samurai*, *Harakiri*, and of course *The Samurai Trilogy* (the fascinating story of the famed swordsman Miyamoto Musashi).

Much later, as a professor of history, my research interests first centered on Japanese commoners and the development of a culture of travel and religious pilgrimage in Tokugawa Japan (1600–1868), before I turned to the samurai and their involvement in one of the most ingenious institutions for political control devised anywhere, the alternate attendance system. Under the requirements of that system, the more than 260 daimyo—the military rulers of the various domains—were required to spend every other year in the Tokugawa shogun's capital of Edo. In fulfilling this feudal duty, they brought with them hundreds, and in some cases thousands, of samurai and support staff members. In writing this history I was surprised by the lack of scholarship on the Tokugawa samurai aimed at a general audience.

The reader might be surprised by the last statement—that there is a shortage of historical writing on the samurai—because the samurai appear in so many areas of our popular culture: in anime, in manga (comic books), even in children's cartoons. In fact, a recent Google search of the word "samurai" produced no fewer than 199 million results (no, this figure is not a typographical error!). In fact, the samurai—at least a popularized version of the samurai—appears to be just about everywhere. Although much of this writing is interesting or entertaining, it is often written by nonspecialists without access to Japanese sources. As a result, much of what is available on the Internet can be sensationalistic and historically inaccurate. In terms of print culture, most books dealing with the samurai tend to be rather narrowly focused on their martial aspects, such as their armor or fighting techniques. These books also tend to cover only a portion of the history of the samurai: either the period of civil wars (the Warring States, or *Sengoku*, period, 1467–1600) or the chaotic period at the end of the Tokugawa period, after the arrival in 1853 of the American commodore Matthew C. Perry and his "black ships." However, the long, peaceful period of more than two-and-a-half centuries in between the period of civil war and the fall of the Tokugawa in 1868 has been largely ignored. This huge omission has provided the incentive for this book. To better situate the Tokugawa period for the reader, though, some material has been provided on the formative period of the second half of the sixteenth century leading to the founding of the shogunate as well as some on the few years after the fall of the Tokugawa (the Meiji Restoration) and the beginning of the Meiji state in 1868.

This encyclopedia aims to provide an overview of the samurai of the Tokugawa period for the general reader that is based on historical scholarship not only in English but in Japanese as well. It also contains much historical material derived from original Japanese source materials (personal diaries, government regulations, literature), some of which exists only in manuscript (brush-written) form. Lastly, it is based on more than thirty years' experience teaching, traveling to historical sites in Japan, and researching Japanese history.

In aiming to write about such a broad span of time within the covers of one volume, many painful decisions necessarily had to be made about what to leave out. No doubt some readers will find that their "favorite" samurai is not included or that some aspect of samurai life has been omitted. Although this is regrettable, it is also inevitable. The aim here is to be comprehensive, but no single volume can be all-inclusive. Having said that, this encyclopedia contains entries on a wide range of samurai, both famous and less well known; their martial as well as cultural pursuits and practices (horseback riding, swordsmanship, and tea ceremony, among many others); the material aspects of their lives (housing, clothing, weapons, and armor); and economic and family life. Each entry contains a list of suggested readings for further information on the given subject; wherever possible, English-language sources have been provided.

The focus of this book is the samurai, who were *by definition* male. Women were members of *bushi* households ("warrior households"), known as *buke*, but they were not samurai, strictly speaking. Of course, these women played important roles in samurai households in various social capacities, and sometimes they exerted political influence within the shogun or daimyo's inner quarters. Many acted as household managers, particularly if their husbands were away serving their overlords; and some made notable achievements as writers and a few as artists. In some domains women in warrior households learned to wield a *naginata* (pole weapon) and in one instance, at the end of the Tokugawa period a small group of women from samurai households actually used them in combat. Some of these stories will emerge from the pages that follow, but a full treatment awaits another volume.

I would like to acknowledge a number of personal and institutional debts incurred in the writing and publication of this book. First, I must recognize ABC-CLIO's continuing faith in me in publishing this, my second volume, with them. In particular I would like to recognize the support of Dr. Vince Burns, vice president, editorial; Mr. George Butler, editor, who encouraged me to take up this project; and Mr. Paul Wells, senior editor, media. My home institution, University of Maryland, Baltimore County (UMBC), has always been enthusiastically supportive of its professors' scholarly mission; in particular I would like to acknowledge the dean of the College of Arts, Humanities, and Social Sciences, Dr. Scott Casper, and the chair of the History Department, Dr. Marjoleine Kars, for their strong support over the years. The Dresher Center for the Humanities at UMBC, directed by Dr. Jessica Berman, also has provided the support of a community of scholars and a space for quiet reflection. Outside of my university, I have benefited greatly from Drs. Thomas Conlan, Amaury Garcia, Morgan Pitelka, Luke Roberts, and Michael Wert's critical reading of the manuscript, either in part or in its entirety. (Of course, I alone am responsible for any errors of fact and interpretation.) In Japan, warm thanks go out to Kurumada Hiroyuki, Ishida Yuri, Shindô Kazuyuki, and Lonny Chick. Special appreciation goes to my late father, Rev. Dr. Nomikos Michael Vaporis, and my brothers, Michael and John, who were there "at the beginning," supporting my fascination with Japan in general and the samurai in particular. My nuclear family, with daughter Michaela and son Aleydis, in its now expanded form with son-in-law Nathan, two heart-warming grandchildren, Lunete and Lysandros, and daughter-in-law Jenna, sustains me. But none of this would have be possible without my love, my wife, and life's partner Maria (*Μαρία*), to whom this volume is dedicated.

Introduction

Samurai have long captured the Western imagination. From a long and proud military tradition dating back to the tenth century, the samurai have gone through numerous changes and today have come to symbolize many things for modern Japanese and the rest of the world.

The earliest samurai, or *bushi*, were provincial fighters who performed essential military services for aristocratic families and the imperial court, in Kyoto. Their political role gradually increased, and at the end of the twelfth century Minamoto Yoritomo established a military-based government, the Kamakura shogunate (1185–1333), in eastern Japan that coexisted with the government of the imperial court in central Japan. From early on, samurai developed a strong sense of identity as professional warriors, one that was characterized by a "cult of honor." Known at this time as either the "way of the horse and bow" or "the way of the bow and arrow," this ethos reflected their identity as mounted warriors whose primary weapon was the bow.

A second military government (the Ashikaga shogunate, 1336–1573) succeeded the first, but central authority broke down during the Warring States period (1467–1568). During this time in particular samurai were not known for their loyalty. On the contrary, they were renown for treachery and lawlessness—whatever it took, including betraying their overlords, to advance their own causes. In this harsh climate, hundreds of warlords or daimyo, served by armies of landed samurai retainers, fought to expand their control of local resources.

Waging a war of attrition during the late sixteenth century, three powerful daimyo or warlords came to dominate the landscape of Japan, one after the other. The first, Oda Nobunaga (1534–1582), waged a violent and relentless military campaign to pacify the realm, unifying nearly one-half of the country before he was betrayed by a close vassal and died at Honnôji temple in Kyoto, likely taking his own life by *seppuku* ("cutting open the belly," a type of ritual suicide) before the temple went up in flames. Picking up his overlord's mantle, Toyotomi Hideyoshi (1537–1598) was able to build on Nobunaga's efforts and by 1590 extend political control across the entire realm. His death without a mature heir led to a military struggle for power that culminated in the Battle of Sekigahara in 1600, one of the largest battles in global history, in which more than 150,000 samurai and other men fought. Three years later, the victorious general, Tokugawa Ieyasu (1543–1616), was appointed shogun by the emperor, thereby founding a dynasty of fifteen hegemons who would rule Japan until 1867.

In 1603, Tokugawa Ieyasu established the third, and final, shogunate, which maintained control over the more than 260 domains across Japan, each headed by a daimyo. These daimyo were semiautonomous rulers who were allowed to administer their domains as long as they acknowledged the shogun as overlord, swore oaths of allegiance, obeyed his laws, and faithfully carried out the requirement to travel to Edo to spend alternate years waiting on his person (a system known as the alternate attendance).

In general, the shoguns asserted a degree of authority over the country on a par with the so-called absolute monarchs (like Louis XIV) of contemporary Europe. They held direct control over one-quarter of the territory in Japan, including the two most fertile plains, the Kantô plain in the east and the Kinai plain in the central part of the county; confiscated the territories of their defeated enemies and transferred daimyo, or warlords, whose loyalties were suspect to disadvantageous locations; took direct control over the major cities of Edo, Osaka, and Kyoto; forced the daimyo to tear down all but one castle in each of their domains; and minted a national currency. The Tokugawa also assumed a monopoly on the use of force—meaning that the daimyo could no longer settle disputes on the battlefield—and maintained a monopoly on foreign policy, including foreign trade. Finally, although the shogun was formally conferred in his position by the emperor, he carefully controlled the imperial institution by isolating the emperor in his palace in Kyoto. The Tokugawa were so effective in maintaining a balance of power that Japan under the military rule of the shoguns, daimyo, and the samurai who served them experienced one of the longest periods of peace in world history. This period was heralded by contemporary Japanese as "*tenka taihei*," the realm at peace, and by historians as the "*pax* Tokugawa." The significance of this extended period of peace was highlighted by the eighth shogun, Tokugawa Yoshimune (1684–1751), who responded in the following manner to one of his retainers, whom he overheard deploring the fact that samurai were pawning their armor:

> All the struggle and pain Lord Ieyasu endured was to bring peace to all Japan. Therefore, it is worthy of celebration that bows and arrows are kept in bags and swords in wooden cases. That the shogun's men keep their armor in merchants' storehouses means that Japan is now enjoying unprecedented peace. The ultimate wish of Tôshôgû [the deified Ieyasu] has been realized. You should not be sorrowful that swords and bows rot in pawnshops. (Tokugawa, 2009, 43)

During much of the sixteenth century (end of the Warring States period), the definition of a samurai was unclear. The line between warriors and farmers was blurred, since farmers would take up arms when needed to defend their villages or to heed the call of the local warlord to fight in his army. But, as the scale of warfare increased and the local powers came to need a permanent, standing army, the daimyo began to pull fighting men off the land by requiring them to live in their castle town headquarters. By the end of the following century, roughly 85 percent of samurai lived in cities, physically separated from the farmers in the countryside over whom they ruled. Also, the collection of swords and other weapons from the countryside (the "sword hunt") in the late sixteenth and early seventeenth centuries made the divisions between samurai and farmer clearer: samurai largely lived in castle towns, where they served their daimyo and had the privilege of wearing the two swords; farmers lived in the countryside and engaged exclusively in tilling the soil and other nonpolitical activities.

The samurai gave Tokugawa Japan its distinctive character. Numerically, they were a large social elite, comprising about 6 percent of the population. They imposed their political will on the country through military force and established a warrior-based form of government that brought peace and stability to the land. Essentially an army of occupation, the samurai remained in place from generation to generation, fully armed and ever-present in the castle towns around the country and in the biennial processions of the more than 260 daimyo rulers who marched back and forth from their domain's castle town to the Tokugawa capital at Edo on alternate attendance.

To rationalize their position in society, samurai intellectuals created an ideology, based on the politically constructed notion of status (*mibun*), that placed them above the peasant-farmers, artisans and merchants, who were ranked in that order. Confucian thinker Yamaga Sokô (1622–1685) articulated the samurai's new social identity, writing:

> The samurai is one who does not cultivate, does not manufacture, and does not engage in trade, but it cannot be that he has no function at all as a samurai. . . . The business of the samurai consists in reflecting on his own station in life, in discharging loyal service to his master, if he has one, . . . and with due consideration of his own position, in devoting himself to duty above all. . . . The samurai dispenses with the business of the farmer, artisan, and merchant and confines himself to practice this Way. (Quoted in Vaporis, 2014, 125–126)

In this manner, Yamaga extolled the samurai as the political and intellectual leaders of Japan, devoted to duty. This reinvention of the social identity resulted in a new flourishing of samurai thought and culture, including the code of *shidô*, the "way of the warrior" (later known as *bushido*). Since samurai were to act as moral exemplars, it is not surprising that they were also subject to strict codes of behavior, as children and as adults, and that this extended even to the realm of leisure activities (samurai were, e.g., enjoined from attending the kabuki theater or the pleasure quarters).

Despite the long years of peace that characterized the Tokugawa period, samurai remained keenly aware of their earlier traditions and were expected to maintain their military skills through the pursuit of martial arts (*bugei*). Throughout the period, though, a persistent tension existed between this heritage of martial skills or training (*bu*) and the cultivation of letters, or the "civil arts" (*bun*)—the so-called "twin ways." Written codes for the samurai in earlier historical periods typically included statements about the importance of both elements, but it was only during the Tokugawa, when samurai had to fulfill bureaucratic functions, that so much emphasis was placed on the civil arts. One result of this increased emphasis on the civil arts was the creation of a new definition of masculinity among the samurai. The extended peace meant a lack of opportunity for samurai to demonstrate their martial skills and bravery on the battlefield. As a result, samurai became hypersensitive in defending their honor. An ideology of honor violence developed and manifested in occasional acts of interpersonal violence by samurai against other samurai and samurai against commoners.

The samurai stood out from other members of their society in a number of ways, particularly in terms of the social and legal privileges they enjoyed. In physical terms, their two swords, one long (*tachi*) and one short (*wakizashi*), were the most obvious markers that set them apart from the other status groups, as did the hip-forward posture and stride that was required because of the two blades suspended through their waist sash on their left side. They were also distinguished in a variety of other ways, including dress (particularly in their formal wear, with its stiff-shouldered jackets and skirt-like trousers); their special hairstyle (the shaved pate and topknot, known as *chonmage*); their right to use a surname (family name); their treatment in criminal law; and perhaps most famous in their so-called "license to kill" (*kirisute gomen*), which meant their authorized use of their swords on commoners who were insubordinate. In principle, they were also not to engage in any manual trade.

The samurai's existence, however, was defined by two major paradoxes, one of which was evident in the quotation above from Shogun Tokugawa Yoshimune. For one, once the realm was pacified the samurai were largely forbidden from exercising the military functions that had been central to their identity. As a result, the samurai necessarily reinvented themselves as a civil administrative elite, one that expressed loyalty to the lord through bureaucratic service rather than through military prowess on the battlefield. Also, having been drawn off the land by the daimyo's policies, the samurai's independent authority based on control of land was undercut, making them a bureaucratic elite dependent on the lord for their livelihood. Thus, samurai became largely stipended—that is, salaried—retainers who served in the daimyo's military and government administration. A second major paradox that defined the samurai as a social group was the growing gap between their high formal social status at the top of the formal status system, with its attendant social privileges, and the erosion of their social condition over time. By the end of the Tokugawa period, there is evidence that some commoners found the pretentions of the samurai intolerable, although they had to express their dissatisfaction discretely, given the samurai's ability to inflict lethal violence.

The Tokugawa period was remarkable for the long duration of its peace and the fact that this peaceful society was presided over by an elite group of two-sworded and educated warriors. The social tensions that existed in Tokugawa society after 250 years were exacerbated by the forced opening of Japan by Western powers in the mid-nineteenth century, resulting in the Meiji Restoration and the overthrow of the Tokugawa shogunate. The new Meiji government that followed ended the samurai's monopoly on state-sanctioned violence and made military service a duty of all male citizens. Through this and several other measures the samurai was "unmade" and Japan became a nation, in principle, in which all citizens were equal. Adjusting to change was not without its difficulties for the former samurai, but they continued, by virtue of their education and skills, to play an important role in the new age. They live on today, in a sense, through their frequent appearance in popular cultural forms across the globe.

DEFINITIONS

The term *bushi* often is used synonymously with "samurai," as for example in the term *bushido*, or "way of the warrior" or "way of the samurai." One of the most authoritative texts on Tokugawa Japan, *The Cambridge History of Japan*, vol. 4: *Early Modern Japan*, equates the two, referring to "the *bushi* or samurai" (p. 4) in the introduction and in the index directing the reader looking for information on *bushi* to look up "samurai class": "*bushi* (warrior class), *see* samurai class" (p. 814). Although the terms are often used interchangeably, it is important to understand that there are differences between them if one uses a strict definition of "samurai."

Bushi is composed of two Chinese characters, *bu* or "military" or "martial," and *shi*, which means "gentleman," "scholar," or "warrior." As a compound, the term is used to refer to members of "warrior households," or *buke*. When the Meiji government (1868–1912) tried to calculate how many former male members of warrior households it had to remunerate with interest-bearing bonds, it arrived at a figure of 408,823 households, with a total of 1,892,449 people, dependents included, living in those households. Since the total represented about 6 percent of the population, members of warrior households constituted a very large privileged elite, one that had to be supported through the labor of the other three status groups.

The term "samurai" is often used in a generic sense to connote all members of "warrior households." There are two potential problems with this. First of all, during the Tokugawa period the term "samurai" referred to only the top portion of a daimyo's retainer corps—to those with the rights of an audience with the lord and whose names were listed in the domain's military registers (*bugenchô*). Some writers seek to avoid this issue by referring to the upper portion of a daimyo's retainer corps, which were divided into many ranks, as "full samurai" or "upper samurai" and the lower half of the retainer corps, which was similarly divided into a number of ranks, as "lower samurai." This accommodation is complicated by the fact that the dividing line between "upper" and "lower" differed in many domains. A second issue that one confronts when using "samurai" in a generic sense is that the term includes women. In a strict sense, women were not samurai, but they were members of "warrior households." In Japanese the term most often used to refer to these women were *buke no onna* or "women of the warrior households."

Due to the widespread acceptance of the generic use of the term "samurai," this encyclopedia also follows that practice, but when necessary to clarify whether someone was a retainer with rights to an audience and listed in the domain register or not, the qualifying terms "full samurai" or "upper samurai" will be used. Similarly, "lower samurai" will be used to refer to members of the lower portion of the daimyo retainer corps.

Having now equated samurai with *bushi*, it is important to ask who were the samurai, particularly since the perquisites of rank, two swords and a surname (*myôji taito*), were granted to some villagers and townsmen? We might consider three definitions: the first covers all people (specifically men) considered as *bushi* in the contemporary Tokugawa context. Such a definition would include *rônin*, who despite the lack of formal attachment to a lord and stipend often displayed the symbols of the status group. This definition would also include Confucian scholars

(*jusha*) and physicians attached to a daimyo, even though they might not serve a daimyo permanently. This is the definition that this encyclopedia employs. A second definition stresses the importance of a formal relationship between a retainer and overlord that required the performance of service—not necessarily military service—in return for a stipend. Confucian scholars, physicians, privileged merchants, and artisans could also be included under this rubric. A third definition limits membership in the samurai status group to those whose income was paid for by an overlord in return for military service obligations; such a definition would exclude ancillary groups such as those listed in the second definition above. Under this definition Confucian scholars and doctors attached to daimyo would be excluded or at most might be considered "quasi-samurai."

FURTHER READING

Hall, John Whitney, ed. *The Cambridge History of Japan*, vol. 4: *Early Modern Japan*. Cambridge: Cambridge University Press, 1991.

"The Social Estates: Yamaga Sokô on 'The Way of the Samurai.'" In Constantine Nomikos Vaporis, *Voices of Early Modern Japan: Contemporary Accounts of Daily Life during the Age of the Shoguns*, 125–126. Boulder, CO: Westview Press, 2014.

Tokugawa, Tsunenari. *The Edo Inheritance*. Translated by Tokugawa Iehiro. Tokyo: International House of Japan, 2009.

Timeline of Japanese History Related to the Samurai, from the Mid-Sixteenth Century through the Tokugawa and Meiji* Periods, 1543–1889

1543	Matchlock muskets are introduced into Japan by the Portuguese.
1568	Oda Nobunaga enters Kyoto and installs Askikaga Yoshiaki as shogun.
1571	Oda Nobunaga attacks and burns Enraykuji temple on Mt. Hiei.
1573	Ashikaga Yoshiaki, the last Ashikaga shogun, is expelled from Kyoto and flees in exile to Shikoku Island.
1575	Battle of Nagashino: the forces of Oda Nobunaga, employing volley fire for the first time, defeat rival Takeda Katsuyori.
1576	Oda Nobunaga begins the construction of Azuchi Castle.
1582	Oda Nobunaga dies in surprise attack by his former vassal Akechi Mitsuhide (Honnôji Incident). Toyotomi Hideyoshi defeats Mitsuhide in the Battle of Yamazaki and rises to power. Hideyoshi initiates a national survey of lands and their productive capacity (*Taikô kenchi*).
1583	Toyotomi Hideyoshi defeats Shibata Katsuie in the Battle of Shizugatake; begins the construction of Osaka Castle.
1587	Toyotomi Hideyoshi hosts grand outdoor tea ceremony at Kitano Shrine in Kyoto at which Sen no Rikyû and Tsuda Sôgyû officiate.
1588	Hideyoshi issues edict prohibiting possession of weapons by commoners (sword hunt).
1590	Toyotomi Hideyoshi destroys the Hôjô family, completing pacification of Japan.
1592	Toyotomi Hideyoshi launches the first of two invasions of Korea.
1597	Hideyoshi launches second invasion of Korea.
1598	Hideyoshi dies, and Japanese armies retreat from Korea with Korean potters (who establish Arita, Hagi, and Satsuma wares).

* The Meiji period ran through 1912 but the timeline covers through 1889 only.

TOKUGAWA PERIOD, 1600–1889
(WITH JAPANESE-ERA NAMES)

1600 **(Keichô 5)**	The Battle of Sekigahara: Tokugawa Ieyasu establishes military hegemony over Japan; first Dutch ship (*Liefde*) arrives, with Englishman Will Adams as pilot, who later is appointed a bannerman by Shogun Tokugawa Ieyasu.
1602 (Keichô 7)	Spanish galleon *Espiritu Santo* blown off course to Japan; Tokugawa Ieyasu, seeking trade with Spain, releases crew.
1603 (Keichô 8)	Tokugawa Ieyasu receives the title of *sei-i-tai shôgun* and founds the Tokugawa shogunate. Ieyasu orders daimyo to supply labor and materials to expand castle and city.
1605 (Keichô 10)	Ieyasu retires as shogun, is succeeded by son Hidetada, but continues to rule as retired shogun (*ogosho sama*). Miyamoto Musashi begins his "warrior pilgrimage" (*musha shugyô*); fights in and wins more than sixty duels before the age of thirty.
1607 (Keichô 12)	Donjon (castle keep) is completed at Edo Castle.
1609 (Keichô 14)	Satsuma domain forces, with Tokugawa approval, invade the Ryûkyû Islands, making them a vassal state of Satsuma in 1611.
1611 (Keichô 16)	Dominicans begin missionary activities in Japan; a Dutch trade factory is established at Hirado.
1612 (Keichô 17)	Shogunate decrees ban on Christianity in Tokugawa territory.
1613 (Keichô 18)	Date Masamune (daimyo of Sendai) dispatches embassy led by Hasekura Tsunenaga to Spain to petition Philip III (unsuccessfully) to establish trade with New Spain (Mexico).
1614 (Keichô 19)	The First Osaka campaign (Winter War) begins. The ban on Christianity is extended nationwide by Tokugawa Ieyasu, who limits foreign trade to the ports of Hirado and Nagasaki.
1615 (Genna 1)	Second Osaka campaign (Summer War): Tokugawa forces defeat those of Toyotomi and Osaka Castle falls; Hideyoshi's son and appointed heir Hideyori commits *seppuku*; shogunate issues first set of *Laws for the Military Houses* (*buke shohatto*), the Regulations Concerning the Emperor and the Nobility (*Kinchû narabi ni kuge shohatto*); also issues the order limiting castles to one per domain (*ikkoku ichijô rei*).
1616 (Genna 2)	Tokugawa Ieyasu dies. Trade with Europeans is confined to the southern ports of Hirado and Nagasaki.
1617 (Genna 3)	Tokugawa Ieyasu's remains are interred at Nikkô shrine; he is deified as Tôshô Daigongen, "Illuminator of the East, August Avatar of Buddha"; the construction of a mausoleum at Nikkô for Tokugawa Ieyasu begins.
1620 (Genna 6)	William Adams, first Englishman in Japan and Tokugawa bannerman, dies.
1623 (Genna 9)	Hidetada retires as shogun, Tokugawa Iemitsu becomes third shogun; first senior councilors (*rôjû*) appointed; shogunate decrees that masterless samurai, merchants, and artisans may not live on daimyo estates.

1624 (Kan'ei 1) English factory in Hirado closes due to poor business. Spanish ships prohibited from calling at Japanese ports. Persecution of Christians intensifies.

1629 (Kan'ei 6) Tokugawa Ieyasu's granddaughter ascends to the imperial throne as the sovereign Meishô.

1632 (Kan'ei 9) Tokugawa Iemitsu begins construction of Taitokuin mausoleum for his predecessor, Hidetada.

1633 (Kan'ei 10) First so-called *sakoku* edict, overseas travel prohibited, foreign ships permitted entry only at Nagasaki.

1634 (Kan'ei 11) Iemitsu begins to reconstruct Nikkô Shrine, Ieyasu's mausoleum; construction of Dejima begins; the second *sakoku* edict is issued; Shogun Hidetada visits Kyoto with a large military force.

1635 (Kan'ei 12) *Laws for the Military Houses* (*buke shohatto*) are revised; alternate attendance is enforced for the outside lords (*tozama daimyo*); the third *sakoku* edict is issued; overseas travel by Japanese is prohibited; Japanese residents abroad are prohibited from returning to Japan; the capacity of newly constructed ships is limited to 500 *koku* (49 gross tons); all foreign shipping is restricted to Nagasaki, but the Dutch trade factory remains in operation in Hirado.

1636 (Kan'ei 13) Fourth *sakoku* edict is issued. Construction of buildings on man-made island of Deshima is completed, and the Portuguese, who had lived freely in Nagasaki since 1571, are restricted to it.

1637 (Kan'ei 14) Shimabara Uprising (1637–1638) begins.

1639 (Kan'ei 16) Fifth *sakoku* edict is issued; Portuguese ships are banned from Japan and Portuguese merchants expelled from Deshima: all Westerners except the Dutch are prohibited from entering Japan.

1641 (Kan'ei 18) Dutch trading post moved from Hirado to Deshima, an artificial island in Nagasaki harbor.

1651 (Keian 4) Tokugwa Ietsuna (Iemitsu's eldest son) becomes shogun at age of ten; samurai Yui Shôsetsu plots unsuccessful uprising against the Tokugawa shogunate.

1656 (Meireki 2) Yamaga Sokô writes on the "way of the warrior" in his *Bukyô yôroku* (*Essentials of the Warrior Code*)

1657 (Meireki 3) The "Meireki Fire" ravages Edo for three days, killing more than 100,000 and burning roughly half of the city; compilation of national history *Dai Nihonshi* (*History of Great Japan*) is begun at direction of daimyo Tokugawa Mitsukuni.

1658 (Manji 1) Shogunate organizes four samurai firefighting squads for Edo.

1665 (Kanbun 5) Registers of Religious Investigation (*shûmon aratame*) implemented: shogunate requires daimyo to conduct yearly inquisition of religious affiliation to eradicate Christianity.

1680 (Enpô 8)	Tokugawa Tsunayoshi (fourth son of Iemitsu) becomes fifth shogun, nicknamed the "dog shogun."
1685 (Jôkyô 2)	First of shogun Tokugawa Tsunayoshi's Edicts on Compassion for Living Things (*shôrui awaremi no rei*) are issued.
1688 (Genroku 1)	Beginning of Genroku period, widely viewed as a cultural highpoint of Tokugawa era and the first flowering of urban culture. Yanagisawa Yoshiyasu is appointed *soba yônin* (grand chamberlain) to the shogun Tokugawa Tsunayoshi.
1690 (Genroku 3)	The German physician Englebert Kaempfer arrives on Deshima, where he stays for two years; later he writes the influential *History of Japan* (published posthumously, 1727).
1701 (Genroku 14)	Lord Asano of Akô domain wounds shogunal official Kira Yoshinaka in Edo Castle and is ordered to commit ritual suicide; by this date, Edo is probably the largest city in the world.
1702 (Genroku 15)	Former retainers of Akô domain carry out revenge killing of Kira Yoshinaka (part of Akô Incident).
1708 (Hôei 5)	Jesuit missionary Giovanni Sidotti arrives in Japan but is arrested, transported to Edo, and interrogated by Confucian scholar Arai Hakuseki.
1709 (Hôei 6)	Tokugawa Ienobu succeeds brothers Tsunayoshi and Ietsuna as sixth shogun; Arai Hakuseki becomes a key adviser to shogun.
1713 (Shôtoku 3)	Tokugawa Ietsugu becomes shogun as minor (age four) and rules only three years.
1716 (Kyôhô 1)	Tokugawa Yoshimune, great-grandson of Tokugawa Ieyasu, member of Kii branch of Tokugawa family, becomes eighth shogun; Kyôhô Reforms (1716–1745) launched; Yamamoto Tsunetomo completes *Hagakure* (*In the Shadow of Leaves*).
1720 (Kyôhô 5)	Shogun Tokugawa Yoshimune lifts the ban on imported Western books.
1721 (Kyôhô 6)	A suggestion box (*meyasu bako*) is posted in Edo to receive commoners' appeals to the shogun.
1722 (Kyôhô 7)	Shogunate lifts ban on importing Western books, except those dealing with Christianity.
1732 (Kyôhô 17)	Kyôhô Famine (1632–1633) begins.
1742 (Kanpô 2)	Shogunate compiles the *kujikata osadamegaki*, a codification of its legal codes.
1745 (Enkyô 2)	Tokugawa Ieshige becomes ninth shogun, but Yoshimune remains the central authority for the first two years of Ieshige's rule.
1748 (Kan'en 1)	The first performance is held of the puppet play (*jôruri*) drama *Kanadehon chûshingura* (*Chushingura: The Treasury of Loyal Retainers*), based on the 47 Rônin Incident of 1703.
1760 (Hôreki 10)	Tokugawa Ieharu becomes the tenth shogun (rules 1760–1786).

1767 (Meiwa 3)	Tanuma Okitsugu becomes *soba yônin* (grand chamberlain) and attempts to increase the shogunate's income through expansion of commerce; he falls from power 1786.
1774 (An'ei 3)	*Kaitai shinsho* (*New Book of Anatomy*), a Japanese translation of a Dutch text on anatomy, is published by Sugita Genpaku and Maeno Ryôtaku—the first complete Japanese translation of a Western medical text.
1782 (Tenmei 2)	Tenmei famine (1782–1787) begins, with national death toll estimated between 200,000 and one million.
1787 (Tenmei 7)	Tokugawa Ienari becomes the eleventh shogun, rules for fifty years, the longest of any shogun, and fathers fifty-five children by forty consorts; Matsudaira Sadanobu becomes senior councilor; Kansei Reforms (1787–1793) are initiated.
1789 (Kansei 1)	A debt moratorium is declared to assist shogunal retainers.
1791 (Kansei 3)	The first American ship reaches Japan under hire by the Dutch East India Company during the Napoleonic Wars.
1792 (Kansei 4)	Russian ship led by Adam Laxman and sent by Catherine the Great to establish trade with Japan lands in Ezochi (now Hokkaido); its crew is allowed to spend the winter in Japan, but trade is not permitted.
1793 (Kansei 5)	Matsudaira Sadanobu, author of Kansei reforms, is removed from office.
1799 (Kansei 11)	Tokugawa shogunate establishes the new position of *Hakodate bugyô* (commissioner of Hakodate) and assumes direct control over lands in the southern part of Ezochi.
1804 (Bunka 1)	Russian expedition led by Nicolai Petrovich Rezanov unsuccessfully attempts to establish trade relations with shogunate; rebuffed, Russians raid Japanese communities in Kuriles on return home.
1808 (Bunka 5)	The British warship *Phaeton* enters Nagasaki harbor under a Dutch flag; shogunal official commits *seppuku* in responsibility for this incursion, which exacerbates fears of the threat of the West.
1825 (Bunsei 8)	Shogunate issues *Ikokusen uchiharai rei* (Order for the Repelling of Foreign Ships, known popularly as the "Don't Think Twice" edict) in response to an upsurge in foreign ships intruding in Japanese waters.
1829 (Bunsei 12)	Dr. Phiipp Franz von Siebold placed under house arrest at Deshima for taking into possession maps of Japan from Takahashi Kageyasu; later Seibold is banished from Japan.
1833 (Tenpô 4)	Andô Hiroshige travels Tôkaidô Road with shogun's retinue, begins work on very successful series of prints, *Fifty-Three Stages of the Tôkaidô*; the Tenpô famine (1833–1836) begins, with an estimated 200,000–300,000 deaths nationwide.

1837 (Tenpô 8)   U.S. merchant ship *Morrison* fired upon and forced to leave Japanese waters; first of many unsuccessful attempts by American ships to reestablish trade; Tokugawa Ieyoshi becomes twelfth shogun; shogunal official Ôshio Heihachirô leads a failed rebellion against the Tokugawa.

1839 (Tenpô 10)   A crackdown (imprisonment/execution) of scholars of Western learning (*Bansha no goku*) is initiated by the shogunate.

1841 (Tenpô 12)   The Tenpô Reforms (1841–1843) are initiated by Mizuno Tadakuni, senior shogunal councilor; Tosa fisherman (and later bannerman) Nakahama Manjirô is shipwrecked, rescued by American whaler and taken to the United States.

1842 (Tenpô 13)   1825 Order for the Repelling Foreign Ships is revoked and replaced by shogunal orders for the provisioning of food, water, and firewood to foreign ships.

1844 (Kôka 1)   British and French ships enter Nagasaki harbor and request commercial relations with shogunate; requests denied. Letter from King of Netherlands delivered to shogunate advising it to open Japan to trade; following year shogunate sends letter of refusal; military garrison and battery established at Hakodate in Ezochi.

1853 (Ka'ei 6)   Tokugawa Iesada becomes thirteenth shogun (1853–1858); squadron of four American warships headed by Commodore Matthew C. Perry enters Uraga Bay and presents demands for treaty relations.

1854 (An'sei 1)   An American fleet of seven naval vessels, headed by Commodore Matthew C. Perry, returns to Japan, and anchors in Edo Bay; Treaty of Peace and Amity between the United States and the Empire of Japan (Kanagawa Treaty) is signed.

1855 (An'sei 2)   Ansei Earthquake strikes; more than 7,000 die in Edo; the shogunate opens the *Kaigun denshûjo* (Naval-Officer Training School) in Nagasaki.

1856 (Ansei 3)   U.S. consul general Townsend Harris arrives at port of Shimoda to begin negotiations with shogunate on commercial treaty; *Banshô shirabesho* (Institute for the Investigation of Barbarian Books) established by shogunate for the study of the West; Chôshû samurai Yoshida Shôin establishes private school Shôka sonjuku.

1858 (Ansei 5)   Harris Treaty/Ansei commercial treaties are concluded between the shogunate and the United States, the Netherlands, Russia, Great Britain, and France; Tokugawa Iemochi becomes fourteenth shogun at age twelve (rules 1858–1867), becomes first shogun since Iemitsu (in 1634) to travel to Kyoto; Ii Naosuke becomes *tairô* ("great councilor") to the shogun; beginning of Ansei Purge (1858–1860) of opponents to the shogunate's opening to the Western powers.

1859 (Ansei 6)   Ports of Yokohama, Nagasaki, and Hakodate opened to foreign trade.

1860 (Man'en 1)   Assassination of shogunal regent Ii Naosuke (Sakurada Gate Incident); shogunal mission is dispatched to the United States to ratify the Harris (commercial) Treaty.

1862 (Bunkyû 2)   Shogun Iemochi ends requirement of alternate attendance; British merchant murdered by retainers from Satsuma (Richardson Affair or Namamugi Incident); shogunate dispatches first students (Nishi Amane and Tsuda Mamichi) overseas, to the Netherlands; British warships attack Satsuma domain in retaliation for the Namamugi Incident; radical pro-imperial samurai from Chôshû driven from Kyoto; assassination attempt is made on Andô Nobumasa, leading *rôjû* (senior councilor) of the shogunate.

1863 (Bunkyû 3)   British warships bombard the Satsuma domain in retaliation for the Richardson Affair. Radical pro-imperial samurai of Chôshû domain attempt coup d'etat but are driven from Kyoto.

1864 (Genji 1)   Mito Civil War takes place; pro-imperial samurai and shogunal police (known as Shinsengumi) clash at Ikedaya Inn (Kyoto) (Ikedaya Incident); pro-imperial forces from Chôshû domain attempt to force their way into Kyoto (Kimmon Incident); imperial court orders shogunate to mount a punitive expedition against Chôshû (the first of two Chôshû Expeditions).

1866 (Keiô 2)   Satsuma and Chôshû form secret alliance against the shogunate; shogunate launches the Second Chôshû Expedition, which ends in failure.

1867 (Keiô 3)   Tokugawa Yoshinobu is appointed the fifteenth and final shogun at age thirty; later in the year he resigns his position and "returns" political authority to the emperor (*taisei hôkan*); Tosa samurai Sakamoto Ryôma and Nakaoka Shintarô are assassinated in Kyoto.

MEIJI PERIOD (1868–1912)

1868 (Meiji 1)   Shogun's forces are defeated in the Battle of Fushimi-Toba, marking the end of Tokugawa rule; rebels seize the imperial palace and emperor proclaims restoration of imperial rule; the Charter Oath is pledged by Emperor Meiji; Edo is renamed Tokyo; shogunate loyalist forces lose the Boshin Civil War (1868–1869).

1869 (Meiji 2)   The last pro-Tokugawa forces surrender, ending the Boshin Civil War; Emperor Meiji accepts the return of domain registers from all daimyo; the Meiji government abolishes traditional status groups. Ômura Masujirô, vice-minister of war and proponent of conscription in Japan, is attacked by former samurai from his own domain of Chôshû (dies of his wounds two months later).

1870 (Meiji 3)   Commoners (*heimin*) are permitted to assume surnames.

1871 (Meiji 4)   Meiji government abolishes daimyo domains, creates prefectures (*haikan chiken*); central government becomes responsible for samurai stipends; official government mission (Iwakura Mission) departs for the United States.

1873 (Meiji 6)   A conscription system is adopted; Emperor Meiji announces his opposition to a proposal to invade Korea; Saigô Takamori and other advocates of war resign from the government. Proscription of the practice of revenge-killing (*katakiuchi*).

1874 (Meiji 7)   Samurai rebels in former Saga and Chôshû domains suppressed by forces of the imperial army.

1877 (Meiji 10)   The Satsuma Rebellion, led by Saigô Takamori, begins; Saigô Takamori dies as a result of his wounds; and the rebellion is suppressed by imperial army, with 34,000 casualties on both sides.

1878 (Meiji 11)   Home minister (and ex-samurai) Ôkubo Toshimichi assassinated by a group of disgruntled ex-samurai.

1882 (Meiji 15)   Emperor Meiji issues the Imperial Rescript to Soldiers and Sailors.

1889 (Meiji 22)   Emperor Meiji promulgates the Constitution of the Empire of Japan.

Administrative Headquarters (*jin'ya*)

During the Edo period, *jin'ya* were administrative headquarters or government out-posts. Most were located in territories under shogunal control (house lands, or *tenryô*) and on fiefs held by Tokugawa bannermen (*hatamoto*). Others were located in small daimyo domains. The term was also used, however, to refer to the district headquarters (*gun daikansho*) in large domains.

In Tokugawa territory, *jin'ya* served as the headquarters for intendants (*daikan*) or regional intendants (*gundai*), whose charge it was to maintain law and order and to collect the rice tax. Only one example of a *jin'ya* from Tokugawa territory remains today, in Takayama (present-day Gifu prefecture). The *jin'ya* at Takayama served as a local administrative headquarters for Tokugawa officials from 1692 to 1868;

Main gate (in foreground) and office building (in background) of Tokugawa administrative headquarters in Takayama. The main building was reconstructed in 1816. This is the only remaining local administrative headquarters in Japan. (Photo by Constantine Vaporis)

Office space for Tokugawa government officials at Takayama administrative
headquarters. Officials sat on the tatami mats. Three desks, a box for storing paper,
ink, and brushes for writing, and a large brazier are visible in the first room
(foreground). (Photo by Constantine Vaporis)

previously, the territory was part of Hida Takayama domain. (The Tokugawa
assumed control of the territory in 1692, due in part to the region's rich forestland.)

The headquarters has been designated by the Japanese government as a National
Historic Site and operates as a museum. The complex consists of residential space
for the intendant, a guest room, a reception room, offices, a civil court room, an
interrogation room (for criminal suspects), a room where a designated Buddhist
priest carried out investigations of residents' religious affiliations (Christianity was
prohibited by law), a tea ceremony room, and a large storage area for tax rice.

In addition to the Tokugawa administrative headquarters at Takayama, there are
several *jin'ya* extant, preserved to varying degrees, in areas that were formerly
daimyo domains (e.g., Nabari *jin'ya*, part of Tsu domain, in present-day Mie prefecture); these served as district headquarters (*gun daikansho*) in large domains.
Across Japan a much larger number of this type of *jin'ya* have been reconstructed
based on a variety of historical documentation (e.g., Mikazuki *jin'ya*, in the former domain of Mikazuki domain, in present-day Hyogo prefecture).

Since most *jin'ya* were lower-level administrative headquarters, they were much
simpler than castles in terms of scope, size, and architectural style. Although
some (e.g., Ashimori *jin'ya*, part of Ashimori domain in present-day Okayama
prefecture) had stone outer walls and moats, these were small scale, lacking the

impressive dimensions of most castles. *Jin'ya*, with rare exception, lacked the *donjon* (castle keep) that defined most castles. Given their lesser status relative to castles, *jin'ya* were not prioritized in terms of historic preservation. As a result, the vast majority were destroyed in modern times to make way for newer construction.

The administrative headquarters of small domains, generally those of 30,000 *koku* (1 *koku* = 5.1 bushels of rice) or less, were also referred to as *jin'ya*, and fulfilled the same function as castles for larger domains. One example of a daimyo *jin'ya* involved Matsudaira Nobunari, the adopted son of the daimyo of Sunpu. He was a bannerman with a 4,000-*koku* fief who served as a junior councilor (*wakadoshiyori*) in the Tokugawa shogunate. He was promoted to daimyo status and assigned the territory of Ojima (10,000 *koku*) to the east of Sunpu as his domain. Due to the small size of his domain, he was not authorized to build a castle but instead ruled from his fortified administrative headquarters, the *jin'ya*.

See also: Bannermen (*hatamoto*); Castles (*jôkaku*); House Lands (*tenryô*)

Further Reading

"Historic Government House" (part of Hida Takayama site). http://www.hida.jp/english/activities/sightseeing-information/old-government-outpost. Accessed December 21, 2016.

Paine, Robert Treat. *The Art and Architecture of Japan.* Harmondsworth, England, and Baltimore, MD: Penguin Books, 1974.

Akô Incident

The Akô Incident refers to the historical events surrounding what is perhaps the most celebrated example of samurai loyalty in Japanese history. The incident at the beginning of the story took place at Edo Castle on a spring morning in 1701 when Asano Naganori (1655–1701), a young provincial daimyo from the Akô domain in western Japan, drew his sword and struck Kira Kôzuke Yoshinaka (1641–1703), a senior official and direct retainer (a bannerman, or *hatamoto*) of the shogun. Asano was one of the daimyo appointed by the shogun to receive envoys from the imperial court in Kyoto at Edo Castle, while Kira served as the shogunate's master of ceremonies. The reasons for the attack have been much debated but have remained unclear, providing historians with opportunity for debate and storytellers much space in which to create fictionalized accounts in many different forms such as theatrical performances, oral tales, novels, movies, TV dramas, woodblock prints, and manga. The historical event, together with its various representations in popular culture, is commonly referred to by the term *Chûshingura* (*The Treasury of the Loyal Retainers*), the title of the puppet theater play from 1748 that is the best-known example of them.

In the attack Kira was only slightly wounded, suffering wounds on the shoulder and forehead, before Asano was restrained and taken into custody. Asano was highly criticized by at least one contemporary (Satô Naokata, 1650–1719) not only for cowardice in striking Kira from behind but for his lack of skill in failing to kill him. Asano also showed a lack of martial skill in trying to slash at Kira with his short sword (long swords were forbidden inside the shogun's palace) rather than stabbing Kira.

Judgment came down quickly—some contemporaries would say too quickly—and Asano was ordered to commit *seppuku*, or ritual suicide by "cutting the belly," the same day for his high offense in drawing his sword and spilling blood in the shogun's palace, thus defiling the ritual space. In making this decision, the shogunate made it clear that it did not consider this incident a quarrel (*kenka*) between two samurai, which would have resulted in a judgment of "double (equal) guilt" (*kenka ryôseibai*), but rather a clear case of misconduct on the part of Asano. The deputy inspector general (*ometsuke*) Okado Denpachirô, who was on duty in Edo Castle when the incident occurred and was assigned to question Asano after the event, took exception, calling it a "one-sided punishment." He remonstrated with his superiors but was overruled.

Subsequently, Asano's domain was confiscated by the shogunate and his retainers released from service, making them *rônin* or masterless samurai. In stark contrast, Kira was not punished. In fact, he was praised for his restraint, which in the eyes of Asano's retainers was a great injustice and drove them to take revenge on their lord. Naganori's brother, Asano Daigaku Nagahiro, who served the shogunate as a bannerman, was ordered into a form of domiciliary confinement known as *heimon*, since as a close relation he was deemed complicit in his older brother's crime.

Asano's retainers in Akô debated what, if any, actions to take. Their options were to surrender the castle peacefully; to put up a fight against the military force that would be sent to take the castle if they refused to surrender, and then kill themselves; or to surrender the castle and then disembowel themselves in order to follow their lord in death (i.e., to commit *junshi*). Yet another option, made especially by Asano's retainers in Edo, was to attack Kira at once. In the end, a decision was made that was a variation of two of the options; in other words, to surrender peacefully, ostensibly to try to convince the shogun to restore the Asano family line but to plan to kill Kira.

Indeed, after making elaborate plans, twenty-two months later, forty-six of Asano's retainers attacked Kira's mansion on a snowy night. They were successful in their surprise attack, decapitated Kira, carried his head across town in Edo, and placed it on their lord's grave at Sengakuji temple. During the attack the *rônin* carried a declaration, attached to a pike, that articulated the moral inevitability of their actions in avenging their lord. According to that statement, although his retainers understood Asano's guilt in drawing his sword in the shogun's palace, they felt justified in their attack since their lord had been restrained and was thus unable to complete his vengeance on Kira. Accordingly, they found it "unbearable to live under the same Heaven with the enemy of one's Lord and father" ("Manifesto") and carried out the attack.

Government officials of the shogunate debated how to respond to the revenge plot for a month and a half before coming to a decision. Forty-six *rônin* who participated in the attack were sentenced to death by *seppuku* for the crimes of conspiracy and disturbing the peace of the shogun's capital. Although their actions were criminal, the forty-six were allowed the privilege of dying honorably at their own hands rather being executed like common criminals. The *rônin* were then buried in graves near their lord at Sengakuji temple, at which annual commemorations of the Akô Incident are held every year. They are worshipped by some Japanese as *gishi*, or righteous samurai, and were portrayed as such in a famous series of woodblock prints by the artist Utagawa Kuniyoshi (1797–1861).

Confucian scholars were interested in this incident and engaged in a vigorous debate about the "righteous warriors" of Akô, beginning soon after the event and continuing over the course of a number of years. In their manifesto the *rônin* used the phrase "our lord's enemy" to refer to Kira, but there was some debate among scholars whether in fact that was true. In a vendetta (*katakiuchi*) the victim or someone acting on his behalf would take revenge against the attacker, but in this case, it was Asano who attacked Kira. This mattered little to the *rônin*, though; for them, the fact that Kira, their lord's enemy, was still alive while their lord had been forced to commit ritual suicide meant that they had to attack Kira to defend their honor as samurai. But for Confucian scholars such as Satô Naokata and Dazai Shundai (1680–1747), the actions of the *rônin* could not be justified as revenge; for them it was a type of rebellion against the shogunate. Some scholars questioned why the *rônin* did not attack Kira soon after Lord Asano's *seppuku* (ritual suicide) instead of waiting so long to take action; had Kira died before they acted, Lord Asano could not have been avenged. Others, such as Yamamoto Tsunetomo (1658–1721), author of *Hagakure*, and Satô Naokata, also questioned their motives in not committing *seppuku* after successfully executing their revenge, arguing that they were hoping to gain employment by surrendering to the authorities.

Woodblock print by Utagawa Kuniyoshi (1798–1861) depicting the climactic nighttime attack on Lord Kira Yoshinaka's residence in Edo by the 47 *rônin*. This is just one of numerous representations of the Akô Incident, which was memorialized by many print artists, in books, and in the kabuki and bunraku (puppet) theaters. (V&A Images/Alamy Stock Photo)

Images of the Forty-Seven Loyal Rônin

Utagawa Kuniyoshi (1797–1861), one of the greatest nineteenth-century woodblock print artists in Japan, created a series of fifty-one prints of the forty-seven *rônin* known as *Seichû gishi den*, or *The Faithful Samurai*. The prints use the names of the historical figures as they were referred to in the puppet play. To avoid the Tokugawa censors, who prohibited any mention of contemporary politics, the play was set in an earlier historical era. The names of the *rônin*, both in the play and in other artistic forms such as woodblock prints, had to be altered, although in some cases only very slightly; for example, the leader of the revenge plot, Ôishi Kuranosuke, appears as Ôboshi Yuranosuke in the play and in the above-mentioned woodblock print series.

The fifty-one prints portray all of the forty-seven *rônin* as well as Lord Asano (depicted as Enya Hangan Takasada) and their enemy, Lord Kira (as Kôno Musashi no kami Moronao). Terasaka (as Teraoka Hei'emon Nobuyuki), the controversial forty-seventh samurai, was also included in the series.

Images of the forty-seven *rônin* also appeared in a number of *sugoroku* (color woodblock printed game boards), such as those by Utagawa Kunisada, published in 1835, and Toyoharu Kunichika, published in 1866.

The story of the forty-seven *rônin* has been retold many times, but the earliest known account in the West was contained in the writings of Isaac Titsingh, a senior official in the Dutch East India Company who twice traveled to Japan at the end of the eighteenth century. After Japan was opened to diplomatic relations with the Western nations, the story was rediscovered, for example, by the British diplomat Rutherford Alcock in his 1863 book *Capital of the Tycoon* and A. B. Mitford ("The 47 Ronin") in his 1871 publication *Tales of Old Japan*. During the early twentieth century, Robert Baden-Powell, the founder of the Boy Scout movement in Britain, wrote about the bravery of the *rônin*. Although cautioning he was not suggesting that they were necessarily right in killing their master's enemy, he nevertheless wrote: "It is interesting to see that even in those days people thought a lot of men who were manly and loyal to their leader, and who were not afraid to sacrifice themselves, even by the most painful of deaths, in order to do their duty . . ." (Baden-Powell, 1913, 99). In contrast, during World War II, the incident was often viewed critically as evidence of the militaristic spirit of the Japanese.

Several other debates have emerged related to the historical events surrounding the incident. First, why did Asano attack Kira? What was the cause of his anger? The only clear evidence we have is the testimony of a guard, who reported that before Asano attacked, he yelled, "Do you remember your recent affront?!" (*kono aida no ikon oboetaru ka?*). We also have the important testimony of a Tokugawa official, Okado Denpachirô, who was a witness to the attack. (Okado seems to support Asano, but historians do not understand why.) In fictional accounts of the story such as the puppet play *Kanedehon Chûshingura* (*Treasury of the Loyal Retainers*), Kira is vilified, which invests the story with a certain moral force. Kira *had* to be the villain for the revenge to be seen as valid. In fact, there is historical evidence that Kira was a better ruler than Asano, much revered by the people of his domain for the irrigation works and other public projects that he launched.

There is also a question about the number of *rônin* who participated and the circumstances surrounding the discrepancy. The Akô Incident is often referred to as the story of the revenge of the forty-seven samurai, but in fact only forty-six men were ordered to commit *seppuku* by the shogunate. The controversy surrounds the actions of the forty-seventh *rônin*, Terasaka Kichiemon, who signed the declaration of intensions, the league manifesto, that the men left in a box on a pole in the Kira mansion when they attacked early in the morning on December 15, 1702. There is some debate, however, whether or not he participated in the actual attack on Kira's mansion. The scholar Henry D. Smith has argued persuasively that Terasaka did indeed take part in the attack, evidenced in part by the fact that his name was also on the list of the men the shogunate sent to the four daimyo mansions into whose custody the *rônin* were to be remanded while awaiting judgment (Smith, 2004). The league leadership informed shogunal officials that Terasaka only went as far as the gate of Kira's mansion, but then he disappeared and did not take part. Terasaka's own account contradicts this but states that after the attack he parted company for various, unspecified reasons. Smith argues that Terasaka's low status (*ashigaru*) would have drawn attention to the fact that so many of the league were of low rank, which would have reflected poorly on Lord Asano. Terasaka's presence also would have complicated the shogunate's treatment of the group after their surrender, since it was questionable whether he, as an *ashigaru*, could have been legally sentenced to *seppuku*. The leadership of the league therefore acted in a well calculated, political manner after having achieved success in their mission to take Kira's head, and lied about Terasaka's participation.

There is another, much less discussed, controversy about the small number of retainers overall who participated in the revenge league. The Akô retainer band was about 308 *shibun,* full or upper samurai, which means that only about 15 percent participated in the revenge. If one were to include lower samurai (*kachi*), the retainer band was closer to 500 men (and even larger if one included *ashigaru,* the exact number of which is unknown). The revenge was carried out almost exclusively by *shibun,* with only two lower samurai (one *kachi* and one *ashigaru*). The number of members of the revenge league was about 120 at its peak, in the spring of 1702, but numerous defections followed until the final number reached forty-seven. Viewed from today's vantage point, the low level of participation might beg the question whether samurai values had badly eroded by the early eighteenth century.

In the end, the shogunate's judgment on the forty-six *rônin* seemed to both affirm the unwritten code of samurai honor and loyalty and at the same time uphold the law of the land, as the Confucian scholar Hayashi Nobuatsu (1644–1732) argued. The samurai code was affirmed by allowing the forty-six to die as samurai—to commit *seppuku*, instead of being beheaded as common criminals—and in allowing them to be buried next to their lord at Sengakuji temple. At the same time, however, the rule of law and order was affirmed in that their illegal action in killing Kira was punished; the judgment also confirmed that the shogunate laid exclusive claim to the legitimate use of force.

The Akô Incident thus serves as a key example of transformational change in early modern Japanese society as the role of samurai as a status group was redefined in a time of peace. It reveals the contradictions of Tokugawa society as the samurai underwent a slow transformation from warriors to bureaucratic officials. At the same time, some of the shogunate's actions after the sentencing of the forty-six reveals that at least some officials may have thought the original judgment on Asano too harsh. Five months after the death of Shogun Tsunayoshi, Asano's brother, Daigaku (Nagahiro), was released from house arrest, although he was remanded into the custody of the main branch of the Asano family in Hiroshima. He was later restored to his position as a Tokugawa bannerman, although his stipend was much reduced, from 3,000 *koku* to 500 *koku*. There was also a change in terms of the treatment of the nineteen sons of the forty-six *rônin*. Four of the nineteen were adults and heirs who had been exiled but were pardoned three years later. The rest were minors who would have been exiled when they reached adulthood, but they were allowed to take Buddhist vows and hence were exempted from punishment. There were also some changes in the treatment of the Kira family, for the worse. Kira's adopted son, actually his grandson Yoshichika, was seriously wounded during the fighting with the forty-seven *rônin*, but he was stripped of his landholdings because he had not fought to the death protecting his father. He was placed in the custody of a local daimyo and died of his wounds four years later. Kira's natural born son, who had been adopted out as the heir to the prestigious daimyo family Uesugi, was retired early.

See also: Chûshingura (Treasury of the Loyal Retainers); Double-Guilt Doctrine (*ryô-seibai*); Punishment; Retainer Corps (*kashindan*)

Partial view of the graveyard at Sengakuiji temple in Tokyo, where the Akô *rônin* were buried in 1703. The tombstone of the leader of the revenge plot, Ôishi Kuranosuke, is located in the roofed enclosure. The graves were an important pilgrimage site during the Tokugawa period and remain one of Tokyo's most popular tourist spots today. (Photo by Lonny Chick)

Sengakuji Burial Place of the "Forty-Seven" Rônin

One of the most popular tourist sites in Tokyo is Sengakuji, the temple near Shinagawa station where forty-six of the *rônin* involved in the Akô Incident are buried (one, Terasaka Kichieimon, did not commit *seppuku* and was not buried there). Every year, the Akô gishi-sai, or Festival of the Righteous Samurai of Akô), is held to commemorate the event. The anniversary of their revenge plot to kill Kira Kôzuke Yoshinaka, whom they blamed for the death of their lord, Asano Takuminokami of Akô domain, is celebrated on December 14, even though the actual date was on the fourteenth day of the twelfth month of the lunar calendar, which equates to January 30, 1703, on our present-day calendar. The festival features a memorial service in honor of the men and a reenactment of their historical walk from Ryôgoku to Sengakuji temple, about seven miles, to lay in front of their lord's grave the head of Kira. A museum (*Akô gishi kinenkan*) is also located on the temple grounds, which houses various documents and relics related to the forty-seven. To get a look at the graveyard unobstructed by large crowds, go to https://www.youtube.com/watch?v=nYQNXHaj-Rw. Visitors without fail will find incense burning in front of the graves.

The graves were an important pilgrimage site for many samurai during the Tokugawa period. For example, late-Tokugawa imperial loyalist Yoshida Shôin (1830–1859) visited there, and Tosa samurai Mori Yoshiki not only visited in 1828 but also made a stone rubbing of the grave marker for the leader of the revenge plot, Ôishi Kuranosuke (1659–1703).

References

http://www.japanvisitor.com/japan-temples-shrines/sengakuji-temple (accessed January 6, 2015); http://www.jnto.go.jp/eng/location/spot/festival/gishisai.html (accessed January 6, 2015).

Further Reading

Baden-Powell, Robert. *Boy Scouts beyond the Seas*. London: C. Arthur Pearson, 1913.

Bitô, Masahide. "The Akô Incident of 1701–1703." Translated by Henry D. Smith II. *Monumenta Nipponica*, 58(2) (Summer 2003), 149–170.

De Bary, Wm, Theodore, Gluck, Carol, and Tiedemann, Arthur E., eds. Chapter 31, "The Way of the Warrior II," in *Sources of Japanese Tradition, Volume Two: 1600 to 2000*, 2nd ed., 353–393. New York: Columbia University Press, 2005.

Ikegami, Eiko. "The Vendetta of the Forty-Seven Samurai." Chapter 11, in *The Taming of the Samurai: Honorific Individualism and the Making of Modern Japan*, 223–240. New Haven, CT: Yale University Press, 1995.

"Manifesto of the Retainers of Asano Takumi." Translated by Federico Marcon. http://www.columbia.edu/cu/weai/exeas/resources/pdf/manifesto-retainers-asano-takumi.pdf. Accessed February 22, 2016.

McMullen, James. "Confucian Perspectives on the Akô Revenge: Law and Moral Agency." *Monumenta Nipponica*, 58(3) (Autumn 2003), 293–315.

Smith, Henry D., II. "The Trouble with Terasaka: The Forty-Seventh Rônin and the Chûshingura Imagination." *Nichibunken Japan Review*, 14 (2004), 3–65.

Weinberg, David R. *Kuniyoshi: The Faithful Samurai*. Leiden: Hotei Publishing, 2000.

Alternate Attendance (*sankin kôtai*)

The alternate attendance system, which required the daimyo to attend upon the shogun in Edo, was a linchpin of the Tokugawa control system. It greatly impacted the economic, political, social, and cultural life of the country in general, and the samurai in particular, for more than two centuries. In many ways alternate attendance was a critical institution that defined the Tokugawa period.

Based on the centuries-old practice of the lord requiring the periodic attendance of his retainers by his side, alternate attendance was a type of feudal service (*hôkô*), one of the key forms of military-type service that the more than 250 daimyo owed the Tokugawa shogun. The system also required that while the daimyo was in the domain, his family remain behind in Edo, in effect as hostages, to demonstrate their loyalty to the shogun. This practice of vassals leaving hostages with the lord, too, had its origins in earlier times, as far back as the Kamakura period (1185–1333).

Formally codified in 1635 as part of the *Laws for the Military Houses* (*buke shohatto*), the system would continue largely unchanged, with only one temporary interruption, until 1862. As such, alternate attendance stands in contrast to many of the other control measures of the Tokugawa, which tended to erode over time.

Daimyo, and a certain number of the shogun's bannermen (*hatamoto*) with landed fiefs, were required to travel to Edo and back according to a fixed schedule. Half of the "outside" lords (*tozama daimyô*) alternated during odd-numbered years and the other half during even-numbered years (the months were also fixed). The hereditary lords (*fudai daimyô*), who were incorporated into the alternate attendance system in 1642, and the bannermen who were drawn into the system likewise were divided into two groups that alternated in the timing of their service in Edo.

Given the periodic absence of the lord, alternate attendance led to a split in the structure and operation of domain governments, with branches in the castle town and in Edo. The routine absence of the lord also accelerated the bureaucratization of local power, whereby governance increasingly devolved to his officials. Conflict between the two branches could sometimes occur, leading to the confiscation of a domain by the shogunate.

Although the chief focus of alternate attendance was the daimyo, the system also engendered the less routine movement of retired daimyo, who sometimes continued the pattern of alternating residences between the castle town and Edo, and the ruling daimyo's heir. The alternation of residences by the heir, who was not permitted to be in the domain at the same time as the lord, was not formally fixed by regulation. It was nonetheless customary, at least in the largest domains, and regarded as part of the heirs training via *ominarai*, that is, learning (to rule) by observing.

A form of military service, alternate attendance required the daimyo to travel to and from their castle towns to Edo, a trip that could take as long as a month, one-way. In the case of daimyo whose domains were located on the main island of Honshu, the trip was completely overland. For those located in Shikoku and Kyushu, the trip required a combination of travel by boat and on foot. The lord's attendance in Edo required an entourage of retainers and support staff befitting his status, so processions could be massive in scale. The largest could contain as many as

2,000–3,500 men, in the case of large domains such as Kaga or Tosa, and as few as 100–200 in the case of extremely small domains such as Hachinohe or Ushiku. As a type of troop movement, alternate attendance required order and discipline along the highways. It also required a certain level of conditioning on the part of the samurai and support staffs who accompanied the lord.

During the peacetime Tokugawa era, these trips of alternate attendance replaced troop movements to and from the battlefield as the principal large-scale form of military exercise that involved domain troops. Over time, however, these daimyo processions came to assume a more parade-like nature, subverting their earlier military origins. The processions developed notable theatrical elements, in effect becoming a type of cultural performance as the daimyo entourages traveled from their domains to Edo and back. In effect, the daimyo competed for prestige as they paraded on the highways in service to the Tokugawa shogun.

The expenses incurred in fulfilling the requirements of alternate attendance greatly impacted the Tokugawa economy and at the same time worked to deplete the war-making capabilities of the daimyo. The expenses involved in travel to and from Edo combined with the cost of maintaining sizable support staffs in the Tokugawa capital could consume between half and three-quarters of a domain's disposable income. The high costs attendant to participation in alternate attendance, and the constant movement of the daimyo between castle town and Edo, meant that there was little opportunity to plot against the Tokugawa.

The high level of expenses involved in alternate attendance requirements demanded that the daimyo find ways of cost cutting. The stipends of retainers, who were tied to a lord during the Tokugawa period and unable to switch allegiance to another, were the natural target for this. Accordingly, all retainers in the vassal corps were forced to give back a portion of their hereditary stipends. These give-backs, or forced loans, were euphemistically referred to as "loans to the lord" (*onkariage*), but there was no expectation that they would ever be repaid. Moreover, the periodic reductions, typically for five- or ten-year periods, of between 10 and 50 percent, tended to become permanent in many domains from the early eighteenth century onward. This greatly strained the finances of the vast majority of the retainer corps and over time led to a significant erosion of the economic position of samurai. It also led to a state of chronic indebtedness of many samurai, who had to rely on merchants for loans to survive. (For its impact on one retainer from Tosa domain, see Document 13A.)

Alternate attendance functioned like a compulsory military draft system, though in a time of peace, drawing into it large numbers of domain retainers. Roughly 25–30 percent of the population of Edo, about 250,000–300,000 people in the early eighteenth century, consisted of samurai and support staffs for the multiple residences that each daimyo maintained in Edo. The precise mechanisms of the service are not to be found in any extant regulation, but it is clear that domain officials sought to have some continuity in the forces they sent to Edo by mixing inexperienced men with "veterans" who had served previously in Edo. These retainers who accompanied the lord in his retinue for the most part continued to serve him during the period of residence in Edo (a small number returned almost immediately back to the domain). Another small number of samurai were assigned to remain in

Edo on longer-term postings and were allowed to bring their families with them. The vast majority of retainers assigned to Edo duty, however, were separated from family and home during the period of service. Despite the compulsory element involved in alternate attendance, there is some evidence that a certain amount of volition could also be involved if a retainer wanted to participate in the system. Some domains gave financial incentives for Edo service that might have made it attractive to some retainers. The attractions of life in Edo no doubt also offered incentives to many others, for whom participation in alternate attendance provided what may have been their only opportunity to travel outside the domain's castle town.

Retainers serving in Edo lived in one of the residence compounds (*daimyô ya-shiki*) that the domain maintained in Edo. Most domains had a minimum of two residences, while the largest could have as many as a dozen, including a warehouse for storing supplies sent from the domain. Larger domains maintained in their residences a permanent population of at least 1,000 people, with the largest and most prestigious of them having as many as 2,000–5,000. Smaller domains generally maintained a population of several hundred. Regardless of the size of the domain, the numbers increased significantly when the lord was in town.

According to one contemporary account detailing the life of domain retainers in Edo on alternate experience, the "existence of retainers on duty in Edo involves pleasure and hardships" (Vaporis, 1996, 300). The element of hardship came in part from the above-mentioned separation from home and family. In some unusual cases, a year of service in Edo might be extended if a daimyo was asked to remain in Edo to continue performing some service for the shogun. From the personal diaries kept by samurai serving in Edo, we learn that some of them experienced the birth of children, the death of a parent, or some catastrophe that befell their household during their absence. Single men might have had to delay marriage, too.

There was a good amount of free time in Edo because the duties required of many retainers in Edo were not very onerous. Conditions varied from domain to domain and depended as well on a samurai's rank, but it was not unusual for a retainer to be able to leave the domain's residence on personal business between five and ten times a month. This could lead to boredom and the tendency to drink a lot, something for which samurai on duty in Edo were renown. Boredom could also lead some retainers to engage is questionable behavior, the most common form of which was gambling. Punishment for illicit behavior could lead to domiciliary confinement, a monetary fine, or being sent home in disgrace.

The trip to and from Edo was an educational experience in itself, but Edo was unlike any other city in Tokugawa Japan. With a population that topped one million in the early eighteenth century, Edo dwarfed by many times the castle towns from which they came. For many domain samurai, one of the attractions of Edo no doubt was that the lifestyle there was much less restrictive than in the castle town. There was also much greater opportunity there for leisure activities, which included dining out at restaurants, visiting shrines and temples, festivals, and markets, theater, not to mention the licensed (pleasure) quarters. A period of residence in Edo provided many opportunities for shopping in what was the largest consumer market in the country. Edo not only had its own distinctive products, such as Yamamoto tea and woodblock prints (*Edo-e*), but it also acted as an entrepôt for goods made all over the country.

There were also great possibilities for retainers to take advantage of educational and cultural activities in Edo, both within the domain residences as well as outside of them. These activities tended to take place within certain cultural networks, like the salons of contemporary France. Domain retainers in Edo could participate in groups that formed, for example, for the study of medicinal herbs, literary arts, Dutch studies, Nativist studies (*Kokugaku*), or Confucian studies. Retainers with certain cultural or martial skills could use the year of service in Edo to improve their abilities and perhaps to gain professional certification, whether it be in Western-style painting, medicine, woodblock printing, swordsmanship, or gunnery. In sum, the "Edo experience" could be life changing for large numbers of retainers who were drawn into the alternate attendance system.

See also: Bannermen (*hatamoto*); Castle Towns (*jôkamachi*); Daimyo Residence Compounds (*daimyô yashiki*); *Laws for the Military Houses* (*buke shohatto*); Sakai Banshirô

Further Reading
Vaporis, Constantine Nomikos. "A Tour of Duty: Kurume hanshi Edo kinban nagaya emaki." *Monumenta Nipponica,* 51(3) (1996), 279–307.

Vaporis, Constantine Nomikos. *Tour of Duty: Samurai, Military Service in Edo, and the Culture of Early Modern Japan.* Honolulu: University of Hawai'i Press, 2008.

Ambassadors (Samurai)

Samurai played an important diplomatic role in the country's foreign relations in the late sixteenth century and then again after the opening of Japan to the Western powers in 1853. In the earlier period, the Tenshô embassy (1582–1590) and the Keichô embassy (1613–1620) were diplomatic missions sent to Europe to increase trade ties during a time of relative openness to the West. Due primarily to increasing concerns about the disruptive political and social influence of Christianity, however, Japanese hegemons, first Toyotomi Hideyoshi (1537–1598) and then the Tokugawa shoguns (from 1603), issued regulations that controlled and then suppressed the foreign faith. The anti-Christian political climate in Japan discouraged European leaders from wanting to expand ties with Japan. Furthermore, the Japanese expulsion of all Europeans except the Dutch after 1639 put an end to state-to-state relations between Japan and Western nations until after 1853, when the mission led by U.S. commodore Matthew C. Perry forced the Tokugawa shogunate to establish diplomatic relations with the United States; several European powers followed suit. After negotiating diplomatic and then commercial treaties with the United States and some European countries, the shogunate dispatched diplomatic missions overseas to ratify them in 1862–1863. These were the first overseas diplomatic missions for a Japanese government since the early seventeenth century.

Japan's first diplomatic mission to the Western world occurred in 1582, when four young Japanese samurai were sent to Europe on behalf of three Christian daimyo, Ôtomo Sôrin (1530–1587) of Bungo, Ômura Sumitada (1533–1587) of Ômura, and Arima Harunobu (1567–1612) of Arima. The four samurai were Mancio

Itô (1569–1612), Michael Chijiwa (1567–1633), Martin Hara (1568–1639), and Julian Nakaura (1568–1633). The mission was the brainchild of Alessandro Valignano (1539–1606), the head of the Jesuit mission in Japan, who thought that it would help the Jesuit effort to gain more attention, and more financial support, in Europe from various monarchs and church authorities. The four young samurai were students at a Jesuit school in Kyushu, and during the entire eight-year trip they were under close supervision. This was in large part because Valignano was concerned that they be impressed with Europe so they would give a positive report in Japan to encourage possible converts; hence he tried to limit what they might see or learn that might give them a negative impression. They traveled to Portugal, Italy, and Spain. In Rome they were received by Pope Gregory XIII and participated in the coronation mass of Pope Sixtus V. It appears that the samurai were represented as "princes" or official envoys from Japan, rather than simply the representatives of three daimyo, and accordingly they were received with full-scale ceremonies usually reserved for ambassadors. Back in Japan, to which they returned in 1590, the four samurai were ordained as the first Japanese Jesuit fathers by Valignano.

The embassy had limited success. It did increase knowledge of the Jesuit mission across Europe. Furthermore, while Valignano was promised funding by several sources, the Jesuit monopoly on missionary work in Japan was successful for only a short time thereafter, as Franciscans, Dominicans, and Augustinians began to enter Japan to begin their own missionary work. Anti-Christian policies first instituted by Toyotomi Hideyoshi and the Tokugawa shoguns limited the Christianizing efforts of all the religious orders. The four envoys met different fates on their return to Japan due in large part to the growing anti-Christian climate: Mancio Itô died uneventfully in Nagasaki in 1612; Martin Hara was banished from Japan by the shogunate in 1614 and ended up living in Macao; Miguel Chijiwa left the Jesuit order sometime before 1601 and died in Nagasaki in 1633; and Julian Nakaura was caught and tortured by the shogunate and died a martyr in 1633 (he was later beatified in 2008).

A second embassy to Europe was sent by the daimyo of Sendai, Date Masamune (1567–1636), in 1613. This mission was a result of the opening of relations between the Spanish government and the Tokugawa shogunate. The Spanish, who had developed the famous Manila galleon trade between New Spain (Mexico and present-day California) and the Philippines in 1565, wanted to establish a trade factory in Japan. Tokugawa Ieyasu (1543–1616), as retired shogun, was open to increased international trade ties and approved a treaty in 1609 under which the Spanish were permitted to build a factory. The treaty also allowed Spanish ships to visit Japan in case of necessity and called for the Japanese to send an embassy to the Spanish court. Given its approval by the shogunate, this mission can be considered Japan's first official embassy to Europe. With the backing of the shogun, Date Masamune organized the embassy and named one of his retainers, Hasekura Tsunenaga (c. 1571–1622), to lead it. Hasekura's appointment was both surprising and a testament to his high value to his daimyo, given that he was the son of an official who was ordered to commit suicide over allegations of corruption.

Departing from Sendai in 1613, Hasekura, one of about 180 passengers, including thirty samurai, onboard, traveled across the Pacific Ocean to the west coast of

> **Legacy of the Hasekura Mission Today**
>
> The memory of the samurai Hasekura Tsunenaga and the mission to Europe that he headed in 1613 is still alive today. There are statues of him in a number of places that he visited, such as in Acapulco (Mexico), Havana (Cuba), and Coria del Rio, near Seville (Spain), Manila (Philippines), not to mention several places in Japan such as Tsukinoura (near Ishinokai) and Osato (both in Miyagi prefecture, in what was the former Sendai domain).
>
> Many of the letters and documents from the mission still survive, including the letters from Hasekura to Pope Paul V, but a living legacy also exists in the southern Spanish city of Coria del Rio. A number of Japanese members of the embassy decided to remain there rather than return to Japan, and today their descendants number about 700 people. They have been identified as such because they bear the surname Japon (as in Hasekura de Japon, or Hasekura of Japan).

New Spain, which they crossed overland to Veracruz before traversing the Atlantic Ocean, arriving in Spain in October 1614.

The embassy was well received in Spain and Rome. During the eight months that Hasekura spent in Spain, he was baptized and met twice with King Philip III. He also met with Pope Paul V in Rome (in 1615), to whom he delivered two letters from Date Masamune requesting that Christian missionaries be dispatched to Japan on behalf of the daimyo. Hasekura was granted an honorary certificate of Roman citizenship, which is preserved at Sendai's City Museum. A portrait of Hasekura was painted in Rome and depicts the samurai in magnificent white robes and *hakama* trousers, with the trademark pair of swords at his waist. Despite these positive developments, when Hasekura returned to Spain King Philip II refused to agree to the trade pact that Hasekura had been sent to acquire. During the time the mission had been in Europe, the anti-Christian climate in Japan had intensified and the shogun Tokugawa Ieyasu had issued an edict expelling all Christian missionaries from Japan. This news, while troubling in itself also made the king doubt whether the embassy had the authority to negotiate a trade treaty. As a result he declined to agree on any treaty. Hasekura thus returned empty-handed to Japan in 1620 by the same route taken to Europe, and in his homeland he found that the political climate had indeed turned considerably worse for Christianity. Hasekura died of illness only a year after his return, and tragically, his family and servants were killed during the anti-Christian persecutions of the 1630s–1640s.

More than 200 years later, after the shogunate was forced to open the country to diplomatic and trade relations with the United States and a number of European countries, it sent delegations of samurai to several nations to ratify those treaties. The first such mission was to the United States, in 1860, to ratify the Treaty of Amity and Commerce between the two countries that had been negotiated two years earlier. More specifically, the Japanese envoys were to exchange the signed Japanese-language version of the treaty with the English-language version in Washington, D.C. This was the first official diplomatic group to leave the island country in more than 200 years, and it remained away from Japan for nine months. During this time, the seventy-six samurai, which included three ambassadors, sixteen lesser officials, interpreters, doctors, pike-bearers, armorers, servants, cooks, and barbers, visited Washington, D.C., Baltimore, Philadelphia, and New York. News of their stay in the United States was widely reported across the country, with photographs and illustrations of the samurai appearing in the popular media.

Among the members of the mission were Katsu Kaishû (1823–1899), who would gain further renown for his role in helping to negotiate the peaceful surrender of Edo Castle; Fukuzawa Yukichi (1835–1901), who served as a translator and later became known as the unofficial leader of the "civilization and enlightenment movement" in Meiji Japan; and Nakahama (John) Manjirô (1827–1898), the shipwrecked fisherman who lived in the United States from 1841 to 1851, before returning to Japan, where he was appointed a *hatamoto* (a high-ranking direct retainer of the shogun) for his knowledge of the West.

The delegates spent three weeks in Washington, D.C., where they were received in proper fashion, the Congress having appropriated $50,000 for this purpose. The director of the Smithsonian, Joseph Henry, had urged President Buchanan to make great efforts to impress the Japanese with the "superiority of our civilization and institutions" and to treaty them with dignity. Accordingly, the Japanese delegates were shown evidence of American progress in science, arts, government, and military affairs. Among the many places they visited were Fort Monroe, Mount Vernon, George Washington's tomb, the Smithsonian, and the Washington Navy Yard, where they heard the "Star Spangled Banner" for the first time, and a seventeen-gun salute was fired in their honor. On the procession route to their hotel, the Willard, large cheering crowds of as many as 20,000 (Washington's population at this time was 75,000) came out to see the two-sworded men from afar. On March 28, the ambassadors met with President Buchanan, and two days later they fulfilled their mission by exchanging the instruments of ratification for the treaty between Japan and the United States.

After leaving Washington, the samurai visited Baltimore and Philadelphia briefly, before ending their American trip in New York, where they experienced a whirl-wind of parades and balls, a reception at City Hall, and extensive press coverage in newspapers and the illustrated weeklies. New Yorkers likewise seemed quite anxious to impress their Japanese visitors with this pageantry, which cost an estimated $82,000, and by also taking them on official tours of the city's most modern factories.

The shogunate also sent two embassies to Europe, in 1862 and 1863, to ratify commercial treaties but also to learn about Western civilization and to try to negotiate a delay in the opening of ports and cities to trade and to foreign residence. The first mission, which consisted of roughly forty men, including the Nakatsu domain samurai Fukuzawa Yûkichi as one of two translators, traveled to France, the United Kingdom, the Netherlands, Prussia, Russia, and Portugal. The envoys were successful in concluding an agreement (the London Protocol) for the postponement of the opening of Osaka, Hyôgo, Edo, and Niigata by five years. A second embassy, sent by the shogunate to Europe in 1863, sought from the French the closure of Yokohama harbor to foreign trade. It was not successful, however, despite

Photo of members of the second mission sent to Europe by the Tokugawa shogunate in 1863–1864, taken by Antonio Beato. In this extraordinary image, some of the samurai ambassadors are posing in front of the famous Sphinx, in Egypt, on their way to France. The goal of the unsuccessful mission was to renegotiate some of the terms of treaties recently enacted by the various western powers and Japan. (Chronicle of World History/Alamy Stock Photo)

the growing antiforeign climate in Japan, including the 1863 "Order to Expel the Barbarians" issued by Emperor Kômei and the bombardment of Japanese batteries at Shimonoseki after Western ships had been fired on. On the way to France the mission visited Egypt, where the members were photographed before the Great Sphinx of Giza by Antonio Beato, the brother of the famed photographer of Japan, Felice Beato.

See also: Bannermen (*hatamoto*); Fukuzawa Yûkichi; Katsu Kaishû; Tokugawa Ieyasu; Toyotomi Hideyoshi

Further Reading

Boxer, C. R. *The Christian Century in Japan, 1549–1650*. Berkeley, CA: University of California Press, 1951. (1993 reprint edition)

Cooper, Michael. *The Japanese Mission to Europe, 1582–1590: The Journey of Four Samurai Boys through Portugal, Spain and Italy.* London: Global Oriental (Folkstone), 2005.

Miyoshi, Masao. *As We Saw Them: The First Japanese Embassy to the United States.* New York: Kodansha International, 1994.

Arai Hakuseki (1657–1725)

A Confucian scholar-bureaucrat, Arai Hakuseki served as adviser to the shoguns Tokugawa Ienobu and Ietsugu and helped to influence economic and diplomatic policy during the early eighteenth century. Leaving government service with the death of Ietsugu, Hakuseki began a career as a prolific writer of Japanese history, political thought, military arts, poetry, botany, geography, and philology, among other subjects. He also famously wrote several books on the West based on his contact with the Jesuit priest Giovanni Battista Sidotti and an autobiography.

Born in Edo in 1657, Hakuseki is reported to have shown signs of genius at an early age. Growing up, Hakuseki experienced firsthand some of the many challenges facing the samurai in a time of peace. Not only did both his grandfather and father spend part of their lives as *rōnin*, but Hakuseki himself went through two periods as such, from 1675 to 1682 and from 1691 to 1693. He did serve as a retainer of Hotta Masatoshi (1634–1684), *tairō* (chief councilor) to the Tokugawa shogun, but after Hotta's assassination he left the family's service. He also declined an offer to serve the Maeda daimyo of Kanazawa before finally returning to government in 1693, as an adviser to shoguns Tokugawa Ienobu (1662–1712) and then Ietsugu (1713–1716).

In terms of economic policy, he sought to improve the position of the Tokugawa shogunate and secondarily that of the samurai in general. Although he sought to relieve the economic distress of the samurai, he did not go as far as the samurai scholar Kumazawa Banzan (1619–1691), for example, as to urge the relaxation of the alternate attendance (*sankin kôtai*). Instead he tried, rather unsuccessfully, to apply economic checks to the trend of rising standard of living. To halt inflation he planned a contraction of the currency through recoinage, which led to the unintended consequences of hoarding and depressed conditions. To prevent the continued outflow of precious specie to foreign countries, which Hakuseki saw as a national threat, Hakuseki proposed and implemented a new trade policy that called for an export ban on Tokugawa coinage in 1715. He insisted that Chinese and Dutch merchants be paid in Japanese products, such as silk,

Anonymous portrait of Arai Hakuseki (1657–1725). A noted Confucian scholar, bureaucrat, and shogunal advisor, Hakuseki appears here in formal court attire, including *eboshi* headgear and a fan in his right hand, and sitting on an (imported) tiger skin. (Axis Images/Alamy Stock Photo)

porcelain, and dried sea products, rather than in precious metals. His ability to influence national policy was limited, however, by the fact that Tsushima's trade with Korea and Satsuma's trade with Ryukyu kingdom could not be effectively controlled by the shogunate.

Hakuseki sought to buttress the shogun's status through his political writings. Confucian scholars were divided on the question of the position of the shogun relative to the emperor. The view of Hakuseki, who was less a Neo-Confucian and more of an adherent of the original Confucianism, was that the shogun was the legitimate ruler in his own right. In other words, the shogun was not a sovereign emperor's deputy, but he nonetheless owed the emperor reverence. In support of his views about the political supremacy of the shogun, Hakuseki in his historical writings traced the Tokugawa family's roots back to the Minamoto clan, thus connecting the shogun to a line of imperial descent. Also in support of his efforts to improve the position of the shogun, he proposed changing his title to *koku-ô* ("nation king").

In his position as principle adviser to the shogun Ienobu, Hakuseki had the rare opportunity to interview the last Roman Catholic missionary to land in Japan during the Tokugawa period. Giovanni Battista Sidotti, a Sicilian Jesuit priest who arrived in Japan in 1708, was immediately captured and sent to Edo, where in late 1709 he was questioned on four occasions by Hakuseki. The Confucian scholar welcomed the opportunity to interview Sidotti, whose character and erudition he praised. Hakuseki showed an extremely open mind in exonerating Christian missionaries from subversive political intent, the argument that provided the basis for the anti-Christian campaigns of the early Tokugawa period. He did argue, though, that the spread of Christianity would lead to internal subversion. Hakuseki argued for Sidotti's repatriation, but the Christian cleric was imprisoned in the special prison constructed in Edo for Christians. At first he was not treated harshly, but that changed when he converted two of his caretakers to Christianity, leading to his being confined in a hole in the ground, where he died in 1714. Their conversations became the basis for Hakuseki's book on the West, entitled *Seiyô kibun* (*Record of Things Heard from the West*), which remained an important reference work in Japan until the end of the Tokugawa period.

Hakuseki continued to serve under shogun Ienobu's son and successor, Ietsugu (1709–1716), but his untimely death came only three years into his administration. There is some debate whether or not Hakuseki was slighted by the succeeding shogun, Tokugawa Yoshimune (1684–1751), or pushed out by rival political factions, but it seems clear that he submitted his resignation on his own initiative two days after being informed of Ietsugu's death. According to historian Joyce Ackroyd, "Not only was Hakuseki obsessed with the idea of its being unethical to serve a second lord—he obviously regarded Ienobu as his one and only true lord—but he and the new Shôgun [Yoshimume] were in temperament basically incompatible" (Introduction to *Told Round*, 1980, 8).

Hakuseki's book *Oritaku shiba no ki* (*Told Round a Brushwood Fire*) is arguably the first Japanese autobiography. It is actually one of the rare examples of the genre among samurai in the Edo period, but it is largely an account of his public rather than his private life. In it, for example, he scarcely mentions family, a wife to whom he was married for more than forty years and who was the mother of his nine children (five of whom died in childhood).

See also: Alternate Attendance (*sankin kôtai*); Kumazawa Banzan; Ronin (*rônin*)

Further Reading

Arai Hakuseki. *Told Round a Brushwood Fire: The Autobiography of Arai Hakuseki.* Translated by Joyce Ackroyd. Princeton, NJ: Princeton University Press, 1980.
Arai Hakuseki. *Lessons from History: The Tokushi Yoron.* Translated by Joyce Ackroyd. Brisbane, Australia: University of Queensland Press, 1982.

Armor

Armor is a major category of military tools (*bugu*), which refers to objects used for both offense and defense in battles. It consisted of a helmet, a mask, two shoulder pads, protective sheaths for the arms, a cuirass, various protective elements for the lower abdomen, and thigh and shin guards. Armor had two main components: first, it imparted protection to the warrior; second, it also provided a sense of identity to the wearer. For warriors of high status, armor could provide a sense of individual identity and distinguish him from others on the field of battle. On the other hand, for lower-ranking warriors, particularly foot soldiers, standardized armor and uniforms helped with group identification and a sense of esprit de corps.

Japanese armor is renowned for its extraordinary blend of elegance and function, made possible through the use of two natural elements, silk and lacquer. In general, armor was constructed from thousands of lacquered lames of steel (*kôzane*) or boiled leather, arranged side by side and row by row, and laced together by silk ribbons. The silk was either monochrome or polychrome. Those parts of the armor that needed to be flexible made use of scales that were lacquered before assembly; elsewhere the lacquering was done on the assembled rows of scales, which helped to stiffen them and to prevent them from sagging as the leather stretched. This construction technique resulted in a strong protective barrier and provided excellent freedom of movement, which was necessary for warriors who fought on horseback and then often dismounted and fought on their feet. Japanese armor was thus much lighter and more flexible than the solid metal plates or chain mail often used in contemporary Europe.

Before the fifteenth century there were three main styles of traditional armor, which differed from one another mainly in the construction of the body armor, or cuirass (*do*, in Japanese). The first type was known as *ôyoroi* ("large armor") and was designed for mounted archery. It was notable for the feature that its midsection (*nakagawa*) covered the front, left side and the back, while the right side was protected by a separate, solid plate that was tied to the body before the rest was put on. The entire front section was covered by a single sheet of stenciled leather, which prevented the bowstring from catching on the heads of the metal scales. Since shooting a bow required the use of both hands, large rectangular shoulder guards of lamellar extended down to the elbow to offer protection. Although the remainder of the arms were undefended, some forms of protection such as fabric sleeves covered by plates and mail were later introduced. The lower legs were protected by shin guards of plate, which were later extended to cover the knee. For fighting on foot, the upper legs were further protected with shorts made of mail or more commonly by a type of armored, divided apron. Completing the armor worn was a helmet, or *kabuto*, which consisted of a hemispherical iron bowl (*hachi*), made up of triangular plates fastened to each other by rivets.

The other two main styles of early armor were similar to the *ôyoroi* but were designed for use by samurai on foot. Accordingly, they needed to be more flexible. The midsection of the first of these, the *domaru* (lit. "around the body"), overlapped under the right arm, eliminating the necessity for a separate plate there. Since the armor was designed for foot combat rather than for archery, there was no need for the sheet of leather over the front. To allow the wearer to walk and run, its lower portion was divided into many sections, typically seven or eight. Some armors were equipped with small shoulder guards or more commonly with solid plates that hung over the point of the shoulder. The third, and latest, style of traditional armor was the *haramaki* (lit. "belly wrapper"). The main element that distinguished it from the *domaru* was that the opening ran down the center of the back rather than under the right arm. The gap was similarly protected with a separate narrow plate.

As warfare on foot became more common, the *ôyoroi* was largely abandoned by the late fourteenth century in favor of higher-quality *domaru* and *haramaki*, worn together with a helmet and limb defenses. Armor became more refined, with smaller scales and lacing often done in stripes or blocks of different colors. Helmets, typically, made in the shape of a hemispherical bowl, were constructed with larger numbers of plates held together by a larger number of rivets with smaller heads.

With the spread of warfare during the Warring States period (1467–1568), and particularly with the introduction of guns to Japan in the sixteenth century, innovations in materials and in the construction of armor were made. These changes were necessitated because lamelar armor, while elegant and efficient against arrows, spear, and sword, had its defects. Delicate and easily damaged, lacing often had to be replaced after a battle; it also absorbed water, would become very heavy with rain, and was difficult to keep free of mud and dirt. The introduction of guns also accelerated the shift away from the *domaru* and *haramaki* in favor of *tosei gusoku* (lit.

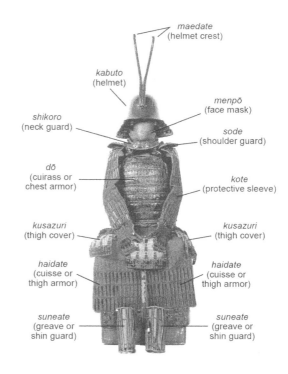

Major components of a *tosei gusoku* suit of armor.

"modern equipment"), eliminating scales in favor of heavier, solid plates, which afforded more protection. Some extant suits of armor from the seventeenth century display dents from bullets fired at the plates to demonstrate their ability to withstand gunfire. The plates in the midsection were divided into hinged segments, for ease in putting on the armor, and the more homogeneous surfaces allowed for more decorative elements such as embossing. There was some experimentation in adopting European armor and incorporating Japanese-style accoutrements in what were called "southern barbarian armor," but in general Western armor was too heavy for Japanese-style warfare. Lacquer was used increasingly not just for its

---

The Red Devils

The samurai of Ii domain were famous throughout the Tokugawa period for their brilliant red-lacquered armor, which gave their military units in battle the name the "Red Devils." The bright color made the troops easy to identify, and hence to organize, on the battlefield. It also was said to have had a big psychological impact on opposing forces. The first daimyo of the Ii family during the Tokugawa period, Ii Naomasa (1561–1602), is said to have borrowed the practice of red-lacquered armor from Yamagata Masakage, a general under Takeda Shingen. He wore the red armor together with a helmet (*kabuto*) topped with giant gilded devil horns at the Battle of Sekigahara (1600), where he was wounded. His troops can be spotted easily in the famous screen of the battle by Kano Sadanobu, which dates from the 1620s.

For a view of some examples of the Ii's armor in the collection of the Hikone Castle Museum, go to http://hikone-castle-museum.jp/en/.

Military Flags (*sashimono*)

As armies grew in size during the late sixteenth century, it became increasingly important that battlefield leaders be able to command them from afar, usually from a hilltop or some other strategic position. For this purpose, it was common for troops to wear a small flag bearing their lord's crest for identification known as *sashimono* or *hata sashimono*. A member of each unit of warriors had a square or rectangular flag that was attached to their cuirass (*do*), the body of their armor, and was fitted with a bracket behind him and a socket to hold it in place at the waist. Some cavalry warriors flew banners, known as *umajirushi*, in special holders on their horses. Different background colors of the flag were often used to distinguish one unit from another. Other functionaries wore distinctive flags for recognition. One such group were battlefield messengers (*tsukaiban*), who wore a set of three feather-like flags or a ballooning cape-like structure (*horo*). These and other types of flags are visible in a multipaneled painted screen depicting the Siege of Osaka (1614–1615). Higher-ranking warriors might wear a flag with a distinctive personal design or crest, but some actually wore carved ornaments attached to a pole as *sashimono*. A seventeenth-century screen depicting the Battle of Nagakute in 1584, for example, depicts warriors wearing a variety of objects, such as guilded buckets, fish, Japanese chessmen (*shogi* pieces), and ears of rice. Other types of very large and narrow banners (*nobori*) required two or three men to hold upright and were used in battle to control the direction of fighting. In the peacetime of the Tokugawa period samurai might wear *sashimono* bearing their family crest during annual horseback riding or other ceremonial occasions.

strengthening properties but as a main decorative element; it allowed for the introduction of color that went far beyond the use of colored silk ribbons used in earlier styles of armor.

Limb armor remained a part of a complete set of armor, although shoulder guards became smaller or were completely eliminated. Armored aprons, worn to protect the midsection, remained largely unchanged, while shin guards were constructed of iron splints connected by mail.

Helmets were also simplified with the introduction of the *zunari kabuto,* or "head-shaped helmet," the main element of which was a wide metal plate running from front to back over the top of the head. This style of armor prevailed during the Tokugawa period, although sometimes suits in the older style were made as a type of retro style.

Not surprisingly, the type of armor worn by warriors differed according to status. The mass of troops, including foot soldiers, wore relatively simple armor, with little ornamentation. On their backs they wore distinctive flags known as *sashimono,* so they could be readily identified from a distance. Higher-ranking samurai, including daimyo or even shoguns, wore richly decorated suits marked with family crests or symbols meant to call on the power of Buddhist or Shinto deities, animals, natural forces, and even insects. The dragonfly, for example, was popularly depicted on armor because of its name *katsumushi* ("invincible insect") and its instinct to fly straight toward its prey. Armor could also serve as a type of signature, as was the case with the first shogun, Tokugawa Ieyasu, and his gold armor, or the Ii family, which was distinguished by its red-lacquered armor.

Sometimes loose jackets and coats were worn over the armor. These camp coats, or *jinbaori,* had wide brocade facings on either side of the opening in the front. The main body of the coats were often made of fabrics dyed with vivid colors, often red, with bold designs, and bore the wearers' family crest or seal (*kamon*)

Front view of *jinbaori* (surcoat), with the crest of the Nagai family. Early to mid-Edo period (17th–18th century), made of leather, lacquer and brocade. Jinbaori were worn over suits of armor and were often decorated elaborately. The inside of the collar and lapels are lined with blue brocade, and the interior is painted with a black wave. (Photo by Brad Flowers/Samurai Collection/The Ann & Gabriel Barbier-Mueller Museum)

Back view of *jinbaori* (surcoat), with the crest of
the Nagai family. Early to mid-Edo period
(17th–18th century), made of leather, lacquer and
brocade. Visible on the back are the family crest
and a *saihai* (signalling baton). (Photo by Brad
Flowers/Samurai Collection/The Ann & Gabriel
Barbier-Mueller Museum)

on the back, often in a contrasting
color. Early examples of *jinbaori*
were of highly water-resistant
wool gauze-weave (*rasha*) or fur,
which provided protection against
cold and inclement weather; the
wools were imported by the Dutch
or by Chinese traders.

Many examples of Japanese
armor remain, particularly of the
Tokugawa period. This is due in
part to the fact that armor was
valued for its utility in war, and
during the more than two centuries of peace it assumed important ceremonial functions. It was
worn during alternate attendance
processions, on ceremonial occasions within the domain, and
likely displayed within the alcove
of a samurai's residence. As a
prized household object, armor
was passed on from generation to
generation. At the same time, in
the early Meiji period many former samurai households were
hard-pressed for funds and sold

Horse Armor

Although warriors in Japan wore armor even in prehistoric times, horses do not seem to
have been protected in any manner until the late Warring States period (1467–1568). Horse
armor dating from the beginning of the Tokugawa period usually consisted of lacquered rawhide scales that were sewn onto a fabric backing; it was lightweight and comparatively strong.

The square scales measured about an inch or half an inch a side. The edges were turned
up, with an embossed dome rising slightly in the center. Each square was pieced with holes
at each corner for sewing. Commonly used colors included gold lacquer, black, brown, and
red. Some examples of horse armor are decorated with the owner's family crest (*kamon*).

Separate sections covered the neck and fastened along the mane. Chamfron (known in
Japanese as *bamen* or "horse mask"), designed to protect the horse's face, were usually caricatures of either a horse or a dragon. Very few of these were made of iron, but the overwhelming
majority were of lacquered rawhide. They were shaped to fit the front of the horse's head and
were tied to the bridle. Holes were left for the horse's eyes. Some of the horse masks have the
added feature of horns and flames flowing from out from either the brows or the nostrils.

Images and accounts of the use of horse armor have not been discovered to date. They
are not, for example, evident in the screen paintings of the Battle of Sekigahara or the
Sieges of Osaka. It appears that they, like the "extraordinary helmets" (*kawari kabuto*) of
the time, were meant for purposes of extravagant display.

them to European and American collectors, which explains the presence of many suits of Japanese armor in Western museums and private collections. Some pieces made their way to Europe during the Tokugawa period as well, through the trade of the Dutch East India Company. Most famously perhaps, the second shogun Tokugawa Hidetada presented King James I with two Japanese armors, which were brought back to England in 1613. One of these has been on display in the Tower at least since 1660.

See also: Armor; Helmet (*kabuto*)

Further Reading

Botomley, Ian. *An Introduction to Japanese Armour.* Leeds, England: Royal Armouries Museum, 2002.

Conlan, Thomas D. *Weapons and Fighting Techniques of the Samurai Warrior 1200– 1877 AD.* New York: Metro Books, 2008.

Samurai. The Way of the Warrior. Florence, Italy: Contemporanea Progetti, 2016.

Bamen (horse mask), late Edo period, 19th century. The leather mask was boiled, molded, and then lacquered gold, black, and red. It was made in the shape of a dragon, with horns, flame-like brows, and threatening mouth. Like the helmets worn by the samurai who would have ridden the horse, the bamen was meant both to protect its wearer as well as to intimidate the enemy on the battlefield. (Photo by Brad Flowers/Samurai Collection/The Ann & Gabriel Barbier-Mueller Museum)

Aru Meiji-jin no kiroku: Aizu-jin Shiba Gorô no isho (Remembering Aizu)

A memoir by Shiba Gorô (1859–1945), a samurai from a high-ranking samurai family in the northern domain of Aizu, this text gives a personal account of the events that befell Aizu domain during the Meiji Restoration of 1868, when it was attacked by the newly formed army of the Meiji government and punished for its support of the Tokugawa shogunate.

Aizu was one of the few domains to support the Tokugawa in the Meiji Restoration, and earlier it had played a prominent role in service to the Tokugawa. The Aizu lord was appointed by the shogun as the Kyoto Protector (*shugoshoku*) to provide a police force to guard the imperial palace from the troops of Chôshû domain. Because of their support for the Tokugawa, Aizu was punished by the forces from Satsuma and Chôshû, who were then acting as the imperial army and set fire to the castle. Tragedy struck close to home for Gorô, whose grandmother, mother, and two sisters committed suicide before the battle, so the male members of the family could concentrate on fighting and not be concerned with their welfare. Gorô's father and four brothers fought in the campaign, but quite against the odds only one brother was killed. The author himself, as a young boy of ten, had been sent away to the countryside, away from the fighting, and was spared as well.

After the fighting ended, the domain lands were confiscated, and its samurai and their families, almost 15,000 people, were sent into exile to the northernmost part of Honshu, where winters were severe. Many members of the 2,797 samurai families, unaccustomed to farming, fared poorly in these conditions and died.

Gorô's firsthand account tells the story of his early life, including his education and family life as the second youngest of eight children, who together with his parents resided close to the castle. It continues with a detailed account of the fate of Aizu domain and the samurai who fought for it against the imperial forces. After a period of exile in the north, his personal fortunes turned for the better. He gained admission first to the Army Cadet School, then to the Officers Academy, and subsequently rose up through the ranks in the military. Gorô played a much-acclaimed role as a colonel in charge of Japanese forces in Peking during the Boxer Rebellion (1899–1901) and later ended his career as a general.

See also: Education

Further Reading

Shiba Gorô. *Remembering Aizu. The Testament of Shiba Gorô.* Edited by Ishimitsu Mahito. Translated, with Introduction and Notes, by Teruko Craig. Honolulu: University of Hawai'i Press, 1999.

Asahi Monzaemon Shigeaki. See *Ômurôchûki (Diary of a Parrot in a Cage)*

B

Bakufu. See Shogunate (*bakufu, kôgi*)

Bannermen (*hatamoto*)

The Tokugawa shogun's retainer band (sometimes referred to as liege vassals) consisted of two groups, totaling about 22,000 men: the bannermen (*hatamoto*) and the *gokenin* (housemen). Officially, the lands granted to the two categories of liege vassals amounted to 2,606,545 *koku* (in 1700), in comparison with the 4,213,171 *koku* held directly by the shogunate. However, due to the shogunate's efforts in withdrawing the *hatamoto* and *gokenin* from the land, by 1722 roughly nine-tenths of them were simply drawing stipends. In other words, their lands were withdrawn and incorporated in the shogunate's domains or house lands; accordingly, those retainers then received stipends that were collected from the government's granaries. When called to service by the shogunate, the liege vassals were supposed to field a total force of 80,000 men; it is doubtful, however, that this level of mobilization was ever possible, even early in the Tokugawa period.

Bannermen such as Oguri Tadamasa and Enomoto Takeaki were loyal to the shogunate to the end. Oguri, in fact, led the call to fight the forces of Satsuma and Chôshû that attacked Aizu domain's castle town in 1868. He was imprisoned for that loyalty and actually put to death—the only shogunal official to be executed during the Restoration. As a result of their loyalty, few bannermen other than Enomoto Takeaki and Katsu Kaishû rose to positions of any significance after the Meiji Restoration.

Bannermen were in effect the bureaucrats and military officers of the shogunate. In number, they ranged between roughly 5,000 (early eighteenth century) and 6,000 (nineteenth century). Their incomes were greater than 100 *koku* (1 *koku* = 5.1 bushels of rice) but less than 10,000 *koku* and also had the important but largely ceremonial right to an audience with the shogun. The status was in principle hereditary, although it could be revoked and, sometimes, special appointments were made, as in the case of the Englishman Will Adams, in 1613, and Nakahama Manjirô (a.k.a. John Manjirô), who was awarded *hatamoto* status by the shogun upon his return from the United States in 1853.

Almost all of the bannermen were descendants of warriors who had helped Tokugawa Ieyasu establish the shogunate in 1603. For example, both the third- and fourth-generation male heirs of the Oguri family fought alongside Tokugawa Ieyasu. The fourth-generation head, Oguri Shojirô, fought beside Ieyasu during the Battle of Anegawa (1570) and actually saved his life when he used his spear to kill an enemy who had caught Ieyasu off guard.

The shogunate, in the early nineteenth century, compiled a record of the geneolo-gies of its retainers, known as *The Kansei Revised Geneologies* (*Kansei chôshû shokafu,* 1812), which included a total of approximately 35,000 bannermen. These retainers qualified for certain positions—actually all but the top sixty or so posts—in the shogunate. In the civil sphere, they held positions ranging from the grand cham-berlain (*sobayônin*) which was directly under the senior councilors *(rôjû)*, to a variety of clerk positions, including financial. In the military sphere, bannermen could serve in positions that ranged from the high-ranking captain of the great guard (*ôba*n) or Edo city magistrate to unranked membership in less prestigious guard units.

A minority of bannermen were enfiefed (i.e., possessed fiefs, or *chigyô*) retainers—about 25 percent of those in the middle- to high-income brackets—and maintained themselves from the tax payments they received directly from the vil-lages in their fiefs. Among these enfiefed bannerman, the average received between 500 and 600 *koku*. Most of these fiefs were located in the provinces around Edo in the Kantô region, but it was unusual for any to consist of a single contiguous terri-tory; for example, in 1711, the fief of Nagasawa Motochika, a master of court ceremonies, was scattered in seven different villages in two different provinces (Musashi and Sagami). The fief of the Oguri family, mentioned above, consisted of eleven villages, which were spread widely across an area that today consists of four different prefectures. Although there was special status attached to holding a fief, these were largely fictive in nature; the source of the enfiefed bannerman's sti-pend may have been different, but otherwise there was little difference between enfiefed and fully stipended bannermen.

Almost all bannermen lived in Edo because of their important military role as the shogun's direct retainer band, but a small, elite, group of bannermen with fiefs known as *kôtai yoriai* actually performed alternate attendance every other year, just like a daimyo. Outside of this elite group, those few with distant fiefs actually had to receive permission to leave Edo to visit them, but in reality most never did. The only contact between a bannerman and his fief might be the visit of a repre-sentative from one of the villages in his fief. In the case of some dispute or conten-tion in a village, the bannerman was likely to send a vassal as his representative to deal with the problem, rather than going himself. From the villages in his fief, a bannerman might demand goods and services other than tax rice, but if he tried to demand too much the villages might protest. The fief holder had to worry, then, about being punished for incompetence by having his fief confiscated, should prob-lems there catch the attention of the shogunate.

The vast majority of bannermen, who were not enfiefed, were paid stipends. In terms of income, according to a record from 1705, 1,268 bannermen received between 100 and 199 *koku*; 1,386 received between 200 and 299 *koku*; 1,298 received between 300 and 399 *koku*; 339 received between 400 and 499 *koku*; and only two received as much as 9,000 *koku*.

Those bannermen who received at least a portion of their stipend in rice were paid three times a year, in February, May, and October. The shogunate paid its ban-nermen in equal installments up through 1722; thereafter the installments were in ratios of 1:1:2. The rice they received in payment was used in two ways: (1) they retained that portion which was consumed by his family and employees; (2) the remainder was converted to cash, at the market price of rice. This was the pattern for the vast majority of bannermen; only a small minority, about a dozen men, were paid entirely in cash, and they were among the lowest-income group. The cash the bannermen received was based on a conversion of their rice stipend into cash, for which the shogunate, since 1652, used what was known as the "posted price." This was in effect a price support system, meant to minimize large fluctuations in the bannermen's income. Typically, bannermen would not go to the shogunate's granary at Asakusa to collect their payments themselves. Instead they hired rice jobbers (merchants) to go to the shogunate's granary and receive the rice on their behalf. The rice jobbers would also be paid to market the rice and upon sale would deliver the cash (or more likely a combination of cash and rice) to the bannerman. As the financial condition of bannermen deteriorated after the beginning of the eighteenth century, many rice jobbers also took advantage of their close personal relationship with them to become their moneylenders.

Bannermen, like all samurai, required cash due to their urban lifestyle and the fact that the Edo-period economy became increasingly monetized and commercialized over time. The cash income a bannerman received was used to purchase consumer goods (household necessities); to pay the salaries of household servants, which included maids, cooks, and handymen; and to pay the salaries of the samurai and nonsamurai employees that bannermen were required by the shogunate to maintain as part of their duty to the shogun. This requirement varied according to income level: According to regulations issued in the mid-seventeenth century, for example, a bannerman with 200 *koku* was to maintain five men, specifically one lancer, one swordsman, and three manservants; at the highest end of the income scale, a bannerman with 10,000 *koku* was required to maintain 235 men, with a breakdown of 20 riflemen, 10 archers, 30 lancers, 16 swordsmen, 10 cavalry men, 3 banner carriers, and 149 manservants. The enforcement of these requirements was relaxed over time but remained officially in effect until 1862.

There is both quantitative as well as indirect, literary evidence that the bannermen suffered "increasing poverty." At the beginning of the period the income of bannermen, and the samurai social group as a whole, was barely sufficient to maintain the living standards of the day. Their real income level was relatively stable over the course of the period, but due to their urban lifestyle and contact with other social groups whose condition appeared to be improving, bannermen often experienced a type of "psychological poverty" (Yamamura, 1971, 376). As early as 1632, the shogunate issued decrees prohibiting luxuries that were aimed to limit their spending and prevent them from falling into debt to moneylenders; the following year it even tried to improve the financial condition of bannermen holding military positions who received less than 1,000 *koku* by increasing their stipends by 200 *koku*, but these measures were insufficient to improve conditions for the general lot.

In the face of this psychological poverty bannermen, who were on a fixed income, were limited in how they could react to try to improve their economic condition. They could not expand their incomes by doing by side work (by-employment); the shogunate permitted this for housemen but not for the higher-ranking bannermen. They could, and did, save funds by reducing household expenditures, in particular by reducing the number of samurai and nonsamurai employees, particularly household servants, they maintained, even if it meant reducing them below the level required by regulations issued by the shogunate. Some rented out their house (as a retainer of the shogun they were allotted a plot of land and a house) and moved to less expensive quarters, despite prohibitions on the practice. There is evidence than some constructed tenement housing on their allotted land and rented it out to commoners; although the bannermen kept the largest dwelling for themselves, they lived as neighbors with their tenants. Even enfiefed bannermen had limited options for improving their household's financial condition. In their fiefs they were bound by tax rates fixed by the shogunate and could not raise them arbitrarily or without permission. Attempts to raise the tax rate on villages in their fiefs could result in peasant resistance. As a result of their general inability to raise their income levels, bannermen often had no option other than to take out loans; in the case of enfiefed bannermen, ironically this sometimes meant taking out loans from wealthier peasants who resided in villages under the bannermen's administrative control. There is documentary evidence (see Document 13B) that peasant lenders sometimes took advantage of this leverage they had to demand that their bannermen debtors take specific measures to reduce their household debt.

Examining the household budgets of actual households allows us to get a sense of the financial conditions bannerman faced. For example, one relatively poor household whose bannerman had a stipend of 300 *koku*, actually had an income of roughly 75 *ryô* once it was converted to cash. Household expenditures, however, exceeded 100 *ryô* that year: this broke down to 38 *ryô* for wages, 10 *ryô* for horse and feed; 12 for firewood; 18 for oil, vegetables, salt, and other daily necessities; and 30 for clothing, paper, and other household goods. The resulting deficit had to be made up through loans, which often created a vicious cycle of debt. Bannermen with higher income levels were not necessarily better off, as their higher status required a commensurately larger household staff. The case of the above-mentioned Nagasawa Motochika, a bannerman with a stipend of 1,960 *koku*, which converted to slightly more than 453 *ryô*, is instructive: in 1711, his household experienced a deficit of 373 *ryô*, which represented more than 83 percent of income. During the eighteenth century, bannermen became increasing reliant on loans to maintain their households.

The shogunate was not unaware of the straightened financial condition of its bannermen. The price support for the conversion of rice to cash, mentioned above, was one means by which it tried to help, but it could not repeatedly increase stipends. The shogunate was also limited in its ability to lend bannermen funds of its own, to prevent them from falling prey to the high interest rates that merchant moneylenders charged. From time to time it imposed a moratorium on hearing court cases of aggrieved merchants trying to recoup their loans from delinquent bannermen debtors, but this strategy could backfire as the moneylenders could retaliate by increasing interest rates or refusing to lend money to those who refused to settle their old debts. The problems faced by the bannermen were not unique to them: the conclusions drawn about their financial difficulties apply in general terms to the retainers of daimyo as well.

See also: Housemen (*gokenin*); Katsu Kaishû; Shogunate (*bakufu*, *kôgi*).

Further Reading

Ôguchi, Yûjirô. "The Reality behind *Musui Dokugen*: The World of the *Hatamoto* and *Gokenin*." Translated by Gaynor Sekimori. *Journal of Japanese Studies,* 16(2) (1990), 289–308

Totman, Conrad. *Politics in the Tokugawa Bakufu, 1600–1843.* Berkeley and Los Angeles: University of California Press, 1967.

Wert, Michael. *Meiji Restoration Losers: Memory and Tokugawa Supporters in Modern Japan.* Cambridge, MA: Harvard University Asia Center, 2013.

Yamamura, Kozo. "The Increasing Poverty of the Samurai in Tokugawa Japan, 1600–1868." *The Journal of Economic History,* 31(2) (1971), 378–406.

Yamamura, Kozo. *A Study of Samurai Income and Entrepreneurship.* Cambridge, MA: Harvard University Press, 1974.

Books of Heraldry (*bukan*)

Books of heraldry in Tokugawa Japan were known as *bukan*, which literally means "Mirrors of the Military [Houses]." These were a type of personnel register or guidebook published by commercial ventures that contained detailed information about prominent samurai households, namely daimyo and *hatamoto*, the shogunate's higher-ranking direct retainers. The first printed *bukan*, dating from 1643, contained information on daimyo only, but from 1659 on the compilers also included information on the officeholders in the shogunal bureaucracy. The registers provided contemporaries (and historians today) with an invaluable source of information about the changing status of Tokugawa Japan's political elite.

Daimyo were listed with the following type of information: daimyo's name; name of his domain; genealogy; family crest; audience hall in Edo Castle where he was usually seated; year he succeeded to the family headship; court rank, honorary office and title; wife or fiancée; assessed land value (*kokudaka*) of his domain; name of his castle; schedule for performing alternate attendance (*sankin kôtai*) and types of decorative lances permitted; and addresses of the domain's residence compounds (*daimyô yashiki*) in Edo, among others. Elizabeth Berry has referred to them as "encyclopedic treatments of lordly anatomy" (Berry, 2006, 104).

There is some difference of opinion on the sources of information for the *bukan*, which were regularly brought up to date. Elizabeth Berry concludes that the shogunate was the "major supplier" of data (Berry, 2006, 110), but Peter Kornicki informs us that the shogunate in 1844 asked the *bukan* publishers Subaraya Mohei and Izumoji Bunjirô the source of their data, which makes it unlikely that the shogunate provided it, or at least all of it. The publishers responded that it was collected from direct observation at the entrance to Edo Castle, but that there were other sources as well. They also indicated that some high-ranking samurai, including the Sô daimyo of Tsushima, "paid to be moved from the beginning of the second volume of the *bukan* to the end of the first" (Kornicki, 2007, 99)

Once Westerners gained entry to Japan after 1863, the shogunate forbade booksellers from selling them maps or *bukan*, given that they both contained politically sensitive information. It appears, however, that the ban was not very difficult to get around, as some foreigners were able to obtain them by using Japanese agents. The British diplomat Ernest Satow, in his personal account of his residence in Japan, recounted how a Prussian diplomat "made a determined stand against the prohibition" by entering a bookseller's shop, demanding a copy of the book, and refusing to leave until he was sold a copy (Satow, 1984, 67–68).

These texts were printed quite prolifically in the Tokugawa period, on the order of tens of thousands of copies annually (and surviving copies can still be seen in considerable numbers in used bookstores in Japan). By the end of the seventeenth century, at least ten different firms were publishing editions, in a variety of formats. The books also circulated via lending libraries.

Various editions of *bukan* were assembled by the scholar Hashimoto Hiroshi in 1935–1936 and published in a thirteen-volume set entitled *Daibukan* (*Great Book of Heraldry*).

See also: Alternate Attendance (*sankin kôtai*); Bannermen (*hatamoto*); Daimyo and Domains

Further Reading

Berry, Elizabeth. *Japan in Print: Information and Nation in the Early Modern Period.* Berkeley: University of California Press, 2006.

Kornicki, Peter. *The Book in Japan: A Cultural History from the Beginnings to the Nineteenth Century.* Leiden, Boston: Brill, 1998.

Kornicki, Peter. "New Books for Old." *Monumenta Nipponica,* 62(1) (2007), 97–105.

Satow, Sir Ernest. *A Diplomat in Japan.* Rutland, VT, and Tokyo, Japan: Tuttle Publishing, 1984.

Boshin War (1868–1869)

The Boshin War (so named because of the name of the year in the sexagenary cycle in which it began) was a civil conflict that resulted in the fall of the Tokugawa shogunate and its allies at the hands of a coalition of domains opposed to it, led by Satsuma and Chôshû, and resulted in the "restoration" of power to the emperor (the Meiji Restoration). It shattered the great peace of the Tokugawa and led to the establishment of the Meiji state in 1868.

The Boshin War was not, however, the bloodless conflict that it is sometimes portrayed. Granted that it was not as long nor as bloody as two other contemporary civil conflicts, in the United States (the Civil War, 1861–1865) and in China (the Taiping Rebellion, 1850–1865), the Boshin War lasted seventeen months, involved the mobilization of more than 100,000 troops, and by one estimate it resulted in casualties on the order of 13,000. The numbers included an estimated 8,200 killed and more than 5,000 wounded. Despite this evidence, ever since the late nineteenth century, Japanese history textbooks have downplayed the violence of the Boshin War. In fact, just a few years after the Meiji Restoration, the former samurai turned politician (and future prime minister) Itô Hirobumi, gave a speech in San Francisco in 1872 in which he asserted that the Tokugawa system had been destroyed without "firing a gun or shedding a drop of blood." In line with Hirobumi, one prominent contemporary Japanese historian has even suggested that the Meiji

Photo of samurai from Satsuma domain who were fighting on the imperial side in the Boshin War (1868–1869). It was taken by the famous travel photographer Felice Beato (1832–1909), who was in Japan during 1862–1885. Notice several of the men in the back row, on the right, are wearing western uniforms but also have topknots and are armed with traditional swords. In general, the imperial side was better able to take advantage of western technology in the conflict with the Tokugawa. (Historic Images/Alamy Stock Photo)

Restoration was unique among revolutions in world history due to its relative low level of violence.

The conflict took place in four phases, as the hostilities moved eastward, beginning in the Kyoto-Osaka region, then to the Kantô region, to the northeast of the main island of Honshu, and concluding in Hokkaido. The first phase, in January 1868, consisted of the Battle of Toba-Fushimi. There, south of Kyoto, a sizable Tokugawa army of about 15,000, part of which was French-trained and included the special police force known as the Shinsengumi, was defeated by a much smaller but well-disciplined force of about 4,500 men—troops of Satsuma, Chôshû, and Tosa domains, fighting under the nominal leadership of an imperial prince flying the "brocade banner." This phase of the conflict came about after the restoration of power to the emperor (*ôsei fukko*) and the move of the former shogun Tokugawa Yoshinobu (1837–1913) from Nijô Castle to Ôsaka Castle in December 1867. Not content to allow the Tokugawa to be a part of any post-restoration political settlement as envisioned by the Tosa plan devised by Sakamoto Ryôma (see Document 15), Satsuma domain's political authorities instigated terrorist activities in Edo to prompt a punitive response from the shogunate in Edo and then the dispatch of forces to subdue the forces of Satsuma in Kyoto. Having lured the Tokugawa into action, Satsuma's forces fired at the shogunate's troops in Toba, beginning the conflict, which lasted from January 3 to 6, 1868. Poor leadership, the betrayal of key putative allies of the shogun (the daimyo of Tsu, Aki, and Yodo domains), and the bestowal of the imperial flag to by the Emperor Meiji to the imperial prince commanding the anti-Tokugawa forces were critical factors in the routing of the Tokugawa's forces. The former shogun fled Osaka by boat and withdrew to Edo.

The victory at Toba-Fushimi emboldened the leadership of the anti-Tokugawa forces to push for a military settlement rather than some form of political compromise. The formal recognition of the Meiji government by foreign ministers no doubt added to their confidence, and in the second phase of the Boshin War, the imperial forces marched north, planning to attack Edo Castle, the seat of Tokugawa authority. However, the leader of Satsuma's military forces, Saigô Takamori, and the head of the shogunate's army, Katsu Kaishû, were able to negotiate the peaceful surrender of the castle on May 3, 1868. No doubt Tokugawa Yoshinobu's approval of the decision to give up the castle saved tens of thousands of lives. Still, several hundred former retainers of the shogun who opposed the negotiated surrender resisted the imperial troops and clashed at Kan'ei-ji temple (a Tokugawa mortuary temple). The pro-Tokugawa forces, known as the *shôgitai*, were easily defeated in a brief, single-day-long conflict known as the Battle of Ueno on July 4, 1868.

With the defeat of the Tokugawa forces and the destruction of Kan'ei-ji temple, armed resistance in Edo ended, and the imperial forces moved north, to defeat the league of domains opposed to the imperial government that had formed under the daimyo of Aizu. The league was assisted by former Tokugawa retainers who had

Shôgitai ("League to Demonstrate Righteousness")

The *Shôgitai* was an elite military unit of the shogunate formed during the *bakumatsu*, or end of the Tokugawa period. Originally established in 1868 by Shibusawa Seiichirô, a retainer of Hitotsubashi domain, they were stationed at the Tokugawa family's Kan'ei-ji temple in Ueno. When the commander of the imperial forces announced the date on which an attack on the *Shôgitai* would take place, almost one-half of the Tokugawa unit deserted. The attack, which led to the conflict known as the Battle of Ueno, came on May 15, with the *Shôgitai* suffering a decisive loss. Some members did survive, however, and either joined other troops supporting the shogunate in the north or put down their weapons and returned to Edo. A memorial tomb for the *Shôgitai* is located in Ueno Park in Tokyo. One of the two main tombstones was erected in 1874 by a surviving member of the group, Ogawa Okisato. The second tombstone was erected in 1869 by one of Kan'ei-ji's priests. The site was named an important cultural asset of Tokyo's Taitô ward in 1990 and subsequently, in 2003, fell under the administration of the Tokyo Metropolitan Government.

survived the previous battles of the conflict. This, the third phase of the war, was drawn out, taking place during the summer and fall of 1868. Although the vast majority of the castles across the country were transferred to the imperial forces with little if any combat, the determined defense of a number of the northern castles slowed down the progress of the imperial forces. At several castles, including Aizu-Wakamatsu, there was intense fighting. For example, the resistance at Wakamatsu castle held out for several weeks before surrendering; famously, a young group of young samurai, known as the *byakkotai* (White Tiger Brigade), committed *seppuku* after returning from a mission and believing that the castle had fallen.

The final phase of the Boshin War took place in the far north, to which the Tokugawa loyalist Enomoto Takeaki (1836–1908) had fled, taking with him the bulk of the Tokugawa naval fleet. Jules Brunet (1838–1911), a member of the French military mission to the shogunate who decided to resign his commission and fight in support of the Tokugawa loyalists, accompanied Enomoto. In Hokkaido, Enomoto, in defiance of the new Meiji imperial government, proclaimed the Ezo Republic, of which he became the elected president. His hopes of gaining recognition of Ezo as a separate regime by the Meiji government and the foreign powers were soon dashed, however, as the imperial forces launched a series of land and sea engagements against his nascent government. From the star-shaped fort Goryôkaku, near Hakodate (seat of the office of the Hakodate *bugyô* or Magistrate's Office), Enomoto and his troops, shielded in part by the winter climate, held out against the imperial troops for almost nine months before their surrender, bringing an end to the Boshin War on June 26, 1869. Although Enomoto was arrested and imprisoned, he was later pardoned, and like numerous former Tokugawa loyalists ended up contributing to the Meiji state.

Both sides in the conflict used a combination of traditional weapons and techniques but also some Western techniques and armaments, either learned or acquired from French, German, Dutch, British, and American military suppliers, or in some cases actually constructed in Japan. In general, the imperial side acquired newer, more effective guns, although the daimyo of Nagaoka, fighting on the Tokugawa side, possessed two Gatling guns. Similarly, some troops, particularly officers, on both sides wore Western-style uniforms, as captured in a famous, hand-tinted color photograph by Felice Beato.

See also: Aru Meiji-jin no kiroku: Aizu-jin Shiba Gorô no isho (*Remembering Aizu*); Foreign-Born Samurai; Magistrates (*bugyô*); Saigô Takamori; Shinsengumi; Tokugawa Yoshinobu; White Tiger Brigade (*byakkotai*)

Further Reading

Sheldon, Charles D. "The Politics of the Civil War of 1868." In *Modern Japan: Aspects of History, Literature & Society*, ed. W. G. Beasley. Berkeley: University of California Press, 1975.

Steele, M. William. "The Rise and Fall of the Shôgitai: A Social Drama." In *Conflict in Modern Japanese History: The Neglected Tradition*, eds. Tetsuo Najita and J. Victor Koschmann. Princeton, NJ: Princeton University Press, 1982.

Wert, Michael. *Meiji Restoration Losers: Memory and Tokugawa Supporters in Modern Japan*. Cambridge, MA: Harvard University Asia Center, 2013.

Budô shoshinshû (The Way of the Warrior: A Primer)

Daidôji Yûzan Shigesuke (1639–1730) lived a long life during a transitional period of the samurai from war to peace and served a number of daimyo as a scholar. Early in the eighteenth century, he authored *Budô shoshinshû*, one of the more widely circulated texts on the "way of the warrior."

Daidôji Yûzan Shigesuke (1639–1730) was of a distinguished lineage, his family claiming descent from the Taira clan through the tenth century Taira Korehira and close relations with the Go-Hôjô family through Shigetoki, the elder brother of Hôjô Sôun (1432–1519), the warring states daimyo (*sengoku daimyô*) of Odawara. It was Shigetoki who took the name Daidôji from the village where he retired. Shigetoki's grandson Masashige committed *seppuku* (ritual suicide) when Odawara Castle was besieged by Toyotomi Hideyoshi in 1590; his son Naoshige became a vassal of the second shogun, Tokugawa Hidetada (1579–1632), and fought in support of the shogunate at the Siege of Osaka in 1615. Yûzan's father Shigehisa served Tokugawa Tadateru (1592–1683), the sixth son of Ieyasu and the younger brother of Hidetada.

Yûzan himself served Tokugawa Tadateru for a time but became a *rônin* (masterless samurai) when Tadateru was dismissed in 1619. After a period of study of literary and military strategy under a number of scholars in Edo, including Obata Kagenori (1572–1663), Hôjô Ujinaga (1609–1670), and Yamaga Sokô (1622–1685), Yûzan took a position as an adviser to the daimyo of Aizu. He retired to Iwabuchi in Musashi province but remained active, lecturing to a number of daimyo around the country. Yûzan lived a long life and witnessed the Akô Incident involving the forty-seven *rônin*, experienced the exciting years of the Genroku period under the shogun Tokugawa Tsunayoshi (1646–1709) and then the period of reform under the eighth shogun, Yoshimune (1684–1751), who sought to reenergize the samurai through his policies emphasizing martial skills.

Compiled in the early eighteenth century, Yûzan's text *Budô shoshinshû* is considered one of the classic texts explicating and extolling the values and practices of the warrior, known contemporaneously as *budô*, *shidô*, and more infrequently as *bushido*. The text, in forty-four chapters, circulated widely during the Tokugawa period, was organized as a series of lessons delivered by a father to his son. It reflects the conditions facing the samurai after a period of extended peace and begins with advice: "One who is supposed to be a warrior considers it his foremost concern to keep death in mind at all times, every day and every night, from the morning of New Year's Day through the night of New Year's Eve. As long as you keep death in mind at all times, you will also fulfill the ways of loyalty and familial duty" (Cleary, 1999, 3). The text circulated more widely than the now-famous *Hagakure* written by Yamamoto Tsunetomo (1659–1719) of Saga domain.

Yûzan was also the author of a number of other texts, including *Iwabuchi yawa* (*Evening Chats at Iwabuchi*); *Ochibôshû*, a history of Tokugawa Ieyasu and Edo; *Taishôden* (*Records of Great Commanders*); and *Goshinron* (*Essays on Five Vassals*).

See also: Akô Incident; *Bushido*; *Hagakure* (*In the Shadow of Leaves*); Ronin (*rônin*); Sieges of Osaka (*Ôsaka no jin*); Tokugawa Hidetada; Warring States Daimyo (*sengoku daimyô*); Yamaga Sokô

Further Reading

Cleary, Thomas, trans. *Code of the Samurai: A Modern Translation of Bushido Shoshin-shu of Taira Shigesuke.* Boston, Rutland, VT: Tuttle Publishing, 1999.

Sadler, A. L., trans. *The Code of the Samurai: A Translation of Daidôji Yûzan's Budô shoshinshû.* Rutland, VT: Charles E. Tuttle, 1988.

Buke giri monogatari (Tales of Samurai Honor), 1688

The merchant writer Ihara Saikaku (1642–1693), *haikai* poet and author of a number of well-known fiction books on townsmen, such as *Kôshoku gonin onna (Five Women Who Loved Love,* 1686) and *Nippon eitaigura (The Japanese Family Storehouse,* 1688), also produced several works about the samurai. The first of those texts, part of a genre known as *bukemono,* or samurai tales, was *Nanshoku ôkagami (The Great Mirror of Manly Love,* 1687). The first half of this work consisted of stories that dealt with the samurai and the practice of male-male love (*nanshoku*). A second work, *Budô denrai ki (The Transmission of the Martial Arts,* 1687), which appeared only three months after the first, consisted of thirty-two stories about samurai vendettas (*katakiuchi*). In his third work on the samurai, *Buke giri monogatari (Tales of Samurai Honor,* 1688), Saikaku broadened his focus to cover the entire sweep of samurai life.

Giri, often translated as "duty" or "obligation," connotes the moral path that men are to follow in their relations with others and provides a unifying theme for Saikaku's stories in *Buke giri monogatari.* Although each status group was obligated by *giri,* it was particularly important for samurai. Saikaku's stories reinforce this idea and echoed Yamaga Sokô (1622–1685), who in his work *Shidô (Way of the Warrior)* wrote that, "The business of the samurai consists in reflecting on his own station in life, in discharging loyal service to his master if he has one, in deepening his fidelity in his association with friends, and, with due consideration of his own position, in devoting himself to duty above all" (Quoted in Vaporis, 2014, 125). Although almost half of the twenty-seven stories in this volume were set in the period before the Tokugawa, when civil war prevailed, the remainder focused on daily life and behavior of samurai during the seventeenth century to show how *bushi* tried to devote themselves to *giri* during a time of peace.

The twenty-seven stories present a wide range of accounts, and in them Saikaku often uses humor and exaggeration to good effect. Just a few of the stories are didactic in purpose, extolling the samurai as self-sacrificing models of behavior. There are some stories of vendettas, others that highlight the loyalty between male samurai lovers, as well as some that reveal the resolve of women belonging to *bushi* households. He was realistic in revealing that a samurai's devotion to *giri* could be calculating and self-serving, as in the tale "A Surprise Move: The Heir's Killer Replaces Him." In this story the father of a boy who was killed in a duel adopts the victor as his son. The father explained to his wife, "Although he is only thirteen, this boy is much better at the military arts than our own fifteen-year-old son was" (Saikaku, 1981, 67). Although it was common sense that a *bushi* father would want the best possible heir, his calculation would have struck Edo-period readers as ridiculous. In other stories, though, Saikaku greatly simplified the code by which samurai lived, thereby exaggerating the good qualities of the samurai's code of behavior, particularly *giri*, to comic effect. His use of exaggeration, however, was never in a completely unrestrained manner. Perhaps this restraint was due to the fact that as a commoner he was under certain social and political pressures not to be too critical of his putative social superiors. Still, according to the translator of his samurai tales, "he did not hold back when dealing with individual *bushi* who erred by over-enthusiasm when putting their code into practice. Furthermore, at times he seems to poke fun at the rigidity and sanctimoniousness of the code itself" (Callahan, 1979, 4).

Saikaku ends his collection of stories on a light but critical note, using humor and a happy but ironic ending. The final story, "A Boy's Beauty Flowers When His Forelock Is Unshaven," ends with praise for the shogunate for maintaining "this well-governed realm where the sword remain forever sheathed and peace reigns eternal." But there is irony in the ending as well, for a cowardly samurai who challenged the hero of the story backs out at the last moment, offering only a transparent excuse. The hero and his friend laugh as they walk away, which casts the final sentence in a different light. Saikaku seems to be suggesting that if the "sword remains forever sheathed," then the peace has been eroding the samurai spirit.

See also: Male-Male Love (*nanshoku*); Revenge-Killing (*katakiuchi*)

Further Reading

Callahan, Caryl. "Tales of Samurai Honor. Saikaku's *Buke Giri Monogatari*." *Monumenta Nipponica,* 34(1) (1979), 1–20.

Saikaku, Ihara. *Tales of Samurai Honor.* Translated by Caryl Ann Callahan. Tokyo: Sophia University, 1981. *Monumenta Nipponica* monograph.

Vaporis, Constantine Nomikos. *Voices of Early Modern Japan: Contemporary Accounts of Daily Life during the Age of the Shoguns.* Boulder, CO: Westview Press, 2014.

Bushi

The term *"bushi"* often is used synonymously with "samurai." One of the most authoritative texts on Tokugawa Japan, *The Cambridge History of Japan*, vol. 4: *Early Modern Japan*, equates the two, referring to "the *bushi* or samurai" (p. 4) in the introduction and in the index directing the reader looking for information on *bushi* to look up "samurai class": *"bushi* (warrior class), *see* samurai class" (p. 814). Although the terms are often used interchangeably, it is important to understand that there are differences between them if one uses a strict definition of "samurai."

"Bushi" is composed of two Chinese characters, *"bu"* or "military" or "martial," and *"shi,"* which means "gentleman," "scholar," or "warrior." As a compound, the term is used to refer to members of "warrior households," or *"buke."* When the Meiji government (1868–1912) tried to calculate how many former male members of warrior households it had to remunerate with interest-bearing bonds, it arrived at a figure of 408,823 households, with a total of 1,892,449 people, dependents included, living in those households. Since the total represented about 6 percent of the population, members of warrior households constituted a very large privileged elite, one that had to be supported through the labor of the other three status groups.

The term "samurai" is often used in a generic sense to connote all members of "warrior households." There are two potential problems with this. First of all, during the Tokugawa period the term "samurai" referred to only the top portion of a daimyo's retainer corps—to those with the rights of an audience with the lord and whose names were listed in the domain's military registers (*bugenchō*). Some writers seek to avoid this issue by referring to the upper portion of a daimyo's retainer corps, which were divided into many ranks, as "full samurai" or "upper samurai" and the lower half of the retainer corps, which was similarly divided into a number of ranks," as "lower samurai." This accommodation is complicated by the fact that the dividing line between "upper" and "lower" differed in many domains. A second issued that one confronts when using "samurai" in a generic sense is that the term includes women. In a strict sense, women were not samurai, but they were members of "warrior households." In Japanese the term most often used to refer to these women was *"buke no onna"* or "women of the warrior households."

Due to the widespread acceptance of the generic use of the term "samurai," this encyclopedia also follows that practice, but when necessary to clarify whether someone was a retainer with rights to an audience and listed in the domain register or not, the qualifying terms "full samurai" or "upper samurai" will be used. Similarly, "lower samurai" will be used to refer to members of the lower portion of the daimyo retainer corps.

Having now equated samurai with *bushi*, it is important to ask who were the samurai, particularly since the perquisites of rank, two swords and a surname (*myōji taito*), were granted to some villagers and townsmen? We might consider three definitions: the first covers all people (specifically men) considered as *bushi* in the contemporary Tokugawa context. Such a definition would include *rōnin*, who despite the lack of formal attachment to a lord and stipend often displayed the symbols of the status group. This definition would also include Confucian scholars (*jusha*) and physicians attached to a daimyo, even though they might not serve a daimyo permanently. This is the definition that this encyclopedia employs. A second definition stresses the importance of a formal relationship between a retainer and overlord that required the performance of service—not necessarily military service—in return for a stipend. Confucian scholars, physicians, privileged merchants, and artisans could also be included under this rubric. A third definition limits membership in the samurai status group to those whose income was paid for by an overlord in return for military service obligations; such a definition would exclude ancillary groups such as those listed in the second definition above. Under this definition Confucian scholars and doctors attached to daimyo would be excluded or at most might be considered "quasi-samurai."

See also: Bushido; Retainer Corps (*kashindan*); Status System (*mibunsei*)

Further Reading

Hall, John Whitney. *The Cambridge History of Japan*, vol. 4: *Early Modern Japan*. Cambridge: Cambridge University Press, 1991.

Bushido

A Japanese term meaning "the way of the warrior," it refers to the ideals of *bushi* (usually referred to in the West as the samurai), usually stretching back as early as the Kamakura period (1185–1333) and running through the Tokugawa period. The term, however, was not often used during the Tokugawa period and only became popularized in the twentieth century, when it became associated with the rise of nationalism at the end of the nineteenth and early twentieth centuries and then closely linked with Japanese militarism in the 1930s and 1940s. Many historians critique the term as an invented tradition, arguing that there was no comprehensive or consistent articulation of a samurai code of behavior. Nonetheless, the term continues to be widely used—indeed a recent Internet search of the term yielded more than 15 million hits.

During the Kamakura and Muromachi eras (1185–1573), the ideals of samurai behavior were described in terms of "the way of the horse and bow" (*kyûba no michi*), which distinguished them from the practices of the court aristocrats. These idealized values included but were not limited to courage, honor, and most importantly loyalty to one's overlord, and a willingness for self-sacrifice in battle or through ritual suicide. The behavior of samurai was glorified in the numerous war chronicles (*gunki monogatari*) of the time. A study of the many warrior house codes of the period reveals the lack of a universal standard of behavior for samurai of the pre-Tokugawa periods. By examining other contemporary records historians have shown that loyalty and honor were largely driven by selfish motives of personal gain rather than observance of a code of behavior. The term *bushido* does appear in some texts attributed to the late-sixteenth-century texts, but their idealization of loyalty indicates that it was more often lacking; in fact, foreign visitors to Japan in the sixteenth century remarked about the lack of loyalty among samurai, who changed lords according to circumstances in order to improve their individual or family's positions.

During the Tokugawa period, the samurai underwent a transformation during the long years of peace, losing their battlefield skills, which developed into the martial arts, and becoming overwhelmingly a service bureaucracy. The nature of loyalty changed, too, becoming unconditional in nature, as samurai were no longer easily able to change lords. Yamaga Sokô and other scholars turned their attention to defining a new role for the samurai in an age when there was little opportunity to risk their lives on the battlefield. He and other Confucian scholars such as Kaibara Ekken and Nakae Toju used the term *shidô* or *budô* (both translated as "way of the warrior") in elaborating their views on the expected behavior of samurai. The samurai were enjoined to develop their martial skills while serving as scholar officials and acting as role models for the other social groups.

The term *bushido* appeared only infrequently in Tokugawa-period texts. It is used in the often-quoted *Hagakure* (1716), written by Saga domain samurai Yamamoto Tsunetomo (1658–1719), which is known particularly for its opening sentence: "The way of the warrior lies in death." The *bushido* that he was writing about, however, was an idealized form of loyal service to a daimyo through self-sacrifice that was out of date in the peaceful conditions of his lifetime.

Ironically, the term *bushido* became popular only in the late nineteenth century, when the samurai no longer existed. Observers in Japan and abroad wrote about *bushido* as a set of clearly articulated values that was passed on by the samurai to the modern Japanese. It was popularized in Japan by writers such as Ozaki Yukio,

Uemura Masahisa, and Inoue Tetsujirô, and in the West by Nitobe Inazô, who wrote the English-language book *Bushido: The Soul of Japan* (1899). Although Nitobe wrote that *bushido* was an unformulated teaching in his book, *Bushido: The Soul of Japan,* nonetheless he enumerated the so-called "seven virtues of bushido," which have been quoted widely ever since and even found their way into publicity material for the American film *The Last Samurai* (2003).

The British author Basil Hall Chamberlain was highly critical of Nitobe's book, and his criticism is quite similar to today's academic critique of *bushido* as an invented tradition:

> So modern a thing is it that neither Kaempfer, Sielbold, Satow, nor Rein—all men knowing their Japan by heart—ever once allude to it in their voluminous writings. The cause of their silence is not far to seek: Bushido was unknown until a decade or two ago.
> *The very word appears in no dictionary, native or foreign, before the year 1900.* Chivalrous individuals of course existed in Japan, as in all countries at every period; but Bushido, as an institution or a code of rules, has never existed. The accounts given of it have been fabricated out of whole cloth, chiefly for foreign consumption. (italics in original; quoted in Powles, 1995, 114)

The concept of *bushido* as articulated by Nitobe and other Japanese developed as a nostalgic discourse and borrowed much from the contemporary European ideals of chivalry and "gentlemanship." It represented a rediscovery of tradition, although an invented one, after a period of Westernization after the Meiji Restoration (1868). *Bushido* was used by nationalists, particularly in the 1930s and first half of the 1940s, to instill bravery and loyalty to the emperor and nation. Anthropologist Ruth Benedict wrote in her influential book *Chrysanthemum and the Sword* (1946) that *bushido* was a "publicist's inspiration" turned into a "slogan of the nationalist and militarists." It is still much discussed and written about by right-wing nationalists in Japan today.

See also: Budô shoshinshû (*The Way of the Warrior: A Primer*); Yamaga Sokô

Further Reading
Benesch, Oleg. *Inventing the Way of the Samurai: Nationalism, Internationalism, and Bushido in Modern Japan.* New York: Oxford University Press, 2014.

Hurst, G. Cameron, III. "Death, Honor, and Loyalty, the Bushidô Ideal." *Philosophy East and West,* 40(4) (1990), 511–527.

Powles, Cyril H. "Bushido: Its Admirers and Critics." In *Nitobe Inazô: Japan's Bridge Across the Pacific*, ed. John F. Howes, 107–118. Boulder: Westview Press, 1995.

C

Castle Abolishment Law (*haijôrei*) and the Reconstruction of Castles

After the Meiji Restoration, in 1873, the Meiji government adopted the Castle Abolishment Law (*haijôrei*), and by 1875 at least 100 of the 170 Edo-period castles had been dismantled or torn down. By the end of the nineteenth century, however, there was a resurgence of pride in native Japanese culture and a reevaluation of castles as positive symbols of the country's martial heritage. As a result, no additional castle keeps (donjons) were torn down after 1891. Moreover, from late in the Meiji period (1868–1912) through the end of World War II, the urban spaces where the former Edo-period castles stood gradually were taken over by the Japanese army as garrisons. Public sentiment arose in Osaka during the 1920s, calling for the transformation of Osaka castle into a castle park that would be open to the public. Although this was achieved only in 1931, additional reconstructions of castles were delayed until after the end of World War II. Today there are roughly sixty castles extant, or partially extant, across the country, with original or reconstructed castles, and whose grounds house a variety of public institutions.

In 1615, the Tokugawa shogunate issued the "one province, one-castle" decree (*ikkoku ichijô rei*), ordering the daimyo to destroy all castles in their domains other than the one where they were to reside. More than two centuries later, after the shogunate was overthrown, the leaders of the new Meiji government in 1873 ordered the abolishment of castles. The castles were placed under the jurisdiction of the finance ministry for "disposal" (*shobun*), as its officials saw fit. This meant that mostly they were either torn down or repurposed for use by the imperial army. Whenever possible, castle complexes that were dismantled were also recycled for other buildings, typically schools or administrative structures. As a result of the 1873 law, more than 150 castles were destroyed in the 1870s and 1880s; this included castles whose domains fought in the civil war of 1867–1868 (Boshin War) on the side of the Tokugawa (e.g., Aizu Wakamatsu), as well as those who fought to topple the shogunate (e.g., Chôshû). Today's most famous castle in Japan, Himeji, was slated to be pulled down, but the costs for disassembling the structure proved too costly and the plan was abandoned. The imperial army took over forty-three of the largest castles and set up garrisons in the biggest of them. Nagoya-jô (Nagoya Castle), the largest of the extant castles, was one of these; its keep was scheduled to be pulled down, too, but the German envoy Max Von Brandt, who was in Japan at the time, convinced the Japanese officers posted at Nagoya to abandon the plan.

From the late 1880s in Japan there was a resurgence of pride in Japanese culture and a move away from indiscriminate Westernization, across many sectors of society. Part of this movement included a gradual appreciation for Japanese castle

Photo of Hagi Castle remains, with stone walls, moat, and base for castle keep (in the center, background). Since Chôshû was one of the leading domains in the Meiji Restoration, it was one of the first to dismantle its castle keep, in 1874, as a demonstration of loyalty to the new Meiji government. More than 100 castle keeps across Japan were dismantled by 1875. (Photo by Constantine Vaporis)

architecture, and although castles were not officially protected until the 1930s, no castle keeps were torn down after 1891. Moreover, positive views of Japan's castle heritage were evident at a number of industrial and cultural expos that were held in different parts of Japan from the late Meiji period onward. As a result, twenty donjon survived into the twentieth century; their castle grounds were controlled by the military and largely inaccessible to the public. Thousands of troops were garrisoned in them, and the grounds of one castle, Osaka, was the site of the largest arms factory in Asia, employing some 60,000 workers. Despite this military use for Osaka Castle, civil society groups were able to negotiate with local government and military officials to build a permanent keep inside a new castle park that would be open to the public. This work was completed in 1931, with the keep built from steel-reinforced concrete in place of wood.

Since the Castle Abolishment Law, many more castles, including the largest of them, Nagoya, were destroyed by fires, earthquakes, and World War II. Today only twelve original castle main keeps remain: of this number, Matsumoto-jô (1596), Inuyama-jô (1601), Hikone-jô (1606), and Himeji-jô (1609) have all been designated National Treasures by the Japanese Ministry of Education and Culture (Monbushô); Maruoka-jô (1576), Matsue-jô (1611), Marugame-jô (1660), Uwajima-jô (1665),

Bitchu-Matsuyama-jô (1684), Hirosaki-jô (1810), and Matsuyama-jô (1854) have all been designated Important Cultural Properties.

The majority of castles have lost most of their original grounds and peripheral buildings, but with the above-mentioned reevaluation of these sites as of great historical and cultural value, many old castle main keeps, turrets, and castle gates were reconstructed. As mentioned, the first main keep to be reconstructed, of concrete, was Osaka-jô in 1931. Two others—Gujô Hachiman-jô (1933) and Iga Ueno-jô (1935)—followed soon thereafter, but the pace of reconstruction increased rapidly only after the postwar recovery, beginning with Toyama-jô and Kishiwada-jô in 1954.

Today, there are roughly forty-five reconstructed donjons, in addition to the twelve original ones. The reconstructed main keeps are generally made of concrete and have been reconstructed with various degrees of authenticity. Some castles, for which there exists no documentation, have been reconstructed using another castle as a model or in replication of some generic conception of the castle form. An example of the former is Otaki Castle (Chiba prefecture), which was modeled on Uwajima Castle (Ehime prefecture), while Fushimi Momoyama Castle (Kyoto) was based on a generic plan of a Japanese castle without reference to any specific historical donjon. Many of the reconstructed donjon serve as museums, housing artifacts related to the daimyo and the domain in which they were located, or, less commonly, museums of local history and culture.

The inner baileys of the castles "have been transformed into civic parks shaded by stands of pine and cherry trees, with gravel paths meandering among decorative stones, flower beds and ornamental bushes, and black or white swans gliding about the still waters of the castle moats" (Ehrentraut, 1995, 223). Other parts of the castle grounds have been put to a variety of uses, housing schools, public parks, museums, civic centers, Shinto shrines, state hospitals, municipal swimming pools, amusement parks, and even in one case (Odawara) a zoo.

See also: Boshin War; Castle Towns (*jôkamachi*); Castles (*jôkaku*)

Further Reading

Benesch, Oleg, and Zwigenberg, Ran. *Japan's Castles: Citadels of Modernity in War and Peace.* Cambridge: Cambridge University Press, 2019.

Ehrentraut, Adolf W. "Cultural Nationalism, Corporate Interests and the Production of Architectural Heritage in Japan." *Canadian Review of Sociology and Anthropology,* 32(2) (1995), 215–242.

Castle Towns (*jôkamachi*)

The administrative and economic center of a daimyo domain, castle towns were a distinctive and dominant urban form in Japan from the late sixteenth century until the end of the Tokugawa period in 1868. The antecedents of castle towns can be found during the Warring States period (1467–1568), when contending warlords (*sengoku daimyô*) built a wooden fortress on mountains or hilltops, from which they tried to secure control of the surrounding area through military force. In the sixteenth century they developed into urban settlements, as the daimyo's vassals and supporting troops were either persuaded or forced to take up residence around the lord's castle. Merchants and artisans were also encouraged to follow the samurai into the settlements to serve the needs of the growing market centered on the daimyo's retainers. During the Tokugawa period almost all of the largest urban settlements in Japan, with the notable exception of Kyoto, were castle towns. Although the shogunate was toppled from power in 1868 and the system of domains was abolished three years later, the former castle towns continued to exist thereafter and remained important urban centers. In fact, the majority of cities in Japan with populations of more than 100,000 today are former castle towns.

During the late Warring States period the most successful daimyo were able to convert their small defensive settlements into full-blown urban centers, centering on a castle complex, that served as military, administrative, and commercial headquarters for their domains. They did this through the enforced resettlement of their retainers (the so-called "separation of warrior and peasant," or *heinô bunri*), but also by moving their castles from mountain or hilltops to more strategic positions on the plains, near rivers, or the coast, from which they could better mobilize the area's resources. The further concentration of population and economic activity in the castle town was unintentionally promoted by the Tokugawa shogunate's "one castle, one province" (*ikkoku ichijô*) decree in 1615, by which all castles other than the one the daimyo was residing in were to be dismantled. Although some exceptions to the decree were allowed, it served to centralize administrative and commercial functions in the castle towns that stabilized between 200 and 250 in number.

In the late sixteenth and early seventeenth centuries the daimyo used their political authority to construct their castle towns as garrison cities and the military headquarters of their domains. Samurai quarters were grouped close to the castle, whose castle keep stood prominently as a symbol of the daimyo's authority. The urban layout around the castle reflected the status hierarchy, as lot size and the size of the residence, as well as proximity to the center (the castle and the daimyo), were directly related to a samurai's rank. Some samurai districts have been well preserved and can be seen today in cities such as Hagi (Chôshû domain, present-day Yamaguchi prefecture) and Kanazawa (Kaga domain, present-day Ishikawa prefecture).

The layout of the castle town reflected the military concerns of daimyo in the early seventeenth century, the country just having emerged from a century-long period of civil wars. The samurai district was an important line of defense, just like the castle. The roads of the castle town, particularly close to the center, would curve or bend intentionally at a right angle to confuse and bottleneck an attacking enemy. Buddhist temples, too, had a strategic function: they were often located beside roads leading into the castle town; their open spaces and surrounding walls could be utilized by the daimyo's military forces in times of emergency. An elaborate moat system served a defensive function for the daimyo and his retainers and also separated samurai and townsmen areas of the city. Unlike cities in China, the castle towns did not have walls enclosing the entire city.

Although the military function of the castle town figured prominently in the early phase of its development, with peacetime conditions other functions—administrative

Photo of a *masugata* (right-angle turn in the road) in the former Hagi castle town. They were constructed at different points in the castle town for defensive purposes, to bottleneck a potential invading force, and sometimes were gated. (Photo by Constantine Vaporis)

and commercial—assumed greater importance. In Kôchi (Tosa domain), for example, this is evident from the development of the townsmen areas of the castle town, which were grouped to the east and west of the samurai districts (the original city was constructed in the area between two rivers, the Enokuchi and Kagami). Leading merchants and artisans were encouraged to move here from the Yamauchi's previous domain in central Japan as well as the former lord Chôsogabe's castle town of Urado, which was located nearby. Merchants and artisans were motivated to move to Kôchi with land grants; and in some cases with stipends, the right to an audience with the lord, and a degree of authority over other merchants. A number of these merchants were given monopolies over the rights to make and sell certain products; for example, the Pak family, originally brought to Japan as captives from Toyotomi Hideyoshi's invasion of Korea in the 1590s, were granted a ward, Tôjin-machi ("foreigner's ward"), to administer and a monopoly on the rights to manufacture and sell tofu in the castle town. Other merchants were similarly organized into protected occupational wards, organized according to occupation, skill or art—for example, paper merchants ward, blacksmiths ward, and sake brewers ward. Property taxes in townsmen areas were based on the width of road frontage, so the tendency was for artisans and merchants to build narrow street-facing buildings that doubled as home and shop.

Although there were various types of urban communities in Japan, including the imperial capital of Kyoto—commercial towns developed around temples and shrines, market towns, and post stations—the castle town was the most important urban center in Tokugawa Japan. As a result of the policies that daimyo pursued to centralize political and economic functions in the castle towns, Japan in 1700 was one of the most urbanized countries in the world. Five to seven percent of the Japanese population at that time lived in cities of more than 100,000 (and all but one of these, Kyoto, were castle towns), while only 2 percent did so in Europe.

The population of castle towns varied considerably, but as a general rule, however, about 10 percent of a domain's population lived in the castle town. In the early 1700s Kanazawa and Nagoya had populations in excess of 100,000 each, rivaling in size the European cities of Rome, Amsterdam, Madrid, and Milan. These two Japanese cities were part of two of the largest domains: Kanazawa, part of Kaga domain (with an official listed productive capacity of one million *koku*) and Nagoya (with a *kokudaka* of almost 620,000 *koku*). Smaller domains had correspondingly smaller castle towns. The castle town of Tosa domain (with a *kokudaka* of 202,626 *koku*), Kōchi, had approximately 22,000 residents in the mid-seventeenth century: 17,054 townspeople and an estimated 5,000 samurai (formal census data were gathered from commoners but not from the samurai). Other examples of castle town populations (commoners only), from 1714, include: Hiroshima (37,155), Hakata (19,468), Karatsu (3,972), Kokura (18,065), Morioka (14,797), Akita (21,313), Matsumoto (9,578), Hikone (7,814), and Okayama (30,296; figure from 1721). Although also castle towns, Edo (population of one million in 1731) and Osaka (roughly 500,000 in the early eighteenth century) were outliers, as Edo was not just the administrative center of the shogunate, but also in a sense the capital of Tokugawa Japan, due to the forced migrations of the daimyo to the city on alternate attendance. Osaka, on the other hand, was a national commercial center.

One of the distinctive features of Tokugawa Japan's castle towns was the large number of samurai residing there, a result of daimyo policies spanning from the late sixteenth to the mid-seventeenth centuries to separate warrior and peasant. As a result, on average samurai accounted for roughly one-half of the castle town's entire population. In outlying regions of Japan the percentage was often higher. In Sendai, for example, statistics from the 1872, after the end of the Tokugawa period, reveal that the former samurai comprised 29,000 of the 50,000 total urban population (58 percent). In Tottori 25,000 (71 percent) of the 35,000 total population in 1810 were samurai. Edo had as many as 500,000 samurai in the mid-eighteenth century, roughly one-half of its total urban population there. In contrast, Osaka had a much smaller percentage of samurai: only 10,000 in contrast with the 400,000 townsmen that resided there in the eighteenth century.

Urban growth in castle towns was intense during the period from the late sixteenth century through the first half of the seventeenth century. The original seven townsmen wards planned in Kōchi, for example, had risen to twenty-five by the 1640s and twenty-eight in 1665. However, by the early eighteenth century most castle towns reached their peak in populations, as population growth shifted to outlying areas, including smaller "rural towns." To a certain extent this was because urban growth shifted to the territory outside the original administrative city borders—what today we would refer to as "urban sprawl." The castle town remained important, however, as a center of consumption focus on the daimyo and his retainers; merchants and others who moved to the outlying regions around the castle towns likely did so to escape castle town controls and restrictions. Large numbers of retainer households may also have moved to these outlying villages, as evidence from Kôchi suggests.

See also: Castles (*jôkaku*); Daimyo and Domains; Samurai Residences (*buke yashiki*); Separation of Warrior and Peasant (*heinô bunri*); Yamauchi Katsutoyo

Further Reading

Hall, John W. "The Castle Town and Japan's Modern Urbanization." In John W. Hall and Marius B. Jansen, eds., *Studies in the Institutional History of Early Modern Japan*, 169–188. Princeton, NJ: Princeton University Press, 1968.

McClain, James L. *Kanazawa: A Seventeenth-Century Castle Town*. New Haven, CT: Yale University Press.

Roberts, Luke S. *Mercantilism in a Japanese Domain: The Merchant Origins of Economic Nationalism in 18th-Century Tosa*. Cambridge: Cambridge University Press, 1998.

Smith, Thomas C. "Premodern Economic Growth: Japan and the West." *Past & Present*, 60 (1973), 127–160.

Castles (*jôkaku*)

There is evidence that local powers in Japan from dating back to prehistoric times (specifically, during the Yayoi period, 300 BCE–300 CE) sought to defend themselves by constructing defensive structures such as forts and surrounding them with moats. Before the sixteenth century, fortifications in Japan typically were made of earth and wood. During the Warring States period (1467–1568), there were an estimated 3,000 castles of varying sizes. These consisted of forts or castles built on hilltops, such as Takeda Castle in Hyôgo prefecture (made famous by Hayao Miyazaki's film *Castle in the Sky*), but also several temple towns that were surrounded by a moat. The introduction of firearms in the mid-sixteenth century, likely from European and Chinese sources, impacted castle construction, and led to the construction of massive stone castles with towering wooden keeps (*tenshu*), or donjon, at the center. The height of castle construction occurred in the roughly half century spanning the end of the Warring States period and the beginning of the Tokugawa period, 1580–1630. Castles were meant to protect the lord, his retainers and their families, not the townspeople; the surrounding castle town was not encircled by stone walls. Ironically, these castles were constructed during the period when Japan transitioned from war to peace. Few of them ever saw conflict and were little more than symbols of power and authority.

THE EVOLUTION OF CASTLES PRIOR TO THE TOKUGAWA PERIOD

During the Warring States (*sengoku*) period, local military leaders (*sengoku daimyô*) seeking to control their territories built small "hilltop castles" (*yamajirô*). Typically, these were located on mountaintops or hilltops and were only used as strategic lookouts or as a last line of defense against an enemy; in other words, the lord or daimyo of the castle typically did not reside in the castle. In the case of the above-mentioned Takeda Castle, it was situated 354 meters above sea level, and during foggy weather today appears to float in the air.

As daimyo were able to unify larger amounts of territory, they moved their castles from mountain or hilltop locations down to lower hilly areas or at the foot of mountains. The most famous example of this type of castle, known as a "flatland mountain" castle (*hirayama-jô*), is Azuchi, located in present-day Ômi Hachiman City (Shiga prefecture). Built by Oda Nobunaga (1534–1582) over the course of three-and-a-half years, 1576–1579, Azuchi represented a revolution in the conception and design of the Japanese castle. It sat on a hilltop on the eastern banks of Lake Biwa (in Ômi Hachiman city, Shiga prefecture), a strategic location that allowed him significant control of traffic on overland routes and on the lake itself.

Azuchi Castle itself was meant to be a political statement of Nobunaga's authority. According to one authority, "Nobunaga's castle was the first major citadel to give priority to a grand display of personal power and glory. It announced a new era in which the lord's physical surroundings would become an integral part of his rulership, and interior decoration would reinforce statecraft" (Wheelwright, 1981, 87). The main keep, the first ever five-level tower, which had six interior stories, sat on the most extensive stone base theretofore constructed and rose 138 feet from the base to the roof ridge. The hill that the tower sat on itself rose 360 feet above Lake Biwa, meaning that the keep commanded quite a view of the surrounding area and likewise must have been an imposing structure from ground level. The first three floors contained audience halls, private residential chambers, offices, and a treasury, which made it more like a royal palace than just a military structure. Its residence function distinguished it from other castle keeps of its time as well as those constructed during the Edo period. The first three floors of the interior were constructed in the *shoin-zukuri* style (i.e., aristocratic mansion architecture), with a symmetrical arrangement of rooms around a central main structure. The center of the keep rose without a ceiling up to the level of the fifth floor, almost sixty-two feet from the ground. Jutting out into the open space on the third floor was a stage for theatrical performances, primarily Noh theater, leading some specialists to speculate that the design might reflect some European influence, possibly from the vaulted churches of Europe; Nobunaga maintained close relations with several Jesuit priests and would have been exposed to European culture through them. Others have argued that the design of rooms surrounding a central open vault resembled the fully developed *shoin-zukuri* style.

Azuchi Castle's interior walls, sliding doors, and partitions were covered in gold leaf and decorated by elegant paintings by renown artists of the Kano school of artists. The gold leaf not only added beauty but also helped to reflect light in the interior space of the keep. Furthermore, interior form was imbued with meaning: for example, the fifth floor of the keep was an octagon represented heaven while the quadrangular sixth floor represented the philosophies of Taoism and Confucianism. The castle did not long outlast its ruler and was burnt to the ground in the conflict between the forces of Nobunaga's second son and those of Akechi Mitsuhide (1528–1582), Nobunaga's vassal who turned traitor. Although short-lived, Azuchi Castle provided a model for the larger structures that were to follow. The importance of Azuchi Castle, together with Fushimi-Momoyama Castle, is evident from the fact that they lent their names to the cultural historical period known as Azuchi-Momoyama, spanning between 1573 and 1603/1615. The castles and the luxurious artwork painted onto gold leaf covered walls and sliding doors defined the period.

EARLY MODERN CASTLES

From the end of the Warring States through the early Tokugawa period, as daimyo authority and control over territory increased, they began to construct castles in open plains, known as "plains" or "flatland" castles (*hirashirô*) or on low hills overlooking a plain (*hirayama-jirô*); these, together, are known as the "early modern" (*kinsei*) type of castles. The daimyo also laid out the area around the castle for the construction of settlements, the castle towns. Toyotomi Hideyoshi's Osaka Castle (1583–1597), which was built on top of the ruins of the Jôdo shinshû (True Pure Land sect) temple complex, Ishiyama Honganji, is considered as the first example of such a flatland castle. For strategic purposes, some daimyo located their castles on the coast (Hagi Castle), or more commonly close to a river leading to the sea (as with Okayama and Matsuyama Castles). Many of the castles constructed by the daimyo

Photo of the donjon of Matsue Castle, known as the "black castle," located in Matsue (Shimane prefecture). Constructed in the early 17th century, it is one of the few original castles (not a reconstruction) in Japan today. (Photo by Constantine Vaporis)

acquired nicknames related to their appearance. Matsue Castle, completed in 1611, was covered in black lacquer, earning it the name "Black Castle." Himeji Castle, completed in 1609, was known as the "White Heron Castle" due to its graceful, curving gables and the white fire-proofing plaster that covered its exterior.

Early modern castles were created with stone walls and earthen rampart walled foundations, over which were erected wooden superstructures. One of the notable characteristics of the castles of this time is the different materials used to construct the foundations and the structures. In contrast, in Europe often stone or brick were utilized for the entire structure. Stone was used in Japan for the foundations, but because the country is earthquake prone, mortar was not used; a variety of construction techniques (e.g., discontinuous horizontal joints) were utilized for the stone walls to absorb movement when earthquakes did occur. Stone superstructures also were not necessary because while matchlock guns, bows, spears, and swords were weapons commonly used in battle, cannons were rarely utilized.

The number of castles across Japan was sharply reduced after the summer campaign of the Sieges of Osaka Castle in 1614–1615, when the Tokugawa shogunate issued its "one castle, one province" (*ikkoku ichijô*) law. This decree limited each daimyo, in principle, to one castle. Chôshû domain, for example, which spanned two provinces, under these regulations was permitted only one castle. The daimyo, Môri Terumoto (1553–1625), after consultation with Tokugawa officials, decided in 1604 to construct a new castle at Hagi, on the coast of the Sea of Japan, rather than in Hôfu or Yamaguchi, two other sites that were under consideration. In large domains, particularly those that spanned more than one province, the daimyo

---

Himeji Castle

Known as the "White Heron Castle" (*shirasagi-jô*) due to its white plastered main tower complex and upturned gables, Himeji has the most remaining original structures of any castle in Japan. The main castle keep, the surrounding sub-keeps (*kotenshu*), and corridor-like tower (*watari-yaguya*) are National Treasures, and seventy-four other structures are registered as National Important Cultural Properties. In 1993, Himeji Castle and Hôryûji Temple (in Nara) became the first of Japan's World Heritage Sites.

A castle was constructed on the site by Toyotomi Hideyoshi in 1581, but the present complex, much expanded from the original one, dates from 1601 to 1609. It became the castle of Tokugawa Ieyasu's son-in-law, Ikeda Terumasa (1564–1613). It is a classic example of a flat-plains castle (*hirayama-jô*) and has the largest original Edo-period keep, standing 31.5 meters high, on top of a 14.8-meter high stone base.

Long shots of the castle often appear in period films set in the Tokugawa period. Himeji was also a setting, a ninja-training headquarters, in the 1967 James Bond film *You Only Live Twice*.

The castle reopened in 2015 after undergoing a major renovation for five-and-a-half years that cost 2.4 billion yen. Its white plastered walls were cleaned to counter the effects of dirt, grime, and general air pollution. As a result, some web-based commentators, playing on words, remarked that the *shirasagi* (White-Heron) castle was now *shirosugi* (too white). It is the most visited castle in Japan, receiving almost three million domestic and foreign visitors in 2015.

Himeji (known as the White Heron) Castle in Himeji (Hyôgo prefecture), with the main castle keep at center and sub-keep visible to its left. Designated Japan's first World Heritage Site in 1993, it has the largest original Edo-period keep in Japan. This photo was taken in 2017, after the completion of a major renovation project. (Photo by Constantine Vaporis)

selected one castle to retain as the domain's administrative headquarters and dismantled the others. In some cases, the dismantling simply meant tearing down the central turret, or donjon. Most but not all of the domains complied with the Tokugawa's orders. The Maeda family of Kaga domain, for example, maintained at least six castles in operation through 1638. However, when the daimyo Maeda Toshitsune ordered some repairs made to Kanazawa Castle in 1631, the Tokugawa interpreted this as a hostile act, bringing the domain to the brink of war with the Tokugawa. Fortunately, negotiations followed and the dispute was resolved. The powerful Shimazu daimyo, whose Satsuma domain was located at a distance from Edo, in the southern part of Kyushu, was able to defy the Tokugawa orders by maintaining a dense network of castles (called *tojô*), which allowed them to maintain tight control over their population. Similarly, the Satake (Kubota or Akita domain, in present-day Akita prefecture) were able to maintain three castles, the main one at Kubota but also at Yokote and Ôdate. Despite exceptions, as a result of the one-castle, one-province decree, the Tokugawa were able to reduce the number of castles across the country, with approximately 170 in existence during the remainder of the Tokugawa period.

As the national hegemon, the shogun had the authority to order the daimyo to contribute to the construction of castles in the Tokugawa's domain (the house lands). Most notably, this was the case with Edo Castle, to which the daimyo were ordered to contribute manpower and material after Ieyasu became shogun in 1603. This represented a further expansion of the castle begun in 1590 at Edo, after Tokugawa Ieyasu (1543–1616) had been awarded the Kanto region as a fief by Toyotomi Hideyoshi. The castle stood on the site of a castle established in 1457 by Ôta Dôkan (1432–1486). Under Ieyasu the white-walled castle keep was built to a height of 48 meters, but his two sons Hidetada (1579–1632) and Iemitsu (1604–1651) each rebuilt it higher. Under Iemitsu the now black copper-plated keep stood 51 meters high. A major fire destroyed it soon thereafter, in 1657, and it was never rebuilt. Nevertheless, the castle remained the largest not only in Japan but in the world; its outline matches that of the modern-day central Chiyoda ward of Tokyo.

Osaka-jô was also part of the Tokugawa network of castles. It was reconstructed by the Tokugawa shogunate, with the assistance of many daimyo, after it had burned down during the summer Siege of Osaka in 1615. The castle was built over the remains of the castle constructed by Toyotomi Hideyoshi, as if to wipe out his memory. Over a period of more than a decade, in excess of sixty daimyo from northeast and western Japan were ordered to contribute to the work of building the moats and stone walls. The order may be interpreted as punitive in character in a sense, since these daimyo had received Hideyoshi's patronage. More than an estimated one million stones were used in the construction of the castle. Archaeological evidence has been found of numerous sites across Japan, including numerous islands in the Inland Sea, where stone was quarried by daimyo to fulfill their assigned quotas for the construction of Osaka Castle.

With the castle of the Toyotomi buried deep in the ground by the Tokugawa, the Osaka Castle, reconstructed by order of the second shogun Hidetada (1579–1632) after the Siege of Osaka, was built 1.5 times larger. Its foundation stood at an elevation of 32.8 meters, and the white plastered castle keep rose up approximately 58 meters up from its stone base, making it the second largest keep in the country, after Edo, at the time of its construction.

Not all castles during the Tokugawa period had central keeps or donjon (*tenshu*)—at least not for their entire histories. Edo is perhaps the most famous such example. Although an impressive keep was constructed in 1607, it burned down in the great Meireki Fire, which destroyed over half of the city in 1657 and resulted in the death of about 100,000 people. Due to the pressing need to rebuild the city and to assist large numbers of city dwellers in need, not to mention the lack of easy availability of sufficient supplies of wood, the decision was made not to reconstruct the keep. Given the climate of peace that pervaded Japan by this date, the decision was made in the inner councils of the shogunate not to spend precious resources rebuilding what had become largely a "symbol tower" rather than a military necessity. Osaka Castle's keep also burned down, in 1665, and was not rebuilt during the Tokugawa period (a ferro-concrete version was built in 1931). Nijô Castle, constructed early in the seventeenth century for the shogun, while visiting Kyoto, and his representative in the city, the Kyôto shoshidai, originally featured a five-story donjon but was not rebuilt after it burned down in 1750 due to a fire caused by a lightning strike. From Nijô the Tokugawa could keep watch over the emperor, who resided in the imperial palace. In the early seventeenth century, Nijô Castle served as an important base for the Tokugawa shogunate in western Japan, particularly while Toyotomi Hideyori was still alive and occupying Osaka Castle.

Although far less well known than Edo or Nijô, Akô is another example of a donjon-less castle—one without a castle keep for its entire history. There had been a number of castles on this site since the fifteenth century, but when Asano Naganao, the grandfather of Asano Naganori of Chûshingura fame, received Akô as a domain, he began building a new castle on the site. Unlike many castles in Japan, Akô's was built by the sea and was designed as a flatland fortress (*hirayamajô*). At the time of its construction, which was completed in 1628, it was possible to set sail from docks located on the castle grounds. A stone base was constructed for the main tower, which was planned to be five stories in height, but the shogunate did not give permission for its construction. Another distinguishing feature of Akô Castle is its shape. It has sharply angled walls, with many corners, like the Goryokaku fort at Hakodate (constructed 1857–1864), which increased its defensive capabilities. Castle gates were constructed in two layers, which meant that once a person passed through a small gate he found his way blocked by a bigger watchtower gate.

COMPOSITION OF THE CASTLE COMPLEX: THE CASE OF HIMEJI CASTLE

As the best preserved of the twelve original castles that remain today, Himeji serves as a good prototype for examining the composition of a Tokugawa-era castle. Located in Hyôgo prefecture, Himeji was situated at the top of a 45.6-meter-high hill called Himeyama. The main keep stands 31.5 meters high and consists of seven floors, although only six are visible from the outside (the first or ground floor was contained within the stone foundation). Structurally, Himeji, like Kumamoto or Inuyama Castles, is known as a "lookout tower type" (*borogata*) of keep: that is, an irregularly shaped stone foundation on top of which stand a one- or two-story-based building, with a gable-and-hip style roof and a two- or three-story watchtower on top of that. (The other type of structure is a multileveled tower type, or *sotogata*, of which Matsumoto and Hirosaki are examples; this type of keep has a foundation that is nearly square and above which each level is the same shape but slightly smaller than the previous.)

In some castles the main keep stood alone or was directly connected to a smaller tower, but in Himeji the main keep was part of a complex. This network consisted of a large tower keep (*daitenshu*), connected by a corridor-like tower (*watari-yagura*) to the western sub-tower keep (*nishi kotenshu*), the northwest sub-tower (*inui kotenshu*), and the eastern sub-tower keep (*higashi kotenshu*). This combination creates a box-like configuration surrounding a central courtyard. The main keep contained a main hall for receiving visitors, officers for the lord's administrative staff, a watchtower, weapons storage area, kitchens and food stores, and small enclosed rooms where defenders could hide themselves and surprise an enemy entering the keep. The third and fourth floors have platforms from which stones and other objects could be thrown at attackers. The top floor features *shoin*-style architecture, which is an indication of the formality of the keep, and a panoramic view of the surrounding area.

Although the keep occupied the highest ground and served as the symbolic center of a Japanese castle of the Tokugawa period, it was only one part of an elaborate network of walls, moats, gates, and buildings. Himeji Castle, for example, was surrounded by an outer moat (*sotobori*) of 11.5 kilometers, a central moat (*nakabori*), and an inner moat (*uchibori*). Visitors to Japan who alight at Japan Railway's Himeji Station will be standing where the outer moat and main gate once were.

The castle complex was designed to foil an invading force. Moving from the outer moat to the keep required passing through nineteen fortified gates, along a maze-like layout meant to confuse and confine any enemy. There are also switchbacks, zigzags, sudden descents, and dead ends—all meant for the same purposes. At times you appear to be moving toward the keep, but this is only an ingenious optical trick, and in fact you are moving in the opposite direction, away from it. There is even a passageway through which an invading force would be required to pass; once the attackers were in this confined space, the defended above could remove hidden panels and thrust downward with their weapons. At the end of this labyrinth-like route stood the four linked keeps (described above), from which the approaching enemy could be observed and attacked via many windows and special openings, through which guns could be fired or rocks could be dropped (the former known as *teppô-zama* and the latter *ishi-otoshi*). In addition, water-filled moats were located at various points in the castle complex to deter invaders. The curvature and steep gradient of the stone foundations of the keep were yet another deterrent to the enemy, should they be able to proceed that far. Of course, Himeji was completed near the end of the period of castle building (roughly 1568–1615) and never actually experienced a military assault during the entire Tokugawa period.

The inner moat contained a series of three enclosures. The keep complex was contained within the innermost of the three, known as *honmaru* (main enclosure or bailey), with the main keep at the center of this first enclosure, at the highest point in the castle grounds. Typically, two additional enclosures—the *ninomaru* (second bailey) and *sannomaru* (third bailey) spiraled outward from the center. Each of the baileys was protected by a series of entranceways and gates refered to as the "tiger's mouth" (*koguchi*), the purpose of which was to ensure that the passage of an enemy through the castle complex was not straight. To enter the bailey the enemy had to pass through what is a box-like enclosure: two gates, at right angles, connected by stone walls that formed a square. Should the enemy breach the first gate they would enter a courtyard surrounded by high walls forming a box around them. They would also face at a right angle a larger, stronger wall-gate, from which defensive fire from guns or arrows could be directed down on the enemy, trapped in the courtyard.

In terms of function, the daimyo's official business was conducted in the first enclosure or bailey, while the family residences were located in the secondary ones. At Himeji, the lord's residences, or *goten* (sometimes referred to as the "palace"), and most of the other wooden buildings of the inner bailey, do not remain; as elsewhere these were torn down during the Meiji period although in some other cases they burned down during the Pacific War. The *goten* was divided into two separate spaces: a private residence (*oku*), which contained the lord's official living quarters, a private area for the lord's immediate family that was off limits to men besides the lord himself; and an area for official duties (*omote*). The official space consisted of audience chambers, meeting rooms, and domain administrative audiences.

ORIGINAL CASTLE KEEPS

Twelve castle keeps in Japan today are considered originals. The first five (shown in Table 1) are considered National Treasures; the remaining seven keeps have been designated Important Cultural Properties.

See also: Castle Abolishment Law (*haijôrei*) and the Reconstruction of Castles; Castle Towns (*jôkamachi*); Firearms; *Laws for the Military Houses* (*buke shohatto*); Nijô Castle (*Nijô-jô*); Oda Nobunaga; Sieges of Osaka (*Ôsaka no jin*); Toyotomi Hideyoshi

Further Reading

Gerhart, Karen M. *The Eyes of Power. Art and Early Tokugawa Authority.* Honolulu: University of Hawai'i Press, 2000.

Mitchelhill, Jennifer. *Castles of the Samurai. Power and Beauty.* Tokyo, New York, London: Kodansha International, 2003.

Motoo, Hinago. *Japanese Castles.* Tokyo: Kodansha, 1986.

Schmorleitz, Morton S. *Castles in Japan.* Tokyo: Charles E. Tuttle, 1974.

Wheelright, Carolyn. "A Visualization of Eitoku's Lost Paintings at Azuchi Castle." In George Elison and Bardwell L. Smith, *Warlords, Artists, & Commoners: Japan in the Sixteenth Century*, 87–111. Honolulu: University of Hawai'i Press, 1981.

Table 1   Original Castle Keeps

	Name of Castle	**Location**	**Construction Year/Period**	**Height (meters)**
1	Himeji	Himeji city, Hyôgo pref.	1608	31.49
2	Inuyama	Inuyama city, Aichi pref.	1601	18.16
3	Hikone	Hikone city, Shiga pref.	1606	15.53
4	Matsumoto	Matsumoto city, Nagano pref.	1615	25.25
5	Matsue	Matsue city, Tottori pref.	1611	22.43
6	Maruoka	Sakai city, Fukui pref.	1576	12.53
7	Kôchi	Kôchi city, Kôchi pref.	1747	18.60
8	Uwajima	Uwajima city, Ehime pref.	1664–1665	15.34
9	Matsuyama	Matsuyama city, Ehime pref.	1804–1859	16.10
10	Hirosaki	Hirosaki city, Aomori pref.	1810	14.46
11	Bitchû Matsuyama	Takahashi city, Okayama pref.	1681–1683	10.91
12	Marugame	Marugame city, Kagawa pref.	1643–1660	14.66

Source: Jcastle. Guide to Japanese Castles. http://jcastle.info/view/Home. Accessed July 1, 2018.

Can You Own a Castle in Japan?

In Europe there are many historic castles that can be purchased to live in, or rented, but what about in Japan? The short answer is—probably not. Most castles in Japan are owned by the national or local governments. Himeji Castle, for example, is owned by the national government while Osaka Castle is owned by Osaka city. However, there have been a small number of castles that were or are privately owned. Inuyama Castle (located in Inuyama city) is one example. In 2004 it was the only privately held castle, owned by the Naruse family. In that year the owners decided to donate the property to a charitable organization. Nakatsu Castle (in Oita prefecture), the headquarters of the domain of the samurai Fukuzawa Yukichi (1835–1901), remained in the hands of a company run by the descendants of the Okudaira daimyo family until 2010, when they sold the castle (but not the land) to a Saitama prefecture-based company.

Despite the difficulty of owning a real castle, it may be possible to purchase a replica, given sufficient funding. For example, a replica of a castle in the outskirts of Matsuyama city (Ehime prefecture), built in the 1980s, was up for auction in 2016. However, the property, a former love hotel designed in the form of an Edo-period castle, failed to generate much interest despite the minimum bid of 39,240,000 yen (approximately $370,000 U.S. dollars). Another replica, in Hokkaido, used as a doll museum, also went up for public auction in 2011, but similarly failed to sell.

Websites

Hyôgo International Tourism Guide. "Akôjô ato [The Ruins of Ako Castle]." http://www.hyogo-tourism.jp/English/castle_town. Accessed May 2, 2017.

"J Castle. Guide to Japanese Castles." http://jcastle.info.Accessed December 23, 2017.

"Osaka Castle Wall Stone Quarry Remains." http://archaeology.jp/sites/2011/ishikiri.htm. Accessed May 5, 2017.

"UNESCO World Heritage Site Nijo Castle (Nijo-jo)." https://www2.city.kyoto.lg.jp/bunshi/nijojo/english/index.html. Accessed May 5, 2017.

Chûshingura (Treasury of the Loyal Retainers)

Chûshingura refers to the historical events surrounding the actions of forty-seven *rônin*, or masterless samurai, of Akô domain to avenge the death of their lord, the daimyo Asano Takumi-no-kami Naganori. The story, which took place between 1701 and 1703, has been retold countless times since then. Most often the term *Chûshingura* refers to fictionalized accounts of the historical event, as depicted in literature, theater, film, and the arts. Accordingly, the term is an anachronism, since it first appeared only in 1748, in the title of the puppet play *Kanadehon Chûshingura*. Nevertheless, *Chûshingura* has proved to be one of the most enduring mytho-historical accounts in Japanese history. Its enduring popularity is widely regarded as due to the story's role in reinforcing Japanese values of loyalty and self-sacrifice and its treatment of the conflict between duty (*giri*) and human emotion (*ninjô*).

The basic outline of the historical events surrounding the forty-seven *rônin* is straightforward. The incident at the beginning of the story took place on April 21, 1701, when Lord Asano Naganori was placed in charge of a reception of imperial envoys from Kyoto at the Edo palace of the fifth shogun, Tokugawa Tsunayoshi. He was to be instructed in his duties by the shogun's protocol officer, Kira Kôzuke-no-suke Yoshinaka. For reasons that remain unclear, on the day of the ceremony, Asano drew his sword and attempted to kill Kira. However, he was successful only in wounding him only slightly on the shoulder and forehead before Asano was restrained. For the crime of drawing his sword in the shogun's palace, Asano was ordered to commit *seppuku* (ritual suicide) the same day, while Kira was not punished. Furthermore, the shogunate confiscated Asano's domain, which made all of the members of his retainer band masterless samurai. Twenty-two months later, in 1703, Ôishi Kuranosuke, the top official who had been in charge in Akô during the lord's absence in Edo, together with a group of forty-six other retainers, carried out their plot to avenge their lord. As a result, Kira's residence was raided and he was beheaded on the spot. The men then marched through Edo, presented Kira's head at the grave of their lord, and later turned themselves in the shogunal authorities. Some political commentators were critical of them for not immediately committing *seppuku*, since they had achieved their revenge, suggesting that they were hoping to benefit from their act of loyalty. After a month and a half of deliberation, Tokugawa officials sentenced the forty-six to commit *seppuku*, for the crimes of conspiracy and disturbing the peace of Edo. They all carried out the sentence on the same day (February 4) in 1703. The *rônin* were granted the honor of burial in the same graveyard as their lord, at Sengakuji temple.

Perhaps the most popular fictionalized account of *Chûshingura* is the story *Kanadehon Chûshingura*, which has been told in kabuki and bunraku (puppet) theater, stage plays, films, novels, and various other media. The title means the "*Kana* Practice Book Treasury of the Loyal Retainers" and refers to the fact that the number of *rônin* matched the number of characters in the *kana* syllabary, 47. The titles thus liken the *rônin* to a warehouse full of treasure.

The first fictional incarnation of the story was a play written for the bunraku theater. It was authored by Takeda Izumo (1691–1756), Miyoshi Shôraku (c. 1696–1772), and Namiki Senryû (c. 1695–1751) and was first performed in 1748 at the

---

Ôishi Shrine (Ôishi jinja)

Standing within the grounds of the Akô Castle site is Ôishi Shrine (located in Akô city, Hyôgo prefecture). It was established to enshrine the spirits of the forty-seven *rônin*or masterless samurai who avenged their lord, Asano Naganori, by killing the man they held responsible for his death, Kira Kôzunosuke. Their bodies, of course, were buried in Edo at Sengakuji temple. The approach to Ôishi Shrine is lined in two parallel columns with stone statues of the forty-seven, facing each other, armed and in full battle gear, as if they were about to attack Kira's mansion in Edo in 1703. Ôishi occupies a place of honor at the end closest to the shrine's main precinct. A small museum on the grounds contains many historical artifacts related to the forty-seven as well as to the Asano daimyo family.

Images of the shrine are available on its official, Japanese-language website (http://www.ako-ooishijinjya.or.jp, accessed April 30, 2017). An embedded Google map of the shrine allows you to follow the statue-lined path to the shrine.

Woodblock print from the first half of the 19th century depicting a scene from Act 11 of the kabuki play *Chûshingura*. The print shows a portion of the group of 47 *rônin* beginning the attack on Lord Kira Yoshinaka's residence, an attack that would end in his death and beheading. *Chûshingura* has remained a popular story in the theater and the arts since the Edo period. (Library of Congress)

Takemoto-za theater in Osaka. A kabuki adaptation of the play appeared later that year. The play is performed every year in both the bunraku and kabuki theaters, usually at the end of the year, in commemoration of the time when the actual revenge took place, and remains a perennial favorite. Due to its great length, typically only some select acts are performed.

Given the Tokugawa prohibition on any public discourse related to contemporary politics, in the early eighteenth century the story had to be "disguised" to avoid censorship. As a result, the historical account had to be fictionalized by setting it in an earlier time, the Muromachi period (1333–1568), and by changing the names of the principal characters, though only slightly so in some cases. Not many people would have failed to recognize, for example, that the character Ôboshi Yuranosuke in the theatrical forms of the story was none other than the historical Ôishi Kuranosuke. In other cases the names were less obvious—for example, Kô no Moronao is Kira and Enya Hangan is Asano—but became clear through identification with the historical characters.

The play necessarily adds much fictional detail and numerous fictional subplots to create a compelling drama with characters that are capable of moving the emotions of the audience. Although interpretation of the character and behavior of the two principal historical actors, Asano and Kira, has been much debated, in the play, Enya (Asano) is a sympathetic character who is goaded by Moronao (Kira) into drawing his sword. The audience also gets to witness Enya's *seppuku* ceremony and to hear him call out to his chief retainer Yuranosuke that he wants to be avenged for his wrongful death. During the course of the play Yuranosuke seems to devolve into a life of drunken debauchery, even breaking with a taboo not to partake of animal flesh on the death anniversary of his lord, but he and the other retainers together make careful preparations to attack Moronao's residence and kill him.

Chûshingura-themed productions also regularly appear in film and on television. In fact, the story of the forty-seven *rônin* has been a staple of period films in

Japan, making it to the screen more than 140 times. Two of the classic filmic versions of the story are Mizoguchi Kenji's (1898–1956) two-part black-and-white epic *Genroku Chûshingura* (*The Forty-Seven Rônin of the Genroku Era*), which is based on the play by Mayama Seika (1878–1948). Commissioned by the Japanese military, the films were made in 1941–1942, at the beginning of the Pacific War, and thematically were in line with the 1939 Film Law's stipulation that films were to elevate national consciousness. Accordingly, this version draws attention away from the dramatic attack on Lord Kira's mansion—in fact, this is not even depicted. Rather, it emphasizes the sacrifice of the forty-seven *rônin*, not to mention their submission to the state's authority, by focusing on their ritual suicide. In general, other *Chûshingura*-themed films such as the second classic, Inagaki Hiroshi's visually stunning color production *Chûshingura* (*Chushingura: The Loyal Forty-Seven Samurai,* 1962), end with the *rônin* marching triumphantly through the streets of Edo with the severed head of Kira on their way to deliver it to their lord's grave. Although Mizoguchi's film begins with Asano's attack on Kira, giving the viewer no context for the conflict, Inagaki's version goes to great lengths to make the view empathize with Asano by presenting him as an honorable, morally upstanding leader, while Kira is depicted as a lecherous, corrupt, and greedy villain. This portrayal of the two characters serves to rationalize for the viewer Asano's action in drawing his sword and the righteousness of his retainers in seeking to avenge his death. Asano is seen as having forfeited his life, and the well-being of his retainers, in order to protect his name and honor. In a way, this telling of the story obscures the nature of samurai loyalty during the Tokugawa period, which was unconditional. A samurai retainer could not change lords if he did not respect or like him. Loyalty to the daimyo was required, regardless of who he was. This was a type of loyalty to a symbol, the occupant of the position of the daimyo, regardless of his personal merits. But for film and theatergoers, a story with an unsympathetic lord Asano would make for a far less rewarding revenge and a less compelling drama.

Chûshingura has also appeared numerous times as television drama. Three separate NHK Taiga Drama series, each a year long, have taken up the story. The third of these, *Tôge no gunzô* (*Figures on the Mountain Pass,* 1982) starring Ogata Ken as Ôishi Kuranosuke and the renowned director Itami Juzo as Kira, offered a psychological explanation for Asano's attack, depicting him as having suffered from temporary insanity due to the taunting that Kira allegedly inflicted on Asano.

It can be argued that the story of *Chûshingura* has retained a hold on the national imagination for more than three centuries because in it many Japanese have seen a reaffirmation of native values. Westerners, too, since the late 19th century have seen much to praise in the forty-seven *rônins'* loyalty and dedication to their lord, but during World War II and its immediate aftermath it was seen in a negative light, as evidence of the fanaticism of the Japanese; in fact, during the occupation of Japan, the American authorities banned performances of the story until 1947.

See also: Akô Incident; *Bushido*

Further Reading

Keene, Donald, trans. *Chûshingura: The Treasury of Loyal Retainers*. New York: Columbia University Press, 1971.

The Disloyal Rônin?

Although the story of the forty-seven *rônin* is often heralded as evidence for the importance of the ideals of loyalty and honor among samurai, there are dissenting views as well. For example, popular manga artist Inoue Hisashi has parodied the forty-seven in his series *Treasury of Disloyal Retainers* (*Fuchûshingura*, May 1980–December 1984), which consists of nineteen portraits of retainers of Lord Asano's who did *not* participate in the revenge league. His humorous portraits work against the well-established mythologizing of the forty-seven and reveal that they, as real-life human beings, had various motivations in choosing whether to participate or not.

The writer Taketsuka Tôshi parodied the forty-seven in a different manner. In 1814, he created a story that was illustrated by the famous woodblock print artist Utagawa Kuniyoshi (1798–1861) entitled *Gobuji Chûshingura* (*The Chushingura with a Happy Ending*) in which all forty-seven lived long, happy lives.

Smith, Henry D., II. "The Capacity of Chûshingura." *Monumenta Nipponica*, 58(1) (Spring 2003), 1–42.

Smith, Henry D., II. "Chûshingura in the 1980s: Rethinking the Story of the Forty-Seven Rônin." In Kevin J. Wetmore, Jr., ed., *Revenge Drama in European Renaissance and Japanese Theatre: From Hamlet to Madame Butterfly*, 187–215. New York: Palgrave Macmillan, 2008.

Civil and Military Arts (*bunbu*)

In Tokugawa Japan a certain tension existed between the "twin ways" (*ryôdô*) of military training (*bu*, also known as the "arts of war" or "martial arts") and the "civil arts" (*bun*, also known as "the arts of peace" or "letters"), both of which were deemed as necessary for effective governance. This tension was intensified by the dual role required of samurai as military men *and* civil administrators. *Bun* ranged from basic literacy to advanced scholarship, while *bu* referred to a range of martial activities such as archery, swordsmanship, fencing, riding, wrestling, and even swimming, as well as military science and tactics.

The Japanese adopted the notion of *bun* and *bu* as complementary ideals necessary for effective rule from ancient Chinese thought. Mastery of literature and military skills were seen as important for those who served the imperial throne during the Heian period (794–1185). The term was also uitilized by warrior families during the Kamakura shogunate (1185–1333). At that time, *bunbu kyûba no michi* (the way of the civil and military arts, along with the way of the horse and bow) was a term commonly used for warriors' educational ideals. Although the need for military skills went without saying, the letters were also seen as an important tool of power. This was made clear in an early fifteenth-century document (letter) issued by the son of a military governor, Imagawa Ryôshun, who formally admonished his son, Nakaaki, "As you do not understand the Arts of Peace, your skill in the Arts of War will not, in the end, achieve victory" (Steenstrup, 1973, 295). A century later, an article from the law code of the Warring States daimyo Hôjô

Sôun (1432–1519) stated, "It is not necessary to write here about the 'Arts of Peace and War, including Archery and Horsemanship,' for to pursue these is a matter of course. From of old, the rule has been, 'Practice the Arts of Peace on the left hand, and the Arts of War on the right.' Mastery of both is required" (Steenstrup, 1974, 301).

The message conveyed in these various injunctions and codes found its way into the *Laws for the Military Houses,* first issued by Tokugawa Ieyasu in 1615 and then reissued periodically with minor modifications by his successors. In fact, the very first line of the Code in 1615 stated, "The study of literature and the practice of the military arts, including archery and horsemanship, must be cultivated diligently" (see Document 2). The annotation for this article, which was included in the *Laws,* stated: "Literature on the left, and martial arts on the right": this is an ancient law. Both must be cultivated at the same time. Archery and horsemanship are essential for the military houses. It is said that war is a curse but sometimes it is an unavoidable necessity. In times of peace do not forget that disturbances may arise. How can we not train ourselves for war? This message was further reinforced through the widespread use of the above-mentioned Imagawa letter as a primer for the education of the sons of samurai during the Tokugawa era.

Despite the message conveyed in the various laws about the balance between the twin ways, the primacy of the military arts did not readily give way. During the Warring States (1467–1568) and unification periods (1568–1600), *bu* remained the more highly valued skill set, for the obvious reason that it was necessary for self-preservation and was regularly tested on the battlefield. Only higher-ranking warriors were likely to have been literate, and the civil arts were viewed with suspicion in some quarters. This actually remained the case for much of the seventeenth century. Nakae Tôju (1608–1648) wrote that, "According to popular opinion, scholarship is a matter for bookish priests, or monks, and so forth and not an occupation for samurai. . . . If among the samurai someone pursues scholarship, he is, to the contrary, abused" (Bodart-Bailey, 2006, 15).

It was only gradually during then, that samurai, charged as they were with civil administration, came to give more priority to the development of the "arts of peace" and education. Still it became evident by the late seventeenth or early eighteenth century that a subtle shift had taken place. Part of this no doubt had to do with the basic fact that it became more difficult to maintain martial skills in a time of peace, and increasingly difficult to rationalize spending the time to try to do so, given the fact that for many retainers advancing their careers was dependent on administrative skills. As a result, martial skills deteriorated over time and drew the attention of contemporary observers and government officials at the highest reaches.

The eighth shogun, Tokugawa Yoshimune (1684–1751), the former daimyo of Kii domain who was adopted into the Tokugawa main line, sought to revitalize the martial arts, which he thought essential to raise the morale of samurai. He called for this as part of a broader program of social reform (the Kyôhô Reforms, 1716–1736). His various efforts in terms of the martial arts can be seen as part of program to "reassert a militarized masculinity" (Walthall, 2011, 41). Although the first three shoguns had understood the importance of both the martial and literary arts, their successors showed little or no interest.

Yûbikan martial arts training hall at the Meirinkan, Chôshû domain's official school for samurai. It contained practice halls for sword fighting and lance (with a pond behind it for training in swimming). It has been designated a national historic site by the Japanese government. Military training remained an important part of samurai identity throughout the Tokugawa period. (Photo by Constantine Vaporis)

In contrast, Yoshimune was a practitioner and patron of various martial arts, including hunting and falconry. He hunted throughout his career and revived the large-scale hunts that the first three shoguns had conducted. He and his entourage hunted quail and pheasant on horseback with bows on numerous occasions; on one occasion, in 1718, 3,000 peasants were employed as beaters to flush the animals out into the open. He also organized large-scale deer hunts; during those he organized east of Edo in 1725 and 1726, Yoshimune dressed himself in the style of the first Kamakura shogun, Minamoto no Yoritomo (shogun, 1192–1199). The eighth shogun was also quite adept at marksmanship and is known to have shot many boar, some of them in locales not far from the castle.

Not just an ardent practitioner of the martial arts himself, Yoshimune also encouraged their practice among the samurai as a whole. He ordered his officials to test the shogunal troops' gunnery skills and established prizes and bonuses for good performance. Occasionally, he would watch displays of marksmanship, make surprise inspections of the guns that guards were carrying at Edo Castle's gates, watch guard units ride horseback, and attend spear and sword matches at Edo Castle. He was, however, particularly keen on reestablishing the practice of mounted archery (*kyûba*); the formal performance of mounted archery at shrines was known as *yabusame* and is said to have ceased some time before the Tokugawa period, before Yoshimune reintroduced the ceremony.

Striking a balance between *bun* and *bu* remained difficult. Hinatsu Shigetaka, a samurai in service to the daimyo of Sasayama and the author of *Honchô bugei shôden* (1714), the oldest narrative survey of the marital arts in Tokugawa Japan, wrote that:

> The relationship between the cultural arts and the martial arts is like that between night and day or *yin* and *yang*. In heaven and earth, there cannot be a single day without the cultural [meaning *bun*, or the literary] and martial arts. Yet in the everyday world a person well versed in the cultural arts all too often knows nothing of the martial arts; conversely, if he is good at the martial arts, then he is poor in the cultural arts. (Hinatsu, 1990, 261)

As the author noted, most samurai tended to privilege one or the other, the literary or the martial arts. It was most likely upper samurai, meaning those of (*shi*) status, who had the time and financial resources available, that were best able to balance both arts. For example, Asahi Monzaemon Shigeaki (1674–1718), a retainer from Nagoya domain with a stipend of 100 *koku*, practiced several military arts, including sword fighting, sword drawing (*iai*), archery, and spearmanship (*sôjutsu*). On the literary side, he engaged in scholarship and wrote poetry, in both Chinese and Japanese. Mori Kanzaemon Yoshiki (1768–1807), a retainer of 200 *koku* from Tosa domain, similarly engaged in a number of military pursuits, including horsemanship, gunnery, horseback archery, and military tactics; in the cultural realm, he practiced the way of tea (*sadô*), the way of incense (*kôdô*), stone tray arrangement (*bonseki*). He also wrote poetry in Japanese and engaged in scholarship and studies' rites and comportment (*kojitsu*).

Yoshimune's grandson, Matsudaira Sadanobu (1759–1829), as the chief councilor (*rôjû*) of the shogunate and then shogunal regent, initiated a major reform movement at the end of the 18th century (Kansei Reforms, 1789–1801) to address a range of problems, including boosting samurai morale by encouraging frugality and focusing on their cultivation of both *bun* and *bu*. Sadanobu, too, idealized the rural origins of the samurai and even took his own retainers on excursions into the countryside. This program was pushed quite forcefully, one result of which was that it was satirized by a range of writers, including the low-ranking samurai and writer Ôta Nanpo (1749–1823).

Despite the best efforts of Tokugawa Yoshimune, Matsudaira Sadanobu, and others, the (relative) decline of martial skills was inevitable, given the peaceful conditions of the time. Even during Yoshimune's time, the author of *Hagakure*, Yamamoto Tsunetomo, wrote that the samurai of his day had lost interest in the "way of the warrior" and were concerned only with money, clothes, and women. Decrying the decline in swordsmanship, he wrote, "That there are few men who are able to cut well in beheadings [i.e., as *kaishaku*, or seconds, during seppuku rituals] is further proof that men's courage has waned. . . . [I]t has become an age of men who are prudent and clever at making excuses" (Yamamoto, 1979, 24), Echoing Yamamoto's remarks a century later the samurai Buyô Inshi, in 1816, wrote: "The military Way that was laid with great care at the start of Tokugawa rule is now 70 or 80 percent lost" (*Lust, Commerce, and Corruption*, 2014, 94). In the closing years of the shogunate, Chôshû samurai Takasugi Shinsaku (1839–1869) wrote that "the stipendiary samurai have become soft and indolent through yars of peace

Table 2   Selected List of Samurai Artists, Writers, and Tea Masters

Name	Life Dates	Status/Position	Skills
Furuta Oribe	1544–1615	Daimyo	Celebrated tea master, founder of Oribe school (Oribe *ryû*) of tea; instructor to Shogun Tokugawa Hidetada in tea matters
Hiraga Gennai	1728–1780	Takamatsu domain retainer, then *rônin*	Dutch scholar, Western-style painting, physician, inventor, author of *Hohi ron* (*A Theory of Farting*)
Kakizaki Hakyô	1764–1826	Matsumae domain councilor	Painter, famous for his portraits of Ainu leaders
Katagiri Sekishu	1605–1673	Shogunate official	Founder of Sekishu school of tea, the main school for samurai, including daimyo; teacher master to Shogun Tokugawa Ietsuna
Kobori Enshu	1579–1647	Daimyo	Tea master; garden designer; tea house designer; painter; poet; tea instructor for Shogun Tokugawa Iemitsu
Matsudaira Fumai	1751–1818	Daimyo (Matsue domain)	Famed tea master; compiled guide to famous textiles associated with tea ceremony; teahouse designer; Zen practitioner
Matsudaira Sadanobu	1759–1829	Daimyo; senior councilor of shogunate	Scholar; writer, including his memoirs (*Uge no hitokoto*) and a satirical piece *Daimyô katagi* (*Portrait of a Daimyo*)
Miyamoto Musashi	1584–1645	*Rônin*	Philosopher, writer, painter (ink monochrome)
Odano Naotake	1749–1780	Hachinohe domain retainer	Western-style painting
Ôta Nanpo	1749–1823	Tokugawa houseman	Poet, comic poetry (*kyôka*)
Ryûtei Tanehiko	1783–1842	Tokugawa bannerman	Comic novelist; wrote parody of *Tale of Genji*
Sakai Hôitsu	1761–1828	Son of daimyo of Himeji domain	*Rinpa* (decorative style) painting; wrote comic verse under the satirical pen-name: "Burnt Buttocks Monkey Man" (*Shiriyake sarundo*)
Satake Yoshiatsu (Shozan)	1748–1785	Daimyo of Akita	Western-style painting; founder of Akita ranga school
Satake Yoshimi	1749–1800	Castlelan of Hachinohe domain	Western-style painting (Akita ranga school)
Takebe Ayatari	1719–1774	Hirosaki retainer, then *rônin*	Literati (poetry, prose, painting)

Table 2   Selected List of Samurai Artists, Writers, and Tea Masters (continued)

Name	Life Dates	Status/Position	Skills
Takizawa (Kyokutei) Bakin	1767–1848	Gave up service to Matsudaira (shogunal retainer) family to become *rônin*	Wrote *gesaku* (comic) fiction
Watanabe Kazan	1793–1841	Domain councilor for Tahara domain	Literati (*bunjin*) artists, portraiture, landscape painting
Watanabe Shiko	1683–1755	*Rônin*	*Rinpa* (decorative style) painting

and idleness. Their martial prowess has been dulled . . ." (Quoted in Norman, 1943, 50).

Due to the decline in military skills, both real and perceived, a number of prominent figures late in the Tokugawa period sought to promote their revitalization. A sense of urgency in revitalizing the samurai's martial skills and strengthening the spirit was felt by samurai such as Chôshû's Yoshida Shôin (1830–1859) and Kumamoto domain's Yokoi Shônan (1809–1869), with the increasing intrusion of Western ships in Japanese waters in the nineteenth century, particularly after the forced opening of Japan in 1853. Together with Takasugi Shinsaku, Yokoi, writing in 1860, actually argued that trained peasants could make for a more effective fighting force than the "degenerate" samurai. Despite these criticisms of the samurai, many of them were still skilled combatants who were greatly feared by Westerners who came to Japan after 1854. There was indeed reason for this fear, as a number of Westerners met their deaths at the hands of samurai assasins.

Some samurai greatly prioritized *bun* over *bu* and gained reputations as scholars, writers, and artists. This was true of a number of daimyo, too. (A selected list of samurai artists, writers, and tea masters can be found in Table 2.) Moreover, some *rônin* were able to gain employment with a daimyo due to their special skills.

See also: Education; *Honchô Bugei Shôden* (*A Short Tale of Martial Arts in Our Country*); *Laws for the Military Houses* (*buke shohatto*); Tokugawa Yoshimune

Further Reading
Bodart-Bailey, Beatrice. *The Dog Shogun: The Personality and Policies of Tokugawa Tsunayoshi.* Honolulu: University of Hawai'i Press, 2006.

"Excerpts from Articles of Admonition by Imagawa Ryôshun to his son Nakaaki." http://afe.easia.columbia.edu/ps/japan/imagawa.pdf. Accessed October 13, 2016.

Hesselink, Reinier H. "The Warrior's Prayer: Tokugawa Yoshimune Revives the Yabusame Ceremony." *Journal of Martial Arts,* 4(4) (1995), 41–49.

Hinatsu, Shigetaka. "*Honchô bugei shôden.*" *Monumenta Nipponica,* 45(3) (1990), 261–284.

Lust, Commerce, and Corruption. An Account of What I Have Seen and Heard, by an Edo Samurai. Translated by Mark Teeuwen, Kate Wildman Nakai, et al. New York: Columbia University Press, 2014.

Norman, E. Herbert. *Soldier and Peasant in Japan: The Origins of Conscription.* New York: Institute of Pacific Relations, 1943.

Steenstrup, Carl. "The Imagawa Letter: A Muromachi Warrior's Code of Conduct Which Became a Tokugawa Schoolbook." *Monumenta Nipponica,* 28(3) (1973), 295–316.

Steenstrup, Carl. "Hôjô Sôun's Twenty-One Articles. The Code of Conduct of the Odawara Hôjô." *Monumenta Nipponica,* 29(3) (Autumn 1974), 283–303.

Walthall, Anne. "Do Guns Have Gender? Technology and Status in Early Modern Japan." In Sabine Fruhstuck and Anne Walthall, eds., *Recreating Japanese Men*, 25–45. Berkeley: University of California Press, 2011.

Yamamoto Tsunetomo. *Hagakure: The Book of the Samurai.* Translated by William Scott Wilson. New York: Avon Books, 1979.

Clothing

In Tokugawa Japan's status-based society, social identity was marked on the bodies of individuals in a number of ways. Walking down a street in a castle town of the time, it would have been easy to identify a samurai and to distinguish him from a male townsman (merchant or artisan) or a peasant farmer. A samurai's society identity was inscribed on his body in his distinctive hairstyle (*chonmage*), his two swords, his gait (a hip-forward posture and stride that was a function of wearing two swords through a waist sash worn on the left side). His identity was also marked by his clothing, including footwear. (Although armor might be considered a type of clothing, it is considered in a separate entry.)

Despite the diversity in clothing that was worn by members of the different status groups, one article of it that was common to all, male and female, was the *kosode*, or kimono, as it came to be known in the eighteenth century. The *kosode* cut across status and gender lines because it was an efficient form of clothing: easy to create (from rolls of cloth material) and adaptable to all body types. Typically, an undergarment made of cotton was worn underneath and often was dyed a color (since white easily soiled). The two garments were tied with a sash. For men, a loincloth (*fundoshi*) was also worn beneath the undergarment.

When a samurai went out of his residence into the streets of the castle town he would wear *hakama* (wide, ankle-length, flowing trousers that resemble a split skirt) and *haori* (a long-sleeved coat) over the *kosode*. In many domains clothing was coded by status. Aizu domain samurai Shiba Gorô (1859–1945) reported that each of the eleven ranks of samurai in his domain "were identifiable at a glance by the color of their clothes" (Shiba, 1999, 34). Of course, his two swords would have been thrust into his waist sash, on the left side, before setting foot outside. For footwear, he would put on socks called *tabi* and wear *zôri*, a type of flat and thonged sandal often made of leather, which was more formal than the inexpensive straw *waraji* sandal that was typically worn on long trips. Typically, headgear was not worn.

If the samurai was heading to the castle for audience, was attending some official event, or making the rounds of officials seeking an official position, he would don formal or ceremonial dress, the exact type of which was prescribed by the event. In general, though, a formal outfit, known as *kamishimo* (lit., "upper" [and] "lower"), consisted of a formal kimono (with an undergarment worn underneath), tied with a sash; a lower garment known as *hakama*, a type of trousers; and a sleeveless upper garment with stiffened shoulders (*kataginu*) that was tucked into the lower garment. The two pieces of the *kamishimo* could be, but were not necessarily, composed of the same material, and the quality of the material, often hemp, would reflect the status of its wearer. In terms of color, during the first half of the Tokugawa period colors typically were not regulated, but from the middle of the period onward, colors such as indigo, deep brown, and light brown were most commonly worn.

High-ranking samurai attending ceremonial events at the castle would wear the *kataginu* over his kimono, which was marked with small white family crests on the back center of the garment, on the back of both sleeves, and on each side of the front, over the chest. For inside wear, an extra-long *hakama*, known as *nagabakama* (lit., "long *hakama*"), was worn together with the *kataginu*. A short sword and folding man were also mandatory on such occasions. Walking in this outfit required some skill: with the hands would be placed inside the gaps on either side of the *nagabakama*, the samurai had to lift his foot and pull the leg up and forward to create enough slack to move without misstep. Hemp and silk were fabrics commonly used for ceremonial attire.

In general, the clothing worn by the shogun, the daimyo, and the shogun's bannermen (direct vassals known as *hatamoto*) were patterned after that of the imperial court nobility. Since they also held court titles as well, their official garments were in keeping with their court rank. The type of fabric and the color carried according to subtle and complex regulations and varied with the wearer's age, status, and the season. Typically, daimyo wore *naga-hitatare*, which consisted of a long-sleeved jacket and long hakama, as ceremonial wear. For the highest-level ceremonies, including the accession of a new shogun, the daimyo wore an even more formal outfit known as *sokutai*. Silk, of varying grades, was the fabric of choice.

The *kosode* (kimono) worn for everyday use typically was made of cotton, which could be purchased or spun at home. Samurai households often spun raw cotton, which they purchased, into yarn. Those households that could afford it had the yarn dyed and woven; others had the yarn dyed but wove it at home; those households that were the most financially challenged might skip the dying process and weave the fabric themselves. Sober colors were often selected for the dyed cloth, for example, indigo, brown, gray, and gray-blue.

Although cotton clothing was commonly worn, silk became increasingly popular over the course of the Tokugawa period. As a result, domain governments during the late Tokugawa period often prohibited the wearing of silk garments in an effort to force samurai to economize. For example, in Mito domain, after the new daimyo succeeded to his position in 1829, regulations were issued stating that:

> Item: His lordship has heard that in recent years customs have grown exceedingly extravagant, with people drawn to what is splendorous and losing a sense of sobriety. Thus he is ordering all his retainers to wear clothes made of cotton. (Yamakawa, 1992, 40)

Despite the prohibition, samurai (and their wives and daughters) were permitted to wear undergarments made of silk or pongee. This exception gave undergarments new importance as fashion.

Fire Protection Clothing

Fires broke out frequently in Tokugawa Japan's castle towns, due to the flammable nature of construction materials that were used for buildings and the frequency of earthquakes. In Edo they occurred so often that the city was characterized by a contemporary expression, "Fires and fights are the flowers of Edo." Various types of firefighting organizations were organized in cities across Japan, but when a fire became a concern samurai, including daimyo, would don special fire protective clothing (known as *kaji shôzoku*, lit., "fire clothing") for reasons of security. Images of this clothing can be seen in woodblock prints and photographs, the latter from late in the Tokugawa period when the camera was introduced from abroad. Early in the Tokugawa period the protective clothing, often a bold color like red or vermillion, was usually made of leather, but later wool and wool-silk blends were utilized. A fire protection outfit consisted of a helmet—most commonly a *jingasa* ("camp hat") and in the case of high-ranking samurai or daimyo, a *kabuto* (helmet)— fire protection jacket (*kaji haori*); chest protector (*muneate*); neck protector (*shikoro*), which was a kind of fabric cape attached to the base of the helmet; a sash (*obi*); and *hakama* (pleated skirt-like pants). All parts of the outfit for the upper body were marked with the samurai's family crest. The helmet typically is constructed with lacquered leather, which made it lightweight and gave it a fire-retardant quality.

Clothes were a valuable commodity for a samurai household (and for wives, an invaluable personal source of wealth). Although new clothing might be woven for the New Year, old clothing was reworked (recycled) for continued use, with worn portions, particularly collars, replaced with new material. Used clothing was routinely purchased as well, as evidenced from visual images of the time [e.g., Kuwagata Keisai's scroll *Artisans of Edo* (*Edo shokunin zukushi ekotoba*, c. 1803)] and diaries written by samurai. Domain samurai stationed in Edo during their lords' alternate attendance trips to the Tokugawa capital could shop for secondhand clothing in the Yanagiwara area.

See also: Armor; Bannermen (*hatamoto*); Family Crests (*kamon*); Hairstyle; Status System (*mibunsei*)

Further Reading

"Costume Museum." http://www.iz2.or.jp/english. Accessed July 20, 2018.

Gluckman, Dale Carolyn, and Sharon Sadako Takeda. *When Art Became Fashion: Kosode in Edo-Period Japan.* Los Angeles: Los Angeles County Museum of Art; New York: Weatherhill, 1992.

Shiba, Gorô. *Remembering Aizu: The Testament of Shiba Gorô.* Edited by Ishimitsu Mahito. Honolulu: University of Hawai'i Press, 1999.

Yamakawa, Kikue. *Women of the Mito Domain: Recollections of Samurai Family Life.* Translated by Kate Wildman Nakai. Tokyo: University of Tokyo Press, 1992.

Coming of Age (*genpuku*)

Child rearing varied to some extent across Tokugawa Japan in terms of practice and timing, but it is still possible to discuss general patterns while acknowledging the existence of regional differences in custom. In terms of samurai male youth, it was custom for them go to through a coming-of-age ceremony, or the rites of manhood. This occurred generally around the age of fifteen, but it could be as early as seven and as late as seventeen; future shoguns Tokugawa Iemitsu (1604–1651) and Tokugawa Tsunayoshi (1146–1709), for example, went through the rites at the age of thirteen and seven, respectively.

A samurai's formal transition to adulthood was preceded by various stages of childhood growth, many of which were marked socially by ceremonies involving friends and family. The birth itself had to be reported to the political authorities—that is, to the domain or to the shogunate, depending on the father's affiliation. About a week after birth, a baby entered into the social world with a naming ceremony; this name would be changed upon adulthood and likely several times after that during the course of his life. On the 32nd day, the boy would be taken to a Shinto shrine for the first time. On the 110th day after birth the baby would be fed solid food for the first time. The child's first New Year's Day and first *sekku* (*tango no sekku*), also known as Boy's Day, were particularly festive occasions. The baby's head was shaved until the age of three, when a new stage of life, toddlerhood, was marked with a ceremony known as *kamioki*, which meant that the boy's hair was allowed to grow out. Between the age of five and seven, he might begin his education outside the home; this stage would also be marked by the boy's donning his first pair of formal, pleated pants (*hakama*) and his receipt of a short sword (*wakizashi*), which he would subsequently wear as part of his normal attire.

In many places across Tokugawa Japan, between the age of ten to twelve, a boy transitioned to a youth, and at this time he was allowed to modify his forelocks somewhat, into a hairstyle known as *sumimaegami*. This stage was referred to, in many places, as *hangenpuku*, an intermediate stage between childhood and adulthood. It was during this stage, as a youth, when the person was sexually available to an adult male. It was not unusual for samurai male youths to form intimate bonds that were of a romantic and/or sexual nature. These relationships always were between a youth and an older, adult partner; they were generally understood to be temporary, ending when the younger partner went through the coming-of-age ceremony, thus becoming an adult.

The custom of coming of age marked a male samurai's transition to adulthood. It had a number of markers, and these did not necessarily occur in a coordinated fashion, nor at strictly prescribed ages. In terms of practice, coming of age involved both sartorial and tonsorial changes: an exchange of clothes from wide-sleeved robes (*furisode*) to more narrow, adult garb, appropriate to a samurai's rank; second, it involved shaving the front of the head, the forelocks. The rest of the hair was grown long and dressed in a topknot, a hairstyle known as *chonmage*. The transition to adulthood also meant the selection of a new, adult, name. One of the above-mentioned shoguns, for example, changed his name from Tsurumatsu to Tsunayoshi. Youth from families of high rank who were eligible to have audiences with the daimyo would also have their first audience, which was official confirmation of the son as his father's heir. At this time he might also be given his first commission—a type of internship where he would work and receive a minimal stipend. As noted above, being treated as an adult also necessitated changes in a youth's romantic or sexual practice. After a youth's forelocks were shaved, marking his transition to adulthood, he could then initiate sexual activity with a wife, a prostitute, or a male youth. (A samurai could not be married until he went through *genpuku*.)

The transition between stages of development—from child to youth to adult— were not consistent everywhere in Tokugawa Japan, nor were they always clear- cut in any one place. In Tosa, for example, one samurai, writing in 1803, noted that practices there were changing and markers of transition were becoming less clear-cut:

> Previously young samurai of the household still wore the round forelock hairstyles of children until around age fourteen or fifteen, and none of them walked around wearing two swords. Instead, they wore just one short sword when they left the house. It was proper for all of them to start wearing two swords when they trimmed cor- ners into their forelocks and sewed up the open underarms of their kimonos in a "half- adulthood" ceremony showing they would soon take on the appearance and duties of an adult. But in recent years, little boys aged five or six with their hair still up in toddler-like buns cannot go out of the house for even a minute without wearing two swords. Their parents and elder brothers say that of course it is a sign of being born into a warrior house, that they are born into precocious excellence and should wear two swords like adults. (Minoura Yukinao, Quoted in Roberts, 2017, 41)

See also: Education; Hairstyle; Names (Samurai); Swords; Tokugawa Iemitsu, Tokugawa Tsunayoshi

Further Reading

Leupp, Gary P. *Male Colors: The Construction of Homosexuality in Tokugawa Japan.* Berkeley: University of California Press, 1995.

Ôta Motoko. *Edo no oyako: chichioya ga kodomo o sodateta jidai* [Parents and children of the Edo period: An era when fathers helped raise children]. Tokyo: Chûô kôron, 1994.

Ravina, Mark. *The Last Samurai. The Life and Battles of Saigô Takamori.* Hoboken, NJ: John Wiley & Sons, 2004.

Roberts, Luke S. "Growing Up Manly: Male Samurai Childhood in Late Edo-Era Tosa." In Sabine Fruhstuck and Anne Walthall, eds., *Child's Play: Multi-Sensory Histo- ries of Children and Childhood in Japan,* 41–59. Berkeley: University of Califor- nia Press, 2017.

D

Daimyo and Domains

A term composed of two Chinese characters, *dai* (great or large) and *myô* (meaning *myôden* or "name land"), *daimyô* was an informal designation applied to the largest military lords in premodern Japan. Usage of the term varied in earlier historical periods, but during the Tokugawa it assumed a more precise definition and referred to warriors who ruled over domains of more than 10,000 *koku* (1 *koku* = 5.1 bushels) and who were vassals of the shogun. The position of daimyo, of which there were approximately 260 at the end of the Tokugawa period, was abolished after the Meiji Restoration of 1868 with the return of daimyo domains to the imperial government and the reorganization of the country into prefectures in 1871.

HISTORY PRIOR TO THE TOKUGAWA

The term *daimyô* appears in historical documents as early as the eleventh century, but it was only during the Muromachi period (1338–1573) when it was applied to officials appointed by the (Muromachi) shogunate who were given jurisdiction over one or more provinces. The source of their authority of these officials, who were known as *shugo daimyô* (*shugo* meaning "military governor") rested largely on their appointment by the government rather than on the basis of their landholdings; they often held only a small proportion of the land in the province to which they were assigned. The *shugo daimyô* were given authority to collect taxes and to settle disputes over land in the countryside. The most powerful of them were able to add to their landholdings and to convert local landed warriors into their direct retainers. Some of the major *shugo daimyô* of the fifteenth century were the Hosokawa, Uesugi, Takeda, Kyôgoku, Ôuchi, and Shimazu.

The Ônin War (1467–1568) weakened the authority of shogunate and most of its *shugo daimyô*. Although the Muromachi shogunate (1336–1573) continued to exist during these years, it was weak, and political authority became extremely fragmented. Local military men, the *sengoku daimyô* (Warring States daimyo), rose to fill the vacuum of political power in the provinces. Some of the *shugo daimyô* who returned to the provinces after the Ônin War were able to shape their former jurisdictions into autonomous domains. Other daimyo rose up from positions as agents of the former *shugo*, known as *shugodai* or originated from local roots and were known as *kokujin*, or "men of the provinces." The *shugo daimyô, shugodai, and* to a lesser extent the *kokujin* fought among themselves to gain control of the territories over which they had exercised some administrative authority and to expand that control over other areas. Historians generally argue that by the 1550s, the *sengoku daimyô* had gained considerable independent control over their territories.

During the second half of the sixteenth century, the scale and technological sophistication of warfare increased as the daimyo were able to amass larger armies and to equip portions of those armies with muskets. They fought among themselves for regional hegemony, but in turn three military leaders—Oda Nobunaga (1534–1582), Toyotomi Hideyoshi (1537–1598), and Tokugawa Ieyasu (1543–1616)—emerged in succession. In 1568, Oda Nobunaga and his military forces occupied Kyoto, the imperial capital and political center of the country, and drove out the last of the Ashikaga shoguns. Neither he nor Hideyoshi assumed the title of shogun, choosing instead to govern through the institutions of the imperial court. (The Tokugawa would later imbue the position of shogun with utmost significance.) Together they were quite effective in subjugating the other daimyo. Hideyoshi was able to vanquish the remaining daimyo that resisted his authority and unified the country in 1590. In recognizing Nobunaga and then Hideyoshi as overlord the daimyo gained some security of tenure and were able to extend their capacity to rule their domains, but also lost some autonomy. These conditions continued under the Tokugawa.

THE DAIMYO UNDER TOKUGAWA RULE

Building on his success in the Battle of Sekigahara (1600), Tokugawa Ieyasu (1543–1616) gained imperial appointment as shogun in 1603, becoming the first of fifteen Tokugawa rulers, and institutionalized what modern historians commonly refer to as the *bakuhan* (*bakufu*, or military government, meaning the shogunate) and *han* (domain) system. The Tokugawa established a strong national authority with a range of powers over the daimyo, but at the same time the daimyo were able to extend their own controls, locally, over the domains.

Tokugawa authority rested in part on control of territory. After Sekigahara, Ieyasu confiscated 3.83 million *koku* in land from daimyo who had opposed him. This pattern of confiscation or attainder continued under his two successors, Hidetada (1579–1632) and Iemitsu (1604–1651), who between the two of them added another 8.38 million *koku*. Much of this land was distributed to allied daimyo, but post-Sekigahara the Tokugawa and its direct vassals, the bannermen (*hatamoto*) and housemen (*gokenin*), held roughly 8.5 million *koku* directly, with 16 million *koku* resting in daimyo hands. By the time of the third shogun Iemitsu's death in 1651, war was a distant memory and the frequency of confiscation and transfer were greatly reduced, giving the daimyo much greater security of tenure.

Under Tokugawa rule, the daimyo were classified according to their relationship to the shogun's household, by their resources as well as by size. The *fudai*, or hereditary, daimyo were reputedly descended from retainers who were followerss of the Tokugawa prior to Sekigahara while the *tozama*, or "outside," lords, only recognized Tokugawa authority after 1600. Those daimyo families who were relatives of the Tokugawa and traced their lineage to Ieyasu by way of his sons were known as *shinpan*, or "related" daimyo.

The related daimyo houses were subdivided into a number of categories. The three greatest *shinpan* families were known as the *gosanke* (three houses): Mito, Nagoya, and Wakayama. They were descendants of three of Tokugawa Ieyasu's sons and substantial domains (see Table 3) with imposing castles. In principle they acted as advisers to the shogun, but in reality they were excluded from holding administrative positions in the government. However, they had an important function to provide an heir to the shogun when needed. This occurred on three occasions during the Tokugawa period: Tokugawa Yoshimune (daimyo of Kii), Iemochi (son of daimyo of Kii), and Yoshinobu (son of daimyo of Mito, then adopted heir of Hitotsubashi house) all became shogun. Another group, the Three Lords (*sankyô*)—the houses of Tayasu, Hitotsubashi, and Shimizu—were descended from two sons and a grandson of shogun Tokugawa Yoshimune (1684–1751). Descendants of sons of the first three shoguns and branches of the Three Houses, such as the daimyo of Fukui, Matsue, Aizu, Saijô, and Takamatsu, were known as *kamon* ("within the gate").

Size, in terms of productive capacity (*kokudaka*), was also an indicator of status and prestige for a daimyo. Table 3 lists the sixteen largest domains in terms of output. Of these domains, Kaga alone exceeded a million *koku*, making its Maeda rulers the most prestigious of the daimyo, after the Tokugawa. Despite the fact that daimyo service to the Tokugawa in terms of provided military support or corvee labor was assessed based on a domain's official listed productive capacity

Table 3   The Great Domains of Tokugawa Japan

Castle Town/ Domain	Province	Daimyo Family Name	Official Listed Productive Capacity (*omotedaka*) (in *koku*)	Actual Recorded Product (*jitsudaka*) (in *koku*)	Category or Status of Daimyo
Kanazawa	Kaga	Maeda	1,022,700	1,353,300	*tozama*
Kagoshima	Satsuma	Shimazu	770,000	869,500	*tozama*
Sendai	Mutsu	Date	625,600	958,400	*tozama*
Nagoya	Owari	Tokugawa	619,500	. . .	*shimpan*
Wakayama	Kii	Tokugawa	555,000	539,400	*shimpan*
Kumamoto	Higo	Hosokawa	540,000	721,000	*tozama*
Fukuoka	Chikuzen	Kuroda	520,000	. . .	*tozama*
Hiroshima	Aki	Asano	426,000	488,000	*tozama*
Hagi	Chôshû	Môri	369,000	713,600	*tozama*
Saga	Hizen	Nabeshima	357,000	. . .	*tozama*
Mito	Hitachi	Tokugawa	350,000	. . .	*fudai*
Hikone	Ômi	Ii	350,000	. . .	*fudai*
Tottori	Inaba	Ikeda	325,000	428,100	*tozama*
Tsu	Ise	Tôdô	323,000	. . .	*tozama*
Fukui	Echizen	Matsudaira	320,000	. . .	*shimpan*
Okayama	Bizen	Ikeda	315,000	469,100	*tozama*

Source: Albert Craig, *Chôshû in the Meiji Restoration* (Cambridge, MA: Harvard University Press, 1961), 11.

(*omotedaka*), at least one domain (Tosa) actually sought to increase its listing because of the increased prestige it would bring. A different measure of size—whether a daimyo ruled an entire province or more—was also an indicator of status. Eighteen lords had the further distinction of being known as the "eighteen province-holding houses" (*jûhachi kunimochi ke*), and almost all were of distinguished ancestry; the Yamauchi, in contrast, stand out as upstarts. These lords who ruled over an entire province stand in stark contrast to those on the lowest end of the spectrum, with domains that were 10,000 *koku*, or slightly more, but which were portfolios of widely scattered villages rather than compact territories.

Of course, all daimyo, regardless of category were sworn vassals of the shogun and formally received investiture of their domains from him. The shogun drew from his allied daimyo and direct vassals to staff his government, the shogunate, while excluding the *tozama* and *gosanke* from participation.

One result of the confiscation of lands by the first three shoguns was a redistribution in the number of daimyo of the several categories. Daimyo attainders up to 1651 resulted in an increase in the number of *fudai* and *shinpan daimyô* at the expense of the *tozama*. The descendants of only three of Ieyasu's enemies at Sekigahara, the Shimazu, Môri, and Nabeshima, still held major domains. Indeed, a major transfer of some three million *koku* of landholdings from *tozama* to *fudai* and *shinpan* took place between 1616 and 1651. During this time, of the twenty-four great *tozama* houses, nine had been confiscated, one reduced in size, and four transferred. In contrast, a number of new *fudai* houses were created, raising their numbers from sixty-nine in 1601 to ninety-one in 1616 and 115 by 1690. By 1700, the shogun and his direct vassals controlled roughly 6.8 million *koku*, the *fudai* and *shinpan* daimyo 9.3 million *koku*, and the *tozama* lords 9.8 million *koku*, which meant that about three-quarters of the country was administered by the daimyo.

Through confiscations and transfers the Tokugawa aimed to realign the political map of Japan to its advantage, gradually reducing the size of domains and placing more of them under the control of daimyo whose legacy in theory predisposed them to support them. The average size of a domain fell from 93,000 *koku* in the early seventeenth century to slightly more than 65,000 *koku* a century later. Their overall numbers increased, though, from 192 in 1614 to 229 in 1654 and to 262 in 1720, after which there was little change.

The Tokugawa developed a full range of political and economic controls over the daimyo. Confiscation and transfer, or the threat to carry out these actions, were among the most powerful of the political controls at the disposal of the Tokugawa and they, as noted above, were exercised with some frequency before 1651. In addition, the daimyo were required to swear absolute loyalty to the shogun; to follow the shogun's basic laws; to provide military services to the Tokugawa when needed; to provide men and material, upon demand, for the construction of castles, riverine, and other public works projects; to perform the alternate attendance (to attend upon the shogun in Edo) according to a fixed schedule; and, to perform coastal defense. Many of the levies imposed on the daimyo were based on the standard of the officially listed productive capacity of the domain (*omotedaka*), which generally remained fixed during the Tokugawa period, rather than the actual recorded product (*jitsudaka*). All daimyo were to follow the provisions of the *Laws for the Military Houses* (*buke shohatto*), which were first issued under Ieyasu in 1615 and reissued periodically thereafter. These *Laws* were aimed particularly at the personal behavior of the daimyo, instructing them to study the "twin ways of literature and the military arts," to avoid drinking parties, to perform the alternate attendance, and not to arrange marriages without the approval of the shogun.

The *Laws for the Military Houses*, however, did not provide a detailed list of regulations on how the daimyo should rule. The daimyo were instructed to follow the Tokugawa's *Laws* in general terms, enjoined from building new castles or repairing existing ones without permission, and given vague instructions that they were to select men of ability for office; however, they were largely given free administration of their domains. Within their domains, the daimyo held rights of taxation, law enforcement, and criminal justice (however, disputes that spilled over into another domain would fall under the shogunate's authority).

Although some scholars emphasize the range and strength of the Tokugawa's controls over the daimyo and define the polity as a "Tokugawa state," others argue that Japan was a "compound state" of domains in which the daimyo were largely independent rulers. Regardless of the size of the domain, though, no daimyo dared reject the authority of the Tokugawa, for example, by refusing to swear allegiance

Daimyo graveyard of the Môri clan of Chôshû at Tôkôji (Obaku Zen) temple in Hagi (Yamaguchi prefecture). Many of the now moss-covered lanterns were donated by retainers of the Môri in honor of their clan and its lords. (Photo by Constantine Vaporis)

Daimyo Graveyards

  Most domains in Tokugawa Japan established a graveyard exclusively for their daimyo and their spouses. Chôshû was unusual in that it had two, both located in the outskirts of the castle town, Hagi, but at some distance from one another. The first to be established was on the precincts of the Zen temple Daishôin, where the founder Môri Terumoto (1563–1623) is buried as well as the even-numbered daimyo that followed him, together with their spouses. Leading up to the tombs are 603 stone lanterns donated by domain vassals. The second graveyard is located behind Tôkôji temple, a Zen temple belonging to the Obaku sect, and was founded in 1691 by the third Chôshû lord, Môri Tsunahiro (1651–1682). He and the odd-numbered daimyo who followed him (3, 5, 7, 11) are buried in the middle of the thickly forested hillside, together with their wives. (The thirteenth and final Tokugawa-era daimyo is buried elsewhere, in Yamaguchi city.) Five hundred stone lanterns donated by domain vassals are arranged in a way that draws the visitors up the slope toward the monumental graves of the daimyo and their spouses.

  During Obon, an annual Buddhist festival for commemorating one's ancestors, all the stone lanterns are lit and a festival is held to welcome the spirits of the dead, on August 13, and then to send them back to the nether world two days later, on August 15.

or failing to perform the alternate attendance. On the other hand, it must be acknowledged that after 1651 the daimyo "came to be treated with notable forbearance, receiving, in the main, the lightest of reproofs for offenses that would have cost their fathers and grandfathers dearly. Open dissension among one's vassals, a misdemeanor that had cost at least seven daimyo their fiefs in the first fifty years of the Tokugawa period, was now usually punished with a reprimand, or at most a brief period of house arrest; only the really spectacular cases attracted anything more" (Bolitho, 1991, 207).

THREE EXAMPLES: KAGA, TOSA, AND BIZEN

  A few examples of individual daimyo domains will be illustrative of the administrative development of this basic unit of political organization: Kaga (Maeda family), Tosa (Yamauchi family), and Bizen (Okayama, the Ikeda family).

  The Maeda settled permanently at Kanazawa in the 1580s (the domains are sometimes also referred to by the name of their castle town). Having fought on the Tokugawa side at Sekigahara, Maeda Toshinaga (1562–1614) was confirmed in his landholdings of over 1 million *koku* (an officially listed productive capacity of 1.022 million *koku* and an actual recorded product of 1.35 million *koku*), making it the largest domain in Japan after the shogun's, covering the three provinces of Kaga, Noto, and Etchû. Toshinaga further demonstrated his loyalty to the shogun by becoming the first daimyo to build a residence in the Tokugawa capital of Edo for his use during alternate attendance. In addition, in 1614–1615 the Maeda led a large army to Osaka to support the Tokugawa's Sieges of Osaka Castle. Upon his retirement in 1639, Toshitsune ordered that the domain be divided and as a result, two branch domains (*shihan*) were established: 100,000 *koku* was designated for his younger son Maeda Toshitsugu to form a new (branch) domain, Toyama, and 70,000 *koku* was alloted to his third son, Maeda Toshiharu, to form Daishôji, another branch domain. A large and bustling castle town, Kanazawa's finances were challenged by the costs of alternate attendance as well as the periodic fires that ravaged it (and most castle towns). Large fires in 1631 and 1635 allowed domain authorities to rearrange samurai and townsmen housing to create more order and physical division between the status groups. Like many lords, the Maeda issued legal codes, in 1637 and 1642, for civil administration and criminal punishment. From the mid-seventeenth century, the government promoted a program of land reclamation to open new fields to cultivation. During the 1650s the Maeda also carried out major reform of rural administration by taking direct control of vassals' fiefs, thereby undercutting their independent authority while strengthening that of the daimyo and improving tax collection. Through a spate of new legislation, the Maeda also tried to increase government control over castle town life. In particular, the Maeda, like daimyo across Japan, issued sumptuary regulations to curtail the consumptive behavior of townsmen and to deal with growing samurai indebtedness to merchants. Across Japan, including in Kaga, the basic shape of domain administration was settled by the end of the 1660s.

Another *tozama* domain, Tosa, was situated in the southern half of Shikoku, with an officially listed productive capacity of 202,627 *koku* (in 1603). For his support of the Ieyasu at Sekigahara, Yamauchi Katsutoyo (1545–1605) was awarded the domain of Tosa, a substantial increase over the 60,000-*koku* fief that he held under Hideyoshi. Its ruling daimyo family, the Yamauchi, were not native to the area and faced the hostility and outright opposition of some of the retainers of the previous lord, the Chôsogabe. It was only with the assistance of the forces held by a trusted Tokugawa vassal, Ii Naomasa (1561–1602), that Katsutoyo was able to suppress local opposition and begin to reorganize his new domain. Given that the Yamauchi were new to the area, Katsutoyo and his immediate successors were better able to control their vassals, as they did not have to deal with trying to remove vassals from traditional local bases of power. It was relatively easy, then, to concentrate many low- and middle-ranking vassals in the castle town of Kôchi. The vast majority of the agricultural land was distributed as fief to his more substantial retainers, including five senior vassals, who held fiefs ranging from 1,100–10,000 *koku*. Below them were more than one hundred samurai with fiefs from 20 to 7,000 *koku*; they were also granted residences in the castle town. Even when awarding new fiefs, Katsutoyo was careful to grant landholdings that were dispersed so as to prevent them from building up local power bases. Katsutoyo was also able to double the amount of land under his direct control (relative to that held by his predecessor) to 45,000 *koku*, from which he paid stipends to hundreds of lower-ranking retainers.

Like many daimyo, the Yamauchi exerted great effort to create a large castle town. In Katsutoyo's case, he determined that the current castle, constructed by the Chôsogabe, at the mouth of Urado Bay, was inadequate, as it allowed little room for future development. Instead, Katsutoyo decided to build a new castle on the Kôchi plain, between two rivers, giving the domain easy access to water transport, which was critical to the economic development of the domain. Katsutoyo's successor completed the construction project in 1611, but much of the original castle burned down a century later, in 1727, and had to be rebuilt; the main keep of the castle, one of only twelve original castle keeps in Japan and designated an Important Cultural Asset, dates from this time (1729–1753).

In contrast to the Yamauchi, who ruled Tosa from the very beginning, and for the entire duration, of the Tokugawa period, the Ikeda became rulers of Bizen (Okayama) domain only in 1632, after the termination of the Kobayakawa family line. Ikeda Terumasa (1565–1613), who was married to one of Ieyasu's daughters, sided with the Tokugawa side at Sekigahara and was rewarded with the strategic castle of Himeji (Harima province) before the house was reduced by the shogunate in 1632 to two branches of almost equal size, the 320,000-*koku* domain of Tottori and Okayama, which was assessed at 315,000 *koku.*

The first Ikeda to rule Okayama was Mitsumasa (1609–1682), who married Katsuhime, a granddaughter of the second shogun, Tokugawa Hidetada (1579–1632). During the 1630s–1640s, Mitsumasa not only engaged in reorganizing domain administration and establishing firm policies on taxation and fiscal management, but he was one of the first daimyo to establish a domain school (*hankô*) where his retainers could study. He hired the Confucian scholar Kumazawa Banzan (1619–1691) to serve as his adviser, and when hidden Christian communities were found in the Nagoya area (Christianity had been proscribed in Japan as early as 1587 by Toyotomi Hideyoshi and then again, more forcefully by the Tokugawa in 1614), Mitsumasa promoted Confucianism in education, promoted Shinto, requiring everyone to register at Shinto shrines (rather than at Buddhist temples, as occurred across most of Japan), and tore down about half the temples in Bizen. His successors, as elsewhere, sought to improve domain finances by encouraging land reclamation and riparian work, and improving port facilities to encourage trade.

Although there were important differences in the histories of the individual daimyo families and the domains over which they presided, there were also many common patterns in daimyo rule. Across Japan, the daimyo dealt with similar problems in trying to cope with the demands of service to the Tokugawa, to improve finances by expanding their tax bases and encouraging trade, tightening control over their retainers and the general populace, all while maintaining the peace.

See also: Alternate Attendance (*sankin kôtai*); Bannermen (*hatamoto*); Education; Housemen (*gokenin*); *Laws for the Military Houses* (*buke shohatto*); Retainer Corps; Sekigahara, Battle of; Warring States Daimyo (*sengoku daimyô*); Yamauchi Katsutoyo

Further Reading

Bolitho, Harold. "The *Han.*" In John Whitney Hall, ed., *The Cambridge History of Japan*, vol. 4: *Early Modern Japan.* Cambridge: Cambridge University Press, 1991.

Brown, Philip C. *Central Authority & Local Autonomy in the Formation of Early Modern Japan: The Case of Kaga Domain.* Stanford, CA: Stanford University Press, 1993.

Craig, Albert. *Chôshû in the Meiji Restoration.* Cambridge, MA: Harvard University Press, 1961.

Hall, John Whitney. *Government and Local Power in Japan: A Study Based on Bizen Province, 500 to 1700.* Princeton, NJ: Princeton University Press, 1966.

Jansen, Marius B. "Tosa in the Seventeenth Century: The Establishment of Yamauchi Rule." In John W. Hall and Marius B. Jansen, eds., *Studies in the Institutional History of Early Modern Japan.* Princeton, NJ: Princeton University Press, 1968.

McClain, James L. *Kanazawa: A Seventeenth-Century Japanese Castle Town.* New Haven, CT: Yale University Press, 1982.

Roberts, Luke S. *Mercantilism in a Japanese Domain: The Merchant Origins of Economic Nationalism in 18th-Century Tosa.* Cambridge: Cambridge University Press, 1998.

Woodson, Yoko. *The Samurai: The Legacy of a Daimyo Family.* San Francisco: Asian Art Museum, 2009.

Daimyô katagi (Portrait of a Daimyo)

Matsudaira Sadanobu (1759–1829) was the great-great-great grandson of Tokugawa Ieyasu and the grandson of Tokugawa Yoshimune, the first and eighth shoguns of the Tokugawa dynasty, respectively. He was born in Edo Castle as a member of the Tayasu branch (one of the cadet branches of the shogun's family, or *gosankyô*) of the Tokugawa house. His family promoted him as a candidate for adoption as the next shogunal heir, but their attempts were blocked by a rival political faction led by Tanuma Okitsugu, the chief senior councilor. He rose from the position of daimyo to chief senior councilor of the shogunate and is remembered as the main architect of the Kansei Reforms (1787–1793). He was also the (anonymous) author of a satirical piece of writing known as *Daimyô katagi*, which was quite out of character for this moralizing reformer.

Sadanobu was adopted by Matsudaira Sadakuni, the head of another Tokugawa cadet branch, which ruled Shirakawa domain in northern Japan (Mutsu province, present-day Fukushima prefecture). There he succeeded to the position of daimyo of this famine-stricken and financially strapped Shirakawa domain in 1783. He enacted strict reforms that did much to restore the domain's finances and agricultural productivity. His success in Shirakawa made his reputation as a "model ruler" and drew the attention of the shogunate. As a result, he was appointed chief senior councilor in 1787 and the following year regent to the shogun Tokugawa Ienari (ruled 1787–1837), serving from 1787 to 1793. During his tenure with the shogunate he oversaw the famous Kansei Reforms of 1787, which have been viewed by some scholars as a reactionary response to the excesses of administration under Tanuma Okitsugi, the chief councilor of the previous shogun, Tokugawa Ieharu, who ruled from 1760 to 1786. Sadanobu enjoyed some success as an economic reformer but was hampered by natural disasters, such as famine and floods, during his tenure as well as a national security crisis. The latter occurred when a Russian expedition led by the military officer Adam Laxman intruded in Japanese waters and foreigners set foot in Japan in 1791, using the return of two Japanese castaways as a pretext to establish trade relations. This broke with the principle of the so-called "closed country" edicts of the early seventeenth century under which all Westerners except the Dutch were proscribed entry to Japan.

Sadanobu was also known as a writer and a moralist. He composed a number of texts under the pen name Rakuô, including his memoirs (*Uge no hitokoto*). Far less well known, however, is that in 1784 he wrote, anonymously, a parody of a daimyo, entitled *Daimyô katagi*. Apparently, he had second thoughts about the manuscript and destroyed it. In doing this he was following a long-standing pattern of promoting a certain image of himself and only allowing those texts that fit his self-image as a model Confucian official to be made public. Unbeknownst to him, however, a number of different attendants of his made copies. Today at least four separate copies of *Daimyô katagi* exist in public collections in Japan. The manuscript was virtually ignored by scholars until an American academic, Haruko Iwasaki, wrote about it in 1983.

The text *Daimyô katagi* itself can be thought of in terms of two parts. The first half "is a tongue-in-cheek portrait of a naïve and over-zealous daimyo who goes from one extreme to another in his pursuit of the proper Way" (Iwasaki, 1983, 8). At first, the daimyo is preoccupied with the martial arts (*bu*), and as a result his retainers encourage him to shift to the literary arts (*bun*). They are too successful, and so the lord goes overboard in reciting the Confucian classics. At a loss, his retainers consult a doctor who "prescribes" a dose of *tsû*, an ideal of sophistication that was current in popular Edo culture. They take the lord to a kabuki theater, but as a result the lord becomes in turn obsessed with it. The second half of the text is much different in tone and akin to a didactic public sermon, which was popular at the time.

Sadanobu appears to have written the text for his own pleasure and had no intention of sharing it with anyone else. Seen in that light, the text could be seen, at least in part, as a type of self-admonishment. Accordingly, the daimyo protagonist can be seen as a caricature of himself. For example, the daimyo in the text poses as a "tough" smoker: "Let's start with the daimyo's tobacco. A tough guy smokes strong tobacco, and so he would smoke the strongest kind, take one or two puffs, and then quickly knock it out. 'What strong stuff your Lordship likes!' admired his subjects, but behind his back they all laughed at him, saying, 'The way the Boss purses his lips when he puffs—why, he could even smoke nettles'" (Matsudaira Sadanobu, 1983, 20). In this passage, the real-life daimyo, Sadanobu, was perhaps making fun of his own self-professed fondness for smoking, which had been a habit from a young age. As an adult, Sadanobu was also quite preoccupied with the martial arts, particularly with the *jûjutsu* that he practiced. From another written account of his we know that he tried to convince his retainers to become similarly involved. In creating a fictional daimyo who tries to bully his retainers into becoming *jujutsu* enthusiasts, he was poking fun at his own infatuation.

Daimyô katagi is significant for several reasons. First of all, it reveals something of the character of Sadanobu, whom previous scholarship "tended to characterize as a gifted but humorless and didactic proponent of Confucian virtue" (Iwasaki, 1983, 2). The story that he wrote was a type of satire, one that falls into the literary category of *gesaku*, a genre of witty, popular fiction that he had officially opposed in his role as official of the shogunate in implementing the Kansei reforms. Second, the text also gives evidence of the influence of influence of Edo popular fiction late in the eighteenth century, among commoners *and* samurai. Third, it also forces a reconsideration of Sadanobu's crackdown on *gesaku* in the Kansei Reforms. Given his apparent affinity for *gesaku* in private, it appears that his repression of it may have been motivated by a desire to silence certain *gesaku* writers who were critical of his reform program rather than as a result of a strident moralism.

See also: Civil and Military Arts (*bunbu*); Daimyo and Domains; Shogun (*shôgun*); Tokugawa Ieyasu; Tokugawa Yoshimune

Further Reading

Iwasaki Haruko. "Portrait of a Daimyo: Comical Fiction by Matsudaira Sadanobu." *Monumenta Nipponica,* 38(1) (1983), 1–19.

Matsudaira Sadanobu. "Daimyô katagi" (English translation). *Monumenta Nipponica,* 38(1) (1983), 20–48.

Ooms, Herman. *Charismatic Bureaucrat: A Political Biography of Matsudaira Sadanobu, 1758–1829.* Chicago: University of Chicago Press, 1975.

Daimyo Residence Compounds (*daimyô yashiki*)

Daimyô yashiki were compounds maintained in Edo, Kyoto, and Osaka by the daimyo, to house the men who accompanied the daimyo on alternate attendance plus a permanent staff. They were also erected in some cases primarily to store commercial goods. Approximately 600–900 in number (they varied over time), the compounds were constructed in Edo by the daimyo, since the demands of *sankin kôtai* (alternate attendance) required that they alternate their residences between the domain and Edo and also maintain their wives and children as hostages in Edo. With the daimyo spending large amounts of time in the shogun's capital, the compounds became the physical setting for a branch of the domain's administrative organization in Edo, with the main administration being back in the domain castle town. During the Meiji Restoration (broadly speaking, 1868–1890), many of the compounds—then also referred to as *hantei* or "*han* (domain) residences"—were converted to other uses or torn down. Today, a few visual reminders of the daimyo compounds in Edo can still be seen in several locations across Tokyo, but much of the city's green space can also be traced back to its early modern origins as *daimyô yashiki*.

To make it possible for the daimyo to attend his person in Edo, the shogun bequeathed land to them on which to build residences, which served as a kind of embassy for the daimyo while in the capital. The vassal daimyo (*fudai daimyô*) were generally located to the northeast of the castle while the outside lords (*tozama daimyô*) were mostly placed to the southwest, particularly along what became known as Daimyo Avenue (*daimyô kôji*). The daimyo built their principal or main residences (*kami yashiki*), which fulfilled administrative, diplomatic, and economic functions for the domain, close to the Edo Castle. The main residences were built in the early 1600s in the extravagant Momoyama style of architecture, visual evidence for which can be seen in the Edo screens known as the *Edo-zu byôbu* (see below reference to "Views of Edo (*Edo zu*) Pair of Six-Panel Folding Screens," National Museum of History). After the fire, due to economizing measures, they were rebuilt in a plainer style, but Daimyo Avenue remained a remarkable sight, one that new visitors to Edo were sure not to miss.

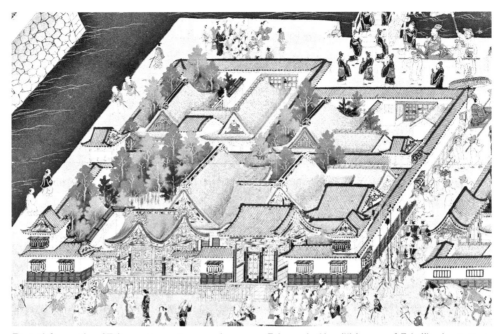

Detail from the 17th-century six-panel screen *Edo-zu byôbu* ("Views of Edo"), depicting the main residence of Matsudaira Tadamasa (1597–1645), daimyo of Fukui domain (Fukui prefecture). Daimyo built residence compounds in Edo to house their retainers while fulfilling the requirements of the alternate attendance system. The screen captures the opulence of many of the daimyo residences in Edo before the Meireki Great Fire of 1657. (The Picture Art Collection/Alamy Stock Photo)

The compounds varied somewhat in function. The principal compound was where the daimyo and their immediate families, chief officials, and many other retainers resided. Many domains maintained at least one other, secondary compound ("middle residences," or *naka yashiki*), usually at some distance from the castle. Their use was quite fluid: they provided a second residence in case the main compound burned or was being repaired, but also functioned as the residence of the daimyo heir, the retired lord, or the mother of the current lord and a support staff. Many domains also built tertiary or supplemental compounds (*shimo yashiki*), which were typically located on the outskirts of the city. These did not house substantial numbers of people but were used as holiday villas or retreats. In addition to the three above-mentioned types of residences, most domains purchased space along the waterfront of Edo Bay on which to build large warehouses where commodity goods could be stored or shipped from. Some of the largest domains maintained a network of compounds in Edo. Tosa domain (202,600 *koku*), for example, had as many as twelve in the early eighteenth century.

The Edo residences of the daimyo also served as cultural centers. In the main compounds, and often in the "middle residences" as well, they constructed theatrical stages for performances of the Noh and Kyôgen theater. Confucian scholars, artists, and teachers of the martial arts lived in the domain compounds, on

---

The Red Gate of the University of Tokyo

The foreign tourist in Tokyo today will likely see the famous red gate (*akamon*) of Tokyo University, Japan's top university. Its origin is perhaps much less well known. The campus of Tokyo University was the site of several daimyo residence compounds (*daimyô yashiki*), including that of the Maeda, the most powerful lord after the Tokugawa. The color red signified close ties with the Tokugawa—permission to build them was given only when a shogun's daughter married a daimyo, one from a powerful domain. In the case of the Tokyo University gate, it marked the marriage of the daughter of the eleventh shogun, Tokugawa Ienari (1773–1841), to the Kaga daimyo Maeda Nariyasu (1811–1884) in 1823. The red gate served as an entrance to the new bride's quarters in the compound and was a popular site for tourism even in the Tokugawa period.

---

rotation from the home domain, where they studied, created, and taught. During the late Tokugawa period, many domains also established schools in the residence compounds for the retainers in residence.

Regrettably, there are no fully intact daimyo compounds in Tokyo. There are, however, a number of remnants of them that give us some indication of their former state. The most famous vestige of the daimyo compounds is the Red Gate (*akamon*) of Tokyo University, on the site of Kaga domain's main residence in Hongô, which was built in 1827. Another remnant of the daimyo compounds is the "black gate" (*kuromon*) of the Ikeda daimyo compound, so-called because of the dark color of the wood. This branch of the Ikeda family were daimyo of Tottori domain, and while his domain was much smaller than that of the lord of Kaga (325,000 *koku* versus 1.25 million *koku*), the gate, with its two bow-shaped guard boxes, is quite impressive. Originally located in the Marunouchi area, where many of the other main residence compounds were concentrated, it was used as the gate for the Tôgû Palace and then for the residence of an imperial prince before it found a more permanent home in Ueno, close to the National Museum of Art, in 1954.

Besides the architectural structures mentioned above, several gardens belonging to the former daimyo compounds still remain in Tokyo. Korakuen, established in 1629, is Tokyo's oldest garden and was part of the *yashiki* of the lord of Mito, one of the Three Houses, distinguished Tokugawa branch families who were called on to supply an heir to the shogunal line, if needed. It is a strolling-type garden, developed by Zhu Shun Shui (1600–1822), a refugee scholar from Ming China. A second example of a garden in Tokyo that was originally part of a daimyo compound is the Kyu Shiba Rikyu Garden, which was established in 1686 as part of the compound of the lord of Odawara domain, Ôkubo Tadatomo (1632–1712).

Many other parks and gardens have some connections to the former daimyo compounds. Shinjuku gyoen (Shinjuku Park), for example, was on the site of a daimyo compound (that of the Naitô lord of Tsuruga domain) that was destroyed during World War II; the current garden only dates to 1949. An even more famous example is Hibiya Park, which is a large public park located close to the Imperial Palace; it sits on land that where the former residence compounds of the Môri and Nabehima lords were located.

Significant numbers of daimyo also maintained compounds, known as *kura ya-shiki* or warehouse compounds, in other cities such as Osaka, Kyoto, and Fushimi. Daimyo located in western Japan maintained compounds in Osaka in which to store rice sent from the domain before selling it in the local market. The lords and part of their entourages also stayed in the compound for several nights on the way to and from Edo for alternate attendance. By the end of the seventeenth century there were nearly one hundred compounds. About 130 domains also maintained residences in Kyoto, mostly in the Shijô-Kawaramachi area. The residence might house the lord on his alternate attendance trip, if he received special permission to stay overnight in the imperial capital; otherwise he would stop at a residence maintained in nearby Fushimi for that purpose. Maintaining a compound in Kyoto allowed the domain to remain connected, in economic and cultural terms, to the Kyoto region.

See also: Alternate Attendance (*sankin kôtai*); Daimyo and Domains; Shogun (*shôgun*)

Further Reading and Viewing

Coaldrake, William H. "Edo Architecture and Tokugawa Law." *Monumenta Nipponica,* 36(3) (1981), 235–284.

Coaldrake, William H. *Architecture and Authority in Japan.* London and New York: Routledge, 1996.

"Daimyo Yashiki." https://edoflourishing.blogspot.com/2013/08/daimyo-yashiki.html. Accessed December 21, 2017. (Clicking on the image of the residence at the top of the page takes the reader to a page with a variety of different images of *daimyô yashiki*).

Vaporis, Constantine Nomikos. *Tour of Duty: Samurai, Military Service in Edo, and the Culture of Early Modern Japan.* Honolulu: University of Hawai'i Press, 2008.

"Views of Edo (*Edo zu*) Pair of Six-Panel Folding Screens." National Museum of History. https://www.rekihaku.ac.jp/english/education_research/gallery/webgallery/edozu/l32.html. Accessed December 21, 2017.

Disrespect Killing (*burei-uchi*)

Samurai were able to demonstrate their collective superiority over commoners through their legal right to execute a person of lower status such as a commoner or a servant, for rudeness. This act was known as *burei-uchi* ("disrespect killing") or *kirisute gomen* ("permission to cut down"). The ostensible purpose of such violence was to exact justice and to enforce respect for the status system. For the exercise of lethal violence against a commoner to be recognized as *burei-uchi* two conditions had to be met: one, the commoner's act had to be deemed truly offensive to the samurai; and two, the samurai had to have killed the commoner on the spot, not at a later time.

Samurai-directed violence toward people of lower status could take place in several types of social settings: in Japan's castle towns, which were populated by samurai and townsmen (the latter term meaning artisans and merchants); and, on the highways and post-towns that the daimyo processions, with their entourages of samurai and support staff, utilized on the lords' required biennial trips to Edo as part of the alternate attendance system. In contrast with the relative physical proximity of samurai and townsmen in urban centers, samurai would not have had much opportunity to interact with peasants, who resided in the countryside. In most domains the samurai-based government maintained a minimal presence in rural areas in the form of a lightly staffed intendant's office. In fact, in many places samurai were required to obtain official permission to travel into the countryside. Nevertheless, the occasions when samurai and peasants did meet were fraught with opportunity for conflict and violence.

Offensive acts toward samurai that arose most commonly occurred when samurai and members of the other status groups physically passed by one another, resulting in chance physical contact. They also could occur simply by virtue of a commoner not showing adequate social deference in creating a buffer zone between the samurai and himself. It was for that reason, for example, that the townsman code from cities like Kanazawa instructed that it is "forbidden . . . to walk along the street next to samurai" (Vaporis, 2014, 90). Similarly, in the countryside in Tokushima domain, on Shikoku Island, a farmer carrying a bucket of urine (used as fertilizer) on a path at the edge of a rice field did not give way to a samurai and was summarily cut down. (Of course, this example begs the question of why the samurai was in the countryside, but no further information is available.)

Disputes between samurai and commoners leading to lethal violence could also result when commercial transactions took place. This could occur whenever a samurai purchased some commodity, such as a horse or a weapon. It might also happen when a samurai engaged a service, such as hiring a packhorse driver. An argument over prices could lead to violence if the samurai felt as if he was being cheated or the commoner became verbally or physically abusive. For example, in 1768, a samurai on his way home from Edo became involved in a dispute with two packhorse drivers who claimed that his load was overweight. They demanded a tip, even after it was determined that the load was under the legal limit. One of the porters verbally taunted the samurai, saying, "There's nothing less interesting than a samurai," and grabbed him by the front of his kimono. The samurai responded by cutting the one porter's head in two and then went after his colleague, who tried to run away, eventually killing him, too. An official investigation followed in which about fifty witnesses were interviewed. The end result was that the packhorse driver's employer wrote a letter of apology to the samurai. In addition, the Tokugawa government issued an official judgment that the samurai was not at fault; in fact, his actions were deemed "praiseworthy."

Although the right to cut down an offending commoner was in principle a samurai's right, it was also in effect, an obligation: if a samurai did not take action to address an insult from a commoner or was not successful in killing the commoner on the spot, there could be negative consequences for him. Moreover, if the samurai did not act immediately to redress the insult, and instead decided at a later time or even date to redress his grievance, this also could result in his punishment. In one case from 1839 the samurai was not able to kill a merchant who had been verbally abusive. The merchant managed to escape, and only later did the samurai track him down and kill him. The result in this case was that the samurai was deemed "incompetent" or "negligent" and sentenced to twenty days of house arrest. In some cases when the offended samurai was unsuccessful in killing the offender, the samurai might feel that he had no choice but to flee from his domain in disgrace. Such an action typically led to the confiscation of his fief or stipend and the extinction of the family line. Because of these requirements for action—immediate action—disrespect killing should be viewed as an act during peacetime that a samurai *must* carry out, rather than one that must be controlled or restricted by the state. Samurai were compelled to act to remedy insults; the failure to do so could impact negatively not only the individual but his relatives as well.

How often did *burei-uchi* take place? Due to the fragmented nature of the Tokugawa state, one with more than 250 domains, there are no national statistics available. However, a study of Okayama, one of the country's largest domains, reveals that there were fifty-one cases over the period 1670–1860. This amounted to roughly one every four years, and there was a notable increase of incidents from the mid-eighteenth century on. Disrespect killings were, in other words, far from a common occurrence, yet the possibility of a male commoner being cut down by a samurai's sword was quite real. The fear was genuine enough that some commoners apparently carried paper amulets to protect them from "sword calamities," likely meaning being killed by a samurai's sword. In addition, popular consciousness of the occurrence of this type of honor violence, and licensed revenge-killing (*katakiuchi*) was likely magnified through the circulation of woodblock prints, which acted as broadsheets, spreading detailed news of these bloody affairs.

Although the legal principle supporting disrespect killing seems quite straightforward, the reality was not as clear-cut. In fact, a samurai's action in killing a disrespectful commoner was not accepted unconditionally. By the early eighteenth century procedures for dealing with disrespect killings were systematized. A samurai's actions had to be reported to a high-ranking official of his domain (usually a house elder), which led to an official investigation to verify the samurai's account. For a samurai to escape some type of punishment for killing a commoner there had to be eyewitness testimony that the commoner had been sufficiently rude to have merited his being cut down. If these conditions were not met, then a samurai was likely to suffer legal punishment for having engaged in what was then classified a "fight" (*kenka*), which was disturbing the public peace, an illegal act that would likely have led to banishment from the domain.

Given the possible punishment that a samurai might face, it becomes clearer why samurai did not exercise their prerogative to cut down commoners as often as one might imagine. According to one authority, "Only if his [a samurai's] conduct were so spotless and the misconduct of the murdered party so obvious that the survivors would not strongly question the justice of the execution, would a samurai escape punishment" (Roberts, 2001, 33). No doubt the cases when samurai were punished for exercising their privilege worked to discourage its frequent exercise. In addition, the social acceptability of *burei-uchi* also seems to have greatly diminished over time, which also discouraged its exercise.

See also: Alternate Attendance (*sankin kôtai*); Intendants (*daikan*); Punishment

Why Did Samurai Favor the Left Side?

Samurai walked on the left side of the road and always on the left of other samurai. Why? Since their swords were also worn on the left, walking on the left side prevented the sheaths of two samurai swords from hitting each other, which could be a cause of a fight that had the potential to lead to both men's death. Due to the samurai's position at the top of the social system, traffic on Tokugawa roads moved forward on the left side of the road. The British merchant Charles Richardson did not understand this and got in the way of a procession of samurai from Satsuma domain while traveling near the village of Nama-mugi (outside of Edo) in 1862 and was cut down by several angry samurai for his lack of discretion.

When a samurai put on his kimono, he also inserted his left arm into its sleeve first. Why? Because the left arm was needed first to begin to take action with whatever weapon a samurai might pick up: a bow, a spear, or a sword. The left hand held the bow (while the right hand held the arrow); the left hand was used to thrust the spear forward (while the right hand manipulated its up-and-down movement); when about to draw his sword, a samurai grasped the hilt with the right hand but at the same time extended the thumb of the left hand to push the sword guard up, to ready the sword for drawing and cutting with the right hand.

Further Reading

Ikegami, Eiko. *The Taming of the Samurai: Honorific Individualism and the Making of Modern Japan.* Cambridge, MA, and London: Harvard University Press, 1995.

Roberts, Luke S. "Mori Yoshiki: Samurai Government Officer." In Anne Walthall, ed., *The Human Tradition in Modern Japan*, 25–42. Lanham, MD: Scholarly Resources, 2001.

Taniguchi Shinkô. "Kinsei ni okeru 'burei' no kannen [The concept of 'disrespect' in early modern Japan]." *Nihon rekishi*, 636 (2001), 54–70.

Vaporis, Constantine Nomikos. *Voices of Early Modern Japan: Contemporary Accounts of Daily Life during the Age of the Shoguns.* Boulder, CO: Westview Press, 2014.

Double-Guilt Doctrine (*ryôseibai*)

During the Warring States period (1467–1568), daimyo sought to consolidate their control over territories and the people living in them through a variety of means. They did this, for example, by building strong military forces, articulating ideological justifications for their rule over their domain, through intermarriage with court aristocrats, through debt moratoria, and through the construction of law codes. Daimyo also sought to undercut the independent power of their subordinates and to bolster their positions as hegemons holding sole regional authority, in particular by issuing laws that discouraged destructive conflict by punishing all parties to a violent dispute, regardless of the circumstances or merit of any party's case. This was known as the "double-guilt" doctrine or "laws punishing both sides in a dispute" (*kenka ryôseibai hô*). Daimyo sought to establish their authority over their followers, who had enjoyed a customary right of self-redress of grievances (*jiriki kyûsai*) in resolving conflicts.

The "double-guilt" doctrine can be found in a number of the daimyo house laws of the sixteenth century, including those of the Takeda house of Kai and Shinano (in 1547 and 1574), the Mori Code (1550), the Date Code (1536), the 100 Article Code of Chôsokabe Motochika of Tosa (1596), and the Imagawa Code (1526). The last of these, which was created in 1526, laid out the basic principle in Article 8:

> In dealing with those who have quarreled, both parties should be sentenced to death, irrespective of who is in the right or in the wrong. In cases where one party to the dispute, although provoked and attacked, controls himself, makes no defense and, as a result, is wounded his appeal should be granted. While it is reprehensible that he should have been a party to the dispute and perhaps contributed to its outbreak, his respect for the law in not returning the attack merits consideration. However, in cases where warriors come to the aid of one or other parties to a dispute and then claim to be an injured party, their claims shall not be entertained, even if they should be wounded or killed. (Satô, 1958, 117)

The language in the Date Code (Article 20) closely follows this in declaring that fault will be round "regardless of reports of right or wrong" and "even in cases of absolute righteousness" (Satô, 1958, 140).

The issue of the double-guilt doctrine was not only relevant to the life of warriors in the centuries before 1600. Although the principle was never codified in the shogunate's law codes, it remained relevant during the Tokugawa period. In one house code, that of the daimyo of Hachisuka, it was referred to as "the great law of the realm." It further stated that "those who are involved in a quarrel or dispute should be punished according to the principle of the great law of the world (*tenka no gohatto*). Without prejudice as to right or wrong, both parties will be executed" (Quoted in Ikegami, 1995, 142). It was, in fact, an important element in the case involving Lord Asano Naganori and Lord Kira Kôzuke Yoshinaka, known as the Akô Incident in 1701. For reasons that will remain forever unclear—we know only that Asano was motivated by a "grudge"—the daimyo Asano drew his sword and attempted to kill Kira, a direct vassal (bannerman) of the shogun, on the occasion of the reception of an imperial envoy in Edo Castle. Asano wounded Kira only slightly—and Kira "did not even lift a hand in the altercation" (Okado Denpachirô, 2006, 355)—before Asano was restrained and taken into custody. Judgment came quickly from the Tokugawa government: Asano was ordered to commit ritual suicide (*seppuku*) the same day, while Kira was not punished. Okado Denpachirô, a deputy inspector (*ometsuke*) and eyewitness to the event, twice protested the shogunate's decision to punish only Lord Asano, baldly stating that Kira must have done something to push Lord Kira "over the limit" and concluding that "[T]he verdict is much too one-sided. Any *tozama daimyô* [like Asano] would be shamed by it" (Okado Denpachirô, 2006, 357). Okado's protestations were ignored, and he was placed under house arrest for a short time.

There is also a legal question about whether Asano's attack was a proper "fight" (*kenka*), since he did not draw his sword, and therefore subject to the customary practice of "double guilt." A group of Lord Asano's retainers, holding Kira responsible for their lord's death, pledged to complete the task that their lord had not been able to complete. Although they never specifically stated that they were invoking the "double-guilt" principle, they did so by implication by pointing out the "one-sided" nature of the judgment. Of course, one might argue that the implicit intent of the principle, to discourage acts of private violence among the samurai, was upheld since Kira did not draw his sword in response. Still, for a samurai not to draw his sword in the face of an attack went counter to customary notions of dignity and honor, and accordingly Kira was criticized in some circles for his inaction.

See also: Akô Incident; *Chûshingura* (*Treasury of the Loyal Retainers*)

Further Reading

Eiko Ikegami. *The Taming of the Samurai: Honorific Individualism and the Making of Modern Japan.* Cambridge, MA: Harvard University Press, 1995.

Okado Denpachirô. "Memorandum." In Wm. Theodore de Bary, Carol Gluck, and Arthur Tiedemann, eds., *Sources of Japanese Tradition, 1600–2000*, pt. 1: *1600–1800*, 2nd ed., 355–357. New York: Columbia University Press, 2006.

Satô Shinichi, Ikeuchi Yoshisuke, and Momose Kesao, eds. *Chûsei hôsei shiryô shû* [Collected Laws of (Japan's) Medieval Period)], vol. 3. Tokyo: Iwanami shoten, 1958.

E

Education

Samurai experienced both informal and formal modes of education. Instruction began at home in a familial context, then continued with private instructors, "play groups" with peers, and, depending on rank, at the official domain school (*hankô*). By the 1860s there were roughly 225 domain schools across the country. Access to domain schools was largely closed to commoners until the end of the Tokugawa period, when some were able to gain access in some domains; most commoners with access to educational facilities generally attended "temple schools" (*terakoya*), private institutions organized by local Buddhist temples. The shogunate from early in the seventeenth century maintained an academy that late became an official school for its direct vassals, the bannermen (*hatamoto*) and housemen (*gokenin*). All of these formal institutions (see Table 4 for a list of the various types of schools and the periodization of their establishment) existed until shortly after the Meiji Restoration (1868), when the Tokugawa were toppled from power and the domains were abolished. Private schools also developed during the second half of the Tokugawa period to meet the needs of samurai for a more diverse education than was offered in the domain schools. Through access to these various types of educational institutions the samurai as a social group were transformed from largely illiterate warriors to a fully literate, well-disciplined, cultured social group—one that had a shared and common intellectual culture.

INFORMAL EDUCATION

Prior to entering a domain school the children of samurai took private lessons with local teachers. Shiba Gorô (1859–1945), the son of a high-ranking retainer of

Table 4   Formal Educational Institutions by Type and Date of Establishment

Year	Private School	Temple Schools	Gôkô*	Domain School
Before 1750	19	47	11	40
1751–1788	38	194	9	48
1789–1829	207	1,286	42	78
1830–1867	796	8,675	48	56
Date unknown	18	–	8	3
TOTAL	1,076	10,202	118	225

Gôkô can be translated as "village fraternity."

Source: Rubinger, 1982, 5.

Aizu domain (present-day Fukushima prefecture), reported that until he entered Nisshinkan, the domain school that was established in 1803, at age ten, he took private lessons with two neighborhood teachers. Under their tutorship he studied the Confucian classics, which he found extremely boring since the pedagogy involved only memorization (only later, usually at the age of fifteen, as students progressed was content actually discussed). Important socialization also occurred in neighborhood groups of sons of samurai known as *asobi no jû* or "play groups"); the boys, aged six to nine years old, were usually organized into groups of about ten individuals. The group met every day in a member's home. The day with the oldest boy reciting a list of rules to the others:

One, you shall not disobey elders;

Two, you shall bow and pay respect to elders;

Three, you shall not lie;

Four, you shall not act in a dastardly way;

Five, you shall not pick on a weakling;

Six, you shall not eat outside the home;

Seven, you shall not exchange words with a female outside the home;

Eight, what must not be must not be. (Shimoda, 2014, 31)

Afterward, each member was questioned whether he had broken any of the rules since the group's last meeting. Each boy was expected not only to confess his own violations of the rules but to report on those of their playmates. The group, as a whole, set punishments appropriate to the violation. In addition to play at home, the boys spent time outdoors climbing hills or swimming in a local river. Gorô thought of this time spent in the company of his peers an important type of "spiritual training."

In Satsuma domain (present-day Kagoshima prefecture), there was a similar youth-based institution such as Aizu domain's Shiba Gorô experienced, but one that was much more developed and provided not only physical training but moral guidance and political indoctrination as well. At these neighborhood schools, which were known as the *gôjû*, older bows taught the younger ones. Emphasis was on group solidarity, discipline, and bravery, and the curriculum included both Confucian studies as well as the military arts, including swordsmanship and sumo wrestling.

DOMAIN SCHOOLS (*HANKÔ*)

Only a small minority of domains, perhaps as few as forty, established formal schools for their retainers prior to the mid-eighteenth century. After that, the number increased steadily, and from the late eighteenth century until the end of the Tokugawa period the number rose rapidly. By the end of the period there were at least 225 schools in existence, with some domains establishing more than one. From the late eighteenth century many of the larger domains even established branch schools (*gôgaku*) to educate the children of retainers living in branch domains or outside the castle town. The larger domains also established branch schools at one of their domain residences (*daimyô yashiki*) in Edo for their retainers who were posted there on short- or long-term assignments. At the end of the Tokugawa period most samurai lived in domains that had official schools, but there were still about ninety-five domains, mostly small ones, that did not. Some of these domains that lacked schools were able to compensate by sending some of their talented samurai to attend schools in neighboring domains that allowed it or to private schools in one of the three big metropolises, Edo, Osaka, and Kyoto, a practice known as *yûgaku* (lit., "traveling to study"). Even those with domain schools, though, sent some of their top students to study outside the domain in order to expose them to talented teachers, particularly in Edo. Late in the Tokugawa period, many samurai traveled to train in swordsmanship, but others went to Edo to study Western studies or military science.

The education offered at domain schools was thoroughly Confucian, involving philosophy, moral training, and Chinese language drill, meant for the cultivation of samurai as moral exemplars, to prepare them to act in accordance with their position in society as members of the top social group in the formal status system (*mibunsei*). The charter of the above-mentioned Nisshinkan promised to "ground students in filial piety and develop their talents through received virtue so as to produce men of character who are useful to the state" (Quoted in Shimoda, 2014, 31). In other words, domain school education was intended to prepare them for the duty of service to which every samurai was born. Students entered the vast majority of domain schools between the ages of eight and ten, but their academic studies largely consisted of recitation of the Confucian classics until they reached the age of fifteen, which was usually the time for the *genpuku* (coming of age) ceremony. Only then did their classes actually turn to an attempt to understand the meaning of the texts. In Hagi, samurai boys entered the school at the age of nine, learning to recite key Confucian texts by heart. From the age of thirteen they began to learn the meaning of those texts. Sometime between the ages of eleven and thirteen they began to learn various martial arts, etiquette, and calligraphy. After their sixteenth year, group study ceased and the young samurai began private tutorials. Mandatory formal education continued until the age of twenty-two, after which they were free—but not required—to stop their studies.

Attendance at the official schools was mandatory and limited to the children of the upper ranks of samurai, although late in the period some domains loosened requirements to allow lower-ranking retainers to attend as well. The level of attendance required varied according to rank. In Mito, for example, the minimum level of attendance required ranged from fifteen days a month for househeads and eldest sons of high-ranking samurai to eight days for younger sons of the lowest rank of full samurai. More frequent attendance was required of higher-ranking retainers because in principle they were to have heavier responsibilities and thus had a great need for education.

Although late in the Tokugawa period a number of domains allowed some non-samurai to attend, most commoners who received formal instruction did so at *terakoya*, or temple schools. The social background of teachers at these institutions was varied and included commoners, Buddhist and Shinto priests, doctors and samurai as well. Samurai may have made up as much as a fifth of the teachers, the income from which supported the livelihoods of lower-ranking samurai.

Some of the most famous domain schools included: Nisshikan (Aizu domain), whose curriculum included astronomy and medicine; the Kôdôkan (Mito domain); Meirindô (Sendai); Jishûkan (Kumamoto); Meirinkan (Chôshû); and Shizutanikô (Okayama), one of the oldest schools, founded in 1670. The Kôdôkan, founded in 1841 by Tokugawa Nariaki (1800–1860) of Mito domain (present-day Ibaraki prefecture) was the largest of the group. The main building, The Seichô ("Correct Government"), has been designated an Important Cultural Property and a photograph of the school, taken in 1975, can be seen at http://www.koen.pref.ibaraki.jp/foreign _language/en/kodokan/index.html. The Meirinkan, founded in 1718 by the sixth daimyo of Chôshû, was greatly expanded in the closing decades of the Tokugawa period; a number of the leaders of the Meiji Restoration from Chôshû attended the school. During the Tokugawa period these schools were known by their names;

The south gate of the Meirinkan, the former *hankô* (domain school) of Hagi (Yamaguchi prefecture), which was named after Mencius. Established in 1718, the school was moved to the lower Hagi Castle area in 1849 and today is on the grounds of the Hagi City Meirin Elementary School. It was one of the three most important domain schools, and Chôshû samurai Yoshida Shôin and Takasugi Shinsaku were both students there. (Photo by Constantine Vaporis)

Meirinkan

Chôshû domain's Meirinkan was one of the top three domain schools in the Tokugawa period—the other two being Mito domain's Kôdôkan and Okayama domain's Shizutani school. Meirinkan (the name referred to the famous Chinese Confucian philosopher Mencius) was established in 1719. It was originally located in the third bailey (enclosure) of the castle, but in 1849 it was rebuilt for the convenience of more samurai at a location in the center of the castle town and on a much larger scale (total area of 50,107 square meters). About 20 percent of the area of the school grounds (9,966 square meters) was designated for military training. At that time the entrance policy underwent reform, and the sons of low-ranking samurai were permitted to study at the Meirinkan for the first time.

One of the martial arts practice halls of the Meirinkan still exists today. (There were four other, smaller, spaces on the school grounds for sword fighting and three others for practice with the lance.) The building, which was known during the Tokugawa period as the *Kensô keikoba* (lit., sword and lance practice hall) had, as its name indicated, one section for sword fighting and another for the lance. In the center of the hall, between the two practice spaces, was a drawing room for the daimyo for those occasions when he came to observe practices. A special bathroom for the lord was also constructed there, with extra thick walls to thwart any assassination attempt. There was also a special section set off in each practice hall for the lord to view demonstrations from. A placard at the site mentions that in 1862 famous Tosa domain swordsman Sakamoto Ryôma traveled to Hagi and during his stay practiced there with various Chôshû samurai. Close by the practice hall the school had a pond (15.5 meters × 39.5 with a depth of 1.5 meters) where samurai practiced swimming and mounting their horses while in under water. It is the only extant swimming pond belonging to a domain school in Japan.

The historic remains of the Meirinkan today—the main gate, the martial arts halls, and the swimming pond—have been designated an official National Historic Site by the Japanese government.

the term "domain school" (*hankô*) actually is a modern invention dating from the Meiji period (1868–1912).

The number of critics of domain school education increased from the late eighteenth century in the face of deteriorating social and economic conditions. In part the complaints stemmed from the fact that students were neither admitted nor advanced on the basis of ability but rather due to their father's hereditary status. The importance of hereditary privilege over merit was reinforced by certain school practices, such as seating arrangements—the sons of high-ranking samurai would sit in the front of the classroom. There was also strong criticism of the curriculum, with calls for the traditional education, which was steeped in the Confucian classics, to expand to included more "practical" subjects. In 1787, for example, an Aizu domain elder named Tanaka Gensai "recommended six special vocational courses for samurai between the ages of twenty-five and thirty who had completed their general training. They were to be in fiscal matters, village administration, ceremonies and protocol, military affairs, criminal detection and law, and public works and utilities. The students . . . [Gensai] said were to read widely in Japanese and Chinese sources but also study contemporary affairs" (Dore, 1965, 205; the phrasing is Dore's).

Although Tanaka Gensai's recommendations were not adopted in Aizu, some domains did gradually introduce "practical" studies to supplement the regular curriculum. Other domains, particularly from the 1830s, chose to expand the curriculum to include Nativist (*kokugaku*) and Mito learning. Also, from this time some domain schools began cautiously to introduce some practical elements of "Dutch learning" (*rangaku*) and "Western learning," particularly Western medicine and military science. After the arrival of the American expedition, led by Commodore Matthew C. Perry, to open Japan in 1853, this trend gained more acceptance.

Military training was also an important part of a samurai's education, and it usually began around the age of fifteen, although in some domains it was earlier. Students spent their mornings performing academic work and devoted the afternoon to military affairs. In some places military training was conducted in establishments separate from the domain school, but a number of fiefs brought the facilities into the school compound, thereby physically manifesting the warrior ideal of *bunbu*, with the literary and the military arts taught in one institution. However, since the military arts were taught on an individual teacher-student basis, the training facilities consisted of various separate areas where a different teacher taught his particular "school" of military art (*bugei*), ranged around the edge of the compound. Typically, there were areas for archery, sword fighting, horse riding, gunnery, and various forms of armed combat (*jûjutsu*). Many schools with military training facilities also had a pond for swimming, which was considered an important martial art. In Tsu domain (present-day Mie prefecture), for example, there were four *jûjutsu* sheds, three for gunnery, one for archery, three for horse riding, one for military strategy, three for lance, three for swordsmanship, and one for the halberd.

THE SHOGUNATE'S EDUCATIONAL INSTITUTIONS

The Tokugawa shogunate also sponsored schools. The first began in 1630, when the shogunate offered official support for the private school of the Confucian scholar Hayashi Razan (1583–1657). It supplied him with a plot of ground and funds to expand it into a center for Confucian studies. Originally located in the Ueno district of Edo (present-day Tokyo), it was moved in 1691 to Yushima in the Kanda district of Edo in 1691, where it was known as the *Yushima seidô*. At first it was open to samurai from other domains, but during the late eighteenth century it became an official shogunal academy, known as *Shôheizaka gakumonjo* or *Shôheikô*, and attendance was restricted to the shogun's direct vassals, the bannermen (*hatamoto*) and the housemen (*gokenin*). The curriculum centered on the Zhu Xi (Chu His) school of Confucianism, which was taught as the official doctrine. The *Shôheikô* became the model for many of the official schools that were established in the domains, but officials there were reluctant to open up the curriculum beyond orthodox Neo-Confucian studies.

The Tokugawa also established a number of other schools in the "house lands" (*tenryô*)—territories that it administered directly. Not all of these were Confucian. Most notably, it took over a center for classical Japanese literature in 1795 that had opened two years before and created a center for Western medicine in 1861. It also established a Western-style military school in 1854 and expanded a small-scale office for the translation of Western books (*Bansho shirabesho*) that was founded in 1856 into a leading center for the Western studies (the *Kaiseijo*) seven years later. After 1853, in the face of the Western military threat, the shogunate opened its educational centers to talented students from the domains.

PRIVATE SCHOOLS (*SHIJUKU*)

From the late eighteenth century private schools played an important role in the mix of educational institutions in that they were open to samurai from across the country, irrespective of domain affiliation; many of them were also open to men (only rarely were women admitted) other than retainers, including *rônin* (masterless samurai) and commoners of all types. They were also significant because they provided a variety of curricula, in addition to the official Neo-Confucian orthodoxy taught at most domain schools. These schools offered a range of fields of study, including Chinese studies, calligraphy, mathematics, Western studies (*yôgaku*),

The small building that served as the *Shôka sonjuku* ("The Academy Among the Pines"), the private school operated by Chôshû samurai Yoshida Shôin for a little more than a year, before his death in 1859. Many leaders of the Meiji Restoration were Shôin's students there. The school is part of a series of "Sites of Japan's Meiji Industrial Revolution" that were designated World Heritage Sites in 2015. (Photo by Constantine Vaporis)

Academy Among the Pines (Shôka sonjuku)

Designated a World Heritage Site in 2015, part of a set of "Sites of Japan's Meiji Industrial Revolution," the Shôka sonjuku, or Academy Among the Pines, was a private school outside the castle town of Hagi that Chôshû doman samurai Yoshida Shôin took over from his uncle. During a period of only thirteen months over the years 1857–1858, while he was under house arrest, Shôin lectured on *Mencius*, military science, and geography, among other subjects. He was intensely curious about the West and earlier in 1853 had tried to stow away American commodore Matthew C. Perry's ship. His lessons were given in a small room in his family's house before another room was added on to create additional space to accommodate the growing number of his students. He attracted a wide range of young men, including a number of nonsamurai. Many of his students went on to become important figures in the Meiji Restoration, such as: Takasugi Shinsaku, who founded a mixed militia of peasants and samurai; Itô Hirobumi, who later went on to become Japan's first prime minister and then resident general of Korea; Yamagata Aritomo, who is widely recognized as the "father" of the Japanese military, and twice became prime minister; and Kido Takayoshi (Kôin), who helped to write the Charter Oath, the first official declaration of the Meiji government in 1868.

Shôin is remembered as a passionate and devoted teacher of political thought, one who encouraged his students to think for themselves, to discuss current events, to build up Japan's military might to resist the West, and to support the cause of imperial loyalism that toppled the Tokugawa government in 1858. Shôin's Academy Among the Pines remains a popular site for Japanese nationalists, including the current prime minister Abe Shinzô.

Dutch studies (*rangaku*), and military studies. Notable private schools included the Kogidô of Itô Jinsai and the Kangien of Hirose Tansô, both led by Confucian scholars, the Tekijuku of Ogata Kôan, which emphasized Western learning, and Yoshida Shôin's Shôka sonjuku, where a number of future leaders of the Meiji Restoration were schooled in imperial loyalism. The low-ranking samurai Fukuzawa Yûkichi (1835–1901) attended the Tekijuku and in his autobiography left an important record of its operation and the dedication of its students to the acquisition of new sources of knowledge from the West.

See also: Civil and Military Arts (*bunbu*); Coming of Age (*genpuku*); Daimyo and Domains; Fukuzawa Yûkichi; Martial Arts (*bugei*); Shogunate (*bakufu, kôgi*); Yoshida Shôin

Further Reading

Dore, R. P. *Education in Tokugawa Japan*. New York: Routledge and Kegan Paul, 1965.

Fukuzawa Yûkichi. *The Autobiography of Yûkichi Fukuzawa*. Revised translation by Eiichi Kiyooka, with a foreword by Carmen Blacker. New York: Columbia University Press, 1980 [1966].

Rubinger, Richard. *Private Academies of Tokugawa Japan*. Princeton, NJ: Princeton University Press, 1982.

Shiba Gorô. *Remembering Aizu: The Testament of Shiba Gorô*. Edited by Ishimitsu Mahito. Translated, with Introduction and Notes, by Teruko Craig. Honolulu: University of Hawai'i Press, 1999.

Shimoda, Hiraku. *Lost and Found: Recovering Regional Identity in Imperial Japan*. Cambridge, MA, and London: Harvard University Asia Center, 2014.

F

Falconry (*takagari*)

Falconry, or *takagari* in Japanese, refers to the practice of hunting with birds of prey. The Japanese term *taka* is most often glossed as "falcon" or "hawk," but the term "raptor," using the scientific name for the entire order of birds of prey, Accipitriformes, is the most precise. Although in Japanese the term *taka* is used most often when referring to birds of prey, sometimes *tobi* (black kites or *Milvus migrans*) and *washi* (eagle, a common name for several genera within the bird family) are also utilized. Falconry in Japanese history was not just a personal hobby or sport—it also often served as a political and cultural tool.

There is evidence from Japan's prehistory that warriors engaged in falconry (*takagari*) from as early as the fifth and sixth centuries. This is based on archaeological finds of clay figurines of falconers uncovered in mounded tombs in Japan. Literary evidence from the *Nihon shoki* (Chronicles of Japan, 720) suggests that the technical skills and equipment may have come from Korea. In that text we learn that Emperor Nintoku employed a man from the Korean kingdom of Paekche who was in Japan to train hawks to be used to hunt pheasants. During the Heian period (794–1185), falconry was practiced by the court aristocracy, but from the Kamakura period (1185–1333), with the establishment of the first shogunate, warriors began to take up the practice as well.

Falconry was, however, a practice associated with privilege and political authority. Acquiring and maintaining the birds of prey, not to mention the training and maintaining of skilled handlers, required substantial financial resources. To engage in falconry also required access to, or control of, large areas of land to train and hunt with the animals.

During the sixteenth century falconry was practiced by both daimyo and court aristocrats. For the daimyo, hunting in this manner involved walking and riding through the countryside, reconnecting him to the land over which he ruled. It also provided an occasion for intelligence gathering. European visitors to Japan in the late sixteenth century made note of the Japanese custom of capturing and breeding birds of prey and training them to use in hunting. Joao Rodrigues, a Portuguese Jesuit priest who was in Japan in the late sixteenth and early seventeenth centuries, relates that:

> The lords and nobles breed in their houses many kinds of birds of prey, such as falcons, hawks, gerfalcons [gyrafalcons], and many other types, both big and small, so that they may go hunting with them. They have special houses where the birds are kept on wooden perches, tied by the leg with handsome cords of crimson silk. There are certain men appointed to breed, feed, and clean the birds, and this they do meticulously. (Cooper, 2001, 110)

Indeed, among daimyo during the sixteenth century falcons were often given in gift exchanges. Takeda Katsuyori, daimyo of Kai province, sent Uesugi Kagekatsu a raptor, calling it a "famous product of this province" (Pitelka, 2016, 100). In fact, a well-known portrait of his father, Takeda Shingen (1521–1573), painted by Hasegawa Tôhaku (1539–1610), depicts him seated, with a hawk on a perch to his side.

Falconry and the exchange of falcons were practiced by the three unifiers, Oda Nobunaga, Toyotomi Hideyoshi, and Tokugawa Ieyasu. The *Chronicle of Lord Nobunaga* informs us that the warlord took up the sport at a young age and was very good at it. He did so in the company of his teacher in the military arts, which indicates that falconry was considered essential to his training as a warrior. The linkage between warfare and falconry is evident in the name that Nobunaga gave one of his favored birds, Randori (plunder). However, to Nobunaga, like his two successors, falconry was also a means by which to impress people with his wealth and his military skills. When he visited the Imperial Court in 1577 at the beginning of a falconry outing, Nobunaga put on a show before crowds in Kyoto, with more than one hundred archers, fourteen men bearing falcons on their arms, as well as Nobunaga with his pages and horse guards. The ceremony was concluded with the emperor himself presenting gifts to the archers and examining Nobunaga's falcon.

Hideyoshi engaged in falconry seemingly with the same enthusiasm that he had for the practice of tea. For one, hunting with falcons provided a form of respite from battle and the struggle for power. In a letter from 1588 addressed to his wife, Kita no Mandokoro, he wrote, "In this period I am engaging in falconry every day and am eating well. Please do not worry. Everything is forgotten but the falcons, and at night I sleep soundly" (Pitelka, 2016, 103). At the same time he used the practice for political purposes, as in 1591 when he engaged in falconry for more than a month. During this period he worked with 150 falcon handlers (*takajô*) and forty-eight falcons, catching as many as 3,000 birds. For his return to Kyoto after his outing Hideyoshi set up seating for the members of the imperial court to admire the return of his victorious procession with all of the spoils from their hunt.

The third of the three unifiers, Tokugawa Ieyasu, was also a falconry enthusiast. According to the *Tales of Mikawa* (*Mikawa monogatari*), his interest began at an early age, while he was a hostage of the warlord Oda Nobuhide. Later, as an ally of Oda Nobunaga's they hunted together on several occasions, helping to further build their alliance and personal relationship. As shogun, from 1603, Ieyasu frequently engaged in falconry and in the exchange of falcons as one important element of his politics of sociability and gift-giving. The birds and other animals that the falcons caught could be sent to allies and vassals, where they were presented at banquets, thus helping to cement political relationships. By doing this one can argue that a lord was literally feeding his inferiors and thereby demonstrating his benevolent authority.

After his retirement in 1606 Ieyasu remained an avid fan of the hunt, including falconry. In 1612, he sent more than seventy birds that he had caught while traveling between Nagoya and Sunpu and sent them to Toyotomi Hideyori and the emperor. Given Ieyasu's appreciation of falconry, it was not surprising that other lords gifted him raptors as well. Satake Yoshinobu (lord of Kubota domain) and Date Masamune (lord of Sendai domain) gave Tokugawa Ieyasu a gift of five falcons in 1615, after his defeat of the Toyotomi forces in Osaka Castle; in fact, for the remainder of the Tokugawa period, the practice of gifting raptors to the shogun became increasingly ritualized. In 1615, two months after destroying Osaka Castle, thereby eliminating the threat posed by Toyotomi Hideyori, Ieyasu departed Kyoto for last time, returning to Sunpu, which was his base as retired shogun. He seems to have spent his final months engaging in the pastime he enjoyed for much of his life.

As falconry enthusiasts, the three unifiers also made considerable efforts to protect falconry habitats, to establish rookeries, as well as to regulate who could practice the sport. Falconry became the prerogative of elite warriors and their retainers. It was one of the many hereditary rights of samurai, but because of the issue of cost, falconry was limited even more to the economically privileged, higher-ranking samurai.

For the early shoguns—Ieyasu (1543–1616), Hidetada (1579–1632), and Iemitsu (1604–1651)—falconry was not only a sport. They also used it to demonstrate and enforce their authority, restricting the right to engage in it to themselves, the daimyo and their specialist falcon handlers. Ieyasu and his descendants revoked the emperor's hawking privileges and demonstrated his authority by sending the cranes that he caught to the imperial court. The size of the early shogun's expeditions resembled military campaigns and gave visual evidence of their political power. That power was also exercised by the shogun in restricting who could hunt which birds: for example, only the shogun could hunt cranes and swans, while the daimyo were restricted to other types of birds, such as geese and ducks. Authority was also asserted in designating large areas of land as falconry fields (*takaba*), entrance to which was highly controlled.

As noted, daimyo were also known to engage in the practice of falconry. A vestige of this practice can be found in place names in Japanese cities that were formerly castle towns. In Kôchi, for example, the ward name Takajô-machi (falconer's town) still exists. It is the location where a residence for the daimyo's falcon handlers was built, together with facilities for housing the lord's falcons.

Given its association with restricted privilege and military prowess, falconry was an ideal subject for warriors who commissioned paintings. Scenes of warriors engaged in falconry, or images of just the falcons themselves, were subjects for screen paintings and hanging scroll paintings that symbolized the owner's authority.

With the Meiji Restoration of 1868 the shogun was removed from power and imperial rule restored. With that political change, the privilege of falconry was restored to the emperor. There is no evidence that he exercised that right, but the change demonstrates that the right to engage in the practice conferred high status.

See also: Firearms; *Mikawa monogatari* (*Tales of Mikawa*); Oda Nobunaga; Tokugawa Ieyasu; Toyotomi Hideyoshi

Further Reading

Cooper, Michael. *Joao Rodrigues's Account of Sixteenth-Century Japan*. London: Hakluyt Society, 2001.

Pitelka, Morgan. *Spectacular Accumulation: Material Culture, Tokugawa Ieyasu, and Samurai Sociability.* Honolulu: University of Hawai'i Press, 2016.

Saunders, Rachel. "Pursuits of Power: Falconry in Edo Period Japan." *Orientations,* 36(2) (March 2005), 82–92.

Family Crests (*kamon*)

Mon (crests) or *kamon* (family crests) are Japanese heraldic emblems that were used to identify an individual or household in Tokugawa Japan, similar to the badges and coats of arms in the European heraldic tradition. Although all samurai households utilized them, some commoners, including merchants and craftsmen, also used them for business purposes from this time onward. In modern times they continue to be used: the *mon* of the imperial institution (the stylized chrysanthemum blossom) or of major corporations such as Mitsubishi (the three water chestnuts) are but two famous examples.

The use of *mon* during the Tokugawa period built on a tradition of battlefield identification going back to the late twelfth century, when various aristocratic families such as the Taira and Minamoto used colored flags, sometimes with different designs or insignias, to distinguish themselves from their adversaries. The practice of *mon* became well established by the Warring States period (1467–1568). Some famous *mon* include the *aoi* crest—three hollyhock leaves pointing inwards within a circle—used by the Tokugawa family; the crane crest of the Mori family (Chôshû domain), which is quite similar to that used by Japan Airlines; the three oak (*kashiwa*) leaf in a white circle crest of the Yamauchi family (Tosa domain); and the cross within the circle crest of the Shimazu family (Satsuma domain). In general *mon* consisted of a number of general categories, such as plants, flowers, trees, tools, birds, insects and animals, abstract patterns and designs, as well as ideographs and symbols.

Kamon (family or heraldic crests), from left to right, of the Tokugawa (three hollyhock leaves inside a circle), Môri of Chôshû domain (three circles, or stars, under the Chinese character for the number one), Shimazu of Kagoshima or Satsuma domain (cross in a circle), and Yamauchi of Tosa domain (three oak leaves in a circle). Family crests, worn on clothing, or appearing on banners and other objects, marked samurai identity in a public manner. The crests of the major daimyo families would have been immediately recognizable to most contemporaries.

Mon were emblems of identification found on flags worn on the back of the armor that samurai wore, known as *sashimono*; individual military units were further indicated by different field colors. The crests might also appear on larger flags; banners, including those worn by horses (*uma jirushi*); streamers; on armor; on ceremonial clothing and personal possessions; and even on roof ridge tiles of residential and castle architecture. There does not exist a definitive collection of family crests, but the *mon* of the daimyo and the high-ranking direct retainers (*hatamoto*) of the Tokugawa were included in the information contained in the *bukan*, books of heraldry published throughout the period.

See also: Books of Heraldry (*bukan*); Daimyo and Domains

Further Reading
Turnbull, Steven. *The Samurai Sourcebook.* London: Cassell & Co., 1998.

Websites
"Japanese Heraldry: Kamon Knowledge & Japanese Insignias Knowledge Base." http://www.thejapaneseheraldry.com. Accessed December 27, 2017.
"Kamon Symbols of Japan." https://doyouknowjapan.com/symbols. Accessed December 27, 2017.
"Kamon World." http://www.harimaya.com/kamon (Japanese only). Accessed December 27, 2017.
"Nihon kamon kenkyûkai." http://www.nihonkamon.com (Japanese only). Accessed December 27, 2017.

Fief (*chigyô*)

It is often repeated in written accounts of Tokugawa Japan that the majority of samurai were drawn off the land and became urban residents, in or around the castle towns, receiving stipends from their lords drawn from the domain's storehouses. The reality is much more complicated and reveals that the relationship between the samurai and the land was far from uniform across Japan. It also reveals that the notion that landed fiefs were a vanishing practice of an earlier time (the Warring States period) is incorrect.

The relationship between lords and their vassals during the Tokugawa period was often defined by the Japanese term *chigyô*, which literally means "management" and which we often translate in English as "fiefs." The term, however, had several meanings: in some cases, it identified a higher status of stipend disbursement, and in other instances it meant a land grant involving some degree of management rights. In either case, the term applied only to full samurai, meaning retainers in the upper half of a daimyo's retainer corps. (As explained below, lower samurai would receive their stipends in *fuchi* or *kippu,* which were "rice tickets," meaning pieces of paper that were exchanged for rice or a combination of rice and money obtained from the domain's warehouse.) The lord bequeathed *chigyô* to a retainer in exchange for military and other services to be performed. In some cases, a high-ranking, enfieffed samurai might also grant a sub-retainer a *chigyô*. In either circumstance, the term *chigyô* was used in terms of daimyo vassals' or a

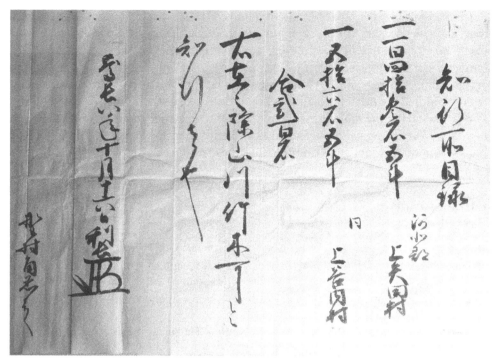

Photo of an original, brush-written document of enfeoffment (list of lands granted in fief), dating from 1603, from the Nomura Samurai House in the former Kaga domain, Kanazawa city (Kanazawa prefecture). The document, written in Japanese, is read from top to bottom, right to left. (Photo by Constantine Vaporis)

sub-vassals' holdings, as defined above. A daimyo's landholdings, on the other hand, which were in theory bequeathed by the shogun as "special favor" (*go-on*), were usually referred to as *ryôchi* or *ryôbun* (territory in fief). In return for his domain, a daimyo was required to pledge loyalty to the shogun and to provide military and other forms of service, including the alternate attendance (*sankin kôtai*).

The practice of landed fiefs (*jikata chigyô*) originated in the Warring States period (1467–1568), when samurai had broad-based, independent authority over these landholdings. In the Tokugawa period, however, many daimyo made great efforts to undercut those rights and make their vassals subordinate to his public authority, meaning domain law. This process was facilitated by the development of the *kokudaka* system in the late sixteenth century, by which yield was measure in terms of *koku* (1 *koku* = 5.1 bushels, or approximately 180 liters, of rice). Accordingly, fiefs could be measured in terms of output, in standardized amounts such as 100 *koku* or 200 *koku*, instead of defined by topography.

Vassals with landed fiefs often resided in the countryside and exerted some legal and economic controls over the peasantry: for example, they determined the level of tax payments and could demand labor services. They often received tax payment in rice directly from the peasants, even if they lived in the castle town.

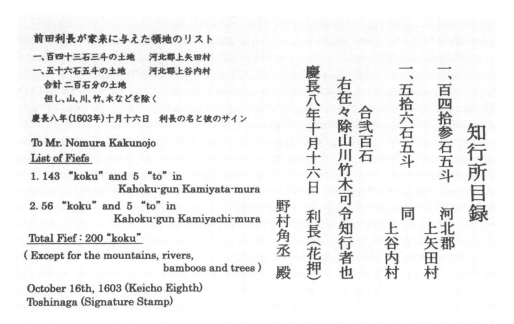

前田利長が家来に与えた領地のリスト

一、百四十三石三斗の土地　　河北郡上矢田村
一、五十六石五斗の土地　　　河北郡上谷内村
　　合計 二百石分の土地
　　但し、山、川、竹、木などを除く

慶長八年(1603年)十月十六日　利長の名と彼のサイン

知行所目録

一、百四拾参石五斗　　河北郡上矢田村

一、五拾六石五斗　　同　上谷内村

合弐百石

右在々除山川竹木可令知行者也

慶長八年十月十六日　利長(花押)

野村角丞　殿

To Mr. Nomura Kakunojo

<u>List of Fiefs</u>

1. 143 "koku" and 5 "to" in
　　　Kahoku-gun Kamiyata-mura
2. 56 "koku" and 5 "to" in
　　　Kahoku-gun Kamiyachi-mura

<u>Total Fief : 200 "koku"</u>

(Except for the mountains, rivers,
　　　　　　　　　　　　　bamboos and trees)

October 16th, 1603 (Keicho Eighth)
Toshinaga (Signature Stamp)

Transcription and translation of the document of enfeoffment on page 106, which was presented by Kaga daimyo Maeda Toshinaga (1562–1614) to his retainer Nomura Kakunojô, in printed form (right), in modern Japanese (top left), and in English-language translation. The document presents concrete evidence of the political and economic relationship between lord and vassal. From the Nomura Samurai House in the former Kaga domain, Kanazawa city (Kanazawa prefecture). (Photo by Constantine Vaporis)

However, some landed fiefs were "paper" or "fictive" fiefs (*kuramai chigyô*), meaning that while the income they received was in principle derived from a designated landholding, the retainer had no personal connection with it. Still, these were more prestigious than outright stipends that were not even nominally related to a landholding.

The majority of a daimyo's retainers were stipended samurai. According to this scheme, tax grain was collected from peasant farmers who worked on so-called "provisioning lands" (*kurairechi*), which were under the daimyo's direct control. The tax rice was stored in a central treasury, from which it was later disbursed to retainers. The salary was measured in rice—in *koku*—but was often paid in a combination of rice or lesser grains and money (specie). A stipend paid largely in rice conferred some prestige on the retainers, whereas a payment in cash was associated with menial status.

The great majority of domains, over 80 percent of them by the end of the seventeenth century, abandoned the practice of granting land in fief to their retainers or granted only "paper fiefs." In Tosa domain (Kôchi prefecture), for example, new allotments of fiefs stopped in 1681; however, all fiefs awarded before that date continued to exist, and samurai on them continued to have a direct relationship with the people of their fiefs and received payments directly from the villages where they lived. In Hirosaki domain (Aomori prefecture), officials there began to convert landed fiefs to "fictive fiefs" or stipends until 1685. Across Japan new land that was brought into production after the late seventeenth century became part of the daimyo's "provisioning lands" and was not dispersed to retainers in fief.

At the end of the seventeenth century landed fiefs existed in about 20 percent of domains across the country. Although this represents a minority of the domains in numerical terms, in fact those in which landed fiefs continued to be granted accounted for over one-half of the assessed productive capacity (*kokudaka*) of all domains. In terms of area, domains in which fiefs were granted comprised the majority of the collective territory held by domains—that is, the territory not held by the shogunate and its retainers—and included nine of the ten largest domains in the country, such as Kaga, Chôshû, Satsuma, Kumamoto, and Fukuoka. Furthermore, the institution of landed fiefs was not restricted to these peripheral areas but was found in all the major regions of Japan, including the Kinai region (around Kyoto and Osaka). All domains over 500,000 *koku* in size maintained landed fiefs, but almost without exception those below 50,000 *koku* abandoned them.

The extent of control that the fief holder held can be broken down into two parts: the rights of a landlord, meaning "private rights," and the right to wield lordly, or "public rights." In the latter category, there are three elements: the rights of taxation, administration, and legislation or jurisprudence. In general terms, over time the daimyo were successful in increasing their central authority by decreasing the amount of land held in fief and in undercutting the private authority of the retainers in areas where they nominally still held onto fiefs. In most domains these policies were pursued in various forms during the 1640s–1660s. For example, domain authorities in Kii introduced a reform in 1646 that allowed the fief grantee to retain direct control of the peasants but removed from them any authority over taxation and jurisprudence; the tax rate for the rice tax and other imposts were set by the daimyo while legal and penal authority was made the responsibility of a magistrate appointed by the daimyo.

These institutional changes left the fief holder only with the power of tax collection. Although this was done according to principles laid down by the domain, the way in which they were applied was left to the discretion of the fief holder. This meant that the fief holder had broad powers: he was responsible for setting the annual tax rate, collecting it, not to mention pursuing policies that would ensure that the peasant cultivators were able to continue to pay taxes (and not become bankrupt and abandon their fields). Although "these powers were exercised as the private authority of the fief-holder, they were supported and guaranteed by the 'public' authority of the domain" (Morris, 1988, 6). In Yonezawa domain (Yamagata prefecture), for example, landed fiefs continued into the nineteenth century, but the rights of the fief holders were regulated strictly. Acceptable tax levels were regulated by domain regulation in 1683. Moreover, tax delinquents were not to be dealt with by the vassal; they were to be brought to the domain intendant, meaning to an official of the daimyo. Fief holders were allowed to impose a variety of taxes in kind, on things such as sugar, rope, and straw, but these tax rates were also set by the domain government. Through these measures, then, the daimyo's government undercut the independent authority of its vassals. Although this might seem like a negative development for those retainers, in giving up some of their private rights they gained increased protection under the lord's authority and no longer had to negotiate with the peasant farmers, which explains why some retainers actively requested that their landed fiefs be converted into stipends.

Another way in which daimyo eroded the independent authority of their retainers was to create shared fiefs (*bunsan aikyû chigyô*). Domains previously administered as a contiguous landholding could be arbitrarily altered by the daimyo by ordering changed in the local location of fiefs measured according to *kokudaka*. In other words, the daimyo physically disbursed formerly contiguous domains into a number of divided fiefs, thereby created villages shared by several different fief holders. In Yonezawa domain, for example, out of the 101 villages in Nagai district, 11 villages were held by only one retainer; 52 villages were held by groups of two to ten retainers; 23 villages were held by groups of ten to twenty; and 9 villages were held by groups that included more than twenty retainers. By creating this complicated patchwork of divided landholdings, the daimyo bolstered his authority and diminished that of his landed retainers.

As a rule, to increase their controls over their retainers, daimyo forbade their retainers from residing in the countryside, requiring them to live in the castle town. In 1653, the shogunate issued an order to all daimyo that echoed the efforts of Kii domain: fief holders should move to the castle town and become stipendiaries. The Tokugawa order may have encouraged daimyo in some domains to follow suit, but many already were pursuing these policies to increase their centralized authority and to diminish local autonomy as well as the possibilities of local revolt. In Chôshû (Hagi) domain (present-day Yamaguchi prefecture), for example, while the majority of tax revenues (57 percent) came from landed fiefs in the early seventeenth century, by the early nineteenth century that figure had fallen to less than a third (28 percent). To some extent this drop in percentage reflected the fact that new land brought into production became nonfief land, but according to one authority, "By 1800, indeed, only a handful of senior families in any domain were likely to hold fiefs in land, except by special dispensation" (Craig, 1961, 110).

In a number of domains, a select number of major retainers had special fiefs that included a moated residence compound (*doi*). In many cases, these were late Warring States period castles whose turrets or donjons had been removed. In Tosa domain, for example, five of the largest fief holders—all domain house elders (*karô*)—were granted landed fiefs in different parts of the domain. In Aki (Aki City, Kôchi prefecture), where the Gotô family held their fief, the residence was encircled by low-lying stone walls and surrounded by a moat. The residences of the Gotô's vassals were arranged around it in a type of small-scale castle town. Although the five elders held their landed fiefs in different parts of the domain, they were also required to maintain residences in Kôchi castle town; the elders performed a type of local alternate attendance in rotating their residences between their fiefs and Kôchi. The same was true in Kubota domain, where the Satake daimyo had five senior retainers, each of whom lived on a fortified estate, in Kakunodate, Yuzawa, Hiyama, Jûniso, and In'nai; one of the senior retainers was the head of a branch family of the Satake lord known as the North Satake and held a fief of 10,000 *koku*, the same as a minor daimyo.

See also: Alternate Attendance (*sankin kôtai*); Daimyo and Domains; Income

Further Reading

Craig, Albert. *Chôshû in the Meiji Restoration.* Cambridge, MA: Harvard University Press, 1961.

Madoka, Kanai. *Han* [Domain]. Tokyo: Shinbundô, 1962.

Morris, John Francis. *Kinsei Nihon chigyô no kenkyû* [A Study of Fiefs in Early Modern Japan]. Ôsaka: Seibundô, 1988.

Ravina, Mark. *Land and Lordship in Early Modern Japan.* Stanford, CA: Stanford University Press, 1999.

Firearms

The standard narrative regarding the introduction of firearms in Japan is that they were brought to Japan by a ship carrying 100 Portuguese who were driven ashore by a storm in 1543 on Tanegashima Island, located to the southwest of the Japanese archipelago. Also on board was a Chinese scholar, and through him the Japanese communicated with the Europeans, two of whom possessed arquebuses. The local daimyo, Tanegashima Toritaka, then ordered his craftsmen to reproduce the weapons. This interpretation is based on the *Teppôki* (*An Account of Arquebuses*), a history written in 1606 at the request of Tanegashima Hisatoki to honor his grandfather, Toritaka, more than sixty years after the purported first arrival of guns in Japan.

Recent research, however, has revealed a complicated history, pointing to more diverse origins for the introduction of firearms to Japan. There is a strong claim that the arquebuses first introduced to Japan were in fact manufactured in Southeast Asia, not in Europe, and were brought to Japan by trader-pirates, known as *wakô*; this statement is based on evidence that the structure of Japanese arquebuses, specifically the location of metal fittings and the shape of bullets, were similar to those of weapons produced in Southeast Asia rather than in Europe. There is also evidence that the Ryukyu kingdom was a conduit for the transfer of guns to Japan in the mid-fifteenth century. In other words, while Tanegashira is often described as the location where guns were first introduced to Japan, in fact the evidence now suggests that this took place in multiple locations.

It was not until the mid-sixteenth century, however, that firearms found their way onto Japanese battlefields. For example, documents dating from 1565 relate that combatants suffered casualties with arquebuses; two years later, in 1567, Môri Terumoto, the daimyo of Aki provinces, hired and dispatched a group of infantry with arquebuses to the battlefront.

The performance of early firearms in Japan left much to be desired. A well-trained archer could fire about ten arrows per minute up to 200 meters. In contrast, an arquebus took several minutes to reload and was accurate only up to 100 meters. However, the virtue of guns was that virtually no training was needed, whereas it took many years to become a skilled archer.

Still, the destructive potential of guns was such that as the technology of guns was improved (many contemporary books on the art of gunnery remain), leading daimyo of the time such as Oda Nobunaga and Takeda Shingen came to recognize the importance of firearms. As early as 1549, Oda Nobunaga placed an order for 500 matchlocks with gunsmiths in Kunitomo, which became a leading center of production, and organized a firearms brigade in his army. Takeda Shingen, in 1555, had 300 firearms in his possession at his fortress at Hitachi, and an order from him dating from 1569 instructed his retainers to bring arquebusiers (gunners) as well as bowmen to battle. Just two years later, in 1571, we see in another order of his a marked shift in preference for guns over more traditional weapons: "From now on, guns will be what we need most" (Stavros, 2013, 4–5). Thus, gradually over thirty of forty years of their introduction to Japan, arquebuses came to be recognized as essential weapons for success in military warfare. Yet, despite the fact that daimyo like Takeda Shingen recognized the importance of guns and used them in battle, many were unable to obtain them in great quantity. As a result, some daimyo in the late sixteenth century competed to intercept or to purchase shipments of new weapons that began arriving with increasing frequency from Europe, mainly via India. Oda Nobunaga, however, had greater economic resources at his disposal and was thereby able to achieve a military advantage through the acquisition of more firearms than his rivals. His vassal and successor, Toyotomi Hideyoshi, was also as dedicated to the procurement, and deployment, of firearms; he was able to amass several thousand of them, which he put to use in his campaigns against the Shimazu family in Kyushu. The early victories of Hideyoshi's forces in Korea (1592–1598) were likely due to the overwhelming number of muskets that his Japanese forces had. For example, he ordered the same daimyo (Shimazu) he had earlier defeated to arm 1,500 of his soldiers to be sent to fight for Hideyoshi in Korea with muskets (in addition to 1,500 with bows and 300 with spears). Given the size of the total force the Japanese dispatched to invade Korea, there may have been more than 10,000 guns in Japanese hands. With this technological advantage, the Japanese forces were able to capture the Korean capital of Pyongyang within twenty days of their initial landing on the Korean Peninsula.

According to George Sansom, in his well-respected *History of Japan*:

> The muskets which they [the Portuguese] carried caused excitement among the rescuers [the Japanese], and for a long time after this event the Japanese name for firearms was Tanegashima. The weapons were soon copied in considerable numbers, but it would be a mistake to suppose that the use of firearms at once brought about a great change in methods of warfare. For although they were used in the major battles of the sixteenth century, they remained in scarce supply for a century or more, and they did not displace traditional weapons—the sword, the bow, and the spear—until an even later date. (Sansom, 1961, 263–264)

Sansom's statement raises an important question, whether firearms brought about a military revolution in Japan. According to some scholars, a military revolution took place in Japan in the sixteenth century as a result of the use of firearms on a large scale, beginning with the Battle of Nagashino in 1575. Others argue that while guns did not radically change the nature of battle, they were significant because they did "allow men to fire projectiles at twice the distance than had been common before. This caused an upswing of casualties among high-ranking warriors. . . . Massed units of pikemen continued to occupy the battlefield" (Conlan, 2008,179). Also, while Nobunaga was certainly an innovator in terms of use of guns on a large scale (1,000 or 3,000 employed at Nagashino, according to two different historical sources), it is not clear that he can be credited with being the first to develop synchronized volley fire at Nagashino, as some historians have claimed.

Hideyoshi sought to pacify the countryside through his sword hunt edict (1587), which called for the confiscation of not only swords but also pikes and arquebuses. Nevertheless, the Tokugawa government allowed many guns to remain in the possession of villagers since they were used to protect agricultural fields from wild animals as well as for hunting by commoners living in mountainous areas. Also, groups of villagers employed by the authorities at a number of checking stations (*sekisho*) on the official Tokugawa road network acted as peasant-reserve forces and were allowed to maintain possession of guns, which were registered at the stations. Thus, while firearms, and weapons in general, were highly regulated by the Tokugawa state, demilitarization of the countryside was not complete.

Besides the villagers who were allowed to possess and fire guns, who else in Tokugawa society used them, and what were social attitudes surrounding their use? In Japan during the Tokugawa period, the sword rather than the gun came to symbolize the soul of the samurai. Nevertheless, skill with guns, which supplemented rather than replaced the bow, came to be seen as a mark of masculine identity. Although women who belonged to the samurai status group did carry daggers and practice fighting with halberds (*naginata*), there is no evidence that they ever fired guns. For shoguns and daimyo, skills with a gun were one manner in which they demonstrated their manhood. For example, Tokugawa Ieyasu and his heir, Hidetada, were known as proficient marksmen. Their reputations were gained, however, through their use of guns on the hunt rather than on the battlefield. Shoguns and the daimyo exchanged guns as gifts. The daimyo also incorporated them into their alternate attendance retinues, which paraded up and down Tokugawa Japan's highways in a very public manner, while the shoguns displayed them in their processions to Nikkô Shrine to worship Tokugawa Ieyasu's incarnation. Guns were even a part of Ieyasu's funeral procession in 1616, suggesting perhaps that guns, like bows, were regarded as having some efficacy against evil spirits. The guns that shoguns and daimyo exchanged as gifts were of great value, enhancing their owners' prestige and serving as a cultural symbol of their masculinity (Walthall, 2011, 31).

Guns carried different symbolic value depending on who was using them. High-value guns meant for the hunt were a part of the life of daimyo and shoguns and "served as tools that assisted in the performance of masculine tasks" (Walthall, 2011, 43). Samurai were known to enjoy shooting guns at targets or in recreational hunts, but when guns were used to earn one's livelihood, as was the case of male foot soldiers or hunters, they were associated with low status. This was particularly true of hunters, due to the pollution associated with their handling of dead animals.

See also: Falcony (*takagari*); Nagashino, Battle of; Oda Nobunaga; Sword Hunt (*katanagari*)

Further Reading

Conlan, Thomas. *Weapons and Fighting Techniques of the Samurai Warrior, 1200–1877.* London: Amber, 2000.

"An Encyclopedia of Guns." The Significance of Anzai Minoru's Collection of Secret Books on the Art of Gunnery in the Museum Collection. *Rekihaku,* 126 (2004): https://www.rekihaku.ac.jp/english/outline/publication/rekihaku/126/witness.html.

Howell, David L. "The Social Life of Firearms in Tokugawa Japan." *Japanese Studies,* 29(1) (2009), 65–80.

Lidin, Olof G. *Tanegashima: The Arrival of Europe in Japan.* Copenhagen: Nordic Institute of Asian Studies, 2002.

Sansom, George. *A History of Japan, 1334–1615,* vol. 2. Stanford, CA: Stanford University Press, 1961.

Stavros, Matthew. "Military Revolution in Early Modern Japan." *Japanese Studies* (2013), 1–18.

Taniguchi, Shinko. "Military Evolution or Revolution? State Formation and the Early Modern Samurai." In Rosemarie Deist, ed., *Knights and Samurai: Actions and Images of Elite Warriors in Europe and East Asia*, 169–195. Goppingen: Kummerle Verlag, 2003.

Walthall, Anne. "Do Guns Have Gender? Technology and Status in Early Modern Japan." In Sabine Fruhstuck and Anne Walthall, eds., *Recreating Japanese Men*, 25–45. Berkeley: University of California Press, 2011.

Foreign-Born Samurai

A number of foreigners (non-native Japanese) during the Edo period were given special status in the form of a fief or stipend and the privilege of wearing two swords. In addition, during the period of unification prior to then (1568–1600), before the status system was established, several foreign-born people were granted a fief or stipend in rice by their lord. It is questionable whether or not these historical figures should be considered *bushi* (i.e., samurai in a general sense of the word).

In the period prior to the Edo period, one foreigner stands out for the service he performed for a Japanese daimyo. An African man, perhaps from Mozambique or Angola, who was either a slave or servant of Alessandro Valignano, the Italian head of the Jesuit mission in Japan, arrived in Japan in 1579. He came to the attention of Oda Nobunaga because of the crowds that would gather to catch a glimpse of him in Kyoto in 1581. As an African, his dark skin would have been quite unusual to the Japanese of the time. The warlord summoned the man, presented him with gifts of money and took him into his service. The *Chronicles of Lord Nobunaga* (Shinchô kôki) detailed their first meeting that year:

> On the 23rd of the 2nd month [in 1581], a black page (*kuro-bôzu*) came from the Christian countries. He looked about 26, 24 or 25 by Western count or 27 years old; his entire body was black like that of an ox. The man was healthy and good-looking. Moreover, his strength was greater than that of 10 men.

Impressed by his physical stature, and likely also due to his ability to speak Japanese, Nobunaga took the African into his service and gave him the name Yasuke. He later followed his lord into battle, and when Nobunaga was entrapped by his formerly trusted vassal, Akechi Mitsuhide, at Honnôji temple in 1582, Yasuke was captured but released. Apparently, his foreign birth saved him, for in releasing Yasuke, Akechi is said to have remarked, "He is not Japanese," perhaps meaning that as such he could not have truly been serving Nobunaga (Quoted in Leupp, 2003, 37). There was no further mention of him in the historical record after his release to the Jesuits.

Two Europeans on board the Dutch vessel, the *De Liefde*, William Adams and Jan Joosten van Loodensteyn, became advisers to Tokugawa Ieyasu (1543–1616), the founder of the dynasty that bore his name. The first, William Adams (1564–1620), was an English pilot who held the position of major pilot on the Dutch East Indies ship *Liefde* (originally named *Erasmus*). After a hazardous journey from Rotterdam around the Straits of Magellan in which they experienced many storms, dwindling supplies, and spreading disease onboard, only eighteen of the more than one hundred crew members remained alive when the ship arrived, in 1600, in Japanese waters, in Bungo province in northern Kyushu (Oita prefecture); four more died in the ensuing days.

The Portuguese Jesuits who had Tokugawa Ieyasu's counsel, fearing the loss of their trade monopoly and personal influence, tried to convince him that Adams and his crew were pirates, but Ieyasu was not so easily swayed—at least until he personally met him. Ieyasu did confiscate the ship and its military cargo on board the *Liefde:* 500 matchlocks, 5,000 cannonballs, 5,000 pounds of gunpowder, and 300 firearrows, not to mention the nineteen bronze cannons that protected the ship, an arsenal that the Tokugawa leader put to good use five months later in the Battle of Sekigahara (1600). Since Adams could speak Portuguese, and with his captain too sick to move, he was transported to Osaka to meet the man he described as "the king," that is, Tokugawa Ieyasu, which he did on three occasions. Adams was imprisoned after his first meeting, while Ieyasu considered how to deal with the foreigner. After a six-week period of confinement, Adams began to tutor Ieyasu in geography, world affairs, math, and gunnery. Adams was unsuccessful, though, in convincing Ieyasu to allow him and his remaining crew members to return to Europe. Accordingly, in 1602 Ieyasu dispersed the crew, giving each member a living allowance, and put Adams to work building an eighty-ton European-style ship.

Through his tutoring and ship building activity (Adams built Ieyasu another, larger, 120-ton ship in 1608 that was sent on a diplomatic mission to the Philippines), Adams seems to have gained Ieyasu's trust. One clear sign of this was the fief that Ieyasu granted him at Hemimura, on the Miura Peninsula (part of the modern naval port of Yokosuke), in Edo Bay. The fief was valued at 250 *koku,* and on it approximately 100 peasant-farmers came under his jurisdiction. Adams also acquired residences in Edo and Hirado, although it is unclear whether he purchased or was granted them. He appears to have prospered in Japan, in large part through his efforts in assisting the Dutch to establish a permanent trading post at Hirado and similar efforts to aid the English in starting up trade relations with Japan, which occurred in 1613.

Ieyasu finally offered Adams his freedom in 1613, but he chose to remain in Japan and married a Japanese woman, the daughter of an Edo innkeeper, and with whom he had two children, Joseph and Susan. He appears to have grown accustomed if not fond of life in Japan, preferring to live in the Japanese residence of the local magistrate in Hirado rather than in Englishman John Saris's English-style quarters. We also know that he wore Japanese dress and became quite fluent in the Japanese language. Adams also profited from his business ventures, going into the employ of the English Trading Company, for which he became the driving force. During the years 1614–1619 he represented the company on a series of voyages for trade to Siam.

Tokugawa Ieyasu died (in 1616), and Adams became the only European in Japan with unrestricted movement in the country. Likely due to his personal association with Ieyasu, Adams fell into disfavor with Ieyasu's son and successor, Tokugawa Hidetada.

Adams died in 1620, the first Englishman to settle in Japan and likely the first in all of Asia. He was buried on his estate with his Japanese wife. He left half of his estate to the family he had left in England and the other half to his Japanese family. He willed his swords to his Japanese son, Joseph. The last words ascribed to Adams, which were inscribed on his tombstone, were: "Having in my wandering come to this land, I have lived in comfort and plenty thanks entirely to the favor of the shogun. Be so good as to bury me on the summit of Hemi Hill, making my grave face to the east so that I may thus behold Edo. My soul being in the underworld, I shall even have in protection this capital city." Due to the location of his fief and final resting place on the Miura Peninsula, Adams remains known to the Japanese today as *Miura anjin* (the Pilot of the Miura Peninsula).

It is questionable whether or not we can consider Adams a samurai. Some have referred to him (and Jan Joosten, below) as a bannerman (*hatamoto*). Certainly, he was an adviser to Ieyasu, although one of a number of foreigners who served Ieyasu in that capacity, including his shipmate, Jan Joosten van Lodensteijn. As noted, Adams was provided with an estate by Ieyasu and thereby became his retainer. He also wore two swords, the customary symbols of samurai status, but he was a man of commerce, an activity that was anathema to warriors. Adams's status was similar to that of doctors, scholars, artists, and others who fulfilled professional or advisorial functions for daimyo or other *bushi* leaders. As such, he belongs in a group of people known as *hogaimono* (lit., "those outside of the [normal] way"), who existed outside the official four-status social hierarchy of samurai-peasant-artisan-merchant. At most, one might consider him, just like other foreigners in the employ of Japanese military leaders, an "honorary samurai."

William Adams was the historical figure upon which James Clavell based the character Blackthorne (*Anjin-san*) in his 1975 novel *Shôgun*, which was made into a television miniseries that aired in 1980 as well as a feature-length movie for release in Japan and on DVD.

We know far less about Adams's crewmate, and second mate of the *Liefde*, Jan Joosten van Loodensteyn (or Jan Joosten, c. 1560–1623). Like Adams, van Loodensteyn became a confidant of the shogun and was granted a residence in Edo, in an area that came to be called "Yayosu Quay" (and today "Yaesu-chô"). He too was allowed to take a Japanese wife and gained the privilege of wearing the two swords. Like Adams, he fared well in Japan, making a fortune in trade between Japan and Southeast Asia, chartering a number of licensed ("red-seal") ships. Also, like

Shôgun, the Miniseries

An American miniseries based on the eponymous novel by James Clavell, *Shôgun* was broadcast in the United States over five nights in 1980. Despite a running time of 547 minutes, the series was highly rated, winning a Peabody Award and several Golden Globes in 1981, and NBC television experienced the highest weekly ratings in its history to date. A much-shortened version (125 minutes) of the miniseries was released in theaters in Europe, North America, and Japan. The film received a poor reception in Japan, where the public seemed to react negatively to the stereotypical portrayal of violent samurai depicted in it.

The miniseries is loosely based on the historical tale of the English navigator William Adams, who was in the employ of the Dutch, and journeyed on the ship *Erasmus* in 1600 to establish trade relations with Japan. He arrived in Japan at a pivotal time in the country's history, just before the critical Battle of Sekigahara. Adams (the fictional pilot-major John Blackthorne in the miniseries/film) becomes a trusted adviser of the soon-to-be shogun, Tokugawa Ieyasu, who makes him a retainer, a *hatamoto*, or bannerman. Adams is of great assistance to Ieyasu in establishing trade relations with New Spain, marries a Japanese woman, with whom he had a son, and lived out the rest of his life in Japan.

The novel and miniseries led to a boom in undergraduate students in the United States studying Japanese. They were both used in classroom settings as well, as a book (*Shogun: Japanese History and Western Fantasy,* edited by Henry Smith) was published in 1980 that facilitate their educational use. It is still freely available on the Internet: http://www .columbia.edu/%7Ehds2/learning/Learning_from_shogun_txt.pdf.

Adams, he was involved in trade with Siam, but unlike Adams he attempted to return home in 1623 and drowned in the attempt. The district of Edo (Tokyo) where he lived has been named Yaesu-chô and the Yaesu side of Tokyo Station also bears his name. A memorial in his and William Adams's memory exists today on Yaesu-dôri in Nihonbashi (Tokyo): http://www.vanderkrogt.net/statues/object.php ?webpage=ST&record=jp006. There is also a bust of Jan Joosten in the Yaesu Shopping Mall in Tokyo.

During the Boshin War (1868–1869) there were several foreigners, such as Jules Brunet and Eugene Collache, who supported the Tokugawa side in the conflict. One of the men (Collache) appears to have worn samurai attire, including the two swords, but in neither case can they be considered samurai.

See also: Bannermen (*hatamoto*); *Bushi*; Sekigahara, Battle of; Tokugawa Ieyasu

Further Reading

Corr, William. *Adams the Pilot. The Life and Times of Captain William Adams: 1564–1620.* Kent, England: Japan Library, 1995.

Diary of Richard Cocks, Cape-Merchant in the English Factory in Japan, 1615–1622, vol. 2. Cambridge, England: Cambridge Library Collection, Hakluyt First Series, 2010.

Leupp, Gary P. *Interracial Intimacy in Japan: Western Men and Japanese Women, 1543– 1900.* London and New York: Continuum, 2003.

Milton, Giles. *Samurai William: The Englishman Who Opened the East.* New York: Farrar, Straus and Giroux, 2003.

Smith, Henry. "James Clavell and the Legend of the British Samurai." In Henry Smith, ed., *Learning from Shôgun: Japanese History and Western Fantasy,* 1–19. Santa

Barbara, CA: Program in Asian Studies, University of California, Santa Barbara. http://www.columbia.edu/%7Ehds2/learning/Learning_from_shogun_txt.pdf. Accessed December 28, 2016.

Tames, Richard. *Servant of the Shogun: Being the True Story of William Adams, Pilot and Samurai, the First Englishman in Japan.* New York: St. Martin's Press, 1981.

Fukuzawa Yûkichi (1835–1901)

The son of a low-ranking samurai from Nakatsu domain, a middle-sized fief in northern Kyushu, Fukuzawa Yûkichi's life straddled the divide between the Tokugawa and the Meiji periods. Breaking free from the low-level bureaucratic position that the hereditary system prescribed for him, Yûkichi became a leading intellectual in various forms of Western learning and was taken into the employ of the Tokugawa shogunate as a direct retainer, a bannerman (*hatamoto*), during its last years, after the arrival of Commodore Matthew C. Perry and the U.S. naval expedition that forced open Japan in 1853. Due to his expertise in things foreign, Fukuzawa was able to join three official government missions overseas before the fall of the Tokugawa shogunate in 1868. Under the Meiji regime (1868–1912) he had an even greater impact on Japanese society through his prolific and wildly popular writings, becoming the unofficial leader of the Western-looking "civilization and enlightenment" movement. His career was tarnished by his advocacy for Japanese imperialism and exceptionalism in general, and his essay "Departing from Asia" (*Datsu-A-ron*), in particular, but he was still honored with his portrait on the 10,000-yen bill, where it has remained since 1984.

Fukuzawa Yûkichi (1835–1901) in traditional costume, including samurai swords, in Utrecht, Netherlands, in 1862. He was hired as a translator for the first mission sent by the Tokugawa shogunate to Europe. Highly critical of Japan's feudal system, Fukuzawa was a major voice for modernization and westernization in early Meiji Japan. (The History Collection/Alamy Stock Photo)

Yûkichi was the youngest of five children born to Fukuzawa Hyakusuke, a lower-ranking samurai serving the Okudaira family of Nakatsu domain, and O-Jun, the eldest daughter of another Nakatsu samurai. He began his life in Osaka, the city to which his father had been posted to serve as overseer of the domain's treasury; many of the domains from the western half of Japan shipped rice to Osaka, where it was stored in warehouses and later sold in the national market for cash or other commercial goods.

Yûkichi's father's clerical position was well suited to a lower samurai, one with a stipend of 13 *koku* of rice. He held the rank of *nakakoshô*, which was among the higher ranks in the lower half of the lord's corps of retainers. Although his work also involved negotiating with merchants in selling the domain's rice and negotiating loans, when needed, for the domain, Hyakusuke was an intellectual by nature and possessed a large library of more than 1,500 volumes.

The death of Yûkichi's father left the family in difficult circumstances, since his elder brother, the family heir, was only eleven years old and not prepared to succeed his father in his position of responsibility. Having no other choice, his mother O-Jun moved the family back to Nakatsu, where life was difficult. The family was forced to economize strictly, and Yûkichi learned to do many household tasks, some of which he performed for others in order to earn additional income for the family.

In addition, the members of the Fukuzawa family faced a tremendous culture shock moving to Nakatsu, a castle town that only O-Jun had known. Not only was Nakatsu a new place for the displaced children, but culturally it was a different world. Osaka was one of the three largest cities in Japan, together with Edo and Kyoto, while Nakatsu was only a remote castle town with fewer than 10,000 people. Fukuzawa and his siblings stood out in Nakatsu due to their dress, hairstyle, and manner of speaking. Their Osaka dialect, in which even a simple "yes" or "no" differed from those used in Nakatsu, immediately gave them away as outsiders. In his autobiography Yûkichi also reveals that they thought of themselves as superior to their neighbors and even their relatives, which no doubt made it even more difficult for them to get along with local Nakatsu folks. Given this high level of discomfort with Nakatsu, Yûkichi and his siblings largely kept to themselves, which only made him more determined to leave the place as soon as it was possible.

Since Yûkichi's older brother was their father's designated heir, Yûkichi could have remained a dependent in his brother's household, which meant that he could not marry and would have to do some odd jobs to help support the household. He also could have elected to renounce his samurai status. Another option, adoption into another samurai household with no son, a common practice in Tokugawa Japan, was the course he and his family decided on. Such an arrangement was made with an uncle, but before the adoption was to go into effect Yûkichi had to renege on it when his elder brother died.

Given the family's low rank and Yûkichi's position as a younger son, he was not eligible to attend the domain school (*hankô*). This was just one aspect of the life for the families of lower samurai that embittered him, leading Yûkichi to write: "To me, indeed, the feudal system is my father's mortal enemy which I am honor-bound to destroy" (*Autobiography*, 1980 [1966], 6). Nonetheless, there were educational opportunities available to samurai like him in private schools. There, the system was for the older students to teach the younger ones, with general oversight and occasional instruction by the scholar-teacher. In this environment, Yûkichi informs us that in four of five years of study he advanced quickly in his studies of the Chinese Confucian classics, which formed the basis of a samurai's education, and had become a senior disciple in his teacher's school. Given Fukuzawa's great success as a scholar, intellect, and writer, there is good reason to believe him, but his autobiography is full of boasting and clearly reflects an inflated sense of ego.

Life in the single-parent Fukuzawa household was challenging. Given the small stipend the househead received, the family could not afford any servants, which meant that they did their own household duties, cooking, and shopping. To improve their financial situation lower samurai were forced to take on handicraft or menial jobs of various sorts. In Yûkichi's case, he learned how to fit out swords—meaning to lacquer the sheath, wind colored cords around the handle, and to put on metal fittings. Although he was, admittedly, not very skilled at this work, as he grew older he was able help out when needed to repair the paper coverings on the sliding doors, to repair wooden clogs and sandals, fix broken doors, change the coverings of the tatami mat flooring, and repair leaks in the roof.

FUKUZAWA AND JAPAN'S OPENING TO THE WEST

The arrival of the American commodore Perry's "black ships" in Japan sent shock waves around the country, but for Yûkichi it provided a way out of his home domain of Nakatsu. Yûkichi's older brother, who had inherited his father's position as househead, saw an opportunity to improve the family's position, offering him the opportunity to learn Dutch. Yûkichi was able to do this by serving as the attendant of the son of a high-ranking samurai who was traveling to study in Nagasaki, located to the southwest of Nakatsu. Yûkichi's application to leave the domain necessarily had to be phrased in terms of traveling to study gunnery, which was necessary for national defense, rather than "Dutch studies," since there was no precedent for the latter. Yûkichi's elder brother Sannosuke hoped that through the Dutch language Yûkichi would be able to master Western gunnery and perhaps thus serve their lord in the near future.

Leaving Nakatsu at the age of twenty, one month before the signing of the first diplomatic treaty between Japan and a Western power, the Treaty of Peace and Amity between Japan and the United States (1854), Yûkichi was determined never to return. During the year that Yûkichi spent in Nagasaki, he studied the Dutch language and fulfilled the expectations of his brother and the domain in learning about the manufacture and technology of guns and cannon.

Yûkichi later studied at the Tekijuku, a school headed by the prominent doctor and scholar of Dutch studies, Ogata Koan (1810–1863); Ogata was himself a lower samurai, from Ashimori domain, who later became the shogun's personal physician. As his was one of the most influential schools in the late Tokugawa period, Yûkichi's acceptance in 1855 was an important achievement for a Nakatsu samurai. Yûkichi and his fellow students from across the country studied a variety of subjects—physics, chemistry, and physiology—and copied and translated Western scientific and technical texts.

As a result of Yûkichi's progress at the Tekijuku, he came to the attention of officials from Nakatsu, who ordered him to open a small school in the domain's secondary mansion in Edo. Fukuzawa taught young Nakatsu samurai Dutch studies in a rather modest setting, but the school would later become quite successful and eventually be transformed into the prestigious Keio University, which still thrives today. In 1858, though, before departing for this assignment, Yûkichi returned home briefly to bid his mother farewell. The news that he would now be receiving a stipend for this position that was almost as much as his stipend as head of the Fukuzawa family, in addition to other benefits such as funds for a servant, must have been welcome news. Yûkichi hired one of his friends to serve as his "servant," and together they made the 300-mile journey from Osaka to Edo, arriving shortly after the commercial treaty between Japan and the United States went into effect in 1858. That agreement opened three ports to the Americans and to the other Western powers that followed. But in Edo a whole new life opened up before Yûkichi.

In the following year, Yûkichi went to visit the foreign enclave of Yokohama, outside of Edo. He was greatly disturbed that he could not read the signs, which were written in English, nor make himself understood. Discouraged at this unexpected turn of events, he was able to find a two-volume book on English conversation and headed for home. In dramatic fashion, he turned his energies to the study of English.

Later in 1859 he was able to obtain a position as the personal servant of Commodore Kimura's, one of the officials that the shogunate sent to the United States to ratify the terms of the commercial treaty of 1858. The delegation comprised seventy-seven samurai, including three official ambassadors, treasury officers, foreign affairs officers, inspectors, secretaries, interpreters, physicians, attendants, and servants. Since this was an official Tokugawa mission, eighteen of the nineteen officers were direct retainers of the shogun. The Tokugawa shogunate, wanting to impress the Americans with Japan's rapid mastery of Western technology, dispatched the Japanese vessel *Kanrin Maru* as an escort to the American steamship *Powhanttan*, which was carrying the three Japanese envoys. This embassy was not only Japan's first official diplomatic mission to the United States but the first such trip overseas after more than two centuries of national seclusion.

Since Yûkichi was not an official member of the embassy, he had to remain in San Francisco while the envoys went on to Washington, D.C., where the U.S. government received them with great ceremony and crowds as large as 20,000 came out to see them. Nevertheless, Yûkichi made good use of his time in San Francisco, witnessed a number of cultural oddities for him, such as carpets on the floor of the hotel and men and women ballroom dancing, and was able to see the wonders of science put into practice. While in the United States Yûkichi was also able to acquire a Webster's dictionary, which greatly accelerated not only his study of English but his study of Western culture.

Upon his return to Japan, Yûkichi was hired by the foreign affairs office of the Tokugawa shogunate due to his natural abilities and growing experience in foreign affairs. His charge was to translate diplomatic documents and to act as a translator on several other missions overseas. In 1862 he was hired as an official translator for officials on the shogunate's mission to Europe, the official purpose of which was to negotiate a postponement of additional port openings for trade and foreign residence and to seek an adjustment in the exchange rate between Japanese and American currencies. Although both goals went unrealized, this was to be Yûkichi's longest overseas trip, lasting an entire year, during which time he traveled with the mission through a number of countries in Europe, namely the United Kingdom, the Netherlands, Germany, Russia, and Portugal. He was an indefatigable note-taker, writing down all the information he could collect into a series of notebooks. This experience in Europe became the basis of his book, *Things Western* (also known as *Conditions in the West*, or *Seiyô jijô,* in Japanese), which became a national bestseller. The first volume, published in 1866, sold out 150,000 copies rather quickly and was even widely pirated.

Several years later, Yûkichi found himself hired as a translator on his second trip to the United States, in 1867, during which time he traveled again to the East Coast, to Washington, and New York City. This mission sent by the shogunate was to negotiate on the as yet unsettled purchase of a warship from the U.S. government. During this stay in the United States, he purchased as many books as his budget would allow. Back in Japan, these would serve as textbooks for students who, like him, had to copy their texts by hand.

See also: Bannermen (*hatamoto*); Education

Further Reading

The Autobiography of Yûkichi Fukuzawa. Revised translation by Eiichi Kiyooka, with a
    foreword by Carmen Blacker. New York: Columbia University Press, 1980 [1966].
Craig, Albert M. *Civilization and Enlightenment: The Early Thought of Fukuzawa Yûkichi.*
    Cambridge, MA: Harvard University Press, 2009.
"Kyuhanjo." Translated by Carmen Blacker. *Monumenta Nipponica,* IX, 1–2 (Tokyo, 1953),
    304–329.
Moore, Ray A. "Samurai Discontent and Social Mobility in the Late Tokugawa Period."
    Monumenta Nipponica, 24(1–2) (1969), 79–91.

Hagakure (In the Shadow of Leaves)

Yamamoto Tsunetomo (1659–1719), a retainer of Saga domain in Kyushu, completed the text *Hagakure* (*In the Shadow of Leaves*) around 1716. It was conceived as a type of manual for samurai and consists of 1,300 short anecdotes and reflections about life. In contemporary times it is often viewed, erroneously, as one of the key texts associated with the "way of the samurai," but it was not well known during the Edo period and circulated only within Saga domain, in manuscript form. It was only published during the Meiji period, but became quite popular in the 1930s and 1940s and remains in print today.

Yamamoto was a middle-ranking samurai who served Saga's second daimyo, Nabeshima Mitsushige (1632–1700), first as a personal page and then as a scribe. When his lord died, Yamamoto had to refrain from committing suicide because Mitsushige, in 1661, had banned the practice of *junshi*, the self-immolation (*seppuku*) of retainers to follow their overlord in death; this was three years before the shogunate took the same step, adding the prohibition to the *Laws for the Military Houses* (*buke shohatto*). Instead, Yamamoto resigned his commission as a retainer, shaved his head, and went to live in seclusion in a small hermitage several miles north of Saga Castle.

It is believed that the text *Hagakure* was actually dictated by Yamamoto to Tashiro Tsuramoto (1678–1748), a fellow scribe who had served Saga's third daimyo Tsunashige, beginning in 1710, about ten years after he went into seclusion, and continuing until his death in 1716.

Hagakure is often regarded as a nostalgic work, written in a time of peace by a retired samurai who longed for a past when the role of the warrior was clear. As a result, he invented a code of utter loyalty that was at odds with a state that committed to the rule of law. Accordingly, he praised the forty-seven *rônin* for their revenge plot to kill Kira Kôzunosuke but criticized them for their long delay (almost two years) in attacking and their unwillingness to kill themselves afterward. Yamamoto's account can also be seen, in effect, as a protest against the bureaucratization of the samurai and the attack on the samurai's independent authority through the lord's attempt to reduce or eliminate independent fiefs. He longed for an earlier time, when the relationship between lord and vassal was a personal, intimate one.

A number of Yamamoto's ideas in *Hagakure* were at variance with the efforts of the ruling authorities and intellectuals like Yamaga Sokô (1622–1685) to create a new identity for warriors in peacetime. For example, Yamamoto did not embrace the study of letters (the *bun* of *bunbu*) that the Tokugawa promoted in its *Laws for the Military Houses* (*buke shohatto*). He expressed a kind of anti-intellectualism in writing, "Learning is a good thing but more often it leads to mistakes," (Wilson, trans., 2000, 37) and "for the most part, we admire our own opinions and become fond of arguing" (Wilson, 2000, 51). He also held in disdain the arts, proclaiming that, "A person who is said to be proficient in the arts is like a fool" (Wilson, 2000, 41). For samurai from Saga, he argued, "the arts bring ruin to the body. In all cases, the person who practices an art is an artist, not a samurai" (Wilson, 2000, 66).

The work is best known for its emphasis on, some would say obsession with, death, particularly in its often-quoted opening line, "The way of the samurai is found in death." Yamamoto continues, "When it comes to either/or, there is only the quick choice of death. It is not particularly difficult" (Wilson, 2000, 17). Given that he lived in a peaceful age, though, in practical terms this meant that a samurai had to "school" his mind about death, "to confront death, if only imaginatively, every day" (Ikegami, 1995, 281–282). It was only by learning how to die honorably, Yamamoto believed, that a man could be a true samurai.

Although the *Hagakure* historically has been viewed as a work that focuses on the concept of absolute loyalty to one's lord, the reality was actually different. Yamamoto argues, in fact, that great loyalty lay with being a remonstrant to his lord; in other words, to advise one's lord to correct his mistakes or blunders and to educate him about the history of his household and the trials and difficulties that his ancestors faced. Yamamoto believed that this knowledge of history was essential to the success of a lord in controlling his retainers and ruling the commoners in his domain.

Hagakure was first published in 1906, just after the Russo-Japanese War (1904–1905), a time when the idea of *bushidô* began to gain a lot of attention. It became well known during the 1930s and 1940s, particularly among nationalists who sought to embrace "the way of the warrior." The book has gone through many editions—the thirty-sixth edition was published in 2007—and remains a popular text today.

See also: Akô Incident; *Bushido*; *Laws for the Military Houses* (*buke shohatto*); *Seppuku* (Ritual Suicide)

Further Reading

Ikegami, Eiko. *The Taming of the Samurai: Honorific Individualism and the Making of Modern Japan*. Cambridge, MA: Harvard University Press, 1995.

Yamamoto Tsunetomo (1659–1719). *Hagakure: The Book of the Samurai*. Translated by William Scott Wilson. New York: Kodansha, 2000.

Hairstyle

During the late sixteenth and early seventeenth centuries, government authorities sought to end the endemic warfare that had wracked Japan during the Warring States period and to bring order to society. The Tokugawa shoguns and daimyo created institutions to govern many areas of life, and therefore it is not surprising that they also sought to inscribe submission or order onto the bodies of adult males, both samurai and commoners. Through social legislation, the Tokugawa fixed hairstyle and proscribed those styles that deviated from the prescribed norm. It became customary for samurai to shave or pluck the hair from the center of their pates

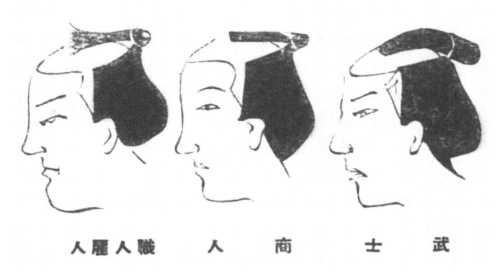

人雇人職　　　人　　商　　　士　　武

Male hairstyle of (left to right) artisan, merchant, and samurai. Generally men were clean-shaven and wore their hair in a *chonmage* ("topknot"), the exact style of which varied according to the *mibun* ("status") of the wearer. (Historic Collection/Alamy Stock Photo)

(*sakayaki*), from the hairline back to the crown. The hair was worn long elsewhere on the head, oiled and tied into a ponytail, which was then folded onto the top of the head. This hairstyle was known as *chonmage* (the shape of the diacritic mark *chon* is said to mirror the bend in the topknot). The face was also to be shaven. In sum, political authorities attempted to make "topknots, shaved pates, and clean-shaven faces the three pillars of normative appearance for men" (Howell, 2005, 164). There were, however, subtle variations in style that distinguished samurai from commoners (and commoners from outcastes); images of some of the variations in hairstyle among samurai and townsmen during different parts of the Tokugawa period were recorded in *Morisada mankô* (*Morisada's Sketches*), a late-Edo account by Kitagawa Morisada. The *chonmage* became a symbol of tradition in the early Meiji period, and therefore the end of its practice was viewed widely as necessary in a modernizing society.

During the Warring States period (1467–1568) and early Tokugawa period, it was customary for warriors to have facial hair. Moustaches, with beards worn thin, were popular, as evidenced by portraiture of the time. Even the first three Tokugawa shoguns had it. Facial hair was seen as a sign of manliness, and so when Toyotomi Hideyoshi, a man who was known to wear a fake beard, called Oda Nobunaga a "bald rat," he was insulting him by questioning his manhood.

During the early seventeenth century Tokugawa authorities turned their attention to the bodies of their male subjects, particularly the samurai, and issued regulations for grooming as well as dress. In contrast to other sumptuary legislation aimed at the general population, these orders aimed at the samurai were only issued early in the period. In 1615, the shogunate issued a series of prohibitions, three of which were concerned with hair (the other four dealt with swords):

1. Shaving far too much of the hair off the top of the head;
2. Wearing one's hair slicked back with oil or having the sideburns meet as a mustache;
3. Wearing beards or facial hair on the cheeks (Quoted in Rogers, 1998, 53–54)

In 1645, a similar list of prohibitions was issued:

1. Wearing one's hair slicked back with oil instead of arranged as a top knot.
2. Wearing excessively long mustaches, beards, or sideburns.
3. Shaving the entire top of one's head, and having the sideburns meet as a mustache.

The net intent of these prohibitions was to standardize hairstyle and to eliminate heterodox styles, as suggested above. In particular, the shogunate banned the two hairstyles, the *ônadezuke* (where the top of the head was left unkempt while the hair was slicked back with oil) and the *chasen* (where the hair was left wild and then gathered up into a ponytail on top of the head, resembling a tea whisk, or *chasen*). Failure to follow these standards for grooming typically resulted in a retainer being punished by being thrown in prison for an undetermined period of time while his commander was assessed a hefty fine (according to the 1615 regulations, generally two pieces of silver but for growing a beard, three). Although these various regulations were issued by the Tokugawa for its retainers, local domains tended to follow its lead in terms of grooming standards, as they did in many areas of legislation.

The regulations standardized a very conservative hairstyle, the topknot, one that dated back perhaps as early as the thirteenth century. No explanations were offered by the Tokugawa for why samurai must wear their hair in a topknot, nor why mustaches were allowed but not beards. Some historians of the Edo period argue that the shaving of the top of the head may have developed as a custom during military campaigns because it allowed a warrior's helmet to fit tightly on the head; it also meant he was able to keep cooler inside the helmet during the summer months. The pony tail was inserted into the opening at the top of the helmet, and when the samurai was not in battle, the hair was neatly tied and folded on top of the shaved head.

Those outside the mainstream wore less orthodox hairstyles: for example, Buddhist priests and some doctors shaved their heads; *rônin* (masterless samurai) often wore a topknot but left the pate unshaved; Confucian scholars sometimes wore beards; and the Ainu and outcastes generally did not bind their hair.

Maintaining one's hair in good order was an important part of a samurai's appearance; conversely, disorderly hair was seen as social nonconformity or deviance. During the late-Tokugawa period, *shishi*, samurai who were imperial loyalists and who disassociated themselves from their domains to pursue their political agendas such as Sakamoto Ryôma or Nakaoka Shintarô, were known to grow their hair out. However, those samurai in service to their lords generally paid to have their hair done (*kamiyui*) by barbers; from samurai diaries we know that low-ranking samurai sometimes developed this skill in order to earn extra income.

The topknot was symbolic of a samurai's identity and honor. Accordingly, those samurai who suffered from thinning hair had to take sometimes unpleasant measures to compensate for this, as was the case for Mito samurai Aoyama Enju. In his fifties "there was no longer enough of his own hair to make a proper topknot. It was necessary to comb the hair from the fringes of his bald pate up to the top of his head, keeping it in place with pomade, and attach a false topknot, which was secured by smoothing what was left of his own hair around it. In hot weather . . . the pomade would melt and the topknot come loose" (Yamakawa Kikue, 1992, 7). The topknot could also be said to embody the person of the samurai. After late-Tokugawa samurai Yoshida Shôin (1830–1859) was executed and buried in Edo, several of his students acquired his topknot to take back home to Hagi for burial in his family graveyard.

As a status marker, hair was also a focal point in the unmaking of status at the beginning of the Meiji period. The new government took a number of steps in this regard: first, formally abolishing the traditional status groups (1869); permitting all former commoners to take surnames (1871); calling on all former samurai to give up sword bearing (1871) and to adopt unbound hair (*sanpatsu dattô rei*, 1871). Although the suggestion regarding swords became an outright prohibition five years later, in 1876, the Meiji government did not issue a legal ban on the samurai's *chonmage*. Men were exhorted to unbind their hair and to wear it in a "cropped" (*zangiri* or *sanpatsu*) style not associated with any specific Tokugawa-period status groups. They were not forced to change their hairstyle on pain of punishment or death, as was the case during the early Qing period in China, when the Manchus imposed their hairstyle (queue) on the Han Chinese population; nor as depicted in a scene without any historical basis in the Hollywood film *The Last Samurai* (2003), in which the samurai Nobutada has his topknot cut off by a group of imperial soldiers sporting Western-style cut hair.

According to a Nagoya newspaper from mid-1873, about 80 percent of the former samurai in Tokyo sported cut hair. In 1873 the Meiji emperor adopted a Western hairstyle, and by the end of the decade it spread throughout the male population; those still wearing the topknot were unusual and perceived as "behind the times." In Japan, as in Korea and China, the cutting off of the traditional hairstyle by men was a symbol of rejection of traditional values and an embrace of modernity. Apparently, the *chonmage* hairstyle struck some European observers as odd; during a shogunal mission to Holland in 1863 two of the men were the subject of public ridicule in a theater for their hairstyle (apparently, they had covered their topknots with hats but had to remove them because they were blocking the view of audience members behind them).

Today, variations on the *chonmage* hairstyle are worn by sumo wrestlers, but they do not shave their pate. Wrestlers of high rank (*sekitori* status, meaning in the top two divisions) are permitted on certain occasions to wear a particular style known as *oicho*, in which the topknot is splayed out in the shape of a fan. Outside of Japan, it became fashionable during the mid-2010s for young men in Europe, North America, and Australia to wear a so-called "samurai bun," although in this hairstyle the hair on top of the head is kept long while on the sides it is worn short or shaven.

See also: Coming of Age (*genpuku*)

Further Reading

Hiltebeil, Alf, and Barbara D. Miller, ed. *Hair: Its Power and Meaning in Asian Cultures.* Albany: State University of New York Press, 1998.

Howell, David L. *Geographies of Identity in Nineteenth-Century Japan.* Berkeley and Los Angeles: University of California Press, 2005.

Kitagawa Morisada. *Morisado mankô*, vol. 2. Edited by Asakura Haruhiko and Kashikawa Shûichi. Tokyo: Tôkyôdô shoten, 1992.

Rogers, John Michael. "The Development of the Military Profession in Tokugawa Japan." PhD thesis, Harvard University, 1998.

Yamakawa Kikue. *Women of the Mito Domain: Recollections of Samurai Family Life.* Translated and with an introduction by Kate Wildman Nakai. Tokyo: University of Tokyo Press, 1992.

Helmet (*kabuto*)

The helmet, or *kabuto*, is one of the most important elements of a samurai's armor. It not only protected the head, but for high-ranking samurai from the late sixteenth century onward it also served as an important marker of individual identity.

The first evidence for helmets in Japan, dating from the fifth century, can be found in excavated mounded tombs (*kofun*). These were imports from the Asian continent or based on models originating there. The basic form of helmet worn by samurai in the early modern period, though, represented an evolution of styles dating from the medieval period, roughly from the twelfth century through the sixteenth century. The basic form of the helmet during the medieval period consisted of a hemispherical bowl made of iron, formed from individual plates fastened with rivets. At the top of the bowl was a hole (*tehen*), surrounded by an ornamental rim. The hole was quite large, allowing for the excess of the cap worn in place of a lining to the helmet to be pulled through. Over time, as helmets began to be fitted with linings, the size of the hole was decreased, although it was still retained for decorative purposes. A continuous iron strip (*koshimaki*) was riveted around the base of the bowl. Attached to this at the front was a small peak (*shinodare*) and on the sides and back a large neck guard (*shikoro*) made of lamellar. The ends of the rows of lamellae that formed the guard were extended and curved out to protect the face. These extensions (*fukigaeshi*) were retained even after warfare ceased and became the site for displaying the wearer's family crest. A final, hornlike forecrest known as *kuwagata* (a hoe-shaped form) completed the helmet.

A number of *kabuto* and armor makers became well known in the sixteenth century. Among the important schools were the Haruta, the Myôchin, and the Saotome. Many of their works are signed, but other, unsigned, pieces are identifiable from their specific features, shape, and style of construction. Both the Myôchin and the Saotome produced the *suji-bachi kabuto* (with a bowl of ridged plates) and the *hoshi-bachi kabuto* (with raised accentuated riveting), which were generally formed by sixty-two to seventy-two or more wedge-shaped plates. The wedge-shaped plates were joined by metal strips, which almost doubled the thickness of the helmet. The Myôchin were also the first to develop an "s"-shaped wedge that when positioned partially one upon the other created a pocket of air between them that acted like a shock absorber. The Saotome soon adapted this technique as well and used it to become the most successful armorers in Japan during the seventeenth and first half of the eighteenth centuries.

During the sixteenth century the production of armor—both body armor and helmets—was transformed through a process of simplification. In terms of the construction of helmets, the number of plates used was greatly reduced in number, from as many as 72–120 to 6 or 8, and held in place by metal rivets. Known as *zunari*, or head-shaped helmets, they were made of a smaller number of plates of heavier steel and thus offered the wearer more protection. This simplification was made possible through the use of a central plate covering the crown that overlapped the plate covering the brow. As before, a *shikoro* hung from the helmet to protect the neck.

Armorers used the simplified *zunari* to create another type of helmet known as the *kawari kabuto* (lit., "transformed helmet"), which is sometimes translated as "fantastic" or "spectacular" helmets. The manufacture of this style of helmet spread during the Azuchi-Momoyama period (1568–1603) and remained popular in the early Edo period as well. It gained in popularity in part because the simplified style of helmet construction led to the problem of identification of warriors of rank on the battlefield. This was a time when larger and larger armies were being fielded and the introduction of firearms, which created clouds of smoke on the battlefield, made conditions more chaotic. The *kawari kabuto*, a plain bowl helmet on top of which a number of unusual shapes were constructed, was made to stand out on the battlefield. It

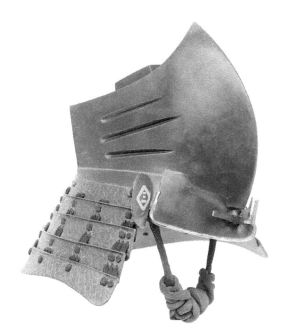

Makiwarinari kawari kabuto (axe-shaped helmet). Signed *Makiwarinari, Muneyoshi o shite kore o tsukurashimu, Kōno Seitsū* ("axe shape, made by Muneyoshi upon the order of Kōno Seitsū"). Early to mid-Edo period, 17th–18th century, iron, lacquer, lacing, bronze, gold, and leather. The axe, a symbol of power and strength, emphasized the martial character of the helmet's wearer, who was (based on the heraldic crest visible on the *fukigaeshi*—the ear-like projection to the right of the neck guard) from Usuki domain (Ôita prefecture). (Photo by Brad Flowers/Samurai Collection/The Ann & Gabriel Barbier-Mueller Museum)

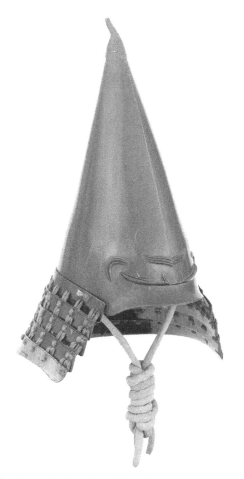

Nasubinari kabuto (eggplant-shaped helmet). Early Edo period, 17th century, made of lacquered leather, iron, gold, lacing, and papier-mâché. It is an example of a *kawari kabuto* ("transformed helmet"). The selection of eggplant, a symbol of prosperity, as a theme for the helmet demonstrates the multi-faceted nature of samurai identity. (Photo by Brad Flowers/Samurai Collection/The Ann & Gabriel Barbier-Mueller Museum)

also served a similar purpose in times of peace, as the helmets helped to identify the warrior.

In a large number of cases more radical changes were made by altering the shape of the helmet so that it assumed an identifiable form. The entire helmet bowl was used as a base on which to attach an unlimited variety of constructions. Some examples of *kawari kabuto* include helmets made in the shape of: rabbit ears, hares being a symbol of longevity; eggplant (a symbol of prosperity), a catfish tail; the arm of a fierce Buddhist deity; Mt. Fuji; Jurôjin, the *kami* of longevity; a crab or lobster, both with protective outer shells; or a Chinese-style helmet. These extreme designs were created by use of lighter materials—wood, bamboo, paper, leather, fabric, lacquer—that were carved or shaped to represent the desired subject. The additions were affixed (with leather ties) to the metal helmet bowl, which thereby served as a base for the sculptural design. The entire design was then consolidated with a filler made of chopped hemp and lacquer (known as *harikake*). As a final step the entire form was lacquered, often in black or some other color. These additions resulted in sculptural forms that might totally obscure the original helmet.

Although the *kawari kabuto*—the helmet transformed in shape—on a basic level protected the head, it also often served to transform the wearer, in the manner that a mask does. *Kawari kabuto* added a performative element to the samurai's attire, in a particularly visible manner, since it adorned his head. Although the transformation did not enhance the protective capacity of the helmet in a physical sense, it could transform the wearer by calling on or inviting some religious force like a

Buddhist deity or natural, including animalistic, forces. Other helmets simply displayed an aura of ferocity, exoticism, or even whimsy—which goes against the rather staid reputation of samurai.

Other helmets with unusual shapes differed from *kawari kabuto* in that their designs were made completely of metal rather than transformed or altered from their original design through additions to the basic helmet bowl. Difficult and unusual forms were hammered from a single sheet of iron, at a time before the invention of pressing machinery.

During the second half of the Tokugawa period, demand for *kawari kabuto* "declined in favor of a return to previous, conventional models" (*Samurai: The Way of the Warrior*, 2016, 56). Also, while samurai of substantial rank might be able to commission or to purchase *kawari kabuto*, most others were likely to settle for the above-mentioned conventional models. However, even these helmets could be customized to a certain extent by replacing the *kuwagata*, the hoe-shaped attachments that often adorned the front of helmets, with other types of frontal pieces (*maedate*) comprised of distinguishing marks such as family crests, animal shapes (e.g., a hare), insects (dragonfly), or even plant forms (snow pea). Low-ranking *bushi* such as foot soldiers (*ashigaru*) were likely to wear simple *jingasa*, a conical "camp-style" hat.

Kabuto were also augmented with face masks (*mengu*), usually made of iron, which "generally covered either the face below the level of the eyes, or only the cheeks and chin, both types having a few plates attached below the chin to defend the throat" (Botomley, 2002, 17). One type of face mask was fitted with a nose-piece that could be removed by means of a turn-button. One extreme form was in the shape of a mythical half-bird, half-human creature. During the peacetime of the Tokugawa period these were largely ceremonial in function.

See also: Armor; Firearms

Further Reading

Botomley, Ian. *An Introduction to Japanese Armour*. Leeds, England: Royal Armouries Museum, 2002.

Conlan, Thomas D. *Weapons and Fighting Techniques of the Samurai Warrior, 1200–1877 AD*. New York: Metro Books, 2008.

Munroe, Alexandra, ed. *Spectacular Helmets of Japan, 16th–19th Centuries*. New York: Japan Society, 1985.

Samurai: The Way of the Warrior. Florence, Italy: Contemporanea Progetti, 2016.

Hiraga Gennai. See *Hohi ron (A Theory of Farting)*

Hohi ron (A Theory of Farting)

An essay written in 1771 by Hiraga Gennai (1728–1780), a low-ranking samurai who became a noted Dutch scholar (*rangakusha*), *Hohi ron* was a literary work that satirized the samurai.

Gennai was a multitalented man, born into a low-ranking samurai family that served the Takamatsu daimyo as a keeper of the domain's rice warehouses. Because of his aptitude for the study of medicinal herbs (*honzôgaku*), Gennai was appointed a pharmacologist in the castle's herb garden. Although his lord supported his studies, Gennai, like a number of other low-ranking samurai during the Tokugawa period, found that the demands of service were too time-consuming and interfered with his intellectual pursuits. As a result, he decided to resign his position in 1761 and live the remainder of his life as a materless samurai (*rônin*). During his career, Gennai was, variously, a student of Dutch studies (*rangaku*) who wrote a number of books on a variety of scientific topics, an inventor, physician, and painter. He also gained some notoriety as an author of satirical and parodic prose literature in the *kokkeibon* (lit., "comical books") and *dangibon* (lit., "lecture books") genres. His work *Hohi ron* (*A Theory of Farting*) falls in the latter category.

A Theory of Farting takes place at Ryôgoku Bridge, an important hub in Edo where many performance artists could be found. The story focuses on one such artist, who drew large crowds because of his skill in farting as a musical talent and to imitate sounds:

> The man's greetings to the audience were clear and unaffected. His opening number, together with the musicians, was a fart version of the Sanbasô blessing dance. He progressed rhythmically with *nô* drums and flutes, *toppa hyoro hyoro, hiih-hiih-hiih*. Then he gave off a rooster's cry at the ruddy eastern sky, *bu-bu-buuu-buu*. Next came a waterwheel. He loosed a sloshing *buu-buu-buu* as he did catwheels and made the exact sounds of water filling the buckets and then pouring out as it pushed the wheel around. (Shirane, 2002, 515)

Gennai employs the character "Crankshaw Stonington, Esquire," a country bumpkin samurai, as a straight man to critique, via parody, the samurai's social values. Crankshaw reproaches the farting artist and the crowd, telling them that the shogunate allowed public performances to teach about loyalty and filial piety, citing the example of the Akô Incident that was the basis for *Chûshingura* (*Treasury of the Loyal Retainers*). Gennai mocks the idea of samurai honor, as Crankshaw states, "Flatulence is, after all, a personal matter and should not be aired in public. Any proper samurai would be mortified to the point of suicide if he were inadvertently to let, uh, fly in polite company" (Shirane, 2002, 518).

When another patron criticizes the farting man as disgusting and disgraceful, the author defends the artist as an original, self-made man, who differs from unoriginal masters of other arts who only imitate the past. Gennai, in turn, mocks the samurai's pursuit of the many "ways" (*dô*) in Japanese culture, such as the way of tea (*sadô*) and the way of archery (*kyûdô*):

> Tomisaburô became a great kabuki star only after he began using the prestigious stage name Kikunojô II. But farts have no hereditary titles, no fans to sleep with, and no rich patrons. They have only themselves, plainly, as they actually are. They ask to be judged for that alone. Using nothing but a two-inch hole, the Farting Man is blowing away all the other shows. Triumfartly, if I may put it that way, he's left the competition flatulented on their backs. How different he is from our professional musicians who go to a certified master to receive secret instruction on the proper way to articulate and chant so they themselves can later charge high fees to their

own students. . . . But look at the Farting Man. He's invented everything by himself, without master or secret oral transmission. With an unspeaking rear end and uncomprehending farts, he's learned articulation and rhythmic breathing, he has natural sense of timbre and pitch at all five tones and twelve semitones, and he's able to make so many clearly distinct sounds that his rear end is clearly superior to the voice of a second-rate puppet-play chanter. Call him one of a kind, call him a wonder. Truly he is the founder of the Way of Farting. (Shirane, 2002, 518).

Having lived the majority of his life as a samurai, Gennai was in a position to view them in a critical light through his own skillful use of satire and parody in *Hohi ron* and other works.

See also: Akô Incident; *Chûshingura (Treasury of the Loyal Retainers)*; Ronin (*rônin*); Tea Ceremony (*sadô*)

Further Reading

Jones, Stanleigh H. "Scholar, Scientist, Popular Author Hiraga Gennai, 1728–1780." PhD dissertation, Columbia University, 1968.

Shirane Haruo. *Early Modern Japanese Literature: An Anthology, 1600–1900*. New York: Columbia University Press, 2002.

Honchô Bugei Shôden (A Short Tale of Martial Arts in Our Country)

This is the oldest narrative survey of the martial arts in Tokugawa Japan. It dates from 1714 and was written by Hinatsu Shirôzaemon Shigetaka, during the period of the Kyôhô reform (1716–1736) of the eighth shogun, Yoshimune. Hinatsu was the son of a master practitioner of the *naginata*, a weapon similar to a European halberd. Not much is known about the author, who also completed several other works on the martial arts. It is unclear why he did not succeed his father (d. 1688), but he served the lord of Sasayama Castle in Tamba province until the latter's death in 1717, after which he served the Sakai family. He died in Edo at the age of seventy-two.

The book is divided into ten chapters, covering nine different martial arts: the arts of military science and strategy (*heihô*); military decorum (*shitsuke*); archery (*shajutsu*), horsemanship (*bajutsu*); swordsmanship (*tôjutsu*); the art of the spear (*sôjutsu*); firearms (*hôjutsu*); armed close combat (*kogusoku*); and unarmed combat (*jûjutsu*), and gives short biographies of a total of 150 famous samurai who founded or practiced the various arts. He devotes particular attention to issues of succession and lineage in the various schools. The book gives the reader "an unsurpassed picture of how the origins of the martial arts were seen by the literati in the mid-Edo period" (Rogers, "Swordsmanship," 1990, 254). Reflecting the trends of the Tokugawa period, Hinatsu's book privileges swordsmanship (*tôjutsu*) over other martial arts, including archery. Its two long chapters on swordsmanship consist of a full one-third of the work.

Hinatsu's work enjoyed wide circulation, was frequently quoted, in other major contemporary histories of the martial arts, and also later appeared in digest form (edited by later writers). In the chapter on archery, Hinatsu is highly critical of practitioners of the bow, who were only interested in shooting for records of distance or number of arrows shot in a given period of time rather than devoting themselves to the study of proper form and tradition.

Despite his efforts, neither Hinatsu nor the shogun Yoshimune, who promoted the martial arts, could do much to stop the inevitable transformation of fighting skills like archery and swordsmanship into something akin to competitive sports.

See also: Martial Arts (*bugei*); Tokugawa Yoshimune

Further Reading

Hinatsu Shigetaka. "Honchô bugei shôden." *Monumenta Nipponica,* 45(3) (1990), 261–284.

Hurst, Cameron. *The Armed Martial Arts of Japan.* New Haven, CT: Yale University Press, 1998.

Rogers, John M. "Arts of War in Times of Peace. Archery in Honchô Bugei Shoden." *Monumenta Nipponica,* 45(3) (1990), 253–260.

Rogers, John M. "Arts of War in Times of Peace. Swordsmanship in Honchô Bugei Shoden, Chapter 5." *Monumenta Nipponica,* 45(4) (1990), 413–447.

Horseback Riding Ceremony (*onorizome*)

Horseback riding was an important skill for samurai during the Tokugawa peace. In many domains, retainers with stipends of 200 *koku* or more were required to maintain one horse, as part of their preparedness for wartime service to the lord. However, with the increasing financial difficulties that most samurai faced from the early eighteenth century on, particularly in the face of daimyo efforts to economize by reducing samurai stipends, it became increasingly difficult for samurai to even own horses. In Tosa domain there is evidence that horses were being shared, or higher-ranking retainers with more than one horse lent them out to others.

Not only was it more difficult for samurai to own horses, but over time there were fewer occasions to exercise their riding skills. One notable exception was in Tosa domain, where samurai had an annual, public, forum for exhibiting their horseback riding skills known as *onorizome* (lit., offical horseback riding ceremony). This ceremony was held every year in Tosa's castle town, Kôchi, during the entire Edo period (and actually beyond, until 1871, three years after the demise of the Tokugawa shogunate). *Onorizome* took place on the eleventh day of the New Year and was a part of a roughly two-week-long period of official New Year's season festivities, during which time there was also one that involved maritime preparedness, known as *funanorizome* (the first boat riding ceremony).

Onorizome provided a venue in which retainers' horseback riding skills were put on view—and put to the test. The annual ritual required the domain's retainers to demonstrate their horseback riding skills on an 860-meter course down a major road near the main gate of Kôchi Castle (where today the trolley lines run, known as *densha dôri*). Participation was for the most part limited to those retainers with full samurai status—that is, those who were included in the domain's official registry of retainers (*bugenchô*). In 1649, however, the event was opened up to *gôshi* (rural samurai), the top rank of the lower samurai, despite the opposition of upper samurai, who wanted to protect the privileges of their rank. At the end of the seventeenth century the event involved close to 1,000 riders, though later in the period that number decreased to 500–600. The breakdown for the event in 1758, in which 598 men participated, was 431 direct retainers of the lord, 60 subretainers (*baishin*), and 107 *gôshi*. During special years—particularly on the occasion of a new lord's first visit to Tosa—the entire retainer core, typically more than 2,000 men, was required to participate. Of course, each retainer was accompanied to the ceremony by the requisite number of attendants as befitted his status, minimally one or two persons, so there were thousands of people involved.

A samurai's misstep or tumble on the course would bring the rider more than a momentary feeling of shame, for the lord (during years when he was back from Edo), and his top officials would be watching from a position of honor about midway in the course. A rider's slip or fall could have significant long-term consequences: the names of riders who had fallen were publicized in a public document, indicating that this possibility of falling or being thrown from the horse was taken quite seriously. After the ceremony the shamed rider also had to endure an interview with the inspector (*metsuke*). There was a clear connection between this and Tosa domain's military law (*Gunpô shohatto*, 1649), which stated that if a mounted samurai was thrown from his horse in battle, he would be demoted (i.e., lose his mounted status—no pun intended) and would be assessed a fine. Whether in wartime or peacetime, a samurai was expected to train his horse, if he owned one, or at least to train on a horse sufficiently to have a firm command of riding skills should he be called on to exercise them in battle. Pleading illness on the day of the ceremony would not save a samurai either, as Shibuya Dennai found out in 1722. His repeated yearly absence due to "illness" (it was unclear whether it was real or feigned) led to an official investigation and the confiscation of his fief of 250 *koku*.

The demonstration of riding skills in the *norizome* ceremony put the samurai in full public view, as even commoners were allowed to watch from the open area on the southern end of the course. The house flags and banners attached to the rider and horse clearly marked his identity in a visible manner. A good showing riding would bolster a samurai's reputation, but the potential for public humiliation made it an event that could not be taken lightly. With no battles to wage, a samurai could demonstrate his loyalty by following the twin ways of the civil and military arts (*bunbu*). The civil arts entailed classical learning, which could be put to good use in bureaucratic service to the lord. Maintaining one's skills in the martial arts was a struggle in a time of peace, as the periodic calls for military reform indicate. But in Tosa and in other domains that held similar ceremonies, the ability to perform on horseback remained an essential part of service to the lord. The writing brush may have maintained its figurative importance in samurai life, but horseback riding and other martial arts could only be ignored at great peril.

See also: Civil and Military Arts (*bunbu*); Martial Arts (*bugei*)

Further Reading
Ôno Mitsuhiko. *Jôka no fûkei. Ryôma no ikita Tosa* [Landscape of the Castle town. The Tosa where Ryôma Lived]. Kôchi: Kôchi shinbun, 2010.

Sôma Nomaoi Festival

A different sort of horseback riding festival than the *onorizome* in the former Tosa domain occurs every summer in Haramachi city (Fukushima prefecture), known as the Sôma-Nomaoi Festival. The four-day event (July 22–25), organized by Ôta Shrine and Odaka Shrine in Minami-Sôma and Nakamura Shrine in Sôma city, recreates a festival involving the residents of what used to be known during the Edo period as Sôma domain. The festival has its origins in a military exercise dating back to the Warring States period (1467–1568) in which a daimyo, an ancestor of the later lords of Sôma domain, released wild horses on a plain for his cavalry to pursue and capture. The horses were then presented as offerings to a local Shinto deity.

Today the highlights of the festival include several activities that take place on the vast Hibarigahara plain. The first is a race over a distance of 1,000 meters by local men dressed as mounted samurai in traditional armor, with long swords at their side and flags bearing family crests streaming from their backs. In the second event, mounted samurai compete to capture banners shot into the air by fireworks. During the final part of the festival a small group of ten mounted samurai pursue unsaddled horses in the sacred precincts of Odake shrine, where young people clad in white clothing capture the horses barehanded to present them as offerings to the deity.

The largest summer festival in the Tôhoku region, it has been designated an Important Intangible Folk Cultural Property. Photographs of the festival and yearly updates are available on a dedicated Facebook page, "Soma Nomaoi Festival, Soma Wild Horse Chase": https://www.facebook.com/Soma-Nomaoi-Festival-Soma-Wild-Horse-Chase-1459773789 15235 (accessed June 7, 2017).

House Lands (tenryô)

The shogunate (Jp., *bakufu* or *okôgi*) was the government through which the Tokugawa administered its house (*ie*) organization and ruled over the more than 260 daimyo. Although the shogunate had national responsibilities in numerous areas, particularly in terms of foreign defense, cross-jurisdictional legal affairs, famine relief, and administration of a central road network (the Gokaidô), it was supported only by the tax income (*kuramai*) drawn from its house lands (*tenryô*), which were scattered over forty-seven provinces and created administrative difficulties for the shogunate.

The house lands consist of the territories in the personal domain of the Tokugawa shoguns and includes both those directly administered by the shogunate as well as that which was overseen by adjoining daimyo on behalf of the shogunate. Broadly interpreted, the term includes all Tokugawa land, but more technically speaking it does not include perhaps what was in the seventeenth century one-third of the total, that which was awarded in fief to the shogun's senior vassals, the bannermen (*hatamoto*), who administered and taxed the land themselves. Over time, though, many of the fiefs of the bannermen were withdrawn (or in some cases the intendants themselves sought to turn over their land) and incorporated into the lands directly administered by the shogunate; these bannermen then drew stipends from Tokugawa-administered granaries. At the end of the seventeenth century the house lands produced a little more than 4 million *koku* of rice, roughly 17 percent of the national total. The breakdown (in the early seventeenth century) was approximately 8.5 million revenue from the Tokugawa's direct holdings, 6.0 million from domains allotted to the hereditary daimyo (*fudai daimyô*), and 10 million for the outside lords (*tozama daimyô*) and other miscellaneous holdings. From the tax on the house lands, which constituted about 40 percent of the crop, the shogun paid his vassals who had no fiefs and operated the shogunate.

The majority of house lands were administered by shogunal officials called intendants or district administrators known as *daikan*. Above them were regional intendants, or *gundai*, who came under the direct authority of the magistrate of finance (*kanjô bugyô*). There were also a number of magistrates (*bugyô*), who were appointed to oversee major cities under shogunal authority, such as Edo and Osaka and cities important to the country's external relations, such as Nagasaki and Hakodate. Governors (known as *jôdai*) were also appointed to oversee a number of castles under Tokugawa control, such as Kyoto, Osaka, and Sunpu.

Although the Tokugawa controlled about four times as much land as the wealthiest daimyo, it was highly fragmented and made for an inefficient tax base. The house lands were scattered over forty-seven provinces, such that the shogunate for convenience came to rely on a total of twenty-six daimyo for administering and collecting taxes on neighboring territories on its behalf; these lands were referred to as entrusted lands (*azukari dokoro* or *azukarichi*). Accordingly, the domains assigned administrative authority over such lands and provided the tax collectors and other officials needed for government there. In 1713, the shogunate under the reforming influence of Arai Hakuseki (1657–1725) sought to reassert control over entrusted lands by abolishing the system, but the reform's impact was only temporary, lasting but seven years before the individual daimyo were given permission to administer them again. In the mid-eighteenth century, 13 to 18 percent of the house lands were administered in this fashion. Almost a century later, in 1838, daimyo-administered Tokugawa territories amounted to a considerable 22 percent of the total house lands. The daimyo-entrusted lands were often in areas distant from the Kantô and Kinai (Osaka-Kyoto) regions, particularly in the northern provinces. Aizu domain (230,000 *koku*) carried the largest burden, administering as much as 880,000 *koku* of Tokugawa territory in adjacent parts of three provinces, followed by Nakatsu domain (80,000 *koku*), in northern Kyushu, which oversaw almost twice as much territory for the shogunate. Over time the *azukari dokoro* system caused the shogunate some problems; for example, a 55,000-*koku* portion of house lands adjacent to Aizu domain by the early nineteenth century came to be regarded by its officials as a legitimate part of its fief.

See also: Arai Hakuseki; Intendants (*daikan*); Shogunate (*bakufu, kôgi*)

Further Reading

Bolitho, Harold. *Treasures among Men: The Fudai Daimyo in Tokugawa Japan.* New Haven, CT, and London: Yale University Press, 1974.

Totman, Conrad. *Politics in the Tokugawa Bakufu, 1600–1843.* Cambridge, MA: Harvard University Press, 1968.

Housemen (*gokenin*)

The term *gokenin* has a long history in Japan, referring to vassals of the shogunate during the Kamakura (1185–1333) and Muromachi periods (1333–1568). Under these two governments some *gokenin* were given land grants and appointments as estate stewards (*jitô*) or military governors (*shugo*) in exchange for military service. During the Edo period, the term referred to one part of the Tokugawa shogun's direct retainer band, which consisted of two groups, totaling roughly 22,000 men: about 5,000 higher-ranking *hatamoto* (bannermen) and 17,000 lower-ranking *gokenin* (housemen).

Although the dividing line between the two categories was not unequivocal, housemen generally held much smaller stipends than those of the *hatamoto*, usually less than 100 *koku* (1 *koku* = 5 U.S. bushels or 180 liters), although they could range from 260 *koku* to just 4 *ryô* in cash; second, they did not possess the largely theoretical right to a shogunal audience *omemie*. Although some *hatamoto* were granted fiefs (*chigyô*), *gokenin* were completely dispossessed of authority over land, receiving only a stipend, payable in rice or a combination of rice and cash.

Katsu Kokichi, the son of famed *bakumatsu* samurai Katsu Kaishû (1823–1899), was a *gokenin* who is remembered today largely for the autobiography he wrote, *Musui dokugen* (*Musui's Story*), which details the exploits and misadventures of an unemployed Tokugawa. Kokichi was born Otani Kokichi, the third son of Otani Heizô, a Tokugawa houseman with a stipend of 100 *hyô* (bales of rice) who served as an intendant (*daikan*). Kokichi's eldest brother, Otani Hikoshirô, was known as a Confucian scholar and a district administrator in the Tokugawa's house lands in Shinano and Echigo, while his other brother was adopted into another samurai family and also served in a similar administrative position.

Since there were two other sons ahead of him in line for succession to the Otani family headship, Kokichi was adopted out into the Katsu family in 1808. From the age of sixteen he attempted to gain a formal position in the shogunate through a labor pool (reserve force) for unemployed samurai (*kobushingumi*) established for low-ranking Tokugawa retainers. Ironically, his finances actually deteriorated as a result of his effort, since he had to purchase the appropriate clothing to appear before officials to present his requests, not to mention give them gifts in hopes of gaining their favor. Despite his repeated attempts, Kokichi was unsuccessful, and he turned to a variety of activities to supplement his family's income, such as dealing in swords (appraising and trading them) and military gear.

Kokichi's experience is indicative of the experience of many *gokenin*, who unlike the higher-ranking *hatamoto*, generally were permitted to work "side jobs," even if they held an official position in the shogunate. From Kokichi's account, we learn that other *gokenin* were earning extra money as instructors in various military arts: for example, his judo instructor held a position as the "head of the office of procurements" (*saikujo*); his riding teacher was a guard at Edo Castle; and his sword master held a position in the household of a Tokugawa consort. Other *gokenin*, particularly those without official posts, engaged in domestic by-employments, making handicraft items such as umbrellas, cricket cages, or lanterns.

The number of *gokenin* increased over time, however, and by 1800 totaled some 20,000. In the face of challenging financial conditions, some *gokenin* were permitted to build rental apartments and let them out, to both other samurai but also to commoners. Many low-ranking *gokenin* lived in barracks-style housing, little different from the backstreet tenements of commoners. The sale of *gokenin* status also became increasingly frequent in the last decades of the Tokugawa period. Thus the divisions between the *gokenin* and townsmen became increasingly blurred in the late Tokugawa period.

See also: Bannermen (*hatamoto*); Shogunate (*bakufu, kôgi*)

Further Reading

Ôguchi, Yûjirô. "The Reality behind *Musui Dokugen:* The World of the *Hatamoto* and *Gokenin*." Translated by Gaynor Sekimori. *Journal of Japanese Studies,* 16(2) (1990), 289–308.

Totman, Conrad. *Politics in the Tokugawa Bakufu, 1600–1843.* Berkeley and Los Angeles: University of California Press, 1967.

Ii Naosuke (1815–1860)

The fifteenth lord (daimyo) of Hikone domain (present-day Shiga prefecture) and great councilor (*tairô*) of the Tokugawa shogunate from 1858 to 1860, Ii Naosuke was responsible for signing the Treaty of Amity and Commerce (Harris Treaty) with the United States, which opened a number of Japanese ports to trade and foreign residence. He was responsible for a resurgence of Tokugawa power and the suppression of antishogunal power in the Ansei purge (1858–1859), which led to a backlash and his assassination in 1860. Historical views of Ii have been mixed due to his having directed the purge, which led to him being branded an imperial traitor, and his opposition to imperial loyalist forces. At the same time, his role in opening Japan to the Western powers has been viewed more positively for having saved the country from colonization.

Born in 1815, the fourteenth son of Hikone daimyo Ii Naonaka and his concubine known Otomi no kata, Naosuke was not in line to succeed his father or to be appointed to a top position in the domain government. He devoted himself to the cultural pursuits, including the tea ceremony, establishing his own branch of the Sekishû school of tea and brushing several philosophical works on tea and the arts. However, due to rather extraordinary circumstances—his elder brothers were either adopted into other family lines or died before Naonaka (1766–1831)—Naosuke found himself elevated to the position of daimyo of one of the most important hereditary (*fudai*) domains in Japan. The Ii were one of the *fudai* families eligible for service on the shogunate's most important governing body, the council of elders (*rôjû*). Four of his predecessors also had served as *tairô* (great councilor), a high-ranking position in the shogunate that was only occupied during times when the shogun was a minor or during a political crisis. Naosuke himself would occupy this position from 1858 to 1860.

Ii became involved in national politics and a leader of a coalition of daimyo who advocated for opening Japan to the outside world. In response to the shogun's unprecedented call for opinions on how to respond to American commodore Matthew C. Perry's demands for diplomatic and trade relations in 1853, Naosuke brushed a now-famous memorial that drew attention to imminent military danger the country faced and called for: a partial opening of the country (only Nagasaki port) to trade with Westerners; and using the Dutch as agents to deal with the other Western powers. Recognizing the danger that Japan faced, given that it was without warships to drive off the Westerners, he urged the shogun to "open the country" (*kaikoku*):

> There is a saying that when one is besieged in a castle, to raise the drawbridge is to imprison oneself and make it impossible to hold out indefinitely; . . . Even though the Shôgun's ancestors set up seclusion laws, they let the Dutch and Chinese to act

as a bridge [to the outside world]. Might not this bridge now be of advantage in handling foreign affairs, providing us with the means whereby we may for a time avert the outbreak of hostilities and then, after some time has elapsed, gain a complete victory? (MIT Visualizing Cultures)

A largely diplomatic treaty (Treaty of Peace and Amity or the Kanagawa Treaty) between Japan and the United States followed in 1854. After shogunate leader Hotta Masayoshi (1810–1864) was unable to acquire imperial sanction for a commercial treaty, shogun Tokugawa Iesada (1824–1858) replaced Hotta with Ii Naosuke as *tairô* (great elder). (A copy of Ii Naosuke's oath as *tairô*, which was submitted to the shogun, can be seen at: http://hikone-castle-museum.jp/en/collection/355.html.) Fearing American retribution for inaction, Ii went ahead and ordered the treaty signed, in 1858. Since the treaties signed with the United States, as well as the Netherlands, Russia, Britain, and France, allowed for foreign residence in Japan, particularly in Hyôgo, which was near the imperial city of Kyoto, imperial loyalists were particularly opposed to it. Ii sought to consolidate his power by purging opponents of his open-country position in a heavy-handed manner that was without precedent in scale. In total, he ordered the detention of seventy-nine people, including nine daimyo such as Mito Nariaki (his second time under house arrest), Shimazu Nariakira, and Yamauchi Toyoshige (Yôdô, who was forced to retire and then restricted to Tosa domain's secondary residence at Shinagawa). Seven of the detainees were executed, including Hashimoto Sanai (Fukui domain) and Yoshida Shôin (Chôshû domain). One, Saigô Takamori, was exiled to a distant island off the coast of Satsuma. At the same time Ii pushed forward his candidate for heir to the ailing shogun, Tokugawa Iesada (1824–1858), the twelve-year-old daimyo of Kii, Tokugawa Yoshitomi (who became the fourteenth shogun Tokugawa Iemochi), whom he could influence and control more easily than the mature Hitotsubashi Keiki, Tokugawa Nariaki's son.

Ii's strong-armed policy of persecution of opposition forces and his ignoring the reforming daimyo's efforts in support of Hitotsubashi Keiki led to a backlash by imperial loyalists and the so-called reformists who were supporting Tokugawa Hitotsubashi Keiki as shogunal heir. That backlash resulted in Ii's assassination in 1860 in the Sakuradamon (Sakurada Gate) Incident, just twenty months after his appointment as *tairô*. Ii's persecution of prestigious daimyo had motivated lower-ranking samurai to take action, and seventeen Mito samurai, together with one from Satsuma, killed him just in front of one of the gates of Edo Castle as he was on his way to meet the shogun (the Sakurada Gate was photographed by famous photographer Felice Beato sometime between 1863 and 1870). Ii's bodyguard was unprepared for an ambush, their weapons covered due to the snow that was falling, and Naosuke was killed easily. News of the assassination spread quickly, even reaching the shogunate mission sent to the United States to ratify the commercial treaty. The story of Ii and his assassination has been retold often in film, most recently in 2010's *Sakurada Gate Incident* (director Satô Jun'ya).

Naosuke was buried at the Ii family temple, Gôtokuji, in Edo (present-day Tokyo, Setagaya ward). This is the same temple that is central to the story of the *maneki neko*, the inviting cat, which adorns the show windows or counters of many restaurants across Japan. Ironically, the grave of Ii Naosuke is located near the shrine dedicated to the memory of Yoshida Shôin (*Shôin jinja*), one of Ii Naosuke's victims in the Ansei Purge (1858–1859).

After Ii's death his heirloom swords and other prized possessions were given to close relatives, prominent daimyo, and even the shogun as "relics" or "reminders" of Naosuke. This was common practice after the death of a lord.

Ii's death incited loyalist samurai to carry out terrorist actions against other members of the shogunate and those who had informed on people targeted in the Ansei Purge. After Ii's death the center of political activity began to shift to Kyoto. The new shogunate advisers for a time promoted policies to improve the government's reputation through close association between the shogunate and the imperial court, in particular through the marriage between Emperor Kômei's younger sister Kazunomiya to the shogun in 1861. The shogunate also later (in 1864) established a police force known as the Shinsengumi to maintain peace in Kyoto, in part by assassinating antishogunal loyalists.

Since his death Ii Naosuke has been variously vilified as traitor to the court and heralded as Japan's savior. After the Meiji Restoration the new government leaders, who were the former opponents of the Tokugawa shogunate, largely controlled the historical narrative, which meant that Ii continued to be viewed as a traitor. Over time, however, Ii has been viewed more positively for his role in signing the treaty that opened Japan to trade with the Western powers in 1858 and saving Japan from foreign encroachment and colonization, as had happened in China. This later trend is evident from public statues of the man that have been erected in Yokohama and in Hikone as well as a Japan Railway's advertisement for Hikone city that contains

Controversial Statues: Ii Naosuke

Civil War statues in the United States have been the subject of controversy in recent years. Japan, too, has had controversies over public statues that go back to the beginnings of the modern period (the Meiji period, 1868–1912). In Japan, many of the controversies have surrounded historical figures involved in the Meiji Restoration. One of the most heated debates surrounded the erection of a statue of Ii Naosuke (1815–1860), the shogunal regent (*tairô*). Ii was branded a traitor and an enemy of the court (*chôteki*) by the Meiji government for having enacted the Ansei Purge of 1858, when several leaders of the antishogunal restoration movement were executed. The effort by formal retainers of Ii to have a statue of him erected in 1881 met with the opposition of members of the Meiji government, a number of whose colleagues had been purged or put to death by Ii. A statue of Ii was only realized in 1909, and it had to be erected outside of the capital, in Yokohama. The statue became acceptable politically because it was to celebrate Ii's decision in 1854 to open Japan's ports (Yokohama was one of the first) to the Western powers. The views of those in power concerning Ii had also softened with time; many of them came to view Ii as a hero, rather than an enemy, for having saved Japan from colonization by the Western powers.

During World War II most of Japan's public statues, including that of Ii Naosuke in Yokohama as well as one in his former domain of Hikone, were melted down in support of the war effort. His statue in Hikone was built in 1949 and was one of the first prewar statues to be reinstated. The inscription on the statue reads: "Pioneer of Japanese-American Friendship." Another statue of him, in Yokohama, followed in 1954.

a large image of Ii and welcomes potential visitors to the festival celebrating the 150th anniversary of the opening of Japan (2008) entitled "Ii Naosuke and the 150th Anniversary of Opening the Country" and refers to Naosuke as "Gateway to the Future."

See also: Saigô Takamori; Shinsengumi; Shogun (*shôgun*); Shogunate (*bakufu, kôgi*); Swords; Tea Ceremony (*sadô*); Yoshida Shôin

Further Reading

Cullen, L. M. *A History of Japan, 1582–1941. Internal and External Worlds.* Cambridge: Cambridge University Press, 2003.

MIT Visualizing Cultures website "Black Ships & Samurai," Lesson 7: Sitequest: Advising the Shogun on a Response to America. http://ocw.mit.edu/ans7870/21f/21f .027/black_ships_and_samurai/cur_student/bss_cur_07_letter02.html (accessed July 23, 2018).

Income

The shogun granted daimyo territories known as domains, in theory in return for their loyal service. In turn retainers received economic support from their daimyo lords in return for their own loyal service, including certain specific military obligations (e.g., maintaining a stipulated number of subretainers, for use in times of war). Economic support from the daimyo mainly took the form of grants in fief (*chigyô*), generally for retainers of middle rank and above; or stipends (*kuramai* or *hôroku*), drawn from the domain's central granary in the castle town; or some combination of the two. Stipended retainers also received support rice (*fuchi*, sometimes referred to as "storehouse allotments"), one unit of which was supposed to support one man for a year. The size of the fief or the stipend was expressed in units of *koku* (1 *koku* was equivalent to 5.1 bushels of rice) or *hyô* (1 *hyô* was equivalent to roughly .35 *koku*). The distinction between the two measures (*koku* being preferable to *hyô*) as well as the amount granted in fief or stipend determined the social standing of a samurai.

In the vast majority of domains (roughy 80 percent) retainers were granted stipends, while in the remainder they were invested with fiefs (although many of these were really "paper" or fictive fiefs, existing on paper only with no real territorial basis). The domains that continued to invest retainers with fiefs (i.e., to subinfeudate) included many of the largest domains, which existed in the peripheries of Japan and comprised roughly half of the land area of the country [see entry Fief (*chigyô*)]. Samurai stipends were measured in *koku* of rice and usually were paid in a combination of rice, other grains (e.g., millet or barley), and specie. Stipends paid exclusively in rice were of higher prestige.

Looking at conditions in one particular domain, for example, in mid-nineteenth-century Mito (present-day Ibaraki prefecture), which had an assessed productive capacity (*kokudaka*) of 350,000 *koku*, fiefs were distributed in the following manner:

1,000 *koku* and above,	11 houses
500–1,000 *koku*,	37 houses

300–500 *koku,*	31 houses
200–300 *koku,*	105 houses
100–200 *koku,*	125 houses

In other words, a total of 425 warrior households were supported with fiefs of 117,820 *koku.* There were also an additional 600 retainers who received stipends of less than 100 *koku,* together they totaled about 80,000 *koku.* This included the stipends of a range of retainers, including foot soldiers, rural samurai (*gôshi*), falconers, and salaries granted officeholders in addition to their regular stipends.

Although stipends were hereditary, in principle, passed from father to son, office salaries were a supplement only as long as the retainer occupied the position. The salary that came with an official position often made a major difference in the standard of living of a retainer's household; accordingly, the competition for positions was quite intense. The Tokugawa bannerman Musui Kokichi writes of his great frustration due to his inability to acquire a position, despite his best efforts—and considerable monies expended in purchasing the appropriate clothing with which to wear when appearing before officials in charge of hiring. Since positions in warrior governments (the domains' and the shogunate's) were pegged to status, meaning that it was required that the officeholder be of minimum rank in terms of income to qualify for a position, a supplemental salary system, known as *tashidaka,* was developed in many domains in the early eighteenth century. This allowed talented but low-ranking retainers to be eligible for certain offices.

The figures listed above for Mito domain retainers do not indicate the actual income received by the fief or stipend holder; rather, they are indicative of official rank standing. The above-mentioned Katsu Kokichi (1802–1850), for example, had a hereditary stipend of 41 *koku,* made up of 23 *koku* of income from his fief and 18 *koku* in granary rice (*kuraichimai*). His actual income, though, was only about 35 percent of the 41 *koku*; this represented the income derived from the land tax on the peasant farmers living plus an equivalent tax assessed on granary rice income. (Tax rates across Japan generally were in the range of 35 to 40 percent.) Katsu's real income came to forty-one bales of rice (1 *hyô* = .35 *koku*), one-third of which was paid in rice and the remainder in cash. Given that during Kokichi's lifetime 1 *koku* of rice was equivalent to about 1 gold *ryô,* his actual income was about fourteen bales of rice and 9 1/2 gold *ryô.* He received his stipend in three installments, with a quarter in the spring and summer, respectively, and the remainder in the winter. As a retainer of the shogunate, Kokichi also was allotted a plot of land and a house to live in, but it appears that he rented out the house, despite regulations prohibiting it, and used the income to rent less expensive accommodations.

Looking at statistics for another domain, Chôshû (with an assessed productive capacity of 369,000 *koku*), allows us to see income distribution at the lower end more clearly. Fiefs and stipends were distributed in the following manner:

Over 100 *koku,*	661 households
Over 70 and less than 100 *koku,*	202 households
Over 50 and less than 70,	339 households

Over 40 and less than 50 *koku,*   472 households
Under 40 *koku,*   4,001 households
TOTALS   5,675 households

From these statistics we see that less than 12 percent of retainers earned 100 *koku* or more; in fact, the vast majority, a full 70 percent of the retainer corps, had an income of 40 *koku* or less.

Samurai income was derived from the agricultural tax, and by the late seventeenth or early eighteenth century, for a variety of reasons, that tax base stopped growing. This meant that samurai began to feel economically hard-pressed, given that the rising consumer demands of an urban lifestyle were difficult to manage on a fixed income. Writing a century later, an anonymous samurai author writing under the pseudonym Buyo Inshi, a "retired gentleman," commented:

> Warriors are impoverished and unable to make ends meet because the world as a whole has become ever more profligate. Everything has become costly, and, since the Way of lending and borrowing is prevalent everywhere, a warrior easily incurs unforeseen debts, and interest is laid upon interest. A warrior who wants to keep his finances in order for the foreseeable future stands no chance unless he dislocates himself from the world at large and maintains a modest and frugal lifestyle. (*Lust, Commerce, and Corruption*, 2014, 55)

Retainers were not the only ones facing difficult household economies. For the vast majority of the Tokugawa period most daimyo also were in financial straits, due to the alternate attendance and the rising costs of their own urban lifestyles. In response, they began to demand that retainers return a portion of their stipends. These forced loans were known euphemistically as *onkariage,* "loans to the lord." In theory they were to be repaid, but in fact they were not, which meant that many samurai were forced to deal with a near-permanent reduction in their stipends.

In some domains, the forced loans were collected only from the samurai, but even in those where commoners also paid, the samurai bore the heaviest burden (one document from early-nineteenth-century Tosa tells us that samurai bore almost 80 percent of the total tax). One of the earliest impositions of this type of levy was in Obama domain (present-day Fukui prefecture) in 1647, but they appeared more widely in the early eighteenth century. In Tosa domain (present-day Kôchi prefecture), the forced loans were first imposed in 1704 at a rate of 10 percent but steadily increased until they reached 50 percent in the 1760s. At first, the domain used the funds to pay for levies (construction duties) imposed by the shogunate but thereafter they were utilized to service the domain's increasing debt to merchants in Osaka.

The political economist Honda Toshiaki (1744–1821) in his treatise *Keisei hisaku* (*A Secret Plan of Government*) warned that the long-term reductions in income would result in retainers' resentment of the lords they served. Samurai would not have felt free to express openly the difficulties the reductions caused, for fear of being perceived as disloyal, but from the letters of Tosa samurai Tani Tannai (1729–1797) we can get a sense of the great difficulties his household faced trying to deal with the forced loans. Tannai received a stipend of 24 *koku* in rice certificates (*kippu*), which was distributed in two equal portions (unlike the Tokugawa bannerman Katsu Kokichi, who received three payments per year), in summer and year-end payments. The forced loans, however, were required to be paid in one sum, deducted from the summer payment. In the mid-eighteenth century, Tosa retainers were required to return one-quarter of their base stipends, which meant that Tannai's was reduced from 24 to 18 *koku*; he received only 6 *koku* (one-half of his nominal stipend payment of 12 in the summer). The forced loan in general, and the payment scheme in particular, forced samurai to live on credit and created a cycle of debt that made samurai dependent on loans taken out from merchants. The purchasing power of the now-reduced stipend of 18 *koku* was of course affected by the market exchange rate for rice, adding to the financial instability that retainers on stipends faced.

See also: Fief (*chigyô*); Rural Samurai (*gôshi*); Supplemental Salary (*Tashidaka*) System and Talent; Tani Tannai

Further Reading

Craig, Albert M. *Chôshû in the Meiji Restoration.* Cambridge, MA: Harvard University Press, 1961.

Craig, Teruko (trans.). *Musui's Story: The Autobiography of a Tokugawa Samurai.* Tucson: University of Arizona Press, 1988.

Kasaya, Kazuhiko. *The Origin and Development of Japanese-Style Organization.* Kyoto: International Research Center for Japanese Studies, 2000.

Lust, Commerce, and Corruption. An Account of What I Have Seen and Heard, by an Edo Samurai. Edited and introduced by Mark Teeuwen and Kate Wildman Nakai, et al. New York: Columbia University Press, 2014.

Roberts, Luke S. *Mercantilism in a Japanese Domain: The Merchant Origins of Economic Nationalism in 18th-Century Tosa.* Cambridge: Cambridge University Press, 1998.

Vaporis, Constantine N. "Samurai and Merchant in Mid-Tokugawa Japan: Tani Tannai's 'Record of Daily Necessities' (1748–54)." *Harvard Journal of Asiatic Studies,* 60(1) (2000), 205–227.

Yamamura, Kozo. "The Increasing Poverty of the Samurai in Tokugawa Japan, 1600–1868." *Journal of Economic History,* 31 (1971), 378–406.

Intendants (*daikan*)

The shogunate appointed officials to oversee Tokugawa house lands (*tenryô*). These officials, who were known as *daikan*—"intendants" or "district administrators," in English—were appointed from among the Tokugawa's direct vassals, mostly from the bannermen (*hatamoto*). In general terms, their job was to supervise and manage its house lands (*tenryô*). *Daikan* were in charge of roughly three-quarters of the house lands; the remaining 22 percent (in 1838), often located in areas distant from the Kantô or Kinai regions, was put under the charge of daimyo who administered the land on behalf of the shogun (hence the designation of those lands as *azukaridokoro*, or "entrusted lands").

The intendants were one of three types of officials who administered lands under Tokugawa control; the other two were *gundai* (regional intendants) and *bugyô* (magistrates), the latter of whom were often appointed to oversee major cities under shogunal authority, such as Edo and Osaka, including those of vital importance to Japan's external relations, such as Nagasaki and Hakodate. From the mid-seventeenth century the system was largely fixed: intendants (*daikan*) and regional intendants (*gundai*) came under the direct authority of the magistrate of finance (*kanjô bugyô*).

Intendants' duties were to keep the peace, to send regular reports on conditions in his local area to the shogunate's finance office, and, importantly, to collect and transmit tax goods from the territory under their administrative control to the shogunate. They kept detailed records of the putative yield of villages under their jurisdiction, based on which they assigned tax bills and corvée labor duties. The tax bills and calls for labor duty were sent by the intendant's office to the village headmen, who were responsible for allocating the tax burden among the residents. Intendants were also responsible for communicating edicts and notices from the shogunate to the villages located on house lands. Other than interceding in disputes in a village or between villages that could not be settled locally, the intendant otherwise left the villages alone to self-manage themselves (a principle known as village "semiautonomy").

The Tokugawa tried to limit the amount of taxes to be retained by the intendants and to limit the amount of corvée labor demands they could impose on the peasants living in the villages under their administrative control. In other words, the shogun moved to limit any inclination among the intendants to exercise independent authority. Even so, when Tsunayoshi became shogun in 1681, he found that many intendants were not sending the expected taxes to Edo, which was damaging the shogunate's fiscal health. After a very careful new survey of house lands thirty-four intendants were dismissed for either underpaying or delaying the payments of tax rice to Edo. This personnel shake-up did much to break up the independent power of the intendants. Another measure with similar intent was taken by the eighth shogun, Tokugawa Yoshimune, who in 1725 abolished what had been the traditional system whereby the intendants deducted office expenses from tax proceeds—a system that was ripe for corruption. From this time onward, intendants were required to transmit all tax goods and were paid an office allowance instead. This step minimized their ability to exploit the peasants living in the territories under their administrative control, making them, in theory, effective appointed representatives of the shogun.

The number of intendants varied considerably at the time. Early in the seventeenth century they totaled as many as 127, but through a process of bureaucratic rationalization where larger areas were put under each intendant, their numbers dropped by the middle of the century to forty (with nine regional intendants). As a result they each were responsible for keeping the peace and collecting the taxes in large assigned areas. In 1838, these areas averaged 77,000 *koku* and in some were considerably more than 100,000 *koku*; in fact, only three intendants were responsible for territories with less than 50,000 *koku*. In other words, intendants were responsible for territories larger than those of most vassal (*fudai*) daimyo.

While intendants were assisted by a manager (if the intendant lived in Edo), assistants and clerks, who performed duties such as record-keeping, carried out technical tasks, conducted inspection tours, the total personnel and authorized office size of the intendancy were not great: for example, an intendant supervising a territory of 50,000 *koku* was permitted to have a staff of twenty-nine men assist him. In comparison, a daimyo with a domain of similar size would have perhaps 1,000 vassals. Largely as a result, the tax rates on these lands generally were lower than in daimyo domains.

The intendant's headquarters itself was an outpost known as *jin'ya* or *daikan-sho*, consisting of a residence (for the intendant or his manager), office space, warehouses, palanquin storage (to store the vehicle in which the intendant was transported), and a garden plot. Only one example of a *jin'ya* in Tokugawa territory remains today, at Takayama.

Some domains also appointed officials called *daikan*, who fulfilled a similar function on the domain level as those appointed by the shogunate. A number of these complexes have been preserved or reconstructed around the country.

See also: Administrative Headquarters (*jin'ya*); House Lands (*tenryô*); Magistrates (*bugyô*); Shogunate (*bakufu, kôgi*)

Further Reading

"Hida Takayama." http://www.hida.jp/english/activities/sightseeing-information/old-government-outpost. Accessed December 17, 2016.

Totman, Conrad. *Politics in the Tokugawa Bakufu, 1600–1843.* Cambridge, MA: Harvard University Press, 1967.

Isoda Koryûsai (1735–1790)

One of only a handful of samurai who were also ukiyoe (woodblock print) artists, Koryûsai was active from 1769 until his death in 1790. As an artist he has been overshadowed in reputation by Suzuki Harunobu and Torii Kiyonaga, but in recent years his creative role has been reevaluated more positively by art historians.

A prolific artist, Koryûsai produced more than two thousand five hundred designs. More than the sheer volume of production, however, his range of interests has been deemed remarkable by art scholars. According to one scholar, "Koryûsai designed one hundred seventy print series—five times the combined output of his predecessors. The four hundred fifty *hashira-e* (pillar prints) he issued constitute nearly forty percent of all extant designs in this format. His production of *kachôga* (flower and bird prints), roughly one hundred eighty designs, was twenty times greater than any artist working before him. In addition to his two hundred plus *ichimai-e* (single sheet designs) and four *ehon* (illustrated books), each consisting of several images, Koryûsai also designed roughly five hundred *shunga* (erotic pictures) for albums of various formats. He was as well, one of the most prolific *ukiyo-e* painters—approximately ninety of his works are known" (Hockley, 2003, 3). Given this output, Koryûsai may have been the most productive artist of the eighteenth century.

Scholars had assumed that Koryûsai became a printmaker by necessity due to his having become a *rônin*, but there is new evidence detailing his career that shows otherwise. Koryûsai had been a vassal of the daimyo Tsuchiya Nobunao, who died in 1735, passing on the family headship to his two-year-old son Atsunao. Apparently, the Nobunao faced tremendous financial challenges in ruling the domain, which was assessed at 95,000 *koku*, as evidenced by the decrease in the number of residences the domain maintained and the switch to a much smaller main compound. After Atsunao died in

Woodblock print by Isoda Koryûsai (active 1764–1788) entitled *Geta no yukitori* ("Removing snow from one's clogs"). The print shows a woman holding an umbrella while a female servant removes snow from her geta. Koryûsai was one of the few samurai who were also *ukiyo-e* artists. (Library of Congress)

1777, his son and successor lived but a year before passing away himself. It appears that it was at this point that Koryûsai became a *rônin*. In other words, Koryûsai had been active as an artist nine years, almost half of his career, before his status changed to *rônin*.

As noted above, Koryûsai produced a very large number of pillar prints. These ranged in topic, from Chinese themes to images of sumo wrestlers to representations of the Buddhis monk Saigyô. A number of his prints depict historical figures from history and mythology, such as Atsumori, Yoshitsune, the Soga brothers, the female warrior Tomoe Gozen, and Empress Jingû. These images were not made necessarily for the homes of samurai, however, since the figures were widely known across social status groups. A number of his flower and bird prints with martial themes, however, involving hawks, tigers, and dragons, for example, are said to have played to samurai tastes.

See also: Kakizaki Hakyô; Odano Naotake; Ronin (*rônin*); Watanabe Kazan

Further Reading

Hockley, Allen. *The Prints of Isoda Koryûsai: Floating World Culture and Its Consumers in Eighteenth-Century Japan.* Seattle and London: University of Washington Press, 2003.

"Isoda Koryusai-1725–1790." https://www.artelino.com/articles/isoda-koryusai.asp. Accessed March 24, 2017.

Marks, Andreas. *Japanese Woodblock Prints: Artists, Publishers and Masterworks: 1680–1900.* North Clarendon, VT: Tuttle Publishing, 2012.

Itô Hirobumi (1841–1909)

Born to a farming family in the village of Tsukari in Chôshû domain (present-day Yamaguchi prefecture), Itô Hirobumi (then known as Hayashi Risuke), was adopted into samurai status, studied under the late-Tokugawa loyalist scholar Yoshida Shôin, played an important role in the Meiji Restoration and a leading role in guiding the Meiji state during its formative years. He was the main architect of Japan's first modern constitution (the Meiji Constitution), served four terms as prime minister, was appointed the first resident general in Korea in 1906, and was assassinated by a Korean nationalist in 1909. His portrait appeared on the 1,000-yen bill in Japan from 1963 to 1984.

A member of the peasant status group, Itô Hirobumi's father Hayashi Jôzô gained employment serving a low-ranking samurai named Itô in the castle town of Hagi (Chôshû domain). The entire family was adopted into the Itô household and given the family's name; hence Hayashi Risuke became Itô Risuke. His given name subsequently changed twice, first to Shunsuke (1858) and then to Hirobumi (around 1869). Hirobumi's experience is

Photo of Itô Hirobumi (1841–1909) in 1890. Itô came from a peasant background but was adopted into a samurai family in Chôshû domain. He served four terms as prime minister and was the main architect of Japan's first modern constitution. (Print Collector/Getty Images)

thus an example of the limited mobility that existed across status lines between commoners (peasants, artisans, and merchants) and samurai.

In 1856, Itô Hirobumi was assigned to guard duty at Edo Bay (now Tokyo Bay) in Sagami province by Chôshû domain, which was like a number of domains under orders from the Tokugawa shogunate to provide men for service to protect Japan's coastline from Western gunships. While serving there, Hirobumi was befriended by the head of the guard unit to which he had been assigned, a Hagi samurai named Kuruhara Ryôzô (1829–1862). Kuruhara introduced Hirobumi to the world of letters and provided him with a letter of introduction to the scholar and imperial loyalist Yoshida Shôin.

Late in 1856, Itô was released from service and returned to Hagi determined to study under Shôin. He was successful in being admitted to Shôin's school, the Shôka sonjuku ("village under the pines"), and was highly motivated to learn. Writing a colleague about the academy, Hirobumi wrote: "Literature is flourishing here. There is no one who is not always reading something. All of Matsumoto village is alive with our academy Shôka Sonjuku. We students read day and night. I urge you, too, to keep reading and studying. I don't for a moment think you are neglecting your studies, but I do believe it is very important" (Quoted in Takii, 2014, 8).

Shôin had a mixed, limited opinion of his student, writing that Itô "is of a petty official rank but enjoys himself with his colleagues. He is not very talented and is slow in learning. But he is serious-minded and modest. I like this very much." He also described Itô as a "negotiator" (*shûsenka*). In other words, he probably would have been shocked, had he lived, to see that Itô would become one of the leading statesmen of the Meiji state.

For his part, although Itô may have sympathized with Shôin's ideology, he did not get entangled with his teacher's plans for radical action, particularly with his plans to assassinate a top Tokugawa official. Still, after Shôin was ordered to Edo and imprisoned by the shogunate in 1859, Itô was able to travel to the same city by gaining employment as an attendant to the samurai Kido Takayashi (Kôin), who also went on to play a major role in the Meiji Restoration. Of course, there was no contact between them while Shôin was in custody, but Itô was in Edo in 1869 when his teacher Yoshida Shôin was executed by the shogunate. Together with a few others, Itô retrieved Shôin's body and buried it on the grounds of one of Chôshû domain's residence compounds in Edo (now the site of Shôin Shrine in Tokyo).

From this point on Hirobumi became actively involved in the "Revere the Emperor, Expel the Barbarian" (*sonnô jôi*) movement, which sought to elevate the position of the emperor and to expel the Western powers from Japan. More directly, for a time he became a terrorist. In 1862, he took part in an abortive attempt to assassinate a high-ranking Chôshû official named Nagai Uta (1819–1863), who was seen as advocating trade relations with the West and conciliation between the shogunate and the imperial court. He also was part of a group that burned the British legation at Goten'yama in Shinagawa (Edo) later in 1862. Furthermore, Itô assassinated the classics scholar Hanawa Jirô Tadatomi (1808–1862), whom he believed—incorrectly so—was trying to find an ancient precedent for dethroning an emperor.

Having been introduced to academic learning by Kuruhara and Shôin, Itô was anxious for more and was selected by the domain as one of five young Chôshû samurai—known as the Chôshû Five—to send overseas to study in the West, as part of a strategy to learn from the West to build a strong Japan that would take its rightful place in the world. However, since leaving Japan was still a violation of Japanese laws, the group had to depart surreptitiously, which they did in 1863. Itô studied at the University College London, and his experience in Great Britain convinced him that Japan needed to adopt radical reforms along Western lines. Writing a letter to his father just prior to departing, Itô explained his reasons for going overseas: "Today there is a pressing need to learn about everything in that country [Britain] and to master naval technology; otherwise there is no hope for us. It is with those thoughts that I go to carry out my tasks, for three years only, before returning home" (Quoted in Takii, 2014, 11)

While studying in Britain, Itô and his fellow students learned in 1864 that Chôshû domain had fired cannons at Western ships in the Shimonoseki Straits while Satsuma domain had exchanged cannon fire with a British naval squadron. Itô and his colleague Inoue Kaoru (1836–1915), who would become one of the Meiji government's *genrô*, or elder statesmen, decided to return home to persuade the domain leaders to stop their attacks on the Western powers. Having lived in Britain briefly, just six months instead of the three years planned, they had quickly come to realize that all attempts to expel the Western powers from Japan would be totally useless.

Returning home with valuable experience overseas, Itô, the son of a farmer, found himself invited to offer opinions before the top domain officials and then the lord (the daimyo) himself. Although he was not able to convince them that the domain exclusion policy should be abandoned, the wisdom of his counsel was fully realized after Chôshû was defeated by the joint naval forces of Britain, France, the Netherlands, and the United States, which then occupied Chôshû's Shimonoseki battery. Itô continued to advocate for opening the country, and his foreign experience was put to good use for the domain in formal peace negotiations with the Western powers.

Itô would travel again to the West in 1871 as deputy ambassador for the Iwakura mission (1871–1873), which traveled around the globe as part of an official effort to raise Japan's profile in the world and to learn the secrets of Western society that might be put to use in building up the Japanese nation.

Appointed the first prime minister of Japan in 1885, Itô served a total of four terms over the following sixteen years. He left politics for a few years before his appointment as head of the Privy Council in 1903. His final government position was as the first Japanese resident general in Korea, in 1905. He is viewed by many as having played an important role in the annexation of Korea, and this led to his assassination by a Korean nationalist while touring in Manchuria in 1909.

See also: Kido Takayoshi (Kido Kôin); Yoshida Shôin

Further Reading
Takii, Kazuhiro. *Itô Hirobumi—Japan's First Prime Minister and Father of the Meiji Constitution.* London and New York: Routledge, 2014.

K

Kakizaki Hakyô (1764–1826)

The fifth son of the Matsumae daimyo, Kakizaki Hirotoshi (better known by his studio name, Hakyô) was adopted out into the Kakizaki family, a collateral family of the Matsumae who served as house councilor (*karô*). He was taken by the Kakizaki househead to Edo in 1773, at the age of nine, and lived for ten years in the Matsumae domain residence. While in Edo Hakyô studied painting in the Nagasaki style, under its premier master there, Sô Shiseki.

Hakyô gained fame for a series of colorful, realistic portraits of twelve Ainu leaders who fought on the Japanese side during an uprising in the eastern part of Ezo (present-day eastern Hokkaido). He painted from living models and paid careful attention to portray realistically the distinctive detail of the chieftains, such as the colorful and highly detailed patterns on their *attush* attire, cherished artifacts, long beards, and curly hair (a sign of beauty). To the ethnic Japanese population, the paintings were surely exotic depictions.

One of Hakyô's earliest portraits, and one that is considered to be the finest contemporary depiction of an Ainu, is of a subject identified only as "Tobu," an Ainu leader. According to art historians, the painting reveals his schooling in the Chinese Nan-pin style, which emphasizes realism and the use of Western perspective. In the painting Hakyô is holding a decorative crest for a warrior's helmet, a highly valuable artifact that the Ainu handed down across the generations.

Hakyô completed this series of paintings, known as *Ishu*

Portrait painting by Kakizaki Hakyô (1764–1826) of Ainu chieftain Ikotoi of Akkeshi, one of a series of 12 realistic portraits of Ainu leaders that he painted in 1790. Hakyô, the son of the daimyo of Matsumae who served as a domain elder, is a notable example of a high-ranking samurai who gained fame in the arts. (The Picture Art Collection/Alamy Stock Photo) *retsuzô*, in 1789 and took it to Kyoto, where it was widely viewed and admired. Even the reigning emperor, Kokaku, viewed and praised the paintings. In Kyoto Hakyô spent time with Maruyama Ôkyo, which led to some contemporaries calling him Kakizaki Ôkyo. While in Kyoto, Hakyô also became friendly with a number of intellectuals there, such as Minagawa Kien, Murase Kôtei, Ban Kôkai, and the priest-poet Rikunyo, all men from commoner backgrounds.

In Edo, too, his paintings achieved notoriety. Many daimyo asked to borrow a painting in order to produce a copy of one of the portraits, which evidence the high regard in which they were held. Hakyô made a number of additional trips to Edo in his forties and fifties, accompanying his lord on alternate attendance.

Hakyô's paintings are still widely viewed and were the subject of a 2016 exhibition at the National Museum of Ethnography in Osaka, Japan. A number of his paintings are in private hands outside of Japan and in foreign museums, including the Besançon Museum of Fine Arts and Archaeology in France.

See also: Alternate Attendance (*sankin kôtai*); Daimyo Residence Compounds (*daimyô yashiki*); Isoda Koryûsai; Watanabe Kazan

Further Reading

Fitzhugh, William H., and Dubreuil, Chisato O., eds. *Ainu: Spirit of a Northern People.* Washington, D.C.: Arctic Studies Center, National Museum of Natural History, Smithsonian Institution, 1999.

Hakyô ronshû kankôkai, ed. *Hakyô ronshû.* Tokyo: Hakyô ronshû kankôkai, 1991.

"Ishuretsuzo, the Image of Ezo: Tracing Persons, Things and the World." http://www .minpaku.ac.jp/english/museum/exhibition/special/20160225ishu/index. Accessed December 27, 2016.

Katsu Kaishû (1823–1899)

Born in Edo in 1823, Katsu Kaishû was the son of an impoverished retainer of the Tokugawa family. He is known primarily for his role in mediating the surrender of the Edo Castle to the imperial forces in the spring of 1868, but he straddled the Tokugawa-Meiji divide and held positions in both governments.

Kaishû, who was also known as Rintarô, became househead at the early age of fifteen because his father, Kokichi, largely led an idle life and was unable to provide for the Katsu family adequately; Kokichi is remembered today largely for the autobiography he wrote, *Musui dokugen* (*Musui's Story*), which details the exploits and misadventures of an unemployed Tokugawa retainer. Although skilled with the sword, Kaishû's instructor in sword fighting encouraged him to pursue Dutch studies seriously, which he did, with a focus on military science. From 1855 to 1859, he studied at the Nagasaki Naval Academy, as one of a select group of thirty-seven Tokugawa retainers.

In 1860, the year after completing his studies in Nagasaki, Kaishû was commissioned an officer in the Tokugawa Navy and was selected to command the *Kanrin maru*, a Dutch-built ship purchased by the shogunate. The vessel made the trans-Pacific journey, escorting Japan's delegation that was traveling to the United States to ratify the Treaty of Amity and Commerce between the two countries. His two-month stay in San Francisco gave him direct exposure to foreign culture and bolstered his commitment to the modernization of Japan.

Upon his return to Japan, Kaishû held a number of high-ranking positions in the Tokugawa Navy, including appointment as vice-commissioner (1862) and commissioner (1863); upon appointment as commissioner he received the honorary title *Awa no kami* (Lord of Awa). In 1863 he founded the Kobe Naval School, where he promoted modernization and attempted to create a national navy. His efforts at the school, however, led conservative opponents to push for his dismissal in 1864. Recalled to Edo, Kaishû was placed under house arrest, his naval school closed, and his stipend reduced. Katsu had also provoked the ire of imperial loyalists as well for his support for opening the country and modernizing Japan. The previous year (1863), Tosa loyalist Sakamoto Ryôma had called on Kaishû with the intention of assassinating him, but after discussion between the two men Ryôma ended up becoming his disciple. In fact, in a letter

Statue of Katsu Kaishû (1823–1899), located in Sumida ward, Tokyo. Katsu was the Tokugawa bannerman who negotiated with Satsuma domain's Saigô Takamori for the peaceful turnover of Edo Castle. He later became commissioner in the Tokugawa navy, where he commanded the *Kanrin-maru*, and escorted the first Japanese delegation to the United States in 1860 for formal ratification of the Harris Treaty. The statue depicts him with his right arm extended, pointing to the Pacific Ocean, as he prepared to depart for the U.S. (Masayuki Yamashita/Alamy Stock Photo)

that Ryôma wrote to his sister in 1862, he wrote that Kaishû was "the most important person in Japan."

Kaishû's punishment ended with his reinstatement in 1866, from which time he was utilized by the shogunate as its major contact with the pro-imperial forces of Chôshû and Satsuma domains, which opposed the Tokugawa. In 1868 he commanded the Tokugawa forces but negotiated with Satsuma's Saigô Takamori (1828–1877) the peaceful surrender of Edo Castle, thereby preventing civil war and preserving the life of the shogun.

Although he followed the last shogun, Tokugawa Yoshinobu (1837–1913), into exile, Kaishû's skills were in demand under the new Meiji government. He became one of the highest-ranking former Tokugawa retainers to serve the Meiji, as Vice Minister of the Navy (1872–1873) and Ministry of the Navy (1873–1878). He was also appointed a member of the Privy Council (1888) and became a count in the new peerage (*kazoku)* system.

Kaishû was a prolific writer—his diary, memoirs, and histories fill twenty-three volumes. A number of his writings are important in preserving the record of the Tokugawa shogunate and in providing a narrative account of the last days of that regime. Numerous photographs of him remain, from both Tokugawa and Meiji times. A statue of him can be found in Sumida ward, Tokyo.

See also: Housemen (*gokenin*); *Musui's Story* (*Musui dokugen*); Punishment; Saigô Takamori; Sakamoto Ryôma

Further Reading

Jansen, Marius B. *Sakamoto Ryôma and the Meiji Restoration.* Princeton, NJ: Princeton University Press, 1961.

Steele, M. William. "Against the Restoration: Katsu Kaishû's Attempt to Reinstate the Tokugawa Family." *Monumenta Nipponica,* 36(3) (1981), 299–316.

Katsu Kokichi. See *Musui's Story (Musui dokugen)*

Kido Takayoshi (Kido Kôin) (1833–1877)

Kido Kôin was a samurai from Chôshû born during the Tenpô era (1830–1843), a time of famine and political unrest that many historians view as marking the beginning of the end of the Tokugawa shogunate. A pro-imperial loyalist, he played an important role in the effort to topple the Tokugawa government and went on to serve the Meiji government in a number of leading roles.

Born Katsu Shôgorô, the son of a physician, Takayoshi was adopted into the Kido family at the age of seven. A decade later he entered Hagi's domain school, the Meirinkan, where he was introduced to the Yamaga school of military studies under the instructor Yoshida Shôin. Three years later, in 1852, he was given permission to travel to Edo, where he studied the *Shintô munen-ryû* style of sword fighting under Saitô Yakurô and rose to a supervisory position. He also established ties there with loyalist samurai from Mito domain. After the crisis prompted by the arrival in Japan of the American naval expedition under Commodore Matthew C. Perry in 1853, Tadayoshi expanded his areas of study to include Western military studies (particularly artillery techniques, under Egawa Tarôzaemon), shipbuilding and, more generally, Dutch studies.

A staunch supporter of the *sonnô jôi* (Revere the Emperor, Expel the Barbarian) movement, he opposed those who worked to advance a union of the imperial court and the shogunate (*kôbu gattai*). At the same time, he managed to maintain personal relationships with a number of leading figures who advocated opening the country (*kaikoku*) to relations with the Western powers, such as Katsu Kaishû, Sakamoto Ryôma, and Yokoi Shônan. Still, his ardent imperial loyalism made him a target for assassination by pro-shogunate forces. In fact, he was supposed to be at the Ikedaya Inn the night it was raided by the Shinsengumi, a police force for the shogunate, but was spared the same fate as Sakamoto Ryôma, who was murdered) when his geisha lover informed him of the impending raid. He successfully hid in seclusion for the next few days.

Kido played an instrumental role in establishing an alliance between his domain, Chôshû, and Satsuma, which joined forces to topple the Tokugawa shogunate in the Boshin War (1868–1869). After the restoration of imperial rule (*osei fukko*) but while the fighting was still ongoing, Kido, as an imperial adviser, engaged in the drafting of the Charter Oath, the founding document of the new Meiji government.

As part of the Meiji government, Kido played an instrumental role in guiding the reforms that swept away the Tokugawa administrative structure and created a centralized state. His diaries, which cover the years 1868–1874, provide the perspective of an insider to the events of the Meiji Restoration. In the new government Kido served variously as education minister, home affairs minister, as a cabinet councilor, and as lead inter-

Photo, dating from 1869, of Kido Takayoshi (also known as Kido Kôin), a Chôshû domain samurai who was one of the most important leaders of the Meiji Restoration. Kido played a major role in instituting many of the modernizing measures of the Meiji government, including the abolition of the domain system. (Chronicle of World History/ Alamy Stock Photo)

mediary for Japan's external relations with Korea. Moreover, Kido was one of the top officials to embark on the Iwakura mission (1871–1873), Meiji Japan's first major diplomatic mission overseas. After returning to Japan, Kido was part of a group of officials who opposed an invasion of Korea, which Ôkubo Toshimichi was promoting, not because he was in principle against the use of force to open Korea to relations with the outside world. Rather, Kido believed the Meiji government should focus on domestic affairs, building up the country, instead of becoming embroiled in costly overseas military campaigns. For his role in restraining "those whose reckless programs threatened to precipitate counter-revolution or to involve Japan in disastrous foreign war," a scholar of Kido has dubbed him a "moderate reformer" or "cautious revolutionary" (Brown, 1956, 151). The following year he resigned from government in protest against the Taiwan Expedition of 1874.

Together with Saigô Takamori and Ôkubo Toshimichi, Kido is regarded in Japan as one of the three leading figures (*ishin no sanketsu*) of the Meiji Restoration. He is buried in the same graveyard in Kyoto at Ryozen Gokoku Shrine as Sakamoto Ryôma and numerous other heroes of the Meiji Restoration. He is also buried next to his wife, Ikumatsu, a former geisha who is said to have saved his life by hiding him in a small closet when a Tokugawa police force came looking for him (presumably to kill him). His family home in Hagi, where he lived until the age of twenty, has been preserved as a historic sight. Inside the visitor can still see the graffiti he left: "Stop only after death" (*shishite nochi yamu*), which relates how motivated he was to change Japan.

Photographs of Kido, one in samurai attire and another in Western dress, are available at the website listed under Further Reading.

See also: Katsu Kaishû; Saigô Takamori; Sakamoto Ryôma; Yoshida Shôin

Further Reading

Beasley, William G. *The Meiji Restoration.* Stanford, CA: Stanford University Press, 1972.

Brown, Sidney D. "Kido Takayoshi (1833–1877): Meiji Japan's Cautious Revolutionary." *Pacific Historical Review,* 25(2) (1956), 151–162.

Craig, Albert M. *Chôshû in the Meiji Restoration.* Cambridge, MA: Harvard University Press, 1972.

Kido, Takayoshi. *The Diary of Kido Takayoshi* (Sidney DeVere Brown and Akiko Hirota, trans.), Vol. 1 (1868–1871), Vol. II (1871–1874). Tokyo: University of Tokyo Press, 1983.

"Kido, Takayoshi." Portraits of Modern Japanese Historical Figures, National Diet Library, Tokyo, Japan. http://www.ndl.go.jp/portrait/e/datas/65.html?c=3. Accessed May 4, 2017.

Kumazawa Banzan (1619–1691)

Banzan was born in Kyoto, the son of a *rônin* named Nojiri Kazutoshi (1590–1680), who had served two different daimyo but who found himself masterless at the time of Banzan's birth, just three years after the death of Tokugawa Ieyasu (1543–1616). Banzan's grandfather had served the daimyo Oda Nobunaga (1534–1582) and Sakuma Jinkurô (1556–1631). His mother, Kamejo, was the daugher of a samurai named Kumazawa Morihisa, who served the daimyo of Mito, Tokugawa Yorifusa. Since Kazutoshi was unable to find a lord to serve, he sent his wife and son to Mito to be cared for by his wife's father. At the age of eight, Banzan was adopted out to his maternal grandfather Kumazawa Morihisa, whose surname he assumed. At about the same time, Banzan's younger brother was adopted out to a Hirado samurai family, which tells us much about the impoverished condition of the Nojiri household.

Through the introduction of a well-connected distant relative, in 1634, at age sixteen Banzan was able to obtain a position as a page under Ikeda Mitsumasa, the

Contemporary portrait of Kumazawa Banzan (1619–1691), the son of a *rônin* who was later able to enter the service of Lord Ikeda Mitsumasa of Okayama. Banzan was a bright scholar and rose high in the domain administration, but his critical views of certain Tokugawa policies and adherence to the heterodox Wang Yang-ming school of Confucianism forced him to withdraw from public life. (Art Collection 3/Alamy Stock Photo)

daimyo of Okayama, whom he served for five years. During this time he traveled to Edo in the lord's entourage on two occasions. His period of service, not to mention the two trips to the Tokugawa capital, gave Banzan important life experience that served him well in his later career. During this time he exhibited great ambition to become a model samurai, as we read the account he left of this time: "When I was about sixteen I had a tendency toward corpulence. . . . So I tried every device to keep myself agile and lean. . . . While on duty at Yedo there were no hills and fields at hand where I could hunt and climb, so I exercised with spear and sword." (See Document 10 for a fuller excerpt.)

For reasons that are unclear, Banzan left the service of Mitsumasa in 1638 and returned home for a time to his grandfather's home in Mito domain. Some scholars have argued that this was likely the first of four times during his career in which he seems to have displeased his superiors. One explanation for his release from service was that in his zeal to join the domain's forces in fighting for the Tokugawa to put down the Shimabara Rebellion in 1638, he is said to have conducted his own coming-of-age ceremony (*genpuku*) and rushed home from Edo to Okayama without permission, both offenses for which he was disciplined. Whatever the actual reason for his dismissal, seven years later the offense had been forgiven, and he entered again into the employ of Okayama's lord.

During the six years that he was home in Ômi province he read widely, primarily in military studies. He appears to have worked with intensity, to the point where he made himself ill. After this he decided to abandon this single-minded focus and to broaden his intellectual life with Confucian studies. For a time he studied under the Confucian scholar Nakae Tôju (1608–1648), the founder of the Yang-ming school (Yômeigaku). This period when he was not in service to a lord was difficult one, as he recounted: "While I was a *rônin*, for five or six years I ate a food of the common people of Ômi called lily gruel, with bran paste as a side dish. I had no soup, fish, sake or tea. I kept out the cold with clothes of Kiyomizu paper and wadded cotton. Forgetting old standards of dress and food, I enjoyed my books" (McMullen, 1999, 78).

His dedication paid off well, as he was able to enter again into the service of Ikeda Mitsumasa in 1645, at the age of twenty-seven, as a petty officer (*keihai*). He also worked as an aid in the domain school, one of the first in Japan. Within two years, though, his scholarship in Confucianism came to the attention of the lord, and in 1647 Banzan was appointed to the position of *osobayaku* (chamberlain), in the lord's personal entourage, with an emolument of 300 *koku*. This promotion was badly needed by the family, and Banzan used it to support his then-widowed mother as well as his brothers and sisters. His position also allowed him plenty of opportunity to study, and he accompanied his lord Ikeda Mitsumasa again to Edo.

Further recognition of Banzan's considerable abilities followed just two years later, in 1649, when he was appointed to the rank of captain of guards (*bangashira*) in Mitsumasa's government, with an income of 3,000 *koku*, and held the position of chief minister. This represented an unprecedented rise in rank, one that made him inferior in rank and stipend only to the senior councilors (*karô*) of the domain. During the seven years (1649–1657) that he held this ministerial position he traveled again to Edo on two occasions (1651, 1653) with Mitsumasa, and gained fame; in Edo, he was invited for audiences by the Lord of Kii (Wakayama domain), one of the Tokugawa collateral families, and even the Shogun Iemitsu. While in Okayama he worked energetically to introduce a series of agricultural reforms in the domain that brought him into conflict with the lord's more traditional-minded top councilors. Those reforms aimed to provide relief to farmers in the countryside suffering the ill effects of both a major flood, in 1654, as well as famine.

It was Banzan's philosophical bent, being a follower of Yômeigaku (the Wang Yang-ming school) rather than the orthodox Neo-Confucianism (*shushigaku*) followed by the Tokugawa shogunate, which brought him into conflict with a number of important Tokugawa officials. In 1657, the political pressure brought to bear on Banzan led to his decision to leave the service of Ikeda Mitsumasa. He went into hiding in Okayama domain for a brief time, before deciding under further pressure from both domain and shogunal officials to leave Okayama. He left, however, with a 200 *koku*-a-year retirement allowance that he received from the lord.

During the years after he left the service of Okayama domain, Banzan wrote extensively, advocating a number of positions that were critical of the policies of the Tokugawa shogunate. He was, for example, critical of the alternate attendance system as it existed; the separation of warriors and peasants (*heinô bunri*), advocating for the resettlement of samurai on the land; and even the hereditary system of privilege itself. He advocated for a political system in which merit would trump hereditary privilege. These were some of the arguments that he made in his most famous work, *Daigaku wakumon* (*A Discussion of Public Questions in Light of the Great Learning*, 1686). As a result of his writings, he spent the rest of his life under the surveillance of the shogunate. Driven out of Kyoto in 1667 by the local Tokugawa official in that city, Banzan went into hiding for two years. From 1669 until the end of his life, at age seventy-four, in 1691, he lived under the control of a several different daimyo, ending his life essentially as the captive guest of Matsudaira Nobuyuki, daimyo of Koga domain.

See also: Alternate Attendance (*sankin kôtai*); Ronin (*rônin*)

Further Reading

Fisher, Galen M. "Kumazawa Banzan: His Life and Ideas." *Transactions of the Asiatic Society of Japan*, Second Series, 16 (1938), 223–258.

Kumazawa Banzan. "*Daigaku wakumon*. A Discussion of Public Questions in the Light of the Great Learning." Translated by Galen M. Fisher. *Transactions of the Asiatic Society of Japan*, Second Series, 16 (1938), 259–356.

McMullen, James. *Idealism, Protest and the Tale of Genji: The Confucianism of Kumazawa Banzan (1619–91)*. Oxford: Oxford University Press, 1999. (See in particular Part II: A Warrior's Life.)

Kurume hanshi Edo kinban nagaya emaki (Scroll of the Life of Kurume Domain Retainers in their Barracks While on Duty in Edo)

This horizontal scroll is a pictorial and textual record of the life of retainers from Kurume domain (Kyushu), who were required to accompany their lord on alternate attendance to Edo around the years 1839–1840. It measures 26.5 cm × 746.5 cm and was the combined work of two Kurume domain retainers. The thirteen paintings comprising the visual text were the work of the samurai-domain painter Kano Shôha (a.k.a. Mitani Masanobu, 1805–1869). The text, which appears at the beginning and at various intervals throughout the work, was written by another man, Toda Kumajirô (1805–1882), an inspector (*metsuke*) at the time of the events depicted.

The illustrations depict the life of a small circle of Kurume retainers associated with Toda Kumajirô in their barracks, or *nagaya*, at the domain residence in Edo. A number of the images are unique in that they depict life inside the barracks (most other images, particularly woodblock prints, only reveal their exteriors). Although the events shown in the scroll took place around 1839–1840, it is apparent from the language used that the images and text were not created until several decades later, early in the Meiji period. In other words, the scroll represents the selective memory of the artist and author looking back on a time in the past when they were obliged to remain in Edo for service, away from home and their families.

The scenes depicted take place inside the Akabane residence compound (*daimyô yashiki*) in Edo, in Shiba Mita-chô, behind Zôjôji, the shogunal temple. According to the written text, the "existence of retainers on duty in Edo involves pleasures and hardships," and the visual images give the viewer some evidence for both. In terms of pleasures, we see the men in the barracks at leisure, talking, eating, drinking, writing, and playing games. In the scroll's first scene we see two samurai talking and enjoying some sake and light food. In another scene, a group of samurai are playing a game called *rakan mawashi*, which involves imitating the hand and facial gestures made by each of the other participants. Other scenes depict individual groups of men composing poetry, conducting a tea ceremony, and drinking and eating.

The hardships involved in a period of duty in Edo are also revealed in several scenes. In one scene, which is unusual in that it is the only one in which a woman appears, two samurai are sitting next to a pot of cooking food, eating and drinking, while a third is at the window. The man at the window was a retainer who had been in Edo for studies for four years on his own (it is unclear whether or not he was married); he is looking outside, in the courtyard, at two women talking. The text informs us that they are members of a family of a retainer in Edo on a long-term assignment, the only retainers who were allowed to bring their families to Edo. The sight of the women outside the barracks may have brought back memories of the man's own family and a longing for home. In the scroll's climactic scene, we see a group of retainers reacting to the bad news that their lord was ordered to remain in Edo an extra year to continue to provide guard service at Zôjôji. The men are clearly upset at this news, which would keep them away from home for another year. At least one group got drunk, smashing a sake bottle and tearing down doors in their barracks.

Although retainers were deployed for military service in Edo, they lived in a time of great peace. Not surprisingly, nowhere in the scroll do we see them engaging in actual martial activities (in one scene, one samurai is shooting a toy bow and arrow at a target inside a room). In a number of scenes we see evidence of the cultivation of the so-called civil arts (the *bun* of *bunbu*): a number of rooms are decorated with hanging scrolls or other artwork, cut flowers in vases, books, writing utensils, and implements for the tea ceremony.

See also: Civil and Military Arts (*bunbu*)

Further Reading

Vaporis, Constantine N. "A Tour of Duty: *Kurume Hanshi Edo Kinban Nagaya Emaki*." *Monumenta Nipponica*, 51(3) (1996), 279–307.

Vaporis, Constantine Nomikos. *Tour of Duty: Samurai, Military Service in Edo, and the Culture of Early Modern Japan.* Honolulu: University of Hawai'i Press, 2008.

Kyûji shimonroku (A Record of Inquiry into Bygone Days)

An oral history of the late Tokugawa period, *Kyûji shimonroku* was undertaken by a research group established in 1890 by Ogawa Ginjirô, the secretary of the organization *Shigaku zasshi* (*Journal of the Historical Association*).

Ogawa was conscious of the importance of recording the history of the last years of the Tokugawa shogunate while the people with firsthand knowledge of its institutions and practices were still alive. In November 1890 he published an article in *Shigaku zasshi* announcing the establishment of a research group that would interview former officials of the shogunate. Notable promoters of the project included Shigeno Yasutsugu (founder of the Department of National History of the Imperial University of Tokyo) and Kume Kunitake (a historian who traveled on the Iwakura mission, 1871, and published a five-volume account of his journey around the world). The project was undertaken at a time, the late Meiji period (1868–1912), when there was a certain nostalgia for the recent past, the Tokugawa era. The interviews were held in 1891–1892, and the transcripts of the interviews were published as a supplement to *Shigaku zasshi* as *Kyûji shimonroku*.

Kyûji shimonroku is a valuable source of information about the workings of the shogunate but also gives the reader a sense of the general spirit of the times. It includes interviews with a wide range of historical figures, including a supervisor of the corps of pages (*koshô tôdori*), a lady-in-waiting from Edo Castle's interior (from the *oku*, the shogun's private quarters), officials of the Finance Magistrate (*kanjôsho*) and the Shogunate's Tribunal (*hyôjôsho*), a former member of the shogun's personal secret guard (*oniwaban*), and a former commissioner for foreign affairs (*gaikoku bugyô*).

The text was largely forgotten until after World War II, when writers of historical fiction and drama discovered it as a rich source for their work. Portions of the Japanese text have been translated into English; specifically, parts of the interview with Yamaguchi Naoki (1830–1895), a Tokugawa bannerman (*hatamoto*) and official who served in a succession of posts as *metsuke* (inspector), *gaikoku bugyô* (commissioner for foreign affairs), and *machi bugyô* (Edo city magistrate). (Beerens, "Interview with a Bakumatsu Official," two parts, 2000, 2002). As *metsuke* he served as a member of the committee that prepared for Tokugawa Iemochi's trip to Kyoto in 1863, the first such visit by the shogun in 200 years. In several of his other positions he had to deal with a variety of foreign-policy issues related to the American and British presence in Japan, including the crisis arising from the various Western powers demanding the opening of the ports of Hyôgo and Osaka. As *machi bugyô* he held one of the most important offices in the shogunate (held concurrently with one other *bugyô*), and was responsible for the commoner population of Edo, with oversight of commercial affairs, civil order in the city, judicial affairs, and firefighting.

See also: Bannermen (*hatamoto*); Shogunate (*bakufu, kôgi*)

Further Reading

Beerens, Anna, trans. "Interview with a Bakumatsu Official. A Translation from *Kyûji shimonroku.*" *Monumenta Nipponica,* 55(3) (2000), 369–398.

Beerens, Anna, trans. "Interview with a Bakumatsu Official. A Translation from *Kyûji shimonroku* (2)." *Monumenta Nipponica,* 57(2) (2002), 173–206.

L

Laws for the Military Houses (buke shohatto)

The second shogun, Tokugawa Hidetada, formally promulgated the thirteen-article code known as the *Laws for the Military Houses* in 1615. The document was compiled, at the retired shogun Tokugawa Ieyasu's direction, mainly by the Zen monk Ishin Sûden (1539–1633). Every succeeding Tokugawa shogun in the Tokugawa dynasty formally reissued the regulations, allowing for them to be amended over time, as needed. They remained, however, the same in general tone and effect. This set of guidelines, or code of conduct, issued by Tokugawa, was aimed at the regional lords, or daimyo, the shogunate's main rivals, not samurai in general; other regulations issued by the shogunate such as the *shoshi hatto* (*Regulations for the Samurai*), despite the title they were given, were aimed specifically at the Tokugawa's direct vassals, the bannermen (*hatamoto*) and the housemen (*gokenin*).

The *Laws for the Military Houses* (see Document 2) were an important step in a series of actions taken by the Tokugawa house to assert its hegemony (military rule) over the other regional lords since its victory over them on the battlefield in 1600, in the Battle of Sekigahara. Three years later, Tokugawa Ieyasu, then simply the head of the Tokugawa house, felt in a strong enough position to demand that the emperor appoint him to the title of shogun. In 1611, Ieyasu was able to demand oaths of allegiance from the daimyo of central and western Japan in Nijô Castle (Kyoto), nearby the castle of Osaka, where the forces of the rival Toyotomi family were concentrated. The following year, similar oaths were obtained from the daimyo of northern Japan. Finally, in 1614–1615, in two separate campaigns, the Tokugawa defeated the forces aligned with the Toyotomi and burned Osaka Castle to the ground (see entry Sieges of Osaka). Months later, the daimyo were assembled in Fushimi and read the regulations (Documents 2A and 2B, described below).

Since the forces aligned with the Tokugawa's rivals, the Toyotomi family, had been defeated only months earlier, the political climate was still quite delicate when the daimyo were called together. The regulations reflected the tense political climate of the early seventeenth century and thus Ieyasu's desire to control the daimyo closely. Ieyasu was aware of the fact that the Tokugawa victory at Sekigahara in 1600 was only sealed with the assistance of key former vassals of the Toyotomi, such as the Kuroda, Fukushima, and Yamauchi—and the treachery of several other daimyo who switched sides during the battle. In other words, he was well aware of the tenuous nature of Tokugawa's hold on power. Even after Sekigahara, there were still powerful daimyo, such as Uesugi, Date, and Shimazu, of whom he had to be wary. There were also masterless samurai and other disaffected warriors who supported the Toyotomi; although they were defeated in the Battle of Osaka, sufficient numbers still remained after the conflict and would support the forces that rose in opposition to Tokugawa-led forces in the Shimabara Rebellion. Of course, Ieyasu had only to remember that in Osaka he broke his own pledge to Toyotomi Hideyoshi to protect and support his son, Hideyori, as Hideyoshi's heir to reaffirm that political loyalties were often short-lived.

The *Laws for the Military Houses* were one of the most important means by which the Tokugawa sought to subject the daimyo to its authority. In this context, the Tokugawa saw the *Laws for the Military Houses,* in the words of the code, as "the foundation of the social order." Since the *Laws* were issued by the Tokugawa they were in essence a declaration of its authority over the daimyo. As issued in 1615, the documents use the *kô* or *oyake* (meaning "public" or "official") in reference to the shogunate, in contrast to the term *shi* (meaning "private" or "personal") in relation to the daimyo, was a further assertion of the Tokugawa's hegemonic power.

The *Laws* represent a codification of rules for the behavior or deportment of the daimyo. The daimyo were admonished to cultivate civilian as well as military skills, report any trouble or troublemakers, restrict contacts between their domain and others, report for duty in Edo, encourage their samurai retainers not to live above their station, and appoint officials who would govern wisely. The *Laws* also made daimyo marriages and castle construction or repairs subject to the shogun's approval. Marriages were of particular concern since during the Warring States period daimyo often used marriage to seal political alliances; the Tokugawa wanted to restrict the daimyo's use of marriage to create alliances that might challenge its authority. Expansion of a daimyo's castle network, or unreported renovations to existing castle structures, could be seen as part of a military strategy to challenge Tokugawa authority and hence were prohibited. Implicit in all of this was the threat that if the daimyo were convicted of breaking any of the regulations the shogun could confiscate their domains, stripping the lord or rank and rendering all of his retainers masterless samurai.

These regulations were part of a broader plan to extend Tokugawa authority over all elites in Japanese society, including the emperor and the court nobility, also issued in 1615, and a series of laws, issued between 1610 and 1614, aimed at the Buddhist church.

The *Laws for the Military Houses* were reissued twice by the third shogun, Iemitsu, in 1629, in exactly the same form as in 1615, and again in 1635. The 1635 version (see Document 2, part B) strengthened and extended Tokugawa controls. Most importantly, it formalized or institutionalized the requirements for alternate attendance for all daimyo, including a system of hostages; the daimyo were required to spend alternate periods, usually a year, in Edo, and when they were away from the city they were to leave important family members behind as security. Several articles also underscore the shogunate's concern for the free flow of communications, calling for maintenance of roads and related transportation infrastructure, such as ferryboats and bridges, while prohibiting toll barriers and the interruption or disruption of ferry services. The 1635 version prohibited the construction of ships with a capacity of over 500 *koku*, essentially meaning ocean-going vessels; this was meant to prevent daimyo from making contacts with foreign powers for independent trade or to build alliances against the shogunate.

The 1635 version of the *Laws* specified that domain laws should follow those of the shogunate in broad terms: "In all matters the example set by the laws of Edo is to be followed in all the provinces and places." This would seem to make an argument for the extraordinary nature of state authority. Yet, to a certain extent, the similarity in governing structures, both the shogunate and domain governments, was the result of the common conditions faced by warrior leaders across the country in the late sixteenth century. From another perspective, many of the articles, as noted above, were directed at the person of the daimyo, with little intervention into the manner in which the daimyo ruled. Accordingly, the *Laws* can be interpreted as an example of a feudal rather than a bureaucratic model of Tokugawa control. By following the Tokugawa's lead, and by pledging allegiance to the shogun, the daimyo benefited greatly. They received confirmation of their right to rule and widespread recognition of the territorial borders.

The edicts were reissued on the succession of each shogun: in 1663, under the fourth shogun, Tokugawa Ietsuna; 1683, under Tokugawa Tsunayoshi; and then in 1710, under Tokugawa Ienobu. Although these versions of the *Laws* evidenced stylistic differences, in terms of substance the amount of change was not terribly great. Among the important changes, however, was a ban on Christianity, included in the 1663 version. The next issue of the *Laws*, in 1683, included language reinforcing the ban on *junshi*, ritual suicide upon the death of one's lord, which had been banned earlier in 1663. Other new articles in these later versions included stipulations on the abuses of power, the acceptance of bribes, the proper succession of daimyo, and sumptuary rules on clothing and housing. The 1683 version was reissued by almost all successive shoguns.

The *Laws for the Warrior Houses* reveal a great deal about the nature of law and the ideal role of the state in Tokugawa Japan. The state not only served as an administrative mechanism in maintaining public order and collecting taxes, but it was also an agent of moral leadership. Through the *Laws* it encouraged the daimyo to behave in certain ways and to follow certain practices, without necessarily having the ability to enforce them. In other words, these *Laws* were not treated as positive law, justiciable and enforceable; rather they were meant largely to exhort good behavior. Only 14 of the 235 cases (6 percent) in which a daimyo was punished with confiscation of his domain by the shogunate were a result of a violation of the *Laws for the Military Houses*; these fourteen cases all involved control of the person of the daimyo, particularly private marriage contracts, concealment of criminals, and unapproved castle repairs. Nevertheless, the *Laws* could be enforced on an as-needed basis, which meant a certain unpredictability of law enforcement and made them a useful tool of control.

See also: Alternate Attendance (*sankin kôtai*); Daimyo and Domains; Shimabara Rebellion (*Shimabara no ran*); Shogun (*shôgun*); Shogunate (*bakufu, kôgi*); Sieges of Osaka (*Ôsaka no jin*)

Further Reading

Brown, Philip C. *Central Authority & Local Autonomy in the Formation of Early Modern Japan*. Stanford, CA: Stanford University Press, 1993.

Hall, John C. "Japanese Feudal Laws III. The Tokugawa Legislation, Part I." *Transactions of the Asiatic Society of Japan,* 38, First Series (1911), 269–331.

Laws for the Samurai (shoshi hatto)

The Tokugawa shogunate issued regulations not only for the daimyo—the *Laws for the Military Houses* (*buke shohatto*)—but also for its direct retainers, the *hatamoto* (bannermen) and *gokenin* (housemen). The first set of *Laws* was promulgated in 1632, the timing perhaps related to the unsettled conditions in Edo after the death of the retired shogun, Tokugawa Hidetada (1579–1632). The nine-article regulations instructed the Tokugawa's retainers to serve their lord faithfully ("The way of the samurai is to take pleasure in his military service, without negligence."), to respect their parents, to pay attention to literary arts, to keep their military gear in good condition, to be frugal, not to get drunk, and not to form political factions. It also prohibited deathbed adoptions under any circumstances, a privilege that was allowed for daimyo in 1651.

Tokugawa Iemitsu (1604–1651), the third shogun, reissued the *Laws* in 1636, adding fourteen additional articles and more than doubling the length of the document. Most of these new articles were sumptuary in nature, aimed at trying to regulate consumption, including housing, by pegging it closely to status. Relatedly, more detail was provided on avoiding luxury, particularly with regard to wedding celebrations, housewares, gift-giving, and dress (for the retainers themselves as well as for their subordinates). The 1636 regulations also contained an article prohibiting samurai from engaging in trade or purchasing excessive goods with an eye to selling them for a profit.

The *Laws* were reissued once more in 1663, under the fourth shogun Ietsuna (1641–1680), virtually unchanged. The contents of the last two sets of *Laws* were so similar in content with the *Laws for the Military Houses* that Tokugawa Tsunayoshi (1646–1709), the fifth shogun, integrated them into the latter.

See also: Bannermen (*hatamoto*); Housemen (*gokenin*); *Laws for the Military Houses* (*buke shohatto*); Tokugawa Hidetada; Tokugawa Tsunayoshi

Further Reading

Hall, J. Carey. "Japanese Feudal Laws III—The Tokugawa Legislation, Parts I–III." *Transactions, Asiatic Society of Japan* (Yokohama: 1910), 286–319.

M

Magistrates (bugyô)

An old term used for officials with formal responsibilities to oversee important government administrative functions, *bugyô* during the Edo period were high-ranking administrators with well-defined duties who typically operated out of an office known as a *bugyôsho* (lit., "magistrate's office"). The most important of these magistrates, or commissioners as they are also known, were so-called "three magistrates" (*sanbugyô*): the Edo city magistrates (*Edo machi bugyô*), the magistrates of temples and shrines (*jisha bugyô*), and the magistrate of finance (*kanjô bugyô*). Each position was filled by multiple officials who served simultaneously. There were two officials in charge of the administrative affairs of Edo, the shogun's capital, the North Edo magistrate (*Kita machi bugyô*) and the South Edo magistrate (*Minami machi bugyô*); five magistrates of temples and shrines, who had jurisdiction over affairs related to Buddhist temples and Shinto shrines; and four magistrates of finance who oversaw the shogunate's budget. In terms of hierarchy, the magistrate of temples and shrines was the highest-ranking official and was selected from among the daimyo. The Edo city magistrate and the magistrate of finance followed in that order and were both staffed from among the lower-ranking bannermen (*hatamoto*).

In addition to the "three magistrates," other important positions of this type include the magistrate of public works (*fushin bugyô*), magistrate of foreign relations (*gaikoku bugyô*), Kyoto city magistrate (*Kyôto machi bugyô*), the Nagasaki magistrate (*Nagasaki bugyô*), and the Hakodate magistrate (*Hakodate bugyô*). The last two positions were for oversight of two cities of critical importance to the

Edo City Magistrate

Perhaps the most famous Edo city magistrate was Ôoka Tadasuke (1677–1752), who served for two decades (1717–1736) during the reign of the eighth shogun, Tokugawa Yoshimune. He held the title Echizen no kami (Lord of Echizen) and is often known as Ôoka Echizen. As Edo city magistrate he fulfilled various administrative roles and served as the modern equivalent of mayor, judge, police chief, and fire marshal. He was particularly famous as an incorruptible judge. Due to his stellar record Ôoka was promoted to magistrate of temples and shrines, in which capacity he served for a dozen years. After more than thirty years of service to the shogunate, Ôoka was elevated in rank to daimyo and was given a small fief, Nishi-Ôhira (10,000 *koku*). He is a major character in historical dramas on Japanese television, such as *Ôoka Echizen* and *Meibugyô Ôoka Echizen*. Ôoka has also figured prominently in young adult fiction, such as Dorothy and Thomas Hoobler's *The Ghost in the Tokaido Inn*.

shogunate's foreign commercial activity and foreign relations, Nagasaki, in the south, and Hakodate, in the north.

The Nagasaki magistrate was an important post because of the position of city as one of the four so-called "gates" of Tokugawa Japan (in addition to Tsushima, Satsuma, and Matsumae), the only one that was Tokugawa territory. The southern port of Nagasaki was prioritized as the probable locus of attack following the enactment of the shogunate's so-called "exclusion edicts" (to expel the Portuguese from Japan) and its refusal to trade with two Portuguese ships in 1647. The importance of this position to Japan's defensive system, which aimed to protect Nagasaki from anticipated attack by Western ships, in enforcing trade restrictions and protecting the Dutch merchants in Nagasaki, is evident from the elevation of the rank of the Nagasaki magistrate during the 1690s. By the end of the century, the position was ranked the highest of all the "distant magistrates" (*ongoku bugyô*),

Lithograph entitled *Bungo or Prefect Hahodadi [Hakodate]*, created by Eliphalet Brown in 1855. Standing behind the seated Hakodate magistrate (on the right) is a samurai retainer of his and (on the left) a spear-holding attendant. The Hakodate magistrate's office played an important role in Japan's foreign relations after the opening of Hakodate port with the signing of the Treaty of Kanagawa in 1854. (Photo by Constantine Vaporis)

even above the highly prestigious post of Kyoto magistrate. Given the importance of his role, the Nagasaki magistrate Matsudaira Yasuhira felt compelled to commit ritual suicide for his role in the failure of Tokugawa and domain forces to prevent the forced intrusion of the British frigate *Phaeton* into Nagasaki harbor in 1808.

On the northern end of Japan, the Hakodate magistrate's office, first established in the early nineteenth century but abolished in 1821, was reestablished in 1855 after the opening of the port of Hakodate to the United States as part of the Treaty of Kanagawa between the two countries the previous year. The magistrate in 1854, Endô Matazaimon, had tried to delay negotiation with the officers whom Commodore Matthew C. Perry had sent to Hakodate to discuss implementation of the treaty, but to no effect. Due to the vulnerable position of the magistrate's office, located as it was close to the port, at the foot of Mt. Hakodate, it was later moved, in 1864, to a secure position inside a newly constructed

---

Bungo (bugyô) or Prefect, Hakodadi (Hakodate)

This image is a lithograph of the Hakodate magistrate (*Hakodate bugyô*), Endô Matazaimon, and two of his retainers. This formal portrait measures 23.5 × 15.8 cm. It is from the Beverley Tucker, Senate Printing (1856) of the official *Narrative of the Expedition of an American Squadron to the China Seas and Japan, Performed in the Years 1852, 1853, and 1854, Under the Command of Commodore M.C. Perry, United States Navy.* Washington: Beverly Tucker, Senate Printer, 1856, between pages 434 and 435. This copy of the lithograph is the possession of the author. Notice that the positions of the swords and the fold of the kimono are on the "wrong side" in the lithograph (they are shown in reverse position). The kimono appear folded right over left, as is done with a corpse, and the swords are tucked into the sash on the right side, which would have made them very difficult to draw for right-handed samurai.

---

fort, Goryokaku (Star-Shaped Fort). Between 2006 and 2010 the office was carefully reconstructed, using old documents, photos, and drawings, and is now open to tourists.

The position title, *bugyô*, was also used in the various domains, for town magistrates (*machi bugyô*), district magistrates (*kôri bugyô*), who oversaw the countryside, and coastal magistrates (*ura bugyô*), in charge of ports and coastal villages.

The title ceased being used after the Meiji Restoration.

See also: Bannermen (*hatamoto*); Daimyo and Domains; Shogunate (*bakufu, kôgi*)

Further Reading

Hakodate Magistrate's Office. Official Website: http://www.hakodate-bugyosho.jp/en. Accessed December 16, 2016.

Totman, Conrad. *Politics in the Tokugawa Bakufu, 1600–1843*. Cambridge, MA: Harvard University Press, 1966.

Wilson, Noell. *Defensive Positions. The Politics of Maritime Security in Tokugawa Japan*. Cambridge, MA: Harvard University Asia Center, 2015.

Male-Male Love (*nanshoku*)

Literally translated as "male colors," *nanshoku* refers to a specific form of homosexuality in Japan. Although the term was first used during medieval times, its heyday in Japan was during the Tokugawa period. The practice has been described succinctly by one reviewer as "characterized by the anal penetration of a youth or a man in the role of a youth by a man who, in the context of the relationship, could be considered the elder. It seldom took the form of mutual masturbation and never involved fellatio. It was thus inherently unequal. It was also impermanent" (Walthall, 1997, 1552). Practiced among samurai as well as townsmen, *nanshoku* was popularized in vernacular fiction as well as in erotic prints (*shunga*) from the Genroku period (1688–1704) onward.

Nanshoku homosexual culture grew out of two historical traditions, monastic Buddhism and the relationships forged by men in warrior bands during the medieval period, when warfare frequently kept men away from their households. The most celebrated male-male relationships, however, were between daimyo and their vassals. Numerous Warring States daimyo, such as Takeda Shingen (1521–1573) and Tokugawa Ieyasu (1543–1616), were known to have enjoyed sexual relationships with subordinates, particularly with male pages. The practice of *nanshoku* continued during the Edo period among samurai, including a number of shoguns, and male townsmen, primarily as a nonexclusive form of sexual activity outside of marriage, the purpose of which was to produce an heir for the household. Two foreign visitors to Tokugawa Japan in the seventeenth century made note of the practice. François Caron (1600–1673), a Frenchman who was employed by the Dutch East Indian Company, in 1636, wrote: "Their Priests, as well as many of the Gentry [i.e., the samurai], are much given to Sodomy, that unnatural passion, being esteemed no sin, nor shameful thing thing amongst them." Later in the century, Englebert Kaempfer, a German similarly employed by the Dutch, on his way to Edo in 1691 wrote that, "Our Bugio, or Commander in chief of our train, whose affected gravity never permitted him to quit his Norimon [palanquin], till we came to our Inns, could not forebear to step out at this place, and to spend half an hour in company with these boys . . ." (Quoted in Pflugfelder, 1999, 97).

Male-male sex, as practiced by samurai, was an activity motivated by erotic desire and characterized by hierarchy, namely a superior-subordinate or mentor-protégé type relationship. It was characterized by an unequal relationship between a senior, adult, "active" male (the "penetrator," or "top") and his "passive" adolescent boy lover (the penetrated, or "bottom"), the latter whom generally assumed a feminine appearance. As a rule there was no possibility for role-switching. *Nanshoku* thus reflected the hierarchical values inherent in Tokugawa society, particularly the feudal elements involved in lord-vassal relationships and the Confucian principle of filial piety. The relationship was to have a mutually ennobling function. It fulfilled a pedagogical function in that the elder provided mentorship in samurai values and skills while at the same time encouraging the elder to prove himself worthy of his partner. The tie between the male partners was widely viewed as a form of personal obligation subject to the codes of loyalty, similar to the bonds between lord and vassal.

Male-male sexual relations were not stigmatized or proscribed in Japan as they were in many other places. As François Caron's comment, above, indicated, the Japanese religions of Shinto and Buddhism did not view male-male sexual practices as particularly sinful. Moreover, unlike what happened in Qing China, or in contemporary Europe, political authorities in Japan did not criminalize male-male sexual relations; there was no legislation banning "sodomy" (anal penetration), as in Europe. In fact, they viewed the illicit coupling between men and women as more threatening to the social order. However, political authorities were concerned about overindulgence in erotic pleasures, regardless of whether it was between men or between men and women. For example, the 1615 *Laws for the Warrior Houses* issued by the shogunate to govern the activities of daimyo warned that "lasciviousness" was a cause of "state ruin" but did not specify the gender of the object of lust.

Nanshoku relationships were generally tolerated as long as they did not threaten social values or social order, power structures, or the greater interests of the household. Both partners were supposed to outgrow the relationship once the youth attained adulthood; the passage to adulthood was physically marked by a coming-of-age ceremony that took place around the age of fifteen and which included the shaving of the boy's forelocks. Male-male relationships were viewed more often as complementary to male-female relationships. Men who engaged exclusively in male-male sex were by far the exception rather than the rule, so for many samurai who engaged in this activity it represented a stage in their human development.

According to one authority, "[m]ale-male erotic ties, although deeply embedded within warrior culture, posed a significant challenge to this hierarchical structure by creating alliances along horizontal lines" (Pflugfelder, 1999, 144). In other words, officials were concerned that male-male relationships between samurai retainers might conflict with the feudal loyalty they owed their overlord. As a result, domain authorities tried to regulate behavior through legal pronouncements such as retainer regulations and directives. For example, as early as 1611, Okayama domain authorities prohibited pages who accompanied the lord's processions on alternate attendance from "going crazy over youths" in Edo, indicating that sex was undergoing a process of commercialization in the shogunate capital (as well as in other urban centers) (Pflugfelder, 1999, 136). Domain authorities were also concerned about young males engaging in violence, fighting, over matters involving male-male relations.

Nanshoku was the subject of many erotic prints (*shunga*) as well as popular vernacular fiction. Among those works of fiction, Ihara Saikaku's *The Great Mirror of Male Love* (*Nanshoku ôkagami*), which belongs to the genre of "floating world literature" (*ukiyo zôshi*), is the best-known example. Published in 1687, the book's first half contains a number of stories involving the samurai and *nanshoku*. In these stories the adult lovers act as mentors for the younger, submissive youth. (Other stories involve monks, kabuki actors, and townsmen.) The texts present male-male love as a "way" (*michi*), a form of practice—*shudô* (the way of loving youths)—that had to be learned, mastered, and perfected. *Shunga*, produced by many of the top woodblock print artists, also circulated widely and included *nanshoku* themes, including the sexual behavior between samurai and teahouse boy–prostitutes.

See also: Coming of Age (*genpuku*); *Laws for the Military Houses* (*buke shohatto*)

Further Reading

Ihara, Saikaku. *The Great Mirror of Male Love.* Translated, with an introduction, by Paul Gordon Schalow. Stanford, CA: Stanford University Press, 1990.

Leupp, Gary. *Male Colors: The Construction of Homosexuality in Tokugawa Japan.* Berkeley and Los Angeles: University of California Press, 1995.

Pflugfelder, Gregory M. *Cartographies of Desire: Male-Male Sexuality in Japanese Discourse, 1600–1950.* Berkeley, CA: University of California Press, 1999.

Walthall, Anne. Review of Gary P. Leupp, *Male Colors: The Construction of Homosexuality in Tokugawa Japan.* In *American Historical Review,* 102(5) (December 1997), 1552–1553.

Martial Arts (*bugei*)

Samurai during the Tokugawa period were supposed to strike a balance between their study of the literary (civil) and the martial arts, a concept known as *bunbu*. Maintaining martial readiness in the early seventeenth century was necessary, as under the new rule of a Tokugawa shogun the country faced political uncertainty and warfare did break out again, 1614–1615, at the Sieges of Osaka Castle. Afterward, as peaceful conditions set in, samurai necessarily began to lose their battle-tested skills, and when those veterans of war passed away they were replaced by samurai who would know only peace during their lifetimes. According to the commonly accepted narrative of the development of the martial arts, over the course of the Tokugawa period the samurai's martial skills were transformed in purpose and technique in three stages: from skills that were aimed at providing self-protection, to skills that were meant for self-perfection (roughly from the 1640s), and then late in the period, roughly from the late eighteenth century, skills that were developed as essentially sport.

Chôshû samurai Takasugi Shinsaku (1839–1867), a staunch advocate for exclusionism and founder of the *Kiheitai* mixed militia, in protective armor for *kenjutsu* (sword fighting) practice. Sword fighting became increasingly popular in the late Tokugawa period, particularly after the arrival of Commodore Perry's fleet in Japan in 1853. (FLHC 40/Alamy Stock Photo)

There were eighteen fundamental martial arts during the Tokugawa period. Sword and spear (lance) fighting, archery, and horsemanship were the principal skills that most samurai focused on. Other skills included in the eighteen were: swimming, sword drawing (*iai*), dagger throwing (*shuriken*), gunnery (*hôjutsu*), fighting with the short sword (*tantô*), the art of stealth and spying (*ninjutsu*), *yawara* (similar to today's *jûdô*), needle-spitting (*fukumibari*), the halberd (*naginata*), the *kusarigama* (a chained sickle), the staff (*bôjutsu*), and restraining techniques with a variety of implements (the *jitte*, or truncheon), the *mojiri*, a staff with barbs on one end, and rope (*torite*).

Considering swordsmanship first, during the seventeenth century there were a few styles (*ryûha*) that were based on combat arts, which developed from the experience of warriors during the civil wars that preceded the Tokugawa. Only with peaceful conditions, though, did swordsmanship become a field of knowledge, one where teachers articulated their art through the written word. The first treatises on sword fighting actually utilized the vocabulary and teaching methodology of other cultural arts, such as the Noh theater and the tea ceremony. In this manner sword fighting also became a (martial) art, with the development of distinct styles or "schools" (*ryû*), which competed with one another. This art was developed in training halls rather than on the battlefield, and without actual combat swordsmanship became, in effect, an activity without purpose. In other words, it became an end in itself, which meant that swordsmanship was akin to the seated meditation of Zen. In fact, some early texts on swordsmanship such as the *Family-Transmitted Book on Swordsmanship* (*Heihô kadensho*, 1632) by Yagyû Munemori, the shogun's swordsmanship teacher, drew from Zen and Noh sources.

Although swordsmanship may have had practical applicability, this was not its primary purpose during this second stage in the development of the martial arts. The emergence of a concept of "martial arts" (*bugei*) reflected these changes and did much to systematize fighting techniques into an art. In this, the above-mentioned *Book on Swordsmanship*, by Yagyû Munemori, played an important role; it consisted of three sections, *Shinrikyô* (A Bridge for Progress), *Setsunintô* (The Murderous Blade), and *Katsuninken* (The Sword of Life). Another notable book on sword fighting from this period was written by Miyamoto Musashi (1584–1645), perhaps the greatest swordsman of his time, known as *Gorin no sho* (*A Book of Five Rings*). Through the practice of sword fighting, which during this time came to be known as *kenjutsu* ("the art of the sword"), samurai learned both etiquette and bodily comportment. Accordingly, practice consisted of formal swordplay—engaging in prescribed drills with wooden swords rather than free-style fencing matches. At the same time swordsmanship was an activity that reinforced status differences among samurai, as low-ranking members did not train beside their superiors. Also, daimyo supported certain martial art styles with official recognition and rewarded its higher-ranking practitioners with allowances to pay for their equipment and training. Lower-ranking retainers also trained in officially recognized styles but did not receive government support for their efforts.

Free-style matches were generally forbidden, and students were required to sign oaths not to engage in matches, particularly with students of other styles, or face expulsion. This was done for two main reasons: to prevent conflicts that could turn violent; and to prevent damage to a style's reputation, and the livelihood of its teachers, should its practitioners perform poorly.

Although most styles of swordsmanship during the eighteenth century continued to emphasize the repetition of forms (*kata*), with set attack and defense sequences, early in the century a new form of swordsmanship emerged using bamboo swords wrapped in leather instead of wooden ones; this allowed for greater freedom for students to attack each other with full force, without risk of great bodily harm or even death. Gradually fencing became more popular than the older form of sword fighting, particularly among low-ranking samurai; fencing even spread among elite commoners from the early eighteenth century onward.

From the mid-to-late eighteenth century, the third phase of development of the martial arts, free-play fencing within swordsmanship rose in popularity among samurai, becoming the dominant trend, akin to a competitive sport. During this time protective equipment, namely bamboo swords, helmets, and padded chest protectors, were widely adopted. These developments were resisted by some of the more traditional styles of sword fighting, but the trend was unstoppable. Fencing that simulated combat, even with protective gear, was much more realistic than formal swordplay with prescribed forms.

By the end of the Tokugawa period it was common for samurai to embark on excursions to challenge practitioners of other training halls, both at domain and private schools. One samurai from Saga domain who spent two years training on the road, with official permission, kept a detailed log of his encounters across the country. Successfully defeating the top students or the teacher of another school was referred to as *dôjô yaburi*, or "destroying a training hall." In his autobiographical account Tokugawa bannerman Katsu Kokichi (1802–1850) describes his frequent challenging of students from other schools and his utter glee when he defeated them (which always happened, if we are to believe him).

Similar trends are also evident in the transformation of archery, from an emphasis on combat skills to a concern for form, and then its emergence as a sport, with the focus of bowmen shooting for records, many of which had little to do with precision or accuracy (e.g., number of arrows shot in a fixed period of time). The rules of archery were codified by the Ogasawara family, who also set the standards for horsemanship; their school, as well as the Takeda school, practiced the art of *yabusame*, or mounted archery. The rules and practices of archery, like those in the other martial arts, were turned into "secret transmissions" (*hidensho*), which often took the form of a precious document or scroll, access to which was restricted by the teacher to a single student who was to carry on the transmitted traditions in turn to his own designated successor. The main school of archery during the Tokugawa period, though, remained the *Heki-ryû* ("military style"), which had its origins during the Warring States period. The Heki school, like the Ogasawara, developed many branches of its own. In total, at least fifty-one identifiable schools of archery existed during the Tokugawa period.

The Ogasawara house also applied the principles of archery to gunnery. Various schools of marksmanship began to appear in the seventeenth century, such as the *Inatomi-ryû, Nakanishi-ryû, Tsuda-ryû,* and the *Tatsuke-ryû*, through which students learned the techniques of killing with a gun as an abstract, theoretical martial art.

See also: Civil and Military Arts (*bunbu*); Education; Firearms; *Honchô Bugei Shôden (A Short Tale of Martial Arts in Our Country)*; Horseback Riding Ceremony (*onorizome*); Miyamoto Musashi; Tokugawa Yoshimune

Further Reading

Hurst, G. Cameron, III. *Armed Martial Arts of Japan: Swordsmanship and Archery.* New Haven, CT, and London: Yale University Press, 1998.

Katsu Kokichi. *Musui's Story: The Autobiography of a Tokugawa Samurai.* Translated by Teruko Craig. Tucson, AZ: University of Arizona Press, 1988.

Rogers, John M. "Arts of War in Times of Peace. Archery in *Honchô bugei shôden.*" *Monumenta Nipponica,* 45(3) (1990), 253–260.

Japanese Samurai Films and Hollywood

Samurai films, particularly those of Kurosawa Akira (1910–1998), have had a huge impact on Hollywood. Kurosawa's *Seven Samurai* (1954), which is set in the late Warring States period, tells the story of villagers who hire six masterless samurai and one peasant farmer posing as a warrior to protect them from marauding bandits, and provided the inspiration for John Sturges's *The Magnificent Seven* (1960). The Sturges film featured a number of top American film stars such as Steve McQueen, Yul Brynner, James Coburn, Charles Bronson, and Eli Wallach. It was remade again in 2016 by director Antoine Fuqua and stars an international cast of Denzel Washington, Ethan Hawke, and Lee Byung-hun, among others.

Kurosawa, who was actually descended from a samurai lineage, studied kendo swordsmanship. During his long career, his samurai films inspired and influenced many other filmmakers, such as Clint Eastwood, Martin Scorsese, George Lucas, and Steven Spielberg. Story elements, filmmaking techniques, not to mention swordfighting scenes from his *Seven Samurai* found their way into the various Star Wars films. It is widely recognized that Kurosawa's *Yojimbo* (1961) was closely imitated by Italian filmmaker Sergio Leone in his *A Fistful of Dollars* (1964).

Rogers, John M. "Arts of War in Times of Peace. Swordsmanship in *Honchô bugei shôden*, Chapter 5." *Monumenta Nipponica,* 45(4) (1990), 413–447.

Wert, Michael. "Swordsmanship and Society in Early Modern Japan." In Rebekka von Mallinckrodt and Angela Schattner, eds., *Sports and Physical Exercise in Early Modern Culture*, 253–268. London: Routledge, 2016.

Memorials and Petitions

In many domains across Tokugawa Japan, only senior officials had the right to submit memorials or petitions (*tangan* or *ikensho*) directly to the lord. However, in a large minority of domains and in various parts of Tokugawa territory, petition boxes, known in Japanese as *sôjôbako* or *meyasubako*, were created to open up channels of communication among a larger segment of the population. The use of this practice generally increased in the early modern period and was continued for a number of years by the Meiji government as well.

An early example of the petition box can be found in Okayama domain, where the daimyo, Ikeda Mitsumasa (1609–1682) created one in 1654 in response to social problems that were aggravated by extensive flooding in his domain. A placard placed above the box explained its purpose: "Because I, my senior officials, and magistrates make proclamations that are not always for the best, we should borrow the wisdom of the whole country. Therefore, I am creating a remonstrance box (*isame no hako*), and people ranging from senior officials down to the least individual may write on any topic, and submit anonymously their petitions into this box" (Quoted in Roberts, 1994, 428).

The overwhelming majority of petition boxes were established from the eighteenth century onward. Such was the case even with the shogunate: Tokugawa Yoshimune, the eighth shogun, introduced one in 1721, during a period of social unrest and reform. In Tosa domain, a petition box was established in 1759. The scholar Miyaji Haruki, among others, had advocated for its establishment because he felt that restricting the right to petition only to senior officials was a major cause for discontent, as government was seen as unresponsive. Miyaji petitioned his lord, the daimyo Yamauchi Toyonobu, in 1759 to express his views on the widespread frustration he sensed in Tosa society:

> The reason your government is in such bad condition is none other than the damming up of the avenues of speech. Nothing causes the decline of government more than the obstruction of communication. The fact that many laws need correcting is an issue peripheral to your main problem: [Proper communication has been obstructed, and] government is in a terrible state. (Roberts, 1994, 436)

Miyaji then expressed how officials obstructed justice unless they were bribed, causing widespread resentment and anger among the people. He ended his petition on an ominous note, hinting at the possible consequences of inaction: "Of old it was said, 'Rebellion has roots in places where hatred collects'" (Roberts, 1994, 436).

Although the Yamauchi lord in Tosa was reluctant at first to change established practice, in 1759 he agreed to the creation of a system of direct appeal, to himself, via a petition box. As part of a broader policy of government reform in Tosa, the right to submit petitions was opened up not just to all *bushi* but to anyone in the domain, regardless of social status. Given the type of documents that were submitted, an argument can be made that the petition box was seen by the lord as a mechanism for diffusing social unrest. Once created, the petition box continued in place until 1873, after the fall of the Tokugawa shogunate. Due to the destruction of World War II, only 149 of these documents survive, spanning the years 1759–1771, but a prewar historian who studied the petitions wrote that at the time there were thousands.

The submission of petitions, which were supposed to be signed, was to open up an avenue for communication. The petitions were to: offer suggestions for improving government or society; provide a vehicle for complaints about government officials as well as their policies; and, present legal appeals directly to the lord about court cases that the petitioners felt had not been dealt with fairly. To encourage submission of petitions in which people could express themselves in an unconstrained manner, the authors were in principle immune from punishment.

A large wooden box was placed across from Kôchi's main castle gate, inside a small building that served as a waiting room for people seeking permission to enter the castle on business. Given the location of the box deep within the *bushi* district of the castle town, one can imagine that it took some courage for a commoner to submit a document. Once a month the box was removed and taken to the chief inspector (*metsuke*). It was his job to break the seal, unlock the box, and then forward the sealed petitions to the senior councilors. The lord received the sealed petitions, unopened, to read.

The petitions covered a wide range of topics and were used by a variety of people to deliver social commentary and political advice to the daimyo. The collection of special levies or taxes was a frequent topic in extant petitions. Other petitions drew attention to the mismanagement of corvée labor taxes, railed against merchants' monopoly rights to purchase paper from village producers, or simply identified corrupt officials. Yet other petitions submitted offered advice on agricultural practices that might be adopted in the domain. One low-ranking samurai named Imakita Sakubei, who also would have been ineligible to offer a formal written opinion before the creation of the petition box system, even called for the inclusion of commoners into the domain government.

See also: Tokugawa Yoshimune

Further Reading

Roberts, Luke S. "The Petition Box in Eighteenth-Century Tosa." *The Journal of Japanese Studies,* 20(2) (1994), 423–458.

Roberts, Luke S. "A Petition for a Popularly Chosen Council of Government in Tosa in 1787." *Harvard Journal of Asiatic Studies,* 57(2) (1997), 575–596.

Roberts, Luke S. "Translation of the Memorial of Imakita Sakubei to the Lord of Tosa, Yamauchi Toyochika." *Early Modern Japan* (Spring 2001), 53–56.

Mibunsei. See Status System (*mibunsei*)

Mikawa monogatari (Tales of Mikawa)

Ôkubo Hikozaemon or Tadataka (1560–1639), a warrior whose life spanned the late Warring States and early Tokugawa periods, was the author of *Mikawa monogatari (Tales of Mikawa)*. It was written in 1622, during the reign of the third shogun, Tokugawa Iemitsu, for the instruction of his son and future descendants, detailing the way that a samurai should live. Its other focus was to chronicle the rise of the Tokugawa clan and the role that his own Mikawa clan played in it. His account also reflects the changed circumstances of samurai society as the country transitioned from war to peace in the early Tokugawa period.

Hikozaemon was born in Kamiwada, in Mikawa province (Aichi prefecture), the eighth son of Ôkubo Tadakazu, who was a vassal of Tokugawa Ieyasu. Two of his elder brothers became daimyo while Hikozaemon was still a child. He saw the first of many battles at the age of seventeen, fighting under his elder brother Ôkubo Tadayo, and fought in his last conflicts in the Winter and Summer Sieges of Osaka Castle, in 1614–1615. Under the third shogun Tokugawa Iemitsu (1604–51), in 1632, Hikozaemon was made a commander of a company of spearmen, a bannerman (*hatamoto*) and thus direct retainer of the shogun; the following year his fief was doubled, to 2,000 *koku*.

The primary theme of *Mikawa monogatari* was the continuous loyalty that his family had shown the Tokugawa. Hikozaemon attributed Tokugawa Ieyasu's success to the close ties between him and his vassals while he was a lord in Mikawa province. To be a good military leader, he wrote that it was necessary: (1) to be fierce in combat but possessing sufficient judgment to be victorious or capable of avoiding conflicts that cannot be won; (2) compassionate, meaning to care not just for one's own vassals but for all who fell under one's temporary command; and (3) to be compassionate not only to townsmen and peasants in one's fief but even to one's enemies. Hikozaemon contended that only if a leader acted in this manner would his men be willing to sacrifice for him in war.

In his work, Hikozaemon focuses on the generosity of the shoguns and the faithful service given by his forefathers in response to this treatment. His discussion of this relationship between lord and vassal was individualistic and sentimental rather than philosophic, but some scholars consider his treatment a forerunner of later treatises on the "way of the warrior."

Although Hikozaemon took great pride in the close relationship between his family and the Tokugawa, toward the end of his life he became disenchanted by what he saw as the much-diminished benevolence of the Tokugawa toward him. Feeling like his loyalty and service had not been adequately rewarded, he wrote, using irony, that to win promotion and gain an increase in fief, one must: (1) betray one's master and come over to the Tokugawa side; (2) behave like a coward and attract others' scorn; (3) behave politely and act tactfully in the office and dining room; (4) be a master of the abacus and skilled at accounting; and (5) be a man whose origins are unknown (Cited in Tokugawa, 2009, 65). He wrote, further, that "it is disappointing to see that a retainer with skillful and ostentatious public behavior would gain some popularity with his lord's household and would eventually be given his own territory" (Quoted in Fukushima, 1984, 71).

See also: Fief (*chigyô*); Sekigahara, Battle of; Sieges of Osaka (*Ôsaka no jin*); Tokugawa Iemitsu; Tokugawa Ieyasu

Further Reading

Bolitho, Harold. *Treasures among Men: The fudai daimyo in Tokugawa Japan.* New Haven, CT: Yale University Press, 1974.

Fukushima, Shoichi. "Bushido in Tokugawa Japan: A Reassessment of the Warrior Ethos." PhD dissertation, University of California, Berkeley, 1984. (This dissertation has extensive quotations translated from the Japanese text *Mikawa monogatari.*)

Ôkubo Hikozaemon. *Mikawa monogatari* [Tales of Mikawa], 2 vols. Translated by Kobayashi Takaaki. Tokyo: Kyôikusha, 1980.

Tokugawa, Tsunenari. *The Edo Inheritance.* Translated by Tokugawa Iehiro. Tokyo: International House of Japan, 2009.

Military Service (*gun'yaku*)

A term that refers to the levies for military service required of vassals by warrior lords, *gun'yaku* existed at least as far back as the Kamakura period (1185–1333) and continued until 1867, just before the end of the Tokugawa period (1603–1868). *Gun'yaku* was perhaps the most important of such obligations, but corvée labor exactions (laborers plus materials for construction projects) could be quite taxing on a daimyo's wealth as well.

Records for *gun'yaku* appear in the historical accounts of the Kamakura period, when the shogunate required the heads of its vassal families to mobilize their kinsmen for military service when called on. During the Warring States period (1467–1568), a vassal's service obligations were determined by the productivity of the lands he held in fief (*chigyô*) and generally were levied in terms of manpower per *koku* (equivalent to about five bushels), or putative yield (*kokudaka*). There is some debate among historians, however, whether military service during this period was always directly proportional to putative yield. One historian argues, for example, that under Toyotomi Hideyoshi (1537–1598) the rate of service a vassal owed was determined for each daimyo individually, based on the daimyo's strength relative to the hegemon's. Also, since his control over his vassals was not absolute, not all portions of a daimyo's fief were subject to military obligation.

The Tokugawa shogunate issued *gun'yaku* regulations for all daimyo as well as for its direct vassals, the bannermen (*hatamoto*) and housemen (*gokenin*) on three occasions during the seventeenth century, in 1616, 1633, and 1649. The first edict followed a year after the defeat of the last rival to Tokugawa authority, Toyotomi Hideyoshi (1593–1615) in the Winter and Summer Sieges of Osaka Castle and the codification of a set of regulations governing the daimyo (the *Laws for the Military Houses*, or *Buke shohatto*, 1615). While the *Lawss* instructed the daimyo on proper military and political conduct, the *gun'yaku* edict directly addressed military service obligations, for daimyo and direct vassals of the shogun both.

The shogun Hidetada (1579–1632) issued the first Tokugawa military service regulations just two months after his father Ieyasu's death. The level of service obligation was made proportional to the putative yield, in *koku*, of the daimyo or direct vassal's land holding or stipend. For example, a vassal with a 1,000-*koku* fief was required to provide one mounted warrior, two musketmen (arquebusiers), one archer, and five pikemen. A daimyo with the minimum 10,000-*koku* fief was required to provide fourteen mounted warriors, twenty musketmen, ten archers, and fifty pikemen.

Hidetada's successor and son, the third shogun Iemitsu (1604–1651), upon assuming full power after the death of his father, overhauled the *Laws for the Military Houses* as well as the Military Service edict. He actually expanded and reissued them in two parts in 1633: the first part set service obligations for the Tokugawa's direct vassals with a land grant between 200 and 900 *koku*; the second edict contained requirements for daimyo, with holdings between the minimum 10,000 *koku* and 100,000 *koku*. Although the Tokugawa imposed military obligations on the daimyo, it left it up to the daimyo to decide how they were distributed within their domains. During Iemitsu's reign, the shogunate utilized the edicts in requiring the daimyo of twelve different domains in Kyushu to provide military men for the composite army (of the shogun and the daimyo) of some 120,000 troops, which after only much difficulty was able to overwhelm the defenders in Hara Castle near Shimabara (the Shimabara Rebellion, 1637–1638).

In 1649 the military service regulations were reissued without significant changes, but the effects of the peacetime economy made it increasingly difficult for the Tokugawa's vassals to maintain the stipulated military service levels. In recognition of this, late in the period, in 1862 and 1866, the shogunate greatly reduced the service requirements.

The *gun'yaku* system was abandoned in 1867, and after the Meiji Restoration (1868) the new Meiji government adopted the principle of universal military conscription (1872).

See also: Bannermen (*hatamoto*); Fief (*chigyô*); Housemen (*gokenin*); Retainer Corps (*kashindan*); Shimabara Rebellion (*Shimabara no ran*); Sieges of Osaka (*Ôsaka no jin*); Tokugawa Hidetada; Toyotomi Hideyoshi

Further Reading
Keith, Matthew E. "The Logistics of Power: Tokugawa Response to the Shimabara Rebellion and Power Projection in Seventeenth-Century Japan." PhD dissertation, The Ohio State University, 2006.

Miyamoto Musashi (c. 1584–1645)

Perhaps the most legendary of all Japanese swordsmen, Miyamoto Musashi lived during the pivotal transition from civil war to the peaceful order of Tokugawa rule. He has been a figure of legendary proportions, from Tokugawa times to the present, and these legends have often obscured the known facts of his life. His text *Gorin no sho* (*A Book of Five Rings*), which contained his thoughts on strategy, tactics, and philosophy, even found a worldwide audience in contemporary times. Although not as well known, Musashi was also an accomplished artist who went by the art name of Niten.

Musashi was born sometime around 1584 in Harima (modern-day Hyôgo prefecture), in west central Japan. His father was Shinmen Munisai, a skilled warrior with

---

Miyamoto Musashi in Film

Musashi has been the subject of numerous filmic interpretations. Among them, director Hiroshi Inagaki's trilogy, produced from 1954 to 1956, is perhaps the best known. Adapted from Yoshikawa Eiji's novel, the films appeared as *Samurai 1: Miyamoto Musashi* (Japanese title, *Miyamoto Musashi*), *Samurai 2: Duel at Ichijoji Temple* (*Zoku Miyamoto Musashi: Ichijoji no ketto*), and *Samurai 3: Duel on Ganryu Island* (*Miyamoto Musashi kanketsuhen ketto Ganryujima*). The first film follows Musashi's life from the battlefield of Sekigahara to his undertaking of a rigorous moral education, changing his name to Musashi and setting out to travel and train himself. It won the Academy Award for Best Foreign Film in 1955. Part 2 continues Musashi's journey to become more than a skilled warrior, as he learns to control his wildness, to learn etiquette and gentleness, and a sense of detachment from the world around him. In a couple of scenes, the film also introduces Musashi's writings from *The Book of the Five Rings* (*Gorin no sho*). The main plot line, though, concerns the feud between Musashi and the Yoshioka school of swordfighters. In the climax of the film, Musashi battles with eighty of the Yoshioka men, skillfully making use of the marsh-like conditions in the rice paddy against the large force to emerge victorious. In Part 3 we see the final stages of Musashi's development: no longer obsessed with fighting and fame, he actually tries to avoid violence whenever possible. Nonetheless, he is unable to avoid a confrontation with the warrior Kojiro, who persistently pursued Musashi to duel. That famous duel, on Ganryu Island, is the fitting climax of the film and trilogy.

the sword and the *jitte* (a short metal truncheon with a blunt end). It was likely that he trained with his father, but there is no evidence of him having studied with any other swordsman during his youth. However, at the age of thirteen he claims to have defeated a noted Shintô-school swordsman named Arima Kihei. Three years later he defeated another swordsman named Akiyama of Tajima province in a duel. After this, Musashi fought in six major battles including Sekigahara, Osaka, and Shimabara.

Musashi traveled for a number of years across Japan trying to perfect his skills and to unify his spirit, a practice known as *musha shugyô*. In doing so he is reputed to have fought, and won, sixty duels before reaching the age of thirty. As a wandering swordsman he followed a path similar to several other figures of this time, Kamiizumi Ise-no-kami, Ittô Ittôsai, and Yagyû Jûbei. While traveling he developed his own style, using both the long and short sword at the same time, known as *nitô ryû* ("two-sword style"). Contrary to what many popular accounts claim, though, he did not use this particular style all the time, and not against very skilled opponents.

One of Musashi's epic duels was against a warrior named Sasaki Kojirô, also known as Ganryû, whom he met while visiting the daimyo of Kokura domain (in Buzen province, northern Kyushu), Hosokawa Tadaoki. Ganryû was the swordsmanship instructor for the Hosokawa house. The two men fought their duel at Funajima (later known as Ganryûjima), a small island at the tip of Honshu Island. Musashi arrived to the duel late and cleverly kept the sun at his back to confuse his opponent, whom he struck and killed with a wooden sword made from an oar.

Later in life Musashi accepted a position in service to the Hosokawa lord Tadatoshi of Kumamoto domain. It was while there, in 1643, that he wrote his text *Gorin no sho*. Quite surprisingly, the English translation of the book became popular among buinessmen in the United States in the late twentieth century.

Woodblock print of a kabuki actor depicting the famous early-Tokugawa samurai Miyamoto Musashi, by Utagawa Kuniyoshi, 1852. The Japanese title is *Mukôjima Miyamoto Musashi* from the series *Tôto ryûkô sanjuroku kaiseki* ("Popular Restaurants in the Eastern Capitol"). Musashi was the subject of numerous kabuki plays and a popular theme in the *musha-e* (warrior prints) of the mid-19th century. (Library of Congress)

Musashi also became an accomplished painter during his career, although exactly how that came about is unclear. He may have been influenced by Kaihô Yûshô (1533–1615), another samurai artist. Regardless of his training, Musashi's painting had an extraordinary power and intensity. He took up subjects such as Zen figures, waterfowl, birds of prey, particularly hawks, and bamboo. Less often he painted landscapes or carved wooden Buddhist images. He also left us, famous, a self-portrait from around 1640.

During the Tokugawa period Musashi became the subject of a number of kabuki plays. He also became a popular theme in the warrior prints (*musha-e*) that were produced in large numbers in the mid-nineteenth century. For example, Utagawa Kuniyoshi's three-panel print *The Warrior Miyamoto Musashi Subduing a Whale* (c. 1847–1850) depicts the legendary swordsman astride a thrashing whale, about to deliver a deadly thrust. To Kuniyoshi, Musashi was a superhero who personified a bygone era but one who he, and no doubt the customers who purchased the print, hoped would inspire the samurai of their present-day to similar feats of bravery in meeting the foreign enemy on Japan's doorstep.

Musashi remained popular among contemporary Japanese through the serialized novels of Yoshikawa Eiji (available in English translation as *Musashi*) in the 1980s and from numerous filmic versions of his story.

Some scholars have attributed Musashi's enduring popularity in Japan to his role as a transitional figure between the skilled warrior of the Warring States period and the bureaucrat-scholar type of samurai of the Tokugawa era. Under the Tokugawa shogunate samurai were severely restricted in their freedom to travel outside their domains, not to mention restricted in challenging practitioners of different schools of swordsmanship, which explains why he is widely perceived as the last wandering swordsman of the era.

See also: Ronin (*rônin*); Sekigahara, Battle of; Shimabara Rebellion (*Shimabara no ran*); Sieges of Osaka (*Ôsaka no jin*); Warrior Prints (*musha-e*)

Further Reading

Addis, Stephen, and G. Cameron Hurst. *Samurai Painters*. Tokyo and New York: Kodansha International, 1983.

De Lange, Willian. *Famous Swordsmen of the Period of Unification*. Warren, CT: Floating World Editions, 2008.

Tokitsu Kenji. Translated from French by Cherad Kodzin Kohn. *Miyamoto Musashi: His Life and Writings*. New York: Weatherhill, 2006.

Modern Legacy of the Samurai in the West

The samurai came into the consciousness of many people outside of Japan with the series of Japanese embassies to the United States and Europe after the opening of the country after 1853. However, after the publicity surrounding the 1860 delegation visit, Japan slipped out of the public consciousness in the United States. Americans became preoccupied with domestic affairs during the Civil War and postwar Reconstruction. It took a series of international expositions to bring renewed interest in Japan among Americans. A series of expositions, held in Philadelphia, New Orleans, Chicago, and St. Louis, were attended by millions of people who came to understand the distinguished cultural legacy of Japan through carefully assembled displays, which included material culture associated with the samurai.

The first of these expositions, in Philadelphia, marked America's centenary in 1876. It was here that many Americans made their first contact with Japanese culture. The Japanese exhibit included samurai armor, along with a teahouse, ceramics, silks, and other traditional wares. The samurai armor displayed in Philadelphia drew a lot of interest, and as a result similar displays were prominently showcased at subsequent international exhibitions, such as in Chicago. For that exhibition—the 1893 Columbian Exposition in Chicago—Japanese officials sent three times the amount of material for display than they had to Philadelphia and more than 27 million visitors were recorded. This exposure to Japanese culture at the fairs led to

Group of mannequins, five of whom are in full combat armor (with the overlord seated in the center). They were originally displayed in 1893 in Japan's exhibit at the World's Columbian Exposition. The samurai remained an important part of Japan's self-identity long after they had been legislated out of existence by the Meiji government. (Smithsonian Institution Archives)

an awareness of the country's distinguished cultural legacy. The exhibitions also led many Americans to begin collecting traditional Japanese handicrafts and samurai-related artifacts, including armor and *tsuba* (sword guards). The presence of samurai armor in the various exhibits pointed to the longstanding military traditions at a time when Japan was trying to show itself as equal to a major western power such as the United States, Germany, Britain, and Russia.

Japan's military victories in wars against China (the Sino-Japanese War, 1894–1895) and the Russo-Japanese War (1904–1905) also brought a lot of international attention to the samurai legacy. Although many Westerners were impressed by the Japanese victories in these two conflicts, the rise of Japan as a military power greatly disturbed some observers. This was evident in the popular media; for example, a syndicated cartoon from the *St. Paul Globe* (1904) depicted a sword-wielding Japanese soldier with a skull for a face and the caption "That Famous Japanese Smile—the Smile That Won't Come Off." For some, praise seemed to go hand in hand with a sense of fear, as seen in the cartoon from the *Cleveland Leader* (March 1904), "Why the Japs Win," in which we see a number of positive attributes written across the face of a young soldier (skill, bravery, skills, determination), but the odd smile with "fatalism" written across his mouth was unsettling. This fear was often expressed in racial terms: the "yellow peril." This term first appeared around the time of the Sino-Japanese War (1894–1895) but came into more frequent use in the popular media with Japan's shocking victory in the Russo-Japanese War (1904–1905). Sensational reports highlighted what was seen as Japanese fanaticism and accounted for the success of Japan's troops as a result of the "Japanese Way of Death," echoing Western notions of *bushido* (the way of the warrior), which was perceived as a calm disregard for death.

This view of the Japanese soldier as modern-day samurai only grew stronger during Word War II. In the context of this bloody conflict, the famous account of the self-sacrifice of the forty-seven *ronin* in avenging their lord in 1703, which was praised in books such as Boy Scout founder Robert Baden-Powell's *Boy Scouts Beyond the Sea* (1913), was reinterpreted as evidence of the bloodthirsty character of the Japanese enemy. Similarly, the "banzai charges" and suicidal attacks on Allied vessels by Japanese kamikaze pilots late in the war were seen as further evidence of that disregard for death (or, conversely, for a contempt of life). In Japan, too, the equation of the Japanese with the samurai was encouraged through works like the Ministry of Education's textbook *Fundamentals of Our National Polity* (*Kokutai no hongi*, 1937), which extolled devotion to the emperor and described *bushido* as an "outstanding characteristic of our national morality."

After World War II the American forces that occupied a defeated and war-weary Japan, from 1945 to 1952, sought to reform Japanese society through a two-pronged strategy of demilitarization and democratization. Not only was Japan to be disarmed, but all identifiable sources of militarism in Japanese society were to be eradicated—from its constitution, its education system, from film and theater, and ultimately, it was hoped, from the minds of the Japanese. Everything associated with the samurai and with "feudal values" such as fanaticism and self-sacrifice were taboo. Samurai films in particular were censored and in some cases destroyed.

Kabuki theater, too, which was seen as extolling samurai values, was also a target for censorship. The Western image of the Japanese soldier as reincarnated samurai disappeared from public media, replaced instead by caricatures of infantile, diminutive, and feminized (de-emasculated) males. Perhaps this was due to a desire to repress wartime memories, but the American media in the 1950s and 1960s often presented postwar Japan as a land of geisha and cherry blossoms, famously as in James Michener's *Sayonara* (1954).

In the same year as *Sayonara*, 1954, however, samurai films began to reappear on Japanese screens, and several of them became quite popular overseas. The first of these samurai films to gain an audience internationally was Akira Kurosawa's film *Seven Samurai* (also 1954). It presented a rather benevolent view of the samurai, though, rather than the ultranationalist version that was predominant during the wartime years. Other films featuring samurai characters also appeared, such as a trilogy on the famous swordsman Miyamoto Musashi (publicized as the *Samurai Trilogy* in the United States, 1954–1956) and *The Hidden Fortress* (1958).

With Japan's postwar reconstruction and high rates of economic growth from the 1960s onward—popularly called an "economic miracle"—a more masculine image of Japan began to reemerge in the West, especially in the 1970s and 1980s. This was evident both in depictions of traditional Japanese culture and in attitudes toward newly assertive Japanese businessmen, who were often ascribed samurai-like characteristics: rigorous loyalty to the group and sublimation of individuality and personal desires. The novels and films of the time brought back the samurai, especially shoguns and ninja, as basic samurai values became the focus once again of interpretations of Japan. For example, Americans in large numbers sought to understand the sources of Japan's economic success by reading the lessons contained in the swordmaster Miyamoto Musashi's *The Book of Five Rings* (*Gorin no sho*, c. 1645), which became popular in the mid-1970s. However, Japan's considerable economic success also stirred up fears in the United States and Europe of Japanese domination that was reminiscent of the "yellow peril" of the early twentieth century.

The samurai has remained a popular image and trope for Japan during the last twenty years. From the 1990s, when Japan's economy fell into stagnation, there has been great interest in the United States, Europe, and Japan in the samurai, as seen in the popularity of manga and anime with samurai themes, such as *Rurouni Kenshi*, *Samurai Champloo*, *Sakamoto Ryôma*, and *Basara Daimyô*, among others. Filmic samurai gained in popularity, too, with a resurgence of the samurai period–film, such as *Twilight Samurai* (*Tasogare seimei*, 2002), *The Hidden Blade* (*Kakushi ken—oni no tsume*, 2004), and the American film *The Last Samurai* (2003), the latter which became a worldwide box office hit. The values ascribed to samurai in the form of *bushido* have been viewed on both sides of the Pacific as an explanation for the Japanese version of baseball, or "samurai baseball." The Japanese national soccer team has been dubbed Japan's "Blue Samurai," and Japanese social commentators like Fujiwara Masahiko, author of *The Dignity of the Nation* (*Kokka no hinkaku*, 2005), write with more frequency of the need to recover the samurai spirit in order to reinvigorate Japan. In this manner the samurai continues to be transformed, but remains very much a part of Japanese and Westerners' views of Japan.

See also: Ambassadors (Samurai); *Bushido*; Miyamoto Musashi

Further Reading

Benesch, Oleg. *Inventing the Way of the Samurai: Nationalism, Internationalism, and Bushido in Modern Japan.* Oxford: Oxford University Press, 2014.

Hirano, Kyoko. *Mr. Smith Goes to Tokyo: Japanese Cinema under the American Occupation, 1945–1952.* Washington, D.C.: Smithsonian Institution Scholarly Press, 1994.

Johnson, Sheila K. *The Japanese through American Eyes.* Stanford, CA: Stanford University Press, 1991.

Musui's Story (Musui dokugen)

Musui's Story (Jp., *Musui dokugen*) is an unusual example of an autobiography by a samurai who lived during the Tokugawa period. It was authored by Katsu Kokichi (1802–1850), a houseman (*gokenin*) of the Tokugawa shogun who lived on the fringes of proper samurai society and frequently mixed with townsmen. Ostensibly he wrote the text to warn his descendants not to live as he had, but he appeared to relish his loose lifestyle. In his account, Kokichi (born Kanematsu) narrates his life's adventures in a lively style, including accounts of his travels. It is an entertaining narrative that is also a valuable resource on the life of Tokugawa vassals, bannermen, and housemen, in the closing decades of the shogunate.

Kokichi was born Otani Kokichi, the third son of Otani Heizô, a Tokugawa houseman with a stipend of 100 *hyô* (bales of rice) who served as an intendant (*daikan*). Kokichi's eldest brother, Otani Hikoshirô, was known as a Confucian scholar and a district administrator in the Tokugawa's house lands, while his other brother was adopted into another samurai family and also served in a similar administrative position.

Since there were two other sons ahead of him in line for succession to the Otani family headship, Katsu was adopted out into the Katsu family in 1808, and given the name Kokichi, at the age of seven, with the understanding that he would later marry Nobuko, the only daughter of the Katsu family. Kokichi thus followed the path of his own father, the third son of a wealthy merchant, who himself had been adopted into the Otani family. Shogunal law mandated that formal adoptions could not take place before the age of seventeen, so Kokichi had to claim to be that age. He also shaved the pate of his head as if he had gone through the rites of manhood (*genpuku*). Nobuko's parents had passed away before Katsu's adoption, so both she and Kokichi were raised in his father's household. Kokichi later married Nobuko, at the age of seventeen, and became the head of the Katsu family. Although Kokichi's adoption was no doubt far more desirable than remaining in the Otani family, where he would have had to remain a dependant of his older brother, in assuming the headship of the Katsu family his stipend was only 41 *hyô*.

Kokichi lived a life that greatly contrasted with that of his elder brother, Hikoshirô, as well as his future son, Rintarô (Kaishû, 1823–1899). He describes himself as a "real hell-raiser" (Craig, 1988, 11) from an early age, when he frequently got into fights and took part in brawls. He also practiced judo, took riding lessons, and studied sword fighting. From the age of twelve he briefly attended school at Yushima seidô, the shogunal academy in Edo, but did not devote himself to his studies and so was forced out of it. On two occasions he ran away from home. The first time, at age fourteen, he traveled to Ise and begged when he ran out of money. After four months he returned home to face his father's punishment.

From the age of sixteen he attempted to gain a formal position in the shogunate through a labor pool (reserve force) for unemployed samurai (*kobushingumi*) established for low-ranking Tokugawa retainers. Ironically, his finances actually deteriorated as a result of his effort, since he had to purchase the appropriate clothing to appear before officials to present his requests, not to mention give them gifts in hopes of gaining their favor. Despite his repeated attempts, Kokichi was unsuccessful. Losing interest in continuing this effort, Kokichi decided to run away from home again, at the age of twenty-one, and after he ran out of money resorted to pawning the sword his father had given him. When he eventually returned home, his father threw him into a bamboo cage the size of three tatami mats in his home and instructed him to take his time thinking about his life. During the three years Kokichi spent under a kind of domiciliary confinement he taught himself to read. After his father released him, Kokichi resumed his effort to gain employment but was no more successful. Once his father died, in 1827, Kokichi gave up on the effort for good. Kokichi was not alone in this, as demand for employment far exceeded available demand; indeed, as a result, a full quarter of the Tokugawa shogun's vassals were unemployed.

Since he never was able to gain an official position, Kokichi, like many other low-ranking Tokugawa samurai, turned to a variety of activities to supplement his family's income. He dealt in swords, appraising and trading them, as well as military gear. His brother occasionally sent him to carry out business for him, as when Kokichi was asked to travel to a particular village in Shinano to determine their tax rate for the coming year. He also helped several of his landlords, who were also Tokugawa vassals, to deal with their financial crises and in one case to throw out tenants who were delinquent in paying their rent (some Tokugawa bannermen supplemented their incomes by renting out to housemen or commoners houses they built on the residence lands in Edo they were granted by the shogun).

Contrary to the ideals of the samurai, though, Kokichi even acted as a kind of mob boss for his neighborhood by offering protection for local teahouses and brothels, lent money at high interest rates, frequented the Yoshiwara licensed quarters, and bragged about stealing money from his brothers. Kokichi constantly got into fights, sometimes it seemed simply to impress or intimidate those around him.

At only the age of thirty-six, Kokichi retired in favor of his fifteen-year-old son, Rintarô (Kaishû), who went on to play a major political role during the final years of the Tokugawa shogunate and the early years of the Meiji government. In fact, it was Kokichi's brother who forced Kokichi's hand to retire by threatening that otherwise he would lock him up in a cage again for his poor behavior. Although he had bragged about his lack of schooling, during these years of retirement he wrote his autobiography *Musui dokugen*, which was translated into English by Teruko Craig; Musui ("dream besotted") was the name that Kokichi adopted in retirement.

See also: Bannermen (*hatamoto*); Housemen (*gokenin*); Katsu Kaishû

Further Reading

Craig, Teruko (trans.). *Musui's Story: The Autobiography of a Tokugawa Samurai.* Tucson, AZ: University of Arizona Press, 1988.

Nakai, Kate Wildman. "The Reality behind *Musui Dokugen*: Introduction to the Article by Ôguchi Yûjirô." *Journal of Japanese Studies,* 16(2) (1990), 285–287.

Ôguchi, Yûjirô. "The Reality behind *Musui Dokugen*: The World of the *Hatamoto* and *Gokenin*." Translated by Gaynor Sekimori. *Journal of Japanese Studies,* 16(2) (1990), 289–308.

N

Nagashino, Battle of (1575)

The military forces of Oda Nobunaga (1534–1582) and Tokugawa Ieyasu (1543–1616) routed those of the daimyo Takeda Katsuyori (1546–1582) in the Battle of Nagashino (*Nagashino no tatakai*), a conflict that took place on June 29, 1575, near Nagashino Castle on Shitaragahara plain (Mikawa province; present-day Aichi prefecture) in central Japan. It was one of the most decisive battles during the late sixteenth century, a time when a small number of leading daimyo were competing to unify the country, and marked a decisive shift in the nature of warfare in Japan. The battle marked the end of the Takeda as a serious threat to Nobunaga's efforts to unify Japan and thus bolstered his own efforts.

Nagashino occupied a strategic location, in effect guarding the entrance to the Tokugawa territory in Mikawa and Tôtômi provinces to the east. Takeda Katsuyori laid siege to the fortress at Nagashino, aiming to recapture the castle he had lost to Tokugawa forces the previous year, which would then serve as a bridgehead into the Tokugawa-controlled province on Mikawa. Katsuyori was also motivated by the fact that Nagashino was under the command of Okudaira Sadamasa, a daimyo who had been a former ally of his before switching sides to the Tokugawa. Okudaira commanded a force of only 500 men but was able to defend the castle effectively, leading the Takeda to change tactics by avoiding further assaults and waiting (starving) out the enemy. However, a low-ranking footsoldier, Torii Sune'emon, was able to slip out of the castle and evade the enemy Takeda forces to notify Nobunaga and Ieyasu of the dire situation. Ieyasu no doubt remembered his recent humiliating defeat at the hands of Katsuyori's father, the well-respected daimyo Takeda Shingen, two years earlier when he acted independently of his ally, Oda Nobunaga. On this occasion, though, Oda Nobunaga assisted the Tokugawa forces, and together they handed Katsuyori a decisive defeat.

For a description of the battle we rely primarily on *Shinchô kôki* (*Chronicle of Lord Nobunaga*), a reliable primary source that was written by a vassal of Nobunaga (and later Hideyoshi), Ôta Gyûichi (1527–1610?). We also have the visual record of a screen painting of the battle dating from the seventeenth century. According to the written account, Nobunaga and Ieyasu fielded an army of 38,000 men to relieve the siege on Nagashino Castle by the Takeda, who had a far smaller force of 15,000 men. Leaving 3,000 of their men to continue the siege and prevent the force in the castle from joining the conflict, the Takeda faced the combined army of Nobunaga and Ieyasu on a battlefield located some thirty kilometers from the castle.

Some scholars argue that a military revolution took place in Japan in the sixteenth century in the use of firearms on a large scale and that it began at Nagashino in 1575. The film largely follows the standard version of the battle in depicting

Nobunaga's strategy in maximizing the effectiveness of his arquebusiers and working to minimize the effectiveness of the famed Takeda cavalry forces. He achieved both through the construction of wooden stockades, behind which he positioned his gunners to attack the Takeda forces in volleys and over which the enemy's horses could not leap. Deploying some 3,000 gunners, divided into three ranks of 1,000, each rank took turns in firing, which allowed time for reloading the muzzle-loading weapons. In this way the gunners were able to effect a form of volley fire, something that was not achieved in Europe until at least 1594 (Parker, 1988, 140). Despite being outnumbered more than two to one, Katsuyori pressed the attack, in four or five waves, with devastating consequences.

This account of the battle is in conflict with description in the *Shinchô kôki* (*Chronicle of Lord Nobunaga*), the above-mentioned reliable history of Nobunaga's battles. According to this source, the combined army of the Oda and Tokugawa had only 1,000 guns, and there is no mention of the gunners shooting in volleys to maintain constant fire. Despite its reliability, the (incorrect) standard version of the battle derives from another text, confusingly entitled *Shinchô ki* (*Chronicle of Nobunaga*), by Oze Hoan (1564–1640), that is a fictionalized and romanticized version of the other text. So appealing was this interpretation that it was even canonized in the Japanese army issued publication, *Nihon senshi* (*A History of Warfare in Japan*, 1910). As a result, we can assert that while Nobunaga was an innovator in terms of use of guns on a large scale, it is not clear that he can be credited with being the first to develop synchronized volley fire at Nagashino.

A visual source on the battle, the *Folding Screen of the Battle of Nagashino* (*Nagashino kassenzu byôbu*), exists but it is likely not contemporary with the battle. The screen at face value seems to confirm that Nobunaga's army was arranged into tight, linear formations, behind the stockades. The stockades provided some protection from the onslaught of the Takeda's cavalry as well as from infantrymen armed with swords and pikes. The wooden barriers were constructed in a staggered and overlapping manner—not in a straight line, as depicted in Kurosawa Akira's film, *Kagemusha*—to channel the Takeda into areas where they would be most vulnerable to attack from multiple directions.

The battle was also recreated for the screen in director Kurosawa Akira's movie *Kagemusha* (*Shadow Warrior*). In the film, it appears that Takeda

---

Popular Cultural Adaptations of the Battle of Nagashino

The Battle of Nagashino is the subject of a number of different popular cultural forms, such as video games, television, and film. The battle comprises the lengthy climax of legendary director Kurosawa Akira's 1980 film, *Kagemusha* (*Shadow Warrior*), which dramatizes the final years of the Takeda clan. It is also the subject of the thirty-eighth episode of the Japanese television series, *Nobunaga, King of Zipangu*, which was the thirtieth NHK Television Taiga Drama, in 1992. There are also a number of video games involving the battle, including the PlayStation games *Samurai Warriors* (*Legend of the Oda/Battle of Nagashino*), *Kessen III*, and the Sega game *Shogun 2: Total War*.

Katsuyori was reckless in pressing an attack on Nobunaga's forces. It is important, however, to remember that the Takeda cavalry experienced great success against the Tokugawa forces years earlier at Mikatagahara, so there was reason to expect that they would enjoy similar success in this battle as well. In ordering his forces to charge, Katsuyori appears also to have been counting on the heavy rain of the previous evening to undercut the effectiveness of Nobunaga's arquebuses by dampening supplies of gunpowder. He was likely also counting on the short distance (about 200–400 meters) that the cavalry had to cross to reach the stockades. It was anticipated that the charging cavalry of the Takeda would cause the Oda forces to break rank. Such was not the case, however, as Nobunaga's disciplined forces stood firm, which allowed them to repel each cavalry charge. Spearmen on the Oda-Tokugawa side used the protection of stockades to attack any horses that made it past the initial volleys of gunfire. Samurai with swords and footsoldiers with spears, engaged in hand-to-hand combat with any Takeda forces that made it past the palisades.

Nobunaga was not the first daimyo to employ arquebuses on the battlefield, but Nagashino was unique in the annals of Japanese warfare on at least two counts. For one, he employed more of these weapons—according to one account as many as 3,000—in a single battle than had ever been done before. Nobunaga's innovation in strategy, however, was to stage his gunners, in all their positions across the battle lines, in several rows. Each row shot rotating volleys of fire. There is no way that Katsuyori could have predicted that the opposing forces would be able to sustain continuous, or near-continuous, fire. Seen in this light, the Battle of Nagashino poses a challenge to an interpretation in global military history (itself the subject of some debate) that the first instance of volley fire was employed in Europe in 1594, meaning almost twenty years after the Battle of Nagashino.

The battle lasted from sunrise until the early afternoon, when the Takeda forces broke. Their remaining forces gathered around Katsuyori and fled. Casualty figures are in dispute. According to *Shinchô kôki*, the Takeda lost between 10,000 and 12,000 of their 15,000 men, which is likely an exaggerated figure. Other contemporary sources put the number much lower, but there is no dispute that Katsuyori suffered a devastating defeat and his Takeda clan eliminated as a serious contender to unify the country. Katsuyori lived to fight another day, but he died in battle less than a decade later, in 1582. For Nobunaga, victory at Nagashino removed the threat of the Takeda as a serious contender for the military unification of the country. He was thus free to mount a military campaign against the forces of the Buddhist Ikkô sect (*ikkô ikki*) in Echizen province (now Fukui prefecture), while Ieyasu was left to contain the remaining forces of the Takeda.

The tactics employed by Nobunaga at Nagashino soon became the standard mode for the conduct of warfare—for example, at Shizugatake, a battle between Toyotomi Hideyoshi and Shibata Katsuie, in 1583. Each side entrenched its forces and waited for the other to initiate hostilities. In the end, Hideyoshi was able to provoke a general under Shibata to break ranks and attack, which triggered an advance of the army's main lines. Here too the attacking force, the Shibata, were devastated by the entrenched, more disciplined, forces (of Hideyoshi).

See also: Firearms; Oda Nobunaga; Toyotomi Hideyoshi

Further Reading and Viewing
Animated Battle Map of Battle of Nagashino. http://www.theartofbattle.com/battle-of
          -nagashino-1575. Accessed February 6, 2016.
Parker, Geoffrey. *The Military Revolution.* Cambridge: Cambridge University Press, 1988.
Stavros, Matthew. "Military Revolution in Early Modern Japan." *Japanese Studies*
          (2013), 1–18.

Names (Samurai)

In Tokugawa Japan the status system (*mibunsei*) impacted society broadly. It even
was reflected in the practice of naming. In principle, only samurai were allowed
surnames. Moreover, naming practices for samurai were a complicated phenomenon and served to distinguish them in many respects from commoners. These differences between samurai and commoners, particularly with regard to surnames,
were eliminated by the Meiji government after 1868.

Although in principle samurai were privileged with *myôji taito*, the twin rights
of a surname and bearing arms (two swords), as was often the case in Tokugawa
Japan, the reality was much more complicated; there was often a difference between
law and custom. Commoners with property that could be handed down likely possessed what is best referred to as a *yagô*, or "house name," rather than a proper
surname. In the case of merchants, some *yagô* might include the name of a province, as in Echigoya (Echigo province + *ya*), or indicate the person's occupation, as
in Minatoya (*minato*, meaning "port" + *ya*). In villages, many peasants who had (or
claimed) a samurai lineage before the juridicial separation of peasants and samurai (*heinô bunri*) continued to use those surnames in unofficial documentation
throughout the Tokugawa period. Sometimes peasants were given permission by
domain or shogunate officials to use a surname (and often, carry a sword); this permission could be given for just one generation or in perpetuity. In villages, however, there were many people without surnames, typically tenant farmers and day
laborers. Also, sometimes official documents would list peasants by surname to
distinguish one from the other; this could be the case even without the people in
question having been given permission to use a surname. Only after the end of the
Tokugawa period, in 1870, did the Japanese (Meiji) government permit all commoners to take surnames; indeed, in 1875, surnames became mandatory.

Many surnames of samurai are derived from a geographical property or point
to some physical property; *Honda* ("original paddy") and *Takeda* ("bamboo paddy")
are representative examples. Typically, they consist of two Chinese characters, or
kanji; but some names used three or more characters, and in a few cases there were
one-character surnames as well.

As with Japanese names today, during the Edo period the surname came first.
For samurai during the course of his lifetime it was followed by a series of names.
Each name carried with it certain significance. Six days after birth, a samurai was
given his first name, known as his "childhood name" (*yômyô*), by which he would
be known until his coming-of-age ceremony (*genpuku*). Ii Naomasa (1561–1602),

one of Tokugawa Ieyasu's top generals, for example, was first known as Manchiyo, while Ieyasu (1543–1616), the first Tokugawa shogun, was given the childhood name of Takechiyo.

At the coming-of-age ceremony, which could take place sometime between the ages of thirteen and seventeen, a samurai typically was given two additional names. (A commoner might also change his given name when reaching adulthood.) The first of these two names was known as *tsûshô* (or *zokumyô*) and almost always consisted of two characters; it was the name by which he was commonly known to his close friends and family and often reflected the numerical order of birth the child had in the family. The *tsûshô* of Yoshida Shôin (1830–1859), the late-Tokugawa samurai from Chôshû domain, for example, was Torajirô, which indicated that he was the second-born son. A samurai might also be given a second name at the time of his coming-of-age ceremony, a *jitsumei* ("true name"; also known as *nanori*). This was a formal, adult name that was used publicly, consisting of two Chinese characters and producing a four-syllable name, pronounced with the "Japanese reading" (or "*kun yomi*"), as in Takamori (e.g., Saigô Takamori, 1828–1877, a late-Tokugawa samurai from Satsuma). The *nanori* name often had an auspicious or felicitous meaning; indeed, in Saigô's case, "Takamori" was written with two Chinese characters, both of which meant "prosperity." Sometimes a father would give his son the front character from their names or that of an ancestor. In the case of the Oda family, this meant the character read "Nobu" (as in Nobunaga). For the Yamauchi family, daimyo of Tosa domain, the character "toyo" was shared by all but the second of fifteen daimyo. For thirteen of the fourteen daimyo with "toyo" in their name it came as the first character (as in Toyomasa or Toyofusa); only in one instance was it positioned second (as in Tadatoyo, who received the first character "Tada" from his father Tadayoshi). A samurai, particularly a man of considerable learning, could have yet another name, known as *azana*. These typically added a literary or cultured feel to the name. Yoshida Shôin, for example, also used the name Norikata. As demonstrated here, a samurai could have many different names over the course of a lifetime, which can make it challenging for scholars or students of history to keep track of an individual samurai's history.

Some samurai, particularly late Warring States daimyo, might adopt a religious (Buddhist) name at some point in their life, typically upon retirement. Some well-known cases of daimyo who adopted Buddhist names (with their better-known, non-Buddhist name, in parenthesis) were Takeda Shingen (Harunobun) and Uesugi Kenshin (Terutora). A final name that some daimyo or high-ranking samurai might assume was a death name, one that was given to him posthumously. In some rare cases this name marked his deification, as in the case of the first shogun, Tokugawa Ieyasu, who was known as *Tôshô daigongen*.

The granting of honorary surnames or a character from a first name to a political subordinate could be one way to cement a political relationship. For example, after the Battle of Sekigahara (1600), the daimyo of Satsuma domain, Shimazu Yoshihiro, who had opposed Tokugawa Ieyasu, was forced to resign in favor of his third son, Tadatsune. In a gesture of magnanimity, Tokugawa Ieyasu allowed Tadatsune to assume the Matsudaira name, which was the old surname of the Tokugawa and the surname of branch families of the Tokugawa in the Edo period. He further permitted Tadatsune to change his personal name to Iehisa, which included the first character, *ie*, of Ieyasu's name. The granting of the Matsudaira surname was also done for powerful outside lords (*tozama daimyô*) to foster political ties.

The Tokugawa took pains to control the imperial institution, and part of this control system involved usurping its former monopoly rights to grant court ranks and office titles, a practice that dated back to ancient times under the *ritsuryô* system. The Tokugawa assumed a monopoly on the right to petition the court for prestigious court ranks and titles, and the court could not refuse its requests. These ranks and titles (or "names") conveyed tremendous prestige to the recipient. Actually, daimyo and high-ranking shogunal retainers (bannermen) who held imperial office were usually addressed by their office titles; for example, the daimyo of Akô domain involved in the Akô Incident was generally known as Asano Takumi no kami (chief of the bureau of artisans), his court title, rather than by his name Asano Naganori (1667–1701); others were granted honorary titles that referred to the province he "held" (honorifically).

Other high-ranking samurai adopted lower-ranking office titles of their own accord as personal names. For example, Ôishi Yoshi, the domain elder (*karô*) in Akô and hero of *Chûshingura*, adopted the office title "Kuranosuke," which literally meant "assistant in the bureau of imperial palace warehouses." It also became common among samurai to adopt a guard title—"emon" as part of their name, as in Hikozaemon.

See also: Akô Incident; Coming of Age (*genpuku*); Status System (*mibunsei*); Warring States Daimyo (*sengoku daimyô*)

Further Reading

Bryant, Anthony J. "Japanese Names." http://www.sengokudaimyo.com/miscellany/names/html. Accessed December 16, 2017. This site focuses on Japanese names during the *sengoku* period.

Wakabayashi, Bob Tadashi. "In Name Only: Imperial Sovereignty in Early Modern Japan." *Journal of Japanese Studies,* 17(1) (1991), 25–57.

Nijô Castle (*Nijô-jô*)

In asserting their political authority over the realm (*tenka*), the Tokugawa built a series of castles across the country, in Osaka, Sunpu, and Kyoto. Nijô Castle, in Kyoto, played an important role in the assertion of that authority early in the seventeenth century, particularly while Toyotomi Hideyoshi's heir, Hideyori, was alive. After Hideyori's death in the Siege of Osaka in 1615, Nijô remained an important administrative center of Tokugawa authority, available for the shogun's residence on the rare occasions when he visited Kyoto. From Nijô the shogunate exercised oversight of the imperial institution, which was located nearby, also in the same city. After the fall of the shogunate in 1867, Nijô became imperial property and remained so until 1939, when it was turned over to the city of Kyoto. Today, the castle and its palace buildings are an important part of Kyoto and Japan's cultural legacy; international recognition of Nijô 's cultural significance came in 1994, when Nijô was registered by UNESCO as a World Heritage Site.

Nijô Castle served as the stage for the opening and closing ceremonies of the Tokugawa shogunate. Its construction began in 1601, and the basic structure was completed in time for the shogun Tokugawa Ieyasu's investment ceremony by the emperor in 1603. After receiving his appointment, the shogun came to Nijô Castle to announce his appointment to the daimyo, who were assembled there for that purpose. Work on the castle and its interior decoration continued over the next two decades. It was finished in time for the visit of Emperor Gomizuno-o (reigned 1611–1629), who was married to the daughter of the second shogun, Hidetada (1579–1632). Nijô Castle served as the shogun's official residence while in Kyoto and as the Tokugawa outpost in the imperial city. From Nijô, the shogun's representative in the city, the Kyôto shoshidai, could keep watch over the emperor, who was essentially restricted to the imperial palace. Envoys from the imperial court would travel to Nijô to meet with Tokugawa officials, as needed.

The castle featured a five-story donjon, which was relocated from Fushimi Castle and reconstructed in the inner bailey (*honmaru*). It shared a fate similar to Edo Castle's donjon. It burned down in 1750, due to a fire caused by a lightening strike, and was not rebuilt. (The base of the keep tower can still be viewed today.) The *honmaru* palace itself burned not long afterward, in 1788, and also was not replaced, until the 1860s.

The main gate leading to the *Ninomaru goten*, the *Karamon* (Chinese-style Gate), together with the *Ninomaru* Garden, "are unique survivals from one of the golden ages of Japanese architecture and design, the early Edo period, known for its ornate architecture and magnificent interiors" ("Former Imperial Villa Nijo-jo Castle," 2017). The palace in the secondary enceinte, the *Ninomaru goten*, was spared from natural disaster and remains today one of the most heavily visited places on the tourist agenda in Kyoto. Many of the rooms were decorated in a lavish fashion, with gold leaf and paintings by the renowned artist Kano Tan'yu, of the Kano school of painting, which enjoyed the patronage of the Tokugawa shoguns. In all, there are more than 3,600 wall paintings inside the palace, many from the Kan'ei period (1624–1644). About a third of this number (1,016) have been designated as Important Cultural Properties. The *Karamon* is notable for its architectural forms— cusped gable to the front and back of the roof, use of cypress bark for the roofing, brilliantly colored carvings of cranes, pine, bamboo, and plum blossoms (all symbols of longevity)—and underwent a major restoration in 2013.

The *Ninomaru* Palace consists of six connected buildings, arranged in a diagonal line from southeast to northwest. Its thirty-three rooms cover 3,300 square meters (over 800 tatami mats). The palace includes the shogun's living quarters, audience chambers, a formal reception room, and a waiting room. The most splendid is the formal audience chamber (*ôhiroma*), where the shogun met with the daimyo and imperial court nobility. The chamber consisted of two rooms, the First Room (*ichinoma*) and Second Room (*ninoma*). During audiences, the shogun sat in the First Room, facing south. In a room to the shogun's left, divided only by sliding doors, bodyguards sat at attention in the *musha kakushi no ma* (Bodyguards' Chamber), in case they were needed to defend him from possible assailants. It was here in the *ôhiroma* that the last shogun, Tokugawa Yoshinobu (1837–1913), had assembled the senior officials of forty of the largest domains on November 8, 1867,

The *karamon* ("Chinese gate") of Nijô Castle in Kyoto. This photo was taken in 2017, after the completion of the gate's reconstruction in 2013. The gate was an important symbol of Tokugawa authority and it remains an important example of the ornate architectural style of the early Edo period. (Photo by Constantine Vaporis)

to announce his decision to return rule to the emperor (*taisei hôkan*). The floorboards of the palace were constructed in such a manner that walking on them creates a sound like the song of a nightingale (hence the appellation the "Nightingale Corridor"). One explanation for this is that this construction was devised for security purposes, to announce the presence of intruders.

A large garden extends outward on the western side of the audience chamber known as the Ninomaru Garden. It was redesigned by Kobori Enshu, who was commissioned for the work on the occasion of the 1626 imperial visit. It is a classic *shoin-zukuri*-style garden, with a large island, symbolizing paradise, flanked by a crane island and a turtle island, both animals being metaphors for longevity.

During the early seventeenth century, Nijô Castle served as an important base for the Tokugawa shogunate in western Japan, particularly while Toyotomi Hideyori (1593–1615) was still alive and occupying Osaka Castle. In fact, a meeting between Tokugawa Ieyasu and Hideyori took place at Nijô Castle in 1611, four years before the Siege of Osaka Castle began. The Tokugawa used Nijô Castle as a base for the planning and execution of those military operations. In 1634, the third shogun, Tokugawa Iemitsu, led a great army of 300,000 men into Kyoto and stayed at

Photograph of Nijô Castle in Kyoto, ca. 1890, showing the southwest tower and east gate. It served as the Tokugawa shogunate's headquarters in the imperial city of Kyoto. It was here that the last shogun, Tokugawa Yoshinobu (1837–1913) announced his resignation and decision to return rule to the emperor, in 1867. (Library of Congress)

the castle. He would be the last shogun to set foot inside Nijô for 230 years, and under very different circumstances. Although Iemitsu's visit to Kyoto and to Nijô in 1635 made a strong statement about the supremacy of Tokugawa authority, the visit of the fourteenth shogun, Tokugawa Iemochi (ruled 1858–1866), in 1863 was evidence of the much-weakened position of the shogunate in the nineteenth century. Iemochi had in fact been summoned by the emperor and traveled to Kyoto with an escort of only 3,000.

In 1867, Nijô provided the setting for the final chapter of the Tokugawa shogunate, whose formation had been publicly announced to the daimyo in 1603. The last shogun, Tokugawa Yoshinobu (1837–1913), succeeded to his position at Nijô Castle and resided there from 1866 until 1868, after the Meiji Restoration, when he moved to Sunpu, the castle town in the Tokugawa's ancestral lands. It was from here, as noted above, that in 1867 he announced the decision to return rule to the emperor (*taisei hôkan*).

After the collapse of the Tokugawa shogunate in 1867, Nijô became imperial property, which it remained until it was gifted to the city of Kyoto in 1939. In 2013, during renovations of the castle's Momoyama-period Karamon gate, workers discovered a metal imperial chrysanthemum emblem on the gate was covering an earlier one, the triple hollyhock crest, of the Tokugawa family.

The historic importance of Nijô Castle has been recognized by the Japanese government, as it has a number of structures dating from the Momoyama period

(1573–1615) and lavish paintings and wood carvings. Specifically, the government has designated six buildings of the Ninomaru Palace as National Treasures and twenty-two buildings, including the main palace (*Honmaru* Palace) and the corner turrets, Important Cultural Properties. The sliding door panels of the secondary palace (*Ninomaru* Palace) were similarly designated Important Cultural Properties as fine works of art in 1982. Lastly, Nijô was registered by UNESCO as a World Heritage Site in 1994.

See also: Castle Towns (*jôkamachi*); Castles (*jôkaku*); Tokugawa Ieyasu; Tokugawa Yoshinobu

Further Reading

"Former Imperial Villa Nijo-jo Castle. World Heritage Site." Kyoto: Nijô-jô Castle Office, 2017.

Hirai, Kiyoshi. *Feudal Architecture of Japan*. New York and Tokyo: Weatherhill/Heibonsha, 1973.

Mitchelhill, Jennifer. *Castles of the Samurai: Power and Beauty*. Tokyo, New York, London: Kodansha International, 2003.

Ninja. *See Ninjutsu (the Arts of Stealth)*

Ninjutsu (the Arts of Stealth)

There is perhaps no greater myth surrounding the samurai than that of the ninja, practitioners of the stealth arts of *ninjutsu*—espionage, sabotage, and assassination. Most of what we think we know about the ninja comes from popular culture in both Japan and the West, from movies, novels, and Japanese Tokugawa-period television shows. Much of this popular culture presents the false notion that ninja and samurai were competing orders or tribes of warriors. Far from this, ninja existed only in the sense that there were samurai who practiced *ninjutsu*, which was one of the eighteen fundamental martial arts during the Tokugawa period (others included archery, sword fighting, swimming, dagger throwing, and sword drawing). *Ninjutsu* also involved the art of intelligence gathering. In short, it was an activity and did not confer on its practitioners a special identity. In this sense, there were no ninja.

In popular culture representations of the ninja are as larger-than-life figures. In many films, novels, and manga they are clad in black garments and endowed with extraordinary acrobatic skills and pinpoint accuracy in throwing a variety of weapons such as *shuriken* (throwing knives), daggers, *fumihari* (small metal pins that were blown from a ninja's mouth through a tube at an adversary's eyes), and *makibishi* (pointed metal objects thrown on the ground to injure the feet of pursuers). A ninja attack appears to be a standard feature of any Western movie about Tokugawa Japan, as in the 2003 Hollywood blockbuster *The Last Samurai* (dir. Edward Zwick). Although there are legends that trace the roots of *ninjutsu* back into ancient Japanese history, it was during the civil wars of the Warring States (*sengoku*) period (1467–1600) that practitioners of spycraft first emerged as a historical phenomenon. During this politically unsettled period, military leaders—the Warring States daimyo—had need of operatives (scouts) to penetrate the enemy's territory in a clandestine manner to obtain intelligence, to observe troop movements, to engage in commando-style raids, or to engage in assassination. There were areas of Japan, such as Iga (from present-day Mie prefecture) and Koga (present-day Shiga prefecture), that had reputations for producing individuals who were skilled in these activities, but there were no real "ninja clans" or secret ninja villages, as presented in movies, comics, and in some books written by contemporary practitioners of martial arts.

With the onset of the Tokugawa peace, *ninjutsu* became systematized as a formal martial art—one of the standard eighteen military arts (*bugei jûhappan*). One of the key ninja manuals was the *Mansen shukai*, compiled by Fujibayashi Samuji in 1676, the aim of which was to preserve knowledge that had been gained during the period from the onset of the Warring States period until the Sieges of Osaka in 1614–1615. A set of manuals on *ninjutsu* by the scholar of military arts Chikamatsu Shigenori (1695–1778), who was already well known as a practitioner of the tea ceremony and author of *Stories from a Tearoom Window*, have recently been identified.

The eighth shogun, Tokugawa Yoshimune (1684–1751) used a group of undercover detectives or spies, known as *oniwaban*, to gather intelligence about daimyo and shogunate officials. They also acted as security guards within Edo Castle. These agents were known as *Iga mono* (people from Iga), even though they originated in Kii domain (where Yoshimune had served as a daimyo before being elevated to the position of shogun).

See also: Tea Ceremony (*sadô*); Tokugawa Yoshimune; Warring States Daimyo (*sengoku daimyô*)

Further Reading

Cummins, Anthony. *In Search of the Ninja: The Historical Truth of Ninjutsu.* Stroud, Gloucestershire, UK: The History Press, 2012.

Fukai, Masaumi. *Edo-jô oniwaban: Tokugawa Shôgun no mimi to me* [The 'Garden Keepers' of Edo Castle: The Shogun's Eyes and Ears]. Tokyo: Chûô Kôronsha, 1992.

Nonaka Kenzan (1615–1663)

A scholar and administrator, Nonaka Kenzan was the chief architect of intellectual, economic, and political policies that established Tosa as one of the great domains in the seventeenth century. Although those policies improved the domain's economic position and increased its self-sufficiency, they also engendered political opposition, which led to his dismissal from office in 1663.

Kenzan was born in the castle town of Himeji in 1615. His father had for a period served the first lord of Tosa, Yamauchi Katsutoyo, as domain counselor, or elder, but at the time of Kenzan's birth found himself a *rônin*, or masterless samurai. When his father died the family returned to Tosa domain, where Kenzan was adopted at the age of four as the heir of his father's cousin, Nonaka Naotsugu.

Kenzan succeeded his adopted father as the domain's chief administrator in 1636, and under the direction of Yamauchi Tadayoshi (1592–1665), the second lord of

Tosa, began to put into place a reform program for the domain's government. First, he pursued several policies to improve the domain's economic development. In the agricultural realm, Kenzan focused on increasing the amount of lowlands under cultivation through extensive reclamation projects and riparian (irrigation) works; this involved increasing levels of corvée labor from the populace. Kenzan also put pressure on village headmen to get the most out of the countryside by incentivizing their cooperation with special land grants. Under Kenzan's energetic direction, "new irrigation canals were cut across the lowlands of Tosa in the 1640s and 1650s. These canals enabled the development of great tracts of rice producing paddies in the ensuing decades" (Roberts, 1998, 66). Production levels increased in many older villages, and as many as thirty new villages, not to mention several market towns and ports, were also created by the end of the century; to improve coastal sea transportation, Tei port (present-day Nangoku city, Kôchi prefecture) was created and is reputed to be Japan's first man-made harbor. In addition to these domain-sponsored land development projects, the domain under Kenzan's administration also promoted private land development by granting the status of *gôshi* (rural samurai) to any man who developed more than 30 *tan* (1 *tan* = 0.245 acre) of land. As a result of these various efforts the plains population increased rapidly and the amount of registered land under cultivation increased by about 40 percent during the second half of the seventeenth century. However, population growth also increased rapidly, putting pressure on the food supply.

During the period of Kenzan's administration, Tosa came under extreme pressure from the Tokugawa shogunate for lumber, one of the domain's abundant resources (it never became a major rice-growing region). In fact, during the seventeenth century the shogunate demanded lumber contributions on thirty-six occasions; in eight years the demands exceeded fifty thousand trees. These demands forced the domain to abandon responsible forest protection policies and put excessive tax demands on Tosa's population. By most accounts, Kenzan became the easy target for people's discontent and was accused of abusing the people for "selfish reasons," leading in part to his dismissal from office in 1663.

Another means by which Kenzan tried to increase the domain government's income to help pay for the large imposition levied by the shogunate in 1662 was by assuming a commercial monopoly over certain commercial products. Under this scheme, the domain created a monopoly on four important products (paper, tea, lacquer, and oil-bearing seeds). Their private sale of these products was banned and under pain of punishment, fines, or prison, domain producers were required to sell these commercial goods to officially designated merchants in the domain's castle town, Kôchi. This policy, too, engendered much discontent, also contributing to Kenzan's fall from power the following year, after which the domain reversed itself and abolished the monopoly.

Kenzan, as the chief administrator, played an important role in negotiating Tosa's border disputes during the mid-seventeenth century with its neighbor, Uwajima, which was ruled by the Date family. The first of these disputes involved an island, Okinoshima, off the coast of the southwestern portion of Shikoku Island, and attendant fishing rights in the coastal waters; the second entailed the land boundary between the two domains in the area of Sasayama mountain. Kenzan played an integral role in rallying support for Tosa's case among influential daimyo, particularly among the members of the shogun's Senior Council, who decided the case in Tosa's favor in the case of Okinoshima. He also played an important role in the land boundary dispute on Sasayama. He had hoped that a Tosa domain samurai with a large fief along the disputed border would have been able to deal with the problem on his own, but when that samurai asked the domain to send an official to the border to help, Kenzan wrote him a letter in disgust: "You have asked the domain administrators to send an official to the border, but *you* have been entrusted with a large fief along that border so that you may deal with such situations as this. If we have to send someone in your stead, then you do not belong there! . . . If you had been thinking, 'I will disembowel myself if there is any injury to my country on my watch,' then this would never have happened! The administrators forwarded on to me your letter to them requesting assistance. I was so disgusted that I tossed it into the fire" (Roberts, 2012, 113). Kenzan had to take control of the situation, and in the end was able to convince his lord that Tosa would lose in the shogun's court if it was a party to a second law suit, regardless of the merits of their case. In making his position clear, Kenzan argued that he was willing to risk his lord's displeasure and likely losing his domain: "I have decided that the clan should not engage in another court case. Even though in arguing this point I must disobey my lord's will and give up my fief, it would be for the benefit of the [Yamauchi] clan . . . and would be the right way of serving the lord and fulfilling my duties as administrator" (Roberts, 2012, 126).

In the end, Kenzan's attempts to bring the local economy under the increasing control of the domain government, the intense labor demands put on the peasantry, and bureaucratic infighting among other Tosa samurai fomented such dissatisfaction with his administration that he was dismissed from his position and forced into retirement in 1663. He died only a year later. Many of his economic controls were lifted after his fall from power, and the domain replaced the system of having a single administrator to a rotation system of domain elders (*rôjû*). Other reprisals against those related to or associated with Kenzan followed. Those who served in office with him similarly dismissed and punished, while anyone with marriage ties to the Nonaka had those relationships dissolved. The final punishment was that his last descendants were sent into exile in an outlying part of the domain and his family line was allowed to die out.

Nonaka Kenzan is also remembered for his efforts to promote Confucian studies in Tosa domain. One scholar has written of him, "It is significant that his search for an ideology of authoritarian and monolithic state control led him to the code of imperial China" (Jansen, 1968, 126). He encouraged Tosa scholars like Yamazaki Anzai and the Tani family line of Confucianists, who developed the southern school (*Nangaku*) of Confucianism.

Despite the harsh measures taken against Nonaka Kenzan, there is recognition today of his positive contributions to the economic development of the Tosa region, tempered by the caveat that he was too harsh in his methods. In terms of a physical legacy, there is a list of his accomplishments in the Kôchi Prefectural Museum of

History; a stone monument in Kôchi marks the location of his former residence, inside the inner moat of the castle; and in Motoyama town (Kôchi prefecture), he is memorialized with a statue in Kizenzan Park.

See also: Daimyo and Domains; Rural Samurai (*gôshi*); Yamauchi Katsutoyo

Further Reading

Jansen, Marius B. "Tosa in the Seventeenth Century: The Establishment of Yamauchi Rule." In John W. Hall and Marius B. Jansen, eds., *Studies in the Institutional History of Early Modern Japan.* Princeton, NJ: Princeton University Press, 1968.

Roberts, Luke S. *Mercantilism in a Japanese Domain: The Merchant Origins of Economic Nationalism in 18th-Century Tosa.* Cambridge: Cambridge University Press, 1998.

Roberts, Luke S. *Performing the Great Peace: Political Space and Open Secrets in Tokugawa Japan.* Honolulu: University of Hawai'i Press, 2012.

Oda Nobunaga (1534–1582)

One of the most famous historical figures of the sixteenth century, Oda Nobunaga rose from a minor warlord during the late Warring States period (*sengoku*, 1467–1568) to become the foremost military power in the country, which contemporaries referred to as "the realm" (*tenka*). In doing so he unified most of the main island of Honshû before meeting his early death in 1582, at the hands of one of his generals. Despite his methods, Nobunaga made great strides toward pacifying the militarized Buddhist church and demonstrated that national unification was possible. He is also renown not only for his use of violence to further his military and political goals but also for his policies to promote economic integration, his use of firearms, construction of castles, political uses of tea culture, and the promotion of the arts.

CAREER

Nobunaga's roots were in the fertile and strategically located Owari province (part of Aichi prefecture), in central Japan, where his family had long exercised power as deputy *shugo*, or deputy military governor. His father Nobuhide (1510–1551) was a warlord in the region, and after his father's death Nobunaga slowly eliminated rival military figures in the area, consolidating his control of the entire province by 1559.

Nobunaga's position in Owari province was soon challenged by a major rival in the neighboring Mikawa province (part of Aichi prefecture), Imagawa Yoshitomo. In a battle widely seen as launching Nobunaga's military campaign to reunify the country, Nobunaga's forces surprised and defeated the vastly larger forces of the Imagawa at Okehazama (present-day Toyoake, in Aichi prefecture) in 1560, during a driving rain, taking not only Imagawa's life but his most prized sword. Nobunaga's troops also marked their victory by collecting about 3,000 heads from the opposing side. Importantly, Nobunaga also entered into alliance with an important follower of Imagawa's, Matsudaira Motoyasu, the future Tokugawa Ieyasu, in order to secure his eastern flank.

In 1567 Nobunaga gave public notice of his ambition to unite the country and rule over it in that he began to use on official documents a seal, similar to a signature, that bore the slogan *tenka fubu*, the "realm under military rule." Indeed, by 1568 Nobunaga was in a strong enough position to march on Kyoto and to retain control of the city. That control was reflected by Nobunaga's installation of Ashikaga Yoshiaki as shogun, whom he sought to use in advancing his own national designs. Yoshiaki, for his part, needed Nobunaga's military backing and thus offered him several positions, which he declined. Instead, Nobunaga requested and received

Portrait of Oda Nobunaga by the artist Kanô Sôshû (1551–1601), from a hanging scroll held at Chôkô-ji temple, Toyota (Aichi prefecture). It is one of the few portraits of this important political leader and is thought to bear the closest likeness to Nobunaga himself. (Tibor Bognar/ Alamy Stock Photo)

control of the critical merchant city and firearms manufacturing center of Sakai the following year.

Nobunaga's march to power met stiff resistance during the 1570s, particularly on the part of rival daimyo, especially the Azai, the Asakura, and later the Takeda, as well as the powerful Buddhist sects. In 1571, Nobunaga's forces laid waste to Enryakuji, burning down the temple complex and killing several thousand monks and laypeople, including women and children, in the process. Nobunaga faced a much more prolonged and difficult campaign, however, against the temple-fortress Honganji, the headquarters of the True Pure Land branch of Buddhism, which resisted his authority in Osaka and in Echizen province. It took him almost a full decade, from 1570 to 1580, before he was successful in suppressing the militant sectarians. The rival daimyo Takeda Shingen also provided great resistance to Nobunaga, defeating the combined forces of Tokugawa Ieyasu's and Nobunaga's allied army at the Battle of Mikatagahama in Tôtômi (now Hamamatsu city, Shizuoka prefecture). After Shingen's unexpected and unexplained sudden death in 1574, Nobunaga drove the shogun Ashikaga Yoshiaki from Kyoto and into exile; although Yoshiaki did not abdicate until 1588, marking the official end of the Ashikaga shogunate, Nobunaga's actions in driving him from Kyoto meant that Nobunaga was now the supreme political authority in the realm.

With Ashikaga Yoshiaki driven into exile, the imperial court sought to curry favor with Nobunaga, bestowing on him court titles and invitations to the imperial palace. In what was clearly a symbiotic relationship, Nobunaga helped to support the court and aristocracy financially; the imperial honors he was awarded and close association with the court helped to bestow legitimacy on his power that was acquired through military means. The court even offered Nobunaga the position of *daijô daijin* (grand minister of state), but he died before he could give an official response.

In the military realm, from early on Nobunaga realized the importance of fire-arms to success on the battlefield. In 1549, he first designated a special unit in his army for them and outfitted it with 500 matchlocks purchased from gunsmiths in nearby Kunitomi (Ômi province, current Shiga prefecture). Muskets played a deci-sive role in Nobunaga's defeat of the Takeda forces under the leadership of Katsu-yori, who challenged Nobunaga after the death of Shingen at the Battle of Nagashino in 1582.

Nobunaga was not unique among the *sengoku daimyô* to build castles. He was, however, arguably the first to realize the political uses of monumental castle architec-ture and art, as well as the first to build a castle town. Azuchi Castle, built during 1576–1579, was constructed not just as a military stronghold but also as his residence and court. The castle complex became the site for public spectacles, including sumo tournaments, tea ceremonies, and a sound-and-light show. A separate palatial build-ing called the Gyokô no Ma (Hall for an Imperial Visit), adorned with paintings entirely in gold, was constructed to demonstrate his wealth and authority. The inside of the donjon (*tenshu*) he decorated with the artwork of Japan's most accomplished art-ists. To build up Azuchi as a thriving town, Nobunaga ordered his vassals to reside at the base of the castle and offered numerous incentives to attract merchants and arti-sans to take up residence there. Such was his new conception of the castle that its name has become a part of the designation Azuchi-Momoyama period (1568–1600), a term used by cultural historians because of its opulence and grandeur.

BETRAYAL AND DEATH

Nobunaga's death came at the hands of one of his former allies, Akechi Mitsu-hide (1528–1582). In the age renown for *gekokujô* (the overturning of authority), this was not uncommon, but it is surprising that Nobunaga allowed himself to be caught unprotected. On his way to campaign in southwestern Japan in 1582, Nobu-naga stopped at Honnôji temple in Kyoto, a Buddhist temple that he had used habitually as his headquarters. Akechi Mitsuhide was supposed to be leading the vanguard of the expeditionary force, but changed plans and caught Nobunaga by surprise in the early morning of June 6. The exact manner in which Nobunaga died is not clear. According to the Jesuit Luis Frois, who was not a firsthand observer, Nobunaga suffered an arrow round in the side but continued to fight until he was hit with another arrow in the arm, at which point he retreated into another cham-ber and shut the doors. Frois reports that at this point either Nobunaga committed *seppuku* ("slitting the belly"), ritual suicide, or simply set the temple on fire. A simi-lar account was related in the chronicle *Shinchô kôki* (*Official Account of Nobu-naga*) in which he retreated to a room to commit ritual suicide. Whatever the exact details of his final minutes, the temple burned to the ground and with it, Nobuna-ga's life was extinguished. His betrayer was chased down and killed by Toyotomi Hideyoshi's forces; for his act of betrayal and quick subsequent death, Akechi is known disparagingly as the "three-day *shôgun*" (*mikka kubô*).

With Nobunaga's death the Oda family suffered decline, as his general Toyotomi Hideyoshi rather than his son Nobukatsu (1558–1630) succeeded him. However, decendants of Nobunaga continued to exist, albeit as minor political forces, during the Tokugawa period. Several branches were minor daimyo while one branch became bannermen (*hatamoto*), retainers of the Tokugawa shogun.

NOBUNAGA AND TEA CULTURE

As seen through his efforts at Azuchi, Nobunaga sought to become "the nation's main cultural patron" (Lamers, 2000, 129). In part he did this through his patronage of the tea ceremony. Although his vassal and successor Toyotomi Hideyoshi is better known in this regard, Nobunaga, too, was deeply involved in the tea world and the politics surrounding it. Sen Rikyu, who later served Hideyoshi, was Nobunaga's tea official and cultural adviser first. Nobunaga used tea implements as rewards to help cement political relationships with his vassals and allies or to appease an enemy. Even his rivals knew of his great love of the tea world. One of his enemies, Matsunaga Hisahide (1510–1577), made peace with Nobunaga by giving him a prize tea caddy. Some eleven years later, after Hisahide had joined a plot against Nobunaga and was about to be attacked, he deliberately smashed a prized tea kettle rather than allow it to fall into Nobunaga's hands. On the other hand, after his triumphant occupation of Kyoto in 1568, and in recognition of his pacification of the realm, he received numerous gifts from daimyo such as Chinese tea caddies and tea jars. After 1568 he appears to have began a two-year campaign known as the Hunt for Famous Objects (*meibutsu gari*), during which he spared no amount of money to acquire at least ten of the most prized tea utensils in Japan. From 1571 he began to practice the tea ceremony himself by hosting small gatherings at his castle in Gifu. At the same time he continued to enlarge his collection of tea objects, particularly Chinese objects, which he showcased during special events. He conspicuously displayed his tea articles to enhance his power and prestige, in the same manner that he and other daimyo used decorative arts and even castle architecture. In these efforts he strove to surpass the Ashikaga shoguns as collectors of Chinese famous objects, thereby seeking another source for the legitimization of his political-military power. A final example of his use of tea for political purposes was that in 1581 he gave his vassal Hideyoshi privileges in three core practices related to the tea ceremony: permission to host tea gathering using the famous tea implements that Nobunaga had given him; permission to hire tea master from the city of Sakai; and permission to gift tea utensils to his vassals.

HISTORICAL LEGACY

The Portuguese jesuit Luis Frois was granted several audiences by Nobunaga, the first in 1569, and left a firsthand account of the ruler. Based on Frois's accounts, we can say that his assessment of the man is generally favorable, although this may have been in part due to Nobunaga's friendliness toward him. Frois describes Nobunaga as "tall, thin, sparsely bearded, extremely war-like and much given to military exercises" (Cooper, 1965). He noted that those around Nobunaga were very obedient and paid him great respect. Frois found Nobunaga quite self-assured in his power and status and unwilling to listen to the advice of others. Nevertheless, he also saw a ruler who could converse with men of all positions in life. Since Frois traveled to Japan to spread the Christian faith, it is no surprise that he concluded that Nobunaga despised the Shinto and Buddhist deities, and noted in great detail Nobunaga's military campaign against the Buddhist monastic complex at Enryakuji on Mt. Hiei in 1570. Subsequently, as Nobunaga enjoyed more success on the battlefield, Frois noted Nobuanga's tendency toward "megalomania" and his desire to be worshipped as more than a mere mortal. In 1582 Frois accused Nobunaga of sacrilege in announcing that he was to be worshipped as a divine being, but this claim is suspect as there is no corroborating evidence from a Japanese source.

A popular haiku dating from the Tokugawa period echoes this view of Nobunaga as a violent man and vividly contrasts the personalities of the three so-called unifiers. According to the haiku, Nobunaga, Hideyoshi, and Tokugawa were watching a cuckoo bird waiting for it to sing, but the bird would not sing. Nobunaga said to the bird, "If you don't sing I will kill you." Hideyoshi said to the bird, "If you don't sing, I'll make you sing." Then Tokugawa Ieyasu said to the bird, "If you don't sing I will wait for you to sing."

The judgment of historians about Nobunaga has been mixed. The noted British scholar and diplomat George Sansom, for example, concluded that Nobunaga "was a cruel and callous brute" (Sansom, 1961, 309–310). He is representative of one group of scholars who have viewed him as the last ruler of medieval Japan, whose tyrannical personality and violent policies doomed him to failure. In contrast, another group sees him as pursuing policies that were necessary, "ruthless and pragmatic" (Lamers, 2000, 232), given the chaos and disorder of his time, thereby setting in motion the processes that moved Japan into the early modern (Tokugawa) period.

Further Reading

Cooper, Michael, ed. *They Came to Japan: An Anthology of European Reports on Japan, 1543–1640*. Berkeley: University of California Press, 1965.

Lamers, Jeroen P. *Japonius Tyrannus: The Japanese Warlord Oda Nobunaga Reconsidered*. Leiden, Netherlands: Hotei Publishing, 2000.

Ôta Gyûichi. *The Chronicle of Lord Nobunaga*. Translated by J. S. A. Elisonas and J. P. Lamers. Boston: Brill, 2011.

Pitelka, Morgan. *Spectacular Accumulation: Material Culture, Tokugawa Ieyasu, and Samurai Sociability*. Honolulu: University of Hawai'i Press, 2016.

Sansom, George. *History of Japan, 1334–1615*. Stanford, CA: Stanford University Press, 1961.

Ogyû Sorai. See *Seidan (Discourse on Government)*

Odano Naotake (1749–1780)

Born in Kakunodate, Odano Naotake was a retainer of the daimyo Satake Yoshiatsu of Akita domain (today, Akita prefecture). The fourth of five children fathered by Odano Naokata, a domain instructor of spearmanship (*sôjutsu shinan*), Nao-take developed an unusual facility with art from an early age. In fact, one of his paintings, which he completed when he was twelve years old, still exists in Kaku-nodate. As a young boy Naotake engaged in the Confucian-based academic stud-ies that most samurai male children undertook but also began his formal study of painting, in the Kano school, from the age of fifteen under the tutelage of Takeda Enseki, an artist in the official employ of the domain.

Odano Naotake's life was changed when he met Hiraga Gennai (1728–1780), a samurai from Takamatsu domain who later became a *rônin*. Gennai was a Dutch scholar, well versed in Western science as well as in Western (oil) painting. He had been summoned from Edo, where he was residing after becoming a *rônin*, to Akita to advise the lord, Satake Yoshiatsu, on copper mining technology. (Akita was a major producer of copper during the Edo period.) As a result, Odano was sent by his lord to study with Gennai in Edo, which he did for five years. Although Oda-no's official mission was to study metallurgy, he ended up devoting the majority of his time in Edo to learning the techniques of Western-style painting and interact-ing there with Gennai and other prominent Dutch scholars.

Odano's study of Western art progressed well, such that in 1774 Hiraga Gennai introduced Naotake to Sugita Gempaku, whom he knew was looking for an artist to produce the illustrations for *Kaitai shinsho* (*New Book of Anatomy*), a Japanese translation from *Anatomische Tabellen* (1725) by the German doctor Johannes Kulm. As a result, Odano did complete the illustrations for the volume, which became an early, influential work on Western medicine and anatomy but also had a larger impact on intellectual thought in Japan.

Odano remained in Edo, where his lord, Satake Yoshiatsu (1748–1785), became impressed by his retainer's progress in acquiring Western artistic skills and asked for lessons during his period of alternate attendance there. A quick study, Yoshi-atsu, who worked under the name Shozan, became one of the time's outstanding Western-style painters. Odano Naotake and Satake Shozan became the center of the Western-style art movement in Akita, known as *Akita ranga*, which included Naotake's brother Naorin and Satake Yoshimi, the castlelan of Kakunodate, a for-tified landed fief within Akita domain. Shozan became one of a small group of daimyo who were proudly infatuated with "things Dutch" (*ranpeki daimyô*) and wrote the first Japanese treatises on Western art.

Odano himself produced a number of paintings, with a broad range of subjects, in the Akita style, which paired traditional Japanese themes and Western techniques of shading and linear perspective. Some of his notable paintings include *Mount Fuji, Irises and a Knife,* and *Children with Dog.* Odano's paintings were the subject of a 2016 exhibition at the Suntory Art Museum in Tokyo. Some images of his paintings can be viewed in the website "List of Cultural Property of Japan—paintings (Akita)."

Naotake returned to Kakunodate at the end of 1777 and reunited, if only tempo-rarily, with his family after a five-year absence. He received an appointment as the lord's painting companion (*oku goyô e oaite*). Together they produced many paint-ings, most of which unfortunately were destroyed in a fire which struck the castle that year. The following autumn, when Satake Yoshiatsu was required to perform

Painting of the iconic Mt. Fuji, color on silk, hanging scroll diptych, by Odano Naotake (1749–1780), a samurai from Kakunodate. He was a leading figure in the western style of painting and helped to spread it in the Akita region. (The Picture Art Collection/ Alamy Stock Photo)

the alternate attendance again, Odano was ordered to accompany his lord to Edo so they could continue their artistic work. In Edo, Odano for some reason drew the ire of his lord, and he was ordered to return home under domiciliary confinement. Some have postulated that lord Satake took this action because of Naotake's relationship with his former teacher, Hiraga Gennai, who murdered a man in Edo in a fit of rage. Odano returned home but died less than half a year later, again under circumstances that remain unclear. His death may have been due to illness, but some scholars maintain that he committed ritual suicide due to his involvement with Gennai. Ironically, the day following Naotake's death a document was delivered to his home lifting his punishment.

Whatever the cause of his death, Odano's promising career was cut short by an early death in 1780, at the age of thirty-one. Nonetheless, he made his mark as the central figure in the new, albeit short-lived, Akita style of painting.

Naotake's family home in Kakunodate burned down in 1900 but was rebuilt in its Edo-period style and plan and operates as a museum today. The residence has been designated by Kakunodate city as a historic sight.

Further Reading
Hayashi Masataka and Takahashi Yûshichi. *Odano-ke: Kakunodate no buke yashiki* [The Odano Household: A Warrior Residence in Kakunodate]. Senboku-shi kyôiku iinkai, 2006.

Nomura Toshio. *Odano Naotake no shôgai* [The Life of Odano Naotake]. Tokyo: Kankôdô, 1995.

Screech, Timon. *The Shogun's Painted Culture: Fear and Creativity in the Japanese States, 1760–1829*. London: Reaktion Books, 2000.

Ômurôchûki (Diary of a Parrot in a Cage)

Asahi Monzaemon Shigeaki, a middle-ranking samurai from Nagoya castle town (Owari domain) with a fief of 100 *koku*, maintained a diary from 1684 to 1717, which he entitled *Ômurôchûki* (*Diary of a Parrot in a Cage*). It traced his life from the age of seventeen until the year before his death at age forty-five, by which time he had become a grandparent. It contains wonderful descriptions of the daily life of Shigeaki and his circle of friends, gossip from all over Japan, copies of regulations and directives issued by the domain, and his own social commentary. The title he selected may seem to infer that he was simply a passive recorder of events, but the fact that he was observing them from a "secured" environment, a cage, may also suggest a critical attitude toward the conditions of his life as a middle-ranking retainer in a large domain, one with close ties to the Tokugawa shogunate.

Indeed, a number of the criticisms that he makes of important people in his social world strongly suggest that Shigeaki's diary was not meant to be read easily by others. This is evident in part from some of the content of the diary (discussed below), but also from the fact that he uses abbreviated language that is sometimes difficult to interpret and "deliberately encoded his language in obscure, incorrectly used or invented *kanji* [Chinese characters], and in a dense pseudo-*kanbun* style" (Roberts, 1995, 25).

Shigeaki was able to record a wide variety of events that came to his attention while residing in Nagoya, the castle town of one of the Three Related Houses (the *gosanke*, namely the daimyo houses of Owari, Kii, and Mito domains), in central Japan. He recorded, for example, lord Asano Naganori's attack on Kira Kosuno-suke in Edo castle in 1701, an event that led to Asano's forced *seppuku* (ritual suicide), confiscation of domain, and forty-six retainers' almost two-year mission to kill Kira (although he does not mention the revenge of the forty-six). Shigeaki mentions the enormous earthquake he experienced while drinking sake at a dinner party that led the following month to a major eruption of Mt. Fuji in 1707. He also recorded news about major fires that occurred in Edo, such as the one in 1695 when almost 400 men and women were consumed by the flames inside the compound of the lord of Kii domain, but also stories about peasant farmers from distant parts of the country.

Although much of the diary consists of observations, there is also a fair amount of political and social commentary, which could have gotten him into serious trouble. Shigeaki was, for example, critical of the policies of the fifth shogun, Tsunayoshi, for his laws of mercy and compassion, which forbade many types of violence against animals but called for severe punishments for humans who broke these laws. When the shogun died, Shigeaki recorded that he failed to obey the injunction against parties or singing; instead, showing great disrespect, he invited friends over to his house and served sake and whale meat. He was also critical of his own lord, the daimyo of Nagoya, for his sexual depravity and greediness, the latter which Shigeaki saw as bringing poverty on his people.

The diary also contains many accounts of questionable activities—some personal transgressions, some illegal activities—which he and his friends carried out themselves. Shigeaki records with some regularity his drinking sake with friends, a pastime which he and his fellow samurai often carried to excess. He even records stories of samurai who were banished, and a daimyo who was disenfeoffed, because of incidents they caused after consuming excessive amounts of alcohol. Shigeaki also frequently gambled, which was prohibited by the domain and strictly but irregularly punished (with banishment or even forced *seppuku*). He couched much of these accounts in obscure language, but it is clear that as a result of his own weakness for gambling that he had to sell one of his swords and later even a suit of armor in order to pay off his debts. He also records his great love of the theater, particularly the puppet theater (*ningyô jôruri*), which samurai, of course, were prohibited from attending, as well as all forms of popular theater. Shigeaki records that he was so engrossed in watching a street performance that he failed to notice that his short sword had been stolen out of its sheath—a true disgrace as a samurai that in another day might have led to his *seppuku*.

Shigeaki himself appears to have been a peaceful, if not timid, person, but he records numerous accounts of street murders (*tsuji kiri*) and other types of murders of a wide range of people, which seems to suggest that below the peace that was taking place at the national level with no wars there was still a fair amount of violence in Tokugawa society.

See also: Akô Incident; *Aru Meiji-jin no kiroku: Aizu-jin Shiba Gorô no isho (Remembering Aizu)*

Further Reading

Bodart-Bailey, Beatrice M. *The Dog Shogun: The Personality and Policies of Tokugawa Tsunayoshi*. Honolulu: University of Hawai'i Press, 2006.

Kôsaka Jirô. *Genroku otatami bugyô no nikki* [The Diary of the Magistrate of the Tatami Mats]. Chûô kôron, 1985.

Roberts, Luke. "A Transgressive Life: The Diary of a Genroku Samurai." *Early Modern Japan* (December 1995), 25–30.

Ôshio Heihachirô (1793–1837)

A samurai who served for a time as a police official (*yoriki*) working under the city magistrate in Ôsaka, Ôshio Heihachirô was a Neo-Confucian scholar of the Wang Yangming (*yômeigaku*) school who led a rebellion against the Tokugawa shogunate in 1837, the first such rebellion since that of Yui Shôsetsu (1605–1651) in 1651.

Ôshio was born to a minor shogunal vassal in Osaka but was raised by a grandmother after his parents' death. He was adopted by a police officer in the same city, one of sixty *yoriki* in the city, and later succeeded to his post. He married the daughter of a wealthy farmer, which perhaps helped sensitize him to conditions in the countryside. As a city police official, he tried unsuccessfully to fight rampant corruption and crime, generating resentment among his fellow officers. Tiring of indifference of his fellow policemen, he resigned his post, ending a fourteen-year career as a dedicated official of the shogunate, and took up a life of teaching and study of Neo-Confucianism of the Wang Yangming school, which called for the unity of thought and action.

Although Ôshio's students were from all social status groups and on a certain level he believed that the true nature of all men was the same, he also believed that he was a sage hero who had a moral duty to save the people. When his petitions to the city magistrate (his former overlord) to distribute reserve rice to the people was rejected, Ôshio sold his library, giving some of the proceeds to the needy and using the rest to buy weapons: a small cannon, a few shoulder arms, and several hundred swords. He then drafted a manifesto, a summons to revolt, addressing it, and distributing it, to villagers and village officials in nearby provinces.

Ôshio's manifesto, entitled *Gekibun* (*A Call to Arms*), is a condemnation of the corruption and immorality of the very government that he worked for—a government which he saw as doing nothing to help the poor and desperate. The crisis that he described, referred to by historians as the Tenpô crisis (after the Tenpô era, 1830–1843), was marked by worsening fiscal problems and harvest failures, the latter occurring in 1833 and 1836:

> Since the time of Ashikaga Takauji [the first Ashikaga shogun], the Son of Heaven has been removed from participating in government and has been deprived of the power to distribute rewards and punishments. Therefore the rancor of the people no longer has a place of appeal and has reached to heaven itself. In response, Heaven has sent down a long series of calamities. Forgetting the "humanness that unites all beings as one body," the officials of the Osaka magistrate's office are conducting the government for their own selfish ends. They send tribute rice to Edo, but they send none to Kyoto, where the emperor himself resides. On top of this, in recent years the moneyed merchants of Osaka have accumulated vast profits from interest in loans to the daimyo and appropriated great quantities of rice, living a life of unheard-of luxury. . . . Knowing no want themselves, they have lost all fear of Heaven's punishment and make no attempt to save those who are begging and starving to death on the streets. ("Ôshio's Protest," 2008)

He chastised the shogunate for shipping rice from Osaka to Edo even when it was scarce and expensive in Osaka and reminded his fellow countrymen that the shogun could lose heaven's blessings if the people were driven to desperation. The document reveals that he believed that the people were full of bitterness and resentment due to the dire conditions they were facing.

Together with his twenty companions, Ôshio's plan was to attack the magistrate's office and set fire to the homes of wealthy merchants. The smoke from the fire would be a signal for villagers in the surrounding area to rise up. Although his plans were betrayed, he launched the rebellion anyway on February 19, 1837. Despite the banners that he followers carried—"Save the People" and "The Great Shrine of the Goddess Amaterasu"—few villagers joined him, and the rebellion was suppressed within a few hours. Nevetheless Ôshio and his men had managed to burn down a quarter of the city before fleeing. Some of his followers committed suicide while Ôshio was apprehended in Osaka about a month later. He committed *seppuku* just before being captured by shogunate forces.

Although shogunate leaders sought to minimize the importance of Ôshio's Rebellion, some villagers in the Kyoto-Osaka area revered him as if he were a deity. Three months after learning of Ôshio's revolt, Ikuta Yorozu, a former samurai from Tatebayashi domain who had become a *rônin* after his calls for radical social reform were ignored, led an attack on a local office of the shogunate in Kashiwazaki; like Ôshio, Ikuta committed suicide before being apprehended by police officials.

Ôshio's Rebellion greatly alarmed samurai officials and contributed to the reform efforts that followed (the Tenpô reforms). His application of Wang Yangming ideas into active revolt was also a source of inspiration for numerous late-Tokugawa political activists.

See also: Shogunate (*bakufu, kôgi*)

Further Reading

Morris, Ivan. "Save the People." In Ivan Morris, *The Nobility of Failure: Tragic Heroes in the History of Japan*, 180–216. New York: Meridian, 1975.

Najita, Tetsu. "Ôshio Heihachirô (1793–1837)." In A. Craig and D. H. Shively, eds., *Personality in Japanese History*, 155–179. Berkeley: University of California Press, 1970.

"Ôshio's Protest." In Wm. Theodore de Bary, *Sources of East Asian Tradition: The Modern Period,* vol. 2, 317. New York: Columbia University Press, 2008.

P

Photographing the Samurai

The camera was brought to Japan in 1854 on Commodore Matthew C. Perry's government-directed mission to open the country to diplomatic and commercial relations. Use of the instrument spread across Japan and allowed foreign and Japanese photographers to record many elements of late-Tokugawa society, leaving us with an important photographic record of the samurai during their closing years. Among those Japanese who became interested in photography, we can include a number of daimyo, such as Shimazu Nariakira (1809–1858) of Satsuma and the samurai and Dutch scholar Sakuma Shôzan (1811–1864).

Photographic studios opened in major urban centers in Japan in the 1850s and 1860s, and although they were largely operated by foreigners, most famously by Felice Beato and Baron Raimund Stillfried von Rathenitz, Japanese were also engaged as photographers under them or operated as freelancers. Ueno Hikoma, for example, was a merchant who purchased a camera from a Dutch merchant in 1860 and photographed various high-ranking officials in Edo (and then Tokyo).

The photographs taken in Japan by both Western and Japanese photographers often were also for foreign (Western) tourists' consumption. The photographers catered to this audience and frequently sought to capture an exotic Japan (e.g., geisha, many in seminude poses, actors, decapitated heads at the execution grounds) that travelers could show people upon their return home. Images were taken of Japanese from all walks of life engaged in "traditional" activities, but one famous set of photographs depicted the "transformation" of the samurai, with one image of the samurai in traditional garb and the other of the same man in top hat, morning coat, wearing white gloves. Indeed, some of the samurai seen in studio images had their photos taken as a type of keepsake because in 1871 the government issued a decree that endorsed the removal of topknots and prohibited sword-wearing.

One observer has noted that in these photographs of people one can see the highly differentiated society that was Tokugawa Japan revealed. According to Haruko Iwasaki, "The samurai on the whole tend to look alert; their eyes have a certain daring which would not be found in their counterparts today, the elite government bureaucrats. In a reflection of their class and training, the samurai in portraits refuse to be mere objects: their looks are powerful and focused, as though they were staring into the face of the challenge of the West. In contrast, the faces of townsmen and peasants are generally impassive, in the pose of deference expected of them" (Iwasaki, 1988, 30).

Samurai were photographed not just in Japan but overseas as well. From 1860 to 1868 the Tokugawa shogunate dispatched seven missions overseas, to the United States as well as to Europe, including France and Holland, and these provided ample opportunities for Westerners to photograph samurai. During the shogunate mission to the United States in 1860 to ratify the commercial treaty (Treaty of Amity and Commerce), a number of samurai were photographed in fashionable studios—for example, Charles D. Frederick's photo of a composed-looking samurai in New York sitting in a chair and wearing Western-style shoes. Low-ranking samurai Fukuzawa Yukichi, who served as a translator for the mission, was captured in posed group photos with fellow members of the mission and in a famous, informal photo taken with a young American woman—a photo that he took with him back to Japan. Two years later, he served in a similar role on the shogunate mission to Europe. A photograph of Fukuzawa with some of his samurai colleagues in Utrecht (Netherlands) was recently discovered in Japan. On the shogunate's second mission to Europe, in 1864, a remarkable group photo of about two dozen samurai was taken on a stopover in Egypt of the men gathered below the Sphinx, in full traditional attire. (The photo was taken by A. Beato, the brother of the famous photographer Felice Beato, who operated in Japan.)

See also: Fukuzawa Yûkichi; Magistrates (*bugyô*); Sakuma Shôzan

Further Reading and Viewing

"Felice Beato's Japan: People. An Album by the Pioneer Foreign Photographer in Yokohama." https://ocw.mit.edu/ans7870/21f/21f.027/beato_people/fb2_essay01.html. Accessed July 12, 2018.

Iwasaki, Haruko. "Western Images, Japanese Identities: Cultural Dialogue between East and West in Yokohama Photography." In *A Timely Encounter. Nineteenth-Century Photographs of Japan.* Cambridge, MA: Peabody Museum Press and Wellesley, MA: Wellesley College Museum, 1988.

"Japanese Old Photographs in Bakumatsu-Meiji." Nagasaki University Library Collection. http://oldphoto.lb.nagasaki-u.ac.jp/en. (Searchable by topic, including "samurai.") Accessed July 12, 2018.

"Portraits of Modern Japanese Historical Figures." National Diet Library, Japan. http://www.ndl.go.jp/portrait/e. Accessed July 12, 2018. Searchable by status (e.g., former daimyo, government official) or by name (e.g., Fukuzawa Yukichi, Shimazu Hisamitsu).

A Timely Encounter: Nineteenth-Century Photographs of Japan. Cambridge, MA: Peabody Museum Press and Wellesley, MA: Wellesley College Museum, 1988.

Punishment

During the Tokugawa period the shogunate formalized many aspects of the social system, including penal practices. Tokugawa institutions reflected the principle of differential treatment according to status (*mibun*). In terms of penal practices, there was a unique set of penalties that applied to the samurai status group and which further distinguished them from members of the other social groups (*mibun*), for whom the shogunate devised a much wider range of punishments and methods of execution. In order of increasing severity, the penalties for samurai included: (1) *enryo*; (2) *hissoku* (contrite seclusion); (3) *heimon* (domiciliary confinement); (4) *chikkyo* (solitary confinement); (5) *oshikomi* (forced confinement), in which a samurai in solitary confinement was placed inside a specially constructed cell, typically a bamboo cage, within the residence; (6) *kaieki* (attainder or disenfeoffment, i.e., loss of fief or stipend); (7) *seppuku* (ritual suicide); and (8) *zanshu* (decapitation), which occurred quite rarely. Other types of punishments not included in the above-mentioned list include loss of position (*yakugi toriage*) and forced retirement (*inkyo*), imprisonment, banishment, and monetary fines. When a samurai was punished, his household was often affected as well, particularly in the case of disenfeoffment.

The first four punishments, all types of confinement (or *kinshin*), varied in terms of the degree of confinement and degree of interaction or social intercourse permitted with the world outside the residence. Under the lightest form of punishment, *enryo* (lit., "restraint"), the retainer was required to remain confined to his residence, the main gate of which must remain closed; however, passage in and out through the smaller, side door (*kuguri to*) was permitted. A punishment one degree more severe than enryo was *hissoku* (contrite seclusion); this required a retainer: (1) to remain confined to his residence; (2) to keep the main gates of his residence closed; (3) foot traffic into or out of the residence during the day was not allowed (but discreet traffic through the smaller, side door was permitted); and (4) it called for a period of circumspection or reflection on one's behavior. In effect, this was a type of public shaming that could last from only a few days to up to fifty (a thirty-day period of seclusion was sometimes referred to as *tsutsushimi*). *Hissoku* served as a warning not to persist in a particular behavior or to allow others under one's authority to act in a socially disruptive manner. A male househead might receive such a punishment for the unruly or disrespectful behavior of his sons. For example, when Teshima Kihachi and a group of his friends approached his father, a Tosa domain official, and appealed "in an overly forceful and disrespectful manner" about some government business, their rude behavior, which broke with protocol in that they acted beyond their station in the social hierarchy, drew the attention of other domain officials (Roberts, 2017, 53). The father was punished with *hissoku* for not properly managing his household. The third most severe degree of confinement imposed was *heimon* (lit., "closed gate"), which could last from 50 to 100 days, and meant absolutely no traffic was permitted into or out of the residence. Exceptions were allowed only for a doctor's nighttime visit, to take a dead body to a graveyard, and in the case of fire. Bamboo poles were affixed across the closed gates and rain shutters were closed. *Chikkyo* was a more severe form of solitary confinement imposed; in addition to the terms specified for *heimon* the samurai was required to remain in a single room during the entire time of his sentence. A still more severe form of punishment, *oshikomi* (forced confinement), required the samurai be placed in an even more confined space within a room, typically in a bamboo cage.

Chôshû samurai Yoshida Shôin experienced several periods of house arrest during his short life (1830–1859) as well as other forms of punishment. As penalty for leaving the domain compound in Edo, where he was supposed to spend a year serving his lord, and traveling to northern Japan without permission, Shôin was ordered to return to Chôshû and remain confined at home until his case was adjudicated. Seven months later he was dismissed from service, stripped of his samurai status and stipend, had his name removed from the domain register of

Museum display showing a mannequin of samurai Yoshida Shôin during his period of incarceration at Noyama Prison (1855), an institution reserved for upper-ranking samurai in Chôshû domain. Shôin was imprisoned several times during his short life (1830–1859) but was treated fairly leniently at Noyama Prison, as he was given access to books, paper, brush, and ink so he could continue to study and write. Yoshida Shôin History Museum (Yoshida Shôin rekishikan), located on the premises of Yoshida Shrine (*Shôin jinja*), Hagi (Yamaguchi prefecture). (Photo by Constantine Vaporis)

retainers, and placed in the custody of his father. (Legally, then, he became a *rônin*.) Although he was later reinstated, Shôin subsequently would experience imprisonment in the shogunate's Denmachô prison for his illegal act in trying to travel overseas on Commodore Matthew C. Perry's ship in 1854, followed by imprisonment back home in Chôshû. A little over a year later his prison sentence was canceled, and he was released back to house arrest. In principle he was to remain in the confines of his small room of several tatami mats, but domain authorities unofficially allowed him some freedom to move about the premises of the family residence and grounds. Roughly two years later, he was arrested by the shogunate and transported in a bamboo cage to Edo for questioning. Under questioning he confessed to a plot to kill a top Tokugawa official, for which he was put to death by decapitation.

Looking at the case of domain retainers serving in Edo during their daimyo's period of alternate attendance, or those stationed in Edo long term, allows us to see some of the range of punishable behaviors that samurai demonstrated. Although retainers in Edo tended to engage in many similar behaviors as their counterparts back home, they appeared to have faced many more temptations in the shogunate's capital city that could result in punishment. The penal code from Wakayama, for example, called for a range of punishments for retainers (and their menials) who were caught attending theater (typically kabuki) performances in Edo, including domiciliary confinement and the loss of position and stipend. Of course, the severity of the punishment varied depending on the extent to which domain officials chose to enforce the letter of the law and the individual's past history. Gambling was also considered a serious form of misbehavior for samurai and often resulted in a retainer serving in Edo being sent home, which no doubt served as a kind of social shaming. Minor infractions, such as when Tosa retainer Yoshimatsu Kogorô failed to obey the gate guard's command to halt and exited the domain compound, could result in domiciliary confinement. Minor dereliction of duty or failure to obey some regulation could result in either a monetary fine or domiciliary confinement. Records for the nineteenth century reveal that three days' confinement was the standard punishment for Tosa samurai in Edo, for a light offense such as leaving one's guard post while on duty. Of course, fighting had more serious consequences. Depending on the circumstances, engaging in a nonlethal quarrel could result in banishment, loss of position, or disenfeoffment. When one party to a conflict was seriously wounded or killed, the other usually committed suicide. A special holding cell appears to have existed in every domain's main compound in Edo; it was likely there that retainers were held in custody until *seppuku* could be enforced.

The shogunate could punish the daimyo in a number of ways and for a variety of reasons. Over the course of the Tokugawa period 195 daimyo were punished with confiscation of their domains: under Ieyasu (1601–1616), forty-one; under Hidetada (1618–1631), thirty-eight; under Iemitsu (1632–1650), forty-six; under Ietsuna (1651–1679), twenty-eight; and under Tsunayoshi (1680–1709), forty-five. The confiscations began after the Battle of Sekigahara (1600), when a large number of daimyo families were destroyed, including the Ukita of Bizen, the Chôsogabe of Tosa, the Konishi, and the Masuda. Other daimyo were punished with the confiscation of large tracts of their domains; for example, the Môri of Hiroshima were reduced from eight to two provinces, while the Uesugi of Aizu lost three-quarters of their landholdings in the northeast. Early in the period, from 1615 to 1650, as many as ninety-five daimyo lost their domains or substantial parts of them. During this period, forty-one daimyo lost their domains and status for failing to produce an heir (or more precisely an heir that the shogunate would accept). In part due to the shogunate's allowance for deathbed adoptions in 1651, but also due to a relative relaxation of Tokugawa controls on the daimyo, the number of confiscations decreased over time: from an average of three per year between 1616 and 1651 to fewer than one a year from 1652 to 1867. Similarly, the number of domain transfers also were greatly reduced over time: from 1616 to 1651, 205 transfers (almost six per year) and a total of 306 (an average of 1.4 per year) over the succeeding 215 years.

A relatively small number (fourteen) of confiscations of daimyo domains were a direct result of an abrogation of the *Laws for the Warrior Houses* (*Buke shohatto*). These *Laws*, which were promulgated periodically beginning in 1615, established a set of guidelines, or code of conduct, for the daimyo. Although they specified that domain laws should follow those of the shogunate, the majority of the articles were directed at the person of the daimyo. They were largely exhortatory, aimed at encouraging the daimyo to behave in certain ways and to follow certain practices. In fourteen instances a daimyo was punished for a violation of the *Laws*, and all of them involved the personal behavior of the daimyo, such as making a private marriage contract, visiting the licensed quarters or other immoral acts, concealing a criminal, or making unapproved castle repairs.

When a daimyo or samurai in general was disenfeoffed, his family line usually was extinguished (*oie danzetsu*). For example, when Lord Asano Naganori was ordered to commit *seppuku* for having attempted to kill Lord Kira Kôzunosuke in Edo Castle in 1701, the Asano daimyo family line was also extinguished. (His brother, the bannerman Asano Daigaku Nagahiro, given his close relation to Naganori, was automatically punished with house arrest and then exile. He was later reinstated as a bannerman but with a much reduced fief. The extinguishment of a daimyo family line, however, did not always mean the samurai in question's death. In some cases while the stipend or fief was confiscated and the family line extinguished, but the daimyo simply became a *rônin*, or masterless samurai.

In general, after 1651 daimyo were treated with notable forbearance. Those who were punished received light reproofs for offenses that likely would have cost their predecessors with confiscation of their domains. Public dissension among a daimyo's vassals resulted in at least seven daimyo their fiefs during the first half century of Tokugawa rule; but thereafter it was usually punished with just a reprimand or brief period of house arrest. The shogunate appeared even to become more tolerant of mental instability or gross misgovernment, as in the case of Matsudaira Sadashige, the daimyo of Kuwana, who in 1710 carried out the execution of not only an official who had been cheating him but of a large number of his family members, including his octogenarian mother. For this, and for banishing or dismissing a large number of other officials, Sadashige was simply transferred to another domain. In only a singular instance during he Tokugawa period was a daimyo beheaded for misrule; such was the case of Matsukura Katsuie, the lord of Shimabara, in whose domain arose the Shimabara Rebellion of 1637–1638.

The reach of the shogunate could extend beyond the daimyo and its direct retainers (the bannermen and the housemen) and impact samurai intellectuals in the domains who expressed opinions publicly at odds with Tokugawa policy or which just happened to displease a shogun or his top officials. Despite having had his opinions solicited by officials of the shogunate in the 1680s, the samurai Kumazawa Banzan was ordered into strict confinement in Koga domain, under the control of the daimyo Matsudaira Tadayuki, after he submitted a lengthy memorial critical of current Tokugawa practice, including a call for a reduction in the period of alternate attendance service and a return of samurai to the land—that is, an end of the policy of *heinô bunri*, or the separation of samurai and peasant. Another well-known samurai who was ordered into domiciliary confinement by the shogunate for his views was Watanabe Kazan. An artist and Dutch scholar (*rangakusha*) who as a boy had served as a playmate for the daimyo of Tahara domain and as an adult held the position of elder (*karô*), Kazan was arrested in 1839. While imprisoned he was interviewed by shogunate officials four times on suspicion of having criticized the Tokugawa in his writing. The verdict was slow in coming and was rather lenient, given his confession. Rather than the beheading that was recommended by one officer, Kazan was ordered into house arrest in his own official residence in Tahara, essentially into exile, rather than in Edo, where he had been living. Due to his straightened financial situation, however, he painted and sold pictures, even though he was likely aware that this activity could lead to his being denounced for improper behavior while under house arrest. He also provided his enemies with ammunition against him by meeting with a constant stream of visitors who came to seek his counsel. Kazan, ever the faithful retainer, grew distressed over the anxiety that his imprudent behavior was causing his lord and decided to end his life, by *seppuku*.

The shogunate could, and did, periodically punish daimyo and domain samurai whose political behavior was viewed as threatening, particularly late in the period when the Tokugawa faced opposition to its foreign policy, particularly its treaties with the United States, Russia, and the other Western powers. During the years 1858–1860, the shogunate's great elder (*tairô*) Ii Naosuke punished more than one hundred people, mostly samurai, forcing men out of positions within the *bakufu* or from domain leadership, placing daimyo such as Mito Nariaki, Hitotsubashi Yoshinobu, Matsudaira Shungaku, and Yamauchi Yôdô under house arrest while executing radicalized domain samurai such as Yoshida Shôin and Hashimoto Sanai.

A daimyo could, however, also face punishment from his own administrative authorities. He could be subject to a type of house arrest mentioned above known as *oshikome* (lit., "forced confinement"). Such action was taken against a daimyo when excessive cruelty was evident or when there was mismanagement on his part in domanial administration. If a daimyo did not heed any warnings from his retainers, he could be imprisoned under the direction of the domain elders. He could be released after a period of time, if he expressed his regrets, or forced to retire in favor of his lawful son, if he was unrepentant. For example, Arima Norifusa, the sixth daimyo of Kurume domain, was forced into retirement by a group of high-ranking retainers in 1729. Norifusa had been attempting to rectify the domain's severe financial problems: by reorganizing the bureaucratic structure of the fief, dismissing forty-eight officials, appointed due to their high rank, and replacing them with lower-ranking ones with financial acumen; abolishing the system of local fiefs, making all retainers salaried; and raising taxes in the countryside. The daimyo's forceful attempts to improve the domain's fiscal condition attacked the authority of his top retainers and increased the tax burden on the countryside, resulting in a peasant rebellion in which 5,800 people participated and the opposition of former top-ranking officials, led by a domain elder, Inatsugu Masasane. Seeing no alternative path, Norifusa stepped down as daimyo in favor of his son. In another case, the seventh daimyo of Okazaki, Mizuno Tadatoki (a cousin of Tokugawa Ieyasu's mother), sought to centralize authority to facilitate the implementation of a drastic reform program. Like Arima Norifusa, Tadatoki similarly challenged the authority of high-ranking retainers, in his case by abolishing the system of hereditary ranks and appointing talented people of low rank. After many high-ranking officials were ordered out of office and forced into retirement, the elders and a group of high-ranking retainers moved in opposition to the lord by refusing to attend the New Year's audience. Dissent spread among all full samurai (retainers who were of sufficient rank to attend an audience with the lord), who also refused to attend. The daimyo contemplated what course of action to take—use military force to crush the opposition, commit *seppuku*, or yield to the retainers' demands—opting to accept their demands and dismiss all of his closest advisers. When Tadatoki reacted to his political defeat by spending much of his time in the Yoshiwara red-light district of Edo and squandering the domain's finances, his retainers faced off with him again. Directly addressing Tadatoki, the domain elders addressed him, baldly stating: "Your conduct is not befitting, and you ought to be more prudent" (Quoted in Kasaya, 2000, 68). They then physically restrained him, took his swords, and placed him in "forced confinement." Having no other option other than *seppuku*, Tadatoki retired, claiming ill health, and was replaced by a relative, Mizuno Tadatô, who had become Tadatoki's adoptive son. Although *oshikome* could be used as a punishment for misconduct, to prevent a daimyo from becoming a poor leader or a tyrant, it could also be used to check the power of the lord vis-à-vis his high-ranking retainers.

Shifting gears from the daimyo to the samurai in general, it is clear that while samurai enjoyed a number of legal privileges, including the customary right to cut down a commoner who acted in a disrespectful manner, they were also held to a higher standard of behavior than members of the other status groups below them. For example, although commoners were executed for theft only if the value of the stolen property was particularly large, for samurai it was customary that any theft was punishable with death "regardless of the circumstances." This principle was clearly stated in a judgment handed down by the shogunate's top legal council in 1819: "Because of their high status, members of the warrior houses who commit thefts or other such evil acts are to be handled differently and punished with considerably more severity than townsfolk or peasants" (Quoted in Botsman, 2005, 72). The best-known example of a status-specific punishment was *seppuku*, death by disembowelment, which was carried out by samurai, who generally were spared the most painful capital punishments inflicted on commoners, burning alive or crucifixion. *Seppuku* was usually conducted within the grounds of a jail complex or in some special cases, as in the punishment of the forty-six Akô *rônin*, behind the walls of a daimyo compound. *Seppuku* was more often than not a ritualized form of beheading, since it rarely involved actual disembowelment: a fellow samurai acting, as second (*kaishakunin*), beheaded the criminal once he reached toward his short sword (*wakizashi*), which in some cases could a symbolic, wooden one.

Also, as one might suspect in a stratified society like Tokugawa Japan, different ranks of *bushi* were treated differently. In some cases, the lowest rungs of the retainer hierarchy were not expected to maintain the same high standards. According to a judgment from the shogunate (1807), "[E]ven among warrior retainers, when foot soldiers and lackeys (*chûgen*), commit theft, they are punished in the same way as townsfolk and peasants" (Quoted in Botsman, 2005, 72). In other cases, though, according to regulations issued in 1792, foot soldiers and lackeys who engaged in gambling were to be automatically banished from Edo. Although this punishment was not as severe as that imposed on higher-ranking samurai for the same crime (they were to be exiled to a distant island), the penalty was more severe than the fines usually used to punish commoners who gambled.

Sons in samurai families were of course subject to the authority of the male head of the household. The Matsushiro domain samurai Sakuma Shôzan (1811–1864), for example, was punished by his father with house arrest for three years after he had cursed the son of a high-ranking samurai, an elder, after the son's father, a domain elder, reprimanded Shôzan's father. Shôzan had a strong personality and occasionally bristled at the strictures of the hereditary status system. His father punished him in hopes that Shôzan would reform himself and become less rebellious. Similarly, when Katsu Kokichi (1802–1850), the son and heir of a Tokugawa bannerman, ran away for a second time he was punished with a more severe form of house arrest, *oshikomi* (forced confinement), and placed in solitary confinement inside a bamboo cage. In doing so, his father said to Kokichi:

> I hope you realize that you've been behaving very badly, because I am ordering you to stay home for a while. I want you to think long and hard about your life. You'll find that the answers won't come easily, so you might as well take your time straightening things out—a couple of years even. And since people ought to have a measure of learning, it wouldn't hurt if you looked at some books, too. (Quoted in Katsu Kokichi, 1988, 68)

Kokichi was thrown in a cage the size of three tatami mats (each about 3×6 feet), where he spent the following three years. Indeed, he did study hard and sought to reform himself by applying for a government post after his release.

See also: Akô Incident; Alternate Attendance (*sankin kôtai*); Disrespect Killing (*bureiuchi*); Kumazawa Banzan; *Laws for the Military Houses* (*buke shohatto*); Separation of Warrior and Peasant (*heinô bunri*); *Seppuku* (Ritual Suicide); Watanabe Kazan

Further Reading

Botsman, Daniel V. *Punishment and Power in the Making of Modern Japan*. Princeton, NJ: Princeton University Press, 2005.

Kasaya, Kazuhiko. *The Origin and Development of Japanese-Style Organization*. Kyoto: International Research Center for Japanese Studies, 2000.

Katsu Kokichi. *Musui's Story: The Autobiography of a Tokugawa Samurai*. Translated by Teruko Craig. Tucson, AZ: University of Arizona Press, 1988.

Keene, Donald. *Frog in the Well: Portraits of Japan by Watanabe Kazan, 1793–1841*. New York: Columbia University Press, 2006.

Roberts, Luke S. "Growing Up Manly: Male Samurai Childhood in Late Edo-Era Tosa." In Sabine Fruhstuck and Anne Walthall, eds., *Child's Play: Multi-Sensory Histories of Children and Childhood in Japan*, 41–59. Berkeley: University of California Press, 2017.

R

Refuge-Seeking (*kakekomi*)

In the Tokugawa political order there was a fundamental tension between the need of the state to maintain civil order and a *bushi*'s identity as a warrior. Under certain circumstances a *bushi* was compelled to avenge the unwarranted killing of a social superior, an act known as *katakiuchi*, but had to seek formal permission to do so. Armed combat between *bushi* under other circumstances was referred to as *kenka* (lit., a "fight"), which was an illegal act. The *Laws for the Warrior Houses* (*buke shohatto*) prohibited giving shelter to *bushi* seeking refuge (*kakekomi*) after committing an act of bloodshed (*ninjô jiken*). However, there is evidence from cases as early as the mid-seventeenth century that this was indeed taking place, as happened when a page in the employ of Ôkubo Tadayori killed his overlord and climbed over the wall into the adjoining daimyo compound. The officials there asked to have the assailant turned over to them, but they were refused. According to the *buke jûyôki*, an early eighteenth-century primer on *shidô* (the way of the warrior), a warrior seeking refuge should not be handed over summarily to his pursuers, even if he has committed an injustice (*fugi*), such as stealing or killing his master. Implicit here is the notion that the granting of refuge should be automatic. That this was generally accepted in *bushi* society is even confirmed by an undated example, discussed in an early-nineteenth-century source, in which the killer was handed over. Two men quarreled; a bannerman (*hatamoto*) struck down the other *bushi* of undetermined status and fled the scene, seeking refuge in the main compound of Kii domain. The shogunate summoned officials from Kii and ordered that the assailant be turned over, but the official from Kii, the domain elder, acting in the lord's absence, refused to comply. Later the lord admonished his official, saying, "I understand that a *bushi* seeking refuge should not be turned over" (*kakekomi mono o dasanu wa mochiron no koto nari*) but cited Kii's special relationship with the shogunate as one of the Three Related Houses (*gosanke*) as compelling them to obey.

According to *Hagakure*, in a similar case that took place in Kyoto in 1697, a *bushi* who reported killing another in a fight sought refuge in the compound of Arima domain. Someone related to the murdered man tracked the assailant to Arima's compound but was told the man was not inside. He demanded to see proof of this with his own eyes but was twice refused. Still declining to take "no" for an answer, domain guards were forced to draw their swords before he would leave. The same occurred in Edo as well: Nambu domain regulations for its Edo compounds dating from 1742 instructed guards to prevent a pursuer from entering the premises to seek revenge on a man given refuge and to say that the man he was looking for was not there, even if the guard knew that the pursuer saw him enter the compound. In the Kyoto case just mentioned, since bystanders had seen the assailant enter the compound the pursuer was not easily put off and took his case to the city magistrate. However, Arima officials assisted the killer by allowing him to escape through the rear gate (and probably by also giving him some money as well). The Kyoto magistrate, a representative of Tokugawa authority, requested entry, which was declined, but he nonetheless accepted the Arima officials' declaration, in writing, without a physical inspection of the premises, that the man was not present there. According to the domain official from Arima, declining to assist a refuge-seeker would "entail a loss of honor" (*gaibun o ushinai sôrô gi, menmoku nashi*).

Granting an assailant refuge implied that he was being pursued by a revenge-seeker. Requesting such assistance, the assailant knew that there was a high probability that he would be protected; in fact, in some cases guards were dispatched to accompany the man away from Edo, even as far as the *sekisho* (barrier) at Hakone. Furthermore, there was the expectation that the assailant would be given money in order to make good his escape. This is evident from cases such as that of a commoner without fixed abode from Iyo Saijô who tried passing himself off as Hayashi Rokuemon, a retainer of Matsudaira Sanuki no kami. In seeking refuge at Kurobane domain's Edo compound he invented a story, stating to officials there that he had borne a grudge (*ikon*) against a man named Nagano Tokurô and had killed him. An investigation revealed his true identity as well as his attempt to commit fraud.

Another example of refuge-seeking involves the famous case of Kawai Matagorô, who killed a fellow retainer of Ikeda domain and fled into the compound of a Tokugawa bannerman in 1630. The Ikeda lord demanded that Kawai be handed over to his authority and even appealed to the Tokugawa when the bannerman refused. The shogunate, however, refrained from involvement in the affair, probably, because the murder was, first of all, a crime against Ikeda, but not Tokugawa, law; and second, due to the principle of the independence or extraterritoriality of the bannerman's compound. Kawai later left the bannerman's compound, was located and then avenged by the murdered man's older brother, but this case particularly highlights the principle of seigneurial autonomy and underscores the multilayered nature of political authority in Tokugawa Japan.

Why were assailants given refuge, sometimes even in spite of frequent prohibitions on the same issued by the domains? From the perspective of the unwritten code of behavior of *bushi*, the victor in a fight was not considered a killer or murderer; instead, he was seen as upholding his honor and having acted according to that code. The assumption that the assailant was being pursued was important; his actions in fleeing from a revenge-seeker after having achieved his goal, victory over an opponent, were not therefore considered cowardly. To shelter and assist such a person would be an act of sympathy, a response that demonstrated a "righteous spirit" (*giki*). That many *bushi* may have acted improperly or committed some offense that led to the bloodshed was not relevant, at least in terms of the initial decision to grant refuge. As an early-eighteenth- century text on *shidô* stated, "From early times, *bushi* seeking refuge were rarely turned out. This is the warrior's law (*bushi no hô*)." Inside the compounds, the notion of sanctuary or extraterritoriality prevailed, revealing in part the multilayered nature of political authority in Edo.

See also: Hagakure (In the Shadow of Leaves); Laws for the Military Houses (buke shohatto)

Further Reading

Ikegami, Eido. *The Taming of the Samurai: Honorific Individualism and the Making of Modern Japan.* Cambridge, MA: Harvard Univesity Press, 1995.

Kasaya Kazuhiko. "Kinsei buke yashiki kakemomi kankô." *Shiryôkan kenkyû kiyô,* 12 (1980), 211–237.

Resettlement of Samurai (*dochaku*)

A number of Tokugawa intellectuals and domain policymakers advocated reversing the late-sixteenth- and early-seventeenth-century policy of separating warrior and peasant (*heinô bunri*) by removing samurai from the castle towns and resettling them on the land, a process known as *dochaku*. Samurai resettlement was pursued in some domains in times of economic crisis, but the policy of separation largely remained in force across most of Japan for the duration of the Tokugawa period.

A number of samurai intellectuals took public positions, in writing, calling for the resettlement of samurai on the land. An early advocate of reform was Kumazawa Banzan (1619–1691), a samurai who served the lord of Okayama but who also found himself a *rônin* during various parts of his life. In his account *Daigaku wakumon (A Discussion of Public Questions in Light of the Great Learning,* 1686), he was critical of the policies of the Tokugawa shogunate, particularly in advocating for the resettlement of samurai on the land. In the mid-Tokugawa period, Ogyû Sorai (1666–1728) in his treatise *Seidan (Discourse on Government)* recommended the same in 1727 to the shogun Yoshimune. Another example, from late in the Tokugawa period, was Mito samurai Fujita Tôko (1800–1860), who wrote a fourteen-page tract entitled *Dochaku no gi (An Argument for the Return to the Soil).* In this policy paper he cited moral, military, and economic reasons in support of his idea. His plan was to set up groups of samurai in small villages in the periphery around the domain's capital of Mito. By relocating them there the samurai would be close enough to be called on quickly should the need arise, but they would also be able to support themselves through agriculture.

Several domains actually experimented in returning samurai to the soil. Hirosaki, located in the far north of the main island of Honshu where agriculture was difficult, was one of them. To increase domain income, government officials in the 1680s offered retainers, as well as rural samurai (*gôshi*), *rônin*, and commoners tax incentives to bring new land under development. Apparently, large numbers of samurai settled in rural areas and worked the land, but the program increased the authority of landed retainers at the expense of the central domain government. As a result, the domain reversed itself in 1685 and began to convert these newly created landed fiefs into salaried stipends and to collect retainers back in the castle town.

Later, in the 1780s, in response to a major famine (the Tenmei Famine, 1781–1789), which hit northern Japan particularly hard, causing hundreds of thousands of deaths, Hirosaki officials tried again to implement a policy of *dochaku* by forcing the resettlement of thousands of its retainers and their families, a total of perhaps 20,000 people, to farming villages. At first the policy was voluntary, but when it failed to produce many volunteers, the domain in 1784 issued a decree compelling certain specifically designated samurai to work on the soil. The chief architect of the program, domain adviser Mônai Giô, argued that there was a precedent for the policy to be found in the seventeenth-century practice in Hirosaki of placing high-ranking retainers in small rural castles. Mônai saw samurai resettlement as a cure for many of the domain's moral and political problems, arguing that the policy would, among other things, encourage military preparedness among samurai, restore the simple habits of the past, and promote rural prosperity. The end result of the policy would be a restoration of the samurai to their former glory and a transformation of relations between samurai and peasant. According to Mônai, who was greatly influenced by the writings of Ogyû Sorai:

> Such people [resettled samurai] would understand the sentiments of the lower classes, know the suffering of the three estates [peasant, artisan, and merchant], and be well acquainted with farming and geography. Thus, if appointed as administrators, they would not oppress the people, but apply themselves ceaseless to farming and the martial arts. Unconcerned with luxury and pomp, they would naturally grow simple and ingenuous. Thus, even when dealing with their farmers and servants, they would show benevolence and justice and [the farmers and servants] would effortlessly come to know the Way of Heaven. (Mônai Giô, Quoted in Ravina, 1999, 131)

Although the policy was well intentioned, given that samurai had no experience—or perhaps inclination—to farm, particularly under the difficult conditions that life in Tsugaru presented, it is not surprising that the policy was a complete failure. Many of the samurai who were a part of this experiment failed at farming and their finances became worse, forcing the domain to bail them out. Rather than improving the domain's finances, then, the experiment actually increased its indebtedness. Moreover, the domain found that some samurai tried to take advantage of their superior social position and imposed (illegal) levies on the peasantry in an effort to shift the burden of their own poverty to them. This was in opposition to the policy that daimyo took to undercut the independent authority of rural warriors and transfer them into a centrally based and stipended group of military men and administrators. Since Hirosaki's experiment also caused strained relations in the countryside, the domain had no choice but to cancel the program. A policy that was promoted by some of its advocates as a means of promoting better relations between samurai and peasant ironically created more tension between then. The policy was abandoned after five years, and in 1798 all retainers in the countryside were ordered to return to the castle town of Hirosaki.

See also: Rural Samurai (*gôshi*); *Seidan* (*Discourse on Government*); Separation of Warrior and Peasant (*heinô bunri*)

Further Reading

McEwan, J. R. *The Political Writings of Ôgyû Sorai.* Cambridge: Cambridge University Press, 1962.

Ravina, Mark. *Land and Lordship in Early Modern Japan.* Stanford, CA: Stanford University Press, 1999.

Retainer Corps (*kashindan*)

The domain was a military and political organization built on the lord-vassal relationship. The organization of all the retainers (*kachû*) in a daimyo household (*ie*) was known as the *kashindan*, or retainer corps. The daimyo was the titular leader of the daimyo household, which depending on the size of the domain was composed of anywhere from several hundred to thousands of warriors and lesser members, such as secretaries and palanquin bearers. The daimyo household was a military organization and an administrative organization, but over time, as the Tokugawa peace settled in, the administrative side of the role of retainers became more important.

The daimyo household was patterned after the organization of households of local warriors going back as far as the Kamakura period (1185–1333) and involved elements of both actual as well as fictive kinship. Accordingly, all warriors who served the daimyo became retainers in the daimyo's large household (*ie*) and normally remained as such their entire lives. With the Tokugawa peace, retainers (with the possible exception of scholars, artists, and doctors) could not easily change lords, and therefore they became totally dependent on their daimyo. This gave all samurai an interest in promoting the success of the daimyo housechead (the lord).

During the long Tokugawa period, the parallel forms of organization—military and administrative—continued to exist, but with peace the military side of it tended to fossilize over time. In examining the military side of the organization, however, there were two major levels to the retainer corps, upper and lower. In Awa (present-day Tokushima prefecture), a powerful domain with an assessed productive capacity of 270,000 *koku*, the upper level consisted of mounted warriors and was organized in the following order: *daimyô, ichimon/karô, kumigashira, monogashira, hirashi*. Early in the Tokugawa period members of the upper level of hierarchy held their own sub-fiefs; their independent authority was gradually eroded by the daimyo in Awa and across much of Japan, over the course of the seventeenth century, such that the vast majority of upper-level retainers became holders of "fictive" or "paper" fiefs; although there was greater status attached to being a fief holder, even of a fictive fief, in essence they too received stipends just as the lower level of the hierarchy did. [See entry Fief (*chigyô*).] The lower level of the retainer corps served as infantrymen and in order of rank, in many domains, consisted of *kachi, ashigaru, chûgen*, and *komono*; in many domains a number of these were not hereditary in nature.

In the upper level of the retainer corps directly under the daimyo were his chief retainers, a small group of officials (in Awa there were five) known as the domain elders or councilors (*karô*). They handled both military and administrative affairs for the domain. Some of these families, the *ichimon* or collaterals, were related to the daimyo and thus could provide an heir, if needed; also, they were given the privilege of bearing the daimyo surname (in the case of Awa domain, it was the Hachisuka). The majority of the upper level of the retainer corps consisted of *hirashi* or *hirazamurai* (regular warriors). These mounted warriors were organized into *kumi*, which were functional or control units of between twenty to thirty men. A samurai entered the daimyo's service by being enrolled on the service register (*bugenchô*) at a certain rank (*kakaku*) and receiving an assignment to a *kumi*; in Tosa domain (present-day Kôchi prefecture), for example, there were at various times eleven or twelve such groups. After this, the samurai was given an official appointment in the daimyo's army or administration division. As a member of a *kumi* he came under the supervision of a high-level group leader, or *kumigashira*. His treatment within the group was according to rank, and regulations were laid down by the daimyo's administrative staff.

Examining the lower level of Awa's retainer corps, whose members served as infantrymen, the *kachi*, or foot soldiers, who generally were deployed with spears, were the top rank. The core group of infantrymen, though, were the *ashigaru*, who were ranked second; they were armed with either firearms or bows. Both groups, *kachi* and *ashigaru*, were led by talented members of the *hiraishi*, who were upper-level retainers and held appointments as *monogashira* (commander); they held titles such as "commander of the gunners" or "leader of the spearmen." Below the level of *ashigaru* were the *chûgen* and *komono*, both of whom did not engage in battle but rather functioned in a support role, carrying equipment, acting as messengers, and performing a variety of other duties.

Although the daimyo was the top military leader in the domain's military organization, he did not directly command the entire army. Typically, a domain's military organization was divided into between five to ten units, known as *sonae*. In Awa, the five domain elders each held appointments as commanders of one unit; by comparison, in Tosa domain, as noted, there were eleven or twelve. The elders relied on their own retainers to man the inner core of their assigned military unit. Each unit consisted of mounted warrior groups, which were deployed alongside units of *kachi* equipped with spears and units of archers and firearms. In battle, the domain's military force engaged the enemy in three larger groups: the advance group (*sakizonae,* or advance *sonae*); the middle group (*nakazonae*); and then a final group (*hatamotozonae*), typically the largest, which consisted primarily of the army led by the daimyo. The *hatamotozonae* functioned in a largely defensive capacity, serving to protect the daimyo, the domain's top military officer, who planned the course of attack for the entire army. This organization of the army into three major groups was used, in adapted form, as a model for the organization of the daimyo's processions to Edo on alternate attendance.

After the Sieges of Osaka (1614–1615) and the Shimabara Rebellion (1637–1638), Japan experienced peaceful conditions and tremendous economic expansion, which necessitated the further development of the administrative organization through which individual domains could be governed. The civil administrative system, which was an outgrowth of the military administrative organization, continued to evolve in a variety of areas, for example to carry out political duties (such as the creation of laws, judicial decisions, policing), agricultural reform, tax policies, and public welfare activities.

In the civil administrative organization of a domain (Awa domain is detailed in Table 5), military ranks determined a retainer's status (*kaku*), his household's rank, and therefore the administrative positions in which it was possible for him to serve. The rankings became hereditary and therefore very difficult to change. At the top of the organization were the five families who held the heredity status of elders or

Table 5   **Comparison of Samurai Status and Administrative Office in Upper Level of Awa Domain's Retainer Corps**

Status (*kakushiki*) (number of households)	Post (*yakushoku*) (number of positions)
Karô (家老) 5	*Shioki* (仕置) 1
Chûrô (中老) 37	*Toshiyori* (江戸仕置) 9
	Sumoto shioki (須本仕置) 1
	Machi bugyô (町奉行) 1
	Saikyo bugyô (裁許奉行) 1
	Shûmon bugyô (宗門奉行) 1
Monogashira (物頭) 18	*Motojime* (元締) 1
	Metsuke (目付) 1
	Fushin bugyô (普請奉行) 1
	Kôri bugyô (郡奉行) 1
Hirashi (平士) 433	*Kura bugyô* (蔵奉行) 7
	Tsukaiban (使番) 7
	Sakuji bugyô (作事奉行) 6
	Metsuke (目付) 6
	Gundai (郡代) 4
	Ginsatsuba bugyô (銀札場奉行) 2
	Ozenban (御膳番) 6
	Sumoto metsuke (須本目付) 1
	Ataka metsuke (安宅目付) 3
	Umaya metsuke (厩目付) 1
	Aikata (藍方) 1
	Kusurikata (薬方) 2
	Kamikata (紙方) 1
	Ishigaki bugyô (石垣奉行) 1
	Edo rusui (江戸留守居) 1
	Ôsaka rusui (大阪留守居) 1
	Kyôto rusui (京都留守居) 1
	Gakumonsho bugyô (学問所奉行) 1

councilors (*karô*). From among these five families, one person was selected to serve in the highest position in the domain government, a position called *shioki* (executor). Another elder was selected to hold the equivalent position in Edo, where a branch of the domain's government had to be established due to the requirements of alternate attendance, whereby the daimyo were required to split their time between Edo and their domains. Immediately below the elders in status were the *chûrô*, or junior elders, who were some thirty-six or thirty-seven in number. They were from the same families as the elders, also held their positions hereditarily, and were appointed to a number of important offices, such as: adviser to the daimyo (*toshiyori*); judicial magistrate (*saikyo bugyô*), who supervised lawsuits; and magistrate of religious affairs (*shûmon bugyô*), who was in charge of religious affairs, including the suppression of Christianity.

Much of the actual work of domain government was carried out by those retainers who occupied the third level of organization, the *monogashira*. On the battlefield the position was one of great honor (appointees were drawn from the most talented of the *hirashi*); similarly, in the civil administrative side of government that functioned during peacetime, *monogashira* were appointed to some of the most important positions (but only for their lifetime), such as inspectors (*metsuke*), who led criminal investigations; and rural magistrates, who were in charge of the countryside. Although the retainers who occupied the top two ranks in the domain, the elders and junior elders, held their titles hereditarily, many of the *monogashira* were actually chosen on the basis of talent and ability.

Some of the most talented of the *hirashi*, who made up the vast majority of the upper level of the retainer corps, served in several key administrative posts, as noted above. Other *hirashi* occupied the remainder of the important positions in the civil bureaucracy, for example, the magistrate of storehouses, magistrate of construction, and a variety of inspector-type posts.

Status (*kaku*) was used as the basis for appointments to positions in the civil administration in the lower half of the retainer corps as well, although here the focus has been on the upper level only. The shogunate as well as in a number of domains from the early eighteenth century onward adopted a system—the *tashidaka* system—that allowed retainers of low status to be appointed to positions that normally were held by retainers of a higher status. This was done by setting standard levels of stipends (and not simply status) as a guide for determining eligibility for office. Accordingly, through a temporary increase in stipend a retainer of low status could qualify for higher-ranked positions. Retainers also received supplemental income known as *yakudaka*, similar to an office salary, when they served in an administrative post, for as long as they remained in that post.

A retainer's administrative positions changed as he aged and gained more experience. For example, Tosa samurai Mori Yoshiki (1768–1807), a retainer of mounted warrior status (*umamawari*, similar to the *hirashi* of Awa domain), with a fief of 200 *koku*, began his career in domain government at the age of fifteen as a page of the daimyo, Yamauchi Toyochika. When the lord died six years later, he lost his position, but later, in 1795 at the age of twenty-seven, he was appointed to a position as magistrate of ports (*ura bugyô*). He advanced steadily to the highest positions in civil administration (*togawa*) open to a retainer of his status, becoming a chief inspector (*metsuke*) in 1797 and a junior administrator (*shioki yaku*) in 1798. Three years later he became a guardian of the daimyo heir, thus returning to a position related to the lord's family affairs (*kinshû*).

Of course, not all retainers held administrative positions, for there were more retainers than positions; this was true of the shogunate's direct retainers, the *hatamoto* (bannermen) and *gokenin* (housemen), as well. Due to the surfeit of retainers relative to the number of positions, it was common for retainers to share positions, each of them holding it on a rotational basis of several months at a time.

DIVISIONS WITHIN THE RETAINER CORPS

Within the retainer corps there were many gradations in rank and a general division between two categories of a daimyo's retainers that Tokugawa contemporaries and modern historians have referred to as "upper" and "lower" samurai. The terms were often used vaguely during the Tokugawa period, and the meanings of the terms were not precise. Given this, it is not surprising that the number of ranks and the dividing line between the upper and lower categories varied from domain to domain. In Chôshû domain, for example, the 5,675 direct vassals (which excludes sub-vassals) of the daimyo Môri were divided into two groups: *shi* (samurai) and *sotsu* (soldiers). Within each of these groups there were a number of ranks, seventeen of *shi* and twenty-three of *sotsu*. In contrast, in Tosa domain there were five ranks of samurai in the upper half of the retainer corps and five levels of retainers in the lower half.

In the general literature on the samurai all the members of the retainer corps are referred to as samurai; the members of the various ranks in the upper half of the retainer corps are often referred to as "upper samurai" or "full samurai" and those in the lower half as "lower samurai." In fact, though, in most domains none of the members of the lower half of the retainer corps were considered samurai. [In some domains such as Tosa, however, *gôshi* ("rural samurai"), who occupied the top rank of the lower half of the retainer corps, held an anomalous position in that in some respects they were treated as members of the upper half of the retainer corps. For example, *gôshi* had the right to an audience with the lord and had the right to participate in the annual horseback riding ceremony known as *onorizome* along with the *shi*.] The term "samurai" or "shi" was restricted to members of the upper half of the retainer corps; in most domains only they had the right to an audience with the lord and were listed in the official registry of direct retainers of the lord, the *bugenchô*. (Upper) samurai were likely to possess fiefs and subretainers; the domain actually stipulated how many rear vassals an upper samurai was to maintain based on the size of his holding. In seventeenth-century Chôshû, for example, 2.3 vassals were to be maintained for every 100 *koku* of a samurai's holding or stipend; later, in the nineteenth century, this was reduced to two rear retainers for every 100 *koku*. Reality, however, often differed from official regulations; some of the larger fief holders in Chôshû maintained larger numbers of rear vassals than required by domain law while small houses of 100 or less *koku* of income had none. The Masuda house, domain elders with a fief of 12,063 *koku*, for example, maintained 538 vassals of their own (rear vassals); most of these rear vassals received their incomes in stipends, but a few actually possessed fiefs within the Masuda's fief.

It is important to note that in the domain's status system, a rear vassal of *shi* status was lower than a *shi* direct vassal but higher than a direct vassal who was of *sotsu* status. Moreover, a vassal of *sotsu* status was higher than a rear vassal of *sotsu* status.

We can also learn a great deal about the differences between the two main categories of retainers, "upper" and "lower" samurai, from the writings of Fukuzawa Yûkichi (1835–1901), a low-ranking samurai from Nakatsu domain in Kyushu.

Fukuzawa noted that within the two categories "there were as many as a hundred different minute distinctions between their social positions and official duties" (Fukuzawa Yûkichi, 1953, 309). The first, meaning upper, group comprised all samurai from the top councilors down to the Confucian scholars and members of the *koshogumi*, who were attendants to the daimyo. The second, lower group, which made up two-thirds of the retainer corps, included everyone else, men who fulfilled support roles as grooms and stablemen, guards, and foot soldiers. Yûkichi was from one of the top ranks among the lower samurai.

Emphasizing the huge gap that existed between the two groups, Yûkichi wrote that a "lower samurai, whatever his merit or talents, could never rise above an upper samurai." Thus, "[a] lower samurai might therefore aspire to promotion within his own class, but he would no more hope to enter the ranks of the upper samurai than would a four-legged beast hope to fly like a bird" (Fukuzawa, 1953, 310). As a lower samurai, Yûkichi personally felt the inequities of the social system. He explained this in personal terms, writing that, "When within the domain I met some illustrious high retainer or samurai, I was always treated with contempt; even as a child I could not help but feel resentment" (Fukuzawa, 2009, 185). Indeed, as a child he remembers that he and other children of lower samurai "had to speak to those of higher rank in a respectful manner," while those children used an "arrogant" form of address to them. "Then what fun was there in playing together?" he asked, rhetorically (*Autobiography,* 1980 [1966],18). Furthermore, he noted, when a lower samurai encountered an upper samurai on the road, the lower samurai always had to prostrate himself on the ground. Even if it was raining, the lower samurai had to take off his *geta* (footwear resembling clogs) and prostrate himself by the roadside.

There were also great distinctions between upper and lower samurai in a variety of other areas of life, including marriage, education, income, household economy, general rights, and a variety of customs, and these were maintained through regulations issued by the domain. In terms of clothing, when upper samurai went out at night they always wore *hakama* (formal trousers) and were always accompanied by an attendant carrying a lantern; neither of these applied to lower samurai. Most telling of the social hierarchy were differences in permissible modes of transportation: lower samurai were required to travel on foot while upper samurai could own horses and ride on horseback; lower samurai were allowed to ride only when in performance of their official duties. Upper samurai were allowed to hunt boar and to fish, whereas lower samurai did not have those privileges. Yûkichi concluded that, "There were minute distinctions of rank within both the upper and lower classes, yet these were not rigid and immovable. The broad distinction between the upper and lower classes, however, was accepted unquestioningly, almost as though it were a law of nature rather than an invention of man" (Fukuzawa, 1953, 311).

RELATIONSHIP BETWEEN DAIMYO AND VASSALS

The relationship between lord and vassal changed a great deal during the Tokugawa period in relation to the Warring States period (1467–1568). In general

Woodblock print by Hishikawa Moronobu (1618–1694) from the series *Yoshiwara no tei* ("*Scenes in the Yoshiwara*"), ca. 1680. Two samurai (one wearing a sedge hat that disguises his identity) speak to a courtesan in the lobby of a brothel while their attendants (squatting) wait for them; in the foreground, another samurai and his attendant have walked past the brothel but are looking back at a courtesan and her attendants. Samurai were not supposed to visit the licensed quarters but many did, often in disguise. (Art Collection 2/Alamy Stock Photo)

terms, we can say that the relationship during the earlier period was conditional and personal and during the Tokugawa period became unconditional and impersonal. The ties between lord and vassal became unconditional in that with peace it was no longer possible to change lords (with some exceptions, as noted above); during the Warring States period a warrior might change lords in order to advance his career, and he was more likely to have a personal relationship with that lord. During the Tokugawa period a retainer's relationship to the lord became increasingly impersonal and bureaucratic. An upper samurai officially might have the right to an audience with the lord but typically, except for the lord's personal advisers and attendants, the audience would be with a large group of other retainers. He would be able to view the lord (more accurately the lord would be able to view him because the retainer's head would be face down in a bow during the audience), but the relationship would not be intimate.

As loyalty became institutionalized within the structure of Tokugawa society it became increasingly directed toward the daimyo as a status that symbolized the domain. Accordingly, if an individual daimyo acted in a manner that was against the best interests of the daimyo house (*ie*) or threatened the continuation of the domain, a retainer might remonstrate with the lord to correct his behavior or a group of retainers might work together to force the lord to retire. Thus, the retainer's

---

Did Samurai Ever Retire?

There are two main elements to this question. First, in some domain, the head of a samurai household (*buke*) was required to retire, meaning to turn over his position to a son, upon reaching the age of sixty (*kanreki*). He could retire earlier than this age if granted permission by the domain. A head of household could also be forced to retire by the domain or pressured to retire by branch family members. There is, however, no truth to the popular notion that a samurai had to retire when he went bald and could no longer tie his hair in a topknot.

Second, a samurai could also "retire" in the sense of relinquishing his hereditary position and becoming a *rônin*, or masterless samurai; similarly, he could be released from service and lose his hereditary status, a punishment known as *kaieki*, and become a *rônin* by his overlord as punishment for some crime or for failure in the performance of his assigned position (job). Some samurai relinquished their samurai status freely to take up a trade or to pursue a career in the arts free from any obligations to a lord.

---

loyalty toward the lord might be thought of as free-floating in nature—directed to a status and not a person.

See also: Alternate Attendance (*sankin kôtai*); Bannermen (*hatamoto*); Fief (*chigyô*); Horseback Riding Ceremony (*onorizome*); Housemen (*gokenin*); Military Service (*gun'yaku*); Rural Samurai (*gôshi*); Sieges of Osaka (*Ôsaka no jin*); Supplemental Salary (*Tashidaka*) System and Talent

Further Reading

The Autobiography of Yûkichi Fukuzawa. Revised translation by Eiichi Kiyooka, with a foreword by Carmen Blacker. New York: Columbia University Press, 1980 [1966].

Fukuzawa Yûkichi. *An Outline of a Theory of Civilization.* Translated by David A. Dilworth and G. Cameron Hurtst III. New York: Columbia University Press, 2009.

Fukuzawa Yûkichi. "Kyuhanjo." Translated by Carmen Blacker. *Monumenta Nipponica,* IX(1–2) (1953), 304–329.

Hall, John W. "Rule by Status in Tokugawa Japan." *Journal of Japanese Studies,* 1(1) (1974), 39–49.

Kasaya, Kazuhiko. *The Origin and Development of Japanese-Style Organization.* Kyoto: International Research Center for Japanese Studies, 2000.

Roberts, Luke S. "Mori Yoshiki: Samurai Government Officer." In Anne Walthall, ed., *The Human Tradition in Modern Japan,* 25–42. Lanham, MD: Scholarly Resources, 2001.

Revenge-Killing (*katakiuchi*)

Samurai were legally permitted to exercise lethal means against another living person in Tokugawa society under certain conditions. (They could also obtain permission to test a new sword on a corpse.) They could, for example, cut down a commoner who was acting in an offensive manner toward them, a practice known as *burei-uchi*, or "disrespect killing." Such occurrences must have given commoners good pause before trying to cheat a samurai, get in his way on the road, or be verbally abusive. A samurai was also permitted to end the life of his wife (and her lover) if she committed adultery. Yet a third legalized form of lethal violence was revenge-killing (*katakiuchi*), which was sometimes referred to as "vendetta." This meant that a samurai could petition for official permission to carry out a revenge-killing—to avenge the death of a social superior, meaning his father or elder brother who had been murdered by another samurai; a father could not do the same for a son, nor an elder brother for a younger one. There were more than one hundred known cases of legalized revenge during the Edo period, and news of them spread widely through the country through woodblock prints, literature, and the theater; revenge-killing was almost exclusively restricted to samurai, but in a few exceptional cases the Tokugawa shogunate gave permission for a commoner to carry one out. If a samurai avenged someone without permission, or engaged in some other unsanctioned form of violence, he became liable to legal punishment for having engaged in a "fight" (*kenka*).

The most famous case of a revenge-killing, the Akô Incident (1702), strictly speaking, was not a *katakiuchi*, because the forty-seven *rônin* from Akô domain took revenge on a man (the Tokugawa bannerman and master of ceremonies, Kira Kôzunosuke) who did not directly cause the death of their lord (the daimyo Asano Naganori of Akô). Often heralded as an example of the resilience of old notions of feudal loyalty, the Akô Incident, viewed differently, can be regarded as evidence for the deterioration of the same values, for only 46 out of the more than 300 full samurai opted to band together to kill the man they held responsible for their lord's death. Their allegedly selfless devotion in acting, has been questioned, too, by contemporaries and historians alike.

The Tokugawa and domain authorities did want to uphold the values of loyalty to one's overlord by sanctioning authorized revenge-killing. In the case of the forty-six masterless samurai from Akô domain, mentioned above, while shogunal officials compelled them to commit *seppuku* after they took the like of Kira Kôzunosuke, their loyalty to their lord was rewarded in that they were allowed to commit *seppuku* as samurai rather than to have been beheaded (as would have been appropriate to their masterless status); their loyalty was also rewarded in that they were buried by their lord's side at Sengakuji temple in Edo.

Nevertheless, political authorities did not want to encourage multigenerational family feuds. Accordingly, secondary vengeance, or retaliatory revenge, was prohibited by law: once a legally sanctioned vengeance had been carried out, the family of the original killer was not allowed to take any action against the avenger or his family. If a samurai avenged someone without permission, or engaged in some other unsanctioned form of violence, he became liable to legal punishment for having engaged in a "fight" (*kenka*). This, depending on the status of the person killed, could lead to banishment or forced *seppuku*.

It sometime took a samurai seeking revenge a long time to complete his mission, and some in fact never found their man at all. Others were in fact prevented from doing so when the would-be avenger was killed, preemptively, by his intended victim. In the case of Kume Kôtarô (see Document 9A), he was not able to succeed until almost thirty years after having received permission to set out to avenge his father, which itself was ten years after his father's death.

The practice of *katakiuchi* occurred through the Tokugawa period and was abolished by the Meiji government only in 1873. Even after that date, however, there were several occurrences of revenge-killing, although the samurai had ceased to exist as a legal status category.

See also: Akô Incident; Disrespect Killing (*burei-uchi*); Unmaking (Abolition) of the Samurai; Women in Samurai Households (*buke no onna*)

Further Reading and Viewing

"Hana" [Tale of a Reluctant Samurai], dir. Koreeda Hirokawzu, 127 minutes, 2006. Available in DVD. The fictional story of a young samurai named Soza who demurs from avenging the death of his father, despite the social pressure to do so, preferring to live a life of peace and reconciliation.

Ikegami, Eiko. *The Taming of the Samurai: Honorific Individualism and the Making of Modern Japan.* Cambridge, MA, and London, England: Harvard University Press, 1995.

Masahide Bitô, "The Akô Incident of 1701–1703." Translated by Hendry D. Smith II. *Monumenta Nipponica,* 58(2) (2003), 149–170.

Mills, D. E. "*Katakiuchi*: The Practice of Blood-Revenge in Pre-Modern Japan." *Modern Asian Studies,* 10(4) (1976), 525–542.

Ronin (*rônin*)

A samurai could become masterless samurai, or *rônin*, in one of four ways: through the extinction of his lord's family; through his release from service by his lord, sometimes as punishment for an offense committed; by the voluntary renunciation of his ties, and vows of loyalty, to his lord; and, being born the son of a *rônin*. The Japanese term *rônin* literally means "wave person," which indicates that by being released from service, or voluntarily releasing oneself from service, a samurai was breaking ties to his structured political and social life, to be cast adrift on the waves of the society around him. The term predates the Edo period; as early as the Nara period (710–784) it was used to refer to peasants who had moved away from their land, but by the Warring States period (1467–1568), it was used to denote warriors whose employment and income had ceased through loss of their lord. Like samurai, *rônin* wore the same two swords as when they were serving a lord, but they existed outside the formal four-status system. Notable examples of Edo-period *rônin* include Miyamoto Musashi, Arai Hakuseki, Kyokutei Bakin, Kumazawa Banzan, Hiraga Gennai, Yamada Nagamasa, Sakamoto Ryôma, Kiyokawa Hachirô, Yoshida Shôin, and of course the forty-seven *rônin* involved in the Akô Incident.

During the first half of the seventeenth century there was a great deal of social dislocation caused by warfare and the various political actions taken by the first three Tokugawa shoguns. After the Battle of Sekigahara (1600), Tokugawa Ieyasu confiscated from the daimyo on the opposing side landholdings valued at 3,830,000 *koku*. However, he also confiscated the domain of Fukushima Masanori, one of

Ieyasu's most trusted generals, for disobeying his orders. Further attainders (confiscation of domains) and reductions of daimyo domains occurred under Ieyasu's successors, Tokugawa Hidetada (reigned 1616–1623) and Tokugawa Iemitsu (reigned 1623–1651): after the fall of Osaka Castle (Seige of Osaka Castle) and defeat of the forces aligned with the Toyotomi, in 1614–1615. Moreover, as many as sixty daimyo lost their domains simply due their failure to name an heir in accordance with the rules established by the Tokugawa shogunate. All of these events added further to the number of *rônin* created.

Some samurai went in an out of service of a lord, becoming *rônin* at different periods of their life. For example, Nojiri Kazutoshi, the father of Kumazawa Banzan (1619–1691), lived in Kyoto, unable to find a lord to serve. As a result, he had to send his family to Mito to be cared for by his wife's father, who served the daimyo of Mito domain, Tokugawa Yorifusa. Nojiri was able to find a temporary position with Itakura Shigemasa (1588–1638), a hereditary vassal of the Tokugawa, fought at Shimabara on the Tokugawa's side, and was wounded in battle. Six years later, in 1643, he was again released from service but unable to find another lord to take him into service for the rest of his life. The father was then supported by his son, Banzan, who was successful in entering the service of the Ikeda Mitsumasa, daimyo of Okayama.

The large number of samurai who lost their livelihoods in becoming masterless samurai posed a risk to social order early in the seventeenth century. Many of them traveled to Edo to seek new work; and many of them failed to find that work, leading some of them turned to a life of crime, forming street gangs in the shogun's capital. After the Sieges of Osaka (1614–1615), great numbers of *rônin* collected in Kyoto, prompting the highest-ranking official in the city, the Kyôto shoshidai, to issue orders in 1623 to drive them out of the area. One article of the order read: "All rônin trying to enter into the employ of another daimyo should be expelled." The shogunate also included a similar prohibition in its *Laws for the Warrior Houses* (*Buke shohatto*) in 1631 and 1635, admonishing daimyo not to harbor men who had been dismissed by their lords.

Rônin faced numerous difficulties. The shogunate sought to banish them from major cities and prohibited them from taking up new employment with a different lord. Kumazawa Banzan (1619–1691), himself a *rônin*, wrote in his text *Daigaku wakumon* (*Questions on the Great Learning*) about the difficult conditions faced by masterless samurai during the seventeenth century:

> Today the worse off of these people are rônin. There are innumerable cases of their starving to death during the frequent famines. Even rich harvests and the consequent lowering of the price of rice would not give much relief to those who are already hard up. Every year there are many cases of starvation which are unknown to the general public. This is due to the impoverished condition of the feudal lords who are thus forced to stop giving allowances to some of their retainers. The retainers in turn cut off their dependents. (Kumazawa Banzan, 1958, 379)

Some *rônin* were able to live settled lives by pursuing other lines of work other than service to a lord. For example, those with sufficient education could teach in a temple school for commoner children (*terakoya*) or even engage in handicraft wage labor by making commodities such as fans, umbrellas, insect cages, just as some low-ranking domain samurai and Tokugawa housemen did. Others, with considerable martial skills, traveled around the country, engaging in *musha shugyô* (lit., warrior training"), and teaching those skills to commoners. There were also a few cases of *rônin* who traveled overseas, one of whom, Yamada Nagamasa (1590–1630), actually became the governor of a province in Thailand.

Despite what was on the face of it a hardline policy against *rônin* on the part of the shogunate, some ex-samurai of talent were hired by other daimyo, particularly by daimyo who were rewarded with larger territories. Nonetheless, many had to live by their wits or their swords. The latter group took up weapons and joined forces opposing the Tokugawa at Osaka in 1614–1615 and during the Shimabara Rebellion in 1637–1638. Perhaps as many as 100,000 *rônin* joined the Toyotomi forces in Osaka, and as many as 500,000 *rônin* existed during the reign of the third shogun, Tokugawa Iemitsu (reigned 1623–1651). That masterless samurai remained a major problem fifty years after the Battle of Sekigahara is evident from the fact that in 1651 Yui Shôsetsu, an instructor of martial arts, and his co-conspirator Marubashi Chûya, organized a group of *rônin* with the intent of blowing up the shogunate's arsenal in Edo. His plan was to do this on a windy night so that the resulting fires would spread through the city and cause sufficient chaos for Yui and his band of *rônin* to raid Edo Castle and murder high-ranking shogunal officials. Apparently, there were also secondary plans to similar action in Sunpu and Kyoto. Yui's plot was discovered and Chûya was arrested in Edo, while Shôsetsu and some of his accomplices disemboweled themselves once police forces of the shogunate surrounded them in Sunpu while others were captured and later put to death. In the end, thirty-four plotters, in addition to their families and relatives, were put to death.

The plot took the shogunate's senior councilors by surprise. They debated what steps to take, beyond putting those responsible to death. At first the majority advocated for a hardline approach, including expelling all *rônin* from Edo, but in the end the view of councilor Abe Tadaaki prevailed to try to take steps to reduce the number of *rônin*. Perhaps they were in part swayed by the note that Yui left, which explained that he had been forced to take action to bring the hardships of the *rônin* to the shogunate's attention. In any case, Abe successfully advocated for moderating its policy of confiscating domains due to issues with daimyo adoption of heirs. Tokugawa officials also made some efforts to employ more *rônin* in the shogunate, but in large part the problem was solved by the passage of time. By the end of the seventeenth century the number of *rônin* was small.

Later in the Tokugawa period, some samurai actually voluntarily became *rônin* by renouncing their ties to a lord, for a variety of personal reasons. Three notable examples of these voluntary *rônin* are Hiraga Gennai, Takizawa (Kyokutei) Bakin, and Uragami Gyokudô. Hiraga Gennai (1728–1780), a low-ranking samurai from Takamatsu domain on Shikoku Island, formally requested to give up his hereditary responsibility to his family and domain in order to pursue his various interests in Western ("Dutch") studies, or *rangaku*, including Western science and oil painting. He passed on his position as family head to a cousin or brother-in-law and made a formal request to his lord to give up his position as overseer of rice storehouses in Shido-ura, his native area. Gennai's lord granted his petition, freeing him of his responsibilities to Takamatsu, but forbidding him from entering the service of any other domain. By becoming a masterless samurai, Gennai had the freedom to travel to Edo to pursue his various interests and to interact with scholars and artists from around the country who were gathered there. Kyokutei Bakin (1767–1848) decided to renounce his allegiance to Matsudaira Nobunari, a bannerman elevated to the position of daimyo of Ojima domain, and eventually became an accomplished writer; his works often centered on themes related to the samurai, such as loyalty and honor. The third example, Uragami Gykudô (1745–1820), renounced his ties to the daimyo of Bizen Okayama, in order to travel around Japan for seventeen years playing his *ch'in* (Chinese seven-string zither) and developing his considerable talents in painting.

At the end of the Tokugawa period (*bakumatsu*), certain loyalist samurai, known as *shishi*, often renounced their vows of loyalty, freeing themselves of the constraints of service to their lords and left their domains in order to pursue a political agenda in what was perceived as the national interest. Many of these men were antishogunate loyalists, whose slogan was "Revere the Emperor, Expel the Barbarian" (*sonnô jôi*). Yoshida Shôin (1830–1859) was one of the more notable antishogunal loyalist *rônin*, but he was actually dismissed from service by Lord Môri of Chôshû for leaving the domain without written permission. He not only lost his hereditary position at the domain school, the Meirinkan, but his name was removed from the samurai register, and he was placed in the custody of his father, Yurisonuke. Not all late-Tokugawa *rônin* were antishogunal, though; in fact, the shogunate hired a

---

Seven Samurai (Shichinin no samurai)

Seven Samurai (1954) is one of Japanese director Kurosawa Akira's best-known movies. The story is set in the late sixteenth century, prior to the Tokugawa family's establishment of a military government (shogunate). It was a time of chaos, when roving groups of bandits routinely victimized peasants living in villages. It was also a time when Japanese daimyo were waging military campaigns against one another and many samurai found themselves without a lord to follow. These masterless samurai wandered around the countryside searching for employment. In desperation the peasants in one village decide to hire a group of seven men—six samurai and one other man who is accepted as such. The seven men must use all of their resources to defend the village, its crops and people, and defeat the bandits. In the end, the seven prevail, but only three survive the conflict. The villagers celebrate at the end, singing while planting their crops, but for the remaining samurai it was a pyrrhic victory. The leader of the group laments the course of events: "In the end we lost this battle too. The victory belongs to the farmers, not to us."

Seven Samurai has been widely viewed as one of the best Japanese films ever made. The masterfully staged fight scenes were choreographed by martial arts masters of two schools of sword fighting, the Ono-ha itto ryû and the Tenshin shôden katori Shintô–ryû. Kurosawa's movie won the Silver Lion award at the 1954 Venice Film Festival and was nominated for two prizes at the Academy Awards in 1957. It was remade in 1960 as an old Western–style film, *The Manificent Seven*, with an all-star cast. More recently (2016) it was remade again, retaining the same name, with another all-star cast, including Denzel Washington, Chris Pratt, Ethan Hawke, and Peter Sarsgaard, among others.

group of *rônin*, known variously as the Rôshigumi and Shinsengumi, to protect Tokugawa interests. Also, a group of loyalist samurai from Mito domain became *rônin* when they rebelled against the policies of domain leaders who were acting in the name of the daimyo.

A number of *rônin* figure prominently in Japanese period films (*jidaigeki*), such as in the following three works by Kurosawa Akira: *Seven Samurai* (1954), *Yôjimbô* (1961), and *Sanjurô* (1962).

In modern times, the term *rônin* has come to refer to high school graduates who are unaffiliated with a degree-granting institution of higher learning but are trying (in some cases, repeatedly) to pass the examinations necessary to gain admission therein.

See also: Isoda Koryûsai; Kumazawa Banzan; Miyamoto Musashi; Sakamoto Ryôma; Sekigahara, Battle of; Shinsengumi; Sieges of Osaka (*Ôsaka no jin*)

Further Reading

"Kumazawa Banzan." In Ryusaku Tsunoda, Wm. Theodore de Bary, and Donald Keene, eds., *Sources of Japanese Tradition*, vol. 1, 378–381. New York: Columbia University Press, 1958.

Sansom, George. *History of Japan: 1615–1867*. Stanford, CA: Stanford University Press, 1963.

Rural Samurai (*gôshi*)

During the Tokugawa period, *gôshi* was a general term that referred to several types of people who had rights to use surnames and carry two swords. One type of *gôshi* were low-ranking samurai who lived in the countryside and supported themselves through farming, by-employments, and from landholdings, which in general they oversaw personally. Often they had a claim of descent from warrior stock. They were an important social element in *tozama* (outside) domains largely in the peripheries of Japan rather than in the central areas of Honshu Island; and in domains with a large number of retainers per commoner, such as Satsuma, Tosa, Chôshû, Wakayama, Sendai, and Yonezawa. In all of these places *gôshi* were often involved as officials in the management of the countryside. In some localities *gôshi* was a title awarded to rural elites, including many village headmen, by a local lord in exchange for a contribution of money or some local service performed. In the late Tokugawa period there was a rise in the number of *gôshi* who wanted to learn swordsmanship, and large numbers of *gôshi* were active during the Meiji Restoration, many of them imperial loyalists who opposed the Tokugawa shogunate. Some other *gôshi* were responsible for proto-industrial developments in their villages.

Gôshi were of diverse origins: some were warriors who remained on the land, bridging the social gap between farmer-cultivators and sword-bearing samurai. They were exceptions to the efforts of local daimyo and other rulers of the late sixteenth century, particularly Toyotomi Hideyoshi (1537–1598), to separate warriors and farmers (*heinô bunri*) functionally and to draw the warriors off the land and into castle towns. Others were granted the rank as an incentive for their land reclamation efforts. Still others, wealthy farmers and even merchants, were able to purchase the rank, particularly during the second half of the Tokugawa period.

The position of *gôshi* varied in terms of rank and status from domain to domain, but they were below the castle town samurai everywhere. Nevertheless, in Tosa domain (Kôchi prefecture) *gôshi* were hugely important and added greatly to the domain's military strength—particularly late in the Tokugawa period, after the arrival of the American naval force led by Commodore Perry in 1853. They occupied the highest of five ranks of "lower samurai" (*kashi*), meaning the top position in the lower half of the retainer corps. All *gôshi* had the right to wear two swords and to use a surname (*myôji taito*), but in Tosa they had special status largely denied to *gôshi* elsewhere: they were permitted to participate just like the "upper samurai" in an audience with lord as well as the *onorizome* (First Horseback Riding Ceremony) during the New Year's festivities. They also were given administrative-military assignments and sometimes accompanied the Yamauchi lord on his alternate attendance trips to Edo.

Despite *gôshi's* special position in the domain retainer corps, there were social tensions between them and the castle town samurai, who tended to look down on them as "country samurai." There is also evidence that the *gôshi* were self-conscious, proud, and resented the arrogance of the castle town samurai. The domain created a number of regulations that created clearly visible distinctions between the *gôshi* and castle town samurai, which added to the tensions: for example, *gôshi* were not permitted to wear *bokuri* (wooden clogs), to carry a sun parasol when walking in the castle town. When they encountered a castle town samurai they were to remove their headgear and show reverence (e.g., by removing to the side of the road).

In terms of social origins, many *gôshi* in Tosa domain were members of the Chôsogabe clan, which had been on the losing side at the Battle of Sekigahara in 1600. Due to sporadic resistance to the new daimyo (Yamauchi Katsutoyo), who was awarded the Chôsogabe's former fief, a number of the former lord's retainers who remained in Tosa were allowed to retain their arms and to administer landholdings in the countryside that produced between 30 and 250 *koku*. However, to help dilute any remaining animosity toward the Yamauchi, in the mid-seventeenth century *gôshi* status was opened up to those men who could reclaim a minimum of 30 *tan* (1 tan = 0.245 acre); as a result, by 1685 there were 747 *gôshi*, controlling 23,498 *tan* as fief. Initially, *gôshi* status was limited to those who could show samurai origins, but a century later anyone without a criminal record, even those of lowly merchant status, could qualify. Sakamoto Ryôma (1836–1867), the Tosa man who played an important role in the Meiji Restoration, is a famous example of a *gôshi* with merchant origins. His grandfather was a wealthy sake brewer and had purchased *gôshi* rank in 1771. This avenue has been described as a type of "backdoor entry" into samurai status and occurred despite prohibitions on such issued by the Tokugawa shogunate. As a result, about 10 percent of *gôshi* (about eighty-two families) in Tosa were residents in or close to the castle town of Kôchi, making them absentee landlords. In the nineteenth century it was even possible to sell the *gôshi* title freely in Tosa domain; in fact, a survey of conditions in the 1860s found that most of the 212 *gôshi* who had entered the rank since 1830 had done so through purchase.

Gôshi in Satsuma domain (Kagoshima prefecture) were also quite remarkable. The families of some were quite old, dating back as far as the twelfth century (Kamakura period). They were quite numerous—as many as 20,000 according to a mid-eighteenth-century census—and scattered widely throughout the domain. In Satsuma *gôshi* were not only landowners but also served both military and administrative functions: they were in charge of villages and served at highway and domain border checkpoints. By locating the *gôshi* in the countryside through the *tojô* (lit., "outer castle") system, Satsuma domain authorities were able to keep a tight grip on the peasanty, effectively suppressing agrarian unrest.

See also: Alternate Attendance (*sankin kôtai*); Sakamoto Ryôma; Separation of Warrior and Peasant (*heinô bunri*)

Further Reading

Jansen, Marius B. "Takechi Zuizan and the Tosa Loyalist Party." *Journal of Asian Studies,* 18(2) (1959), 199–212.

Jansen, Marius B. "Tosa in the Seventeenth Century: The Establishment of Yamauchi Rule." In John W. Hall and Marius B. Jansen, eds., *Studies in the Institutional History of Early Modern Japan,* 115–130. Princeton, NJ: Princeton University Press, 1968.

Norman, E. Herbert. *Soldier and Peasant in Japan: The Origins of Conscription.* New York: Institute of Pacific Relations, 1943.

S

Saigô Takamori (1828–1877)

A low-ranking samurai official from Satsuma domain (present-day Kagoshima prefecture), Saigô Takamori ended up playing a pivotal role in the Meiji Restoration, leading the new Meiji army against the Tokugawa shogunate and negotiating the peaceful handover of Edo Castle in 1868. After a brief period of service in the Meiji government, Saigô returned to Kagoshima and in 1877 became the leader of the unsuccessful Satsuma Rebellion, the largest former samurai uprising against the new regime. Despite being denounced as a traitor and rebel, Saigô became a mythic character, one of the most celebrated figures in Japanese history, and has been lionized as the "last samurai." He was later pardoned by the Meiji government and his imperial court rank restored.

The eldest of seven children, Saigô was born in Kagoshima, in southern Japan, and was educated at the Zôshikan, the domain school. After suffering a serious injury to his right arm in a fight with another youth, Saigô concentrated his energies more on the literary or civil arts (*bun*) than the martial side of his education (*bu*). Later, during a tour of duty in Edo serving his lord as an attendant on the alternate attendance in 1854–1855, he discovered Mito learning, which celebrated the importance of the emperor and would greatly influence his life.

Exiled twice (in 1858 and 1862) due to his political affiliations and political activities, Saigô was sent to remote islands to the south of Kyushu, where he lived simply, taught local children, and studied and wrote poetry. Just prior to his first period of exile, Saigô had attempted to drown himself to follow his lord, Shimazu Nariakira, in death. During his second period of exile he was kept under house arrest, though legends later developed that he had been kept in a bamboo cage for a year and a half.

In 1864, finally pardoned by the new Satsuma lord, Hisamitsu, Saigô was appointed commander of Satsuma's troops in Kyoto to work on behalf of the domain in its relations with the imperial court. Leery of the shogunate's efforts to punish Chôshû domain and to pit Chôshû against Satsuma, Saigô worked to negotiate an alliance between the two domains in 1866 and then became one of the top leaders of the political and military campaigns against the Tokugawa. He commanded the imperial forces at the Battle of Toba-Fushimi and then led them on a march toward Edo. Together with Katsu Kaishû, the leader of the Tokugawa forces, Saigô, despite his initial opposition to a negotiated settlement, agreed to the peaceful surrender of Edo Castle in 1868.

Following the toppling of the shogunate, Saigô became one of the leaders of the new Meiji government. He was nonetheless ambivalent about the new state that he had helped create, particularly about the abolition of the domains and the daimyo.

Woodblock print (triptych) by Tsukioka Yoshitoshi, 1877, entitled *Rebel Insurrection at Kagoshima*. The print depicts an idealized Saigô Takamori (he was in fact very corpulent), the leader of the Satsuma Rebellion, which was defeated by the Meiji government's new conscript army. Yoshitoshi's prints of Saigô and the Satsuma Rebellion were extremely popular. The Satsuma clan crest (a cross in a circle) adorns the flag at bottom right. (Art & Archaeology, Inc./Corbis via Getty Images)

Although a number of the top officials left Japan in 1871 to travel to the United States and Europe, the Iwakura Mission, Saigô remained behind as a key figure in the caretaker government. After the members of the mission returned to Japan in 1873, the government became divided over a number of issues, particularly over a proposal to invade Korea (over a perceived diplomatic insult of Japanese imperial envoys) that Saigô supported. Failing to convince his colleagues, Saigô left the government and returned late in 1873 to Kagoshima, where he established a private school.

Although Saigô did actually support a number of the boldest modernizing reforms of the new government, including gradually eliminating samurai stipends and a conscript army, he became a symbol of traditional values to many disaffected samurai in southern Japan, who rallied around him to oppose the Meiji regime. In 1877, he led these men in the Satsuma Rebellion, the largest uprising by former samurai against the Meiji government; it followed three other unsuccessful revolts by former samurai in southern Japan, the Saga Rebellion (1874), the Akizuki Rebellion (1876), and the Hagi Rebellion (1876).

During the final stand of the Satsuma Rebellion, on Shiroyama in Kagoshima (the historical basis for the climactic final battle scene in the 2003 Hollywood film *The Last Samurai*), Saigô was shot in the hip. Legend has it that he committed *seppuku*, but one scholar (Ravina, 2004, 4–5) has surmised that he was probably crippled by the shot, in shock, and unable to slit his own abdomen in ritual suicide. Saigô's friend, Beppu Shinsuke, acted as the second and severed Saigô's head from his body, which was found with no wounds to the abdomen. Although the head might have been hidden by Saigô's manservant

---

The Last Samurai

Edward Swick's highly acclaimed 2003 film *The Last Samurai* centers on a character named Captain Nathan Algren, an American colonial military officer who is hired by the emperor of Japan to train Japan's first modern army. The army that Algren is training is charged with wiping out the samurai who oppose the emperor's army and the forces of modernization. During a battle between the two forces, Algren is taken captive, but his life is spared. Living among the people who support the opposing side, led by the samurai leader Katsumoto, Algren learns to respect, and eventually tries to emulate, the ways of the samurai. In the end, Algren decides to fight for the samurai against the emperor's army. The character for Katsumoto, who commits *seppuku* in the climactic final battle scene of the film, is based loosely on the historical figure Saigô Takamori. Algren's character, in turn, is influenced by the story of Jules Brulet, a French army captain who fought in the Boshin War (1868–1869) alongside Enomoto Takeaki. There were no Americans who fought during this conflict.

A Samurai and His Loyal Dog

A bronze statue of Saigô and his loyal dog was commissioned by the Meiji government in 1893 and unveiled in 1898. The statue was positioned to face the Imperial Palace and thus promotes his earlier role as a hero of the Meiji Restoration who led the imperial army in its peaceful takeover of Edo Castle and not as the leader of the 1877 Satsuma Rebellion against the Meiji government. Members of Saigô's family, including his widow, were present at the ceremony. Apparently, when the statue was unveiled, she was greatly shocked and let out a shriek. She claimed that it looked nothing like him and was also taken aback by the portrayal of Saigô dressed informally in a common kimono rather than in the formal attire of a samurai or in military uniform (a more recent statue of Saigô built in Kagoshima has him in military attire).

Even though Saigô had been pardoned in 1889 for having opposed the Meiji government in the Satsuma Rebellion (1877), there was still heated public debate over a commemorative statue. As a result, it took almost ten years before the statue was completed, and the planned site for it had to be shifted from in front of the imperial palace (a site associated with the emperor) to Ueno Park (a site associated with the shogunate).

The statue, designed by Takamura Kôun (1852–1934), is located in the entrance to Ueno Park in Tokyo and serves as a popular and well-known spot for people to meet: aboutjapan.japansociety.org/saigo_takamori_statue (accessed July 17, 2018).

Photographs of the statue as it appeared in 1910 can be viewed at: http://www.oldtokyo.com/the-statue-of-saigo-c-1910 (accessed July 17, 2018).

A bronze statue of Saigô Takamori and his loyal dog, designed by Takamura Kôun, commissioned by the Meiji government, and unveiled in 1898. The statue, located in the entrance to Ueno Park, is a popular meeting spot for people in Tokyo. (Mrnovel/Dreamstime.com)

immediately after his death, it was later reunited with his body. With Saigô's death, the rebellion ended and with it the final organized samurai opposition to the Meiji regime.

While Saigô was a physically imposing man, standing about six feet tall, he also possessed an unpretentious character. He enjoyed hunting with his dogs; making his own straw sandals and fishing lures; played the *biwa*, an instrument considered effeminate in many other parts of Japan; and writing poetry, under the name Saigô Nanshû. It was his simple, unassuming character that drew other samurai to him, seeking his leadership.

A portrait of Saigô can be found on the Japanese National Diet Library website: http://www.ndl.go.jp/portrait/e/index.html (accessed July 17, 2018).

Statues of Saigô can be found in Tokyo, at Ueno Park, and in Kagoshima, his hometown.

See also: Boshin War; Civil and Military Arts (*bunbu*); Katsu Kaishû; *Seppuku* (Ritual Suicide); Unmaking (Abolition) of the Samurai

Further Reading

Morris, Ivan. *The Nobility of Failure: Tragic Heroes in the History of Japan.* New York: New American Library, 1975.

Ravina, Mark. *The Last Samurai: The Life and Battles of Saigo Takamori.* Hoboken, NJ: Wiley, 2004.

Yates, Charles. *Saigo Takamori: The Man behind the Myth.* New York: Kegan Paul, International, 1995.

Sakai Banshirô (1833–?)

A retainer from Kii Wakayama domain with a stipend of 30 *koku*, Sakai was twenty-eight years old when he was given the assignment to serve his lord in Edo in 1860. During his posting in Edo he kept a diary for a period of seven months, which is rich in detail about the daily life of a lower samurai from the domain who accompanied his lord on alternate attendance to serve in the Tokugawa capital city. While in Edo, Sakai was assigned to the domain's secondary (middle) residence at Akasaka, where he shared a room with his uncle and one other retainer whose relationship to them was unclear.

Sakai's assignment in Edo essentially was to shadow his uncle—to observe and assist him—a kind of on-the-job training, similar to an internship, with the understanding and the hope that he would succeed the uncle at a later date. The uncle held the position of *okuzume goemon kata*, meaning that it was his responsibility to instruct the women in the private part of the residence in all matters related to their dress. Another part of his job description was responsibility for the placement of screens in the interior. Sakai's account corroborates other evidence from other diaries that retainers' duties in Edo were not terribly demanding. According to Sakai, retainers only worked on average eight days a month and no more than thirteen. He himself worked no more than half a day about every third day.

Sakai also kept detailed notations about his diet that reveal that even a lower samurai such as himself could afford a plain but healthy diet. He was able to consume a number of types of protein, such as sardines (either fresh or dried), which were quite inexpensive; tofu, which he ate in various forms about once every five days; and miso soup. Based on his diary, he ate thirty different types of fish during his stay in Edo. He also ate a variety of seasonal vegetables, such as bamboo shoots during the spring and eggplant during the late summer and autumn. Sakai also writes that he and his roommates in the domain barracks would often pool their rice allowances to make rice gruel to share among them.

When Sakai was off duty, he left the domain compound on average ten times or more a month, and usually in the company of three or four other retainers, to engage in a variety of activities. His most favorite activity seems to have been eating inexpensive meals, such as soba or other noodles, at local restaurants. Sometimes the noodles were accompanied with sushi or one-pot dishes. While out of the compound he made pilgrimages to famous temples and shrines—a total of thirty-six during a nine-month period. Other places he went sightseeing included the domain compounds of some of the largest domains and the gravesite where the forty-six *rônin* from Akô were buried. He visited the Ryôgoku area, where a variety of entertainment was available, and the Yoshiwara pleasure district, although he does not provide any details about what he might have done there other than to view a procession of courtesans. He also went to the public bath forty-three times, saw plays six times, and went to listen to storytellers eight times. Like many retainers on Edo duty, Sakai took advantage of his time in the Tokugawa capital to study the *shamisen*, an activity that likely would not have been looked favorably upon back in the domain.

Sakai, like most retainers on a posting in Edo, received a special allowance for that service, which amounted to 39 *ryô* per year. This allowed him to save enough money to support his family back home in Wakayama. He was frugal with his allowance, eating simply and not spending a lot on gifts. Although he enjoyed the leisure activities available in Edo, Sakai was greatly pained when he had to spend money unexpectedly. In his diary he made notations to complain about high prices when he was forced to pay them.

Examining his budget while in Edo, Sakai spent: on entertainment and miscellaneous expenses, 18.9 percent; on clothing, 20.2 percent; on food, 20.2 percent; on social expenses (gifts for friends and social superiors), 16.2 percent; on household expenses (mainly firewood and charcoal for cooking and warming, candles, and ceramic ware), 4.9 percent; and for health and hygiene, mainly for trips to the public bath, 2.9 percent.

Sakai's account ends during the eleventh month of 1860. After this we know from historical records that he served again in Edo in 1865, arriving in the city during the second month. However, due to the Tokugawa shogunate's dispatch of a second punitive military expedition to Chôshû in 1865, which Wakayama participated in, Sakai returned to Wakayama in the fifth month and then shortly thereafter headed to Chôshû with his domain's contingent. Although he participated in the fighting during that campaign, Sakai was not wounded and returned safely to Wakayama to continue his service. A portion of the diary that he kept during that period of his life has also been discovered. Unfortunately, this is the last historical record of Sakai's life.

Due to the richness of Sakai's account of life in Edo, there has been great interest in his diary and life in Japan, not only among academics but also the public at large. In 2010 the Edo-Tokyo Museum in Tokyo held a special exhibition based on the diary. The following year (2011) a much-acclaimed film short entitled *Bakumatsu tanshin funin* ([*A* Bushi *on*] *A Solo Posting during the End of the Tokugawa Period*) was produced by Maehara Yasutaka for the Kyôto Eiga Company. In 2014 a historical comic book based on Sakai's diary was created by Tsuchiyama Shigeru entitled *Bakumatsu tanshin funin bushi meshi* (*The Culinary Life of a* Bushi *on Solo Posting in Edo during the Late Tokugawa Period*) and appeared in the comic magazine *Komikku ran* (*Comic Disorder*). In 2016 the title was changed to *Kinban gurume bushi meshi* (*The Gourmet Life of a* Bushi *Serving in Edo*), and the magazine continues its run to this date.

See also: Akô Incident; Alternate Attendance (*sankin kôtai*)

Further Reading

Sakai Banshirô. "Edo e hassoku nikki chô" [Diary of a Trip to Edo]. In *Chizu de miru Shinjuku-ku no utsurikawari-Yotsuya hen* [Changes in Shinjuku Ward as Seen through Maps. Yotsuya Edition]. Tokyo: Tôkyô-to Shinjuku-ku kyôiku iinkai, 1983.

Shimamura Taeko. "Bakumatsu kakyû bushi no seikatsu no jittai" [The Realities of the Life of a Lower Samurai during the Late Tokugawa Period]. *Shien,* 21(2) (1972), 45–68.

Sakamoto Ryôma (1836–1867)

A low-ranking samurai from Tosa domain (present-day Kôchi prefecture), Sakamoto Ryôma (1836–1867) was a major figure in the movement to overthrow the Tokugawa shogunate. He achieved this in part by negotiating a secret alliance between the rival Chôshû and Satsuma domains that led to the military defeat of the shogunate. He was also instrumental in the negotiations that led to the voluntary resignation of the last Tokugawa shogun, Yoshinobu, in 1867, which resulted in the Meiji Restoration. In contemporary Japan he remains a popular figure among ordinary people and politicians for his ability to bring together opposing sides and because he is perceived as having worked for Japan's future, to build a "new nation" (a term he used), and not for personal gain.

Ryôma's family had commoner origins. His ancestors were wealthy sake brewers (see the biography of Tani Tannai, a samurai to whom Ryôma's merchant ancestors acted as financier) and his great-grandfather, who formed a branch family (the Sakamoto), purchased the rank of *gôshi,* or "rural samurai," which in Tosa domain was the highest rank of the lower half of the samurai retainer band. Later in life, when his life was under threat, he would use the old family name, Saitani, together with the given name Umetarô, as an alias.

Displaying a talent for the military arts (*bugei*) rather than the literary arts (*bun*), Ryôma

Portrait of Sakamoto Ryôma (1836–1867) of Tosa domain (Kôchi prefecture), one of the most popular historical figures in Japan today. Despite his low status as *gôshi* (rural samurai), Ryôma became a master swordsman. He gained greater fame as a peacemaker, though, helping to forge the alliance between Satsuma and Chôshû and for devising the "Eight-Point Program While Shipboard," a plan for imperial restoration. (Chronicle of World History/Alamy Stock Photo)

enrolled in fencing classes at the age of fourteen, and several years later, in 1853, he received permission from the domain to travel to Edo to train further as a swordsman for a period of one year. In Edo, he enrolled at the famous training school Hokushin ittô-ryû hyôhô operated by Chiba Sadakichi, and later he received a license from the school and became an assistant instructor there. The same year that Ryôma enrolled, the American fleet of ships under the command of Matthew C. Perry arrived in Japan. In reaction to the appearance of the Western ships, Ryôma was appointed to a guard position at Tosa domain's Edo residence in Shinagawa, which was located on Edo Bay. In a letter written to his family in Tosa, he wrote, "If it comes to war, he would take a foreign head and bring it home with him (Miyaji, 2003, 46).

The following year Ryôma returned home, but when an opportunity arose in 1856 to travel again to Edo he took it. Back at the Chiba school, he engaged in further training and teaching before returning to Tosa again in 1858. In Kôchi, Ryôma became involved in local politics, joining the Tosa Loyalist Party, which was dedicated to the principles of *sonnô jôi* (revere the emperor, expel the barbarians). He broke away from the group, though, before they carried out an assassination of a conservative domain government official, Yoshida Tôyô (1816–1862). Ryôma decided to leave the local politics of Tosa behind and to seek a role in the national politics of the country in Edo, leaving the domain without permission (*dappan*) in 1862; this was an illegal act that led to his family being punished, leading one of his sisters to commit suicide due to the shame that his actions had brought on the family.

In Edo, now as a *rônin* due to his illegal departure from the domain, Ryôma decided to work against the Tokugawa shogunate. His first major act was to attempt to assassinate Katsu Kaishû, a high-ranking Tokugawa official who was an advocate for modernizing Japan and opening it up to Western contacts, a position known as "open country" (*kaikoku*). In a now-famous confrontation, Katsu was able to convince Ryôma that they both actually were proponents of strengthening Japan militarily to meet the foreign threat. Instead of killing Katsu, Ryôma became his disciple and, ironically, protected him from other radicals who wanted to murder him. In 1863, Katsu received permission from the shogunate to open the Kobe Naval Training Center, and Ryôma became a head teacher there. From Katsu, Ryôma learned not just about naval science but also about economics and democracy, among other subjects. Later that year, Tosa officials forgave him for fleeing the domain, but when they ordered him to return to Kôchi in 1864, and he refused, his punishment was reinstated. Thus he became a *rônin* for a second time.

Under increasing pressure from pro-Tokugawa forces in Edo that wanted to kill him, Ryôma fled to Satsuma, where he was able to negotiate a secret alliance between that domain and Chôshû, two traditional enemies. (The shogunate had been successful in maintaining its paramount position by playing the one domain against the other, but together, Satsuma and Chôshû, would prove too powerful for the Tokugawa.) Although the pact between the two domains was still secret, Tokugawa authorities in Kyoto, to which Ryôma had returned in 1866, sought to arrest or kill Ryôma for his actions in going back and forth between Satsuma and Chôshû. A Tokugawa police force aimed to do that while Ryôma was staying in Fushimi at an inn called Teradaya, but a maid name Oryô heard the assailants break in and jumped out of a bathtub, barely throwing on a robe, to warn him. Although Ryôma was wounded on his right hand—the one that holds the sword—he was able to escape with his life. (He later married Oryô.)

Ryôma was recalled to Tosa domain (and pardoned again) in 1866, after Chôshû domain's defeat of the Tokugawa forces (the Second Chôshû Expedition). Tosa's domain leaders sought Ryôma's assistance in obtaining a negotiated settlement between the shogun and the emperor, one that would prevent Satsuma and Chôshû from taking military action to overthrow the Tokugawa by force. Ryôma came up with a plan—the so-called "Tosa Plan—that led to the voluntary resignation of the shogun, Tokugawa Yoshinobu, in 1867, effecting the Meiji Restoration.

Ryôma's legacy today is largely as a forward-looking modernizer. Often regarded as the founder of the imperial Japanese navy, Ryôma worked under the direction of Katsu Kaishû to create a modern naval force and founded the private navy and trading company *Kameyama shachû* (later renamed *Kaientai* or "Naval Support Fleet"). He also studied Western political models and wrote a blueprint for a future

Japanese government known as "Eight Point Program While Shipboard" (see Document 15).

Ryôma incurred the wrath of pro-Tokugawa forces for his pro-imperial stance as well as his role in bringing together Satsuma and Chôshû domains. As a result, he experienced the constant threat of assassination and two actual attempts. The first attempt occurred in 1866, when Ryôma was attacked at the Teradaya inn in Fushimi, outside of Kyoto, by a large group of assailants from the Tokugawa's Fushimi magistrate's office. In defending himself he fought with sword and his famous Smith & Wesson pistol but sustained a hand injury before escaping to the residence of Satsuma domain (in Fushimi). While nursing his wounds there, he sent a letter to his brother Gonpei, discovered only in 1867, in which he wrote that he "had a big laugh" over the failed assassination attempt with Saigô Takamori and Komatsu Tatewaki, two important Satsuma retainers. Also according to the letter, when Sakamoto went back to Kyoto he was escorted by Satsuma retainers. Some Tokugawa samurai spotted him and shouted, "Kill him!" but they were not given permission to attack because the magistrate's office was afraid of starting an all-out war with Satsuma.

Although Ryôma was proud of surviving this attempt on his life, he was not successful the second time the following year. He and his friend Nakaoka Shintarô were staying at the Ômiya inn in Kyoto. His assassins overpowered his sumo wrestler bodyguard at the front door of the inn and charged upstairs to Ryôma's room, where they cut down both men. (Ryôma died that night, at the age of thirty-one, while Nakaoka died of his wounds two days later.) The assassins were never identified conclusively, although Kondô Isami, one of the leaders of the Shinsengumi, was accused and executed on charges of assassination.

In contemporary Japan, Ryôma remains a very popular figure, the subject of a yearlong NHK drama, *Ryôma-den* (*The Story of Ryôma*) in 2010, and whose likeness appeared the same year on a 1,000-yen commemorative coin issued by the Japan Mint to celebrate the sixtieth anniversary of the Local Autonomy Law. Japan's lawmakers often invoke Ryôma to gain political support: for example, Ozawa Ichirô, the former secretary general of the Democratic Party of Japan, said in a 1996 speech that he would "like to follow Ryôma's example" and work toward a government "restoration." Several "new" letters written by Ryôma were discovered in 2017 and made national headlines. Several photographs of Ryôma exist—all with

---

Did Samurai Fly?

Well, no. But an airport in Japan was named after a samurai. In 2003, Kôchi renamed its airport Kôchi Ryôma Airport (KCZ), after its famous local son, Sakamoto Ryôma (1836–1867). It was the first airport in Japan to be branded with the identity of a historical person. The airport's official website (www.kochiap.co.jp/en) prominently displays a photograph and short biography of Ryôma, together with a cartoon image of him sitting astride an airplane.

a full head of hair as he was a *rônin* at the time—and these are frequently reproduced in the national media. His reputation is especially high in his local area, Kôchi, where in 1991 the prefecture opened a Sakamoto Ryôma Memorial Museum, outside of which his status stands, overlooking the Pacific Ocean.

See also: Civil and Military Arts (*bunbu*); Katsu Kaishû; Punishment; Retainer Corps (*kashindan*)*;* Ronin (*rônin*); Rural Samurai (*gôshi*); Sakamoto Ryôma; Shinsengumi; Tani Tannai; Tokugawa Yoshinobu

Further Reading

Jansen, Marius B. *Sakamoto Ryôma and the Meiji Restoration.* Princeton, NJ: Princeton University Press, 1961.

Miyaji Saichirô. *Ryôma no tegami* [Ryôma's Letters]. Tokyo: Kôdansha, 2003.

Sakamoto Ryôma Memorial Museum (Kôchi kenritsu Sakamoto Ryôma kinenkan): http://ryoma-kinenkan.jp (accessed July 12, 2018).

Sakuma Shôzan (1811–1864)

A politically minded samurai from Matsushiro domain (present-day Nagano prefecture), Sakuma Shôzan was a scholar of Dutch studies (*rangaku*) who became a prominent figure in the late-Tokugawa period (*bakumatsu*) and teacher to a number of other important samurai of the time, including Katsu Kaishû, Sakamoto Ryôma, and Yoshida Shôin. He was a proponent of strengthening Japan's coastal defenses and an advocate for opening Japan's ports to foreign trade and learning from the West. Shôzan also worked with the Tokugawa in trying to achieve a union of the imperial court and the shogunate (*kôbu gattai*). Ultimately, he met a violent death, assassinated for his political views by imperial loyalists.

Born the son of Sakuma Shinken, a low-ranking samurai from Matsushiro domain with a stipend comparable to a fief of 30 *koku* with a cash supplement of 5 *ryô*, Shôzan was reputed to have been a precocious child, able to recite the entire sixty-four hexagrams of the *Iching* by memory at the age of two. His father earned enough money to allow Shôzan to pursue his studies by supplementing his income by teaching fencing and acting as an adviser to a wealthy commoner. Shôzan's education was broad-based, including the traditional Chinese classics, military arts, but also, quite unusually, mathematics, which he thought important for both political and military affairs. In samurai society mathematics was not widely deemed appropriate for samurai, but Shôzan later was able to use this foundational knowledge in order to gain an understanding of Western mathematics and science after the Opium War (1839–1842) between Britain and China. In Edo, to which Shôzan was able to travel for the first time in 1833, he became a student of the noted Confucian scholar Satô Issai. Despite his succession to the headship of the Sakuma family in 1828, Shôzan was more interested in studying than in serving within the domain government. Matsushiro officials saw his promise, however, and permitted him three additional periods of study in Edo.

Shôzan drove himself hard, with little sleep, and was determined to learn as much as possible in order to have an impact on his society, but he was also quite difficult to get along with. He could also be quite arrogant, particularly in questioning the status-based order of his society, which led to him being punished several times. The first time came at the age of twelve, when he cursed the son of a high-ranking samurai, an elder. When the elder reprimanded Shôzan's father, he punished his son by keeping him at home for three years. Later, his stubborn refusal to comply with another elder's request to submit a list of his father's disciples, organized according to rank, led to his being ordered into confinement. Always confident and proud of his abilities, Shôzan famously wrote (in 1854), "After twenty, I realized that I had a part to play in the affairs of my *han* [domain]. After thirty, I realized that I had a part to play in the affairs of the entire country. After forty, I realized that I had a part to play in the affairs of the world" (Quoted in Chang, 1970, 104).

After China's humiliating defeat in the Opium War, Shôzan dedicated himself to the study of Western gunnery, under notable teachers such as Egawa Tan'an (1801–1855) and Takashima Shûhan (1798–1868). This included the study of the Dutch language in order to read Western texts himself. After Shôzan's lord, Sanada Yukitsura, was appointed senior councilor in 1841 Shôzan became his adviser in matters of maritime defense and was able, through his lord, to submit a memorial to the shogunate on adopting Western military methods, entitled *Eight Plans for Naval Defense*. Through his writing he gained some notoriety and became sought after as a teacher by other forward-looking samurai such as Katsu Kaishû and Sakamoto Ryôma.

Dutch studies had a big impact on Shôzan's life. Through Dutch translations of Western scientific texts, Shôzan was able to make a glass, magnets, thermometers, cameras, and telescopes. He also learned about electricity and created Japan's first telegraph, five years before Commodore Perry gifted one to Japan from the U.S. government. Shôzan came up with a formulation that became famous about how Japan could use foreign learning to modernize Japan, "Japanese ethics, Western science" (*wakon yôsai*).

In 1853, with the arrival of Commodore Matthew C. Perry and the American naval force in Japan, Sakuma was appointed military adviser for Matsushiro domain. In this capacity he submitted a memorial that argued in part that regardless of whether peace or war would result from the talks between the representatives of the two countries, Japan should dispatch men of talent overseas to study conditions in foreign countries, to purchase large ships (through the Dutch), and to learn navigation technology. If this proposal were to be accepted, he recommended that Chôshû samurai, Yoshida Shôin, a disciple of his, be among those selected.

When Perry returned in early 1854, Matsushiro domain was selected, together with Kokura domain, for coastal-defense duty in the Yokohama area. Sakuma took up residence there as supervisor. He opposed the opening of Shimoda as a treaty port, thinking its location too strategic, and recommended Yokohama in its place. Shôzan was arrested in connection with Shôin's failed attempt to stow away on Perry's vessels (shogunate officials discovered the connection between the two men because when he was apprehended Shôin was carrying on his person a farewell poem written by Shôzan) and was sentenced to house arrest, where he remained for nine long years.

Once his punishment was over, in 1863, Shôzan was offered employment by Chôshû and Tosa domains, but he declined both. The following year he was appointed by the shogunate as military and naval adviser and sent to Kyoto. Because of his *kaikoku* ("open the country") views, and his efforts to improve relations between the imperial court and the shogunate, Shôzan was a target for assassination. He knew that his life was in danger and always kept a revolver (a gift from Katsu Kaishû) on him during the day and beside his pillow at night. Despite his precautions, he was cut down by a half-dozen antiforeign, imperial loyalists (*sonnô jôi*) while returning on horseback to his lodgings in Kyoto in 1864.

See also: Katsu Kaishû; Punishment; Sakamoto Ryôma; Yoshida Shôin

Further Reading
Chang, Richard T. *From Prejudice to Tolerance: A Study of the Image of the West, 1826–1864.* Tokyo: Sophia University, 1970.

Samurai. See *Bushi*

Samurai Residences (*buke yashiki*)

The layout of castle towns reflected the social hierarchy of Tokugawa Japan, a society which formally privileged samurai over peasants, artisans, and merchants in the formal status system (*mibun*). The castle complex, where the lord (daimyo) resided, occupied the visual center of the castle town, particularly as the castle keep (donjon) towered over the surrounding areas. The daimyo kept his samurai retainers in close proximity to the castle to facilitate their service to him; in large part this was so they could staff the domain's administrative offices, but also because their quarters served as another layer of defense for the castle. The size and proximity of a samurai's residence to the castle, not to mention its architectural style, also reflected his rank in the daimyo's retainer corps. As has been the case with castles, many samurai residences have been restored across Japan and given varying degrees of protection by the Japanese government at the local, regional, or national level.

Generally, all samurai, including samurai with landed fiefs, kept their formal home in the castle town, near the castle (though some low-ranking samurai, including rural samurai (*gôshi*) were allowed to live outside the castle town). In principle, samurai residences were the property of the daimyo (or in the case of the Tokugawa bannermen and housemen, the shogun), granted to the retainer along with his fief or stipend in exchange for their service, but their residents were responsible for upkeep. Over time, though, in some places samurai were able to treat their residences as if they were personal property by leasing them and finding more modest dwellings to rent as tenants, as an economizing measure.

Low-ranking samurai such as *ashigaru* often lived in row houses rather than in independent dwellings. For example, a row house built for *ashigaru* in Kôchi (Tosa domain, present-day Kôchi prefecture), known as the Yamauchi house lower residence row house (*Yamauchi-ke shimo yashiki nagaya*), was a 33-meter-long building with two floors, containing five apartment-style residences.

STRUCTURE AND ORGANIZATION OF
SAMURAI RESIDENCES

Although the size and location of a retainer's residence in the samurai quarters varied according to his status in the domain hierarchy, all samurai residences had certain features in common. For one, only samurai were allowed to have walled (generally earthen-walled) and gated compounds, which were thus a symbol of their status. In addition to the main gate and walls, the samurai residence—that is, the compound where the samurai resided—of a middle- or upper-ranking retainer consisted of a home, a formal garden, a vegetable garden, and one or more storehouses. It might also have a stable, if the samurai was of sufficient status to own a horse (generally, samurai with a fief or stipend of 200 *koku* were required to maintain a horse).

The front gate distinguished samurai from commoner residences and were, together with the walls that extend out from it, the "public" face of the samurai residence. There were two main types of gates: *nagayamon* and *yakuimon*, and in some castle towns there seemed to have been a preference for one type over the other. The *nagayamon* (lit., "barracks gate"), which were part of the residences of middle- and upper-ranking retainers, was a common type of gate with one or more

Nagayamon ("barracks gate") of the residence of Ôishi Yoshio (Kuranosuke), chief retainer of Akô domain who served Lord Asano Naganori, located in Akô city (Hyôgo prefecture). Asano's retainers from Edo are said to have brought Ôishi the news of the Akô Incident here in 1701. The *nagayamon* and several of the other buildings in the compound survived a major fire in 1729. (Photo by Constantine Vaporis)

rooms built into either side of the gate that served as quarters for lower-ranking samurai and/or menials or for storage, and sometimes a stable. From the *naga-yamon* menials such as *chûgen* (a valet or footman) monitored the outside and controlled access into the residence. This type of gate can be seen in most of the extent gates in Hagi (present-day Yamaguchi prefecture) and Matsushiro (present-day Nagano prefecture) castle towns (see Table 6). The gate actually consisted of a main gate, used in principle only when a higher-ranking official visited, and a side gate that was used for routine traffic and ordinary household affairs.

The house itself also had multiple entrances: a more ornate front entrance for greeting visitors of equal or higher rank and for the master of the house to use on formal occasions. A smaller, unadorned door to the right of the front entrance was used by others. The formal entrance area, known as the *genkan*, has a tatami-matted room with a wooden level below it (*shikidai*) where guests were greeted formally or sent off. A second type of front gate was the *yakuimon*, which was a simple gate, without the attached barracks or other rooms; this type of gate is representative in Kakunodate (present-day Akita prefecture) and Kaminoyama (present-day Yamagata prefecture).

Samurai houses were generally single-story structures and were built in the *shoin-zukuri* style of Japanese domestic architecture and became the prototype for traditional Japanese homes during the modern era. As a style of architecture, *shoin-zukuri* appeared in the Kamakura period and derived from Zen Buddhist monastic dwellings. Its basic elements included the *shoin* itself (a study alcove), *tokonoma* (alcove for the display of art objects), and *chigai-dana* (staggered shelves built into the wall for decorative purposes). The style developed gradually during the Muromachi period (1336–1573) as the older *shinden* style (*shinden-zukuri*) of the Heian period (794–1185), which was developed for the palaces and residences of the aristocracy, died out. During the Tokugawa period, the "mature style" included a *genkan* (formal entry), tatami (rush-mat flooring), *fusuma* (sliding wall panels), and *shoji* (paper-covered sliding doors). In many homes built in the *shoin* style the *shoin*, *tokonoma*, *chigai-dana*, and decorative doors were located on a raised floor area (*jôdan*), one step above the surrounding space.

The *shoin* style fulfilled two needs for the samurai: the need for more formal meeting and reception rooms; and, their desire for a more comfortable style of housing. It thus encompassed both formal and domestic architecture as the style developed during the seventeenth century. The best-preserved and most magnificent example of the *shoin* style in formal architecture is the Ninomaru Palace of Nijô Castle, in Kyoto, which dates from the early seventeenth century. It was widely used, however, in the formal spaces of castles and daimyo residences.

In the domestic sphere, the residences of samurai "were more often patterned after the less rigid style of the teahouses, termed *sukiya*, but they still adhered to the principles of the *shoin* style, usually containing all of its major features" (Hanley, 1997, 32). In contrast to the dwellings of commoners in the countryside, which were built with whole logs for posts and beams, were well enclosed, and meant to protect the inhabitants from the outside elements, samurai homes made more use of boards and hence less material overall. The built-in decorative elements and the use of wood panel ceilings and sliding doors did require skilled labor to construct.

Table 6   Selected Samurai Residences from Former Castle Towns

Name of Samurai Residence	Castle	Extant Features	Designation	Location (city, prefecture)
Aoyagi	Kakunodate	Gates, house, storehouses, garden	Prefectural Historic Site	Senboku, Akita prefecture
Ishiguro	Kakunodate	Gates, house, garden	Local Historic Site	Senboku, Akita prefecture
Kuchiba	Hagi	*Nagayamon*, house, garden	City Important Cultural Property	Hagi, Yamaguchi prefecture
Matsue	Matsue	Gates, home, garden	City Tangible Cultural Property	Matsue, Shimane prefecture
Sanada	Matsushiro	Gates, home, storehouses, garden	National Historic Site	Nagano, Nagano prefecture
Nomura	Kanazawa	Gates, home, garden	City Tangible Cultural Property	Kanazawa, Ishikawa prefecture
Okawa-suji	Kôchi	*Nagayamon*, house	City Tangible Cultural Property	Kôchi city, Kôchi prefecture
Tajima	Sakura	Home, garden	Registered Tangible Cultural Property, Local Historic Site	Sakura, Chiba prefecture
Yamada	Kaminoya	House, garden	Local Historic Site	Kaminoyama, Yamagata prefecture
Yokota	Matsushiro	Gates, house, storehouse, garden	City Important Cultural Property	Nagano, Nagano prefecture

The rooms were also more efficiently designed in that they were all part of one floor plan inside, not in a series of rooms connected by corridors, as was the case in the earlier *shinden* style. Extant houses throughout Japan give evidence that this *sukiya* style was employed throughout Japan. Although the more formal parts of the home had finished ceilings, as noted above, the kitchen and other less formal areas were usually left bare to the rafters.

A formal survey from the of samurai housing in one domain, Tsugaru (Aomori prefecture) in the mid-eighteenth century reveals that (of the 797 houses for which there is detailed information), 80 percent had a formal guest room (*zashiki*), 66 percent had a guest room (*hiroma*), and 53 percent had a formal entrance (*genkan*). It is likely that the 18 percent of the houses with no formal rooms belonged to low-ranking samurai, who probably had no need nor financial ability to receive formal guests. Moreover, the decorative style in most guest rooms was quite sparse, consisting only of a *tokonoma*.

The garden (*teien*) was a crucial part of the residence and a focal point for entertaining visitors in the formal guest room. The size of the garden, given the expense they entailed, necessarily varied according to a samurai's status, and some lower-ranking samurai lacked them altogether. Many samurai residences also had vegetable gardens, typically located in the back of the property.

SAMURAI RESIDENCES TODAY

After the Meiji Restoration (1868) many samurai residences shared a fate similar to castles—they were allowed to fall into disrepair or were sold off. The historical significance of samurai homes was not widely recognized, particularly in the early decades of the Meiji period (1868–1912), when Japan's "feudal past" was under attack in many quarters in Japanese society. Many of these residences were destroyed over the years to allow for the construction of new homes. Others were destroyed by natural disasters or the Allied aerial bombing of sixty-six of Japan's urban centers, most of them former castle towns. Fortunately, some samurai residences were donated or sold to local governments for historic preservation and can be viewed today. There is no architectural survey or overall count of them, but at least hundreds of them exist. In some former castle towns, just one or two residences might remain, while in others an entire district of them has been preserved, as in Hirosaki (Aomori prefecture), Kanazawa (Ishikawa prefecture), Kakunodate (Akita prefecture), Chiran (Kagoshima prefecture), and Kitsuki (Ôita prefecture) (see Table 6).

Other examples of samurai residences exist outside the former castle towns, on the former fiefs of large landed samurai, such as the Gotô, who served as hereditary domain councilors (*karô*) for the Yamauchi. In Aki city, where the Gotô's fief was located, a number of samurai residences remain; many of these were separated from one another not by earthen walls but with bamboo fences or green hedges. Of course, the Gotô themselves had a residence in Aki, located within a moated and walled enclosure (*doi*), but also maintained a residence in Kôchi Castle town

---

Nagamachi Samurai Residences, Kanazawa

Designated a "Landscape District" in July 2014, Nagamachi is the area in Kanazawa, the castle town of the Maeda family, where a number of historic residences of upper samurai have been preserved. The residence of the Nomura family, a samurai household of 1,200 *koku*, is particularly popular with tourists and renown for its beautiful garden (images of the residence can be seen on its official website, Japanese only: http://www.nomurake .com). The alleys and the mud walls of *nagayamon* gates (row house gates) still maintain a sense of nostalgia, but most of the walls have required restoration due to the harsh winters in the area. Many of the houses have beautiful gardens, with streams fed by the Onosho-yosui canal.

Garden attached to the Nomura family samurai residence in the Nagamachi district of Kanazawa. The Nomura were retainers of the Maeda daimyo and held a fief of 1,200 *koku*. The garden was a crucial part of the residence for the Nomura, and upper samurai in general, and was visible from different rooms in the house. In 2003, it was voted one of the top three gardens in Japan by *The Journal of Japanese Gardening*. (Photo by Constantine Vaporis)

(Kôchi prefecture). Other well-preserved samurai districts outside of the former castle towns exist in Chiran (Satsuma domain, present-day Kagoshima prefecture) and Kakunodate (Akita prefecture). In Chiran, there were more than 500 samurai residences in the late-Tokugawa period; those that remain in the preservation district have beautiful dry landscape (*kare sansui*) gardens that are said to reflect the influence of Ryukyu, the southern kingdom which Satsuma invaded in the early seventeenth century.

The extent to which the historical integrity of samurai residences has been maintained varies greatly from place to place. Since Japanese homes were made primarily with perishable materials (wood and paper, with stone foundations), they were continuously being renovated. Some of the residences designated "samurai homes" today have been repeatedly reconstructed such that very little of their Tokugawa-era materials remain. In others, where people have been residing in them until recently, modern conveniences such as electricity, interior lighting, and glass windows have been installed.

The extent to which the various parts of samurai residences remain also varies. In many places only the *nagayamon* exists. In others, only the home remains; in yet others, the *nagayamon* and the home; and in places where the home remains, often a garden still exists as well.

The residence of a high-ranking samurai could be quite impressive. The example of the residence of the Shiomi family of Matsue (present-day Shimane prefecture) is perhaps representative of them. A high-ranking samurai who served in the important position of city magistrate held a fief of 1,000 *koku*. The Shiomi residence, the largest remaining samurai residence in the castle town, was built in 1730. It stands across the moat from Matsue Castle, which has one of the twelve original donjon in Japan today (see Table 7). The main house consists of twenty-one rooms, including the *shikidai* front and official front hall (*genkan*) where official guests were greeted; a guest room; a room for the servants of guests; separate private sitting rooms for the master of the house and his wife; a guard room (*musha kakushi*), where a secret guard was maintained, which adjoined the master's room (found only in the homes of high-ranking samurai); a room for the tea ceremony; a room for the family Buddhist altar; a bathing room; a kitchen; and a bathroom. The formal entrance and guest rooms are elegant or refined, in contrast with the plainness

Table 7   Description of Rooms in Shiomi Residence

Room No.	Description of Room
1	Palanquin storage space
2	*Nagayamon* with room attached
3	Servants' waiting room
4	Private front door for family only
5	Entrance hall for private use
6	*Shikidai* front, for official use or high-ranking samurai's use
7	Official front hall, used for official guests
8	Room for the servants of guests
9	Guard room
10	Guest room
11	Toilet, for visitors only
12	Sitting room for family use
13	Sitting room for master of house
14	Sitting room for lady of the house
15	Small room for miscellaneous use
16	Tea ceremony room
17	Room for Buddhist altar
18	Storage room for household utensils, *tansu* (chest)
19	Family dining room
20	Bathing room
21	Kitchen
22	Room for visitors to rest; previously used to make miso (bean paste) or for other household work

of the private quarters of the family, reflecting the distinction between the public (official) and private spheres of a high-ranking samurai. The house, of course, stood in behind the *nagayamon*, which contained the front gate and several attached rooms, one for servants and another a storage area for a palanquin (the head of the house used this when he needed to travel on official business).

Lower-ranking samurai such as *ashigaru* often lived in tenement or row houses rather than in independent dwellings. For example, a row house built for *ashigaru* in Kôchi (Tosa domain, present-day Kôchi prefecture), known as the Yamauchi house lower residence row house (*Kyû Yamauchi-ke shimo yashiki nagaya*) was a 33-meter-long building with two floors, containing five apartment-style residences; a bathing room. A larger example remains in Matsusaka Castle (present-day Mie prefecture), where Kii domain samurai were stationed as guards. The structure was built late in the Tokugawa period, in 1863, to house twenty castle guards, their families, and staff. The tenement consists of two main buildings with a road running between them. Each of the tenement houses had a garden space; other structures, such as a small shrine and a warehouse, were shared by all the residents.

See also: Castle Towns (*jôkamachi*); Castles (*jôkaku*); Daimyo Residence Compounds (*daimyô yashiki*); Nijô Castle (*Nijô-jô*); Tea Ceremony (*sadô*)

Further Reading and Viewing

Hanley, Susan B. *Everyday Things in Premodern Japan: The Hidden Legacy of Material Culture.* London: University of California Press, 1997.

Hashimoto, Sumio. *Architecture in the Shoin Style: Japanese Feudal Residences.* Translated and adapted by H. Mack Horton. Tokyo: Kodansha International, 1981.

Hirai, Kiyoshi. *Feudal Architecture of Japan.* Translated by Hiroaki Sato and Jeannine Ciliotta. New York, Tokyo: Weatherhill/Heibonsha, 1980.

"Samurai Residences." In *Jcastle: Guide to Japanese Castles.* http://www.jcastle.info/view /Samurai_Residences. Accessed August 5, 2018.

Kakunodate Samurai District

One of the most popular samurai districts for Japanese tourists is Kakunodate, where eighty-six households of samurai serve the high-ranking (*karô* or senior councilor) samurai of the North Satake family, a branch family of the Satake lord of Kubota (also known as Akita) domain in present-day Akita prefecture. The North Satake held a landed fief of 10,000 *koku* and gathered their retainers around them in a castle town–like setting (minus the castle). The district's wide streets and large courtyards are shaded by many weeping cherry trees, which bring droves of tourists in early May every year. Of the numerous samurai houses that remain, six are open to the public and allow visitors to experience how middle- and upper-ranking samurai lived. The residences' gates in Kakunodate were of a simple style (*yakuimon*) rather than the *nagayamon* with built-in rooms seen in many other places, such as Hagi and Matsushiro. The residences, particularly those of the Aoyagi and Ishiguro families, are quite impressive for their size and quality. The home of the Odano family (see entry Odano Naotake) is also located here and was notable in that it had a partial second floor. Several of the residences double as museums, with samurai swords, armor, clothing, documents, household utensils, and toys on display.

Seidan (Discourse on Government)

Perhaps the most famous text written by the noted Confucian scholar Ogyû Sorai (1666–1728), *Seidan* is a multivolume treatise in the genre of political economy in which the author proposed a number of reforms to make the Tokugawa state more prosperous. Written late in his life, during the Kyôhô era (1716–1735), while in the employ of the eighth shogun Tokugawa Yoshimune (1684–1751), Sorai sought to counter the ill effects of the commercial economy and the separation of samurai and townsmen from the countryside. In *Seidan* he elaborates on many proposals that he made in a much more abbreviated manner in the work *Taiheisaku* (*A Policy for Great Peace*). His writings were written in support of Tokugawa rule, as advice to the shogun to correct the problems that he saw in society.

Sorai was born the second son of a samurai who served as the personal doctor of Tokugawa Tsunayoshi while he was daimyo of Tatebayashi, before he became the fifth shogun. He studied the Zhu Xi school of Song (Neo-)Confucianism and was hired into the service of Yanagisawa Yoshiyasu (1658–1714), a senior vassal of Tsunayoshi's, in 1696. After Tsunayoshi's death in 1709 he left Yanagisawa's service, turned away from Zhu Xi to develop his own philosophy that represented a return to the ancient works, to history, and to the study of language.

In *Seidan*, Sorai was concerned with what he saw as the spiritual impoverishment of the samurai that was a result of economic decline. He blamed urbanization for the negative impact that it had on the samurai's lifestyle and standard of living. Living in cities, he emphasized, leads to samurai spending money "as if living in an inn." He, like his fellow Confucian scholar Kumazawa Banzan (1619–91), advocated for moving the samurai back to the countryside (*dochaku*), where they could return to a self-sufficient lifestyle, live a simpler life, free from the negative influence of the urban, commercialized economy. Thus, by returning to the land the samurai could relearn the values of an earlier age.

The focus of most of volume one is an analysis of the socioeconomic situation in Edo. His commentary here is wide-ranging, from his complaint about the prevalence of burglary and assault; he advocates for stricter controls on menial workers in the city and for greater restrictions on the movement of commoners both within the city and on the highways of Japan. With no clear borderline between city and countryside, he points out, Edo continues to spread outward and, with it, commerce has crept into the countryside, impoverishing the people. In the final chapters of the volume Sorai focuses on warrior households. He advocates for samurai to be removed from Edo in order to live a simpler life in the countryside. In addition, he argues that the alternate attendance system should be reformed, with the periods of service in Edo reduced (but not eliminated).

In volumes two and three Sorai elaborates in detail on how to eliminate the impoverishment of the samurai, which he sees as the root of all social evil. Impoverishment, he argues, leads to the decline and fall of a dynasty. The reforms he offers represent the perspective of the samurai ruling class. He envisioned that if the situation was alleviated for the samurai, then the situation would also necessarily improve for the other social groups. By returning the samurai and the townsmen back to the countryside, the pernicious effects of the commercial economy, with its focus on profit, could be countered. Regulations could be issued to suppress luxury, which would stop the process of impoverishment, eliminate the economic power of the merchants, and allow for status distinctions (between samurai and commoners) to become clear again. By reducing the period of residence in Edo, the daimyo on alternate attendance and their samurai would not feel they had to live up to styles considered proper for their station. They would no longer feel as if they were "living in an inn." Returning the samurai to the countryside, where they would live among the peasants, would improve relations between the two social groups. Given that Sorai saw commoners as ignorant, he felt the samurai could then resume their natural role as teachers and leaders.

See also: Alternate Attendance (*sankin kôtai*); Kumazawa Banzan; Tokugawa Tsunayoshi; Tokugawa Yoshimune

Further Reading

Lidin, Olof G. "Ogyû Sorai's Civil Society (*Seidan*)." *Japan Review,* 5 (1994), 3–13.

McEwan, J. R. *The Political Writings of Ogyû Sorai.* Cambridge: Cambridge University Press, 1969.

Seji kenbunroku (Matters of the World: An Account of What I Have Seen and Heard, 1816)

Seji kenbunroku (or in an alternate reading, *Seji kenmonroku*) is a late-Edo period account, written in 1816, during the rule of Tokugawa Ienari (r. 1787–1837). Its author was an anonymous samurai who referred to himself as Buyô Inshi, a pseudonym that means "A Retired Gentleman of Edo." Based on an analysis of the text, most scholars believe that the author was a direct vassal of the shogun, meaning either a bannerman (*hatamoto*) or a houseman (*gokenin*). The work, which initially circulated only in manuscript form and was only published in 1926, has been described as "among the Edo period's most sustained attempts to examine society critically in its entirety, from the shogunal worthies at the top to outcasts of various kinds at the bottom" (Introduction to *Lust, Commerce, and Corruption,* 2014, 2). A modern edition of the text, in Japanese, runs a full 440 pages.

Buyô Inshi begins the account with a chapter on the samurai, before moving on to the farmers and the townspeople, and covers a wide range of topics from the medical profession, the blind, pariahs and outcasts, kabuki, the pleasure districts and prostitutes, lawsuits, the economy, the land, and Japan's identity as a divine land. Throughout the text, Buyô Inshi is a tireless critic of his society and decries the decline in people's customs and morality. He is particularly determined in revealing the details of the corruption that permeated Tokugawa society.

Although the author's exact identity is unknown, there is no doubt that he was a samurai, based in Edo, and one who identified closely with the shogunate. He was likely retired at the time that he wrote the account, as he appeared to be in a position of relative independence that gave him the opportunity to look at his world with some detachment. It also afforded him the time to observe his society firsthand, as he noted himself (*Lust,* 2014, 35). He also appears to have had intimate knowledge of a broad spectrum of society, much more than one would expect from a high-ranking samurai. His intimate knowledge of moneylending and lawsuits indicates that he may well have had some affiliation or connection with a type of legal aid who helped plaintiffs bring suits involving debts and loans in shogunal courts.

Buyô Inshi's account, however, is far from objective or balanced. He idealized the simpler times of the early seventeenth century, just after Tokugawa Ieyasu had established the shogunate, and what he referred to as the "military way" reigned supreme. This was before the economy became commercialized and the pursuit of money corrupted people. In his mind, money took over the world and destroyed social balance, throwing both farmers and samurai into debt to merchants. Despite his ideological perspective, Buyô was a keen observer and pointed out the many social and economic contradictions around him.

As a warrior, what particularly concerned the author was the plight of the samurai. He descried the declining relevance of the status system (*mibunsei*), as commoners were able to purchase warrior status from samurai; and commoners threatened to upend the system by filing lawsuits against samurai over financial matters. Samurai, however, had to be concerned about maintaining their reputation and, showing great weakness, put up with townspeople disrespecting them to keep the matter from becoming public knowledge. To Buyô, the challenge to samurai authority by townspeople posed an existential threat. He asked, rhetorically, "Might it not come to their even bringing the warrior down?" (*Lust*, 2014, 217)

See also: Bannermen (*hatamoto*); Housemen (*gokenin*); Shogunate (*bakufu, kôgi*); Status System (*mibunsei*)

Further Reading
Katsu Kokichi. *Musui's Story: The Autobiography of a Tokugawa Samurai.* Translated by Teruko Craig. Tucson: University of Arizona Press, 1988.

Lust, Commerce, and Corruption: An Account of What I Have Seen and Heard, by an Edo Samurai. Edited and introduced by Mark Teeuwen and Kate Wildman Nakai, et al. New York: Columbia University Press, 2014.

Sekigahara, Battle of (1600)

Sekigahara was the decisive armed conflict that led to the rise of Tokugawa Ieyasu to power and the establishment of a military government, or shogunate, in Edo three years later. After the death of Toyotomi Hideyoshi in 1598, the main daimyo split into two major groups, one led by Ishida Mitsunari and the other under Ieyasu. On October 21, 1600, the two armies, consisting of more than 150,000 men, met in a narrow valley near the village of Sekigahara (in Mino Province, present-day Gifu prefecture). As a result of the battle Ieyasu was able to solidify political and military control over the country, and in a position of strength to demand his appointment as shogun by the emperor. Although Ieyasu's victory was decisive, there still remained political forces opposed to his new government who rallied around Hideyoshi's son, Hideyori; this opposition was finally eliminated in the Battle of Osaka in 1614–1615. The Battle of Sekigahara represents the culmination of the rising scale of warfare during the sixteenth century. The increasing cost of warfare in economic as well as human terms likely encouraged warring daimyo to accept the political accommodation of a semiunified (hybrid) state under Tokugawa rule.

After the death of Toyotomi Hideyoshi in 1598 there was an uneasy peace between the daimyo, but during the summer of 1600 the major political forces around the country coalesced around two rival daimyo, Tokugawa Ieyasu and Ishida Mitsunari, both of whom were part of the group of five regents appointed over Toyotomi Hideyoshi's son, Hideyori. The two sides—a 75,000-strong force (Eastern Army) led Tokugawa Ieyasu and a slightly larger 80,000-man force (the Western Army), led by Ishida Mitsunari—met in a narrow valley just to the west of Sekigahara, in Mino province (now Gifu prefecture) in 1600. It was the largest battle to date in Japanese history and decisive in nature, but it lasted a mere six hours. The Western Army had the initial advantage, but the tide of the battle shifted when the 15,000-man strong force of the powerful western daimyo, Kobayakawa Hideaki, defected to the eastern side. This plot was conceived before the battle, but during the course of the conflict Kobayakawa hesitated to take action as planned, leading Ieyasu to order his troops to fire on Kobayakawa's forces before the daimyo would switch sides. This encouraged the defection of as many as five other daimyo and resulted in the routing of the Western Army. The course of the battle might have been quite different had the putative commander of the Western Army, Môri Terumoto, not failed to participate and a number of troops on both sides, including the force led by Tokugawa Ieyasu's son, Hidetada, not failed to arrive at Sekigahara in time to participate due to other battles.

Several visual depictions of the battle were created. One of them, a pair of eight-fold screens, were given by Tokugawa Ieyasu to his adopted daughter as part of her dowry when she married the daimyo Tsugaru Nobuhira. A single six-panel screen by the artist Sadanobu Kanô dates from the 1620s and was in the possession of Lord Ii of Hikone.

A literary account of the battle, *Oan monogatari*, was written from the perspective of an elderly woman looking back on her experience as a teenager. It was written by a daughter of a retainer of Ishida Mitsunari and describes the chaos and bloody nature of warfare, including the firing of cannons, the making of bullets by the wives and daughters of warriors, and the dressing of the severed heads of enemy warriors. Although she was able to escape along with her father and pregnant mother, and herself went on to live a long life, Oan's fourteen-year-old brother was hit by a bullet and died.

The exact number of casualties is not known, but estimates range from 4,000 to 8,000 men to as many as tens of thousands for the Western Army alone, including the daimyo Shimazu Toyohisa and Shima Sakon. Ôtani Yoshitsugu committed suicide and three other daimyo, including the leader of the Western Army, Ishida Mitsunari, were publicly executed. Large numbers of the gibbeted heads from the losing force were also displayed publicly. The *rônin* Miyamoto Musashi may have been present at the battle as part of the forces of Ukita Hideie, part of the Western Army, but there is no hard evidence to prove it conclusively. The level of casualties was no doubt considerable due to the large number of matchlock firearms employed. For example, 1,200 men under Date Masamune, the daimyo of Sendai domain, were armed with guns (in addition to the 420 horsemen, 200 archers, and 850 carrying long spears that he brought to battle).

After the battle, Ieyasu was well aware of the fact that his victory at Sekigahara was only sealed with the assistance of key former vassals of the Toyotomi, such as the Kuroda, Fukushima, and Yamauchi and the treachery of several other daimyo who switched sides during the battle. Even after Sekigahara, there were still powerful daimyo, such as Uesugi, Date, and Shimazu, of whom he had to be wary. There were also masterless samurai and other disaffected warriors who supported the Toyotomi; although they were defeated in the Battle of Osaka, sufficient numbers still remained after the conflict and would support the forces that rose in opposition to Tokugawa-led forces in the Shimabara Rebellion. It would take three more years before Ieyasu felt confident enough in his consolidation of power over the Toyotomi and other daimyo before demanding that the emperor appoint his shogun.

The political results of Sekigahara were far-reaching. As a result of the victory, the Tokugawa were able to redraw the political map of Japan and increase his family's landed wealth from 3 million to almost 7 million *koku* of rice. Outside lords (*tozama daimyô*) who were friendly to the Tokugawa were moved to strategic positions where they hedged in domains that had opposed Ieyasu. For example, Lord Hosokawa (at Kumamoto) and Lord Kuroda (at Fukuoka) were placed to wedge in Satsuma and Saga domains; while Lord Ikeda (at Okayama) and Lord Asano (at Hiroshima) were relocated to surround Chôshû. Moreover, while not a vassal of Ieyaus's in 1600, Yamauchi Kazutoyo, a minor daimyo who had supported the Tokugawa side at Sekigahara with only a small army of slightly more than 2,000, was richly rewarded. In moving him from central Japan to the southern portion of Shikoku Island, Katsutoyo's new domain of Tosa represented a more than threefold increase in size, from 60,000 *koku* to 242,000 *koku*, as he was moved. In Tosa he replaced Chôsokabe Morichika, who had sided with the Western Army, had his domain confiscated, and was sent into exile.

In general, domains that opposed the Tokugawa were punished while those who supported them were rewarded. However, even Chôshû, whose Lord Môri Terumoto who was ambivalent about fighting Ieyasu and sat out the battle, was punished. Môri found his domain severely reduced, from its original seven provinces to just two. In terms of productive capacity this represented a drop from 1.2 million *koku* to 298,480 *koku*. Morover, Môri lost his castle at Hiroshima, and as a result had to construct a new one, at Hagi, at great cost. At the same time Ieyasu also sought to draw Môri closer to him by marrying his adopted granddaughter to Terumoto's son.

On the other hand, the Tokugawa did not take punitive action against the daimyo of Satsuma, Shimazu Yoshihiro, even though he had opposed the Tokugawa at Sekigahara. Although the reasons for leaving the domain intact were not made explicit, it can be hypothesized that the Ieyasu wanted to avoid what would have been a costly and perhaps drawn-out military campaign at the far reaches of the archipelago had he decided to order to reduce the Shimazu's territory. Wisely, after Shimazu Yoshihiro fled the battlefield back to Satsuma, his brother put him under confinement while two vassals made an appeal to the Tokugawa for clemency, which Ieyasu granted. Although he may have done this, in part, to avoid a costly, drawn-out military conflict in faraway Satsuma, it was also in an act of magnanimity designed to win over others who had opposed him.

The historical memory of Sekigahara was long-lasting, and the anti-Tokugawa sentiments of two of the largest losers in the political settlement that followed it, were institutionalized in a number of ways. In Chôshû, these sentiments were crystallized into specific practices such as the New Year's audience before the lord in which the domain councilors ritualistically would ask the daimyo, "Has the time come to begin the subjugation of the bakufu?" The daimyo would then reply, "It is still too early; the time is not yet come" (Quoted in Craig, 1961, 22). Another comparable custom, with a more domestic setting, involved the mothers of samurai in Chôshû, who were said to have their boys sleep with their feet pointing east, in the direction of Edo, as a form of insult to the Tokugawa, and who enjoined them "never to forget the defeat at Sekigahara, even in their dreams" (Quoted in Craig, 1961, 22). In Satsuma, the battle was memorialized with a special ceremony on the anniversary of the defeat in which the domain's samurai would don their armor and go to a temple near the castle town to meditate on the loss. On the following day, they returned to the castle town to listen to a recounting of the military account of the conflict, "The Military Record of the Battle of Sekigahara" (*Sekigahara gunki*). For more than 250 years, then, the two domains kept the memory of their loss alive. Although it is difficult to judge the extent to which these formalized rituals directly affected the sentiments of the retainers, these were the two key domains that were most responsible for the overthrow of the shogunate in 1868.

See also: Shimabara Rebellion (*Shimabara no ran*); Shogunate (*bakufu, kôgi*); Sieges of Osaka (*Ôsaka no jin*); Tokugawa Ieyasu

---

Remembering the Battle of Sekigahara

As Japan's most celebrated battle, Sekigahara has been the subject of numerous novels, historical films, television shows, and video games, and is popular among historical reenactors in Japan. The battle is depicted at the beginning of director Inagaki Hiroshi's 1954 film *Samurai I,* the first of his samurai trilogy, serves as a backdrop to James Clavell's novel (later turned miniseries and film) *Shogun,* and is the subject of Harada Masato's 2017 period drama (*jidaigeki*) *Sekigahara.* The author (and former director of the Economic Planning Agency) Taichi Sakaiya has written a bestselling novel *Oinaru Kuwadate* (*The Great Scheme,* 1984) based on the conflict. Manga, anime, board games, and video games (such as *Kessen* and *Total War: Shogun 2*) have appeared. There is even a historical theme park, Sekigahara War Land, in Sekigahara city (Gifu prefecture). At this site, measuring more than 30,000 square meters, more than 200 life-size statues of participants have been erected, recreating the atmosphere of the conflict. In 2000 there was a calendar of events commemorating the battle's quadricentennial, including a reenactment of the battle with 800 participants in full battle attire. At its conclusion, a religious service was held for the repose of the men who had lost their lives in the battle. Further commemorations and exhibitions of the event followed in 2015, the 400th anniversary of Tokugawa Ieyasu's death.

Further Reading

Bryant, Anthony. *Sekigahara 1600: The Final Struggle for Power*. Oxford: Osprey Publishing, 1995.

Craig, Albert M. *Chôshû in the Meiji Restoration*. Cambridge, MA: Harvard University Press, 1961.

"O-An Monogatari." In Haruo Shirane, *Early Modern Japanese Literature: An Anthology, 1600–1900*, 39–41. New York: Columbia University Press, 2002.

Sadler, A. L. *The Maker of Modern Japan: The Life of Tokugawa Ieyasu*. London: George Allen & Unwin, 1937.

Sansom, George. *A History of Japan, 1334–1615*. Stanford, CA: Stanford University Press, 1961.

Sekijô nikki (Sekijô Diary)

A picture diary kept by Oshin domain (present-day Saitama prefecture) samurai Ozaki Sekijô, *Sekijô nikki* provides a visual record of his life over the course of 178 days over the years 1861–1862. It is an important resource for understanding the daily life of a low-ranking domain samurai late in the Tokugawa period.

Sekijô, also known as Junnosuke, was born the second son of Shônai domain's Edo-based retainer Asai Katsu'eimon, but he was adopted out to the Ozaki family of Oshin domain. There in Oshin he was a middle-ranking samurai, of mounted warrior (*umamawari*) status, and held a stipend of 100 *koku*. He was also a prolific writer of miscellanies and poetry, as well as a talented artist who painted pictures on scrolls, screens, and *fusuma* (a type interior sliding door typically covered in cloth). Sekijô amassed a large collection of more than four hundred books, which included ancient Chinese texts, Japanese poetry, books on military affairs, including one on *seppuku* (ritual suicide).

At the age of twenty-nine he submitted a politically sensitive memorial on domain government to Oshin authorities; the exact content of the document is unknown, but it appears that it contained some pro-imperial loyalist sentiments. The domain's response was to punish him with a type of domiciliary confinement known as *chikkyo* ("solitary confinement"). This was not the most severe type of confinement; although the shutters of the windows of his residence had to remain shut during his period of punishment, he was allowed to receive guests after dark; an image of him with several friends is contained in the diary. However, he was also demoted significantly, dropping to a position as a low-ranking retainer. His stipend was reduced drastically to one-fifth of its former level. This was not sufficient to maintain his household, but he was able to survive financially at this time by selling his art and teaching calligraphy. Sekijô completed his diary at the age of thirty-three while living at the residence of his married sister (he appears to have been driven out of the Ozaki residence after his punishment).

Sekijô nikki contains images (paintings) and detailed written descriptions of the meals he consumed at home and at restaurants, the drinking and socializing he did, festivities attended, and many other elements of his daily life. The diary is a particularly valuable record of a lower-samurai's diet. His family's meals were quite frugal, often consisting of soup, pickled vegetables, and rice with green tea poured over it (*chazuke*). On some days he recorded eating green tea over rice for all three meals. Sometimes his diet was supplemented with tofu or boiled vegetables, but he only consumed an egg a week. Fish was an extravagance. Even on New Year's Day, a major holiday in the Japanese calendar, there were no special dishes other than boiled pounded rice (*mochi*) served in vegetable soup.

Sekijô nikki appears to be an honest historical account of Sekijô's life, for he did not always present himself in the best light. He was openly quite fond of sake, and on several occasions he writes of his mishaps when he was drunk; for example, one time his *kozuka*, a knife attached to a sword sheath, fell out and cut his finger; another time he slipped and fell.

See also: Punishment; Retainer Corps (*kashindan*); *Seppuku* (Ritual Suicide)

Further Reading and Viewing

Ôoka Toshiaki. *Bushi no enikki. Bakumatsu no kurashi to sumai no fûkei* [A samurai's picture diary. His life and lifestyle in the late Tokugawa period]. Tokyo: Kadokawa, 2014.

"Sekijô nikki." https://kmj.flet.keio.ac.jp/material/sekijou_diary/sn_01.html (images and Japanese-only text). Accessed July 25, 2018.

Separation of Warrior and Peasant (*heinô bunri*)

During the late 1580s and 1590s, Toyotomi Hideyoshi issued a series of edicts that sought to bring order to a society that had been wracked by warfare for more than a century. In 1588 he issued the so-called "sword hunt," which called on all villagers to surrender their weapons, including all bows, swords, spears, and firearms, and instructed officials to implement the edict. Three years later, in 1591, he ordered that censuses be taken in the countryside to prevent military men from taking refuge in them. Third, he also decreed in effect that the social order be frozen: no peasant could become a samurai and vice versa, no samurai could settle in secret in the countryside as a peasant. This is known by historians as the "separation of warrior and peasant," or *heinô bunri*.

Although Hideyoshi's order was intended as an edict to be implemented nationwide, it reflected the policies that many daimyo already were pursuing in their individual domains. In those domains, samurai found themselves pulled from above by the daimyo and at the same time pushed from below by forces within the village. To stabilize their military power, daimyo sought to control the warriors under them and to forge them into a retainer corps dependent on their authority. They did this in part through the forced removal of many warriors from the land to the new castle towns being constructed as domain headquarters across the country. They also worked to break the ties of their powerful vassals to the land by conducting cadastral surveys of their domains, through which the daimyo were able to measure their vassals' lands and to assign a value to their income. By doing this, the daimyo were able to substitute income from the land from an actual landholding, thereby making it easier to transfer their more important vassals and to undercut their vassals' ties to ancestral landholdings.

The removal of the samurai from the land was also a result of the "push" from below by villagers, who sought to reduce or to eliminate the control that the samurai had over their lives. In some cases, daimyo even encouraged actions on the part of villagers to accelerate the process. No doubt there were samurai who welcomed these changes, as samurai who drew income while residing in the castle towns were spared having to deal with the villagers and enjoyed the promise of a steady income source.

Breaking warriors' ties with the land was easy enough to do with minor vassals who held only small landholdings. These samurai were simply ordered to surrender their lands, to move into the daimyo's castle town, and take a stipend instead. In Owari domain, for example, retainers of 300 *koku* or less were ordered to surrender their fiefs and draw a salary; in other domains, such as Sendai, the figure was 100 *koku*. It was more difficult, however, to control more important vassals, with larger landholdings. Nevertheless, those vassals whose daimyo were assigned new domains after Hideyoshi's military unification of the country or after the Battles of Sekigahara (1600) and Osaka (1614–1615) inevitably had their ancestral ties to landholdings severed.

As a result of these various social and political forces, not to mention the political decrees issued by Hideyoshi, samurai and peasant became functionally as well as physically separated: peasants farmed and lived in the countryside; samurai lived in the castle towns, bore arms (a long and a short sword), and assumed new social and political functions that came to be known as the way of the warrior (*shidô*). As the Confucian scholar Ôgyû Sorai wrote early in the eighteenth century, "At present members of the military classes are forbidden to go into the country for a distance of more than five *ri* [about 12 miles], for it is feared that they might behave in a disorderly manner because there are no members of the military class resident there" (McEwan, 1962, 60).

The removal of the samurai from the land was a gradual process that occurred over roughly a half century, but it was by no means complete. In fact, in about thirty-five domains (less than 20 percent of the total), mostly in the periphery of the archipelago, no major attempts were made to do so. Although central Japan was largely free of independent samurai holdings, in the north (e.g., in Sendai) and in the west (e.g., Chôshû), a large percentage, but not a majority, of land remained in vassals' hands. In Satsuma no real effort was made to separate farmer and warrior at all: samurai there were allowed to remain scattered throughout the domain. In other words, sub-infeudation remained in practice in these areas, which were usually outside (*tozama*) domains. In the case of the Tokugawa, who were of course the largest of the daimyo houses, the family's direct vassals, bannermen (*hatamoto*), and housemen (*gokenin*) were largely kept in Edo, where they could serve the shogun and his government. Only a minority of the more than 5,000 bannermen were enfiefed—that is, possessed actual fiefs (*chigyô*), and these were located in the provinces around Edo in the Kantô region. They lived in Edo but could travel, with permission, to their fiefs as needed. All of the housemen, the lower-ranking group of direct vassals who were, as just noted, set apart from the bannermen in terms of income and status, resided in Edo, essentially as salaried employees of the shogunate.

Samurai who lived in castle towns could obtain permission from their domain government to be allowed to live temporarily outside of the urban settlement. This was possible if a samurai petitioned to be declared officially "poverty stricken" (*hissoku*). In Chôshû domain (1669), for example, samurai with fiefs or stipends under 200 *koku*, which meant the vast majority of the retainer corps, were allowed to petition for this temporary status. In Okayama domain the policy was enacted even earlier, prior to the 1654 flood that devastated the area.

Although many, if not most, samurai experienced financial difficulties, in being declared by the domain government officially "poverty stricken" a retainer was given permission to live temporarily outside the castle town, as well as to withdraw from official duties and contacts (known as *zaigô kanryaku*). From the domain's perspective, this permission was given for the purpose of allowing an insolvent retainer's household time to try to recover its economic health. As Tosa samurai Tani Tannai explained, by being declared "poverty stricken" and moving out of the castle town to a residence closer to the mountains that ring Kôchi, where the cost of living was lower, he could lower his household's expenses. Outside the castle town the rent would be cheaper, he explained in a letter he wrote to his merchant financier, and his manservant could gather firewood in the mountains, rather than having to pay for it as he did in the city.

The measure to allow samurai to live in rural areas was intended as a temporary expedient. Ikeda Mitsumasa (1609–1682), the daimyo of Okayama, made it clear that it was "disloyal" for his vassals who were given permission to reside in the countryside "to have an attitude of enjoying domestic sufficiency" (Quoted in McMullen, 1999, 98). He also threatened to punish with *seppuku* (ritual suicide) any retainer who contracted further debts while living in the countryside and used this as a pretext to be excused from further service obligations to the lord.

A number of Tokugawa intellectuals, such as Kumazawa Banzan (1619–1691) and Ogyû Sorai (1666–1728), advocated ending the separation of warriors and peasants by resettling the samurai on the land, a phenomenon known as *dochaku*. Despite the efforts of several domains to settle samurai in the countryside during the second half of the Tokguawa period, and the opposition of some intellectuals to keeping samurai gathered in the castle towns, the policy of "separating warrior and peasant" was not reversed. In the mid-nineteenth century, some domains charged with coastal defense moved military units to coastline areas to defend against foreign ships, but *heinô bunri* remained in effect for the remainder of the period.

See also: Bannermen (*hatamoto*); *Budô shoshinshû* (*The Way of the Warrior: A Primer*); Castle Towns (*jôkamachi*); Kumazawa Banzan; Resettlement of Samurai (*dochaku*); Rural Samurai (*gôshi*); Sword Hunt (*katanagari*); Tani Tannai

Further Reading

Birt, Michael P. "Samurai in Passage: The Transformation of the Sixteenth-Century Kanto." *Journal of Japanese Studies,* 11(2) (1985), 369–399.

McEwan, J. R. *The Political Writings of Ôgyû Sorai.* Cambridge: Cambridge University Press, 1962.

McMullen, James. *Idealism, Protest and the Tale of Genji: The Confucianism of Kumazawa Banzan (1619–91).* Oxford: Oxford University Press, 1999. (See in particular Part II: A Warrior's Life.)

Seppuku (Ritual Suicide)

Seppuku, a more formal term for *harakiri*, is a suicidal practice by "cutting the belly." It is believed that the abdomen was chosen because of the ancient notion that it was the places where the soul resides. The first literary evidence for the practice can be traced back to the early eighth century, but recorded instances of *seppuku* became more frequent with the rise of the samurai as a social force in the twelfth century. During the Tokugawa period *seppuku* was just one of many practices of the samurai that experienced profound change, as it underwent a process of institutionalization and ritualization. It was formally abolished in 1874, after the end of the Tokugawa period, but continued to be practiced occasionally thereafter by military officers and ultranationalists during World War II and most recently and infamously by the writer Mishima Yukio in 1970.

Prior to the Tokugawa period, samurai most often committed *seppuku* to avoid the disgrace of falling into enemy hands. For example, in the twelfth-century war chronicle *The Tale of Hōgen*, the exiled Minamoto Tametomo withdrew into his private room and disemboweled himself in a standing position rather than yield to the 300 warriors sent to kill him; he then proceeded to throw his intestines at the enemy before collapsing. Many samurai committed *seppuku* during the Mongol invasions of the late thirteenth century in order to show their valor in the face of

Staged scene depicting *seppuku* ("ritual suicide"), also known as *harakiri*, from the late 19th century. A samurai in white death robes has opened a cut in his abdomen while his *kaishakunin* ("second") stands behind him, ready to cut off his head. Two officials sit nearby as witnesses. Such staged photos depicting an "exotic" Japan were often sold to western tourists in souvenir albums. (Image Broker/Alamy Stock Photo)

the foreign enemy, to avoid capture, and to assume responsibility for mistakes in battle or for local defeats. During the internecine civil war that was the Sengoku period (1467–1600), *seppuku* remained a form of suicide practice by samurai on the battlefield to demonstrate their valor and avoid capture. A samurai might also be ordered by his lord to kill himself to atone for some offense. Similarly, a defeated daimyo might be called on to commit ritual suicide as part of a peace agreement, as was the case in 1590 when the daimyo Hôjô Ujimasa was instructed by Toyotomi Hideyoshi to do so after the Hôjô's defeat at Odawara in 1590.

During the peaceful Tokugawa era *seppuku* was variously institutionalized, ritualized as well as standardized. Before carrying out *seppuku* the samurai bathed, dressed in white (death) robes, and ate a final meal, which included sake (white rice wine). He was also given the opportunity to write a death poem before carrying out the ceremony before what was generally a small number of official spectators. The samurai was assisted in this act by a second, or *kaishakunin*; ideally it was a close friend of the principal or someone who excelled as a swordsman, being able to cut the neck in such a way that a small band of flesh kept the head attached to the body, hanging in front, rather than rolling unceremoniously away. Few had such skills, which meant that the principal was usually decapitated.

An agreement was made beforehand by the principal and second as to when decapitation would take place. Usually, this occurred when the short sword (*wakizashi*) was plunged into the abdomen, rather than waiting for complete disembowelment to take place; but as the practice became even more ritualized, it could take place as soon as the principal reached for the sword. In some cases the sword was done away with altogether, replaced with something symbolic like a fan.

Seppuku also underwent a basic change in purpose, as it became a type of penalty prescribed by political authorities for samurai, and only for samurai; as such, *seppuku* was the most severe of the various grades of penalties to which they were subject. Members of the other status groups (peasants, artisans, and merchants) convicted of a capital offense were put to death by beheading or crucifixion. As befitting their status at the top of the status system, samurai were given the privilege of committing *seppuku* for their crimes rather than being executed by others. It was thus a type of "conferred death" (*ishi*). The four to six former retainers of Lord Asano Naganori, who was forced to commit *seppuku* for drawing his sword in the shogun's palace in an attempt to kill Kira Kôzunosuke in 1701, were granted permission to commit *seppuku*, as samurai, even though they were *rônin* and therefore technically not qualified for the privilege.

There were numerous types of *seppuku*, as outlined in Table 8. The practice can be divided into two main categories. It was performed as an act forced on an individual for criminal punishment (*tsumebara*) or as a voluntarily act of self-destruction (*jijin*). In the former category we can include *junshi* (*seppuku* performed to follow one's lord in death), *memboku* (*seppuku* performed to prove one's innocence), *kanshi* (in protest again some action taken by a samurai's lord), and *inseki* (performed to assume responsibility for some mistake). The second category includes three types of forced *seppuku* for punishment. The vast majority of *seppuku* was committed in the sitting position (*suwaribara*), while standing *seppuku* (*tachibara*) was

Table 8   Typology of *Seppuku*

General Category	Type	Motives
Jijin (voluntary *seppuku*)		
	1. *Jiketsu*	Defeat in battle
	2. *Inseki*	Assuming responsibility for mistakes
	3. Sacrifice	To save one's own group
	4. *Kanshi*	To protest against misconduct of one's lord
	5. *Menboku*	To prove one's innocence
	6. *Junshi*	
	a. *Sakibara*	To precede one's lord or someone else in death
	b. *Atobara*	To follow someone else shortly after or later
	c. *Oibara*	To follow someone else immediately after
	7. *Oibara*	
	a. *Gibara*	Committed because of *giri* (duty/responsibility)
	b. *Ronbara*	To save one's face
	c. *Shobara*	For the future benefits of one's posterity
Tsumebara (forced *seppuku* for punishment)		
	1. *Munenbara*	Mortified suicide for unfulfilled objectives
	2. *Funbara*	Assuming responsibility legally and morally for someone else
	3. *Keishi*	Legal punishment for crime

Source: Toyomasa Fuse, "An Institutionalized Form of Suicide in Japan," *Journal of Intercultural Studies,* 5 (1978), 54.

committed when facing an enemy during battle, which means that during the peaceful Tokugawa years it was quite uncommon.

There were primarily two forms of disembowelment, and at times both could involve the samurai taking out his intestines and other internal organs. In the most common form (*ichimonji-bara*) the belly was slit with a single line (*ichimonji*), with the blade, held in the right hand, thrust into the left side a few inches below the rib cage and then pulled sideways to the far right. Should the samurai have no second to cut off his head, he might use the same blade to then slash his own throat or to stab himself in the heart. The second most common form, *jumonji-bara* ("cross-forming *seppuku*"), involved adding a vertical cut from the upper center of the rib cage down to below the navel after the aforementioned horizontal single line, thus forming a cross. This type of disembowelment was common in battle; it required a great deal more determination and fortitude to perform, and as peaceful conditions set in during the early seventeenth century it went out of practice.

Although *junshi* occurred occasionally during the medieval period in Japan, usually after a battle when the samurai lost his lord in battle, its practice was quite noticeable once peace set in during the early Tokugawa period. Deprived of the means to show their bravery and loyalty on the battlefield, some samurai felt the need to demonstrate their loyalty when their lord died, of natural causes or illness, by committing ritual suicide. In fact, *junshi* became somewhat of a fad. For example, when the Lord Date Masume died in 1636, fifteen samurai followed him in death by their own hands. Actually, six of the fifteen men were rear vassals (or subvassals) whose masters had committed *junshi* upon the death of Lord Date. Twenty-six samurai followed Lord Nabeshima Katsushige in death in 1657. A samurai who performed *junshi* not only demonstrated his skill in the marital arts but was usually honored posthumously and his heirs well rewarded. Sometimes *junshi* was also related to the socially sanctioned sexual relationship that sometimes existed between lord and vassal.

Since the practice of *junshi* resulted in the removal from service, through death, of valuable retainers who could be of use to the new lord, it came to be viewed as an obstruction to orderly government, leading several daimyo to ban the practice. The Tokugawa shogunate itself moved to ban the practice in 1663, and it was rigorously enforced when, for example, Sugiura Uemon, a vassal of Lord Okudaira Tadamasa, committed *junshi* in 1668. The heirs of both the lord and his vassal were punished. The prohibition was further reinforced through its inclusion in the *Laws for the Military Houses* of 1683. Both codification of the *Laws* and active enforcement acted to stymie this samurai custom. The abolition of *junshi* is interpreted by many historians as an important sign of a shift from a military-based society to a more civil one.

Westerners first wrote about *junshi* during the late sixteenth and early seventeenth centuries. Perhaps the first mention was by the Portuguese Jesuit priest Luis Frois (1532–1597), who wrote: "In Europe when the master dies, his followers weep and send him to the grave, while in Japan some people cut their stomach and many

---

Even the Loyal Cat Committed Junshi *(Following the Lord in Ritual Suicide)*

When the lord of Hagi domain, Môri Terumoto (1553–1625), died his retainer Nagai Motofusa, followed his lord in death, committing *junshi*, a category of ritual suicide carried out after one's lord's passing. He was honored posthumously for his loyalty by being buried nearby his lord at Tenjuin, the lord's retirement place that was subsequently converted to a family temple. As the placard at Nagai's grave explains: "Motofusa had a beloved cat. After Motofusa's death, the cat would not leave from his master's graveside. Following the forty-ninth day of mourning, the cat killed itself by biting its tongue out of grief." According to local lore, because of the cat's loyalty, this area of Hagi gained the informal name "Cat Town" (Nekono-chô). Thus, according to this local lore, the cat was a paragon of virtue, its loyalty echoing that of its master, Motofusa, who was in turn loyal to his lord, Môri Terumoto.

people cut off the tip of their little finger and throw it into the fire which is burning the corpse" (Quoted in Kakubayashi, 1993, 217). François Caron (1600–1673), a Frenchman in the employ of the Dutch East India Company, also wrote about the practice during his more than twenty years of residence in Japan in his book, *A True Description of the Mighty Kingdoms of Japan and Siam* (1636) (excerpted in Document 7).

During peacetime samurai served their lords in a variety of ways, and when they failed to perform their job properly often took responsibility by committing *seppuku*. One notable example of this type of *seppuku* occurred in 1754 when a group of fifty-one samurai from Satsuma killed themselves to take responsibility for a delay in completing a riverine flood-control project in central Japan (Mino province) that Satsuma domain had been ordered to undertake by the Tokugawa shogunate. A local samurai from Mino and a Tokugawa supervisor also committed *seppuku*. Another example involved the Nagasaki magistrate Matsudaira Yasuhira, who committed *seppuku* in 1808 after failing to prevent the entry of the British frigate *Phaeton* from Nagasaki harbor. During the Edo period the Dutch were the only Westerners permitted to trade in Japan. Matsudaira, as the top government official in Nagasaki, was unable to stop the vessel from entering the harbor and also unable to destroy it afterward (the harbor defenses were inadequate relative to the firepower onboard the *Phaeton*). To prevent a criminal investigation for violating Tokugawa law, which would likely have led to the punishment of family members as well, Matsudaira committed *seppuku*. Before doing so he left a memorial, a written account, in which he explained the circumstances of the incident. By taking these actions he was able to preserve both personal and family honor.

After the opening of Japanese ports to Westerners in the mid-nineteenth century, news about *seppuku* made its way to Europe and to the United States due to a number of violent encounters between samurai and foreigners that were reported in the press. For example, the *seppuku* of one of the three samurai held responsible for the murder of two British officers in Kamakura in 1864 was publicized in the *Illustrated London News*. The British diplomat Ernest Satow and Algernon Mitford both published reports of the *seppuku* ceremony they had witnessed in 1868; after a confrontation between two French sailors and a large group of samurai from Bizen the commander of the troops, Taki Zenzaburô, took responsibility with his own death (see Document 7). Perhaps the most notorious incident from the perspective of foreigners involved a group of French sailors who skirmished with twenty samurai from Tosa domain who were stationed near Osaka in early 1868. Armed with both guns and their swords, the samurai shot dead eleven Frenchmen who had landed ashore from their ship, apparently to purchase some fruit, but without a permit. The French government demanded punishment, but since it was unclear whose shots had actually killed the men, the shogunate decreed that twenty men must kill themselves. Both leaders of the two units volunteered for *seppuku*, and lots were drawn for the other eighteen slots. With French officials present at the formal *seppuku* ceremony, one by one eleven samurai calmly went to their deaths by slitting their bellies. Both astonished at the stoicism of the men in going to their deaths and horrified by the gruesome nature of their deaths (some of the samurai pulled out their entrails and taunted the Frenchmen; in other cases it took multiple attempts to decapitate the men), the French official present stood up and to took his leave after the eleventh man had taken his life. The official said he ended the proceedings, which had already gone on for two hours, as a gesture of leniency, while the Japanese largely interpreted it as a sign of the weakness of foreigners. This interpretation was popularized in Japan by the Meiji writer Mori Ôgai in the short story "*Sakai jiken*" ("The Incident at Sakai," 1914).

After the Meiji Restoration of 1868, the status of *seppuku* was debated in the early national legislative body created. In that body, Ôno Seigoro advocated for the abolition of *seppuku*, arguing that "it is a practice unheard of in the civilized West, and it is also an obstacle to social justice. If someone wants to prove his innocence, he should do so at the court of law . . ." (Quoted in Fuse, 1978, 54). Nevertheless, 200 of the 209 members of that body voted against the proposed ban of a custom that was referred to in the debate as "the very shrine of the Japanese national spirit." One of the three men who voted for the motion (there were six abstentions) actually was murdered not long after the debate. Only in 1873, and with a far different parliament in place, was a ban put in place.

There were, as noted, some instances of *seppuku* after this time, but as the case of General Nogi Maresuke and his wife, who committed *junshi* following the death of the Meiji emperor in 1912, the Japanese public viewed the act with mixed emotions. In the Japanese press, while some praised their deaths as acts of loyalty and bravery in modern times, others criticized their deaths as a barbaric tradition that should be left in the past.

See also: Akô Incident; Punishment; Document 6; Document 7

Harakiri, *the Film*

Harakiri, the Japanese term for ritual suicide as it is best known outside of Japan, is also one of the most renowned period-dramas (*jidaigeki*) and films ever made on the samurai. Director Kobayashi Masaki's 1962 black-and-white film, known in Japan as *Seppuku,* is a 133-minute-long epic, produced by Shochiku, which received the Special Jury Prize at the 1963 Cannes Film Festival. More recently, film reviewer Roger Ebert included it in his list of "Great Movies."

The film, set in the early 1600s, tells the story of a masterless samurai named Tsugumo Hanshirô, who arrives at the residence of the daimyo family Ii and asks for a space within the courtyard to commit ritual suicide. To dissuade him from doing so the senior councilor of the domain tells Tsugumo a story of a man, Chijiiwa Motome, who had previously arrived there with a similar mission. Although Tsugumo claims not to know the man whom the elder speaks of, through a series of flashbacks, the viewer learns that Tsugumo is Chijiiwa's father-in-law and knowing that Chijiiwa had been forced to commit hara-kiri with a bamboo sword had come to the Ii residence seeking some justice for him. The film ends with Tsugumo's own bloody murder–*seppuku*, but only after he has exposed the hypocrisy of the Ii clan and its perversion of the informal samurai code of behavior.

The full storyline, reviews, and trivia about the film can be found on the Internet Movie Database: http://www.imdb.com/title/tt0056058.

Further Reading

Fuse, Toyomasa. "*Seppuku*. An Institutionalized Form of Suicide in Japan." *Journal of Intercultural Studies,* 5 (1978), 48–66.

Ikegami, Eiko. *The Taming of the Samurai: Honorific Individualism and the Making of Modern Japan.* Cambridge, MA: Harvard University Press, 1995.

Kakubayashi, Fumio. "An Historical Study of Harakiri." *The Australian Journal of Politics and History,* 39(2) (1993), 217–225.

Mori, Ôgai. "The Incident at Sakai." In David Dilworth and J. Thomas Rimer, eds., *The Historical Fiction of Mori Ôgai,* 129–152. Honolulu: University of Hawai'i Press, 1991.

Rankin, Andrew. *Seppuku: A History of Samurai Suicide.* Tokyo, New York: Kodansha International, 2011.

Seward, Jack. *Harakiri: Japanese Ritual Suicide.* Rutland, VT: Tuttle Publishing, 1968.

Shimabara Rebellion (*Shimabara no ran*) (1637–1638)

An uprising of peasants and *rônin* (masterless samurai) that took place in 1637–1638, in what is now present-day Nagasaki prefecture in southwestern Japan, the Shimabara Rebellion was the last major armed conflict during the Tokugawa period until the 1860s. The uprising was suppressed with great loss of life on the part of the local population, but only after a period of four months and with the assistance of Dutch firepower. The difficulty with which the insurrection was put down led some contemporary observers to bemoan the decline of the samurai's martial skills, only twenty-odd years after the Sieges of Osaka. The shogunate attributed the disturbance to the pernicious effects of Christianity, giving it the pretext to enforce the ban on the foreign religion even more strictly and to expel the Portuguese from Japan, leaving the Dutch as the only Westerners allowed in the country.

Although the shogunate attributed the uprising to Christianity, its origins lay in the oppressive tax policies of lords (daimyo) who had been reassigned to domains on the Shimabara peninsula and Amakusa Islands. The local lord, Arima Harunobu, was a Christian, and as a result many of the people in his domain had also converted. In 1614, he was replaced by Matsukura Shigemasa, who was not an adherent of the foreign faith. There was also a change in leadership of the Amakusa Islands, which were part of Karatsu domain, from the Konishi family to that of the Terasawa (Katataka). Both new lords tried to extract greater taxes from the local population; in the case of the Matsukura, it was to pay for the costs of building a new castle at Shimabara. Matsukura also strictly enforced the persecution of Christianity, which greatly antagonized the local population.

Due to the effects of heavy taxation, famine conditions, and discontent against government persecution of Christianity, the peasants of the region, together with discontented former samurai who had been made *rônin* with the change in daimyo of Shimabara and Karatsu domains, began to meet in secret and plot against the local political authorities. A local domain official for Shimabara, the intendant (*daikan*) Hayashi Hyôzaemon, was killed, and the rebellion spread to the outlying Amakusa Islands. The rebels attempted to lay siege to several of the local castles but were repelled repeatedly. Finally, they occupied the abandoned site of Hara

Castle, which had been left unoccupied by the Arima clan before its move to Nobeoka, and built up the defenses as best as they could.

The shogunate called on the local daimyo to contribute troops to put down the rebellion. Military units from four daimyo domains in Kyushu—Shimabara, Saga, Kurume, and Yanagawa—were mobilized and made the first attacks on Hara Castle. The lord of Saga, Nabeshima Katsushige, led the attack on Shimabara Castle, before the shogunate gave the official order to do so. He likely did so in an effort to make up for the shortcomings of his father, who had belatedly joined Tokugawa Ieyasu at Sekigahara in 1600, and for this he was later punished. After several unsuccessful attacks on the castle, a second group of eight additional domains were called on to contribute forces, and the shogunate dispatched two additional generals to direct the siege. In total, an estimated 120,000–140,000 troops were mobilized for the combined shogunate's composite forces, with Kumamoto (28,600), Saga (22,003), and Fukuoka (20,9024) providing the largest number (Keith, 2006, 109). Shogunal officials came to the siege with much smaller numbers of forces, as was the case with the Nagasaki commissioner, who arrived with only 603 men.

Inside Hara Castle, an estimated 35,000 people, villagers and *rônin*, resisted the onslaught of the military force sent against them. The insurgents, led by a charismatic sixteen-year-old named Amakusa Shirô, used a number of banners utilizing Christian symbols, which gave their effort a religious color (that was perhaps inspired by rebellions in the Buddhist *ikkô* tradition). The rebels in their small fortress were able to hold out against the shogunate-led forces, despite the assistance of the Dutch, who were ordered to shell the castle. The Dutch were reported to have fired about 426 rounds at the castle over a period of fifteen days, from guns on board the Dutch vessel *de Ryp* and from a shore battery, but without apparent great effect. The use of foreign firepower resulted in the dispatch of a contemptuous message from the defenders to the attacking force: "Are there no longer courageous soldiers [i.e., samurai] in the realm to do combat with us, and weren't they ashamed to have called in the assistance of foreigners against our small contingent?"

In the end, though, the defenders were starved into submission after four months and wiped out in a final onslaught. Between those who were killed in Hara Castle and any escapees, who were later hunted down, as many as 37,000 people were slaughtered. After the rebellion was put down, the daimyo of Shimabara domain was actually beheaded in Edo for his misrule, the only instance of this type of punishment being imposed on a lord during the Tokugawa period.

See also: Daimyo and Domains; Intendants (*daikan*); Ronin (*rônin*); Sekigahara, Battle of; Shogunate (*bakufu, kôgi*); Sieges of Osaka (*Ôsaka no jin*)

Further Reading

Doeff, Hendrik. *Recollections of Japan*. Translated and Annotated by Annick M. Doeff. Victoria, B.C.: Trafford, 2003.

Keith, Matthew E. "The Logistics of Power: The Tokugawa Response to the Shimabara Rebellion and Power Projection in Seventeeth-Century Japan." PhD dissertation, The Ohio State University, 2006.

Murdoch, James. *A History of Japan*, vol. II. Introduction and Bibliography by John L. Misch. New York: Frederick Ungar Publishing Co., 1964.

Shinsengumi

A special police force organized by the Tokugawa shogunate in 1864 to maintain peace and order in Kyoto during the turbulent *bakumatsu* ("end-of-the-*bakufu*") period, the Shinsengumi ("newly selected corps") were known for their violence but also as loyal defenders of the Tokugawa, even past the regime's end in 1868. They are often credited with delaying the eventual victory of the imperial loyalists over the Tokugawa regime.

Following the arrival of the American naval expedition under the command of Commodore Matthew C. Perry in 1853, increasing numbers of antishogunate imperial loyalists rallied under the slogan *sonnô jôi* ("Revere the Emperor, Expel the Barbarian"). These men became increasingly active after the ports were opening to foreigners in 1859 and then in the following year when the shogunate's top official (*tairô,* or "great elder"), Ii Naosuke, was assassinated by a group of samurai from Mito and Satsuma domains in 1860. At the end of 1862, the shogunate decided to organize its own group of armed men in support of the regime, *rônin* (masterless samurai) drawn from sword schools in Edo, in an effort to suppress the loyalists operating in the imperial capital of Kyoto. This group of about 250 men, known as the Rôshigumi, or "*rônin* squad," was dispatched to Kyoto in 1863, but the discovery that a large number of them had questionable loyalty to the shogun led to a split in the group. The majority of the group returned to Edo under the leadership of Shônai retainer and imperial loyalist Kiyokawa Hachirô (1830–1863), while the other remained in Kyoto in support of the shogunate. This latter group became known as the Shinsengumi.

Under the leadership of Matsudaira Katamori (1835–1893), the daimyo of Aizu who served as military governor of Kyoto (*Kyôto shugoshoku*), the Shinsengumi patrolled the streets of Kyoto in the name of the shogunate from 1863 to restore order. In 1864 thirty men from the Shinsengumi attacked a group of Chôshû loyalists lodging at the Ikedaya Inn in Kyoto, who may have been planning to burn the city. In the attack eight Chôshû men were killed and twenty-three arrested, while the Shinsengumi lost three men. The squad's success gave them increasing notoriety and promoted recruitment efforts. The following year, 1865, after Chôshû forces that had been occupying the imperial court were driven from Kyoto by samurai from Tokugawa, Aizu, and Satsuma, the Shinsengumi were also charged with assisting Aizu in guarding the gates to the imperial court. Members of the Shinsengumi may have been responsible for the murder of Tosa loyalists Sakamoto Ryôma and Nakaoka Shintarô at the Ômiya Inn in Kyoto in 1867. Although Kondô Isami was later executed for the murders, it is not clear that he was indeed responsible for the act.

The Shinsengumi originally were under the command of two men, Kondô Isami (1834–1868) and Serizawa Kamo (1826–1863), but after a power struggle between them Kondô took firm control of the group after Serizawa was assassinated by Hijikata Toshizô (1835–1869), who was loyal to Kondô and became his vice-commander. At its peak the group had as many as 300 members and included samurai as well as nonsamurai. In 1867 all members of the group were made shogunal retainers.

The Shinsengumi in Popular Culture

The Shinsengumi, a group of young swordsmen recruited by the shogunate to protect Kyoto from radical imperial loyalists in the tumultuous 1860s, has been romanticized in popular Japanese culture, including film, theater, television, anime, manga, and video games. In the postwar era, it has been the subject of at least sixteen feature films, including 1969's *Shinsengumi* (directed by Sawashima Tadashi and starring the famed actor Mifune Toshiro as the group's leader, Kondô Isami). More recently, in 2003, the director Takita Yojiro's took up the subject in his *Mibu gishi den* (*When the Last Sword Is Drawn*), a film that won the Picture of the Year by the Japan Academy. The Shingensegumi has also been the subject of at least ten television shows or series, including the 2004 yearlong NHK Taiga Drama series. Noted writer Shiba Ryôtarô's 1969 novel *Shinsengumi keppûroku* (*Record of Shinsengumi Bloodshed*) did much to popularize it, and the novel was made into an eleven-part television series of the same name in 1998. Individual members, particularly Kondô Isami and Hijikata Toshizô, frequently appear in manga, anime, and video games: for example, in manga artist Nobuhiro Watsuki's *Rurouni Kenshin*, Nanae Chrono's *Peacemaker Kurogane*, Playstation 2 action game *Fû-un Shinsengumi* (*Winds and Clouds Shinsengumi*), and as a stand-alone expansion for *Total War Shogun 2: Fall of the Samurai*. In the latter game, the Shinsengumi are recruitable agents used for assassination and bribery.

In 1867, after Tokugawa Yoshinobu, the last shogun, resigned his position, returning authority to the emperor, and withdrew from Kyoto, the Shinsengumi also left the city. They joined the pro-Tokugawa forces outside the city and fought in the Battle of Toba-Fushimi, which marked the onset of the Boshin War, losing almost one hundred men. Their leader, Kondô, suffered a gunshot in the battle but escaped, only to fight again at Kôshû-Katsunuma and be captured by imperial forces. He was later beheaded at the Itabashi execution grounds in Edo in 1868, his head put on a spike and displayed publicly for three days; incredibly, his head was salted and moved to Kyoto for further public display at the Sanjô Bridge. Other Shinsengumi members sided with Aizu forces in defending their castle town from the imperial army, which was advancing north, and joined the forces of the Republic of Ezo. Hijikata Toshizô was wounded at the Battle of Utsunomiya Castle and later decided to go to Hakodate, where opponents to the new Meiji government made their last stand. Hijikata was shot and killed at the Battle of Hakodate in 1869. The last commander of the Shinsengumi, Soma Kazue, surrendered, effectively marking the end of the group.

The historical reputation of the Shinsengumi is quite varied. Some have viewed them as Tokugawa loyalists, as evidenced by Hijikata Toshizô's moving poem: "Though my body may decay on the island of Ezo, My spirit guards my lord [the shogun] in the east" (Clements, 2010, 298). They also gained renown in some quarters for their strict code of behavior, the penalty for its abrogation being *seppuku*, and their distinctive uniforms. Their outfits consisted of a light blue *haori*, or jacket, and *hakama* (a type of trousers) worn over a kimono, with a white cord crossed over the chest and tied in the back; they also wore a light chainmail suit under their robes, a light helmet made of iron, and a headband inscribed with the word *makoto* (sincerity). Others, though, have disparaged them as vigilantes—infamous for their brutality, including the use of torture on their opponents.

See also: Boshin War; Shogunate (*bakufu, kôgi*)

Further Reading

Clements, Jonathan. *A Brief History of the Samurai*. Philadelphia: Running Press Book Publishers, 2010.

Hillsborough, Romulus. *Shinsengumi: The Shogun's Last Samurai Corps*. North Clarendon, VT: Tuttle Publishing, 2005.

Totman, Conrad. *The Collapse of the Tokugawa Bakufu, 1862–1868.* Honolulu: University of Hawai'i Press, 1980.

Shogun (*shôgun*)

An abbreviation of *sei-i-taishôgun*, which literally means the "barbarian-quelling general," the title of *shôgun* originated in the eighth century with the temporary commissions given by the Japanese emperor to a designated military figure to lead expeditions against tribal groups that occupied the northeastern portion of the main island of Honshu. Four centuries later the title became regularized with the imperial appointment of Minamoto Yoritomo as shogun, in 1192. The warrior-based government that he established is known to us today as the *bakufu* ("tent government"), which is commonly translated in English as "shogunate." The term, however, was not commonly used during the Tokugawa era—*kôgi* or *kokka* being the terms that were generally employed. There were three shogunates in Japanese history: the Kamakura (1192–1333), with its headquarters in the city of Kamakura, near present-day Tokyo; the Ashikaga (1338–1573), who moved their headquarters to Kyoto; and the third, the Tokugawa (1603–1868), who built their great capital in Edo (now Tokyo).

The primary basis for the Tokugawa shogun's authority was the superior military power that he had at his disposal, both that of his own Tokugawa family as well as from daimyo allied with him. In theory his direct vassals, the bannermen (*hatamoto*) and the housemen (*gokenin*), together with their sub-vassals and support staff, were supposed to constitute an army of 80,000 men. On top of this, the shogun in theory could call on his allied daimyo (*fudai daimyô*) and those related to the Tokugawa family, the "related daimyo" (*shinpan daimyô*). In 1634, Tokugawa Iemitsu led an army of 300,000 from Edo to Kyoto and paraded through the streets of the imperial capital in a massive display of military power meant to cower the court and the assembled daimyo. In reality, though, the shogun rarely needed to assemble an army after the Sieges of Osaka (1614–1615), due to peaceful conditions.

In theory, the shogun's authority rested on his appointment by the emperor, which came in the form of a patent of authority. However, this was largely a formality, for the imperial institution was not in a position to oppose the Tokugawa. Nevertheless, when Tokugawa Ieyasu seized political authority away from Hideyoshi's heir Hideyori in 1600, he made use of the imperial court's authority to bolster his own: "As military ruler he used the imperial appointment and rank of shogun, and as civilian ruler he used the high civil office of minister of the emperor's government" (Roberts, 2012, 23). It became customary for the shogunal heir of the Tokugawa dynasty to ascend through the imperial ranks, from minister of the

---

Writing Their Own History

The Tokugawa house commissioned the compilation of a dynastic history—the history of the shoguns and their government, the shogunate—known as *Tokugawa jikki* or *Ojiki* (*Veritable Records of the Tokugawa*), which covers the period from its founding in 1603 through 1786. This corresponds to the reigns of the first ten shoguns, from Ieyasu to Ieharu. It was compiled from 1801 to 1849 and was modeled on the great official histories of Chinese dynasties. The final five shogunal reigns were covered in a second series, *Zoku Tokugawa jikki*, or *Supplemental Veritable Records of the Tokugawa, Supplemental Edition*. Both series contain mostly routine notices related to the appointment, promotion, and dismissal of officials and records of the ritual observances of the regime; but it also contains some political commentaries, battle reports, and materials on institutional reforms. Both series are notable for their focus on the Tokugawa house rather than the emperor; indeed, the history is organized into chapters by shogunal rather than imperial reign. Nevertheless, the imperial role in bestowing appointments on the Tokugawa as shoguns is acknowledged. Furthermore, the person of the emperor is treated with respect, as he is usually referred to as lord (*shujô*).

---

interior, to minister of the right, to minister of the left, and then usually upon retirement or posthumously to grand minister. All shoguns also received the status rank of senior first rank, which was equal to the emperor himself. It is important to note, however, that although we commonly refer to the head of the Tokugawa house as "shogun," the term was used infrequently during the Edo period, most famously in the imperial patent of authority mentioned above. Instead, the Tokugawa referred to themselves as *kubô*, a term meaning "person in charge of the public" that had designated shoguns since the Muromachi period. The title *taikun*, or "great prince," was used by the shoguns in diplomatic correspondence with the Yi dynasty in Korea during the seventeenth century, and then again in the late Tokugawa period with the Western powers. The shogunal adviser Arai Hakuseki (1657–1725) argued successfully that the term was problematic, and in the early eighteenth century the term *Nihon kokuô* ("king of Japan") was used in its place.

The early Tokugawa shoguns sought legitimacy and authority in a number of ways other than their sheer military power. First, he was head of the Tokugawa house, the foremost warrior house, which claimed descent from the Minamoto family. His role as in service to the emperor and through imperial court titles was also important, as noted above. Accordingly, the shoguns paid respect to the imperial institution, gave it monetary support, but carefully controlled it in order to prevent other daimyo from using it to challenge Tokugawa authority. A certain legitimacy was also conferred upon the Tokugawa because of their ability to create a dynasty. Whereas the late-sixteenth-century hegemons Oda Nobunaga (1534–1582) and Toyotomi Hideyoshi (1536–1598) had been unable to pass on their positions of leadership to their heirs, Tokugawa Ieyasu and Hidetada both decided to retire formally, to become "retired shogun" (*ôgosho*) while still active and healthy, and to bequeath their titles to their sons. By doing this each shogun did his part to help cement the position of his successor, and collectively they did what previous military hegemons had not: a long succession of shoguns from a single, extended

Shogun and Emperor

Tokugawa rule was in theory legitimized by the emperor, who appointed the shogun, but the reality was that the shogun's authority, backed by military might, was supreme. The Tokugawa sought to control the emperor and his courtiers' lives through law, by issuing the *Regulations for the Imperial Palace and the Court Nobility* in 1615. The third shogun, Iemitsu (1604–1651), also used intimidation to keep the emperor in line, bringing a substantial force of 300,000 men with him on his trip to Kyoto in 1634. Yet another mechanism of control was through marriage—by marrying women from the shogunal family into the imperial family. For example, shogun Tokugawa Hidetada's fifth daughter, Masako (1607–1678), who was Tokugawa Ieyasu's granddaughter, was married to the future emperor Go-Mizuno'o in 1620; when Go-Mizuno'o became emperor in 1611, the shogunal and imperial lines were united. In fact, when Masako and Go-Mizuno'o's daughter Meishô ascended to the imperial throne in 1629, the granddaughter of a shogun had become empress.

family, whose rule was stable and long-lasting. Through their monopoly control of foreign policy, the Tokugawa shoguns were able to claim legitimacy within a Neo-Confucian discourse as enlightened rulers whose virtue extended across the seas, as evidenced by the embassies from Korea and the Ryukyu kingdom that were paraded up Japan's highways to pay homage and bring tribute to the shoguns in Edo. The merchants of the Dutch East Indian Company (V.O.C.) were similarly paraded up the highways from Nagasaki for a similar purpose.

Further legitimacy was conferred on the shoguns through the deification of the founder of the dynasty, Tokugawa Ieyasu, as a Shinto deity *Tôshôgû daigongen*, which gave him divine protective powers. His body and spirit were enshrined at Nikkô Tôshôgû, a shrine that was rebuilt on a grand scale beginning in 1634 by Ieyasu's grandson and shogun Tokugawa Iemitsu. Other Tôshôgû shrines where constructed on the grounds of Edo Castle and in many domains across the country. In this way Ieyasu "became the spiritual protector not only of the Tokugawa lineage, but of his capital city at Edo, of the Kanto, and of Japan as a whole" (Walthall, 2006, 349).

According to some scholars the Tokugawa ruled not so much by force but by the image of force. They also ruled by the performance of power—meaning through the Tokugawa's "flamboyant" authority (Brown, 1993, 233) and "theaters of power" such as the processions that were a part of the required performance of alternate attendance—more than its use on the battlefield, although the threat of the use of violence remained in place throughout the Edo period.

The Tokugawa shoguns also ruled in a sense by making use of "strategies of concealment and secrecy" (Walthall, 2006, 347) as well as stasis. Shoguns exhibited their power in a material sense through the massive nature of Edo Castle, but they concealed their persons, not only from commoners, but also in terms of their relations with the daimyo and foreign emissaries. The shoguns, with two notable exceptions (in 1623 and 1865), did not travel around the country to demonstrate their military authority nor to be seen by the people, as many European monarchs did; it was the daimyo who were required to travel to Edo to wait on the shogun every other year on alternate attendance. Moreover, in Edo for their audiences with the shogun, most daimyo were unlikely to catch even a glimpse of him. The daimyo waited in reception rooms until they were signaled to prostrate themselves while the sliding doors were opened and the shogun looked out over a "sea of backs" (Walthall, 2006, 349). He observed them but only the daimyo of highest rank glimpsed his face, while the rest kept their eyes trained on the floor. The shogun also did not speak during these audiences; his silence bespoke dignity and authority.

The Tokugawa shogun's responsibility for protecting Japan and protecting the imperial institution from perceived insults by foreign powers undermined his authority in the mid-nineteenth century, as the British, American, and Russian powers pressured the shogun to open up Japan to Western diplomatic relations. Domains that had historically opposed the Tokugawa such as Satsuma and Chôshû, not to mention individual radicalized samurai from other domains, used this weakness in calling for the overthrow of the shogun-led government under the guise of the slogan "Revere the Emperor and Expel the Barbarian." To avoid a civil war, the fifteenth shogun, Tokugawa Yoshinobu, gave his resignation to the emperor and formally stepped down ten days later, thus formally returning power to the imperial institution. Satsuma and Chôshû, however, were opposed to the compromise plan that had been worked out prior to Yoshinobu's resignation whereby he would resign as shogun but continue to preside over a governing council of daimyo. Accordingly, they took up arms against Yoshinobu, an action that would lead to the Boshin War, and manipulated the imperial court to strip him of all titles and land. Then, on December 9, 1867, the fifteen-year-old Meiji emperor issued a formal edict declaring the restoration of imperial rule (*ôsei fukko*).

List of Tokugawa Shoguns

Name	Life Dates	Period of Official Rule
Ieyasu	1542–1616	1603–1605
Hidetada	1579–1632	1605–1622
Iemitsu	1603–1651	1622–1651
Ietsuna	1639–1680	1651–1680
Tsunayoshi	1646–1709	1680–1709
Ienobu	1662–1712	1709–1712
Ietsugu	1709–1716	1713–1716
Yoshimune	1677–1751	1716–1745
Ieshige	1712–1761	1745–1760
Ieharu	1737–1786	1760–1786
Ienari	1773–1841	1786–1837
Ieyoshi	1792–1853	1837–1858
Iesada	1824–1858	1853–1858
Iemochi	1846–1866	1858–1866
Yoshinobu (Keiki)	1837–1913	1866–1867

Zôjôji, Burial Ground of Shoguns

Tokugawa Ieyasu made Zôjôji the family mortuary temple in 1598, eight years after Toyotomi Hideyoshi transferred him to the Kanto region and five years before he became shogun. Ieyasu chose the location south of Edo Castle because it guarded the entrance to the Tôkaidô highway that ran from Edo to Kyoto and also protected one of the four cardinal directions. Six shoguns are buried there, including Hidetada (the second shogun), Ienobu (sixth shogun), Ietsugu (seventh shogun), and Iemochi (fourteenth shogun), but Ieyasu and his grandson Iemitsu, the third shogun, were both buried at Nikkô Tôshôgû Shrine, north of Edo. Some notable wives of shoguns were also buried here, including imperial princess Kazunomiya, who was married to the fourteenth shogun, Iemochi, and Gô, the wife of the second shogun, Hidetada.

The shogunal graves were relocated within the grounds of Zôjôji in 1958, which gave an unprecedented opportunity to scientists and historians to view the remains. Ienobu's body was the best preserved of the shoguns buried there and provides evidence for how they functioned as guardians of the state even after their deaths. Ienobu's embalmed body was sealed inside multiple coffins—two wooden ones, placed in a copper one, and then placed inside a stone chamber—all or which were packed with ash and lime. His hair is in a topknot, and he is dressed in the formal court robes of a chief minister, with a mace in his hands.

Felix Beato's late-Tokugawa photograph of the gate of Shogun Ienobu's burial ground can be viewed at: http://oldphoto.lb.nagasaki-u.ac.jp/en/target.php?id=1444 (accessed March 27, 2017).

For more information about the temple, please visit its official website: http://www.zojoji.or.jp/en (accessed March 27, 2017).

A second Tokugawa family mortuary temple is Kan'eiji, where six other shoguns are buried. The fifteenth and final shogun, Yoshinobu, is buried at Yanaka Cemetery in Tokyo.

See also: Alternate Attendance (*sankin kôtai*); Boshin War; Shogunate (*bakufu, kôgi*); Tokugawa Hidetada; Tokugawa Iemitsu; Tokugawa Ieyasu; Tokugawa Tsunayoshi; Tokugawa Yoshimune; Tokugawa Yoshinobu

Further Reading

Brown, Philip C. *Central Authority & Local Autonomy in the Formation of Early Modern Japan: The Case of Kaga Domain*. Stanford, CA: Stanford University Press, 1993.

Roberts, Luke S. *Performing the Great Peace: Political Space and Open Secrets in Tokugawa Japan*. Honolulu: University of Hawai'i Press, 2012.

Walthall, Anne. "Hiding the Shoguns: Secrecy and the Nature of Political Authority in Tokugawa Japan." In Bernard Scheid and Mark Teeuwen, eds., *The Culture of Secrecy in Japanese Religion*. New York: Routledge, 2006.

Shogunate (*bakufu, kôgi*)

The term "shogunate" refers to the samurai-led governments that existed during three periods in Japanese history, the Kamakura (1185–1333), Ashikaga (1336–1573), and the Tokugawa (1603–1868). Japanese historians have often used the term *bakufu*, which means "tent government," to signify them, but it was not commonly used during those eras. During the third period of samurai rule, the term most commonly used to refer to the government led by the Tokugawa house was *kôgi,* or "public authority." *Bakufu* was used by scholars in the Mito school to draw a contrast between their vision of Japan as an imperial country (*kôkoku*) under the authority of an emperor and the Tokugawa's military-based government. During the mid-nineteenth century, particularly after the opening of Japan to the West in 1853, the term was used by imperial loyalists in opposition to the Tokugawa, whom they saw as usurpers of the emperor's authority.

The Tokugawa shogunate was the most powerful of three military governments and exercised its authority over the daimyo domains and the people residing on Tokugawa-controlled territory (the so-called "house lands," or *tenryô*) through an elaborate administrative system that was headed by the shogun, whose formal title through imperial appointment was *sei-i taishogun* (barbarian-quelling general). In addition to its responsibilities in national defense, the shogunate assumed responsibility for creating laws and relatedly acting as moral arbiter. The Tokugawa took measures to unify the currency; standardize national weights and measures; construct a national highway network; issue laws for the daimyo (*Laws for the Military Houses,* or *buke shohatto*), its direct vassals (Regulations for the Samurai, or *shoshi hatto*), Laws for the Imperial Court and Nobility (*kinchû narabini kuge shohatto*); and to instruct the daimyo to follow precedents set by Tokugawa when making up laws for their own domains. The Tokugawa's authority at the center of national law was manifested in the *Hyôjôsho,* or Judicial Council, that was established to deal with cross-jurisdictional suits (those that that spilled over domain borders) and other complex disputes; under the eighth shogun Yoshimune (1684–1751) an extensive legal code, *Kujikata osadamegaki* (1742), was compiled and influenced legal systems across the many domains. Through legal codes and moral suasion the shogunate aimed to direct the conduct of the Japanese people: for example, through sumptuary legislation, which targeted consumptive habits and material culture; through censorship of the printed word, art, and theater; and through controls on religion, particularly the proscription of Christianity and outlawed forms of Buddhism such as the *Fuju fuse* sect; and controls on some varieties of Neo-Confucianism.

The shogunate was built up gradually and assumed its basic form under the third shogun, Iemitsu (1604–1651). Some of the major positions in the administrative hierarchy are detailed below:

Senior Councilors (*rôjû*): Except on the rare occasion when a great councilor (*tairô*) was appointed, the senior councilors served as the top administrators in the Tokugawa shogunate. Usually four or five in number, they served the shogun in rotation, for a month at a time, but important matters were usually dealt with in a conciliar manner. Usually appointees were men of middle-level hereditary, vassal daimyo (*fudai daimyô*) status, and were responsible for most other shogunal officials through whom they supervised the daimyo, the imperial court and nobility, the direct landholdings of the Tokugawa, foreign policy, and religious institutions. Their counterparts in the domain governments were known as domain elders or councilors (*karô*). *Tairô* were actually appointed on twelve occasions during the Tokugawa period, during emergencies or during the minority of a shogun.

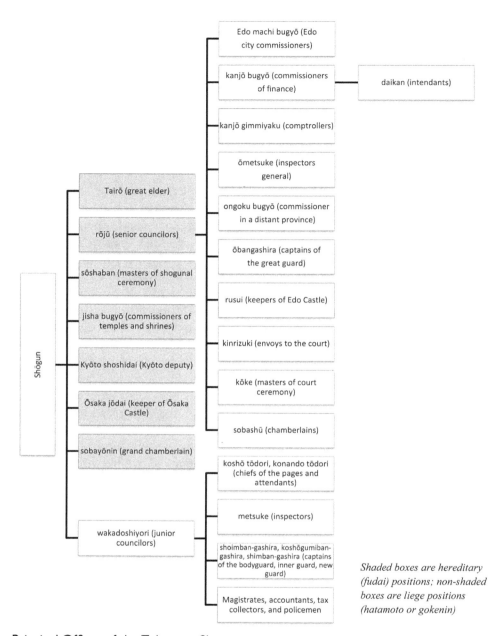

Shaded boxes are hereditary
(fudai) positions; non-shaded
boxes are liege positions
(hatamoto or gokenin)

Principal Offices of the Tokugawa Shogunate

Junior Councilors (*wakadoshiyori*): These were ranked below the senior councilors and were charged with authority over the inspectors (*metsuke*), who reported to them about the *hatamoto* (Tokugawa bannermen, high-ranking direct vassals of the shogun). They also oversaw various other lower-ranking shogunal officials such as the commissioners of lesser engineering works (*kobushin bugyô*), (Edo) castle guards (*shoinban*), page corps (*koshôgumi*), bannermen firemen (*jô-bikeshi*), commanders of archers and musketmen (*sakite kumigashira*), arson and theft inspectors (*hitsuke tôzoku aratame*), and commissioner of workhouses (*yoseba bugyô*). The junior councilors, like the senior councilors, were chosen from among the *fudai daimyo* but wielded much less power.

Magistrates of Shrines and Temples (*jisha bugyô*): These officials, usually four in number, handled all affairs related to temples and shrines, including their landholdings as well as the lawsuits of people under the direct jurisdiction of religious institutions.

Kyoto Deputy (*Kyôto shoshidai*): This official with a support staff of about 150 men was charged with overseeing the activities of the imperial court in Kyoto. The shogunate performed a balancing act of sorts with the imperial institution, seeking to control it, but at the same time honoring its traditional role in legitimizing samurai rule.

Directly under the authority of the senior councilors were a number of positions, including the inspectors general (*ômetsuke*), magistrates of finance (*kanjô bugyô*), magistrates of engineering works (*fushin bugyô*), magistrates of building (*sakuji bugyô*), great guard units (*ôbangumi*), and city magistrates (*machi bugyô*). The inspectors general position was created in 1632 by the third shogun, Tokugawa Iemitsu (1604–1651); *ômetsuke*, who were intelligence officers, oversaw important internal affairs such as the activities of the daimyo, the highway system, and any groups that posed a potential threat to the regime, such as Christian missionaries and their Japanese followers. Generally, four in number, the inspectors general were drawn from among the shogun's bannermen (*hatamoto*) and reported directly to the senior councilors; they were supported by sixteen subordinates, called *metsuke,* who were directly responsible to the junior councilors. Magistrates of finance were also selected from the bannermen and were accountable for the government's financial matters. The "great guard" (*ôban*) was one of the three main guard forces of the shogunate and was responsible for the samurai districts of Edo outside of the castle grounds, as well as the defense of Osaka and Nijô (in Kyoto) Castles. Two city magistrates (*machi bugyô*) were appointed for the major urban centers under Tokugawa control, such as Edo, Kyoto, and Osaka (and typically were on duty alternate months). Two different officials were charged with construction: the magistrate of engineering works (*fushin bugyô*) was responsible for civil engineering projects such as land reclamation projects, for the construction of castle walls, and the excavation of moats and canals; the magistrate of building (*sakuji bugyô*) held responsibility over construction of buildings and architecture.

Under the junior councilors (*wakadoshiyori*) were also a number of administrative positions, including the inspectors (*metsuke*), commissioner of lesser engineering works (*kobushin bugyô*), castle guards (*shoinban*), page corps (*koshôgumi*), bannermen firemen (*jô-bikeshi*), commanders of archers and musket men (*sakite kumigashira*), arson and theft inspectors (*hitsuke-tôzoku aratame*), and commissioners of workhouses (*yoseba bugyô*). The inspectors were particularly important and had a large support staff of about fifty associate inspectors and one hundred assistant inspectors. Although foreign observers described them as "spies," their observation and monitoring of other officials in the shogunate was quite open. It was their charge to root out corruption and to seek out criminal activity. Although they were under the authority of the junior councilors, they had the right to report directly to the senior councilors or even to the shogun. The castle guards (*shoin-ban*) and page corps (*koshôgumi*) oversaw the defense of Edo Castle and the shogun's person.

A number of officials from different parts of the government administration were also tasked with serving on the *Hyôjôsho*. Its members were comprised, among others, of the senior councilors, the Edo city magistrate, the magistrates of shrines and temples, and the magistrate of finances (*kanjô bugyô*).

The shogunate was funded primarily on the house land rice tax (*kuramai*), meaning the rice tax derived from the shogun's house lands (*tenryô*), which constituted roughly one-quarter of the assessed arable land in the country. That land was scattered over forty-seven provinces, though, and because the shogunate's administrative machinery was not large enough to govern the entire country, it relied on neighboring daimyo to administer on its behalf scattered holdings of house lands, particularly in northern Japan. The Tokugawa also controlled gold and silver mines in Sado and silver mines in Iwami. Its various control on foreign trade gave the government a steady though not large source of income. Income was also derived from the granting of monopoly patents to merchants and from forced contributions from merchants, but the shogunate did not tax commerce effectively.

The shogunate was supported by the military force of the shogun's direct retainers, the bannermen (*hatamoto*), about 5,000 in number, and the housemen (*gokenin*), who numbered about 17,000. Between the two types of direct retainers and the support troops the bannermen were required to provide for military service, it is estimated that, in principle, the shogun could field a total force of 80,000 men. In reality it was questionable whether this number could actually have been attained and if so how effective this ad hoc army might have been. The military supremacy of the shogunate therefore rested on the support of the vassal daimyo (*fudai daimyô*) and related daimyo (*shinpan daimyô*). Perhaps the greatest strength of the shogunate lay, however, in its capacity to prevent a military conflict from starting through its political and economic controls on the daimyo, especially the alternate attendance (*sankin kôtai*).

See also: Bannermen (*hatamoto*); Daimyo and Domains; *Laws for the Military Houses* (*buke shohatto*); *Laws for the Samurai (shoshi hatto)*; House Lands (*tenryô*); Housemen (*gokenin*); Shogun (*shôgun*); Tokugawa Hidetada; Tokugawa Iemitsu; Tokugawa Ieyasu

Further Reading

Beerens, Anna, trans. "Interview with a Bakumatsu Official: A Translation from *Kyûji shimonroku*." *Monumenta Nipponica,* 55(3) (2000), 369–398.

Katô, Takashi. "Governing Edo." In James L. McClain, John M. Merriman, and Ugawa Kaoru, eds., *Edo and Paris: Urban Life and the State in the Early Modern Era,* 41–67. Ithaca and London: Cornell University Press, 1994.

Totman, Conrad. *Politics in the Tokugawa Bakufu, 1600–1843.* Cambridge, MA: Harvard University Press, 1968. (Appendix B contains an extensive list of offices in the shogunate, with information on office salary, number of officials, career path, and subordinates.)

Watanabe Hiroshi (Luke Roberts, trans.). "About Some Japanese Terms." *Sino-Japanese Studies,* 10(2) (1998), 32–35.

Sieges of Osaka (*Ôsaka no jin*) (1614–1615)

Also known as *Ôsaka no jin* (the Battle of Osaka) in Japan, the Sieges of Osaka Castle were two military campaigns in 1614 and 1615 in which Tokugawa Ieyasu's forces destroyed those aligned with Toyotomi Hideyori (1593–1615). By eliminating Hideyori, Ieyasu solidified his earlier military success at the Battle of Sekigahara in 1600 and eliminated the last major military opposition to him and political threat to his legitimacy as shogun.

The origins of the military conflict that led to the Sieges of Osaka Castle date to the time of Toyotomi Hideyoshi (1536–1598), Ieyasu's overlord, who appointed him as one of his son's five guardians. By securing victory in the Battle of Sekigahara

Detail from a folding screen which depicts the Summer Siege of Osaka Castle (1615). As many as 100,000 may have died, including large numbers of civilians, some of whom can be seen in the foreground trying to flee. The Siege was the last major pitched battle of the Edo period, until the mid-19th century. (Werner Forman/Universal Images Group/Getty Images)

(1600), Tokugawa Ieyasu became the paramount military leader in the country, but his position was not secure while Hideyoshi's son, Hideyori, was alive. Moreover, Ieyasu's position was undercut by the fact that he had pledged to Hideyoshi to protect and support his son, Hideyori. Accordingly, while Ieyasu worked to strengthen his position, he allowed Toyotomi Hideyori to retain Hideyoshi's castle, Osaka, as his residence. However, by 1614, Ieyasu, who had formally stepped down as in favor of his son, Tokugawa Hidetada, but still retained effective control, felt secure enough politically to attack Hideyori directly.

The pretext for Ieyasu's attack was an alleged insult engraved on a bell that Hideyori was to have dedicated at Hôkôji, the temple where his father had constructed a giant Buddha statue. An inscription on the bell was interpreted by Ieyasu as suggesting that peace would only come to Japan with his death. Despite the apologies Hideyori sent through his personal vassals, Ieyasu refused to be placated, denounced Hideyori for his subversive action (known as the Shômei Incident), and mobilized his forces to attack.

THE WINTER AND SUMMER CAMPAIGNS

Hideyori, from the large castle at Osaka that his father had built, prepared for Ieyasu's onslaught together with his immediate vassals. His mother, Yodogimi, tried to rally daimyo to her son's cause but was not successful. A large number of unemployed samurai (rônin) did join Hideyori, seeing an opportunity for themselves in supporting him against the Tokugawa. Ieyasu and Hidetada amassed a force of 160,000 men and won several victories in skirmishes fought in surrounding areas before the siege on the fortress began.

During this first siege, known as the "winter campaign" (fuyu no jin), the defenders were able to repel the attacking forces repeatedly, despite Ieyasu's use of artillery, some of which were imported, not to mention attempts to dig under the castle's walls. Osaka Castle proved impregnable to the Tokugawa onslaught, leading to a temporary peace treaty between the warring parties. Under the terms of that treaty, Hideyori agreed not to rebel against the Tokugawa. He further permitted the outer layer of defensive walls to be torn down and the outer moat filled in. Ieyasu agreed to withdraw his forces, only to prepare for a second military campaign. Taking advantage of the situation, Ieyasu ordered his work crews to fill in not only the outer but also the inner moats. Hideyori's protests were futile, and when he declined to either leave Osaka Castle or disperse the army under his command, Ieyasu mobilized another army. This time, with both moat systems now defunct, the Tokugawa forces were able to pressure Hideyori's army to engage them in the field. The defending army was easily crushed in several battles and the castle fell, ending the second, "summer campaign" (natsu no jin). Hideyori's wife, who was the daughter of the shogun Hidetada, had been sent out of Osaka Castle before it fell to the Tokugawa's forces. She tried unsuccessfully to convince Ieyasu to spare her husband's life. The day after the castle fell, both Hideyori and his mother Yodogimi committed suicide. Parts of the castle burned, as depicted in an illustration in the Frenchman François Caron's book, A True Description of the Mighty

Kingdoms of Japan & Siam, 1663). It was not, however, totally destroyed, and would be rebuilt in subsequent years by the Tokugawa.

Our knowledge of the conflict at Osaka benefits from the account of foreigners, not to mention contemporary woodblock prints. The head merchant in the British East India Company, Richard Cocks (1566–1624), made a number of entries in his diary from four days in June 1615. In those entries (see Document 3) he recounted news that was communicated to him about the fall of Osaka Castle, where the forces allied with Toyotomi Hideyori (1593–1615), in opposition to the Tokugawa shogunate, were held up. He reported that the castle had fallen to Ieyasu's forces, despite the substantial force of 120,000 whom he said were in the castle and had cost 100,000 lives on both sides. He further stated that men on the Toyotomi side were cutting off the heads of some of their better-known colleagues who had fallen in battle to prevent their severed heads from falling into the hands of the Tokugawa side. Possession of the heads would have allowed the Tokugawa to identify the corpses and to take revenge against the mens' friends and families. Exposing the heads was also a way of publicly humiliating those who had opposed the Tokugawa. Lastly, Cocks reported the rumor that Hideyori had secretly escaped, since his body had not been found, but also gave his opinion that he thought this false.

Several contemporary pictorial accounts of the sieges exist. The first image, one of the earliest broadsheets of the Tokugawa period, informs the reader of the events surrounding the fall of Osaka Castle. In the top right of the page, which is known by the headline "The Battle of Abeno, Siege of Osaka Castle" (*Ôsaka Abeno gassen no zu*), the castle is depicted in flames. Below the castle, and within the enclosure, are written the names of the generals who died along with Hideyori and Yodogimi. Depicted to the left of the castle, within the enclosure, are women offering their clothing and begging for their lives. Below the enclosure we see the forces of the Eastern Army (Tokugawa forces) battling the Toyotomi forces. At the bottom of the print are listed the names of the generals serving under the titular leader, the shogun Hidetada, and the retired shogun, Ieyasu. Later in the Tokugawa period a daimyo named Matsuura Seizan (1760–1841) reported that the print had been sold in the Osaka area after the battle and had been purchased by many members of the Tokugawa forces, as a "souvenir" or remembrance of the event. Another image is a six-paneled screen painting of the summer campaign. It was commissioned by one of the generals who fought on the Tokugawa side, Kuroda Nagamasa. He is reported to have taken painters with him to the battle site, and they depicted the scene from actual visual experience.

AFTERMATH OF THE SIEGES

Rumors that Hideyori survived the onslaught at Osaka Castle continued for some time, but they were quite unfounded. Indeed, he was among the 100,000 men who lost their lives in that battle, which drew to a conclusion the two military campaigns of 1614–1615. It is reported that Hideyori took his own life. Most of the generals on Hideyori's side were either killed in battle or committed suicide as the castle fell. Large numbers of Toyotomi supporters were decapitated, and thousands of their heads displayed on planks on the road between Kyoto and Fushimi, for all passersby to see the cost of opposition to the Tokugawa. Even Hideyori's son—the shogun Hidetada's grandson—was beheaded. His daughter, however, fared better: she was spared and sent to live in Tôkeiji convent in Kamakura.

In taking control of Osaka, the Tokugawa were able to project their power more firmly into western Japan after 1615. In defeating Hideyori, the most visible rallying point of opposition, Ieyasu did much to secure the Tokugawa dynasty, which would last for two and a half more centuries; in fact, it was Ieyasu's final military campaign, and the last time that two armies of samurai would fight in a pitched battle. Some observers have argued that the twin campaigns marked the end of the Warring States period (typically dated from 1467 to 1568) and the beginning of the Tokugawa peace.

See also: Sekigahara, Battle of; Shogun (*shôgun*); Tokugawa Ieyasu; Toyotomi Hideyoshi

Further Reading

Cocks, Richard. *The Diary of Richard Cocks, Cape-Merchant in the English Factory in Japan, 1615–1622: With Correspondence.* London: Hakluyt Society, 1883.

Foster, William, ed. *Letters Received by the East India Company from Its Servants in the East,* vol. IV (1616). London: Sampson Low, Marston & Company, 1900.

McClain, James L., and Wakita Osamu, ed. *Osaka: The Merchants' Capital of Early Modern Japan.* Ithaca, NY: Cornell University Press, 1999.

Turnbull, Stephen. *Osaka 1615: The Last Battle of the Samurai.* Oxford, England: Osprey Publishing, 2006. Ithaca, NY: Cornell University Press, 1999.

Websites

"History of Osaka Castle." Welcome to Osaka Castle. http://www.osakacastle.net/english. Accessed September 12, 2010.

"The Siege of Osaka Castle." *National Geographic Magazine.* http://ngm.nationalgeographic .com/ngm/0312/feature5/zoomify/main.html. Accessed December 29, 2017.

Status System (*mibunsei*)

Given that warfare had wracked Japan for so long during the Warring States period (1467–1568), the Tokugawa rulers placed high priority on establishing and maintaining political and social order. To bring order to society they sought to minimize social mobility and to clarify social roles. Tokugawa political leaders from the seventeenth century found status (*mibun*) to be a useful concept in creating a schematized social system based on hereditary occupational categories.

This notion of a social order was derived from a body of thought called Neo-Confucianism, which had supported imperial rule in China for nearly half a millennium. Under this doctrine emphasis was placed on a hereditary-based, four-tiered system of status groups or "estates." In Japan the status system (*mibunsei*) was defined by *shinôkôshô*: samurai, peasant, artisan, and merchants. The merchant writer Ihara Saikaku explained the system in the preface to his *Buke giri monogatari* (*Tales of Samurai Honor,* 1688): "Wearing a long sword makes a man a samurai. . . . A man who grips a hoe is a farmer, one who wields a hand-ax is a craftsman, and one who calculates sums on an abacus is a merchant. Everyone should realize the overwhelming importance of occupation in determining his life" (Saikaku, 1981, 27).

According to the *shinôkôshô* paradigm, the samurai were Tokugawa Japan's counterpart to China's scholar-officials, who similarly occupied the highest rung in the social system. Samurai were to act as the political-military leaders and role models for the rest of society. They were to eschew trade and to pursue the "twin ways" of martial skills and the literary arts, particularly Neo-Confucian studies. In this hierarchy of "estates" or occupations, the peasants came next, followed by the artisans (craftsmen) and merchants, in that order. This hierarchy reflected the ruling samurai's perspective and was based on the concept of service or formal duties (*yaku*) that accompanied membership in the status group; accordingly, peasants were positioned second, after *bushi* because they tilled the earth, produced crops from the elements of soil, water, and sunlight, which fed the population. Artisans came third because they fashioned natural resources into products that were useful to society in general and samurai in particular, such as armor, helmets, bows, arrows, writing brushes, and tatami matting. Merchants found themselves at the bottom of this idealized vision of society because, while necessary for the circulation of goods, they pursued profit, which was held in disdain according to Confucian morality. It was not the case that peasants per se were more important than the other two social groups but rather that their agricultural work was valued more highly than the work of artisans and merchants.

According to the ideology that undergirded the status system, members of each social group were supposed to act according to their social role. It was the ruler's responsibility to act with humanity and benevolence toward the people—to create a just society in which the people could live in comfort. Similarly, as the political and moral leaders, samurai were not to engage in behavior unbefitting their status, such as acting or even attending the kabuki theater (at least openly doing so). At the same time the lower three estates were to follow faithfully those above them in rank. There were also familistic overtones to this ideology, with the rulers fulfilling the role of parents and the samurai and other status groups that of the family members.

Status was a universal construct or universal category of social organization, transcending the village, city, or domain. In fact, "no other institutional categories existed above status to unite all Japanese as members of the same political community" (Howell, 2005, 26). At the same time, because membership in a status group was usually mediated through the household, not the individual, women and other dependents were not usually seen as independent social actors. As a result, status was gendered, in effect, as male: "adult men, as household heads or potential household heads, always displayed salient markers of status identity—swords or distinctive hairstyles or clothing—while women and children did not necessarily bear such clear marks" (Howell, 2005, 27).

The status system was established through the various policies of the unifiers, particularly those of Hideyoshi, in what amounted to a "sixteenth-century revolution." The sword hunt (1588) largely took weapons out of the hands of the peasantry; together with the daimyo's efforts to draw the samurai off the land and into the castle towns (*heinô bunri*, or the "separation of warrior and farmer"), this resulted in the physical and functional separation of samurai from the peasantry. Farming and military service became exclusive occupations. Peasants were not to take up arms, which had been a means for social mobility. Also, according to Hideyoshi's edicts of 1591, peasants were not to abandon their fields and go into trade or wage labor, and samurai were not to return to the land, thus "freezing" the social order.

Status categories, in principle, were hereditary in nature, but movement among the lower three rungs was common. A peasant, for example, might move into a castle town or other urban settlement and take up a trade. Movement into the *bushi* category—usually into its lowest ranks—was more difficult, but not uncommon, particularly late in the Tokugawa period. Adoption was one means by which some commoners were able to gain entry into the lower ranks of the *bushi* status group.

Different regulations and laws were applied by the samurai rulers to the various status groups; as a result, historians view "rule by status" as one of the defining characteristics of the Tokugawa period. For *bushi*, for example, there were the *Laws for the Military Houses (buke shohatto)* and the *Laws for the Samurai (shoshi hatto)*. Separate regulations were issued for commoners living in villages and for those (merchants and artisans) living in urban centers. Similarly, punishments differed for *bushi* and for members of the other three status groups: for example, capital punishment for commoners could consist of beheading or crucifixion, depending on the crime, but for *bushi* a death penalty was to be self-inflicted through *seppuku*, or ritual suicide.

Political authorities tried to maintain status distinctions through regulations, particularly through sumptuary legislation, which dictated consumption habits and lifestyle. In particular, sumptuary legislation focused on clothing, food, housing (architecture), and entertainment. One list of prohibitions concerning clothing for Edo townsmen (1719), for example, proscribed townsmen from wearing wool capes, using gold or silver leaf in their dwellings, building three-story homes, dressing in an outlandish fashion, and allowing their servants to wear silk. Since clothing was openly visible, attempts to dress in a manner inappropriate to one's social station were especially subject to the law. They were also enjoined from wearing long swords, which only *bushi* were permitted. In addition, in Tosa only *bushi* were permitted to wear parasol hats in Kôchi castle town. This caused some resentment among the townsmen due to the hot sun in that southern domain. One man assuming the alias "Miyata Bunsuke" submitted a petition to the government expressing his dissatisfaction with this state of affairs, depositing it anonymously in the domain's petition box. In his petition, he warned that "it is not a sign of benevolent government to have your people roast under the hot sun" (Quoted in Roberts, 1994, 452). The petition amazingly had its intended effect, and in 1760 this status distinction was eliminated, allowing commoners to use parasol hats in the city just like samurai.

Sumptuary legislation was designed to preserve the social order by maintaining differences in appearance, which were to be in line with distinctions in function (occupation). In other words, they were not simply a way to keep social inferiors in place, but rather they were meant to align with the Confucian principle of the "rectification of names"—that is, the people should act as befits their status. In general, the regulations were aimed at preventing pretentious displays of wealth, which could reveal a disparity between status and wealth. The frequency with which such laws were reissued over the course of the Tokugawa period suggests that the government relied more on exhortation, warnings, and threat than on actual penalties.

Status differences were also made concrete, and made visible, in a number of other ways. The overwhelming domination by samurai of the physical space of Edo was a clear reflection of their dominant position in the Tokugawa social system. In terms of land use, for example, in the early eighteenth century *bushi* occupied the vast majority of space in Edo, almost 69 percent of the total urban area, while townsmen, who were about 46 percent of the population, only occupied about 12.5 percent. This meant that townsmen areas of the city were far more densely populated that *bushi*-occupied areas: it has been estimated that population density for the *bushi* population in Edo (650,000 in 1721) was 16,816 people per square kilometer, roughly one-fourth the figure for the townsmen population of 600,000 (67,317 people per square kilometer). There was also a qualitative difference in the type of land occupied, as townsman land tended to be low-lying, much of it having originally been landfill, while much of *bushi*-occupied land was on higher ground.

Government officials also tried to maintain status distinctions in terms of architecture, which established a type of visual logic to samurai-based political power. As early as 1613, edicts forbade Edo townspeople from building gateways and warned them with severe punishment for disobeying. Other edicts restricted the type of building materials that could be used and the style of internal construction of rooms. It should be noted, however, that the shogunate also issued other types of edicts to maintain visual differences in architectural construction between its own bannermen (*hatamoto*) and daimyo.

This idealized conception of a society based on a hierarchy of estates and natural order was prescriptive rather than descriptive. Accordingly, it was in many ways inconsistent with social realities. To begin with, while there were four status groups, the basic division in Tokugawa society was between samurai and nonsamurai. For most purposes, peasants, artisans, and merchants were considered a single status group of commoners. In village population registers, for example, no distinctions were made between those who were strictly farmers and others who were merchants or artisans. Second, while merchants were positioned at the bottom of the social scale and despised according to the official ideology, in fact they played an essential social function. As a result, many of them became quite wealthy. Third, there was no standard for internal differentiation within status categories. Each status group encompassed a wide range of socioeconomic stratification. For example, a daimyo's upper-ranking vassal and a low-ranking vassal both belonged to the *bushi* status group, but a largely unbridgeable social gulf separated the two. The wealthy head of the Mitsui family and a street peddler were both merchants but again had little in common with one another; the same was true in the countryside of the landholding peasant and tenant farmer.

Yet another problem with the status system was that large numbers of people did not fit, or fit neatly, into any of these four categories, such as the emperor and court nobility, the Shinto and Buddhist clergy, physicians and scholars, actors, prostitutes, itinerant entertainers, sumo wrestlers and outcastes, and the Ainu. Looking at the example of Okayama domain in the mid-nineteenth century, we can see that *bushi* comprised 5.8 percent (23,000 people) of the population of 398,000 people; peasants 84.2 percent (335,000 people); merchants and artisans (townsmen) 9.5 percent (30,000 people); while the "other" category comprised 2.5 percent (10,000 people).

The line between *bushi* and commoner was also sometimes blurred, for as indicated above, there was some limited mobility across the dividing line, particularly late in the Tokugawa period, through adoption. Also, in some domains wealthy peasants were able to purchase the samurai's rights to a surname and two swords (*myôji taito*), but this did not make them real *bushi* in the sense that they did not become retainers of a lord.

The occupational differentiation that defined the status system also became blurred over time, as lower-ranking *bushi* in many domains, not to mention the Tokugawa shogun's own housemen (*gokenin*), were permitted to engage in the production of handicrafts to supplement their stipends; handicrafts were, in theory, the preserve of artisans. Moreover, a number of domains experimented with returning *bushi* to the land and allowing, or even encouraging, them to engage in agriculture, which was the activity that defined the peasant status group.

The status system was dependent on the maintenance of samurai supremacy. Although there was no difficulty maintaining it early in the seventeenth century, under peacetime conditions over time it grew increasingly out of sync with economic power. As a result the low-ranking vassal mentioned above might have more in common with a townsman than with a higher-ranking samurai. Accordingly, during the latter half of the Tokugawa period, the social pretensions of many samurai seemed out of line with their difficult economic position, which declined in overall terms relative to the other social groups. The samurai were handicapped by prohibitions on their engaging in trade or farming and by their rulers' fixed notion of the ideal economy as an agrarian-based one. Since samurai had the prerogative of wearing the two swords, one would imagine that as a group they would be able to improve their economic lot by demanding more taxes from the peasantry. On the contrary, we find that the samurai as the ruling class were not able, or willing to try, to extract more taxes from the countryside from about the early eighteenth century, perhaps to avoid social unrest. As a result, commoners but not samurai benefited from increased agricultural production and commercial trade. Most samurai experienced economic difficulties, particularly as many daimyo attempted to cope with the increasing costs of alternate attendance from the early eighteenth century by taking a percentage of their stipends. In short, the uneven distribution of economic growth contributed to an inversion of status and economic power, one result being the creation of an increasingly wealthy and educated commoner population.

See also: Laws for the Military Houses (*buke shohatto*); *Seppuku* (Ritual Suicide)

Further Reading

Coaldrake, William H. *Monumenta Nipponica*, 36(3) (Autumn 1981), 235–284.

Howell, David. *Geographies of Identity in Nineteenth-Century Japan.* Princeton, NJ: Princeton University Press, 2005 (especially Chapter 2, "The Geography of Status").

Ihara Saikaku. *Tales of Samurai Honor.* Translated by Caryl Ann Callahan. Tokyo: Sophia University, 1981. *Monumenta Nipponica* monograph.

McClain, James L., John M. Merriman, and Ugawa Kaoru. *Edo & Paris: Urban Life & the State in the Early Modern Era.* Ithaca, NY, and London: Cornell University Press, 1994.

Roberts, Luke S. "The Petition Box in Eighteenth-Century Tosa." *The Journal of Japanese Studies,* 20(2) (1994), 423–458.

Supplemental Salary (*Tashidaka*) System and Talent

Education gave samurai the intellectual and moral training necessary to carry out their social mission and administrative duties. Yet, at the same time, education called attention to ability and thereby revealed a fundamental ideological conflict: the disjunction between theory and practice regarding merit or talent (*jinzai*) and hereditary rank. After the early Tokugawa period, appointment to positions in the government bureaucracy were made mainly on the basis of social rank, but the spread of samurai education through domain schools in the latter half of the period made it harder to conceal this discrepancy between privilege and ability. Confucian scholars in particular, aware as they were of the Chinese examination system, were highly critical of the lack of use of the principle of merit, or human talent, in official appointments in Japan.

Although the merit principle was highly regarded—one of the articles of the 1615 *Laws for the Military Houses* urged the selection of men of talent—it was rarely applied. One reason for this was that there were many more samurai who wanted office than there were positions available; holding office was a source of power and prestige—in a time of peace the only means to advance in income and rank. Moreover, most importantly, the tradition of birth as the main criterion for status and authority dictated that rank be the foremost criteria for appointment.

By the 1720s, however, there was some change, due to a sense of moral and financial crisis, in particular due to problems caused by an increasingly commercial economy and the spread of corruption in the government bureaucracy. The merit principle was promoted by the eighth shogun, Tokugawa Yoshimune, with the establishment of the supplemental salary (*tashidaka*) system in 1723. This system set standard levels of stipends as a guide for the appointment of retainers to certain key offices. For example, the standard stipend required for an official to serve as city magistrate of Edo or finance magistrate was 3,000 *koku*. The *tashidaka* system was designed to open up positions to samurai who were of lower rank than normally qualified for certain posts by granting them a salary supplement. If a samurai with demonstrated talent whose household held a stipend of only 1,000 *koku* was appointed to either of the above-mentioned magistrate positions, he would be granted a supplemental salary of 2,000 *koku*, thereby qualifying him for the post. After the *tashidaka* system was implemented, more than one-half of shogunate officials appointed to the post of finance magistrate required a 500-*koku* increase in stipend in order to qualify for the post. Although appointments to prestigious military positions such as chamberlain (*sobashū*), keeper of Edo Castle (*rusui*), or captain of the guard (*ōbangashira*) remained firmly in the hands of samurai from higher status families, the *tashidaka* system was utilized by the shogunate in filling important administrative positions, like the two magistrate posts, that required considerable administrative talents. Men of relatively low rank were thus able to gain these offices.

The one part of the shogunate that particularly benefited from the *tashidaka* system was the office of the finance magistrate. The late-eighteenth-century record of observations, *Okinagusa*, written by Kanzawa Tokô, a midlevel official in the Kyoto city magistrate's office, reveals that the supplemental salary system was applied for all the posts in the office. As Kanzawa reported, "Thereafter, all of the employees in the finance ministry applied themselves with great diligence to their work. Ordinary workers in the finance ministry desired to rise in their appointments in that ministry" (Quoted in Kasaya, 2000, 130–131). As a result, lower-level retainers with 100-*koku* stipends were able to rise through the ranks through merit to become finance magistrate, with a 3,000-*koku* stipend. Given the important of the finance office, which carried out not just financial affairs but also important civil and judicial functions, the effective implementation of the *tashidaka* system there is quite notable. Many other offices, however, had no permanent staff and selections for staffing were made by officials on the basis of feudal ties (i.e., they selected their own vassals) rather than on talent.

Overall, however, there were drawbacks to the supplemental salary system. First of all, appointments made as a result of the *tashidaka* system were only for an individual's lifetime. Once the term of office was completed, the appointment official's status reverted to the original level. It thus actually served to limit the amount and duration of upward social mobility and thus may have unintentionally fueled discontent by giving power and responsibility without the prerogatives that normally went with office.

The *tashidaka* system removed the obstacle to the use of men of talent, but it certainly did not assure their use. In fact, the *tashidaka* system had a limited impact because the shogunate largely chose to fill offices with men who required little or no salary supplement. In addition, few domains elected to adopt the system. This is not to say that merit was not considered in appointments, but it was often applied only when two applicants for a position were of equal rank.

Even when the *tashidaka* system was utilized, it did not threaten the existence of the status system (*mibunsei*), since appointments were only temporary in nature and not inheritable. In fact, it can be argued that the supplemental salary system actually helped to maintain or bolster the status system by allowing for a mechanism to make use of individuals of merit when circumstances necessitated.

The principle of merit was also important in cases of adoption, the use of which increased steadily throughout the Tokugawa period. According to a sample of samurai households from four domains (Hikone, Kaga, Owari, Sendai) across the entire period, from one-fourth to more than a third made use of adoption. Adoption thus provided a means of channeling fresh blood and talent into the system while maintaining the principle of hereditary status. Through adoption talented younger sons, who were unlikely to succeed their father, were able to succeed to the headship of other families, usually of similar rank. This practice thus "served as an outlet for the energies of younger sons, which probably reduced the possibility of dangerous pressures building up and threatening the closed character of the class" (Moore, 1970, 619–620). Adoption, however, was not a major mechanism for upward social mobility, since it normally occurred between families of roughly the same ranks in the samurai hierarchy.

Late in the Tokugawa period there was renewed emphasis, both by the shogunate as well as the domains, on recognizing the principle of human talent in the recruitment of government officials. This was due to the sense of crisis felt in Japan resulting from the growing threat posed by Western gunships in East Asian waters, particularly the British, who defeated the Chinese in the Opium War (1839–1842).

Further Reading

Dore, Ronald P. "Talent and the Social Order in Tokugawa Japan." In John Hall and Marius Jansen, eds., *Studies in the Institutional History of Early Modern Japan.* Princeton, NJ: Princeton University Press, 1968.

Kasaya, Kazuhiko. *The Origin and Development of Japanese-Style Organization.* Kyoto: Nichibunken, 2000.

Moore, Ray A. "Adoption and Samurai Mobility in Tokugawa Japan." *The Journal of Asian Studies,* 29(3) (1970), 617–632.

Sword Hunt (*katanagari*)

The sword hunt was one of a number of policies put forth by political leaders in the late sixteenth and early seventeenth centuries. These policies were aimed at bringing order to society, which had been wracked by more than a century of warfare and great social fluidity during the Warring States period (1467–1568), and building stable governmental rule over the entire country. It was issued in 1588, at a time when occupational categories were blurred: when called on by a local military leader, a peasant might put down his farming tools and take up a sword to fight in the leader's army. Or, a farmer might take up arms with other farmers and or military men to resist a local military leader. It was also issued at a time when there was still widespread warfare, with about a dozen daimyo vying to expand their regional alliances in hopes of unifying the country. By the year the document was issued, 1588, Hideyoshi had conquered most of the country, with just one major daimyo in the east, the Hôjô, still holding out in opposition against him.

Hideyoshi was not the first warlord of the late Warring States period to collect weapons from the countryside, but he was the first to attempt to disarm it on a national scale. As a result, the sword hunt put its stamp on Tokugawa Japan in that, together with policies that largely separated warrior (samurai) and peasants in physical terms, with samurai living in castle towns and peasants living in the countryside, it was instrumental in helping to clarify social occupations. The sword hunt played an important role in helping to distinguish between samurai and the peasantry, the latter of whom were to devote themselves exclusively to agricultural work and not to bear arms. All of these policies were key in the creation of what historians refer to as the status system (*mibunsei*) and to the promotion of civil peace. It is notable that the decree was not addressed to a single individual or official; Hideyoshi, apparently, is addressing the nation as a whole.

The intent of the decree is clear from the first article: "The farmers of the various provinces are strictly forbidden to possess long swords, short swords, bows, spears, muskets, or any other form of weapon. If there are persons who maintain unnecessary implements, cause hardship in the collecting of annual taxes, and [thus] foment uprisings, or commit wrong acts toward the retainers, they shall, needless to say, be brought to judgment. Since [in such cases] the paddies and dry fields of the places concerned will not be cultivated and the fiefs will be wasted, the lords of the provinces, the retainers, and the representatives shall therefore strictly collect all these weapons mentioned and deliver them [to us]" (Quoted in Berry, 1989, 102). In other words, although this decree has gone down in history as the "sword hunt," it did not have a formal title, and as is evident from the first article, all types of weapons, including muskets and bows, not just swords, were collected. As the Jesuit Luis Frois, a Portuguese Jesuit missionary who visited Japan, wrote: ". . . And he is astutely planning to possess himself of all the iron in Japan, having ordered that all the mechanics and common people should leave off wearing swords and carrying and other sort of weapon (with which such people are here always well provided), and bring them to a place indicated for the purpose to be converted into the iron work necessary in the temple. Thus the populace is disarmed, and he the more secure in his arbitrary domain" (Murdoch, 1903, 369).

It is also significant that Hideyoshi rationalized the collection of weapons, the disarming of commoners, in religious terms. The weapons, he decreed, were to be used "as rivets and clamps" in the construction of a Great Buddha statue. By turning over their weapons, the decree affirmed, "the farmers will be saved in this life, needless to say, and in the life to come" (Berry, 1989, 102). Moreover, by engaging exclusively in agriculture, it was promised that they and future generations would prosper.

The sword hunt edict surprisingly met with no widespread resistance. Although not immediately enforced across the entire country, Hideyoshi's designated officials, known as "sword-collecting magistrates," and local daimyo collected large caches of weapons and sent them to Kyoto. For example, from just one district in Kaga domain, located on the Sea of Japan, 2,613 long and short swords, 700 daggers, and 160 spearheads were collected. Apparently, daimyo were only too willing to obey Hideyoshi's order, because removing weapons from the countryside meant that peasants would find it more difficult to create disorder, by resisting the collection of annual taxes, by fomenting uprisings or impeding the rule of local officials. Also, by confiscating the weapons carried by the soldier-monks of the large monasteries such as Kôyasan and Tônomine, Hideyoshi ensured that the Buddhist church would not further oppose him, as it had Oda Nobunaga earlier.

Later, in 1591, Hideyoshi followed up the sword hunt with a new edict that prohibited movement between the three occupational orders of peasant farmer, townsmen (merchant and artisan), and warrior (samurai). This too aimed at a clear separation of peasants and warriors.

The thoroughness of Hideyoshi's policy regarding swords is questionable, however, given the fact that sword collection edicts were issued again in 1618, under shogun Tokugawa Hidetada, and in 1685, under shogun Tokugawa Ietsuna. However, by the beginning of the Tokugawa period (1600–1868), the countryside was largely pacified, and by the end of the seventeenth century the wearing of two swords had become an unquestionable marker of samurai status.

See also: Status System (*mibunsei*); Swords; Tokugawa Hidetada; Tokugawa Ietsuna; Toyotomi Hideyoshi

Further Reading

Berry, Mary Elizabeth. *Hideyoshi*. Cambridge, MA: Council on East Asian Studies, Harvard University, 1989.

Boscaro, Adriana, ed. and trans. *101 Letters of Hideyoshi: The Private Correspondence of Toyotomi Hideyoshi*. Tokyo: Sophia University, 1975.

Murdoch, James. *A History of Japan. Volume 2: During the Century of Early Foreign Intercourse (1542–1651), pt. 1*. Kobe: 1903. Reprinted by Routledge & Kegan Paul, Ltd., London, 1964.

Swords

The Japanese sword has acquired mythical significance in the history of Japan. It is an image cultivated by popular culture in Japan and in the West, as evidenced by *chanbara* (sword-fighting movies) not to mention Hollywood movies (in the opening segment in the blockbuster film *The Last Samurai* the spear is erroneously replaced with the sword in the retelling of Japan's foundation myth). The sword was employed on Japanese battlefields since ancient times, but it only became the primary weapon of samurai during the great Tokugawa peace, once all wars had ceased. The samurai's swords became instruments that helped to clarify social status—to elevate the samurai above the other social groups, the peasants, artisans, and merchants.

Chanbara, Japan's "Sword-Fighting" Movies

A rough cultural equivalent to the western cowboy and swashbuckler films, Japanese *chanbara*, or sword-fighting movies, are usually set in the Tokugawa period or in the period of civil war just before it. Famous examples of this action genre, typically with lots of stylized sword fighting, include many films by legendary filmmaker Kurosawa Akira, such as *Seven Samurai* (1954), *Yojimbo* (1961), and *Sanjuro* (1962). Numerous other directors have also made films in the genre, which featured not just heroes but also antiheroes, such as the merciless swordsman in Okamoto Kihachi's *The Sword of Doom* (1966). The characters portrayed in these films are often solitary figures such as masterless samurai who are engaged against an enemy that requires them to make frequent use of their considerable martial skills, usually with the iconic sword. Although *chanbara* lost much of their popularity in the 1980s, more recently they have experienced something of a revival with films such Yôji Yamada's triology, *The Twilight Samurai* (2002), *The Hidden Blade* (2004), and *Love and Honor* (2006).

American and European directors have borrowed many of the conventions and plots of *chanbara*, but Japanese directors in turn have borrowed from American and Italian westerns (so-called "spaghetti westerns").

The influence of *chanbara* can also be seen in Japanese *anime* and *manga*, such as *Rurouni Kenshin* and *Samurai Champloo*.

THE SWORD PRIOR TO THE TOKUGAWA PERIOD

The weapon most associated with the Tokugawa samurai is the curved, single-cutting-edged long blade known as the *katana*. It represents the culmination of the evolution of Japanese swords beginning in prehistoric times, as evidenced by the long, straight-edged swords (*tsurugi*) found in excavations of Yayoi-period (300 BCE–250 CE) sites and the mounded tombs (*kofun*) of regional chieftains during the Tomb period (250 CE–538 CE). These early swords were made with techniques brought from the Asian continent and were similar to those found in China and Korea.

The straight-edged sword gave way to a one with curvature and a single cutting edge, known as a *tachi*, perhaps as early as the middle of the Heian period (794–1185). The long, curved blade, worn edge downward, was better suited to mounted warfare and allowed for a much more effective cutting technique. The *tachi* generally was longer than the *katana* of the Tokugawa period and was worn slung across the left hip, with the signature on the tang (the part of the blade that is concealed inside the hilt) facing outward when worn. Typically, the *tachi* was worn with a short sword with no hand-guard (*tsuba*), known as *koshigatana* ("waist sword") or a dagger (*tantô*). Already by the Muromachi period (1336–1573) Japanese swords, made of steel and carbon, were valued highly not just in Japan but more broadly in East Asia, as hundreds of thousands of them were traded to Ming China. During the Warring States period (1467–1568) the *tachi* was superseded by a shorter weapon, the *katana*, which was worn thrust through the sash and with the cutting edge upward. With the edge positioned thus the samurai could deliver a deadly sword stroke simply in drawing his weapon up, out of its scabbard, in a single motion. It was this weapon, worn together with a short sword known as the *wakizashi*, that would come to define the samurai during the Tokugawa period. The combination of *katana* and *wakizashi*, which became known as *daishô* (lit., "big, small"),

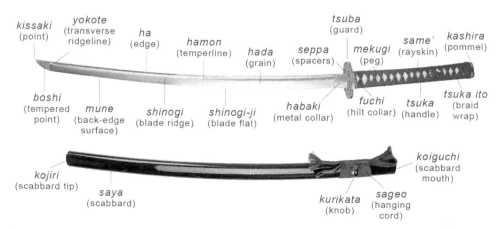

Parts of a *katana* (samurai sword) and its *koshirae* (mountings).

The Sword as Aesthetic Object: Sword Mountings

During the Tokugawa peace the sword was transformed from a tool into something that was also an aesthetic object. This is evident from the great variety and high quality of sword mountings (*koshirae*) that were created during the period. Mountings include all the fittings related to the sword (but exclude the blade); some of the major types are the scabbard (*saya*); sword guard (*tsuba*), which could have a variety of small blades (*kozuka, kogai*) that fit through slots in the face of the tsuba; hilt or handle (*tsuka*); hilt ornaments (*menuki*); and pommels (*kashira*). These various mountings allowed a samurai to personalize—to accessorize—his sword and thus to demonstrate his aesthetic sense. Covering a sword handle in rayskin (from a shark or ray), for example, was one way that a samurai might update and beautify his sword; another was to replace the sword guard. The sword guard had the function of protecting the right hand, which held the sword, from an attacker's blade, but they were also objects of art. There were an almost unlimited number of designs and themes for the sword guards: cherry blossoms (a symbol for and of the samurai because of their short life), dragonflies (popular because they only fly forward, like a samurai toward his enemy), dragons (powerful creatures), or historical themes from Japanese or Chinese history. Most *tsuba* were made of iron, to which attractive patinas in a variety of tones were sometimes added; other decorative features using copper, bronze, silver, and gold could be also be added. *Tsuba* became collectibles both during and after the Tokugawa period: Tosa domain samurai Mori Masana, for example, collected more than twenty sword guards during a year's service in Edo in 1828; collecting *tsuba* has remained a popular hobby or business for Japanese and others ever since, as a quick Internet search of "tsuba collections for sale" will reveal! The same is true for *menuki*, or hilt ornaments.

---

thrust through the waist sash on the left side, were worn with blades facing upward and positioned either parallel or crossing each other, almost perpendicularly. To one foreigner in Japan in 1853, the wearing of two swords seemed to be just for "pomp" or "mere show" (Heine, 1990, 71), but both swords had important functions, the short one being used when necessary for ritual suicide (*seppuku*).

Despite the importance that the sword later acquired in the Tokugawa period, prior to then it was only a secondary weapon of the warrior in Japan. The *naginata* (a bladed pole weapon, similar to a glave) and the bow were the primary weapons before the Warring States period; the bow was the preferred weapon of mounted samurai, who would typically use a sword—either the long *tachi* or a shorter dagger (*tantō*)—only after dismounting from his steed or when his bow failed him for technical reasons. During the Warring States period the spear came to dominate the large massed battles of the time. The introduction of firearms in the sixteenth century also meant that the sword would remain a secondary weapon of the warrior.

THE SWORD AND THE TOKUGAWA SAMURAI

The sword hunts of the late sixteenth century, particularly Hideyoshi's attempt to impose one on a national scale in 1588, was intended to bring peace to the land by disarming peasants in the countryside. After the Tokugawa assumed power, though, the shogunate did not immediately issue any laws that made swords the prerogative of the samurai. It was only in the period 1640–1680 that the shogunate gradually worked out policies that closely regulated the carrying of weapons.

The first law that imposed restrictions on commoners and thus served to help clarify status distinctions between samurai and the three other social groups (peasants, artisans, and merchants) was issued in 1648. According to the Edo ordinance:

> Regarding commoners—
>   who wear long swords,
>   who wear short swords which are unnaturally long,
>   who impersonate members of the military class,
>   who appear strange [*kabuki-taru*] outlandish
>   who act unruly or without propriety
> Immediately upon noticing such persons, the authorities should apprehend them and explain to them that they are neither to impersonate samurai nor wear the long sword; instructing them so that henceforth they shall not in any of their affairs act in such an unthinkable and improper manner. (Rogers, 1998, 18)

Nevertheless, Tokugawa policy was not consistent. Despite the earlier sword hunts, commoners for much of the seventeenth century were still allowed to wear both long and short swords in rural areas, when traveling, or in urban areas during outbreaks of fire, or in "other extraordinary circumstances." It was only in 1683 that commoners were strictly forbidden from wearing the long sword; the regulation did not ban the short sword, however. This meant that the wearing of two swords, long and short, became a samurai privilege, although some townsmen and village leadership with special privileges were allowed to wear the two swords and use a surname publicly, rights known as *myôji taito*.

Daimyo in the provinces followed the Tokugawa lead, prohibiting the wearing of the long sword. Regulations from Shibata domain (present-day Niigata prefecture) in 1720 make clear their intention in clarifying social roles—that is, making clear differences between samurai and commoners:

> 1. Farmers "should cease the owning of arms, the study of military drill, and all imitation of the customs of samurai." Punishment for any farmer of townsman caught wearing a long sword: The sword is to be confiscated and the offender shackled for a period of ten days. (Rogers, 1998, 22)

Similarly, authorities in Morioka in 1808 issued the following decree:

1. Any farmer or townsman who, on his own authority, wears a long sword. Punishment: Both long and short swords are to be confiscated and the offender banished to a distant part of the domain.

2. Any servant of a low-ranking samurai who assumes a surname and wears a long sword without permission. Punishment: banishment to the most extreme regions of the domain.

3. Any farmer or townsman who, while traveling or the like, falsely assumes a samurai name and wears the long sword. Punishment: His swords are to be confiscated and he is to be fined heavily. (Rogers, 1998, 21)

In other words, although commoners were prohibited from wearing the long sword, there was no such prohibition on wearing a short sword alone. However, from early in the seventeenth century the shogunate was concerned with regulating sword length—specifically (first in 1615), it wanted to ban commoners from wearing "unnaturally long short swords." Later, in 1638, it actually specified the length of both long (33.4 inches) and short (20.3 inches) swords. These mandated lengths changed slightly later, but the effect—to allow samurai, with their long sword to have a clear advantage over any commoner who might think about using a short sword against him—remained the same.

Of what use, then, was a sword to a samurai during the Tokugawa period? If he was alive during the first half of the seventeenth century, he might have had occasion to carry it into battle (at the Battle of Sekigahara, the Sieges of Osaka, or the Shimabara Rebellion). As indicated above, once status boundaries were clarified, the two swords that he wore immediately marked his identity and signaled to commoners to show him social deference. If a commoner did not show deference and acted out against a samurai, he could in principle strike down the commoner for his insolence, which was known as "disrespect killing" (*burei-uchi*). Should a samurai's father or elder brother be murdered by another samurai, he could apply to the authorities for official permission to carry out a revenge-killing (*katakiuchi*). Should he bring shame on himself or his family, he could turn his short sword on himself and commit ritual suicide (*seppuku*). If a samurai did not have an official appointment, he might buy and sell swords on the side to supplement his stipend, as the Tokugawa bannerman Katsu Kokichi (1802–1850) did. A samurai might also give another samurai, particularly his overlord, the gift of a beautiful sword on a special occasion or in an attempt to expunge an offense or scandal. Finally, while at home he could display it on a rack, particularly if it was a fine blade with a documented history, to impress visitors to his home.

Japanese Swords and Japan's Self-Defense Forces

In May 2016, Japan's Ground Self-Defense Force (GSDF) unveiled a new insignia in which the *katana* figures prominently. The new "cherry blossom sword" insignia, which comes in three different shapes—round, square, and in the form of a shield—features the symbol of the rising sun (used in the Japanese national flag) above a samurai sword, which is itself above a gold cherry blossom–shaped star. The cherry blossom is a well-known symbol for the samurai and a common motif in GSDF uniforms and paraphernalia; the brevity of the life of a cherry blossom on the bough is said to reflect the samurai's acceptance of death in the pursuit of loyal service to a lord. The *katana,* also associated with the samurai, is depicted crossed with its scabbard at the center, with the scabbard positioned on top. The new insignia has caused some controversy overseas, however, since the *katana* is also associated by some with World War II and Japanese officers who carried swords. (Of course, the sword is part of the dress uniform of some military men in other countries, such as the U.S. Marines.) A GSDF spokesperson said that the samurai sword was used because it is a Japanese symbol of strength and not due to any links to past Japanese military organizations.

"Emburemu ni tsuite" [Concerning the Emblem]. Japan Ground Self-Defense Forces website. http://www.mod.go.jp/gsdf/about/emblem. Accessed September 12, 2016.

See also: Armor; Disrespect Killing (*burei-uchi*); Firearms; Miyamoto Musashi; Revenge-Killing (*katakiuchi*); *Seppuku* (Ritual Suicide); Status System (*mibunsei*); Sword Hunt (*katanagari*)

Further Reading

Heine, William. *With Perry to Japan: A Memoir.* Translated by Frederic Trautmann. Honolulu: University of Hawai'i Press, 1990.

"The Japanese Sword Museum." https://www.touken.or.jp/english. Accessed August 2, 2018.

Katsu Kokichi. *Musui's Story: The Autobiography of a Tokugawa Samurai.* Translated by Teruko Craig. Tucson, AZ: University of Arizona Press, 1988.

Rogers, John Michael. "The Development of the Military Profession in Tokugawa Japan." PhD thesis. Cambridge, MA: Harvard University, 1998.

"Secrets of the Japanese Sword." http://www.pbs.org/wgbh/nova/ancient/secrets-samurai-sword.html. Accessed August 3, 2018. (Transcript of PBS Nova television show that aired October 9, 2007.)

Warner, Gordon, and Donn F. Draeger. *Japanese Swordsmanship: Technique and Practice.* New York and Tokyo: Weatherhill, 1982.

Yumoto, John. *The Samurai Sword: A Handbook.* Rutland, VT: Tuttle Publishing, 2002.

T

Takebe Ayatari (1719–1774)

Born into a samurai family from Hirosaki during the mid-Tokugawa period, Takebe Ayatari (Ryôtei) rejected his hereditary place in society in becoming a *rônin* (masterless samurai), after which he gained notoriety as a literati (*bunjin*) for his pioneering approach to a variety of aesthetic activities, including poetry, prose, and painting.

Takebe Ayatari, the nom de plum he later adopted, was in fact the son of Kitamura Kôi Masakata (1682–1729), a senior official of Hirosaki, a domain in northern Japan. He was related, through his grandmother, to two renowned military theorists, Yamaga Sokô (1622–1685) and Daidôji Yûzan (1639–1730). At the age of nineteen he was cut off by his family and banished from the domain, apparently for scheming to run away with his elder brother's wife, with whom he was having an affair. As the second son of a high-ranking official Ayatari likely would have been adopted into one of the lesser families of the domain, or perhaps he would have been given permission to form a branch family. His actions, however, lead to his forced departure from home and domain, to which he never returned, leaving him without a means of support.

Despite his background in military studies—his brother had even encouraged him through an intermediary to take up a career teaching *naginata* (a bladed weapon with a long wooden handle) and sword fighting—Ayatari rejected his military background (*bu*) and became a priest for nine years (1740–1749). After this he decided to embrace the civil arts (*bun*), first beginning a career as a *haikai* poet, which he continued for the rest of his life and gave him critical acclaim. He also took up the study of *kokugaku* (nativist learning) with the famous scholar Kamo no Mabuchi in Edo and in 1750 tried his hand at painting in the *nanga* style, which was patterned after Chinese literati painting. He apparently was a talented artist, for a couple of years later he received sponsorship as a *nanga* painter from the lord of Nakatsu, Okudaira Masaatsu (1724–1758), thus bringing Ayatari back into contact with his former life as a samurai. His efforts to promote an archaic style of Japanese poetry, however, were not successful. The same year his daimyo sponsor died, Ayatari also tried his hand at prose and wrote a three-part, fictionalized narrative, *Nishiyama monogatari* (*Tale of Nishiyama*), a tale that was inspired by a real-life tragedy involving two ill-fated lovers.

See also: Civil and Military Arts (*bunbu*); Ronin (*rônin*); Yamaga Sokô

Further Reading

Marceau, Lawrence E. *Takebe Ayatari: A* Bunjin *Bohemian in Early Modern Japan.* Ann Arbor, MI: University of Michigan Center for Japanese Studies, 2004.

Young, Blake Morgan. "A Tale of the Western Hill: Takebe Ayatari's *Nishiyama Monogatari.*" *Monumenta Nipponica,* 37(1) (1982), 77–121.

Tani Tannai (or Mashio) (1729–1797)

A member of one of the three top scholarly families in Tosa domain, Tani Tannai, like his grandfather Jinzan and his father Kakimori, was an outstanding figure in the cultural history of region during the Tokugawa period. The Tani family was well known for its wide scholarship, such as Shinto studies, astronomy, the study of ceremonies and customs, and poetry, but Tannai's reputation rested particularly on his literary abilities. His poetic skills were recognized in a number of contemporary works, including the early-nineteenth-century *Nanroshi*, a collection in which concluded one hundred of his poems. When Tosa domain established an official school for its retainers in 1759, known as the Kôjukan, he was appointed one of its four professors.

He frequently accompanied the daimyo of Tosa on his biennial trip to Edo, where he served as a Confucian lecturer to the lord or to his heir. The Tani family became dependent on the subsidies granted for Edo service in their attempts to keep the household financially solvent.

Tani Tannai also compiled a historical document that reveals a great deal about the general financial condition of samurai in the mid-Tokugawa period. His *Record of Daily Necessities* (*Nichiyô beien roku*, 1748–1754), which literally means "Record of the daily necessities of rice and salt," is a collection of letters exchanged between Tannai and the merchant Saitaniya Hachirôbei Naomasu (1705–1779). Tannai actually copied a number of examples of their correspondence into his ledger. In addition, he also recorded therein various budgets and memos to himself. The ledger itself reflected his attempts at thrift, for several of the pages and the cover of the original document were written on paper that already had been used on one side. This may be an indication that he meant the ledger to be a personal record, though perhaps he also kept it as a useful guide and/or warning to his son.

In one letter (see Document 13A) Tannai wrote Saitaniya, who was both his creditor and his student, asking for another loan to carry him over until his next stipend payment. This was because Saitaniya had turned down his request to break out of the spiral of increasing debt by restructuring his considerable debt load from previous years by treating it as "old debt" (i.e., a no-interest loan). In an attempt to convince Saitaniya of his seriousness in cutting expenses, Tannai even proposed moving his residence just north of the castle to a location closer to the mountains that ring the castle town of Kôchi, which would have improved his household economy. Such a move would have required permission for the domain, for retainers normally were required to reside in the castle town to be available for service to the lord at any time. More specifically, Tannai would have had to be declared by the domain "poverty strickened" (*hissoku*) to be granted permission to make such a move for a temporary period of time. In many ways, Tannai's plight seems quite modern: falling prey to a cycle of debt, from which he seemed unable to break away. Tannai and Saitaniya's correspondence also make it clear that the merchant had the dominant position in their relationship, despite the official status hierarchy that put samurai at the top and merchants at the bottom.

By the mid-eighteenth century, the Yamauchi lords of Tosa, like most daimyo, who were themselves in financial straits, commonly demanded that samurai return a portion of their stipends to the domains as forced loans. These were known euphe-mistically as "loans to the lord" (*onkariage*), even though there was no expectation that they would ever be repaid. Forced loans generally were deducted in one sum, from one of the two yearly payments retainers received, which made keeping to a budget very difficult for samurai like Tannai. Samurai also became dependent on merchants due to the multimetallic monetary system of the time, which required converting from one type of currency to another, the variable rate for converting rice to cash, not to mention the stipend-payment system. In Tosa, and many other domains, stipended samurai were paid twice-yearly, and since the forced loans to the domain were deducted from a single payment, this forced them to borrow money to live on until the next payment. The forced loans thus inadvertently added to sam-urai's cycle of debt.

In terms of income, Tannai was a lower-ranking samurai, earning 24 *koku* in rice. In most domains income distribution was concentrated in the lower end: for example, in Hirato domain, about one-third of the retainer corps received stipends in the range of 10–30 *koku*. Tannai, thus, would have been right in the middle of this group. Both Tannai and his father, Tanshirô, also received support rice (rice allowances) for the services they performed as Confucian scholars for the domain, in addition to their basic stipends. What rice was not consumed by the household had to be converted to cash to pay for the other necessities of life. Merchants were also needed for this and received a commission for their services.

Further Reading

Katsu Kokichi. *Musui's Story: The Autobiography of a Tokugawa Samurai.*Translated by Teruko Craig. Tucson, AZ: University of Arizona Press, 1988.

Vaporis, Constantine N. "Samurai and Merchant in Mid-Tokugawa Japan: Tani Tannai's *Record of Daily Necessities* (1748–54)." *Harvard Journal of Asiatic Studies,* 60(1) (2000), 205–227.

Yamamura, Kozo. "The Increasing Poverty of the Samurai in Tokugawa Japan, 1600–1868." *Journal of Economic History,* 31 (1971), 378–406.

Tea Ceremony (sadô)

At its most basic level, the tea ceremony was nothing more than the preparation and serving of a bowl of green tea. However, during the Kamakura period (1185–1333), the monk Eisai (1141–1215), returning from a period of study in China to found Zen as an independent sect in Japan, brought with him the tea ritual practiced in Bud-dhist temples there. This involved the drinking of powdered, unfermented green tea, which was whisked in individual bowls. He also carried with him the tea seeds from plants that became the source of the tea grown in Japan since then. During the Muromachi or Ashikaga period (1336–1573), tea drinking developed into the "way of tea"—*sadô*—a practice in which great artistic and spiritual meaning was found in the highly ritualized actions prescribed for preparing and serving the tea. Large-scale tea gatherings were often hosted by the Ashikaga shoguns, some of whom hired cultural advisers to guide them in selecting tea implements. These imple-ments included tea caddies, which held the powdered tea; iron kettles, for heating the water; curved bamboo tea scoops, used to extract the powdered tea from the tea caddy; bamboo whisks, with which to mix the water and powdered tea; and, last but not least, tea bowls. The instruments used to prepare and serve the tea became objects of beauty; they began to be collected not just by shoguns but more widely among daimyo and wealthy merchants.

The tea ceremony was transformed over time from a simple act of drinking tea to an experience removed from the everyday and drew the attention of Western visitors to Japan in the sixteenth century. According to Alessandro Valignano (1539–1606), the head of the Jesuit mission in Japan, "[I]n every part of Japan they drink a brew made of hot water and a powdered herb, called *cha*. They greatly esteem this drink and all the gentry [meaning, high-ranking samurai] have a special room in their houses where they make this brew" (Quoted in Cooper, 1965, 260). They also understood that there was a greater purpose to the tea ceremony than simply drinking tea and talking. Joao Rodrigues (1561–1633), a Portuguese Jesuit, noted that it "is not for the guests to deliver long speeches, but rather that they may calmly and moderately contemplate within themselves the things they see there; this they do, not to compliment the host on them, but rather to understand in this way the mysteries which are enclosed therein. In keeping with this purpose, everything employed in the ceremony is as nature created it—rustic, unrefined, and simple, as would befit a lonely country hermitage" (Quoted in Cooper, 1965, 264–265). Western visitors also noted the tremendous monetary value that the warlords, the *sengoku daimyô,* attached to various tea implements, particularly the tea caddies and tea bowls, items that appeared quite ordinary in their own eyes.

The drinking of tea had become a part of the lives of Japanese of all classes by the sixteenth century, and the tea ceremony itself grew in popularity during the course of the Tokugawa period. The tradition of Sen Rikyû (1522–1591), the most famous of all tea masters, who was sponsored by the powerful daimyo Oda Nobunaga and Toyotomi Hideyoshi in the late sixteenth century, was carried on by his successors. That tradition was known as *wabi-cha* ("*wabi* tea," *wabi* meaning literally "forlorn"), which emphasized the aesthetic values of simplicity and rusticity. After the death of Rikyû's grandson, Genpaku Sôtan (1578–1658), the family line split in three, forming the Urasenke, Omotesanke, and Mushakôjisenke schools or streams of tea, each professing to teach the original tea ceremony that Rikyû had founded. Building on Rikyû's innovation of making the tea in front of guests (rather than preparing it in one room and serving it in another), they did much to make the tea rituals less exclusive. Patronage thus shifted from the dominance of daimyo to include samurai more broadly, but also artisans, merchants, and other commoners.

In other words, during the Tokugawa period, the practice of the tea ceremony cut across status lines, and it was not unusual for samurai to study it. Some chose to study it as a means of advancement when other, more traditional avenues were closed off to them. Others studied it for purely personal reasons. Retainers were particularly likely to indulge in the tea ceremony when their lord practiced it. The tea ceremony also provided a space in which samurai of different rank could participate and share a moment of contemplation and reflection.

Chikamatsu Shigenori (1695–1778), a retainer of the Tokugawa daimyo in Owari, was one of the above-mentioned samurai who studied the tea ceremony for purely personal reasons. He practiced the Sen school of tea. Shigenori not only studied and practiced *sadô* diligently, but in 1739 he compiled a manuscript on the subject, entitled *Legends of the Tea Ceremony*. This work consisted of seven volumes, with 305 stories and anecdotes based on things either that Shigenori saw himself or that were recounted to him. It remained in manuscript form until well after his death, when the book was published in 1804 under the title *Stories from a Tearoom Window*. It met with some success, and a second edition was published in 1816.

His purpose in writing *Stories from a Tearoom Window* was to restore the tea ceremony to the ideals of Sen Rikyû, meaning to restore simplicity and rusticity as basic elements of the ritual. He decried the rigidity, the excessive detail paid to technique, and the extravagance to which it had fallen. However, that basic tension between the original aesthetics of the tea ceremony and its later development remained, even with the publication of Shigenori's book.

See also: Oda Nobunaga; Toyotomi Hideyoshi; Warring States Daimyo (*sengoku daimyô*)

Further Reading

Chikamatsu Shigenori. *Stories from a Teahouse Window.* Edited by Toshiko Mori and translated by Kazoburo Mori. Rutland, VT: Charles E. Tuttle, 1982.

Cooper, Michael. *They Came to Japan: An Anthology of European Reports on Japan, 1543–1640.* Berkeley and London: University of California Press, 1965.

Graham, Patricia Jane. *Tea of the Sages: The Art of Sencha.* Honolulu: University of Hawai'i Press, 1998.

Sen, Sôshitsu. *The Japanese Way of Tea: From Its Origins in China to Sen Rikyû.* Translated by V. Dixon Morris. Honolulu: University of Hawai'i Press, 1998.

Rivals in the Tea Ceremony

The competition between two samurai, both students of the tea ceremony, to rise in position in their domain, forms the backdrop to puppet play *Gonza the Lancer* (*Yari no Gonza*), by Chikamatsu Monzaemon (1653–1725). Sasano Gonza, an expert lancer, and his rival, Bannojo, compete for the honor to perform a special tea ceremony to celebrate the birth of an heir to the lord of their domain while their tea master is in Edo serving the lord. To gain an advantage in the competition, Gonza arranges to have Osai, the wife of the tea master, show him a set of sacred tea scrolls. To gain this permission, however, Gonza must promise to marry Osai and the tea master's daughter. He agrees to do so in order to get an advantage over his rival, even though he is already engaged to the sister of one of his fellow retainers. While Gonza is studying the scrolls with Osai, Bannojo sneaks into the house and steals their kimono sashes (*obi*). He then proceeds to run through the castle town, proclaiming falsely the two as adulterers. As a result, Gonza and Osai flee and the tea master is forced by custom to return to the domain to hunt them down and punish them by killing them himself. The story was made into a movie *Yari no Gonza* (*Gonza the Spearman*) by Shinoda Masahiro in 1984.

Testing a Sword on a Cadaver (*hiemontori*)

For the vast majority of the Tokugawa period, peaceful conditions prevailed. Samurai could engage in sword fighting in practice halls at domain schools, where and when they existed, or in private academies. For actual experience using a real blade, however, there were few opportunities. Except for cases in which samurai cut down commoners for certain acts of disrespect (*burei-uchi*), which apparently was not very common [see entry Disrespect Killing (*burei-uchi*)], and the even more unusual cases when some samurai killed for sport, a samurai might never have occasion to draw his sword on another person. The practice of *hiemontori* was the exception, although the human being involved was actually a corpse.

The practice of *hiemontori* was unusual enough to catch the attention of Englebert Kaempfer, the German in the employ of the Dutch East India Company who visited Japan in the early 1690s. Kaempfer reported that young samurai were allowed to test the effectiveness of their swords on corpses at the execution grounds, a practice known as *hiemontori*. He reported that they did so "until they [the corpses] have been cut into pieces half the length of a finger" (Kaempfer, 1999, 223). In Satsuma domain there was a competition among young samurai in neighborhood schools known as *gojū*, the winner of which gained the right to be the first to use his sword on a cadaver. In practice, the elder group of boys in the school would gather at the domain prison and wait for the executioner to sever the head of the condemned person "and then rushed forward to seize the corpse. The first to bite off an ear or finger and show it to his companions was deemed the winner and awarded the first round of practice on the cadaver" (Ravina, 2004, 32). In contrast, Tosa samurai Mori Masana used a less lethal method of testing his blade. While in Edo due to the alternate attendance, Masana wanted to test the effectiveness of a newly purchased sword. Accordingly, he and several friends purchased a boar's head from a local market to test them on. When they had finished their test cuts—during which time one of his friend's blades chipped—they cooked the animal's head and ate the meat.

Killing for Pleasure?

Although Tokugawa Japan was a relatively peaceful society, there were occasions when samurai used violent means to address insults to their honor [see entry Disrespect Killing (*burei-uchi*)]. There were also samurai who apparently killed for sport or "pleasure." This we learn from *Ōmurōchūki* (*Diary of a Parrot in a Cage*), the diary of the low-ranking samurai Asahi Shigeaki (1674–1718), who noted that this occurred among some groups of young, unemployed samurai (*rōnin*). As part of this type of behavior, which was known contemporaneously as "street murders" (*tsuji kiri*), passersby were killed with swords and robbed. Even some daimyo were reputed to have engaged in this activity, including Tokugawa Mitsukuni, the lord of Mito domain, during his youth. The Tosa samurai Mori Masana while traveling to Edo in 1829 reported stories that the retired lord of Wakayama would go out at night with four or five attendants, enter people's homes, and kill them. He is reputed to have killed hundreds of people in this way.

The practice of *hiemontori* is one of the subjects in Hiroshi Hirata's manga, *Satsuma Gishiden* (*Tales of Righteous Satsuma Samurai*), vol. 2 (Milwaukie, OR: Dark Horse Publishers, 2007).

See also: Disrespect Killing (*burei-uchi*); Education; Swords

Further Reading

Kaempfer, Englebert. *Kaempfer's Japan: Tokugawa Culture Observed.* Edited, translated, and annotated by B. M. Bodart-Bailey. Honolulu: University of Hawai'i Press, 1999.

Mori Masana. ms. "Edo nikki" (10 vols., 1828–56), vol. 2, folios 34–35. Kôchi: Kôchi Prefectural Library.

Ravina, Mark. *The Last Samurai: The Life and Battles of Saigo Takamori.* Hoboken, NJ: John Wiley & Sons, 2004.

Tokugawa Hidetada (1579–1632)

Born the third son of Tokugawa Ieyasu, Hidetada succeeded his father as the second shogun and ruled from 1605 until he retired in 1623. Although he handed the formal reins of power to his son Iemitsu (1623–1651), he continued to exercise authority until his death in 1632. Hidetada was thus the second of the three shoguns under whom Tokugawa rule was established and solidified—a dynasty that would last 264 years.

As the third son, Hidetada was not the obvious choice to succeed his father Ieyasu. However, his eldest brother Nobuyasu and his mother Lady Tsukiyama were implicated in a plot to assassinate Ieyasu, and Nobuyasu was forced to commit ritual suicide (*seppuku*). His second eldest brother, Kamehime, who was also born to Ieyasu's first wife, Lady Tsukiyama) had been adopted out as Toyotomi Hideyoshi's heir, which left Hidetada, whose mother was Ieyasu's concubine Lady Saigô (or Saigô no tsubone), to succeed. As heir to Ieyasu, Hidetada was sent to serve as a hostage to Toyotomi Hideyoshi (1537–1598) during the Odawara campaign against the Hôjô lord. While under Hideyoshi's oversight, Hidetada went through *genpuku*, the coming-of-age ceremony, and received the Chinese character "Hide" to use in his name (in contrast with Hidetada's son, Iemitsu, who was given his grandfather's character "ie").

Like his father, Hidetada had experience of the battlefield. He was charged with conducting operations during initial stages of the Sekigahara military campaign in 1600 but was distracted by the determined resistance of the Sanada daimyo at Ueda Castle in Shinano; as a result, he arrived at Sekigahara too late to contribute to the victory of the Tokugawa-led Eastern Army, which earned him a stern rebuke from Ieyasu.

Despite his major mishap at Sekigahara, Hidetada was named shogun in 1605, although as noted Ieyasu continued to exert influence from his retirement at Sunpu Castle (in Sunpu). Hidetada was able to redeem himself later by playing an active role in the two Sieges of Osaka Castle, in 1614–1615.

Hidetada's reign was defined by institutional consolidation of the shogunate. For example, he built on the progress Ieyasu had made in strengthening the position of the shogunate in relation to the daimyo. While Ieyasu had confiscated from the daimyo lands worth 3.83 million *koku*, Hidetada took even more—the most of any shogun—4.53 million *koku*. Second, in 1615, he issued administrative orders regulating the powers and duties of the emperor and the imperial court, known as *Kinchû kuge shohatto* (*Rules for the Imperial Palace and Court*). Following Ieyasu's death in 1616, Hidetada took further steps to strengthen the position of the shogunate over the imperial court through marriage. He did this by arranging the betrothal of his daughter to Emperor Go-Mizunoo. The daughter that resulted from this union assumed the throne in 1629 as Empress Meishô, thus briefly uniting the shogunal and imperial lines. Third, Hidetada reorganized the executive organs of the shogunate. Fourth, he took steps to regulate Christianity and foreign trade more closely. He took stern measures against Christianity, repeating the 1597 ban on the foreign faith, but also forcing daimyo who had converted to apostatize, banning the importation of books concerning Christianity, and executing fifty-five Christians in Nagasak in 1622; his son, the shogun Iemitsu, would take his policies even further, with stepped-up persecution of Christianity and the expulsion of Europeans (with the exception of the Dutch) from Japan.

Hidetada married the youngest daughter of the daimyo, Asai Nagamasa (1545–1573), Oda Nobunaga's brother-in-law. She was known as Oeyo or Gô and bore Hidetada four children: Iemitsu, the third shogun; Tadanaga, who was daimyo of Kôfu; a daughter, Senhime, who married Toyotomi Hideyori and was allowed safe exit out of Osaka Castle before it fell to the forces of the Tokugawa in 1615; and another daughter, Tôfukumon-in, who was married to Emperor Go-Mizunoo and gave birth herself to a daughter that later became Empress Meishô. Hidetada's wife Oeyo is reputed to have been very protective of her position and did not allow other women to be a part of the household. This was very unusual for a shogun or daimyo. Hidetada's father, Ieyasu, for example, was reported to have had eighteen concubines. Although Hidetada did father children with other women, they were not

Gifting Armor to a King

Japanese armor and military hardware, particularly swords, were important tools of diplomacy between Japan and Western nations. In the process of Britain negotiating for trade rights with Japan in the early seventeenth century, there was an exchange of gifts between the two countries. According to the Englishman captain John Saris, who was in the employ of the British East India Company and brought the armor back to England in 1614, "the young king at Edo [Tokugawa Hidetada] made us present of two entire suits of Japan armour, finely varnished and a long sword and Waggedash [*wakizashi*] for my self." The gift was to King James I, and it appears to have been put on display in the Royal Armouries by 1662, when according to one contemporary record, "Many persons of quality went to the armoury in the Tower of London to see that most noble and strong defence for the body, the suit of armour sent from the emperor Mougul [the shogun] which suit was presented to His Majesty the King of England." The armor was made by Iwai Yozaemon, the personal armorer of Tokugawa Ieyasu (https://collections.royalarmouries.org/object/rac-object-30423.html; accessed July 28, 2018).

The suit of armor and other gifts from the shogun to the king were on display at the Royal Armouries in 2013 for the 400th Anniversary of Japanese-British relations.

permitted to remain in the household. Hoshina Masayuki (1611–73) was one such example. Although he was Hidetada's son, he was adopted out of the Tokugawa family and into that of the Hoshina, becoming the lord of Aizu; later he would serve as shogunal adviser and regent to the minor Tokugawa Ietsuna, the fourth shogun.

Following his father's precedent, Hidetada also retired in favor of his (eldest) son, Iemitsu, in 1623, but continued to exercise authority as ôgosho (retired shogun), in essence ruling jointly with Iemitsu until his death in 1632. Hidetada and his wife, Oeyo, are buried together in the Taitoku-in Mausoleum at the Tokugawa funerary temple Zôjôji in Tokyo. His posthumous Buddhist name is Daitoku-in.

See also: Coming of Age (*genpuku*); Sekigahara, Battle of; Shogun (*shôgun*); Sieges of Osaka (*Ôsaka no jin*); Toyotomi Hideyoshi; Tokugawa Iemitsu; Tokugawa Ietsuna; Tokugawa Tsunayoshi

Further Reading

Bodart-Bailey, Beatrice. *The Dog Shogun: The Personality and Policies of Tokugawa Tsunayoshi*. Honolulu: University of Hawai'i Press, 2006.

Sansom, George. *A History of Japan, 1615–1867*. Stanford, CA: Stanford University Press, 1963.

Totman, Conrad. *Politics in the Tokugawa Bakufu, 1600–1843*. Cambridge, MA: Harvard University Press, 1967.

Tokugawa Iemitsu (1604–1651)

The third shogun of the Tokugawa dynasty, Iemitsu was the son of Hidetada and the grandson of Ieyasu. He was the first shogun born after the establishment of the shogunate in 1603 and the first to die in office, without having retired and handed over the formal reigns of power to his heir. During Iemitsu's reign, shogunal rule was solidified and the administrative system assumed much of the form it would retain for the duration of the Tokugawa period. He regularized control mechanisms over the daimyo, particularly by imposing alternate attendance on all of them, and issuing a series of edicts in the 1630s to regulate strictly foreign relations, including trade.

Born as Takechiyo in 1604, Iemitsu (the name he would be given on reaching adulthood) was the son of the second shogun Hidetada and his wife Oeyo (or Gô). As a child, he was sickly, "withdrawn and handicapped in his speech" (Bodart-Bailey, 1999, 13). Iemitsu also had a rival in his brother, Tadanaga, who was only two years younger, healthy, intelligent, and more adept in military skills. There were two other siblings: the one sister, Senhime, married Toyotomi Hideyori (1593–1615) and was allowed safe passage out of Osaka Castle before it fell to the forces of the Tokugawa in 1615; she later married the daimyo Honda Tadatoki. Iemitsu's other sister, Masako, married Emperor Go-Mizunoo and later became known as Tôfukumon-in.

Iemitsu went through the rites of adulthood in 1617 and assumed the position of shogun five years later, in 1623. His ascension was far from assured, as his parents had been grooming his younger brother Tadanaga as shogunal successor. It is reputed that Iemitsu's wet nurse Lady Kasuga (Kasuga no Tsubone), who was the subject of a 1989 NHK Taiga Drama, played an important role in his being selected as shogun over his younger brother Tadanaga. Although Hidetada formally retired in favor of Iemitsu, he continued to exert political influence as *Ôgosho* (retired shogun). It was during this period of regency that relations with the emperor, Go-Mizunoo, deteriorated due to the Purple Robe Incident (in which the emperor, in 1627, went against the regulations earlier imposed by the Tokugawa to limit his authority to bestow honorific purple robes to Buddhist clergy); this led to the abdication of Go-Mizunoo and the ascension of Iemitsu's niece Meisho as empress.

Upon Hidetada's death in 1632 Iemitsu took steps to consolidate his authority and to create a strong, centralized administration. First, he eliminated his brother and rival Tadanaga, whose domain he confiscated after charging him with insanity and then forced to commit *seppuku* (ritual suicide). Second, Iemitsu dismissed his father's advisers and appointed his own childhood associates in their place. Third, at the same time he took steps to increase the prestige and authority of the Tokugawa dynasty by erecting a grand mausoleum for his father (called the Taitokuin Mausoleum) at the family's funerary temple, Zôjôji, and by expanding Nikkô Tôshôgû (1634–1636), where his grandfather Ieyasu was enshrined; another symbol of Tokugawa authority, Nijô Castle, was also renovated. The same year that the expansion project at Nikkô Tôshôgû began, Iemitsu also put on public display Tokugawa authority over the realm by leading the largest military procession of the Tokugawa period, on the order of 300,000 men, to Kyoto for the accession of his niece as Empress Meishô. This display dwarfed by far the entourage of 100,000 men that his father Hidetada had led to Kyoto in 1605 and was meant in particular to both impress and cow the outside lords (*tozama daimyô*) and the imperial court; it would be the last shogunal procession to Kyoto until 1863. Last, to more firmly control the daimyo, Iemitsu regularized the requirement of alternate attendance (*sankin kôtai*) as part of the new (1635) version of the *Laws for the Military Houses* (*buke shohatto*). Just seven years later, in 1642, he extended the alternate attendance requirement to all daimyo, including the hereditary daimyo (*fudai daimyô*). Also, breaking with the precedent set by Ieyasu, the shogun distanced himself from them by first greeting the outside lords during their shogunal audience in Edo Castle and not personally meeting them on the outskirts of Edo upon their arrival for alternate attendance. Third, Iemitsu pursued a policy of tight control of foreign relations, which included stepped-up persecution of Christians, particularly after the Shimabara Rebellion (1637), which shogunal-led armed forces brutally suppressed.

The assumption of centralized controls of Japan's foreign relations took place through a number of steps taken in the 1630s. This occurred primarily through the issuing of a series of five regulations between 1633 and 1639, misleadingly referred to as the "seclusion edicts." These documents actually were directives sent to the shogunate's magistrates (*bugyô*) in Nagasaki that limited trade and the scope of Japan's foreign relations. The substance of the edicts was to prohibit Japanese from traveling overseas, to impose the death penalty on any Japanese returning home after being abroad, and to regulate all foreign commerce through Nagasaki. The fifth and final edict, in 1639, essentially an addendum to the previous one, called for the exclusion of the Portuguese. The series of edicts built on earlier ones that limited the size of vessels permitted to be built (in essence prohibiting the construction of ocean-going vessels), in 1605, and which restricted European traders to Nagasaki and Hirado, in 1616. In sum, the edicts allowed Iemitsu to solidify control over the country, and after 1639 the only Europeans permitted to remain in Japan were the Dutch, who were not interested in converting Japanese to Christianity. The "closed country" edicts were not in fact aimed at closing Japan off to the outside world; they were rather meant to stop the threat that Catholic missionaries posed to the shogunate's nation-building and to gain control of foreign trade, in particular to prevent potentially hostile daimyo from trading with Europeans for military arms. Japan's trade with East Asia (Korea, China, Ryukyuan kingdom) actually increased after the Portuguese were expelled and continued to grow until the early eighteenth century, when it was reduced largely due to bullionist concerns.

Iemitsu died in 1651 and was succeeded by his eldest son, Tokugawa Ietsuna. He was interred at Nikkô Tôshôgû, the only shogun other than Ieyasu not to have been buried at one of the two Tokugawa funerary temples, Kan'eiji and Zôjôji.

See also: Alternate Attendance (*sankin kôtai*); Daimyo and Domains; *Laws for the Military Houses* (*buke shohatto*); Shimabara Rebellion (*Shimabara no ran*); Tokugawa Hidetada; Tokugawa Ietsuna; Tokugawa Ieyasu

Further Reading

Bodart-Bailey, Beatrice. *Kaempfer's Japan: Tokugawa Culture Observed.* Honolulu: University of Hawai'i Press, 1999.

Sansom, George. *A History of Japan, 1615–1867.* Stanford, CA: Stanford University Press, 1963.

Totman, Conrad. *Politics in the Tokugawa Bakufu, 1600–1843.* Cambridge, MA: Harvard University Press, 1967.

Totman, Conrad. *Early Modern Japan.* Berkeley: University of California Press, 1993.

Tokugawa Ietsuna (1641–1680)

The eldest son of Tokugawa Iemitsu and the great-grandson of Tokugawa Ieyasu, Ietsuna became the fourth shogun at the age of ten upon the death of his father. Given his youth, Ietsuna was assisted by a group of five top-ranking vassals, in addition to one man who had been selected by Iemitsu for the task, Hoshina Masayuki, Iemitsu's half-brother. He was the first shogun to assume the position as a minor and thus did not have the benefit of a period of tutelage under a retired shogun, as had been the case with his father Iemitsu and his grandfather Hidetada. Ietsuna was also the first to die without issue. In short, Ietsuna was the first figurehead shogun, preferring to allow his ministers to rule, which earned him the nickname *sayô-sama* (Lord So-Be-It). During his tenure, the shogunate underwent a transition from a military to a civil orientation in the nature of its operation; reflecting this change, Confucian learning was encouraged. According to one scholar, Ietsuna as shogun "continued poor in health and mild in spirit, but showed an engaging, gentle character, if one may judge from some of his letters which have been preserved" (Sansom, 1963, 53).

The child of Tokugawa Iemitsu and his concubine Oraku no kata (later known by the name she adopted when she became a nun at Kan'eiji temple, Hôjuin), little is known of Ietsuna's childhood other than the fact that he was a frail child, a condition that continued into adulthood. This no doubt increased the influence of his advisers, who acted as regents until he came of age and helped to preserve Tokugawa authority when the dynasty was at risk with a minor as shogun. During the period of regency, the shogunate faced several crises. The first problem the new administration had to face was a planned uprising by two *rônin* (masterless samurai) named Yui Shôsetsu and Marubashi Chûya in 1651. Later known as the Keian Uprising, the plan was to start a fire in the city of Edo that would cause chaos and allow the instigators and their followers to raid Edo Castle and execute a military coup. Similar uprisings were planned for the other two major cities, Kyoto and Osaka. The plan was uncovered soon after the death of Iemitsu and was brutally suppressed by Ietsuna's regents, but the following year the regents faced another uprising by a group of 800 *rônin* on Sado Island. This disturbance, too, was also suppressed effectively. After this there were not any major disturbances, and the problem posed by masterless samurai was in part solved by the passage of time. The shogunate did introduce a reform, allowing daimyo the right to adopt heirs at a late age, which meant that fewer samurai became *rônin* upon the death of their lord; this was a clear sign of a loosening of the harsh attitude of the first three shoguns toward the daimyo.

Another crisis the regency faced was the Meireki Fire of 1657, which burned about half of the city of Edo and killed an estimated 100,000 people, including Ietsuna's concubine Oyo. It took roughly two years to rebuild the city, and given the serious crisis facing the urban population after the fire, Ietsuna's advisers made the decision not to rebuilt Edo's castle keep, which would have consumed diverted resources badly needed to reconstruct the city. The regents' decision was also influenced by their consensus that the keep was largely a symbol tower and no longer necessary to Tokugawa rule.

The shogunate under Ietsuna also had to face a major, and prolonged, succession dispute from 1660 to 1671 in Sendai domain, the largest northern domain in Japan, where the Date family ruled. This was one of a number of similar events, known as *oie sôdô* ("disturbances among the noble families") across the country in the late seventeenth century and reflected the changing nature of a society transitioning from wartime to peacetime rule. They were also caused by the trend among the daimyo in the larger domains to centralize more power in their hands, at the expense of the landed interests of their larger vassals. In this instance, one political faction intervened with the shogunate to force the reigning daimyo to step down. However, the feud between rival factions continued even thereafter, leading to bloodshed and more intervention by the Tokugawa. These disputes became literary fodder for the majority of the plays written by Chikamatsu Monzaemon (1653–1724), the greatest Japanese dramatist of the period.

The regency formally ended in 1663, when Ietsuna twenty-two years old. His advisers, however, continued to play an active role in ruling, as Ietsuna was often ill. In fact, in 1679 Hotta Masatoshi (1634–1684) was appointed to the special position of *tairô*, or head of the shogunate's council of elders (*rôjû*) in recognition of his important advisory role. Nonetheless, there were occasions when the shogun left his personal mark, such as in 1663 when he was the force behind the decision to abolish *junshi*, following one's lord in death by committing *seppuku*.

A dispute over succession emerged during the last year of Ietsuna's life. Despite a plethora of shogunal concubines, Ietsuna had not successfully fathered an heir. Three male children, and one female child, all died in utero. Sakai Tadakiyo, one of the former regents, proposed that the son of Emperor Go-Sai succeed Ietsuna as shogun, following a precedent of the Kamakura period (when in 1252, Munetaka, the son of Emperor Go-Saga, was appointed shogun). Sakai saw himself playing a role similar to that of the Hôjô regents of the thirteenth century, acting as the unofficial power behind the scenes, but had to give up on the idea due to the opposition of Hotta Masayoshi. In the end, Tadakiyo was forced to retire from office, and Ietsuna was succeeded by his younger brother, Tokugawa Tsunayoshi (1646–1709).

Later joined by five other shoguns, Ietusna was buried at Kan'eiji, one of the Tokugawa family's funeral temples (along with Zôjôji). The tomb was partially destroyed by Allied bombing in 1945, but its formal gate and handwashing station survived and have been designated Important Cultural Properties.

See also: Seppuku (Ritual Suicide); Shogun (*shôgun*); Tokugawa Iemitsu; Tokugawa Tsunayoshi

Further Reading

Bodart-Bailey, Beatrice. *The Dog Shogun: The Personality and Policies of Tokugawa Tsunayoshi*. Honolulu: University of Hawai'i Press, 2006.

Murdoch, James. *A History of Japan*, vol. 3. Foreword and selected bibliography by John L. Mish. New York: F. Ungar Pub. Co., 1964.

Sansom, George. *A History of Japan, 1615–1867*. Stanford: Stanford University Press, 1963.

Totman, Conrad. *Politics in the Tokugawa Bakufu, 1600–1843*. Cambridge, MA: Harvard University Press, 1967.

Tokugawa Ieyasu (1543–1616)

The third of the three unifiers, Ieyasu established a dynasty of fifteen shoguns who ruled from 1603 to 1868—the last warrior regime in Japan's history. The son of a petty warlord from Mikawa province in central Japan, Ieyasu allied himself, in succession, with the first two unifiers Oda Nobunaga (1534–1582) and then with his successor, Hideyoshi (1537–1598), before establishing his military dominance at the Battle of Sekigahara in 1600. Receiving imperial appointment as shogun in 1603, Ieyasu stepped down from office two years later in favor of his son, Tokugawa Hidetada (1579–1632), but remained in power until his death in 1616. Posthumously enshrined at Nikkô Tôshôgû as Tôshô daigongen (Great Deity of the East Shining Light), Ieyasu established a firm foundation for the Tokugawa regime, which played an important part in shaping institutions and cultural practices that continue to influence Japan to the present day.

Born Matsudaira Takechiyo, Ieyasu was the son of a relatively minor daimyo, Matsudaira Hirotada (1526–1549), whose domain in Mikawa province (present-day Aichi prefecture) was sandwiched between those of two stronger rivals, the Imagawa to the east and the Oda to the west. As a result of the Matsudaira's insecure strategic position, Hirotada sent Ieyasu first to the Oda and later to the Imagawa, where

This portrait of Ieyasu (1534–1616), the first Tokugawa shogun, depicts him in formal court attire. He founded a dynasty that lasted 264 years. The peace he helped establish was forged in war, though, as evidenced by his battle-scarred ear. (Art Collection 3/Alamy Stock Photo)

he served for much of his childhood as a political hostage, a common practice of the sixteenth century; and on both occasions Ieyasu was treated well. Under the Imagawa he received an education, and when he officially came of age in 1556, his given name was changed to Motonobu in a ceremony presided over by his host, Imagawa Yoshimoto, from whom he received the character "Moto." A year later he changed his name again to Motoyasu, married his first wife, Lady Tsukiyama (a relative of Imagawa Yoshitomo's), and was allowed to return to his family's domain of Mikawa to support the Imagawa's military campaign against the Oda.

After Imagawa Yoshitomo was defeated, and killed, in Nobunaga's surprise assault at (the Battle of) Okehazama in 1560, Motoyasu allied himself with the Oda and consolidated his power in Mikawa. In pacifying Mikawa, Motoyasu had to fight several battles to suppress the militant monks of the *ikkô ikki*, a political-religious movement associated with the Jôdô shinshû sect of Buddhism. In one battle, he was struck by two bullets, though he survived as neither penetrated his armor.

His political influence growing, in 1567 he changed his name again, to Tokugawa Ieyasu. The Tokugawa surname was changed through petition to the imperial court, thereby establishing a (claimed) line of descent from the Minamoto clan, which had established the first military government, or shogunate, in Japan during the Kamakura period (1185–1333). Ieyasu also received the honorary court title of Mikawa no kami, together with the court rank of junior 5th rank, lower grade.

The main threat to Ieyasu's power base came from the Takeda clan, which allied itself with the Odawara Hôjô. In 1572 Takeda Shingen dealt Ieyasu a major defeat at the Battle of Mikatagahara, in which the Tokugawa leader barely escaped with his life, but the Takeda leader died the following year, leaving Ieyasu to deal with his successor, Katsuyori. In 1575 Katsuyori pressed the attack on Ieyasu at Nagashino Castle (Mikawa province). With the support of Nobunaga's substantial army, the combined Oda-Tokugawa force of 38,000 men was able to deal the Takeda a stinging defeat, one from which it never was able to recover. Greatly weakened militarily, Katsuyori plotted to assassinate Nobunaga, whose daughter was married to

Ieyasu's son and heir, Nobuyasu. When the plan was exposed, Ieyasu had his wife put to death and forced his son to commit *seppuku*; this left his third son, Tokugawa Hidetada, as heir, since his second son had been adopted out to the family of Toyotomi Hideyoshi. The final, crushing blow for Takeda Katsuyori came at the hands of the combined forces of the Oda and Tokugawa in 1582 at the Battle of Tenmoku-zan, after which he and his heir committed *seppuku* (ritual suicide).

Oda Nobunaga did not live long after this battle, as he was betrayed by his vassal Akechi Mitsuhide and died at the Honnôji temple in Kyoto in 1582. At first resistant to Nobunaga's successor, Ieyasu eventually allied himself with Toyotomi Hideyoshi, although he never became formally his vassal. Ieyasu supported the Toyotomi war effort, however, and in 1590 sent a substantial force of 30,000 men in support of Hideyoshi's massive army of 160,000 that was laying siege to the Hôjô clan's Odawara Castle. The defending force was starved into submission after six months, after which Hideyoshi offered Ieyasu the Hôjô's domain, the eight provinces of the Kantô. This land grant meant that Ieyasu now had a fief even larger than Hideyoshi's, over 1 million *koku* (1 *koku* being roughly equivalent to five bushels). However, assigning Ieyasu to the Kantô provinces meant that he had to give up control of his five provinces along the eastern seaboard and move to a relatively undeveloped territory that was located farther from the political center of the country.

Ieyasu spent most of the 1590s developing his new domain, particularly constructing the new castle town of Edo (present-day Tokyo), which within a century would become the largest city in the world, and Edo Castle itself, which had the largest donjon (*tenshu*) in Japan (until it burned down in 1657). Given the degree of isolation of his domain, and his position as an ally of Hideyoshi, Ieyasu was able to maintain a high degree of autonomy from his rule. Although called on to serve in Hideyoshi's headquarters in Kyushu for his two military campaigns in Korea (1592–1593, 1597–1598), off and on for about five years, Ieyasu did not contribute troops or financial resources, which left him in a much stronger position vis-à-vis his rivals after Hideyoshi's death in 1598.

Before his death, Hideyoshi had established a Council of Five Elders, who were to act as regents for his young son, Toyotomi Hideyori (1598–1615). The five men selected included Ieyasu, Maeda Toshiie, Môri Terumoto, Ukita Hideie, and Uesugi Kagekatsu. After Hideyoshi's death there was much jockeying for power among the regents and also another powerful daimyo named Ishida Mitsunari (1560–1600), who unsuccessfully attempted to assassinate Ieyasu in 1599.

By 1600, two rival camps had formed, an "eastern" one around Ieyasu and a "western" one around Ishida. The two sides, which fielded as many as 150,000 men, met on the battlefield near Sekigahara (in present-day Gifu prefecture). Ieyasu's climactic victory in what was one of the largest and most important battles in Japan's premodern history, established his position as the paramount military leader in the country. Victory in battle allowed him to confiscate the lands of many of the daimyo on the opposing side, to redistribute land to those who fought for him, and to move daimyo domains around to improve the Tokugawa's strategic control of the country. The vassals who had pledged allegiance to Ieyasu before Sekigahara came to be known as *fudai daimyô* (vassal daimyo), a number who served in the administration of the Tokugawa government (the shogunate).

Three years later, at the age of sixty, he received the appointment as shogun (formally known as *sei-i taishôgun*, or the "barbarian-quelling general") from the emperor, Go-Yôzei. Ieyasu not only outlasted the other great daimyo of his time, men such as Nobunaga, Hideyoshi, Shingen, and (Uesugi) Kenshin, but he was successful in passing on his title and authority to his son; he did this by stepping down as shogun in favor of Hidetada in 1605, while remaining in control as the retired shogun (*ôgosho*), with his headquarters in Sunpu, until his death in 1616. By doing so he ensured his heir's succession, increasing the power and authority of the Tokugawa house.

Ieyasu took other steps, personal and political, to ensure the continuation of the Tokugawa bloodline, wanting to avoid the obvious problems that Nobunaga and Hideyoshi had had. First, he married twice (the first wife, Lady Tsukiyama, died in 1579) and had nineteen concubines, with which he had eleven sons and five daughters. Three of his sons were allowed to form cadet houses or branches of the Tokugawa family (*Gosanke* or "Three Houses," namely Owari, Kii, and Suruga), which meant that they could provide heirs to the shogun should the main line fail to do so.

Although his victory at Sekigahara was decisive, Ieyasu did not have the loyalty of all the daimyo. There still remained among them those loyal to Hideyoshi's heir, Hideyori, who made Osaka Castle his headquarters from 1598, after his father's death. By 1615 Ieyasu was confident enough in his regime's political and military standing to move against Hideyori. Amassing a large force of roughly 160,000 men, Ieyasu was able to eliminate Hideyoshi's heir as a threat to his power by overwhelming the defenders in the second of two campaigns (the so-called Winter and Summer Sieges, 1614–1615). With Osaka Castle destroyed and the Toyotomi lineage terminated, Ieyasu departed Kyoto for the last time, returning to his retirement base at Sunpu Castle. During the final months of his life, which ended in 1616, Ieyasu is said to have enjoyed himself, relaxing by engaging in falconry, one of his favorite pastimes.

During his tenure as shogun and retired shogun, Ieyasu directed the expansion of his clan-based government into one with national concerns and created regulations to control the imperial court (the *Regulations for the Court Nobility*, or *Kuge shohatto*, in 1613 and *Regulations for the Imperial Palace and the Court Nobility*, or *Kinchû narabi ni kuge shohatto*, in 1615) and the daimyo (*Laws for the Military Houses, or buke shohatto,* 1615). His successors, his son Tokugawa Hidetada (1579–1632) and his grandson Tokugawa Iemitsu (1604–1651), would continue the institution-building and solidify shogunal rule.

Ieyasu was concerned with far more than domestic affairs. He also supervised foreign relations with a number of European countries: England, Spain, Portugal, and the Netherlands. He met frequently with the English shipwright and pilot, William Adams, who instructed him in geography, math, and other subjects, and upon Ieyasu's command built for him several Western-style ships. Adams made diplomatic overtures on behalf of Ieyasu to the Spanish governor of the Philippines with an eye to establishing direct trade contracts with New Spain and sailed ships to Southeast Asia under shogunal authority. Ieyasu grew concerned, however, about the spread of Christianity in Japan and its possible connection to Spanish territorial ambitions in Japan, leading him in 1614 to ban the practice of Christianity and to expel foreign missionaries from the country.

Closer to home, Ieyasu also restored diplomatic relations with Korea, which had been severed due to Hideyoshi's two invasions in the 1590s, and permitted private trade with China (official relations were eschewed because they would have compromised the Tokugawa's sovereign position as shoguns).

Despite his substantial achievements in establishing a dynasty that ruled Japan for more than two-and-a-half centuries, Ieyasu's historical legacy is not without debate. To some he is a heroic figure, a "founding father" of the Tokugawa regime, which left a big mark on political and cultural institutions in Japan down to the present day. One of his earliest biographers in the English language saw him as the most important of the three unifiers and "unquestionably one of the greatest men the world has yet seen" (Sadler, 1978, 9–10). The same biographer also held that as a military figure and statesman, he was more brilliant than many contemporaries such as Henry VIII, Elizabeth, Akbar, Ivan the Terrible, and Suleyman the Magnificent. Others see him as an opportunist who was able to take advantage of his overlord Hideyoshi's death and his heir Hideyori's youth to seize control of Japan for himself. In this light, Ieyasu is seen as appropriating Nobunaga and Hideyoshi's successes not only in pacifying and unifying the country militarily but also in terms of political and social policies, such as the sword hunt, the separation of warrior and peasant (*heinô bunri*), and the pacification of the Buddhist church.

Part of Ieyasu's historical legacy also rests with a portrait of him as a colorful historical personality, renown for his patience and craftiness. The latter quality is epitomized by the nickname he received: *tanuki oyaji*, the Old Badger or raccoon dog, a likable animal also known for being clever and devious. His quality of patience is evidence in a famous set of Edo-period *haiku*, the first and third (final) lines of which are: "If you don't sing" and "Nightingale." The second line differs for each of the three unifiers. For Oda Nobunaga, the second line is "I'll kill you" and for Toyotomi Hideyoshi, "I'll make you sing." In contrast, for Ieyasu the line is "I'll wait until you sing." Thus, rather than killing an uncooperative bird, or otherwise forcing it to sing, Ieyasu patiently waited until it sang. He is also reputed to have been prone to laughter, but this and other assessments about his personal habits are based on hagiographic texts written or compiled long after Ieyasu's death.

See also: Daimyo and Domains; Falcony (*takagari*); Firearms; *Laws for the Military Houses* (*buke shohatto*); Nagashino, Battle of; Oda Nobunaga; Sekigahara, Battle of; Sieges of Osaka (*Ôsaka no jin*); Tokugawa Hidetada; Toyotomi Hideyoshi

Further Reading

Boot, Willem Jan. "The Death of a Shogun: Deification in Early Modern Japan." In John Breen and Mark Teeuwen, eds., *Shinto in History: Ways of the Kami*. London: Curzon Press, 2000.

Cooper, Michael, comp. and ann. *They Came to Japan: An Anthology of European Reports on Japan, 1543–1640*. Berkeley: University of California Press, 1965.

Pitelka, Morgan. *Spectacular Accumulation: Material Culture, Tokugawa Ieyasu, and Samurai Sociability*. Honolulu: University of Hawai'i Press, 2016.

Sadler, A. L. *The Maker of Modern Japan*. Rutland, VT: C. E. Tuttle Co., 1978.

Sansom, George. *A History of Japan, 1334–1615*. Stanford, CA: Stanford University Press, 1961.

Totman, Conrad. *Tokugawa Ieyasu: Shōgun*. San Francisco: Heian, 1983.

Tokugawa Tsunayoshi (1649–1709)

The fifth hegemon of the Tokugawa dynasty, Tsunayoshi served as shogun from 1680 to 1709. He was the fourth son of the third shogun, Tokugawa Iemitsu (1604–1651). His father, to avoid competition between Tsunayoshi and his older brothers, provided him with a largely Confucian, literary based education rather than one with a more traditional military orientation. He later served as the daimyo of Tatebayashi domain (Kōzuke province), from 1661 to 1680, before unexpectedly succeeding his elder brother, Tokugawa Ietsuna (1641–1680), who died prematurely. Tsunayoshi's rule largely overlapped with the Genroku period, which was characterized by affluence, some would say extravagance, and the flourishing of the arts. He is a controversial figure, criticized by samurai authors associated with the regime of his successors and more contemporary scholars for his *Edicts on Compassion for Living Things* as well as for his purported autocratic tendencies.

Tsunayoshi was the son of Tokugawa Iemitsu by one of his concubines, named Otama. She was a commoner birth, the daughter of a Kyoto greengrocer, and was later adopted by an aristocratic family, through whose connections she was later able to enter the Inner Quarters (*Ōoku*) of the shogun Iemitsu as a concubine. After Tsunayoshi's birth he lived with his mother in her private residence in Edo Castle and was deeply influenced by their close relationship, securing for her the highest court rank despite her commoner background. According to one of Tsunayoshi's biographers, because of his close relationship with his mother he came to hold a sympathetic view of the lower classes of Tokugawa society, and this later influenced his policies as shogun. As a child, though, Tsunayoshi apparently distinguished himself by intellect and liveliness—so much so that his father, the third shogun, Iemitsu, became fearful that he might usurp the position of his duller elder brothers. Iemitsu thus ordered that Tsunayoshi not be brought up as a samurai/warrior but rather be trained as a scholar. His early education in the Confucian classics would later guide his period of rule as shogun.

Shortly before his death, Tokugawa Iemitsu enfeoffed Tsunayoshi and his elder brother Tsunashige as daimyo, each with domains of 150,000 *koku* each. By doing this he provided a secure future for both of his sons who were not designated his heir, an honor that went to the eldest, Ietsuna. With the exception of Tsunayoshi (perhaps because of his commoner mother's stronger genetic makeup), Iemitsu's children were sickly. Ietsuna (1641–1680) died prematurely at the age of thirty-nine, while Kamematsu (1643–1647) at the age of five (according to the contemporary Japanese system of counting age whereby a child is one year old at birth), and Tsunashige (1644–1678), who had been given away in adoption at birth, was hunchbacked, and died at the age of thirty-five.

Despite outliving his elder brothers, Tsunayoshi did not come to power until after a power struggle in which one of Ietsuna's top advisers suggested that the succession pass to one of the sons of the emperor, as occurred during the Kamakura shogunate (1185–1333). A rival adviser to Ietsuna, Hotta Masatoshi (1634–1684), pushed for Tsunayoshi, as the former shogun's brother, and Tsunayoshi's appointment was secured in 1680. Because of uncertainty over his succession, however, Tsunayoshi had the roads around Edo Castle secured and special troops stationed near several important gates leading to it. Dutch records, too, make note of the great political insecurity surrounding the succession.

Although Tsunayoshi adopted a firm policy toward the daimyo, confiscating a total of 1.4 million *koku* of land during his reign (in contrast with the 0.77 million of his predecessor), he is remembered most—and criticized most—for his *Edicts on Compassion for Living Things*, particularly for laws directed at the protection of dogs. According to one anonymous account written after his reign, Tsunayoshi was led to protect dogs, allegedly, because after his only son died in infancy a Buddhist priest persuaded his mother that since Tsunayoshi was born in the year of the dog he must have committed some offenses against dogs in a previous life. Although the veracity of this account is questionable, Tsunayoshi was responsible for a large number (135 by one count) of regulations protecting not only dogs, but cats, horses, and birds—laws to ensure that people treated all animals kindly. He also ordered local governments to assist orphans. In some sixty-nine cases people were tried and punished according to these laws, but a scholar associated with the succeeding shogun greatly exaggerated their numbers, claiming there were hundreds of thousands, to discredit him. Due especially to the edicts protecting dogs, Tsunayoshi was lampooned by the famous playwright Chikamatsu Monzaemon (1653–1724), who wisely transposed the plot of his play *Sagami nyûdô senbiki no inu* (*The Thousand Dogs of the Sagami Priest*) in an earlier historical period to avoid censure. Tsunayoshi thus became known pejoratively as *inu kubô* (the dog shogun), a title that has stuck to the present day.

A recent biographer of the fifth shogun has argued that this negative reputation is undeserved. She (Beatrice Bodart-Bailey) argues that contemporary accounts used by later historians were highly biased, as they were written by the very samurai whose power Tsunayoshi curbed. She accounts for Tsunayoshi's policies being a result of a struggle between an "outsider" shogun pursuing his political ideas and a military aristocracy fiercely defending their traditional rights. Having been raised steeped in Confucian education, Tsunayoshi attempted to create a more humane society; this applied to himself as well, and after becoming shogun he never hunted again.

The laws directed at animals might have been excessive (at one point there were more than 50,000 dogs being held in kennels in Edo, eating food at the expense of the taxpaying commoners), but they were part of a milder, more civilized ethic that he was trying to promote to counter the martial values that predominated in the samurai-led Tokugawa society of his time. According to this perspective, the laws of compassion might be thought of an attempt to extend what we today call human rights even to commoners. Although those laws were largely overturned by the next shogun, the regulations requiring local governments to assist providing for the care of orphans did survive and became a part of the legal code drawn up by the eighth shogun, Tokugawa Yoshimune (1668–1751).

Tsunayoshi's rule largely overlapped with the Genroku period, a kind of "golden age" that was characterized by commercial development and affluence, not to mention a flourishing of the arts and literary studies. Tsunayoshi promoted Chinese studies (*kangaku*), including the Neo-Confucianism of Zhu Xi, and Ôbaku Zen, a Chinese sect of Zen that was newly introduced to Japan during his reign. The shogun commissioned or funded the publication of Confucian texts and himself delivered 240 lectures on Confucian themes from 1693 to 1700 in Edo Castle.

During Tsunayoshi's reign, the German doctor Englebert Kaempfer traveled to Edo with the Dutch East India Company, which he served and was able to witness, and later record in writing, his account of the company's audience with the shogun in 1691. It was during this audience that the Dutch merchants were asked to talk and sing with one another, for Tsunayoshi and the ladies of the court, who sat behind reed screens.

Tsunayoshi was also criticized for the outside influence on his rule by Yanagisawa Yoshiyasu (1658–1714), a samurai who became a personal favorite of the shogun, rising from the position of a page (*koshô*) to become a chamberlain (*sobayônin*) and great elder (*tairô*). Yanagisawa may have played a large role in the decision to punish Lord Asano Naganori of Akô domain with *seppuku* on the same day that he attempted to kill Kira Yoshinaka in Edo Castle, while exonerating Kira, leading to the revenge of the forty-seven *rônin* (the Akô Incident) in 1702.

On the other hand, Tsunayoshi has been viewed positively for his efforts in support of the imperial court and imperial traditions. He was responsible, for example, in reviving the Daijôsai (First Fruits Festival), a ritual that had not been

---

Keishôin (1628–1705), Shogun Tsunayoshi's Mother

The daughter of a Kyoto greengrocer, Tama (later known as Keishôin) experienced a kind of rags-to-riches story, eventually becoming the concubine of the shogun Iemitsu (1604–1651) and the mother of Tsunayoshi, the fifth Tokugawa shogun.

When Tama's father died, her mother found employment in the household of Honjô Munetoshi, a Kyoto aristocrat, and she, Tama, and an elder sister moved in together. When Tama's mother bore the head of the household a son, he adopted into the family the two girls. Later, Tama, who is best known by the Buddhist name she took later in life, Keishôin, became an attendant to the daughter of a court noble, Rokujô Saishô Aritsuna, and moved into Edo Castle to serve her. Keishôin caught the attention of the shogun Iemitsu's powerful nursemaid Kasuga no Tsubone, who had her appear before the shogun. Iemitsu was apparently taken with Keishôin, and she bore him a son, the future shogun Tsunayoshi.

There is usually very little information available regarding the lives of the women of the shogun. In the male-dominated world of the shogun's castle, such information was perhaps not considered worth recording. There is some question whether Keishôin was the mother of one or two of the shogun's sons (the other being Kanematsu, 1645–1647). However, based on anthropological research on Keishôin's bones, which were interred in the shogunal mausoleum at Zôjôji until they were cremated after World War II, it appears that Keishôin may have caught Iemitsu's eye because the shape of her face was different than that of other women of the inner quarters (*Ôoku*).

performed for many centuries. He also sponsored efforts to identify and restore imperial mounded tombs; as a result of this effort sixty-six out of seventy-eight tombs that today are considered to be imperial tombs acquired their imperial designation during his reign.

Since Tsunayoshi's only son Tokumatsu died at the age of five, he named his nephew Tokugawa Ienobu (1662–1712) his heir. He was survived by two (adoptive) daughters, Yaehime, who married Tokugawa Yoshizane of the Mito Tokugawa family, and Takehime, who married the daimyo of Satsuma domain, Shimazu Tsugutoyo.

Tsunayoshi was buried at the Tokugawa ancestral temple of Kan'eiji in Edo. His tomb was damaged during the Meiji Restoration and then destroyed by aerial bombing during World War II, but the lavish gate leading to the tomb still remains today (and has been designated an Important Cultural Property).

See also: Akô Incident; Falcony (*takagari*); Tokugawa Iemitsu; Tokugawa Yoshimune

Further Reading

Bodart-Bailey, Beatrice. "The Laws of Compassion." *Monumenta Nipponica,* 40(2) (1985), 163–189.

Bodart-Bailey, Beatrice, ed. *Kaempfer's Japan: Tokugawa Japan Observed.* Honolulu: University of Hawai'i Press, 1999.

Bodart-Bailey, Beatrice. *The Dog Shogun: The Personality and Policies of Tokugawa Tsunayoshi.* Honolulu: University of Hawai'i Press, 2006.

Seigle, Cecilia Segawa. "Tokugawa Tsunayoshi and the Formation of Edo Castle Rituals of Giving." In Martha Chaiklin, ed., *Mediated by Gifts: Politics and Society in Japan, 1350–1850.* Leiden, The Netherlands: Brill, 2017.

Shively, Donald H. "Tokugawa Tsunayoshi, the Genroku Shogun." In Albert M. Craig and Donald H. Shively, eds., *Personality in Japanese History.* Berkeley: University of California Press, 1970.

Tokugawa Yoshimune (1684–1751)

The eighth shogun, Yoshimune was born the third son of the daimyo of Wakayama, a branch of the Tokugawa family, and became daimyo when his two elder brothers died. In 1716, the main branch of the Tokugawa family came to an end with the death of the child shogun Ietsugu (1709–1716), who died without heir. Yoshimune provided some stability to the Tokugawa regime after the very brief periods of rule of Ienobu (the sixth shogun, r. 1709–1712) and Ietsugu (the seventh shogun, r. 1713–1716). His tenure as shogun lasted for thirty years and was notable for his various attempts at political, social, and economic reform (the Kyôhô Reforms). He is remembered as one of the best Tokugawa shoguns.

Yoshimune was a member of the Kii cadet branch of the Tokugawa family and not the son of any previous shogun. He was chosen as shogunal heir at the age of thirty-two, after Ietsugu died without heir; Ietsugu had come into power at the age of three, married at the age of four to Yoshiko no Miya (1714–58), who was only one year old, but died early, before the marriage could be consummated and children produced. It was for this contingency that the founder of the Tokugawa dynasty,

Ieyasu, had created the cadet branch system. Yoshimune was actually the third son of Tokugawa Mitsusada, Ieyasu's grandson, the daimyo of Kii Wakayama domain, a substantial domain of 550,000 *koku*, and only became daimyo because his two older brothers had died.

Yoshimune brought with him as shogun a reputation as a reformer. As shogun, he made considerable efforts to implement governmental reforms, particularly to the legal and finance systems, as well as his attempts to address what he saw as the decline of the samurai's martial skills. These were later known as the Kyôhô Reforms, which took their name from the Kyôhô era (1716–1736) when they were introduced. In the area of governmental reform, Yoshimune sought to restore the financial solvency of the shogunate and to root out corruption. Coming into office as an outsider, he swept out a number of officials who had served the previous two shoguns, most notably Manabe Akifusa and Arai Hakuseki, and formed his own group of personally selected advisers. He also sought to avoid becoming overly dependent on this new group of advisers by periodically bypassing them to confer directly with their own subordinates. He also formed what was in effect his own intelligence agency, a group of officials known as the *oniwaban* who were charged with providing him with information about shogunal officials and daimyo. Also as part of his effort to root out corruption, in 1721 Yoshimune instituted a petition box system, allowing for anonymous communication with the shogun. This both helped to expose corruption but also provided a mechanism by which new ideas could be proposed without fear of potential political consequences. Again, this worked to enhance his personal authority. To improve civil administration, in 1723 Yoshimune encouraged the appointment of officials on the basis of talent alone, rather than hereditary status, a system known as *tashidaka*.

Economic reforms were pursued by Yoshimune and his advisers in a number of areas. First, the shogunate encouraged frugality to counter the profligacy of the two previous shoguns, particularly Tokugawa Tsunayoshi (r. 1680–1709), his second cousin. Also, to quickly improve the shogunate's financial situation, he ordered the daimyo to make contributions of rice (*agemai*), which were used to assist the bannermen (*hatamoto*), who were experiencing dire economic difficulties. In exchange for this unprecedented step, the shogun temporarily reformed the alternate attendance system for a period of eight years (1722–1730), allowing the daimyo to reduce the required period of residence in Edo by half. Another important economic policy that he pursued was to limit the volume of exports of precious specie, copper, and silver, by decreasing the importation of sugar, silk, and ginseng. He did this through a policy of import substitution, encouraging the domestic production of these goods. Also, in terms of commerce, he allowed merchant groups to form guilds (*kabunakama*), which helped to improve Tokugawa finances through their payment of fees in exchange for certain monopoly rights to produce and distribute certain commercial goods. The shogunate also increased tax receipts by encouraging cultivators to open new lands for production, but Yoshimune's attempts to shore up the falling price of rice, which earned him the nickname "the rice shogun," were not very successful; this was, however, in no small part due to famine in the 1730s, leading to the first so-called rice riot in Edo. Overall, Yoshimune experienced some real successes in terms of economic policy, and by the end of his period of direct rule the shogunate's tax receipts were at the highest level in its history.

The shogun's reform program was wide-ranging. It also targeted the legal system, with the codification of laws and an attempt to create an impartial legal system. Importantly, in 1720 Yoshimune also relaxed the ban on the importation of foreign books that had been in place since 1640. By lifting the ban on foreign books, so long as they made no mention of Christianity, an influx of Western books into Japan ensued, which encouraged the translation of foreign texts and the development of "Dutch studies" (*rangaku*, or the study of the West, primarily via the Dutch language).

The eighth shogun was a strong leader, both in terms of his ability to rule as well as his personal constitution. These points were corroborated by the direct observation of a Korean envoy, Shin Yu-han, who visited Japan in 1719. In his *Record of a Journey Across the Sea,* Shin wrote that, "Yoshimune's character is dauntless, superior and wise, and this year, he is thirty-five years old. He is of sturdy spirit and has a dignified bearing. He is a lover of the martial arts but finds no joy in literature. He respects economy and rejects extravagance. . . . He loves the hunt. He often carries thirty kin [almost 40 lbs.] iron canes and climbs hills. When he has time, he puts a hawk on his arm and goes to the city's outskirts" (Lewis, 1985, 32). Shin went on to note that at his shogunal audience he "was unable to examine his [Yoshimune's] face very closely. Roughly speaking, he appeared very fierce, lean and muscular, and his seated appearance was towering" (Lewis, 1985, 35).

As Shin's comments suggest, Yoshimune was keenly interested in the martial arts, more so than the civil arts (*bun*), which his predecessors as shogun Tsunayoshi and Ienobu had cultivated. In contrast with these cultivated men, Yoshimune sought to revitalize the martial arts (*bu*), as he thought this essential to raise the morale of samurai; this attempt to correct what he saw as an imbalance between *bun* (scholarly learning) and *bu* (martial skills) was part of a broader program of social reform (the Kyôhô Reforms, 1716–1736). His various efforts in terms of the martial arts, particularly hunting, falconry, and horseback riding, can be seen as part of program to "reassert a militarized masculinity" (Walthall, 2011, 41). Although the first three shoguns had understood the importance of both the martial and literary arts, their successors showed little or no interest.

In contrast, Yoshimune was a practitioner and patron of various martial arts, including hunting and falconry. He hunted throughout his career and revived the large-scale hunts that the first three shoguns had conducted. He and his entourage hunted quail and pheasant on horseback with bows on numerous occasions; on one occasion, in 1718, 3,000 peasants were employed as beaters to flush the animals out into the open. He also organized large-scale deer hunts; during those he organized east of Edo in 1725 and 1726, Yoshimune dressed himself in the style of the first Kamakura shogun, Minamoto no Yoritomo (shogun, 1192–1199). The eighth shogun was also quite adept at marksmanship and is known to have shot many boar, some of them in locales not far from the castle; he also was known to serve (and to consume) the meat.

Not just an ardent practitioner of the martial arts himself, Yoshimune also encouraged their practice among the samurai as a whole. He ordered his officials to test the shogunal troops' gunnery skills and established prizes and bonuses for good performance. Occasionally, he would watch displays of marksmanship, make surprise inspections of the guns that guards were carrying at Edo Castle's gates, watch guard units ride horseback, and attend spear and sword matches at Edo Castle. He was, however, particularly keen on reestablishing the practice of mounted archery (*kyûba*); the formal performance of mounted archery at shrines was known as *yabusame* and is said to have ceased some time before the Tokugawa period, before Yoshimune reintroduced the ceremony.

Yoshimune lived a relatively long life (sixty-six years) and was able to sire four sons and a daughter with four of his concubines, the eldest, Ieshige (1712–1761), becoming the ninth shogun. Moreover, following the precedent of Tokugawa Ieyasu and Hidetada, Yoshimune stepped down, becoming *ôgosho* (retired shogun), allowing his son to succeed in 1745. Given his origins as a member of a cadet branch family, Yoshimune decided to expand the pool of possible candidates for shogun by establishing a second set of three cadet families (known as *gosankyô*). Two of his sons and a son of his successor Ieshige became the founders of the Tayasu, Hitotsubashi, and Shimizu lines; the Hitotsubashi line in particular was important as it later provided several shoguns.

Yoshimune held the title of *ôgosho* for the remainder of his life, from 1745 to 51, and was buried at Kan'eiji in Edo, one of the two Tokugawa funerary temples.

See also: Civil and Military Arts (*bunbu*); Firearms; Supplemental Salary (*Tashidaka*) System and Talent; Tokugawa Tsunayoshi

Further Reading

Lewis, James. "Beyond Sakoku: The Korean Envoy to Edo and the 1719 Diary of Shin Yu-Han." *Korea Journal,* 25(11) (1985), 32–41.

Tsuji Tatsuya. "Politics in the Eighteenth Century." In John Whitney Hall, ed., *The Cambridge History of Japan, vol. 4: Early Modern Japan*, 425–477. Cambridge: Cambridge University Press, 1991.

Walthall, Anne. "Do Guns Have Gender? Technology and Status in Early Modern Japan." In Sabine Fruhstuck and Anne Walthall, eds., *Recreating Japanese Men*, 25–45. Berkeley: University of California Press, 2011.

Tokugawa Yoshinobu (Keiki) (1837–1913)

Yoshinobu was born the seventh son of Tokugawa Nariaki, the daimyo of Mito domain, one the collateral houses (*gosankyô*) of the Tokugawa family from which shogunal heirs could be selected when the main line failed to produce one. Born in Edo, Yoshinobu (also known as Keiki) became the fifteenth and final shogun in 1867 but ironically never stepped foot in the Tokugawa capital as shogun. Although he made a determined effort to reform the shogunate in the face of the foreign threat and rising domestic opposition, he accepted a plan to return his authority as shogun to the emperor (*taisei hôkan*) in order to prevent a civil war. Nevertheless, Satsuma and Chôshû, and several other domains seized the opportunity, announced a restoration of the monarchy (*ôsei fukko*), in effect beginning the Boshin War. That civil war ended with the defeat of the forces aligned with the Tokugawa who resisted the self-styled imperial forces of the new Meiji government (1868–1912). Yoshinobu, after resigning in late 1867, returned to the ancestral homeland in Sunpu (Shizuoka) and went into retirement, living a quiet life thereafter.

Yoshinobu was born Matsudaira Shichirômaro, the son of the influential Tokugawa Nariaki, the daimyo of Mito domain. He did not bear the Tokugawa name at birth, which was reserved for the son who was designated heir to the Mito lord. He was also connected to the imperial family, as his mother, Princess Arisugawa Yoshiko, was a member of one of its cadet branches. In 1838, his father sent him to be raised and educated in Mito and soon thereafter was adopted out to the Hitotsubashi Tokugawa family, which gave him a better chance of succeeding as shogun. In 1847, having changed his first name to Akimune, he came of age (went through *genpuku*), became family head, received court rank and title, and took the name Yoshinobu.

When Tokugawa Iesada (1824–1858), the thirteenth shogun, became seriously ill, Yoshinobu was proposed as a mature and able candidate to succeed him. His candidacy was supported by a number of leading daimyo, but the opposing faction led by the powerful Ii Naosuke (1815–1860), the shogunate's great elder (*tairô*), successfully promoted a young and pliable candidate, Tokugawa Yoshitomi, who became the fourteenth shogun Iemochi (1846–1866). With his candidate in office, Naosuke initiated the Ansei Purge (1858), placing Yoshinobu and others who had supported him under house arrest (and ordering the death of other political opponents). Yoshinobu was even made to retire as head of the Hitotsubashi family.

Ii Naosuke's heavy-handed actions to suppress dissent lead to his assassination in 1860, and thereafter Yoshinobu was reinstated as family head. Two years later he was nominated and selected as the shogun's guardian. His close allies Matsudaira Yoshinaga and Matsudaira Katamori were appointed to top positions in the shogunate, and together with them Yoshinobu played a leading role in trying to quell political unrest in the imperial city of Kyoto. While for a time they pursued a policy of *kôbu gattai*, seeking political reconciliation between the shogunate and the imperial court. However, in 1866, after Chôshû domain forces attempted to capture the imperial palace (the Kinmon Incident), the shogun Iemochi's government sent a punitive military expedition to Chôshû to punish the domain and to reassert the Tokugawa's authority. The war was not a success, and when the sickly Iemochi died without heir, Yoshinobu succeeded him as head of the Tokugawa family and then shogun (on January 10, 1867).

Assuming his new position as shogun, Yoshinobu set out on an ambitious government reform program that gave great concern to his political enemies, who saw in him the rebirth of Tokugawa Ieyasu (1543–1616), the founder of the Tokugawa dynasty. The British diplomat A. H. Mitford (later Lord Redesdale) described Yoshinobu in quite personal terms: "[He] was a very striking personality. He was of average height, small as compared with Europeans, but the old Japanese robes made the difference less apparent. I think he was the handsomest man, according to our ideas, that I saw during all the years I was in Japan. His features were regular, his eyes brilliantly lighted and keen, his complexion a clear, healthy olive colour. The mouth was very firm, but his expression when he smiled was gentle and singularly winning. His frame was well-knit and strong, the figure of a man of great activity;

an indefatigable horseman, as inured to weather as an English master of hounds. . . . He was a great noble if ever there was one. The pity of it was that he was an anachronism" (Quoted in Sheldon, 1975, 30).

Under Yoshinobu's leadership the reform program appears to have had some success. With the foreign assistance of the British and the French, the shogunate strove to build a modern navy and army, respectively. With the further assistance of the French, shogunate bureaucrats tried to centralize power more, thereby threatening the prerogatives of the daimyo. Whether or not the reform program would have succeeded if the Tokugawa had been left to its own devices is debatable, as suggested by Mitford's comment. However, the pro-imperial daimyo in Satsuma and Chôshû were sufficiently alarmed by it to put their political slogan *sonnô jôi* (Revere the Emperor, Expel the Barbarian) into action by pressuring Yoshinobu to step down. Tosa domain put forward a compromise plan whereby Yoshinobu would resign as shogun but head a council of daimyo under the emperor's authority. Accepting this plan to avoid a civil war, Yoshinobu announced a return of power (*taisei hôkan*) to the emperor at Nijô Castle in Kyoto and then withdrew to Osaka Castle; he was the only shogun never to have stepped foot in the shogunate's capital of Edo while in office.

The leaders of Satsuma and Chôshû, who were opposed to Yoshinobu remaining in any position of authority, secretly obtained an imperial edict (later shown to be a forgery) calling for the use of force against him. The military forces of Satsuma and Chôshû (Sat-chô) moved into Kyoto on January 3, 1868, carried out a coup d'état (the Meiji Restoration), and announced a restoration of the monarchy (*ôsei fukko*). When Yoshinobu dispatched troops to Kyoto to deliver a message to the imperial court protesting against the course of events, Tokugawa forces were attacked by those from Satsuma and Chôshû. This conflict became known as the Battle of Toba-Fushimi, the first clash in the Boshin War (1868–1869). The Tokugawa's forces did not fare well in battle, and Yoshinobu appears to have abandoned them and fled to Edo. When the Sat-chô forces (now the imperial army) marched on Edo, Yoshinobu decided to surrender rather than fight, and the peaceful handover of the city was effected through the negotiations of Saigô Takamori (representing Sat-chô) and Katsu Kaishû (on the Tokugawa side).

Having become shogun at the age of thirty, Yoshinobu served for less than a year (from January 10, 1867 to January 3, 1868). After a brief confinement in Mito he was allowed to settle in Sunpu (Shizuoka prefecture), the castle in the Tokugawa's ancestral lands. In 1897 he moved to Tokyo, where he continued to live in quiet retirement, indulging in a number of hobbies, including hunting and photography. Ironically, he received honors and titles from the Meiji government: in 1902 he was allowed to reestablish his own house as a Tokugawa branch (*bekke*) and received the highest rank of peerage as prince (*kôshaku*) for his loyal service to Japan, sitting in the House of Peers for a number of years before resigning in 1910. One of his daughters, Tokugawa Tsuneko (1882–1939), married an imperial prince, Fushimi Hiroyasu, further connecting the family of the former shogun with the imperial family.

Yoshinobu died in Tokyo in 1913 and is buried there, in Yanaka Cemetery (not entombed or enshrined at the ancestral Tokugawa temples of Kan'eiji or Zôjôji like most of his predecessors).

What Happened to the Tokugawa Family?

Unlike during the French Revolution, after Japan's Meiji Restoration of 1868, there was no "reign of terror" where guillotines were used to execute the monarch and supporters of his regime. Tokugawa Yoshinobu (1837–1913) was allowed to retire and died peacefully. Furthermore, the family line was not extinguished. Yoshinobu was succeeded, in turn, by Iesato (1863–1940), Iemasa (1884–1963), and Tsunenari (1940–). Iesato was born to the Tayasu branch of the Tokugawa family before being adopted by the fourteenth shogun, Tokugawa Iemochi, and was selected as househead after Yoshinobu's retirement (Yoshinobu had no male issue at the time). Iesato did much to restore the Tokugawa family name by serving the country in a number of political roles: in the Japanese Diet as a member and president of the House of Peers; as a member of the Japanese delegation to the Washington Naval Conference; and as head of the Japanese Red Cross Society and Japan-America Society. His son, Iemasa, was the seventeenth hereditary head of the former shogunal branch of the Tokugawa family. Like his father, he too was a political figure, serving in the diplomatic corps as consul-general to the Japanese consulate in Sydney, Australia, and Envoy to Canada, and as ambassador to Turkey. Iemasa's heir, his grandson Tsunenari, is the eighteenth and current head of the main Tokugawa house. Unlike his immediate predecessors, Tsunenari is a businessman and head of the nonprofit Tokugawa Foundation. In 2007 he published a history of the Tokugawa period, entitled *Edo no idenshi* (released in English in 2009 as *The Edo Inheritance*).

See also: Boshin War; Nijô Castle (*Nijô-jô*); Tokugawa Ieyasu

Further Reading

Sheldon, Charles D. "The Politics of the Civil War of 1868." In W. G. Beasley, ed., *Modern Japan: Aspects of History, Literature and Society*, 27–51. Berkeley and Los Angeles: University of California Press, 1975.

Totman, Conrad. *Collapse of the Tokugawa Bakufu, 1862–1868*. Honolulu: University of Hawai'i Press, 1980.

Toyotomi Hideyoshi (1537–1598)

The second of the three so-called unifiers of Japan, Toyotomi Hideyoshi came from rather humble origins and rose in power to complete the task of national reunification begun by Nobunaga. Hideyoshi was a brilliant strategist and shrewd politician who was able to complete the unification of Japan in 1590 by demonstrating great generosity toward his former enemies, but he also gained great renown as a patron and practitioner of the tea ceremony and for the construction of major castles at Fushimi and Osaka. The period of his rule is closely associated with the Momoyama era (1573–1615), a time whose culture is characterized by its grand scale, extravagance, and exotic flavor. Hideyoshi's various social reforms worked to strengthen his hold on the country and established a firm basis for the policies his successors, the Tokugawa, would implement nationwide. His legacy was marred by his proscription of Christianity and persecution of Christians, not to mention his grandiose plans to invade China in the last years of his life, but he was nonetheless a pivotal figure in Japanese history.

RISE TO POWER

Little is known of the earliest years of Hideysohi's life other than he was born the son of a peasant foot soldier in Owari province, the home of the Oda family. He served the Imagawa clan as a servant for a time before joining the Oda clan under Oda Nobunaga, as a foot soldier. He was present at Nobunaga's upset victory over the Imagawa at the Battle of Okehazama (1560) and rose up through the ranks of the Oda organization, eventually serving Nobunaga as a general from 1574 on. While serving Nobunaga, in 1562 he changed his name to Hideyoshi, one of several such changes during his lifetime. Under Nobunaga he displayed some of his legendary abilities as a skilled negotiator to convince rivals to desert the opposing side and side with Oda. When Nobunaga was assassinated in 1582, Hideyoshi hunted down and killed Akechi Mitsuhide, and assumed Nobunaga's mantle of leadership.

After Nobunaga's death Hideyoshi succeeded in a series of military campaigns across a wide area of central Japan and became the first warrior to attain the rank of imperial chancellor (*kanpaku*), in 1585, and the rank of great minister of state (*daijô daijin*), in 1586. (He did not ever assume the title of shogun, and is popularly known as *taikô*, the honorary title for a retired *kanpaku*.) In the latter year, Hideyoshi and Tokugawa Ieyasu came to a rapprochment. Hideyoshi went so far as to use his own mother as hostage to guarantee to Ieyasu his good intensions; and, several years later, in 1590, Hideyoshi would reward Ieyasu with the largest territory in Japan, the six Kantô provinces, in exchange for his former landholdings in central Japan. His accommodation with Ieyasu allowed Hideyoshi to turn his attention to the pacification of the rest of Japan, extending his power to Kyushu in 1587, and then in 1590 waging a campaign against the Hôjô family in the Kantô region. Rather than lay waste to the castle with the twenty cannons Hideyoshi brought for the campaign, his forces laid siege to the Hôjô and their allies in Odawara Castle, cut off their supply lines, and starved them into submission. The lord of the castle, Hôjô Ujimasa (son-in-law of Takeda Shingen) and his heir (and brother) Ujiteru surrendered, left the castle, and committed ritual suicide (*seppuku*) the next day. Their heads were displayed publicly in Kyoto as a visible symbol of Hideyoshi's power.

POLICIES

By 1590, then, Hideyoshi had pacified all of Japan, marking the end of more than one hundred thirty years of fighting across Japan. At the same time he came to peaceful accords with many of his predecessor Nobunaga's staunchest enemies. Through skillful alliance building and the generous treatment of defeated enemies he was able to reduce the amount of opposition to his rule. In this way Hideyoshi introduced the idea of federation, which meant that the daimyo could continue to rule their domains as long as they recognized Hideyoshi as hegemon.

Hideyoshi also sought to bring stability to the land through several social policies. First, he sought to pacify the countryside by carrying out his famous sword hunt in 1588, collecting not just swords but all types of weapons, for the ostensible purpose of using them in the construction of a Great Buddha statue. The order, however, worked to promote his second policy by restricting arms to the samurai.

Through a second policy Hideyoshi sought to freeze the social order through the separation of farmers and warriors (samurai) and preventing movement between them. (There was some irony here in that Hideyoshi himself rose from peasant origins.) Third, he ordered that cadastral (land) surveys be compiled across the country. This gave him knowledge about the productive capacity of the land, which was necessary for taxing it effectively.

The Great Buddha was one of many building projects initiated by Hideyoshi and through which he exercised his authority over the daimyo, who were charged with contributing to their construction. The Great Buddha statue, built between the years 1586–1595, was enclosed in the largest wooden building ever made in premodern Japan. For the statue of the deity, the Vairocana Buddha, rivets and clamps were used from the melted down swords collected from across the country in the sword hunt. Hideyoshi also used the daimyo to contribute to the construction of various castles, including his retirement castle at Fushimi, south of Kyoto, the Jurakutei mansion in Kyoto, and even a stone and earthen wall around the city.

Hideyoshi also went to great lengths to display his authority in other, visible and spectacular, ways. An avid practitioner of the tea ceremony and an ardent collector of tea implements, in the summer of 1587 he held a grand, multiday tea gathering on the grounds of the Kitano Shrine complex in Kyoto that was meant to impress the general public. More than a thousand people attended, and Hideyoshi himself is said to have served tea personally to more than eight hundred guests. His prized tea implements were on display, and several of the most eminent tea masters of the time, including Sen no Rikyû (1522–1591), participated. This was the most spectacular but only one of many displays that Hideyoshi put on in Kyoto to exhibit his cultural credentials.

As Hideyoshi's military campaign to reunify Japan progressed, he began to pay more attention to external threats, meaning the presence of European power in East Asia. Campaigning in Kyushu he became alarmed at the influence of the Christian missionaries and particularly forced conversion of Japanese, notably the common people. In 1587 he put the missionaries on notice by ordering a ban on their activities, but desirous of continued trade with the Europeans did not enforce it. His suspicions became more pronounced in 1597, when the Spanish captain of a shipwrecked trading ship (the *San Felipe*) attempted to recover his confiscated cargo through intimidation, by claiming that the missionaries were there in Japan preparing for an invasion. Hideyoshi thus became the first Japanese ruler to prosecute Christianity. In response to the *San Felipe*, he ordered that twenty-six Christians—three Japanese lay Jesuit brothers, seventeen Japanese laymen, five European and one Mexican Franciscan missionary—be put to death, by crucifixion, in Nagasaki. Hideyoshi's Tokugawa successors would continue the persecution, off and on, with the decree to expel all missionaries coming under the second shogun Hidetada in 1614.

FAMILY LIFE

Hideyoshi left an extensive correspondence, which reveals a great deal about his personality, level of education, and family life. Although he employed scribes, mainly Buddhist monks, for his formal correspondence, which was usually in

Chinese, he brushed many letters himself. This correspondence—which he wrote to his mother, wife, concubines, sons, and other people—was written in the *kana* syllabic script, which was considered the most appropriate for women and children. His lack of formal education is reflected by his frequent use of *ateji*, phonetic equivalents of *kanji* (Chinese characters).

At least 101 of his letters, written from 1570 to 1598, have been translated into English (Boscaro, 1975). Based on a sample of ninety-five letters, one scholar found that three were addressed to his mother, thirty-five to his wife (eighteen to her personally and seventeen to her ladies-in-waiting), twenty to his various concubines (five each to Yodo, Matsumaru, Tora, and Maa), one to his son Tsurumatsu, seven to his son Hideyori, eight to unknown people, and twenty-one to a variety of other recipients.

The translator of Hideyoshi's letters has written that, "The main interest of the letters lies in the sincerity of his expression, in the spontaneity of his repetition, especially when worried about someone's health, and in his deep concern for other people" (Boscaro, 1972, 416). His affection for the women in his life is particularly notable. Although there are very few letters to his mother extant, he entrusted her care to his legal wife O-Nene, or Kita no Mandokoro, from whom he asked for updates on his mother's health. The thirty-five letters addressed to his wife or to her ladies-in-waiting similarly reveal his high regard for her and the close bond of affection between them as husband and wife, which might be regarded as unusual at a time when marriages were often political alliances. What might also be regarded unusual to the present-day reader is the good relations maintained between Hideyoshi's legal wife and his concubines. During the Siege of Odawara in 1590 Hideyoshi even asked his wife to send him his favorite concubine, Yodo: "If Lady Yodo knows that you are communicating [such a thing to her], she will take great care to be ready to make me happy. So please send a messenger saying that I am calling for her with tender feelings" (Boscaro, 1972, 417). The custom of concubinage was well accepted in high warrior society; given that his wife was not able to bear children, Hideyoshi's concubines played an important role in the attempt to pass on Hideyoshi's mantle of leadership to a son.

With Yodo, Hideyoshi had two sons, Tsurumatsu (who died in 1591 at the age of three) and Hideyori, who was born in 1594, when Hideyoshi was already fifty-seven years old. Hideyoshi's letters reveal the great pride that he had in Hideyoshi, a son by birth (instead of the nephew Hidetsugu, whom he adopted in 1592, the year after the death of Tsurumatsu), and his longing for him when separated. Hideyori's birth created a problem of succession. To avert a crisis, however, Hideyoshi exiled his nephew and heir to Hidetsugu to Mt. Kôya, and two years later ordered him to commit suicide. All of Hidetsugu's family members who did not do similarly, including thirty-one women and several children, were murdered in Kyoto.

INVASION OF KOREA (IMJIN WAR) AND DEATH

Late in life Hideyoshi suffered from failing health and exhibited what some would argue were signs of mental instability. To what extent his mental condition explains his decision to conquer China is unclear, but from 1587 he had been in communication with the Joseon government in Korea requesting unmolested passage through the country into China. Having unified all of Japan by 1590, Hideyoshi set his sights on China, which he wanted to conquer and to which he planned to relocate the capital of Japan. Since Korea was a tributary of Ming China, the Korean government refused these demands, which led Hideyoshi in 1591 to order an invasion of Korea.

The following year, a force of as many as 200,000 men, primarily from western Japan, was mobilized for invasion, in what would be Japan's only attack on another polity to that date in its history. Some of Hideyoshi's closest allies, including the daimyo Kato, Konishi, Môri, and Chosokabe sent forces, while other daimyo less loyal to him, including the Tokugawa and Date, did not. The base of operations was a newly constructed castle, Nagoya (present-day Karatsu), located in Hizen province in southern Japan, facing Tsushima Island and the Korean peninsula, and not to be confused with the Nagoya Castle in Owari; the castles shared the same-sounding name but were written with different characters. Hideyoshi remained there rather than directing the invasion from Korea.

The Japanese invading force initially made impressive gains, occupying the capital Seoul, and within four months, most of the remainder of the country. The Korean king, however, requested military assistance from China, and in 1593 a Chinese army of 43,000 troops attacked the Japanese forces at Pyongyang, forcing them to retreat. The Korean admiral Yi Sun-sin enjoyed considerable success against the Japanese forces with his turtle ships, threatening to cut Japanese supply lines. A stalemate ensued and Hideyoshi agreed to a ceasefire, while at the same time demanding the Ming emperor of China send his daughter as a gift to the emperor of Japan. While negotiations were carried out some 70,000 Japanese troops and laborers remained behind in Korea, stationed in the south part of the peninsula. High-ranking samurai and daimyo passed their time in tea ceremony gatherings and other leisure pursuits, while lower-ranking soldiers actually engaged in agriculture. The Ming sent two ambassadors to Japan to meet Hideyoshi in person, and he misinterpreted this as capitulation on their part. When they refused his demands for recognition as an equal (he was addressed humiliatingly as the "king of Japan," i.e., inferior to the Ming emperor), negotiations broke down in failure, and he ordered a resumption of the invasion in 1597.

The second campaign met with little success and a naval force of iron-clad turtle ships led by Yi Sun-sin devastated the significantly larger Japanese fleet, sealing the fate of the invasion. While conflict dragged on, Hideyoshi fell ill and died in 1598, but to prevent panic his death was kept secret by the Council of Five Regents, who had been selected by Hideyoshi earlier in the year to act as regents (guardians) for his son Toyotomi Hideyori (1593–1615). Soon thereafter, Japanese forces were ordered by the council to withdraw to Japan, and the Imjin War came to a conclusion.

The twin campaigns in Korea ended in defeat for the Japanese but resulted in widespread destruction in Korea and significant loss of life. The noses of an estimated 38,000 Koreans, both civilians and soldiers, were collected and brought back to Kyoto, Japan, where they were buried in the so-called "Ear Mound" (*mimizuka*)— the name was changed from its original "Nose Mound" (*hanazuka*) to this inaccurate but perhaps less brutal-sounding name. The noses were collected in place of heads, which were the usual war trophy taken in battle. Together, the two invasions also resulted in the forced removal to Japan of 50,000–60,000 Koreans, in addition to many books and copper movable-type presses. Among the Koreans brought to Japan were potters, who helped to jumpstart various ceramic industries in Kyushu and southern Honshu, particularly those of Karatsu, Arita, and Hagi wares. All of this did much to create a negative legacy for Japan in Korea that was exacerbated by the later period of Japanese colonial rule (1910–1945) and which continues to the present day.

Given that Ieyasu had sworn an oath of fealty to Hideyoshi, he had to honor Hideyoshi's memory and not take any immediate action against Hideyori. Accordingly, Ieyasu honored Hideyoshi by commemorating his spirit at Toyokuni Shrine in Kyoto. There, in 1598, Emperor Go-Yôzei declared Hideyoshi a divinity of the first rank with the title Hôkoku Daimyôjin, or Most Bright God of our Bountiful Country. On the early anniversaries of his death commemorative services were held at the shrine, accompanied by lively banquets, musical recitals, and other forms of entertainment.

The oaths of fealty sworn to Hideyori by the Council of Regents did little to stop their individual ambitions, particularly those of Tokugawa Ieyasu and Ishida Mitsunari, who would fight for supremacy at the Battle of Sekigahara in 1600. After Hideyoshi's death (1598), the Battle of Sekigahara (1600), and Tokugawa Ieyasu's appointment as shogun (1603), Hideyori found himself increasingly isolated in Osaka Castle. Armed conflict finally broke—the Winter and Summer Sieges of Osaka—and Hideyori and his followers met their deaths in 1615 at the hands of a large force led by Tokugawa Ieyasu and his son and successor, the shogun Tokugawa Hidetada. Ieyasu then was able to drop the pretense of honoring Hideyoshi's memory by closing down Hôkoku Shrine.

See also: Oda Nobunaga; Shogunate (*bakufu, kôgi*); Sieges of Osaka (*Ôsaka no jin*); Tokugawa Ieyasu

Further Reading

Berry, Mary Elizabeth. *Hideyoshi.* Cambridge, MA: Council on East Asian Studies, Harvard University, 1989.

Boscaro, Adriana. "An Introduction to the Private Correspondence of Toyotomi Hideyoshi." *Monumenta Nipponica,* 27(4) (1972), 415–421.

Boscaro, Adriana, ed. and trans. *101 Letters of Hideyoshi: The Private Correspondence of Toyotomi Hideyoshi.* Tokyo: Sophia University, 1975.

Elison, George. "Hideyoshi, the Bountiful Minister." In George Elison and Bardwell L. Smith, ed., *Warlords, Artists and Commoners,* 223–244. Honolulu: University of Hawai'i Press, 1981.

Varley, H. Paul, and George Elison. "The Culture of Tea: From Its Origins to Sen no Rikyû." In George Elison and Bardwell L. Smith, eds., *Warlords, Artists and Commoners,* 187–222. Honolulu: University of Hawai'i Press, 1981.

U

Unmaking (Abolition) of the Samurai

The process by which samurai were created—that is, became a socially and legally defined social group—took place at the end of the sixteenth century and continued into the seventeenth century. Samurai were functionally separated from the other three status groups—peasants, artisans, and merchants—and the vast majority of them were physically withdrawn from the countryside to reside in castle towns. They were given special prerogatives (e.g., *myôji taitô*, the right to a surname and to wear two swords) and special treatment under the law. In these and many other ways samurai were distinguished from the other three status groups. However, early in the Meiji period (1868–1912), the samurai leaders of the Meiji Restoration ironically attacked and destroyed the entrenched and privileged position of their fellow samurai over the period of just seven years, 1869–1876. They abolished—"unmade" the samurai—in the name of national need, that is, to build a strong, unified Japan under the centralized power of the Meiji government.

The Meiji leadership took a number of major steps to dismantle the system of samurai privileges, as sketched in the brief chronology below. By taking these steps the new government was released rather quickly from the burden of paying the stipends of the former samurai. It was also able to unleash the energies of "men of talent," samurai who were frustrated by the Tokugawa system that valued hereditary privilege over ability.

1869	Meiji government abolishes traditional status groups (samurai, farmer, artisan, merchant); reclassifies the population as nobility, ex-samurai, and commoners.
1871	Daimyo domains abolished; Meiji government becomes responsible for paying all samurai stipends; all commoners permitted to take surnames; *Taiseikan* Meiji legislative body issues voluntary call on samurai to give up sword-bearing and to adopt unbound hair (*sanpatsu dattô rei*).
1873	Conscription Ordinance promulgated, calling for "unity of soldier and peasant."
1873	Samurai offered taxable, fixed-term, interest-bearing government bonds in place of their hereditary stipends. *Seppuku* (ritual suicide) as judicial punishment abolished; revenge-killing (*katakiuchi*) also abolished.
1876	Prohibition on the wearing of swords (*haitô rei*) by former samurai.
1876	Government announces mandatory plan to replace ex-samurai's hereditary stipends with interest-bearing bonds (*kinroku kôsai*)

It was perhaps because it anticipated resistance to change that the Meiji government leaders adopted an incremental approach to dismantling samurai privileges and customs. As a first step it "leveled" society: in 1869 the government abolished the traditional status groups, and the samurai were reclassified as *shizoku* ("warrior families"), an honorary title without any attendant privileges. However, no changes were made to their hereditary privileges. The same year the government received several indications that there would be conservative resistance to change. The first occurred when in the newly formed deliberative assembly, known then as the Dajôkan, an official proposed that swords not be carried in public by ordinary samurai (only by members of the police, military, and government officials), and he was dismissed from his position and had his life threatened. The second instance occurred when a proposal to ban practice of *seppuku* (ritual suicide) brought before the same assembly in 1869, it was not only easily defeated, by a vote of 206–3, with six abstentions, but the man who proposed the change, Ono Seigorô, was murdered shortly thereafter. During the debate on the matter, *seppuku* was described as "the very shrine of the Japanese national spirit, and the embodiment in practice of devotion to principle," "a great ornament to the empire," "a pillar of the constitution," "a valuable institution, tending to the honour of the nobles, and based on a compassionate feeling towards the official caste," "a pillar of religion and a spur to virtue"—in other words, as an essential part of Japanese culture.

The groundwork for more radical change was laid in 1871, when the Meiji government abolished the domains. At the same time, however, it assumed responsibility for all samurai stipends, which had been paid by the domain governments during the Tokugawa period. The Meiji government also allowed commoners to adopt surnames, thereby removing one-half of the samurai's right to "surname and sword-bearing" (*myôji taitô*). The same year, it issued a voluntary call for the former samurai to cease the customs that provided the physical vestiges of their privileges. This involved unbinding their hair, meaning that they were free to stop wearing the top-knot hairstyle and to cease wearing the customary two swords. As a result, some samurai began to wear their hair unbound and to cut it short, but whether large numbers immediately left their swords at home when in public is more difficult to ascertain. The government pronouncement about hair freed samurai from having to wear the topknot; it should be considered an exhortation to unbind rather than a prohibition. Nevertheless, local officials are known to have pressured men to wear unbound hair. Moreover, in some places the police warned they would haul in anyone without short hair, and this was usually enough to encourage the spread of the new custom. However, there are no records of any samurai having his topknot forcibly removed by police, despite the depiction of such a scene in the popular Hollywood film *The Last Samurai*.

In 1873, the government promulgated the Conscription Ordinance or Law, calling for the "unity of soldier and peasant," which reversed the functional separation of peasant and warrior. In the words of the law, "After living a life of idleness for generations, the samurai have had their stipends reduced and have been authorized to take off their swords, so that all strata of the people may finally gain their rights to liberty. By this innovation the rulers and the ruled will be put on the same basis, the rights of the people will be equal, and the way will be cleared for the unity of soldier and peasant."

From the government's perspective, a critical part of the Meiji Restoration was to reduce the tremendous burden posed by the payment of samurai stipends. The outlay for stipends consumed the vast majority of government revenue, leaving the Meiji leaders with little to implement their reform platform that fell under the slogan "rich country, strong military" (*fukoku kyôhei*). On a national scale, in 1875 about one-third of government revenues went to pay former samurai stipends, but there was great variation at the local level. In the former Kaga domain, for example, over three-quarters of the prefectural budget was consumed by payment of stipends to the ex-samurai. The previous year, in 1874, the government actually began to tax stipends, at graduated rates, but this brought back only a small portion of stipends into government coffers.

In 1873, the government began taxing stipends and at the same time called on the former samurai to convert, voluntarily, their hereditary stipends into interest-bearing government bonds, valued at five to fourteen times their annual stipend, at 5 to 7 percent interest. This was the first of its measures leading to the abolition of hereditary stipends (*chitsuroku shobun*). The interest-bearing bonds did not provide a sufficient income for many. Although some of the former samurai were able to join the new imperial army, others, to survive, were obliged to sell swords and armor to pawnbrokers and curio shops. These were bought by tourists and Western collectors, and many ended up in private collections and museums. In his book *Rambles in Japan* (1895), H. B. Tristram, the canon of Durham, writes about this phenom:

> The collection of old armour and swords in these shops were to me as fascinating as a display of the fashions in Regent Street to an English belle, while the prices, as far as I am able to judge, were extremely moderate. I made many purchases at a price really less than the value of the material. . . . In fact, ancient armour was a drug on the market, many of the poorer Samurai being compelled to part with their treasured accoutrements for rice. (Bottomly and Hopson, 1988, 183)

Having resolved to commute all stipends to income-bearing bonds in 1873, no doubt Meiji leaders felt their government was on a firmer footing so that they could outright abolish certain practices of the samurai that seemed out of date with the new Japan they were trying to establish. Specifically, they targetted *seppuku* (ritual suicide) as judicial punishment and *katakiuchi* (revenge-killing). The government decree announcing the prohibition on revenge-killing stated, "The taking of human life is strictly prohibited by the law of the land, and the right to punish a murderer lies with the Government. However, since ancient times it has been customarily regarded as the duty of a son or younger brother to avenge the murder of his father or elder brother. While this is a natural expression of the deepest human feelings, it is ultimately a serious breach of the law on account of private enmity, a usurpation for private purposes of public authority, and cannot be treated as other than the crime of willful slaughter. Furthermore, in extreme cases the undesirable situation often arises that one person wantonly and deliberately kills another in the name of revenge without regard for the rights and wrongs of the case or the justification for his act. This is to be deplored, and it is therefore decreed that vengeance shall be strictly prohibited. In future, should some close relative unfortunately be killed, the facts should be set out clearly and a complaint laid before the authorities. Let it be plainly understood that anyone who ignores this injunction and adheres to the old customs, taking the law into his own hands to kill for revenge, will be subject to a penalty appropriate to his offence" (Mills, 1976, 525). Several cases of revenge-killing took place over the following decade, but the practice was for all intents and purposes eradicated.

Three years later, in 1876, the government moved from seeking the voluntary cooperation of the former samurai to an outright ban on sword-wearing and made the conversion of hereditary stipends to bonds mandatory; moreover, the bonds were not redeemable for a five-year period, which caused considerable discontent among the former samurai. In terms of sword-bearing, exceptions were made for the military and the police, while government officials were required to wear swords for some special occasions.

Already financially hard-pressed, for some samurai eliminating their right to wear swords was the final, intolerable step that led them to take up arms against the Meiji government. Discontended former samurai led a series of rebellions, beginning in 1876 with the Shinpûren Rebellion (in Kumamoto), which was followed by other outbursts the same year in Akizuki domain in Fukuoka (known as the Akizuki Rebellion), and then in Hagi, one of the principal domains that lead

Partial image from the triptych *Kagoshima bôtô kôsan no zu* ("Surrender of the Kagoshima Rebels"), by Tsukioka Yoshitoshi, depicting the surrender of the samurai force that opposed the Meiji government in the Satsuma Rebellion of 1877. The soldiers in the government army are dressed in western-style uniforms, in contrast to the rebels who are wearing more traditional attire. (Asian Art & Archaeology, Inc./ Corbis via Getty Images)

the Meiji Restoration. The following year, in 1877, the largest of the samurai rebellions took place in Satsuma, the Satsuma Rebellion. All were suppressed militarily, although in the case of the Satsuma Rebellion this was accomplished with some difficulty, after a period of about eight months.

In some cases, samurai discontent targeted specific individuals. As indicated above, the earliest example of this was Ono Seigorô, who was murdered by a former samurai for his 1869 proposal to abolish *seppuku*. The same year, Chôshû samurai Ômura Masajirô (1824–1869), who is considered the "father of the modern Japanese military," was attacked by a group of eight samurai, ironically mostly from his own domain, for his proposals to do away with the privileges of the samurai and to introduce a system of universal conscription; Ômura barely escaped from the attack but later died of his wounds. Similarly, Ôkubo Toshimichi (1830–1878), one of the leaders of the Meiji Restoration, was attacked by a group of disgruntled samurai from Satsuma and Kaga domains while on his way to the imperial palace, nearby the Sakurada gate where the shogunate's official Ii Naosuke had been assassinated in 1860.

Although the Meiji government wanted to abolish the samurai's privileged status in society, they did so to unleash the energies of all the people, not to contain the samurai. They were greatly concerned about the settlement that the former samurai would receive under the Meiji state. Iwakura Tomomi (1825–1883), a courtier, one of the few nonsamurai leaders of the Meiji Restoration, argued that the samurai were essential to the success and prosperity of the new Japan: "For the past 300 years they have been the natural leaders in society; they have participated in governmental affairs, bringing to it a polished purity and virtue. Because of their military and literary accomplishment, this class alone possesses a character that is both noble and individualistic. It is for this reason that the 400,000 samurai of today are the most useful group in society and should be called the spirit of the state" (Quoted in Harootunian, 1960, 258). In 1870, he proposed a plan for the government to encourage samurai to enter business and industry. The prohibition on sword-bearing in 1876 was part of a broader reform package encouraging samurai to take up independent livelihoods. In encouraging the former samurai to change with the times, Iwakura recognized the samurai's unique contributions to the "formation of the proper national character" (Quoted in Harootunian, 1960, 258).

Iwakura Tomomi was far from the only Meiji leader concerned about the role that the former samurai would play in the modern state. In 1870, Kido Takayoshi (from the former Chôshû domain) submitted a petition, *Written Opinions on the Future or Direction of the Samurai,* which argued for the necessity of a rehabilitation plan (*shizoku jusan*), one that would utilize the talents of the samurai, being integrated in tandem with the gradual abolition of stipends. In 1876 the government, at his urging, established an agency to investigate the ways and means by which this could be achieved.

Government policy focused on four general areas: first, the samurai were to be used to manage and assist with large-scale government reclamation projects; second, the ex-samurai were to be employed in government-operated railways and industries, and other sectors of the economy; third, rehabilitation bureaus were to be established at the prefectural level to coordinate policies at the local level; and fourth, the government provided capital for ex-samurai who wanted to start businesses, including agricultural enterprises, to colonize Hokkaido, and to invest in national banks. These policies appear to have been very effective and contributed to the overall growth of an industrialized economy in the early Meiji period.

Given that the samurai were a well-educated social group, their successes in the economic realm in the Meiji period are perhaps not terribly surprising. The influence of the former samurai remained pervasive in across broad areas of society. They dominated, for example, important government offices at the national and local levels, the police, military, and education. That dominance began to ease from the 1880s from the contributions of the former samurai to Meiji society remained important at least through the end of the nineteenth century.

See also: Revenge-Killing (*katakiuchi*)

Further Reading

Bottomley, Ian, and Anthony Hopson. *Arms and Armour of the Samurai.* Lincoln, NE: Bison Books, 1988.

Harootunian, Harry D. "The Progress of Japan and the Samurai Class." *Pacific Review* 3 (1959), 255–266.

Harootunian, Harry D. "The Economic Rehabilitation of the Samurai in the Early Meiji Period." *Journal of Asian Studies,* 19(4) (1960), 433–444.

Jaundrill, D. Colin. *Samurai to Soldier: Remaking Military Service in Nineteenth-Century Japan.* Ithaca, NY: Cornell University Press, 2016.

Kim, Kyu Hun. *The Age of Visions and Arguments: Parliamentarianism and the National Public Sphere in Early Meiji Japan.* Cambridge, MA: Harvard University Asia Center, 2007.

Mills, D. E. "Katakiuchi: The Practice of Blood-Revenge in Pre-Modern Japan." *Modern Asian Studies,* 10(4) (1976), 525–542.

Warring States Daimyo (*sengoku daimyô*)

The Warring States period (1467–1568) was a time of nearly continual military conflict and great social upheaval, characterized by the term *gekokujô* (the overturning of authority). It began with the Ônin War (1467–1477), a conflict during which much of the capital city was laid to waste, and then disorder and warfare spread throughout the country. Although the Muromachi shogunate (1336–1573) continued to exist during these years, it was weak, and political authority became extremely fragmented. Local military men, the *sengoku daimyô* (Warring States daimyo), rose to fill the vacuum of political power in the provinces.

The origins of the *sengoku daimyô* were quite diverse: some were *shugo daimyô*, the military governors appointed by the Ashikaga shogunate, who returned to the provinces after the Ônin War and were able to shape their former jurisdictions into independent domains. Other daimyo rose up from positions as agents of the former *shugo*, known as *shugodai*. Still other daimyo originated from local roots and were known as *kokujin*, or "men of the provinces." In light of the weakness of the shogunate, then, the *shugo daimyô, shugodai, and kokujin* fought among themselves to gain control the territories over which they had exercised some administrative authority and to expand that control over other areas. Historians generally argue that by the 1540s, the *sengoku daimyô* had gained considerable independent control over the territories they held.

Added to the mix of those figures fighting to gain power were a number of men of quite obscure origins, most famous of which was Ise Shinkurô (1432–1519), who likely is better known by his name Hôjô Sôun. To many historians Sôun is the first *sengoku daimyô* and a prime example of *gekokujô*. Serving as a retainer of Ashikaga Yoshimi until 1468, Sôun was likely a masterless samurai (*rônin*) for a time, before becoming a part of the Imagawa clan, where his skills were quickly recognized and he was made a castellan. He remained loyal to the Imagawa but was able to intervene in the succession dispute in the neighboring, Izu province, where he ousted the ruling family and established a strong military base. Although a skilled warrior, Sôun, and his other contemporaries who succeeded, did so also because of their political and administrative abilities. In expanding the territories under his control, he introduced efficient administration, lowering the taxes on the peasants in his lands, conducted cadastral surveys, and promoted economic growth. Sôun is perhaps best known for the house codes attributed to him, known as *Twenty-One Articles by Lord Sôun*. These were a set of precepts for his retainers that exhorted his men to religious piety, encouraged good personal habits, hygiene, frugality, and the practice of the "twin ways" (*bunbu*, or the martial and civil arts). Under Sôun's grandson, Ujiyasa (ruled, 1541–1571), the Hôjô reached the peak of their power, before the domain fell to the armies of Toyotomi Hide-yoshi in 1590.

Like Sôun, the *sengoku daimyô* endeavored to build strong, independent domains. They did so by creating house codes, constructing castles, conducting cadastral surveys, opening up and developing new rice lands, building irrigation systems, and developing efficient transport routes with post stations. The daimyo made great efforts to control their vassals and forge them into a retainer corps dependent on their authority. To do this they tried to undercut their vassals' independent author-ity, in part through the forced removal of many warriors from the land to the new castle towns being constructed as domain headquarters across the country. In addi-tion, by conducting cadastral surveys of their domains, daimyo were able to do much to break their powerful vassals' ties to the land. Through these surveys daimyo were able to measure their vassals' lands and to assign a value to their income. By doing this, the daimyo were able to substitute income from the land from an actual landholding, thereby making it easier to transfer their more important vassals and undercut their vassals' ties to their ancestral landholdings.

Breaking warriors' ties with the land was easy enough to do with minor vassals who possessed only small landholdings, as they were simply ordered to surrender their lands, to move into the daimyo's castle town, and take a stipend instead. However, more important vassals, with larger landholdings, were more difficult to bring under control. They resisted the daimyo's efforts and retained possession of private fiefs. During the peaceful Tokugawa period the daimyo were more suc-cessful in dislodging the vast majority of retainers from their fiefs and making them dependent vassals who largely drew salaries in rice from the daimyo's warehouses.

During the second half of the sixteenth century, the scale and technological sophistication of warfare increased as the daimyo were able to amass larger armies and to equip portions of those armies with muskets. They fought among themselves for regional hegemony, but in turn three military leaders, Oda Nobunaga (1534–1582), Toyotomi Hideyoshi (1537–1598), and Tokugawa Ieyasu (1543–1616) emerged in succession. In 1568, Oda Nobunaga and his military forces occupied Kyoto, the imperial capital and political center of the country, and drove out the last of the Ashikaga shoguns. Although neither he nor Hideyoshi assumed the title of sho-gun, together they were quite effective in subjugating the other daimyo. Hideyoshi was able to vanquish the remaining daimyo that resisted his authority and unified the country in 1590. After this, under the Tokugawa shoguns, from 1603 to 1868, the daimyo lost a good deal more of their independence and became further sub-ject to the authority of the hegemon (i.e., the shogun).

See also: Civil and Military Arts (*bunbu*); Daimyo and Domains; Oda Nobunaga; Toyo-tomi Hideyoshi

Further Reading

Birt, Michael P. "Samurai in Passage: The Transformation of the Sixteenth Century Kanto." *Journal of Japanese Studies,* 11(2) (1985), 369–399.

Elison, George, and Bardwell L. Smith, eds. *Warlords, Artists and Commoners: Japan in the Sixteenth Century.* Honolulu: University of Hawai'i Press, 1981.

Hall, John Whitney. "Foundations of the Modern Japanese Daimyo." *Journal of Asian Studies,* 20(3) (1961), 317–329.

Hall, John Whitney, Nagahara Keiji, and Kozo Yamamura, eds. *Japan before Tokugawa: Political Consolidation and Economic Growth, 1500 to 1650.* Princeton, NJ: Princeton University Press, 1981.

Steenstrup, Carl. "Hojo Soun's Twenty-One Articles. The Code of Conduct of the Odawara." *Monumenta Nipponica,* 29(3) (1974), 283–303.

Warrior Prints (*musha-e*)

A genre of *ukiyo-e* or woodblock prints, *musha-e* (warrior prints), can be traced back to the woodblock-printed books of the mid-seventeenth century. These books were illustrated military chronicles that retold the heroic tales of earlier periods in Japanese history, such as the *Heiki monogatari* (*Tale of the Heike*), *Genpei seisuiki* (*The Rise and Fall of the Genji and the Heike*), and *Taiheiki* (*A Tale of the Great Peace*). The form of *musha-e* developed further from the early eighteenth century, when single-sheet woodblock prints were published, and from late in the same century when colorful triptychs were created.

Due to the shogunate's prohibition on contemporary political issues, any historical subject matter involving the rise of the Tokugawa family, its relationship to the Toyotomi, or any actual political figures of the time could not be reproduced in any artistic form, print or theatrical. As a result, artists were forced to look to the past, prior to the 1590s, for inspiration to avoid censorship; those who did not, faced punishment, as occurred to the famous artist (Kitagawa) Utamaro (1753–1806), who designed two prints depicting Hideyoshi and another depicting his vassal Katô Kiyomasa (1562–1611). Of course, the use of the distant past as subject matter was also necessitated by fact that the Tokugawa era, after 1615, was an overwhelming peaceful age.

Samurai did appear as subject matter in the actor prints (*yakusha-e*) of the Tokugawa period, but these images differed from *musha-e* in that their focus was on the actor playing the role of a warrior rather than on the historical figure himself (or in rare cases, herself). Prints of actors and courtesans of the pleasure quarters enjoyed tremendous popularity; much like fan Facebook pages or movie posters in a pre-Internet age, they captured the celebrities of the day. *Musha-e*, on the other hand, usually dealt with a distant past and occupied what can be described as a niche market. They are notable for their tendency to conflate fact and fiction, history and legend.

In the early eighteenth century, artists such as Torii Kiyomasa and Okamura Masanobu produced crude single-sheet prints depicting samurai. Subsequent artists of the Torii school continued this practice until full-color prints were introduced in 1765. For the several decades thereafter, famous artists such as Suzuki Harunobu, Kitao Shigemasa, Isoda Koryûsai (1764–88), the latter of whom was a samurai artist, and Kitao Masayoshi were active in producing color prints in this genre. Another artist, Katsukawa Shunshô, is credited with producing the first *musha-e* in triptych form late in the eighteenth century.

Musha-e usually depicted the famous battles and famous warrior personalities of several notable periods of conflict. The Genpei War was the earliest conflict to provide thematic material for the prints. Notable battles (the Battle at Uji Bridge, Battle of Miidera Temple, Battle of Yashima, the climactic Battle of Dan-no-Ura) and prominent military figures (such as Benkei, Kumagai, and Atsumori), and the female warrior Tomoe Gozen) were the subject of numerous prints. Revenge stories such as the tale of the Soga brothers were quite popular as well. The personalities of the famous late-fourteenth-century war chronicle *Taiheiki* (*Chronicle of Great Peace*) also became the subject matter or *musha-e*, but the battles and colorful military figures of the late sixteenth century were the produced in far greater numbers. Prints of famous Warring States daimyo such as Katô Kiyomasa and the twenty-four generals of Takeda Shingen were produced along with numerous series of prints of famous conflicts such as the Battle of Okehazama (1560), Battle of Shizugatake (1561), Battles of Kawanakajima (1553–1564), and the Battle of Mitagahara (1573).

Musha-e increased in popularity in the nineteenth century for several reasons. This phenomenon may be attributed in part to the dramatic style of Utagawa Kuniyoshi (1797–1861), who depicted gory scenes, with decapitated heads flying through the air and blood spurting from severed limbs. As a result, Kuniyoshi earned the nickname *Musha-e no Kuniyoshi*, or "Kuniyoshi of the Warrior Prints." His popular 1827 print series *One Hundred and Eight Heroes of the Suikoden* was based on the Japanese adaptation of the fourteenth-century Chinese classic *Tales of the Water Margin* (Shuihuzhuan) and was translated by Takizawa Bakin (1767–1848), a samurai writer who renounced his status. It told the story of 108 bandit warriors and stressed the themes of loyalty and personal justice, thus striking a theme of antiauthority. The increased popularity of *musha-e* may also have been the result of the heightened sense of political crisis created by the Western ships that began intruding in Japanese waters with increasing regularity in the nineteenth century. Yet another reason for the *musha-e* craze might have been the Tenpô Reforms (1830–1842), during which time the Tokugawa shogunate, in an effort to stamp out perceived luxuries banned the popular genres of prints of beautiful women (*bijin-ga*) and actors (*yakusha-e*). In this climate, Kuniyoshi's warrior prints thrived, and he fostered emerging artists such as (Tsukioka) Yoshitoshi (1839–1892). Kuniyoshi's leading pupil, Yoshitoshi became famous for his "bloody prints" of the 1860's, particularly his acclaimed war series *100 Warriors in Battle* (1868), which was inspired by the Battle of Ueno, part of the Boshin War (1868).

See also: Boshin War; Isoda Koryûsai

Further Reading

Hunter, Jack. *The Savage Samurai: Warrior Prints, 1800–1899 by Kuniyoshi, Yoshitoshi & Others*. San Francisco: Shinbaku Books, 2013.

King, James, and Yuriko Iwakiri. *Japanese Warrior Prints, 1646–1905*. Leiden: Hotei, 2007.

"Musha-e." Japanese Architecture and Art Net Users System, 2001. http://www.aisf.or.jp /%7Ejaanus/deta/m/mushae.htm. Accessed March 11, 2017.

Watanabe Kazan (1793–1841)

A well-known artist and Dutch scholar (*rangakusha*), Watanabe Kazan (born Watanabe Sadayasu) was a retainer of the daimyo of Tahara domain (present-day Aichi prefecture). As a boy he had served as a playmate for the lord and as an adult held the position of house councilor (*karô*). He was critical of several of the shogunate's positions and was arrested in 1839 and ordered into house arrest. Not wishing to further harm the name of his lord, Kazan chose to commit suicide. Although Watanabe was attracted to Western learning and believed that Japan could benefit from it, he was also a Confucian traditionalist, believing in the importance of the values of loyalty and filial piety.

As the son of a retainer on a long-term posting in Edo, Watanabe was born and reared in Edo, the shogun's capital. Despite his father's high position in the domain government as a councilor, his low stipend (Tahara was a poor domain) was

Posthumous portrait of Watanabe Kazan (1793–1841), scholar and senior councilor in Tahara domain (Aichi prefecture), completed in 1853. Watanabe was himself a talented artist and experimented with western painting techniques in his own work. (The Picture Art Collection/Alamy Stock Photo)

insufficient to support a family of eleven. Kazan's younger male siblings were adopted out or entered Buddhist temples; his sisters were sent out to serve in other households. As the eldest son, Kazan helped support the family by taking up painting, beginning with images made on lampshades and kites. He studied under a student of Tani Buncho (1763–1840) and eventually under the master himself. The samurai turned *rônin* and fiction writer Takizawa (Kyokutei) Bakin (1767–1848) commissioned Kazan to create illustrations for his works of fiction. By the age of twenty-five Kazan was a well-known painter in Edo.

Although most of Kazan's work was in the approved literati (*bunjin*) style, which he created for profit, he made a name for himself for his portraits, particularly that of the famous Confucian scholar Satô Issai (1772–1859). His portrait of Satô was based on eleven preliminary sketches; it employed Western techniques of shading and is notable for its realism, a touchstone of his art. (An image of the painting can be viewed at: https://www.freersackler.si.edu/object/F1968.66a-e.) Watanabe also did bird-and-flower paintings, nature studies, and travel paintings. On one of his trips, he wrote a travelogue, *Diary of a Journey to Sagami [Province]* (*Yuso nikki*), which reveals that he used the opportunity that travel provided to make contacts with other literati across the country.

In his mid-twenties Kazan also grew interested in Dutch studies (*rangaku*), through which he had access to Western learning. At the same time, he continued to rise in the domain's administrative hierarchy, gaining a promotion to domain senior councilor, his late father's highest rank. His heart, though, was set on devoting all his time to painting. He even petitioned his lord requesting to be relieved of his official duties but was refused.

Watanabe was fearful of Russian and British encroachment on Japan, as he made clear in an essay brushed two years before the Opium War (1839–1841) in which he said: "I wonder how long we shall go on waiting with folded arms for the arrival of an invader?" (Keene, 2006, 160). Accordingly, he defended the shogunate's position of excluding all the Western powers except the Dutch from Japan, but at the same time he advocated for modernizing the country's military with the latest Western technology in order to protect Japan from the West. He wrote two other essays, not meant for public view, that were interpreted as critical of the shogunate's policies toward defending Japan from the Western threat and promoting Western ideas. In these writings he used the expression *seia*, or "the frog in the well," meaning a creature that is not aware of the outside world, which was interpreted as criticism of the shogunate.

While imprisoned he was interviewed by shogunate officials four times, and while one official recommended his beheading, Kazan was ordered into house arrest in his own official residence in Tahara (essentially into exile, rather than in Edo, where he had been living). Due to his straightened financial situation, however, he continued to paint and sell pictures, even though he was likely aware that this activity could lead to his being denounced for improper behavior while under house arrest. He also provided his enemies with ammunition against him by meeting with a constant stream of visitors who came to seek his counsel. Kazan, ever the faithful retainer, grew distressed over the anxiety that his imprudent behavior was causing his lord and in 1841 decided to end his life, by *seppuku*.

See also: Punishment; Shogunate (*bakufu, kôgi*)

Further Reading

Keene, Donald. *Frog in the Well: Portraits of Japan by Watanabe Kazan, 1793–1841.* New York: Columbia University Press, 2006.

"Watanabe Kazan." In Herbert Plutschow, *A Reader in Edo Period Travel*, 282–290. Folkstone, Kent, UK: Global Oriental, 2006.

White Tiger Brigade (*byakkotai*)

A group of young teenage samurai of Aizu domain, the *byakkotai* fought in the Boshin War (1868–1869) against the military forces of the new government (*shinsei*), which waged a campaign against the northern Honshû domains that resisted the control of the new self-styled imperial government. The more than three hundred youths who formed the brigade fiercely resisted the onslaught on Aizu's castle town of Aizu-Wakamatsu (present-day Fukushima prefecture) but were largely decimated. One unit of the brigade, incorrectly thinking that the castle was on fire and their lord dead, committed *seppuku* (ritual suicide). Over time the youths were memorialized and glorified, particularly during the 1930s, for their fierce loyalty, and today they remain part of the popular culture landscape.

The White Tiger Brigade was formed in the Third Month of 1868, after the Battle of Toba-Fushimi, one of the conflicts in the Boshin War. It was designed as a reserve unit to supplement the regular forces of Aizu domain and consisted of young men, mostly sixteen- and seventeen-year-old sons of Aizu samurai, although one youth might have been as young as fourteen. Given that there was so much emphasis on status in samurai society, it is not surprising perhaps that the unit was subdivided into squads based on rank (the rank of their fathers).

The brigade was decimated by the better-armed imperial forces in the Battle of Tonoguchihara, part of the larger conflict known as the Battle of Aizu. One of the squads of high-ranking boys, all pupils at the Nishinkan (Aizu's domain school), while making their way back to Wakamatsu Castle believed they saw the stronghold in flames, which meant that their lord was likely dead. However, the clouds of black smoke that blotted out their vision of the castle actually was coming from the surrounding area; the innermost defenses had not been breached and the lord was not dead. Not realizing this, however, the group committed suicide, some of the boys stabbing each other simultaneously, others putting their swords to their throats before falling forward. One boy (Iinuma Sadakichi) survived the attempt at suicide, however, and lived to serve as an officer in the imperial army; later he was buried near, but not with, the other nineteen members of his squad. He provided testimony about the others' final moments.

More than 3,000 Aizu samurai died in defending their castle town. Many wives of samurai also fought, while others committed suicide before the enemy reached them. The daimyo of Aizu, Matsudaira Katamori (1836–1893), was allowed to take the tonsure and lived the rest of his life as a Shinto priest.

News of the tragedy of the young boys spread slowly after the end of the Boshin War, with local and then national news picking up on the story. During the 1930s as nationalism gained in intensity in Japan, the White Tiger Brigade became objects for glorification. Their fame even expanded beyond the borders of Japan, as evidenced by two gifts from Japan's World War II Allies. The first gift was from the Italian dictator Mussolini, who had been told the brigade's story by a Japanese diplomat. Impressed, Mussolini sent the city of Aizuwakamatsu a bronze eagle, with wings outspread, in tribute "to the spirit of *bushidô*" (*allo spirito del bushido*). The eagle was placed on top of an antique marble column, and after World War II American occupation authorities asked for the inscription to be erased, as part of a more general effort to stamp out militarism in Japanese society. However, they did allow the monument itself to remain. A second monument, a little stele with an iron cross with the inscription "A German to the young knights of Aizu, 1935" (*Ein Deutscher den jungen Rittern von Aizu, 1935)*, was the gift of German diplomat Hasso von Etzdorf. It was removed after the war as a legacy of Nazi Germany by order of the American authorities but put back in its original location in 1953, a year after the occupation's end.

In more recent times, the White Tiger Brigade has become the topic of many different forms of popular media, including plays, books, films, and television in Japan. They also are featured in the popular video game *Total War Shogun 2: Fall of the Samurai.* A museum memorializing the boys, the White Tigers Memorial Hall, lies at the foot of Iimori-yama (Mt. Iimori) in Aizuwakamatsu.

See also: Aru Meiji-jin no kiroku: Aizu-jin Shiba Gorô no isho (*Remembering Aizu*); Boshin War; *Seppuku* (Ritual Suicide)

Further Readings

Rankin, Andrew. *Seppuku: A History of Samurai Suicide.* Tokyo, New York: Kodansha International, 2011.

Shiba Gorô. *Remembering Aizu: The Testament of Shiba Gorô.* Edited by Ishimitsu Mahito. Translated, with Introduction and Notes, by Teruko Craig. Honolulu: University of Hawai'i Press, 1999.

Shimoda Hiraku. *Lost and Found: Recovering Regional Identity in Imperial Japan.* Cambridge, MA: Harvard University Press, 2014.

Women in Samurai Households (*buke no onna*)

Women were not samurai, technically speaking: they were members of "warrior households," or *buke no onna* (lit., "women of warrior households"). Given that women were not samurai, they did not receive fiefs or stipends from a lord, nor obtain posts in the shogunate or domain governments. Some did hold nonhereditary positions as ladies-in-waiting, maids, or nurses in the households of daimyo or the shogun. Of course, within warrior households, women played important social roles as grandmothers, mothers, wives, concubines, and daughters, but sometimes they also exerted political influence within the shogun or daimyo's inner quarters. Moreover, many wives of high-ranking samurai acted as household managers, supervising servants and full-time nannies, who performed much of the household labor; this was particularly true if their husbands were away serving their overlords. *Some buke* women made notable achievements as writers and a few did

Mannequins depicting some of the members of the Ôishi Yoshio (Kuranosuke) family: his wife, Rikuma; eldest daughter, Kûma; and second son Kichijûdai. Exhibit on display at the Ôishi Yoshio Residence Nagayamon in Akô city (Hyôgo prefecture). Notice the contrast between the mother's kimono (with regular-length sleeves) and the unmarried daughter's (with long sleeves). (Photo by Constantine Vaporis)

as artists; in some domains they learned to wield a *naginata* (pole weapon), and in one instance, at the end of the Tokugawa period, a small group of women actually used them in combat.

There is a big distinction between the image of *buke* women and their lived reality, particularly with regard to marriage and divorce. Despite the fact that government regulations aimed at maintaining boundaries between the status groups, commoner women were able to marry into the samurai status group, generally in its lower levels, usually through adoption and marriage. Similarly, the evidence shows that despite popular discourse, mainly instructional texts, which maintained that women should not have two husbands (just as a samurai should not serve two lords), the reality was quite different: divorce and remarriage were possible and occurred with some frequency.

Buke women were expected to become educated through formal instruction, guided by a teacher and sometimes in a school, and through more informal study at home. The formal instruction centered on the acquisition of basic literacy, reading and writing, with a focus on the interpretation of canonical texts, such as *Onna Imagawa* (*Imagawa-Style Admonitions for Women,* 1687) or *Onna daigaku* (*Greater Learning for Women,* early eighteenth century). These and other similar texts instructed women and girls in Confucian-based self-cultivation—in proper

---

History Girls (*rekijo*)

"History girls" (*rekijo*) refers to a pop cultural phenomenon in Japan that peaked around 2009–2010. Sometimes referred to as "history fan girls" in English, *rekijo* are young Japanese women who consume the culture of Japanese history, overwhelmingly of the *sengoku* (Warring States) period or the *bakumatsu* (late-Tokugawa) period. They consume it "virtually," through anime, video games, and television dramas; others also consume it by doing research on the period, reading books and visiting historical sites. In other words, they are female *otaku* (young people who are obsessed with computers or particular aspects of popular culture in Japan) who focus on Japanese history. The *rekijo* typically are attracted to historical figures as if they were rock stars or some other type of popular cultural icon. Such figures include the members of the Shinsengumi, a group of elite swordsmen in the employ of the Tokugawa shogunate in its closing years, Warring States daimyo such as Date Masamune (1567–1636) and Sanada Yukumura (1567–1615), and other late-Tokugawa figures such as Sakamoto Ryôma (1836–1867). Model Watanabe Anne, the daughter of actor Watanabe Ken, is a notable, high-profile *rekijo*.

---

behavior and attitudes, such as filial piety, obedience, compassion, devotion to learning, and diligence, among others.

At the same time, *buke* women were also expected to have broader, more practical household skills (sewing, spinning, weaving) as well as cultivated pursuits (flower arranging, incense appreciation, performing the tea ceremony). The skills and pursuits often were learned in the home, sometimes with the aid of texts and teachers, who were often female family members. In Yamakawa Kikue's account of her mother's reminiscences of life in a samurai household in Mito domain in the nineteenth century, she wrote that, "Upon reaching the age of six a girl, too, began study with a teacher of reading and writing," but they, unlike boys, were not expected learn a large number of Chinese characters (Yamakawa, 1992, 24). When they reached the age of twelve or thirteen, she reported, they were expected to focus on learning how to sew. The essential nature of both elements of women's education were made clear in the early-eighteenth-century text *Onna daigaku takarabako (Treasure Chest of the Greater Learning for Women)*: "Of the many skills necessary to become a woman, sewing is the most important. Along with the inability to wield a writing brush, not being acquainted with the way of needlework is the source of great shame for a woman" (Quoted in Yonemoto, 2016, 67).

Education could also be acquired through service in a household of a higher-ranking samurai. According to one authority, "[B]y cultivating themselves in socially sanctioned ways women were also able to achieve some measure of upward social mobility. In this way, an essentially Confucian notion of improving the self in order to stabilize society became, ironically, a vehicle for social advancement for women through the avenues of work, service, and marriage" (Yonemoto, 2016, 99). Through service in elite households, samurai women acquired practical skills, learned proper social etiquette, and acquired cultural deportment or polish, which was beneficial in marrying above their own station. In marriage, samurai sought status commensurability between spouses; in other words, they sought to maintain or increase their own status through marriage and adoption. For women, though, marriage was an important mechanism for upward social mobility. This generally occurred when women were able to educate themselves well, particularly when their families were not wealthy, thus making themselves attractive candidates for marriage with samurai from families with higher social status.

More rarely, education and upward mobility was made possible through a woman's service in the shogun's inner court. Perhaps the most notable example of a dramatic leap in social position for a woman through service and marriage across status boundaries was the woman known as Kenshôin; she was the daughter of a Kyoto greengrocer who entered into service in the imperial court and later became the concubine of the third shogun, Tokugawa Iemitsu (1604–1651) and the mother of the fifth shogun, Tsunayoshi (1646–1709). Another notable example is the woman known as O-Miyo or Senkôin (d. 1872), the daughter of a low-ranking samurai who entered into service in the household of a middle-ranking bannerman, Nakano Kiyoshige (1765–1842). Nakano was also a confidant of the eleventh shogun, Tokugawa Ienari (1773–1841). O-Miyo was later adopted by him and through his connections became the shogun's favored consort and mother to three of his daughters.

Although government authorities, with some exception, forbade marriage across status lines, it was possible for commoner women to become members of samurai households and thus become a part of the samurai status group through marriage to low-ranking samurai or through the roundabout process of adoption and then marriage to higher-ranking samurai. In the case of a peasant daughter named Yoshino Michi (1808–1883), who came from a village near Edo, she was sent to work in the shogun's capital as a maid-in-waiting to noble women who managed daimyo households, first the daimyo residence compound of the Tayasu lord and then that of the Hitotsubashi, both cadet branch families of the Tokugawa shoguns. Although many elite peasant families spent a great deal of money to send their daughters into service in the residence of a samurai in hopes that they could make good marriages in the rural marriage market, some of them, like Michi, were able to marry a samurai. In Michi's case, her husband, Tamura Motonaga, was a thirty-two-year old, low-ranking samurai doctor who lost his first wife to death or divorce and needed a wife to take care of his son and to manage his household. Michi's many years of training as a maid-in-waiting gave her the necessary preparation to become an appropriate bride for a samurai. When her husband died seven years later, she struggled to maintain both the Tamura household as well as her natal household, with whom she maintained close relations even after marriage. To keep the Tamura household going she had to borrow money from her former Hitotsubashi employers. In addition, when her stepson died without an heir, Michi was able to secure permission for an adopted heir.

The case of Itô Maki, the daughter of a commoner physician, is also instructive, as she was adopted twice and married twice, by which means she and her offspring became *buke*, although among its lowest ranks. At the age of sixteen or seventeen Maki was adopted by her uncle Kôzaemon, who had attained bannerman (*hatamoto*) status but did not have an heir. The adoption of Maki allowed him in turn to adopt in a husband and heir, a practice known as "in-marrying adopted husband," or *muko yôshi*, which happened in 1816 or 1817, a few years after her adoption. As part of a bannerman household, Maki became a suitable candidate for marriage into another bannerman family. In this case the husband, Sugiura Tamesaku, was adopted into the family as husband (to Maki) and heir (to Kôzaemon). Through this marriage Maki gave birth to two children and was able to ensure the samurai status of her descendants. When Tamesaku died in 1823, leaving Maki with two small children, a second marriage was quickly arranged for her. Neither Maki's status as widow or mother of two small children was an impediment to her remarriage. In fact, her second husband, Itô Kaname, was of greater wealth and status than her first. Given the discrepancy in status between her first and second husband, Maki actually had to be adopted into a family of the Itô's status before she could marry him. In this case she was adopted into the Nakamura family, a prestigious lineage with ties to the Tokugawa going back to the early seventeenth century. Thus, Maki, through two adoptions and two marriages, had become a legal member of five different households over the course of her life. The practice of premarital adoption as a marriage strategy for upward mobility was common in late-Tokugawa Japan. Moreover, the process was totally transparent and socially acceptable. As was the case with Yoshino Michi, the case of Itô also reveals how women played an important role in preserving samurai lineages through marriage and remarriage.

Although marriage was a strategy for upward social mobility for some elite commoners and for women born into the lower ranks of the samurai status group, for samurai elites "marriage was a complicated calculus of financial and political costs and benefits" (Yonemoto, 2016, 114). Due to the difficult financial position that many daimyo found themselves in during the course of the Tokugawa period, monetary matters were an important consideration in marriage decisions. Such was the case, for example, in the proposed marriage between the daimyo Sakakibara Masanori of Takada domain (present-day Niigata prefecture) and Sakae-gimi, a daughter of the Nabeshima of Hizen domain (Saga prefecture). The Sakakibara were a powerful allied (*fudai*) daimyo family, whose founder was a top general of Tokugawa Ieyasu. Their domain had an assessed productive output of 150,000 *koku*, which was less than one-half that of the bride's Nabeshima domain, which was assessed at 352,000 *koku*. Despite the stereotype that samurai were unconcerned with monetary affairs or thought that such concerns were vulgar, the Sakikibara negotiated aggressively for a period of two years over the size of the dowry, which was to take the form of a combination of donation and loan of funds for the renovation of the daimyo residence compound where Masanori and his future bride were to live.

According to popular and legal discourse, marriage was supposed to create a lifelong bond, but the evidence shows that remarriage after the death of a husband and remarriage following divorce were frequent among women of all status groups, including samurai. Available statistics confirm that divorce was common among all social groups, perhaps about 10 percent for samurai of all ranks by the end of the Tokugawa period. Furthermore, as a rule neither divorce nor remarriage were stigmatized, and neither were prohibited in shogunal or domain government law. Government officials seemed to prefer that these practices follow local custom. Only when a legal dispute arose from a divorce that the parties were not able to resolve on their own did government magistrates (*bugyô*) get involved. Also, unlike in late imperial China where the practice of widow chastity was deeply entrenched, in Tokugawa Japan marriage after the death of a husband was not problematic. One study of 1,313 women, based on 125 lineages of the Matsudaira family in Mikawa, reveals the prevalence of both of the above-mentioned practices; over the course of the Tokugawa period the combined remarriage rate for widows and divorcees in this sample was 50 percent.

Although government did not regulate divorce, it did seek to protect marriage by punishing offenses against it, mainly adultery. Adultery was defined as sexual relations between a man and a woman when one or both of the parties were married to other people. According to law, both parties were held accountable and subject to punishment, just as both parties in a violent quarrel (*kenka ryôseibai*) were. In both cases, the principle of "double guilt" was applied. In punishing adultery, government officials were most concerned about the threat to social order that adulterous relationships might cause rather than in defending the principle of fidelity in marriage. In fact, the law made no distinction between rape and consensual sexual relationships outside of marriage: both were considered adulterous. In addition, sexual relations outside of marriage was not prohibited for men, as long as another man's wife was not involved.

The line between female household servant and concubine often was not clear. A servant who bore her samurai master's child might be upgraded to concubine status or sent back to her natal home. The child born by a servant or concubine, though, became the wife's child and stayed in the household. Yamakawa Kikue wrote how her great-grandmother had been her great-grandfather's concubine and after his death had married a merchant. Then, after her merchant husband's death she moved back to live with her daughter, and because her position was inferior (as the former wife of a merchant) she addressed her daughter as *okusan*, or "mistress."

The role of samurai women within the household necessarily varied depending on the status of her husband. The households of high-ranking samurai employed attendants, servants, including perhaps full-time nannies, who did much of the work. She did not live an idle life, however: "She waited on her husband and in-laws, prepared special foods, entertained guests, inventoried household goods, decorated the home, sewed clothing, and managed servants. As a girl she had also labored at more menial, taxing chores, including sweeping the yard, pruning bushes, cooking, sewing bedding quilts, and weaving mosquito nets" (Uno, ,1991, 29). Child care, however, was often left almost completely to their servants. Women married to lower-ranking samurai would have had fewer, if any, servants to manage and would have been engaged in secondary occupations, particularly sewing and weaving cloth, to supplement the household's income. Servants or children would be sent to run errands, as it was unusual for samurai women to be seen on the street performing them; their ventures into public space were often limited to visits to their own (natal) family, to the family graves during the annual Obon festival (Festival of Souls), and to the weddings or funerals of relatives.

Although women were not samurai, in some domains they were expected to study the martial art (*bugei*) of *naginata*, a pike-like weapon with a curved blade at the end. Yamakawa Kikue wrote that her mother was given some token training in the weapon as a kind of "spiritual discipline," but did not have much time for

---

Nakano Takeko, Female Warrior

The eldest daughter of an Aizu samurai and skilled in the *naginata* (a pole weapon), Nakano Takeko (1847–1868) was the leader of a unit of women who fought during the Battle of Aizu in 1868. She led an attack by the women against the imperial army, which was well armed with guns. During the charge she was able to kill a number of men with her weapon before being shot. She asked her sister to cut off her head and see to its burial. It as later buried under a pine tree at Hôkaiji temple in Aizu. Nakano and the other women fighters from the unit are commemorated every fall during the Aizu Autumn Festival.

---

reading and writing let alone "something as remote from the needs of daily life as the *naginata*" (Yamakawa, 1992, 20). In fact, Yamakawa noted that by the end of the Tokugawa period "women had almost completely abandoned study of the martial arts" (Yamakawa, 1992, 29). Nonetheless, a group of women in Aizu (later known as the *jôshitai* or "Women's Force"), perhaps as many as thirty, fought in the Battle of Aizu, including in defense of Aizu-Wakamatsu Castle, against the forces of the imperial army that had invaded the pro-Tokugawa domain in late 1868. They fought independently from the domain army so as not to bring shame to the lord, the implication being that the samurai were not enough to defend the domain. Perhaps as many as 200 women in the castle committed suicide so as not to be a cause for concern for their husbands or simply to avoid rape. One woman who did not die was Yamamoto Yaeko (1845–1932), the daughter of a gunnery instructor. She took part in nighttime raids against the imperial government troops using a rifle rather than *naginata* and amazingly survived the battle to live to a ripe old age.

See also: Bannermen (*hatamoto*); Daimyo and Domains; Daimyo Residence Compounds (*daimyô yashiki*); Double-Guilt Doctrine (*kenka ryôseibai*); Magistrates (*bugyô*); Martial Arts (*bugei*); Status System (*mibunsei*)

Further Reading

Seigle, Cecilia Segawa, and Linda H. Chance. *Ooku: The Secret World of the Shogun's Women.* Amherst, NY: Cambria Press, 2014.

Uno, Kathleen S. "Women and Changes in the Household Division of Labor." In Gail Lee Bernstein, ed., *Recreating Japanese Women, 1600–1945,* 17–41. Berkeley: University of California Press, 1991.

Walthall, Anne. "From Peasant Daughter to Samurai Wife." *Annales, économies, sociétés, civilisations,* 54(1) (1999), 58–86.

Yamakawa Kikue. *Women of the Mito Domain: Recollections of Samurai Family Life.* Translated and with an introduction by Kate Wildman Nakai. Tokyo: University of Tokyo Press, 1992.

Yonemoto, Marcia. *The Problem of Women in Early Modern Japan.* Berkeley: University of California Press, 2016.

Yamaga Sokô (1622–1685)

A Confucian scholar and respected leader in the field of military arts or strategy, Yamaga Sokô served briefly as a scholar-adviser in the small domain of Akô, but he made a name for himself through his writings. He gained renown for a series of works he wrote that dealt with the "way of the warrior" (*shidô*) and "the teaching for warriors" (*bukyô*).

Sôkô was the son of a *rônin* who found temporary employment serving a senior retainer of Aizu domain. After his father lost his position upon the change in lords in Aizu, he moved the family to Edo and practiced medicine. In an effort to rebuild the family's fortunes, Sokô's father supported his son's study of the Chinese classics, sending him at the age of nine to become a student of Hayashi Razan, the shogunate's leading Confucian philosopher. He also studied martial arts with other notable teachers. The precocious youth lectured to a number of daimyo, and despite many offers for employment it was only in 1652, at the age of thirty-one, that he accepted a position as military instructor to the daimyo of Akô domain, a post that came with a sizable stipend of 1,000 *koku*. He held the position until 1660, when he relinquished it to return to Edo to write and teach as an independent scholar.

The following year, at the age of forty, he broke away from and challenged the widely accepted views of scholars, including his former mentor, Hayashi Razan, who viewed Neo-Confucianism as the official or heterodox doctrine of the Tokugawa regime. Yamaga argued that to understand Confucius one had to read the original, ancient texts, not the later works of the Song period or later, which were in vogue in both China and Japan. For this, in 1666 the shogunate criticized him for writing "useless books" and ordered him into exile back to Akô domain; there, he was placed in the custody of Lord Asano Nagatomo, daimyo of Akô domain. Among his students was Nagatomo's son, Asano Naganori, who would later be forced by the shogunate to commit *seppuku*, and his son, Nagahiro. Although Yamaga was pardoned in 1675 after an appeal made by the chief abbot of Tôeizan temple and returned to Edo to continue his teachings, he maintained contact with the Naganori and Nagahiro. In 1684 both took the oath as Sokô's disciples in the military arts. Some historians argue that Ôishi Kuranosuke, the retainer who would later be the ringleader in the revenge league for Asano Naganori, was also a disciple; however, most do not believe that Yamaga had any significant influence over Ôishi or any of the other Akô *rônin*.

A great deal of Yamaga's writings were concerned with military science and the welfare of the samurai. His most famous work, *Shidô* (*The Way of the Samurai*), was strongly influenced by Confucianism and defined the new role that the samurai was to play in a time of peace. In justifying a rationale for samurai supremacy, he wrote,

The samurai is one who does not cultivate, does not manufacture, and does not engage in trade, but it cannot be that he has no function at all as a samurai. . . . The business of a samurai is to reflect on his own station of life, to give loyal service to his own master if he has one, to strengthen his fidelity in association with friends and, with due consideration of his own position, to devote himself to duty above all. (Vaporis, 2014, 125)

In other words, in a time of peace the samurai had to discipline himself to fill a new role as political leader and role model. His writings reflect a recognition of the difficulty of samurai pursuing both martial arts (*bu*) and the literary or civil arts (*bun*) in a time of peace. His books include *Bukyô honron* (*A Basic Study of Warrior Teachings*), a study of military tactics in three volumes, and *Bukyô shôgaku* (*Elemental Learning on Warrior Teachings*).

Although his writings were not greatly influential after his death, late in the Tokugawa period they were revived by the imperial loyalist Yoshida Shôin (1830–1859) and other radicalized samurai. In the twentieth century he was viewed by some scholars as a pivotal figure in the development of *bushido*.

His remains were buried at the Sôzô temple in Benten-chô, Ushigome (Edo), where Yoshida Shôin visited his grave several times while he was in Edo. Yamaga, along with Kumazawa Banzan and Yui Shôsetsu, were known as the "Three Great Rônin" of the Tokugawa period. He counted among his students Daidôji Yûzan (1639–1730), author of *Budô shoshinshû*, a popular text on the "way of the warrior."

See also: Akô Incident; *Budô shoshinshû* (*The Way of the Warrior: A Primer*); *Bushido*; Civil and Military Arts (*bunbu*); Kumazawa Banzan; Ronin (*rônin*); Document 8

Further Reading
Tucker, John Allen. "Tokugawa Intellectual History and Prewar Ideology." *Sino-Japanese Studies*, 14 (2002), 35–70.
Uenaka, Shuzo. "Last Testatment in Exile. Yamaga Sokô's *Haisho Zampitsu.*" *Monumenta Nipponica*, 32(2) (1977), 125–152.
Vaporis, Constantine Nomikos. *Voices of Early Modern Japan: Contemporary Accounts of Daily Life during the Age of the Shoguns.* Boulder, CO: Westview Press, 2014.

Yamauchi Katsutoyo (1545–1605)

A warrior who rose up through the ranks to become a *sengoku daimyô* (Warring States daimyo), attaching his fortunes to those of Oda Nobunaga (1534–1582), Toyotomi Hideyoshi (1537–1598), and then Tokugawa Ieyasu (1543–1616), Yamauchi Katsutoyo was the first of fifteen daimyo of Tosa domain during the Edo period.

Katsutoyo was born in Ichinomiya, Owari province (Aichi prefecture), in central Japan. His father, Yamauchi Moritoyo, died in battle against the forces of Oda Nobunaga when Katsutoyo was fourteen years old. After a period as a *rônin* (masterless samurai), Katsutoyo was taken into the service of Oda Nobunaga, from 1565 until his lord's death in 1582, and placed in the unit led by Kinoshita Tôkichirô, who was later known as Toyotomi Hideyoshi. Under Nobunaga, Katsutoyo led troops in numerous battles, including one at Anegawa (1570), where Nobunaga and Ieyasu were first allied; at Ichijôdani-jô (1573), where he prevailed over his opponent despite receiving a heavy head wound; and at Nagashino (1575), where the forces of the daimyo Takeda Katsuyori (1546–1582) were dealt a decisive defeat by the forces commandeered by Oda and Tokugawa. Sometime between 1570 and 1573 Katsutoyo was married to Chiyo (see sidebar), a woman who earned a reputation for her thrift, wisdom, and devotion to her husband.

After Nobunaga's death in 1582, Katsutoyo continued in the service of Toyotomi Hideyoshi, and as his lord expanded his territories he rewarded Katsutoyo with larger fiefs, which necessitated frequent transfers; beginning with a fief of 400 *koku* in Karakuni, he was later transferred (in 1585) to Nagahama in Ômi province, where he became a daimyo of a territory of 20,000 *koku*. He was transferred again, in 1590, after Hideyoshi's campaign in Odawara against the Hôjô, and was rewarded handsomely with a substantial increase, the 50,000-*koku* domain of Kakegawa in Tôtômi province (Shizuoka prefecture) on the coast of Honshû near Shizuoka. That fief was later increased to 60,000 *koku*.

Katsutoyo's career continued its upward trajectory as a result of his strategic decision to side with Tokugawa Ieyasu in the Sekigahara campaign (1600). His forces assisted those of the Tokugawa in the capture of Gifu Castle, prior to the actual Battle of Sekigahara. In that conflict, Katsutoyo's force of 2,000 men held a position in the rear guard, and although his military contribution to Ieyasu's victory was not great, as a nonvassal who sided with Ieyasu he was richly rewarded nonetheless with a fief four times larger than Kakegawa. As his new fief, Katsutoyo received the major domain of Tosa, a province-sized domain on Shikoku Island that had been confiscated from Chôsogabe Motochika, who had opposed Ieyasu at Sekigahara.

As a new lord taking over a domain from the defeated opponent of his allied lord, Katsutoyo arrived in an unfamiliar part of the country, undermanned and facing a hostile climate. As the

Bronze statue of Chiyo (1557–1617), wife of the first daimyo of Tosa domain, Yamauchi Katsutoyo, and the horse she gave him, which stands close to Kôchi Castle. The horse was said to have won the admiration of Katsutoyo's lord, Oda Nobunaga, and led to Katsutoyo's early promotion. She is also credited with later giving Katsutoyo the wise advice to switch allegiance to Tokugawa Ieyasu just prior to the Battle of Sekigahara (1600). (Photo by Constantine Vaporis)

Chiyo (1557–1617)

The lives of samurai women in Tokugawa Japan, even the wives of important political figures, frequently are not well represented in the historical record nor in popular memory. The woman known simply as Chiyo may be exceptional in this regard, but she is most often remembered as "the wife of (the daimyo) Yamauchi Katsutoyo" (1545–1605) and for several stories that made her a model of the "good wife, wise mother" promoted in prewar Japanese society. She is most frequently remembered for her wisdom in promoting her husband's military career. In the first instance, she purchased a thoroughbred horse for her husband with money that she had saved because she felt the horse he had was not befitting a man with aspirations of becoming a daimyo. According to popular lore, she did this right before a formal inspection of the troops by his overlord, Oda Nobunaga (1534–1582), who was greatly impressed by Katsutoyo and his horse and promoted him. Later, prior to the Battle of Sekigahara (1600), while she was held a political hostage by Ishida Mitsunari, Chiyo sent secret letters with important intelligence to her husband to pass on to Tokugawa Ieyasu (1543–1616) to demonstrate his loyalty to him. Of course, Katsutoyo's loyalty (and Chiyo's sagacity) would be richly rewarded after the battle, when Ieyasu awarded him Tosa domain. Chiyo's life has been memorialized in historical drama, in the 1922 silent film *Yamauchi Katsutoyo no tsuma*, and much more recently in the 45th NHK Taiga Drama (2006), *Kômyô ga Tsuji: Yamauchi Katsutoyo no Tsuma*, which is based on the novel of the same name by Shiba Ryôtarô.

Reproductions of her image can be found in a number of places: a bronze statue of her and the horse she gave her husband, which stands near the ascent to Kôchi Castle, close to a statue of her husband on horseback and in full armor; a bronze status of her, holding the reins of the horse, and her husband (perhaps depicting the moment before she gave him the animal), located in the park below Gujô Hachiman Castle (Gifu prefecture); and a portrait of her in retirement, wearing the garb of a Buddhist nun, when she was known as Kenshôin (image in public domain).

daimyo of a small fief, Katsutoyo's military force, by one account, consisted of only 158 mounted warriors, which combined with support personnel (foot soldier units wielding muskets, bows, and lances) likely amounted to fewer than 2,000 men. Knowing he would be vastly outnumbered by the local Tosa forces, Katsutoyo petitioned Tokugawa Ieyasu for assistance. Ieyasu delegated the task to his trusted vassal Ii Naomasa, who just a month after Sekigahara sent a force of eight ships under the command of his vassal Suzuki Hyôe. It took five weeks for Suzuki to suppress local opposition, which he did with a heavy hand, collecting 273 heads to ship back to Ii Naomasa.

Katsutoyo and his men entered Tosa domain in 1601, and to mark the inauguration of his reign sumo wresting matches were held on the beach at Katsurahama. From the village heads and rural samurai in attendance, seventy-three leaders of the resistance were suddenly captured and then crucified, which, along with the exiling of senior Chôsokabe retainers, did much to crush any direct resistance to Yamauchi rule.

After touring his new domain, Katsutoyo decided to build a new castle at the headwaters of Urado bay. The Chôsokabe's castle had been located at Urado point, on a narrow strip of land at the mouth of Urado Bay, a placement that allowed little room for development. The move to the headwaters allowed Katsutoyo and his successors to plan for a much larger urban settlement while still allowing for convenient connection via water transportation for the castle town to other parts of the country. In fact, Katsutoyo himself, together with five of his top retainers, personally inspected the work on a daily basis. By the summer of 1603, enough of the basic construction had been completed that he was able to move in with proper ceremony.

Katsutoyo retained landholdings (his demesne, or *chokkatsuchi*) in the heart of the Kôchi plain that produced roughly 45,000 *koku* (1 koku = approximately five bushels), equivalent to 20 percent of the rated domain income of 202,600 *koku;* from this 45,000 *koku* he paid stipends to hundreds of retainers of lesser status than samurai. Still, the size of Yamauchi's demesne represented a doubling of the amount of lands held directly by the previous, Chôsokabe, lords. His younger brother Yasutoyo was granted a fief of 20,000 *koku* in the western portion of the domain, with Nakamura Castle and daimyo-equivalent status. Five of his top retainers received fiefs of 1,100–10,000 *koku* that were centered on a castle; the castle keeps were demolished after 1615 in response to the Tokugawa's "one-province, one castle decree" (*ikkoku ichijô rei*), but the wall and moats remained. More than one hundred retainers received smaller fiefs, ranging from 20 to 7,000 *koku,* with land grants in the castle town on which to construct residences. Low-ranking retainers received stipends but no fiefs. Since the retainers were not native to Tosa, there were no traditional fiefs to remove them from. It was relatively easy therefore to concentrate many of them in Kôchi. However, with the exception of the five top retainers mentioned above, the Yamauchi were able to prevent those retainers with landed fiefs from building up powerful local bases of power by scattering their landholdings across a number of villages (rather than granting them a fief of contiguous territory).

Katsutoyo did not live long after having taken possession of his new fief. He died in 1605 at the age of sixty, without male issue. Fortunately, his brother Yasutoyo's son, Tadayoshi, succeeded as daimyo and continued the Yamauchi family line.

See also: Castle Towns (*jôkamachi*); Oda Nobunaga; Rural Samurai (*gôshi*); Sekigahara, Battle of; Tokugawa Ieyasu; Toyotomi Hideyoshi

Further Reading
Hirao Michio. *Tosa han* [Tosa domain]. Tokyo: Yoshikawa kôbunkan, 1965. (Japanese)

Jansen, Marius B. "Tosa in the Seventeenth Century: The Establishment of Yamauchi Rule." In John W. Hall and Marius B. Jansen, eds., *Studies in the Institutional History of Early Modern Japan.* Princeton, NJ: Princeton University Press, 1968.

Roberts, Luke S. *Mercantilism in a Japanese Domain: The Merchant Origins of Economic Nationalism in 18th-Century Japan.* Cambridge: Cambridge University Press, 1998.

Yoshida Shôin (1830–1859)

A samurai intellectual from the southern domain of Chôshû, Yoshida Shôin lived a brief but tumultuous life during the closing decades of the Tokugawa period, one whose legacy is still debated today. To many Japanese he was a revolutionary leader, a poet and teacher turned martyred pro-imperial activist. Yet for others, he was a terrorist who glorified the emperor and helped to bring him back into the center stage of Japanese politics, a move that would have disastrous consequences for the country in World War II. Regardless of one's political perspective, Yoshida is a prime example of a samurai who sought to educate and to motivate those around him to rejuvenate the samurai by improving martial skills and by strengthening the spirit. He is also credited with having been a major impact on a number of consequential figures involved in the Meiji Restoration (1868) and the early Meiji government.

Shôin was born in 1830 in Matsumoto, just outside Hagi, the castle town of Chôshû domain, the second son of Sugi Yurinosuke, a low-ranking samurai who engaged in farming. First known by his boyhood name Toranosuke, he later used several other names, including Torajirô and of course Shôin, by which he is the most widely known. As a second son, one who would not succeed to his father's hereditary position, Shôin was adopted out at the age of four to Yoshida Daisuke, one of his father's two brothers. This practice of the Yoshida family to adopt younger sons from the Sugi household was in fact established several generations before Shôin's birth.

The Sugi family was unusual in that it controlled two additional samurai lineages, the above-mentioned Yoshida lineage as well as that of the Tamaki. Consequently, the eldest son in the Sugi family inherited the position of househead of the Sugi lineage, while younger sons were adopted out to the Yoshida and Tamaki lines, respectively. In this manner, Shôin's father and two brothers controlled three lineages at the time that Shôin was adopted out as heir to Yoshida Daisuke.

With the early death of Yoshida Daisuke at the age of twenty-eight, Shôin quite unexpectedly found himself becoming the househead of the Yoshida line at the young age of five. Since the Yoshida househeads were hereditary instructors in military science for Chôshû domain, four men were appointed to act in Shôin's place as instructors while his uncle, Tamaki Bunnoshin, took charge of his education. Under Bunnoshin's tutelage, Shôin made quick progress; his uncle's goal was to prepare Shôin to assume his duties as Yamaga instructor as soon as possible. This intense period of instruction helped to shape Shôin into an educator and activist. At just nine years of age, he gave his first lectures at the Meirinkan, domain school, and the following year (1840), he lectured before the lord, although at least in this case his lecture had been prepared by his uncle. By 1848 Shôin was ready to assume his duties as an independent instructor at the Meirinkan.

Impressed by Shôin's ability, the lord allowed him to travel outside the domain in 1850. Kyushu would be the first of many trips for Shôin over the following two-year period, and during this time he studied for two months at the Yamaga school in Hirado under the direction of a scholar named Hayama Sanai, who was well informed about world conditions, particularly about Western pressure being applied on China. After this, Shôin spent about a month in the open port of Nagasaki, which peaked his interest in Western technology. The following spring, in 1851, Shôin also had the opportunity to travel to distant Edo as part of the daimyo's retinue. There, Shôin studied under the head of the Edo branch of the Yamaga school (Yamaga Sosui), which greatly improved his knowledge of military science and Western learning. Taking advantage of the cultural opportunities that Edo offered,

Shôin also became a student of Sakuma Shôzan's, one of the leading experts in Dutch learning and Western studies.

At the end of 1851 Shôin made a decision that put him at odds with political authorities for the first time, leaving Edo on a four-month long trip across north-eastern Japan without obtaining the requisite written permission. Although he had been granted verbal approval for the trip, he grew impatient at the delay in obtaining the formal, written documentation and departed without it. This action was tantamount to "fleeing the domain" (*dappan*), and after he made his way back to Edo in 1852 he was then ordered to return to Chôshû, where he awaited his punishment while under house arrest; it was during this time that he first began to refer to himself as Shôin (a named formed from two characters, *shô*, which is the alternate reading for Matsu, as in his birthplace Matsumoto, and *in*, meaning "seclusion," which refers to his time under house arrest).

At the end of 1852 Shôin received his sentence. He was dismissed from service, his name removed from the domain register of retainers, stripped of his samurai status and with it his stipend of 57 *koku*, and he was placed in the custody of his father, Yurinosuke. Legally, then, Shôin was a *rônin*. Ironically, one positive outcome of Shôin's act of defiance was that the lord, Môri Takachika, while he had no choice but to punish him also respected Shôin, and thus gave him permission to study anywhere in the country for a period of ten years.

The trip north, while it had resulted in Shôin's dismissal from service, also had a big impact on his life. In Mito Shôin was exposed to the Mito school of learning, which emphasized imperial loyalism. In the far north he wrote of his anger over the arrogance of Western ships intruding into Japanese space by passing through the Straits of Tsugaru. His travels spurred his study of Japanese history, and from that he determined that what he perceived as the aggressive policy of the state in ancient times had "made the Imperial Land the Imperial Land" (quoted in Earl, 1964, 119), safe from foreign aggression.

Having been given permission to leave the domain, Shôin lost no time in returning to Edo, but traveling there in a circuitous manner, via Shikoku, Nara and Ise, Gifu and Gumma, to see as much of Japan as he could. He arrived in the Tokugawa capital just eight days before the arrival of U.S. commodore Perry's ships at Uraga in 1853, and was able to view the ships together with his teacher from Edo, Sakuma Shôzan. The timing of Shôin's stay in Edo coincided with the arrival of a fleet of U.S. vessels under the command of Commodore Matthew C. Perry. Sakuma Shôzan became convinced that some Japanese should travel abroad to study, and Shôin agreed to be the first to attempt it. Since Commodore Perry had already left to spend the winter in the Ryukyu Islands, promising to return to Japan the following year, Shôin traveled to Nagasaki to try to leave Japan on one of the ships of the Russian admiral Putiatin, who like Perry, was also pressuring the shogunate to enter into diplomatic relations with his country. On the way to Nagasaki, Shôin visited Kyoto for the first time and was deeply moved by Emperor Kômei's unhappiness over the domestic and international political situation of the country, and this furthered Shôin's growing feelings of imperial loyalism. The stop in Kyoto delayed him, and as a result Shôin arrived in Nagasaki only to find that Putiatin's ships had departed days earlier. Accordingly, Shôin made a quick U-turn and headed back to Edo, a trip of more than 600 miles.

More determined to travel overseas than ever, Shôin waited in Edo for Commodore Perry's return. He and his friend Kaneko Shigenosuke together wrote a letter, which they entitled "Application for Joining the Barbarians," went to Shimoda, where Perry's ships were anchored, and they rowed themselves out to the ships in the dead of night. They were able to present their letter asking permission to travel on one of Perry's ships to America but were denied permission to remain on board. Shôin actually never had the opportunity to meet Perry, who did not want to risk an incident with Tokugawa officials by allowing Shôin to leave the country, which would have been counter to the terms of the proposed treaty between Japan and the United States. Their boat having drifted away, the two samurai were put back ashore by American sailors. Wanting to confront the shogunate over its policy of not allowing Japanese to travel abroad, Shôin and Shigenosuke actually turned themselves in to the Tokugawa authorities; Sakuma Shôzan was also arrested as an accomplice.

Confined in Shimoda at first, Shôin and Shigenosuke were then transferred to Denma-chô prison in Edo, in a cell right next to Shôin's teacher, Sakuma Shôzan. While in jail, Shôin wrote a letter to his brother in which he equated his defiance of Tokugawa law with that of the forty-seven *rônin* in the famous Akô Incident.

After six months in jail, Shôin and Shigenosuke were sentenced to house arrest and transported to Hagi as criminals, in bamboo cages, to be released to Chôshû government officials. In Chôshû, though, the administration decided to imprison the two men, who were each put in separate jails: Shôin, in a prison reserved for upper samurai and Shigenosuke in a different one reserved for lower-ranking samurai. While in jail, Shôin put his time to good use, studying, writing extensively, and teaching a number of his fellow inmates.

When Shôin's prison sentence was canceled in 1856, he took over as instructor of his uncle Tamaki Bunnoshin's small private school, the Shôka Sonjuku, where he taught military arts and politics. Although technically he remained under domiciliary confinement, he was able to teach and had his students travel in his place and report back to him on conditions elsewhere in Japan.

During this three-year period of confinement, Shôin's imperial loyalism reached its logical conclusion: he became convinced that loyalty to the emperor was the supreme duty and therefore he had no choice but to oppose the Tokugawa shogunate. Although Shôin previously had been critical of the shogunate's weakness in the face of the foreign threat, he was radicalized by the actions of Grand Councilor Ii Naosuke's signing of the commercial treaty with the West in 1858 against the wishes of the imperial court and embraced the anti-Tokugawa slogan "Revere the emperor, expel the barbarian." Anticipating a backlash, Ii Naosuke began to round up activist imperial loyalists in Kyoto, Edo, and in some domains, including many of Shôin's followers, in the so-called Ansei Purge (*Ansei no taigoku*, 1858–1860). Shôin decided to take action: he and a group of his students attempted to assassinate a top Tokugawa official named Manabe Akikatsu. Far from keeping the plot secret, Shôin requested assistance from domain officials, who promptly arrested him and had him placed in the same shogunate prison until he was returned again to Hagi, this time to a prison cell.

In 1859, under pressure from the shogunate to send its radical imperial loyalists to prison in Edo, Chôshû officials dispatched Yoshida Shôin in a bamboo cage to the shogun's capital. In jail, Shôin confessed to the plot to kill Manabe and was executed. According to an account by his executioner, Shôin was composed at the time of his death, which came at the young age of twenty-nine.

Although Shôin failed in many of his endeavors, he is given credit by some scholars for the influence he had on his students; others, however, argue that his influence has been exaggerated. Regardless of one's perspective, it is undeniable that several of his former students went on to high-level positions in the Meiji government. One of his students, Itô Hirobumi, was a major figure in the Meiji Restoration and later became Japan's first prime minister. Others played a role in the struggles leading up to the overthrow of the shogunate. Takasugi Shinsaku, for example, led a mixed militia of commoners and samurai, trained with rifles, against the Tokugawa's army when it attempted to defeat and take over Chôshû domain in 1864.

Yoshida Shôin was put to death at the Denmachô execution grounds in Edo in 1859. His remains were temporarily buried at Eko-in temple, where a monument to him can still be found today. His remains were reinterred by Takasugi Shinsaku, Itô Hirobumi, and other students of Shôin's in 1863 on the grounds of Chôshû domain's residence in Wakabayashi, Edo. After the Meiji Restoration, in 1882, a shrine was erected near his grave where his spirit was enshrined. Shôin's spirit was enshrined in two other religious institutions as well: at Shôin Shrine in Hagi city, Yamaguchi prefecture; and in the now contentious Yasukuni Shrine in 1888. The following year the Meiji government posthumously awarded him the senior fourth rank. Around this time a number of hagiographic-type biographies were written about him and statues erected in his honor in Tokyo, Hagi, and Shimoda. During the 1930s and 1940s, Yoshida Shôin's imperial loyalism became a source of inspiration for radicals in the imperial army.

The historical character of Yoshida Shôin has appeared in a number of Japanese films and television shows, most recently in the 2015's NHK Taiga Drama *Hana Moyu*.

See also: Akô Incident; Itô Hirobumi; Meiji Restoration; Ronin (*rônin*)

Further Reading

Earl, David Magarey. *Emperor and Nation in Japan: Political Thinkers of the Tokugawa Period.* Seattle, WA: University of Washington Press, 1964.

Huber, Thomas M. *The Revolutionary Origins of Modern Japan.* Stanford, CA: Stanford University Press, 1981.

Shôin shrine, Hagi (official website): http://shoin-jinja.jp/en. Accessed February 10, 2017.

Shôin shrine, in Tokyo (official website): http://www.shoinjinja.org. Accessed February 10, 2017.

Stevenson, Robert Louis. "Yoshida-Torajiro." In his *Familiar Studies of Men and Books*, Chapter 5. New York: Current Literature Publishing Co., 1909. Also available online: https://ebooks.adelaide.edu.au/s/stevenson/robert_louis/s848fs/chapter5.html.

Van Staelen, H. J. J. M. *Yoshida Shôin, Forerunner of the Meiji Restoration.* Leiden: E. J. Brill, 1952.

PRIMARY SOURCE DOCUMENTS

Document 1   An Early View of the Japanese, as Seen by St. Francis Xavier (1550)

The author was a Roman Catholic missionary and cofounder of the Society of Jesus. He traveled extensively in Asia to spread the faith, in India, Southeast Asia, and Japan. His goal was to preach the gospel in China, but he died on an island off the southern coast shortly before being able to do so. In Japan, where he remained for more than two years, he experienced difficulties because of the resistance of some political and religious leaders to his foreign faith and due to his own lack of fluency in Japanese. His letters to Jesuit leaders in Europe, from which the excerpt below is drawn, provide a firsthand account of life in Japan and elsewhere in Asia.

The Japanese have a high opinion of themselves because they think that no other nation can compare with them in regard to weapons and valor, and so they look down on all foreigners. They greatly prize and value their arms, and prefer to have gold weapons, decorated with gold and silver, more than anything else in the world. They carry a sword and dagger both inside and outside the house and lay them at their pillows when they sleep. Never in my life have I met people who rely so much on their arms. They are excellent archers and fight on foot, although there are horses in the country. They are very courteous to each other, but they do not show this courtesy to foreigners, whom they despise. They spend all their money on dress, weapons and servants, and do not possess any treasures. They are very warlike and are always involved in wars, and thus the ablest man becomes the greatest lord. They have but one king, although they have not obeyed him for more than 150 years, and for this reason internal wars continue.

Source: Henry James Coleridge, ed., *The Life and Letters of St. Francis Xavier*, 2nd ed., 2 vols. (London: Burns & Oates, 1890).

Document 2   *Laws for the Military Houses* (*buke shohatto*) (1615, 1635)

In July 1615, the daimyo came to Fushimi Castle, outside of Kyoto, where the second shogun, Tokugawa Hidetada, formally promulgated the thirteen-article law code, which was compiled at Tokugawa Ieyasu's direction. Every succeeding Tokugawa shogun in the Tokugawa dynasty formally reissued the regulations, allowing for them to be amended over time, as needed; however, they remained the same in general tone and effect. The Laws for the Military Houses *were reissued twice by the third shogun, Iemitsu, in 1629, in exactly the same form as in 1615, and again in 1635. Only the substantive changes in the 1635 version are included in Document 2.*

Each of the articles was accompanied by a commentary drawn from earlier historical works and laws and often included quotations from the Confucian classics. In the original document the commentary begins on the line after the article, as it does in the translation. To distinguish between the two, the text of the articles, below, is in regular type while the commentary is italicized.

Document 2A   *Laws for the Military Houses* (*buke shohatto*), 1615

1. The study of literature and the practice of the military arts, including archery and horsemanship, must be cultivated diligently.

   "Literature on the left, and martial arts on the right": this is an ancient law. Both must be cultivated at the same time. Archery and horsemanship are essential for the military houses. It is said that war is a curse but sometimes it is an unavoidable necessity. In times of peace do not forget that disturbances may arise. How can we not train ourselves for war?

2. Avoid drinking parties and gaming amusements.

   In our instructions it is laid down that strict moderation in these respects is to be observed. To be addicted to venery and to make a pursuit of gambling are the first steps towards the loss of one's domain.

3. Those who break the law should not be given refuge in the domains.

   Law is the very foundation of social order. Law may be contrary to reason, but reason should not be an excuse to violate the law. Those who disregard the law will not be treated with leniency.

4. The daimyo, the lesser lords, and those who hold land under them should expel any of their retainers guilty of rebellion or murder.

   Savage and unruly retainers are sharp swords that can destroy the state. How can they be tolerated?

5. Henceforth, no social intercourse is to be permitted for residents of your domain with people from other domains.

   In general, the customs of the various domains differ from one another. To divulge the secrets of one's own domain to others or to report the secrets of another domain to people of one's own domain is surely an indication of the intent to curry favor.

6. The castles in the domains may be repaired but this must be reported [to the shogunate]. New construction is strictly prohibited.

   A castle with walls exceeding 100 chi (10 × 30 feet; i.e. 1000 ft. long) is harmful to the domain. Steep walls and deep moats are the causes of great disorder.

7. If innovations are being planned or political factions being formed in a neighboring domain, these must be reported immediately.

   Men have the tendency to form factions, but few ever come to anything. As a result, some of these men fail to follow their lords or fathers and come into conflict with those of neighboring villages. If the ancient prohibitions are not maintained new schemes will be planned.

8. Marriages must not be arranged privately [i.e., without the approval of the shogun].

   Marriage is the result of the harmonious combination of yin and yang. It is therefore not a matter to be undertaken lightly. It is written in the Book of Changes, "Not being enemies they can unite in marriage. While (the elders are) thinking of making advances to the opponent (family), the proper time (for the marriage) is allowed to slip by." Also, it is written in the Book of Odes, "If men and women observe what is correct and marry at the proper time, there will be no widowers in the land." To form political factions through marriage is a source of evil scheming.

9. The practice of the daimyo traveling to attend (*sankin*) the shogun:

   In Chronicles of Japan, Continued (Shoku Nihongi) *it is recorded that: 'Except when entrusted with some official duty, no one is allowed at his own pleasure to assemble his clansmen within the capital, and no one is to go about attended by more than twenty horsemen. Hence it is not permissible to lead about a large force of soldiers. Daimyo whose revenues range from 1,000,000 koku down to 200,000 koku may not exceed twenty horsemen; for those whose revenues are 100,000 koku and under, the number is to be in the same proportion. On occasions of official service, however, the number of followers is to be in proportion to the status of each daimyo.*

10. Regulations governing clothing must be followed.

    The distinction between lord and vassal, between superior and inferior, must be clearly marked by the apparel. Retainers may not, except in rare cases with special authorization, indiscriminately wear silk materials, such as fine white damask, white wadded silk garments, purple silk kimono, purple silk linings, padded silk garments without the bearer's family crest. In recent times retainers and various types of menials have taken to wearing rich damasks and silk. This elaborate display was not allowed according to the ancient laws and it must be kept strictly within bounds.

11. Miscellaneous persons [i.e., persons without sufficient rank] are not to ride in palanquins.

    There are some people who have had the privilege of riding in palanquins without permission, and there are others who have received permission. But lately retainers and their underlings have been riding in them. This is flagrant impertinence. Henceforth the daimyo of the provinces and the distinguished members of their families may ride without special permission. In addition, doctors and astrologers, persons over sixty years of age, and those who are sick or invalid may ride, with permission. If ordinary retainers and their underlings ride it will be considered the fault of their lords. These restrictions however do not apply to court nobles, Buddhist priests, and those who have taken the tonsure.

12. The samurai throughout the domains are to practice frugality.

    When those who are rich make a display of their wealth, those who are poor are ashamed of not being on a part with them. There is nothing as likely to corrupt public morality, and it must be strictly kept in check.

13. The lords of the domains must select for office men of ability.

The way to govern a country is to get the proper men. The merits and faults of the lord's retainers should be closely examined, and rewards or punishments given accordingly. If there are capable men in the administration, that domain is sure to flourish; if there are not any good men, then that domain is sure to go to ruin. This is an admonition which the wise men of old bequeathed to us.

The above-mentioned regulations must be obeyed.
First year of Genna [1615], Seventh Month

Source: Translation adapted from John Carey Hall, *Japanese Feudal Laws. The Tokugawa Legislation* (Yokohama, 1910), 286–319, in conjunction with the Japanese original, published in Shihôsho, ed., *Tokugawa kinreikô* (Consideration of Tokugawa Regulations), vol. 1. (Tokyo: Shôbunsha, 1879), 90–92.

Document 2B   Excerpts from *Laws for the Military Houses* (*buke shohatto*), 1635

2. It is now settled that the daimyo and the lesser lords are to do service, in turns, at Edo. They shall come to Edo every year in the summer during the Fourth month. Recently the numbers of retainers and attendants accompanying them have become excessive. This is wasteful to the domains and districts; moreover it causes the people great hardship. Hereafter, suitable reductions in this regard must be made. When they are ordered to go to Kyoto, the instructions must be followed. When traveling to fulfill an official duty, the number of people accompanying the lord must be appropriate to their status.

4. If an occurrence of any type whatsoever should take place, whether in Edo or in any of the provinces, those (daimyo and their retainers) who are there at the time are to stay where they are and to await the shogun's orders.

6. The scheming of innovations, the forming of parties, and the taking of (private) oaths is strictly forbidden.

13. When the hostages given by sub-vassals to their lords have committed an offense requiring punishment by banishment or death, that punishment should not be carried out before an order consenting to this has been received (from the shogunate). Should it be necessary to cut down a hostage immediately, a detailed account of the matter must be provided (to the shogunate).

15. The roads, post horses, ferry-boats and bridges must be carefully attended to prevent any delays or disruption to services.

16. Private toll barriers are forbidden, as is the discontinuing of any existing ferry service.

17. It is forbidden to build vessels of over 500 *koku* burden.

21. In all matters the example set by the laws of Edo is to be followed in all the provinces and places.

Source: Translation adapted from John Carey Hall, *Japanese Feudal Laws. The Tokugawa Legislation* (Yokohama, 1910), 286–319, in conjunction with the Japanese original, published in Shihôsho, ed., *Tokugawa kinreikô* (Consideration of Tokugawa Regulations), vol. 1. (Tokyo: Shôbunsha, 1879), 93–95.

Document 3   A Foreigner's View of the Battle of Osaka. Richard Cock's Account of the Fall of Osaka Castle (1615)

The first selection is by Richard Cocks (1566–1624), the head merchant in the British East India Company, and comes from his personal diary. In the entries from four days in June 1615 he recounted news that was communicated to him about the fall of Osaka Castle, where the forces allied with Toyotomi Hideyori 1593–1615), in opposition to the Tokugawa shogunate, were holded up. Cocks was also a frequent letter writer, and the second document is from a letter he wrote in 1616 to a fellow merchant, Richard Westby, who was in Jambi, Indonesia, at the time.

The origins of the conflict that led to the burning of Osaka Castle go back to the time of Toyotomi Hideyoshi (1536–1598), Ieyasu's overlord, who appointed him as one of his son's five guardians. After the Battle of Sekigahara (1600), Ieyasu allowed Hideyori to retain his father's castle, Osaka, as his residence. By 1614, the Tokugawa felt secure enough politically to attack Hideyori directly. Although the attack was not successful, Hideyori signed a temporary peace treaty and prepared for a second military campaign the following year, 1615, in which the Tokugawa were successful and laid ruin to the castle.

Document 3A   Richard Cock's Account of the Fall of Osaka Castle: Excerpts from Richard Cocks, *The Diary of Richard Cocks, Cape-Merchant in the English Factory in Japan, 1615–1622: With Correspondence*

June 2[, 1615]. We had news today that Ieyasu hath taken the fortress of Osaka and overthrown the forces of Hideyori. Others say that most of the forces of Hideyori issued out of the fortress, and sallid [to make an attack on an enemy from a defended position] out 3 leagues [three miles] towards Miyako [Kyoto], but were encountered by the Emperor's forces and put to the worse, many of them being slaughtered and the rest drive back into the fortress, etc.

June 5. There came letters from the King of Hirado to Bungo Dono [the daimyo or lord of Bungo], that it is true that the Emperor [Cocks meant the shogun] hath overthrown the forces of Hideyori, and taken the fortress of Osaka, and entered into it the sixth day of this month, Hideyori and his mother with his son having cut their bellies [committed *seppuku*, or ritual suicide], etc.

June 7. After dinner came a Franciscan friar [a member of the Catholic religious order founded by Saint Francis of Assissi in the early thirteenth century], called Padre Apolonario, whom I had seen two or three times in Hirado heretofore. He was in the fortress of Osaka when it was taken, and yet had the good happ [good fortune] to escape. He told me he brought nothing away with him but the clothes on his back, the action was so sudden; and that he marveled that a force of about 120,000 men (such as was that of Hideyori) should be so soon overthrown.

June 19. They say the taking of this fortress hath cost above 100,000 men's lives on the one part and other, and that on the Prince Hideyori's part no dead man of account is found with his head on, but all cut off, because they should not be known, to seek revenge against their friends and parents after. Neither (as some say) can the body of Hideyori be found; so that many think he is secretly escaped. But I cannot believe it.

Source: Adapted from Richard Cocks, *The Diary of Richard Cocks, Cape-Merchant in the English Factory in Japan, 1615–1622: With Correspondence* (London: Hakluyt Society, 1883).

Document 3B   Excerpt from Richard Cock's Letter to Richard Westby, February 1616

"Also we have had great troubles and wars in Japan since our arrival, which hath put us to much pains and charges in sending up and down to save our goods, and yet for all that some is lost and burned, two great cities being burned to the ground, each one of them being almost as big as London and not one house left standing, the one called Osaka and the other Sakai [the port city of Osaka]; and, as it is reported, above 300,000 men have lost their lives on the one part and other. Yet the old Emperor Ieyasu hath prevailed and Hideyori either slain or fled secretly away that no news is to be heard of him."

Source: William Foster, ed., *Letters Received by the East India Company from Its Servants in the East*, vol. IV (1616) (London: Sampson Low, Marston & Company, 1900), 59.

Document 4   A Dutch Audience with the Shogun Tokugawa Tsunayoshi, 1691

This selection is from a history of Japan written by the German physician and naturalist Englebert Kaempfer, who was in Japan in the employment of the Dutch East India Company (VOC). As a result, he accompanied the company's embassy from its base on Deshima, the fan-shaped man-made island where the Dutch were required to live and to do their business, to Edo on two occasions, in 1691 and 1692. In this excerpt, dating from 1691, he relates his account of the audience of the Dutch embassy before the eighth shogun, Tokugawa Tsunayoshi, in his palace within Edo Castle.

The Dutch, after 1639, were the only Westerners allowed in Japan. Furthermore, there were no state-to-state relations between Holland and Japan. The Dutch trade company (or VOC, in Dutch) was allowed to trade with Japan as a private entity. However, the head of the Dutch trade mission—known as opperhoofden, *lit. "supreme headman" in Dutch and* kapitan *in Japanese—was allowed to pay his respects to the shogun, much as the daimyo were required to attend the shogun during alternate years. The annual visits were reduced to once every four years after 1790.*

Document 4 Excerpt from Englebert Kaempfer, *The History of Japan Together with a Description of the Kingdom of Siam, 1690–92*: Audience at Edo Castle, 1691

[The audience hall] opens on one side towards a small court, which lets in the light; on the opposite side it joins to two other apartments, which are on this occasion laid open towards the same court, one of which is considerably larger than the other, and serves for the Counsellors of State [i.e., the Elders, or *rôjû*], when they give audience by themselves. The other is narrower, deeper, and one step higher than the hall itself. In this the Emperor [he means the "shogun"] sits, when he gives audience, cross-legged, raised only on a few carpets. Nor is it an easy matter to see him, the light reaching not quite so far as the place where he sits, besides, that the audience is too short, and the person admitted to it, in so humble and submissive a posture, that he cannot well have an opportunity to hold up his head, and to view him. This audience is otherwise very awful and majestic, by reason chiefly of the silent presence of all the Counsellors of State, as also of many Princes and Lords of the Empire [i.e., daimyo and high-ranking officials in the shogunate], the Gentlemen of his Majesty's Bed-chamber [personal attendants], and other chief Officers of his Court, who line the hall of audience and all its avenues, sitting in good order and clad in their garments of ceremony.

Formerly all we had to do at the Emperor's court, was completed by the captain's [i.e., the head of the Dutch East India Company in Japan] paying him the usual homage, after the manner above related. A few days after, some laws concerning our trade and behavior were read to him, which, in the name of the Dutch, he promised to keep, and so was dispatch'd back to Nagasaki. But for about these twenty years last past, he and the rest of the Dutchmen, that came up with the Embassy to Jedo [Edo], were conducted deeper into the palace, to give the Empress and the Ladies of her court, and the Princesses of the Blood, the diversion of seeing us. In this the second audience, the Emperor, and the ladies invited to it, attend behind screens and lattices, but the Counsellors of State, and other Officers of the Court, sit in the open rooms, in their usual and elegant order. . . . The Emperor himself was in such an obscure place, that we should scarce have known him to be present, had not his voice discovered him, which yet was so low, as if he purposely intended to be there incognito. . . .

The mutual compliments being over, the succeeding part of this solemnity turn'd to a perfect farce. We were asked a thousand ridiculous and impertiment questions. Thus for instance, they desired to know, in the first place, how old each of us was, and what was his name, which we were commanded to write upon a bit of paper, having for these purposes took an European inkhorn along with us. This paper, together with the inkhorn itself, we were commanded to give to Bingo [an honorary title of Makino Narisada, a daimyo and a top official of the shogunate, who held the title "lord of Bingo"], who delivered them both into the Emperor's hands, reaching them over below the lattice. The Captain, or Ambassador, was asked concerning the distance of Holland from Batavia, and of Batavia [Jakarta, Indonesia] from Nagasaki? . . . As for my own particular the following questions were put to me: What external and internal distempers [illnesses] I thought the most dangerous, and most difficult to cure? How I proceeded in the cure of cancrous humors and imposthumations of the inner parts [cancers and internal abscesses]. Whether our European Physicians did not search after some Medicine to render people immortal, as the Chinese Physicians had done for many hundred years? Whether we had made any considerable progress in this search, and which was the last remedy conducive to long life, that had been found out in Europe? . . .

The Emperor who hitherto sat among the Ladies, almost opposite to us, at a considerable distance, did now draw nearer, and sat himself down on our right behind the lattices, as near us as possibly he could. Then he ordered us to take off our Cappa, or Cloak, being our Garment of Ceremony, then to stand upright, that he might have a full view of us; again to walk, to stand still, to complement each other, to dance, to jump, to play the drunkard, to speak broken Japanese, to read Dutch, to paint, to sing, to put our cloaks on and off. Mean while we obeyed the Emperor's commands in the best manner we could, I joined to my dance a love-song in High German. In this manner, and with innumerable such other apish tricks, we must suffer ourselves to contribute to the Emperor's and the Court's diversion.

Source: Adapted from Englebert Kaempfer (trans. J. G. Scheuchzer), *The History of Japan Together with a Description of the Kingdom of Siam, 1690–92*, vol. 3 (Glasgow: James MacLehose and Sons, 1906), 88–94.

Documents 5A and 5B   Weapons Control in Japanese Society: Toyotomi Hideyoshi's "Sword Hunt" (1588) and "A Local Ordinance Regarding Swords" (1648)

The following two documents, one from the sixteenth century and the other from the seventeenth, reveal the concerns of Japanese political leaders with bringing order to their society, which had been wracked by more than a century of warfare and great social fluidity. Although the first document ("Sword Hunt") below predates the seventeenth century, it had long-lasting effects on Japanese society for the entire Tokugawa period. Hideyoshi was not the first warlord of the late Warring States period to collect weapons from the countryside, but he was the first to attempt it on a national scale. As a result, the sword hunt put its stamp on Tokugawa Japan in that, together with policies that largely separated warrior (samurai) and peasants in physical terms, with samurai living in castle towns and peasants living in the countryside, it was instrumental in helping to clarify social occupations. The sword hunt played an important role in helping to distinguish between samurai and the peasantry, the latter of whom were to devote themselves exclusively to agricultural work and not to bear arms. All of these policies were key in the creation of what historians refer to as the status system (Jp., mibun seido) and to the promotion of civil peace.

Document 5A   Toyotomi Hideyoshi's "Sword Hunt" (1588)

1. The farmers of the various provinces are strictly forbidden to possess long swords, short swords, bows, spears, muskets, or any other form of weapon. If there are persons who maintain unnecessary implements, cause hardship in the collecting of annual taxes, and [thus] foment uprisings, or commit wrong acts toward the retainers, they shall, needless to say, be brought to judgment.

Since [in such cases] the paddies and dry fields of the places concerned will not be cultivated and the fiefs will be wasted, the lords of the provinces, the retainers, and the representatives shall therefore strictly collect all these weapons mentioned and deliver them [to us].

2. So that the long and short swords collected shall not be wasted, they shall be [melted down and] used as rivets and clamps in the forthcoming constructing of the Great Buddha. This will be an act by which the farmers will be saved in this life, needless to say, and in the life to come.

3. If farmers possess agricultural tools alone and engage [themselves] completely in cultivation, they shall [prosper] unto eternity, even to [the generations of] their children and grandchildren. [Thus] it is with compassion for the farmers that we rule in this manner. Truly [these orders] will be the foundation of the safety of the country and the happiness of all people. In another country the ruler Yao of China pacified the realm and [then] used precious swords and sharp blades as farming tools. There has been no [such] attempt] in our country. Observing the meaning [of our orders], and understanding their various purposes, the farmers shall invest their energies in agriculture and [the cultivation] of mulberry trees [for silkworms].

Collect the above-mentioned implements without fail and deliver them [to us].

Tenshô 16 [1588], Seventh Month, eighth day [Hideyoshi's red seal]

Source: Mary Elizabeth Berry, *Hideyoshi* (Cambridge, MA: Council on East Asian Studies, Harvard University, 1989), 102–103.

Document 5B   A Local Edo Ordinance Regarding Swords (1648)

Regarding commoners—

who wear long swords,
who wear short swords which are unnaturally long,
who impersonate members of the military class,
who appear strange [i.e. acting and/or behaving in an outlandish manner]
who act unruly or without propriety

Immediately upon noticing such persons, the authorities should apprehend them and explain to them that they are neither to impersonate samurai nor to wear the long sword; instructing them so that henceforth they shall not in any of their affairs act in such an unthinkable and improper manner.

Source: *Machibure*, Shôhô 5 (1648), Second Month, *Ofuregaki Kanpô shû* [Collected Circular Announcements of the Kanpô era] (Tokyo: Iwanami shoten, 1934), edict number 2882, 1305–1306.

Document 6   "An Account of the Hara-kiri," by Algernon B. Mitford, 1871

Harakiri, *also known more properly as* seppuku, *is one of the best-known practices or customs of the samurai. This account is an excerpt taken from an appendix of the book* Tales of Old Japan, *by Algernon B. Mitford, a diplomat in the British foreign service who worked in Japan for several years. It includes a general description of the practice of* seppuku *as well as his eyewitness account of one such ceremony that occurred in 1868.*

Seppuku (hara-kiri) is the mode of suicide adopted amongst Samurai when they have no alternative but to die. Some there are who thus commit suicide of their own free will; others there are who, having committed some crime which does not put them outside the pale of the privileges of the Samurai class, are ordered by their superiors to put an end to their own lives. It is needless to say that it is absolutely necessary that the principal, the witnesses, and the seconds who take part in the affair should be acquainted with all the ceremonies to be observed.

. . .

There are some who say that the perfect way for the second to cut off the head is not to cut right through the neck at a blow, but to leave a little uncut, and, as the head hangs by the skin, to seize the top-knot and slice it off, and then submit it for inspection. The reason of this is, lest, the head being struck off at a blow, the ceremony should be confounded with an ordinary execution. According to the old authorities, this is the proper and respectful manner. After the head is cut off, the eyes are apt to blink, and the mouth to move, and to bite the pebbles and sand. This being hateful to see, at what amongst Samurai is so important an occasion, and being a shameful thing, it is held to be best not to let the head fall, but to hold back a little in delivering the blow. Perhaps this may be right; yet it is a very difficult matter to cut so as to leave the head hanging by a little flesh, and there is the danger of missing the cut; and as any mistake in the cut is most horrible to see, it is better to strike a fair blow at once. Others say that, even when the head is struck off at a blow, the semblance of slicing it off should be gone through afterwards; yet be it borne in mind that; this is unnecessary.

. . .

. . . I may here describe an instance of such an execution which I was sent officially to witness. The condemned man was Taki Zenzaburô, an officer of the Prince of Bizen, who gave the order to fire upon the foreign settlement at Hyogo in the month of February 1868,—an attack to which I have alluded in the preamble to the story of the Eta Maiden and the Hatamoto. Up to that time no foreigner had witnessed such an execution, which was rather looked upon as a traveler's fable.

The ceremony, which was ordered by the Mikado [he actually means the shogun rather than the emperor] himself, took place at 10:30 at night in the temple of Seifukuji, the headquarters of the Satsuma troops at Hyogo. A witness was sent from each of the foreign legations. We were seven foreigners in all.

We were conducted to the temple by officers of the Princes of Satsuma and Choshu. Although the ceremony was to be conducted in the most private manner, the casual remarks which we overheard in the streets, and a crowd lining the principal entrance to the temple, showed that it was a matter of no little interest to the public. The courtyard of the temple presented a most picturesque sight; it was crowded with soldiers standing about in knots round large fires, which threw a dim flickering light over the heavy eaves and quaint gable-ends of the sacred buildings.

. . . [W]e were invited to follow the Japanese witnesses into the *hondo* or main hall of the temple, where the ceremony was to be performed. . . . The seven Japanese took their places on the left of the raised floor, the seven foreigners on the right. No other person was present. After an interval of a few minutes of anxious suspense, Taki Zenzaburô, a stalwart man, thirty-two years of age, with a noble air, walked into the hall attired in his dress of ceremony, with the peculiar hempen-cloth wings which are worn on great occasions. He was accompanied by a *kaishaku* [the "second" in a ritual suicide, the man charged with cutting off the head of the principal] and three officers, who wore the *jinbaori* or war surcoat with gold-tissue facings. . . . In this instance the *kaishaku* was a pupil of Taki Zenzaburô, and was selected by the friends of the latter from among their own number for his skill in swordsmanship.

With the *kaishaku* on his left hand, Taki Zenzaburô advanced slowly towards the Japanese witnesses, and the two bowed before them, then drawing near to the foreigners they saluted us in the same way, perhaps even with more deference: in each case the salutation was ceremoniously returned. Slowly, and with great dignity, the condemned man mounted on to the raised floor, prostrated himself before the high altar twice, and seated himself [i.e., in the Japanese manner, with his knees and toes touching the ground, and his body resting on his heels] on the felt carpet with his back to the high altar, the *kaishaku* crouching on his left-hand side. One of the three attendant officers then came forward, bearing a stand of the kind used in temples for offerings, on which, wrapped in paper, lay the *wakizashi*, the short sword or dirk of the Japanese, nine inches and a half in length, with a point and an edge as sharp as a razor's. This he handed, prostrating himself, to the condemned man, who received it reverently, raising it to his head with both hands, and placed it in front of himself.

After another profound obeisance, Taki Zenzaburô, in a voice which betrayed just so much emotion and hesitation as might be expected from a man who is making a painful confession, but with no sign of either in his face or manner, spoke as follows:—

> "I, and I alone, unwarrantably gave the order to fire on the foreigners at Kobe, and again as they tried to escape. For this crime I disembowel myself, and I beg you who are present to do me the honor of witnessing the act."

Bowing once more, the speaker allowed his upper garments to slip down to his girdle and remained naked to the waist. Carefully, according to custom, he tucked his sleeves under his knees to prevent himself from falling backwards; for a noble Japanese gentleman should die falling forwards. Deliberately, with a steady hand, he took the dirk that lay before him; he looked at it wistfully, almost affectionately; for a moment he seemed to collect his thoughts for the last time, and then stabbing himself deeply below the waist on the left-hand side, he drew the dirk slowly across to the right side, and, turning it in the wound, gave a slight cut upwards. During this sickeningly painful operation he never moved a muscle of his face. When he drew out the dirk, he leaned forward and stretched out his neck; an expression of pain for the first time crossed his face, but he uttered no sound. At that moment the *kaishaku*, who, still crouching by his side, had been keenly watching his every movement, sprang to his feet, poised his sword for a second in the air; there was a flash, a heavy, ugly thud, a crashing fall; with one blow the head had been severed from the body.

A dead silence followed, broken only by the hideous noise of the blood throbbing out of the inert heap before us, which but a moment before had been a brave and chivalrous man. It was horrible.

The *kaishaku* made a low bow, wiped his sword with a piece of paper which he had ready for the purpose, and retired from the raised floor; and the stained dirk was solemnly borne away, a bloody proof of the execution.

The two representatives of the Mikado then left their places, and, crossing over to where the foreign witnesses sat, called us to witness that the sentence of death upon Taki Zenzaburô had been faithfully carried out. The ceremony being at an end, we left the temple.

Source: Adapted from "An Account of the Hara-kiri," in Algernon B. Mitford, *Tales of Old Japan*, 263, 279, 281–284 (London: MacMillan and Company, 1910).

Document 7   An Account of *Junshi*: An Excerpt from François Caron's *A True Description of the Mighty Kingdoms of Japan and Siam* (1636)

Junshi *is a form of* seppuku *(also known as* harakiri*), a well-known practice of the samurai. It was a type of ritual suicide that was performed largely voluntarily upon the death of one's lord. This account is an excerpt from the book* A True Description of the Mighty Kingdoms of Japan and Siam, *written by François Caron (1600– 1673), a Frenchman in the employ of the Dutch East India Company, who lived in Japan from 1619 to 1641.*

When one of these Lords [i.e., daimyo] die, ten, twenty, or thirty of his vassals kill themselves to bear him company: many that do so, oblige themselves to it during their Lord's lives; for having received some more than ordinary grace and favor from him, and fancying themselves better beloved than their companions, they think it a shame to survive their benefactor; and therefore in return of their thanks they usually add, My Lord, the number of your faithful slaves is great, but what have I done to merit this honor? This body, which is indeed yours, I offer you again, and promise it shall not live longer than yours; I will not survive so worth a patron.

For confirmation of this they drink a bowl of wine together, which is solemn; for no covenants thus made are to be broken. Those that thus bind themselves cut their own bellies, and do it as follows: they assemble their nearest kindred, and going to church, they celebrate the parting feast upon mats and carpets in the midst of the Plain, where having well eat and drank, they cut up their bellies, so that the guts and entrails burst out; and he that cuts himself highest, as some do even to the throat, is counted the bravest fellow, and most esteemed. If the Lord cause a wall to be built, either for the King or himself, his Servants often times beg they might have the honor to lie under, out of a belief, that what is founded upon a living mans flesh, is subject to misfortune: This request being granted, they go with joy unto the designed place, and lying down there, suffer the foundation stones to be laid upon them, which with their weight, immediately bruise and shiver them to pieces."

Source: François Caron, *A True Description of the Mighty Kingdoms of Japan and Siam* (translation by Roger Manley of original Dutch version of 1636) (London: Samuel Broun & John de l'Ecluse, 1663), 49–51.

Document 8 Yamaga Sokô on *The Way of the Samurai* (*shidô*)

The following text is an excerpt from a longer work entitled The Way of the Samurai *(Shidô), written by Yamaga Sokô (1622–1685), a noted Confucian scholar as well as an expert in military science. He wrote the text sometime during the middle part of the seventeenth century, after the Shimabara Rebellion, the last major armed conflict for more than two centuries. Given the new conditions of peace, Yamaga was concerned about the inactivity of samurai. Accordingly, he tried to articulate a new role for the samurai, who had a long history in Japan as warriors with a proud martial tradition. Yamaga had been a student of the Chinese Confucian classics since a young age. In this text he applied the Confucian ideal of the "superior man" to the samurai in Japan (he used the same Chinese word,* shi *("superior man" or "gentleman") to describe both of them.*

. . . Generation after generation men have taken their livelihood from tilling the soil, or devised and manufactured tools, or produced profit from mutual trade, so that peoples' needs were satisfied. Thus the occupations of farmer, artisan, and merchant necessarily grew up as complementary to one another. However, the samurai eats food without growing it, uses utensils without manufacturing them, and profits without buying or selling. What is the justification for this? . . . The samurai is one who does not cultivate, does not manufacture, and does not engage in trade, but it cannot be that he has no function at all as a samurai. He who satisfied his needs without performing any function at all would more properly be called an idler. Therefore one must devote all one's mind to the detailed examination of one's calling.

Human beings aside, does any creature in the land—bird or animal, lowly fish or insect, or insentient plant or tree—fulfill its nature by being idle? Birds and beasts fly and run to find their own food; fish and insects seek their food as they go about with one another. . . . None of them has any respite from seeking food, . . . Among men, the farmers, artisans, and merchants also do the same. One who lives his whole life without working should be called a rebel against heaven. Hence we ask ourselves how it can be that the samurai should have no occupation; and it is only then as we inquire into the function of the samurai, that [the nature of] his calling becomes apparent. . . .

. . . The business of samurai consists in reflecting on his own station in life, in discharging loyal service to his master if he has one, in deepening his fidelity in associations with friends, and, with due consideration of his own position, in devoting himself to duty above all. . . . The samurai dispenses with the business of the farmer, artisan, and merchants and confines himself to practice this Way [i.e., "the way of the samurai"]; should there be someone in the three classes of the common people [i.e., farmer, artisan, and merchant] who transgresses against these moral principles, the samurai summarily punishes him and thus upholds proper moral principles in the land. It would not do for the samurai to know the martial and civil virtues without manifesting them. Since this is the case, outwardly he stands in physical readiness for any call to service and inwardly he strives to fulfill the Way of the lord and subject, friend and friend, father and son, older and younger brother, and husband and wife. Within his heart he keeps to the ways of peace, but without he keeps his weapons ready for use. The three classes of the common people make him their teacher and respect him. By following his teachings, they are enabled to understand what is fundamental and what is secondary. . . .

Source: Ryusaku Tsunoda, Wm. Theodore de Bary, and Donald Keene, compilers, *Sources of Japanese Tradition*, vol. 1 (New York: Columbia University Press, 1958), 389–91. Reprinted with permission.

Documents 9A and 9B   Private Vengeance among the Samurai [Documents 9A, "A Letter from a Daimyo's Official in Echigo Province to an Official of the Tokugawa Shogunate" and 9B, "A Letter of Authorization" (1828)]

The following two documents concern the case of two samurai, brothers whose father had been murdered. The first document is a daimyo's official's report to a local official of the Tokugawa shogunate informing him of the request of two brothers from his domain to seek out and kill the man who had murdered their father. It also makes note of the fact that the father's brother had also, separately, sought permission to avenge his slain elder brother. The second document is the letter authorizing the two sons to embark on their mission. A separate letter of authorization—not included here—was sent to the murdered man's brother, praising him, granting him leave and permission to assist his nephews, and giving him an increase in stipend. It also makes note of the fact that domain officials had given the eldest son a valuable sword and a considerable sum of money (20 ryô) to help him achieve his mission.

Document 9A   A Letter from a Daimyo's Official in Echigo Province to an Official of the Tokugawa Shogunate (1828)

Retainers of Mizoguchi Hôki-no-kami:

Kume Kôtarô—son, aged 18
Kume Seitarô—son, aged 15
Itakura Tomegorô—younger brother, aged 43

The father of the above named Kôtarô and Seitarô, Kume Yagobei, was in the twelfth month of 1817 killed in his home town by his associate Takizawa Kyûe-mon, who then made his escape, and although a careful search was made in the neighborhood and even further afield, could not be traced. In the third month of the following year, the affair was reported and registered in the official record. At the time, the brothers were still very young, but now, having grown to mature age, they have recently applied for permission to seek out their enemy wherever he may be, not only in the immediate vicinity but also in Edo or even in some other province, and as soon as they find him to carry out revenge on him. The above-named Tomegorô, being the younger brother of Yagobei, also wishes to avenge his brother, and since the two sons will have no recollection of Kyûemon's appearance, having been so young at the time, Tomegorô has applied for permission to join them. This is hereby registered. Of course, they have been instructed to report to the local officials if they succeed in killing Kyûemon. Therefore, it is requested that the matter should be entered in the official records . . .

28th of the 4th Month of 1828

Kawamura Hatsutarô [retainer to Mizoguchi Hôki-no-kami]

Source: D. E. Mills, "*Katakiuchi*: The Practice of Blood-Revenge in Pre-Modern Japan." *Modern Asian Studies,* 10(4) (1976), 525.

Document 9B   A Letter of Authorization (1828)

Concerning your request that you and your brother Seitarô be given leave to track down and kill Takizawa Kyûemon, the enemy of your late father Yagobei, instructions have been issued that you be given leave as requested. You may set out as soon as you wish. The matter has been duly notified and registered at the local office of the Bakufu [shogunate], the office of the local commissioner, and a copy of the entry is furnished herewith. If all goes well and you succeed in killing your enemy, you must comply with the regulations and report the circumstances to the local officials. In addition, you must report to our own daimyo's mansion in Edo or to this headquarters, whichever is nearer. The allotment of rice to support your family will be continued so that you need have no worries to distract you from the achievement of your goal.

However, you should be careful to avoid violating the sanctity of Edo Castle, the two temples [Zôjôji and Kan'eiji temples, located in Edo, both having important connections to the Tokugawa shogunate], and other such places. Of course if you should receive news that Kyûemon is dead, you should obtain definite proof of that fact and return home.

Source: D. E. Mills, "*Katakiuchi*: The Practice of Blood-Revenge in Pre-Modern Japan." *Modern Asian Studies,* 10(4) (1976), 525–526.

Document 10   Kumazawa Banzan on Samurai Self-Discipline and Training

The author, Kumazawa Banzan (1619–1691), was the son of a rônin. His mother was the daughter of a samurai in the service of the daimyo of Mito domain. Through the introduction of a well-connected distant relative, in 1634, at age fifteen Banzan was able to obtain a position as a page under the Ikeda Mitsumasa, the daimyo of Okayama, whom he served for five years. During this time he traveled to Edo in the lord's entourage on two occasions. His period of service, not to mention the two trips to the Tokugawa capital, gave Banzan important life experience that served him well in his later career. During this time he exhibited great ambition to become a model samurai. He describes some of his efforts at self-discipline and training below, as excerpted from his autobiography. He was motivated largely by the decline in physical readiness that he perceived in samurai. This, he thought, could endanger Japan, should the Manchus, who had just completed their conquest of China, decide to invade Japan as their ancestors, the Mongols, had. At the end of the Tokugawa period, Banzan's ideas were an inspiration to Meiji Restoration leaders who had similar fears of a foreign invasion.

"When I was about sixteen I had a tendency toward corpulence. I had noticed a lack of agility in other fleshy persons and thought that a heavy man would not make a first-class *samurai*. So I tried every device to keep myself agile and lean. I slept with my girdle drawn tight and stopped eating rice. I took no wine and abstained from sexual intercourse for the next ten years. While on duty at Yedo [Edo] there were no hills and fields at hand where I could hunt and climb, so I exercised with spear and sword. When I was on the night watch at my master's residence at Yedo, I kept a wooden sword and a pair of straw sandals in my bamboo hamper with which I used to put myself through military drill alone in the dark court after everyone was asleep. I also practiced running about over the roofs of the out buildings far removed from the sleeping rooms. This I did so as to be able to handle myself nimbly if a fire should break out. There were very few who noticed me at these exercises and they were reported to have said that I was probably possessed by a hobgoblin (*tengu*). This was before I was twenty years old and in my zeal I overdid a little. After that I hardened myself by going into the fields on hot summer days and shooting skylarks with a gun, as I did not own a falcon for hawking. In the winter months I often spent several days in the mountains taking no night clothes or bed quilt with me, but wearing only a lined jacked of cotton over a thin cotton shirt. My little hamper was almost filled by my inkstand, paper and books, and two wadded silk kimono. I stayed overnight in any house I came across in my rambles. In such ways I disciplined myself until I was thirty-seven or eight years old and avoided becoming fleshy. I was fully aware of my want of talent and believed I could never hope to be of any great service to my country, so I was all the more resolved to do my best as a common *samurai*. There are perhaps some old men who remember even yet how active I was in those days."

Source: Galen M. Fisher, "Kumazawa Banzan: His Life and Ideas." *Transactions of the Asiatic Society of Japan*, Second Series, 16 (1938), 230–231.

Document 11   Archery and the Martial Arts: Hinatsu Shirôzaemon Shigetaka's *Honchô Bugei Shôden* (*A Short Tale of the Martial Arts in Our Country*, 1714)

During the years of warfare prior to the Tokugawa period, samurai had frequent occasion to use the weapons with which they trained. However, with the onset of the "Great Peace" under the Tokugawa shoguns there was hardly any occasion for samurai to use their weapons in combat. As a result of peacetime conditions, bat-tlefield skills were transformed into the martial arts, often practiced in interior halls and in a nonlethal manner. This document is from the oldest narrative survey history of the classical Japanese martial arts. It was written by Hinatsu Shirôzaemon Shigetaka, the son of a master practitioner of the naginata, a weapon like a Euro-pean halberd, which consisted of a wooden shaft with a curved blade on the end and a guard, similar to those on swords, between the blade and shaft. The segment that appears below is from chapter three: Archery.

Document 11   Excerpt from Hinatsu Shirôzaemon Shigetaka's *Honchô Bugei Shôden* (1714)

Asaoka Heibei was from Kiyosu in Owari. He studied archery under Chi-kurin Josei. On the 19th day, First Month, Keichô 11 [1606], he succeeded in shooting fifty-one arrows the entire length of the Sanjûsangen-dô. Contending for first place by shooting at the Hall [to see who could shoot the greatest number of arrows successfully] began with Asaoka. Twenty-six archers later became known as the Great Archers of the Hall: Ueda Kakubei, Tsutsui Dembei, Shioya Kakuzaemon, . . .

In a certain book it is written that shooting a fixed number of arrows at the Sanjûsangen-dô does nothing to further the art of archery. This is because study in the art of archery in former times emphasized proper form and did not stress the number of arrows a man could shoot. Technique must be correct for an arrow to hit the target, so those wishing to do this must study and practice the art of archery. Thus as long as archery places its goal on hitting the target, the Way of the bow and arrow will not decline. But seeing how many arrows a man can shoot the length of the hall is a feat accomplished by the strength of the archer and his bow. When a man sets his goal on seeing how many arrows he can shoot the length of the Hall, he stresses strength and does not practice technique; as a result the Way of the bow and arrow cannot but decline. . . .

In the *Analects* it is written, 'In archery it is not going through the leather which is the principal thing;—because people's strength is not equal.' 'Going through leather' refers to the depth to which the arrow penetrates the target. But people today think that being able to shoot scores of arrows the length of the Sanjûsan-gen-dô is true archery. They are quite wrong, for this is merely the Way of strength.

Furthermore, the original purpose of shooting arrows the length of the Sanjû-sangen-dô was not the same as the intention of the people today who try to see how many arrows they can shoot. Shooting at the Hall was originally a test con-sisting of shooting ten arrows so that a man's form could be evaluated. Despite this, people nowadays shoot countless arrows, trying to get as many as possible to travel the length of the Hall. As this is their sole purpose, it goes without saying that the Way of archery as technique will decline. The reason why these archers cannot shoot the length of the Hall is because their form is not right. All the more reason why they should try to correct their form.

Confucius said, 'Shooting the bow is much like the way of the gentleman [refers to the Chinese term *junzi*, or "the superior man," a Confucian term describing the ideal person]. When one misses the mark, one must look for the cause within himself.' It is wrong for those learning archery to set the Sanjûsangen-dô as their goal."

Source: Hinatsu Shigetaka, "Honchô Bugei Shôden." *Monumenta Nipponica,* 45(3) (1990), 282–284.

Document 12   Remonstration of Retainer Asahina Genba, Addressed to Tosa Domain (Heir) Yamauchi Toyofusa (May 18, 1696)

Senior-level retainers had the privilege of submitting written petitions to their over-lord. They might do so to propose a new policy idea, to argue against a current policy, or even to remonstrate against the personal behavior. In the example below, a senior adviser named Asahina Genba is remonstrating not with the lord or daimyo, but rather with the daimyo's heir, Yamauchi Toyofusa, who served as heir from 1689 to 1700 and then later reigned as daimyo from 1700 to 1706. At the time of this peti-tion, Toyofusa had therefore been heir for about seven years, but he had not yet visited the domain of Tosa nor had he even requested official permission from the shogunate to do so, as required. It was customary for heirs to travel to the domains over which they were to rule as part of the alternate attendance system. It was also an expectation of the top domain officials, as the experience was important to the heir's education before becoming the ruling lord. In the document below, Asahina, as Toyofusa's chief retainer, remonstrates with him, telling him that most daimyo heirs of his status had already made a number of trips to the domain. Asahina's language is polite but nonetheless forceful in its message.

"What I will write here is what others have wanted to say, but have been unable to do so. I have refrained from doing so until now, though, as it may seem that I am only recommending this course because I have been given leave to return to Tosa [and hence as his close retainer would selfishly want Toyofusa to return as well]. You have not asked for permission for a leave from your duties in Edo (*oitoma*), but it is already past the time for returning to the domain (*kôtai*). Since there will be no trip this year, I can now offer these words.

Two years ago you had the opportunity to travel to Tosa but because you were sick, did not request permission to do so. This year it is of course already too late. With great deference, I must say that the shogun has no doubt noticed this. Most daimyo heirs of your status [from province-holding daimyo houses] have already been home twice [during the period you have been in Edo], but you have missed the opportunities and have not requested leave, even when you had gone for audi-ences to Edo castle. This may lead to rumors that your illness is grave; or that there is some discord between you and the lord? People may be wondering whether you have postponed making the trip to Tosa because you lack the ability to govern. Surely many think it is suspicious that you have overlooked such an important matter as this. . . .

If you continue to miss opportunities to return to the domain people will think that it is because you lack the ability to govern. There could be nothing worse for a person of your status than if people from across the country begin to criticize you. . . .

Claiming illness, you have not performed your duties for five or six years, and this has caused lord Toyomasa great hardship. Nothing is of greater consequence to our domain than this problem. The lord does not know how this situation will resolve itself, but the future looks dark to him. [I repeat,] there is nothing of greater importance to the domain than this.

I have been in your personal service here in this place [Edo] for five years. The income granted me is abundant and my domestic finances have therefore not been adversely affected by my stay in Edo. I have performed my duty without recourse to loans of rice or silver from our Lord. I have had no concerns about the well-being of my wife and children in Tosa.

There are others, however, who have been here for eight years [that is, since Toyofusa became heir], performing their duty night and day. They have been unable to look after their families' affairs in Tosa and have suffered financial difficulties."

There is, for example, your retainer Nakayama Gen'emon, who has no heir yet and must therefore adopt a son. If other retainers such as Murata Sh|hachi, Miyagawa Seijirô, Shibuya Jihei, Asada Ridayû, and Iwasaki Shôzaemon had been allowed to return home, they would already have married, had children, and been leading settled lives. They would not have to leave the care of their aged parents to their relatives. There is no limit to the number of such stories one hears about the lower ranks of the retainer corps as well. Those of low status (*karuki mono*) are unable to lead normal married lives. While they do not formally sever their matrimonial ties, they are forced to live apart. This brings much grief to several hundred people, who face financial and other serious difficulties. . . ."

Source: Mutô Yoshikazu, compiler and author, *Nanroshi. Tosa kokushi shiryô shûsei.* Yorimitsu Kanji, Akizawa Shigeru, and others, eds., vol. 9, 396–397 (Kôchi: Kôchi Prefectural Library, 1997).

Documents 13A and 13B   Economic Problems Facing Samurai

13A   Letter from Tani Tannai to Saitaniya Hachirôbei Naomasu (1751) 13B Excerpts from a Statement from Three Village Leaders to a Tokugawa Bannerman (1856)

The first document is a letter from the samurai and Confucian scholar Tani Tannai (or Mashio, 1729–1797) to the merchant Saitaniya Hachirôbei Naomasu (1705–1779). The letter was one of a number exchanged by the two men that Tani copied into his ledger, Record of Daily Necessities (Nichiyô beien roku, 1748–1754), which literally means "Record of the daily necessities of rice and salt." In terms of income, Tannai was a lower-ranking samurai, earning 24 koku in rice.

The second selection is a statement from three village leaders to a Tokugawa bannerman, dating from 1856. This bannerman had a fief or domain of 700 koku of rice and was descended from a daimyo; in other words, he was a samurai of some substance. The village leaders were peasants, and their village was part of the bannerman's domain, bequeathed to him by the Tokugawa shogun, from which he derived his income.

Document 13A   Letter from Tani Tannai to Saitaniya Hachirôbei Naomasu (1751)

1751/1/30

To: Saitaniya Hachirôbei

Thank you for your hospitality and the leisurely talk we enjoyed last night. And thank you as well for having sent [my servant] Shin-no-jô to deliver a message from you. When my father Tanshirô returns from Edo he must call on you to pay his respects.

I have thought a lot about what you wrote in your letter (of the previous 6/13) and am resolved to do my best. My repayment scheme is laid out below. Please inform me if I am in error:

The 18 *koku* [a unit of measurement for rice, equivalent to about five bushels] of my stipend which remains after the loan to the lord, at a market rate of 50 *monme/ koku* [a unit of silver; 45 *monme* were roughly equivalent to 1 *koku* of rice], converts to 900 *monme*; divided by 13 months [he includes the intercalary month], this gives me a budget of 69 *monme*/month. Consequently, I will need to borrow 270.68 *monme* for the period from the first day of the Second Month until the middle of the Fifth Month. Please divide the monthly payment in two and dispense the funds to me on the first and sixteenth days.

When my father Tanshirô returns from Edo sometime in the middle of the Fifth Month, he should bring back five or six *ryô* [a unit of gold; 5–6 *ryô* was equivalent to 300 or 360 *monme* silver], and from this the above-mentioned loan will be repaid. If he does not bring back enough money, I will repay you from my Summer payment of 6 *koku*. . . . In this case, I would require another loan until the end of the year.

At the end of the year I will be appointed for Edo duty [i.e., to accompany the daimyo of Tosa to Edo], and will use the 22 *koku* service allowance [a special support allowance for samurai retainers serving their lord in Edo], which at a rate of 50 *monme/koku*, converts to one *kan* 100 *me*, for repayment of my various new loans of 598 *monme*. . . .

Given the above, I will not be able to pay back the old loans next year. Moreover, although I will receive a subsidy for Edo service next year, those funds will be needed to maintain myself there. However, should some money remain from them, it can be applied to the loans—but it probably will not be very much.

If Tanshirô returns from Edo the year after next with some funds, that money can be applied toward my own loans. Should I be appointed again at the end of the year for Edo service, the entire advance payment of 10 *koku* can also be applied to the loan. I am resolved that things will work out in this manner. Moreover, if the forced loans cease, those funds can all be applied toward repayment.

Financial affairs do not ordinarily proceed as planned, but I have nevertheless laid out my ideas above. If my thinking is mistaken, please let me know. Since tomorrow is a fortuitous day, I hope that you can do as I have written and dispense 60 *monme*, one-third of the loan, at that time.

Tani Tannai

Source: Constantine N. Vaporis, "Samurai and Merchant in Mid-Tokugawa Japan: Tani Tannai's *Record of Daily Necessities* (1748–54)." *Harvard Journal of Asiatic Studies,* 60(1) (2000), 25–27. Based on the original document: Tani Tannai, "Nichiyô beien roku" (1748–1754), housed in Kôchi prefectural library, Kôchi, Japan.

Document 13B   Excerpts from a Statement from Three Village Leaders to a Tokugawa Bannerman (1856)

1. Because of your promise to reduce expenditures, we have, during the past years, advanced tax rice and made loans. However, we see no sign of any efforts to achieve necessary reductions in expenditures;

2. Your brother is an immoral idler. As long as such a person is supported by your household, there is little chance of reducing expenditures. Last winter, we asked that some actions be taken against your brother. What is your plan?

3. You have more than six servants including maids and horsemen. Some should be dismissed;

4. Your representative asked us if we could assist in negotiating a further loan. Even if a low interest loan were to be made to you, it would be of little use as long as you have your useless brother. The temple from which you hope to borrow does not know that you already have 200 *ryô* in debt, but you know that you already have a large debt;

5. What is the purpose of your debt? As far as we can determine, you are sufficiently provided for; and,

6. To keep your brother is uneconomical. If no action is taken, we intend to resign our post as village leaders.

Source: Kozo Yamamura, *A Study of Samurai Income and Entrepreneurship* (Cambridge, MA: Harvard University Press, 1974), 47–48.

Document 14   The Gap between Upper and Lower Samurai: Fukuzawa Yukichi's *Kyûhanjô* ("Conditions in an Old Feudal Domain," 1877)

Fukuzawa Yukichi (1835–1901) was a samurai, a retainer of the Lord Okudaira of Nakatsu, a middle-sized domain in the northern part of Kyushu, the southernmost island of Japan. He was one of approximately 1,500 men that made up the retainer corps, but his family was among those households that made up the lower two-thirds. He was a man of great intellectual abilities and was acutely aware of the vast differences between himself, as a lower samurai, and his social superiors. In later sections of the text (not excerpted here) he goes on to describe other differences between upper and lower samurai in terms of education, household economy, and general customs.

Document 14   Differences among the Samurai: Excerpts from Fukuzawa Yukichi's *Kyûhanjô* ("Conditions in an Old Feudal Domain," 1877)

Differences in Rights

A lower samurai, whatever his merit or talents, could never rise above an upper samurai. There were a few examples of men rising from the position of calligrapher, for instance, to that of a member of the *koshôgumi* [from the lower ranks among the upper samurai], but not more than four or five during the whole period of 250 years. A lower samurai might therefore aspire to promotion within his own class, but he would no more hope to enter the ranks of the upper samurai than would a four-legged beast hope to fly like a bird. . . .

An *ashigaru* [lowest rank among lower samurai] always had to prostrate himself on the ground in the presence of an upper samurai. If he should encounter an upper samurai on the road in the rain, he had to take off his *geta* and prostrate himself by the roadside. Even those of the rank of *koyakunin*, superior to the *ashigaru*, were required by law to prostrate themselves on the ground when they encountered the Chief Minister, or indeed any one of the upper samurai with the duties of *yônin* [i.e., high-ranking samurai officials serving in close attendance on the lord]. When a lower samurai came to the house of an upper samurai, he was required to make his salutation in the anteroom before entering the room where the upper samurai sat. When an upper samurai came to the house of a lower samurai, however, he could take his sword with him right into the main front room.

. . . In spoken forms of address all upper samurai, regardless of age, addressed lower samurai as 'Kisama', while lower samurai addressed upper samurai as 'Anata.' . . .

Upper samurai were allowed to have *shikidai* [i.e., a wooden step in the anteroom] in the entrance halls of their houses, whereas this privilege was denied to the lower samurai. Upper samurai rode on horseback; lower samurai went on foot. Upper samurai possessed the privileges of hunting wild boar and fishing; lower samurai had no such privileges. Sometimes it even happened that a lower samurai was refused formal permission to go to another province to study, on the score that learning was not considered proper to his station. . . . Suffice to say that although there were minute distinctions of rank within both the upper and lower classes, yet these were not rigid and immovable. The broad distinction between the upper and lower classes was, however, accepted unquestioningly, almost as though it were a law of nature rather than an invention of man.

Differences in Customs

Upper samurai were sometimes called by the general name of *kyûnin*, while the lower samurai went by the name of *kachi* or *koyakunin*. Under no circumstances was marriage permitted between those of the rank of *kyûnin* and those of the rank of *kachi*. Such alliances were forbidden both by clan [domain] law and by custom. Even in cases of adultery, both parties nearly always came from the same class.

Differences in Income

The differences in rank within the upper class naturally carried with them considerable differences in stipend. The Chief Minister received one or two thousand *koku*, sometimes even more. . . . Generally speaking, however, the average income of an upper samurai was quoted at about 100, 200 or 250 *koku*, and worked out net at anything from 22 to 60 *koku*. . . .

The lower samurai, on the other hand, received stipends of fifteen *koku* plus rations for three, thirteen *koku* plus rations for two, or ten *koku* plus rations for one. Some received a money stipend of even less than this. Those of middle rank and above received a net income no higher than from seven to ten *koku*. At this rate a man and his wife living alone might manage without hardship, but if there were four of five children or old people in the family, this income was not sufficient to cover even the necessities of life such as food and clothing. Hence everyone in the family capable of work, both men and women alike, eked out a poor livelihood by odd jobs such as spinning and handicrafts. These jobs might in theory be mere sidework, but in fact the samurai came to regard them as their main occupation, relegating their official clan duties to the position of sidework. These men were therefore not true samurai.

Source: Fukuzawa Yukichi (trans. Carmen Blacker), "Kyûhanjô." *Monumenta Nipponica*, 9(1–2) (1953), 309–311.

Document 15   Sakamoto Ryôma's "Eight-Point Program While Shipboard", 1867

Sakamoto Ryôma (1836–1867) was a low-ranking samurai from Tosa domain, on Shikoku Island. He was a major figure in the movement to overthrow the Tokugawa shogunate. This he achieved in part by negotiating a secret alliance between Chôshû and Satsuma domains. He was also instrumental in the negotiations that led to the voluntary resignation of the last Tokugawa shogun, Yoshinobu, in 1867, which resulted in the Meiji Restoration. In this document Ryôma listed his proposals for the major reforms he deemed necessary for Japan. These proposals are widely believed to form the basis for the parliamentary system of government implemented after his death. He is also considered by some the "father of the Japanese Navy," and his views on the importance of a strong naval force are evident in his proposals below.

1. Political power of the entire county should be returned to the Imperial Court, and all decrees should be issued by the Court.
2. There should be established an Upper and a Lower Legislative House which should participate in making decisions pertaining to all governmental policies. All governmental policies should be decided on the basis of deliberation openly arrive at (*kôgi*).
3. Men of ability among the court nobles, daimyo and people at large should be appointed as councilors and receive appropriate offices and titles. Those sinecure positions of the past should be abolished.

4. In dealing with foreign countries, appropriate regulations should be newly established which would take into account broadly the deliberation openly arrived at.

5. The laws and regulations (*ritsuryô*) of earlier times should be scrutinized [to preserve only those provisions which are still applicable], and a great new code to last forever should be promulgated.

6. The navy should be properly expanded.

7. An Imperial Guard [directly controlled by the Imperial Court, and not dependent on the *bakufu* or various domains] should be set up to defend the capital.

8. There should be a law established to equalize the value of gold, silver and goods with those of foreign countries.

The above eight-point program is proposed after due consideration of the present state of affairs in the nation. When this is proclaimed both internally and externally to all the countries, it becomes inconceivable to think of engaging in the urgent talk of alleviating the current crisis outside of this program. If with determination these policies are carried out, the fortunes of His Majesty will be restored, national strength will increase, and it will not be difficult to attain the position of equality with all other nations. We pray that based on the enlightened and righteous reason (*dôri*), the Imperial Government will act decisively to undertake the path of renewal and reform of the country.

Source: Iwasaki Hideshige, *Sakamoto Ryôma kankei monjo* [Documents Relating to Sakamoto Ryôma], vol. 1, 1925, 297–298. Tokyo. Reprinted in David J. Lu, *Japan. A Documentary History. The Late Tokugawa Period to the Present* (Armonk, NY: M. E. Sharpe, 1997), 301–302.

Selected Bibliography

Arai, Hakuseki. *Lessons from History: Arai Hakuseki's Tokushi Yoron*. Translated by Joyce Ackroyd. Brisbane, Australia: University of Queensland Press, 1982.

Arai, Hakuseki. *Told Round a Brushwood Fire: The Autobiography of Arai Hakuseki*. Princeton, NJ: Princeton University Press, 1980.

Art of Armor: Samurai Armor from the Ann and Gabriel Barbier-Mueller Collection. Dallas, TX: Ann and Gabriel Barbier-Mueller Museum; New Haven: Yale University Press, 2012.

Beasley, William G., ed. *Select Documents on Japanese Foreign Policy, 1853–1868*. London: Oxford University Press, 1955.

Beasley, William G. *The Meiji Restoration*. Stanford, CA: Stanford University Press, 1972.

Benesch, Oleg. *Inventing the Way of the Samurai: Nationalism, Internationalism, and Bushido in Modern Japan*. Oxford: Oxford University Press, 2014.

Benesch, Oleg, and Ran Zwigenberg. *Japan's Castles: Citadels of Modernity in War and Peace*. Cambridge: Cambridge University Press, 2019.

Berry, Elizabeth. *Hideyoshi*. Cambridge, MA: Harvard University Press, 1982.

Bissonnette, Denise L., coordination; translation, Judith Terry and Shiro Noda. *The Japan of the Shoguns: The Tokugawa Collection*. Montreal: Montreal Museum of Fine Arts, 1989.

Bitô, Masahide. "The Akô Incident, 1701–1703." *Monumenta Nipponica,* 58 (2003), 149–170.

Bodart-Bailey, Beatrice M., ed. and trans. *Kaempfer's Japan: Tokugawa Culture Observed*. Honolulu: University of Hawai'i Press, 1999.

Bodart-Bailey, Beatrice M. *The Dog Shogun: The Personality and Policies of Tokugawa Tsunayoshi*. Honolulu: University of Hawai'i Press, 2006.

Bolitho, Harold. *Treasures among Men: The Fudai Daimyo in Tokugawa Japan*. New Haven, CT: Yale University Press, 1974.

Bolitho, Harold. "The *Han*." In John Whitney Hall, ed., *Cambridge History of Japan*, vol. 4: *Early Modern Japan*, 183–234. Cambridge: Cambridge University Press, 1991.

Botsman, Dani. *Punishment and Power in the Making of Modern Japan*. Princeton, NJ: Princeton University Press, 2005.

Bottomley, Ian, and Anthony Hopson. *Arms and Armour of the Samurai: The History of Weaponry in Ancient Japan*. New York: Gramercy Publishing Company, 1993.

Brown, Philip C. *Central Authority and Local Autonomy in the Formation of Early Modern Japan: The Case of Kaga Domain*. Stanford, CA: Stanford University Press, 1993.

Callahan, Caryl, and Ihara Saikaku. "Tales of Samurai Honor: Saikaku's *Buke Giri Monogatari*." *Monumenta Nipponica,* 34(1) (1979), 1–20.

Cleary, Thomas, trans. *Code of the Samurai: A Modern Translation of the Bushido Shoshinshu*. Boston: Tuttle Publishing, 1999.

Cleary, Thomas, ed. *Training the Samurai Mind: A Bushido Sourcebook*. New York: Random House, 2008.

Coaldrake, William H. *Architecture and Authority in Japan*. London and New York: Routledge, 1996.

Conlan, Thomas. *State of War: The Violent Order of Fourteenth-Century Japan*. Ann Arbor Center for Japanese Studies, University of Michigan, 2003.

Conlan, Thomas. *Weapons and Fighting Techniques of the Samurai Warrior, 1200–1877*. London: Amber, 2008.

Cooper, Michael, ed. *They Came to Japan: An Anthology of European Reports on Japan, 1543–1640*. London: Thames and Hudson, 1965.

Craig, Albert M. *Chôshû in the Meiji Restoration*. Cambridge, MA: Harvard University Press, 1961.

"Diary of an Official of the Bakufu." *Transactions, Asiatic Society of Japan*, Second Series, 8 (1930), 98–119.

Dore, Ronald P. *Education in Tokugawa Japan*. Berkeley: University of California Press, 1965.

Earl, David. *Emperor and Nation in Japan: Political Thinkers of the Tokugawa Period*. Seattle: University of Washington Press, 1964.

Elison, George, and Bardwell L. Smith, eds. *Warriors, Artists, and Commoners: Japan in the Sixteenth Century*. Honolulu: University of Hawai'i Press, 1981.

Fisher, Galen M. "Kumazawa Banzan, His Life and Ideas." *Transactions, Asiatic Society of Japan*, Second Series, 16 (1938), 223–258.

Friday, Karl L. *Samurai, Warfare, and the State in Early Medieval Japan*. New York and London: Routledge, 2004.

Fukuzawa Yukichi. *The Autobiography of Fukuzawa Yukichi*. Revised translation by Eiichi Kiyooka; with a foreword by Albert Craig. New York: Columbia University Press, 2007.

Gerhart, Karen M. *The Eyes of Power: Art and Early Tokugawa Authority*. Honolulu: University of Hawai'i Press, 1999.

Gerstle, C. Andrew. "Heroic Honor: Chikamatsu and the Samurai Ideal." *Harvard Journal of Asiatic Studies,* 57(2) (1997), 307–381.

Hall, John C. "Japanese Feudal Laws III—The Tokugawa Legislation, Parts I–III." *Transactions, Asiatic Society of Japan*, First Series, 38 (1911), 269–331.

Hall, John C. "Japanese Feudal Laws IV—The Tokugawa Legislation, Part IV." *Transactions, Asiatic Society of Japan*, First Series, 41 (1913), 683–804.

Hall, John W. "The Castle Town and Japan's Modern Urbanization." *Far Eastern Quarterly,* 15 (1955), 37–56. (Republished in Hall and Jansen, *Studies in the Institutional History of Early Modern Japan*.)

Hall, John W. *Tanuma Okitsugu, 1719–1788: Forerunner of Modern Japan*. Cambridge, MA: Harvard University Press, 1955.

Hall, John W. "Rule by Status in Tokugawa Japan." *Journal of Japanese Studies,* 3(2) (1977), 365–374.

Hall, John W., and Marius B. Jansen, eds. *Studies in the Institutional History of Early Modern Japan*. Princeton, NJ: Princeton University Press, 1968.

Hall, John W., and James L. McClain, eds. *The Cambridge History of Japan*, vol. 4: *Early Modern Japan*. Cambridge: Cambridge University Press, 1991.

Hanley, Susan B. *Everyday Things in Premodern Japan: The Hidden Legacy of Material Culture*. Berkeley: University of California Press, 1997.

Hashimoto, Fumio. *Architecture in the Shoin Style: Japanese Feudal Residences*. New York: Kodansha International, 1981.

Hesselink, Reinier H. "The Warrior's Prayer: Tokugawa Yoshimune Revives the Yabusame Ceremony." *Journal of Asian Martial Arts,* 4(4) (1995), 41–49.

Hinago, Moto. *Japanese Castles*. New York: Kodansha International, 1986.

Hira, Kiyoshi. *Feudal Architecture of Japan*. New York: Weatherhill, 1973.

Hisako, Hata. "Servants of the Inner Quarters: The Women of the Shogun's Great Interior." In Anne Walthall, ed., *Servants of the Dynasty: Palace Women in World History,* 172–190. Berkeley: University of California Press, 2008.

Howell, David L. *Geographies of Identity in Nineteenth-Century Japan*. Berkeley: University of California Press, 2005.

Howell, David L. "The Social Life of Firearms in Tokugawa Japan." *Japanese Studies,* 29(1) (2009), 65–80.

Huber, Thomas M. *The Revolutionary Origins of Modern Japan*. Stanford, CA: Stanford University Press, 1981.

Hurst, G. Cameron, III. "Death, Honor, and Loyalty: The Bushido Ideal." *Philosophy East & West,* 40(4) (1990), 511–527.

Hurst, G. Cameron, III. *Armed Martial Arts of Japan: Swordsmanship and Archery*. New Haven, CT: Yale University Press, 1998.

Ihara, Saikaku. *Comrade Loves of the Samurai*. Translated by E. Powys Mathers. Tokyo; Rutland, VT: Tuttle Books, 1981.

Ihara, Saikaku. *Tales of Samurai Honor*. Translated by C. A. Callahan. Tokyo: Monumenta Nipponica, 1982.

Ihara, Saikaku. *The Great Mirror of Male Love*. Translated by Paul Gordon Schalow. Stanford, CA: Stanford University Press, 1990.

Ikegami, Eiko. *The Taming of the Samurai: Honorific Individualism and the Making of Modern Japan*. Cambridge, MA: Harvard University Press, 1995.

Irvine, Gregory. *The Japanese Sword: The Soul of the Samurai*. Trumbull, CT: Weatherhill, 2000.

Jansen, Marius B. *Sakamoto Ryôma and the Meiji Restoration*. New York: Columbia University Press, 1994.

Jansen, Marius B., ed. *Warrior Rule in Japan*. New York: Cambridge University Press, 1995.

Japan House Gallery. *Spectacular Helmets of Japan, 16th–19th Century*. New York: Japan Society, 1985.

Kaempfer, Englebert. *Kaempfer's Japan: Culture Observed.* Translated by Beatrice Bodart-Bailey. Honolulu: University of Hawai'i Press, 1998.

Katsu Kokichi. *Musui's Story: The Autobiography of a Tokugawa Samurai.* Translated and with an introduction and notes by Teruko Craig. Tucson: University of Arizona Press, 1995.

Keene, Donald, trans. *Major Plays of Chikamatsu.* Tokyo and New York: Kodansha International, 1961.

Keene, Donald, trans. *Chûshingura.* New York: Columbia University Press, 1971.

Keene, Donald. *Frog in the Well: Portraits of Japan by Watanabe Kazan, 1793–1841.* New York: Columbia University Press, 2006.

King, Winston L. *Zen and the Way of the Sword: Arming the Samurai Psyche.* Oxford: Oxford University Press, 1993.

Lamers, Jeroen P. *Japonius Tyrannus: The Japanese Warlord Oda Nobunaga Reconsidered.* Leiden, Netherlands: Hotei Publishing, 2000.

Lidin, Olof G. *The Life of Ogyû Sorai, a Tokugawa Confucian Philosopher.* Scandinavian Institute of Asian Studies Monograph Series 19. Lund: Studentitteratur, 1973.

Lidin, Olof G. *Ogyû Sorai's Discourse on Government (Seidan): An Annotated Translation.* Wiesbaden: Harrasowitz Verlag, 1999.

Mass, Jeffrey P., and William B. Hauser, eds. *The Bakufu in Japanese History.* Stanford, CA: Stanford University Press, 1985.

Matsudaira, Sadanobu. "Portrait of a Daimyô: Comical Fiction by Matsudaira Sadanobu." Translated by Haruko Iwasaki. *Monomenta Nipponica,* 38(1) (1983), 1–48.

Matsumoto, Shigeru. *Motoori Norinaga, 1730–1801.* Cambridge, MA: Harvard University Press, 1970.

McClain, James L. *Kanazawa: A Seventeenth-Century Japanese Castle Town.* New Haven, CT: Yale University Press, 1982.

McClain, James L., John M. Merriman, and Ugawa Kaoru, eds. *Edo and Paris: Urban Life and the State in the Early Modern Era.* Ithaca, NY: Cornell University Press, 1997.

McEwan, J. R. *The Political Writings of Ogyû Sorai.* Cambridge: Cambridge University Press, 1969.

Mills, D. E. "Kataki-uchi: The Practice of Blood-Revenge in Pre-modern Japan." *Modern Asian Studies,* 10 (1976), 525–542.

Mitchelhill, Jennifer, and David Green. *Castles of the Samurai: Power and Beauty.* London: Kodansha Europe, 2003.

Mitford, A. B. *Tales of Old Japan.* Rutland, VT: Charles E. Tuttle Co., 1966.

Miyamoto, Musashi. *The Book of the Five Rings.* Translated by William Scott Wilson. Tokyo: Kodansha, 2002.

Moore, Ray. "Adoption and Samurai Mobility in Tokugawa Japan." *Journal of Asian Studies,* 29(3) (1970), 617–632.

Morris, Ivan. *The Nobility of Failure: Tragic Heroes in the History of Japan.* New York: Holt, Rinehart and Winston, 1975.

Najita, Tetsuo, trans. "Ôshio Heihachirô (1793–1837)." In Albert Craig and Donald Shively, eds., *Personality in Japanese History*, 155–179. Berkeley: University of California Press, 1970.

Najita, Tetsuo, trans. *Tokugawa Political Writings.* Cambridge: Cambridge University Press, 1998.

Najita, Tetsuo, and J. Victor Koschmann, eds. *Conflict in Modern Japanese History: The Neglected Tradition.* Princeton, NJ: Princeton University Press, 1982.

Nakai, Kate Wildman. *Shogunal Politics: Arai Hakuseki and the Premises of Tokugawa Rule.* Cambridge, MA: Council on East Asian Studies, Harvard University, 1988.

Nakai, Kate Wildman. "The Reality behind *Musui Dokugen*: Introduction to the Article by Ôguchi Yûjirô." *Journal of Japanese Studies,* 16(2) (1990), 285–287.

Nishiyama, Matsunosuke. *Edo Culture: Daily Life and Diversions in Urban Japan, 1600–1868.* Edited and translated by Gerald Groemer. Honolulu: University of Hawai'i Press, 1997.

Ôguchi Yûjirô. "The Reality behind *Musui Dokugen*: The World of the *Hatamoto* and *Godenin*." Translated by Gaynor Sekimori. *Journal of Japanese Studies,* 16(2) (1990), 289–308.

Ôishi, Shinzaburô. "The Bakuhan System." In Chie Nakane and Shinzaburô Ôishi, eds., *Tokugawa Japan: The Social and Economic Antecedents of Modern Japan*, 11–36. Tokyo: University of Tokyo Press, 1990.

Ooms, Herman. *Charismatic Bureaucrat: A Political Biography of Matsudaira Sadanobu, 1758–1829.* Chicago: University of Chicago Press, 1975.

Pitelka, Morgan. "The Empire of Things: Tokugawa Ieyasu's Material Legacy and Cultural Profile." *Japanese Studies,* 29 (2009), 19–32.

Pitelka, Morgan. *Spectacular Accumulation: Material Culture, Tokugawa Ieyasu, and Samurai Sociability.* Honolulu: University of Hawai'i Press, 2015.

Rankin, Andrew. *Seppuku: A History of Samurai Suicide.* Tokyo and New York: Kodansha International, 2011.

Ravina, Mark. *Land and Lordship in Early Modern Japan.* Stanford, CA: Stanford University Press, 1999.

Roberts, Luke S. "The Petition Box in Eighteenth-Century Tosa." *The Journal of Japanese Studies,* 20(2) (1994), 423–458.

Roberts, Luke S. "A Transgressive Life: The Diary of a Genroku Samurai." *Early Modern Japan,* 5 (1995), 25–30.

Roberts, Luke S. *Mercantilism in a Japanese Domain: The Merchant Origins of Economic Nationalism in 18th-Century Tosa.* Cambridge: Cambridge University Press, 1998.

Roberts, Luke S. *Performing the Great Peace: Political Space and Open Secrets in Tokugawa Japan.* Honolulu: University of Hawai'i Press, 2012.

Robinson, B. W. *Arms and Armour of Old Japan.* London: Scribner's, 1951.

Rogers, John M. "Arts of War in Times of Peace: Archery in *Honchô Bugei Shôden.*" *Monumenta Nipponica,* 45(3) (1990), 253–284.

Rogers, John M. "Arts of War in Times of Peace: Swordsmanship in *Honchô Bugei Shôden*, Chapter 5." *Monumenta Nipponica,* 45(4) (1990), 413–447.

Rubinger, Richard. *Private Academies of Tokugawa Japan.* Princeton, NJ: Princeton University Press, 1982.

Sadler, A. L. *The Maker of Modern Japan.* Tokyo and Rutland, VT: Tuttle Books, 1978.

Saikaku Ihara. *Comrad Loves of the Samurai.* Translated by E. Powys Mathers. Rutland, VT: Charles E. Tuttle Co., 1972.

Sato, Hiroaki. *Legends of the Samurai.* Woodstock, NY: Overlook Press, 1995.

Screech, Timon. *The Shogun's Painted Culture: Fear and Creativity in the Japanese States, 1760–1829.* London: Reaktion, 2000.

Screech, Timon, annotated and introduced by. *Secret Memoirs of the Shoguns: Isaac Titsingh and Japan, 1779–1822.* London and New York: Routledge, 2006.

Seigle, Cecilia Segawa. "Konoe Hiroko and Tokugawa Ienobu." *Harvard Journal of Asiatic Studies,* 59(2) (1999), 485–522.

Shimoda, Hiraku. *Lost and Found: Recovering Regional Identity in Imperial Japan.* Cambridge, MA: Harvard University Asia Center, 2014.

Shively, Donald H. "Tokugawa Tsunayoshi, the Genroku Shôgun." In Albert M. Craig and Donald H. Shively, eds., *Personality in Japanese History*, 85–126. Berkeley: University of California Press, 1970.

Smith, Thomas C. "'Merit' as Ideology in the Tokugawa Period." In Ronald Dore, ed., *Aspects of Social Change in Modern Japan*, 71–90. Princeton, NJ: Princeton University Press, 1967.

Steele, M. William. "Against the Restoration: Katsu Kaishû's Attempt to Reinstate the Tokugawa Family." *Monumenta Nipponica,* 34 (1981), 299–316.

Straelen, H. J. J. van. *Yoshida Shôin, Forerunner of the Meiji Restoration: A Biographical Study.* Leiden: E. J. Brill, 1952.

Taniguchi, Shinko. "Military Evolution or Revolution? State Formation and the Early Modern Samurai." In Rosemarie Deist, ed., *Knights and Samurai: Actions and Images of Elite Warriors in Europe and East Asia*, 169–195. Goppingen: Kummerle Verlag, 2003.

Teeuwen, Mark, and Kate Wildman Nakai, ed. *Lust, Commerce, and Corruption: What I Have Seen and Heard, by an Edo Samurai.* New York: Columbia University Press, 2014.

Totman, Conrad. *Politics in the Tokugawa Bakufu, 1600–1843.* Cambridge, MA: Harvard University Press, 1967.

Totman, Conrad. *Collapse of the Tokugawa Bakufu, 1862–1868.* Honolulu: University of Hawai'i Press, 1980.

Totman, Conrad. *Tokugawa Ieyasu, Shogun: A Biography.* South San Francisco: Heian International Inc., 1983.

Tsukahira, Toshio G. *Feudal Control in Tokugawa Japan: The Sankin Kotai System.* Cambridge, MA: East Asian Research Center, Harvard University, 1966.

Tsunemoto, Yamamoto. *Hagakure: The Book of the Samurai.* Tokyo: Kodansha International, 1983.

Turnbull, Stephen R. *The Samurai Sourcebook*. London: Cassell, 2002.

Vaporis, Constantine Nomikos. "A Tour of Duty: *Kurume hanshi Edo kinban nagaya emaki*." *Monumenta Nipponica,* 51(3) (1996), 279–307.

Vaporis, Constantine Nomikos. "To Edo and Back: Alternate Attendance and Japanese Culture in the Early Modern Period." *Journal of Japanese Studies,* 23(1) (1997), 25–67.

Vaporis, Constantine Nomikos. "Digging for Edo: Archaeology and Japan's Premodern Urban Past." *Monumenta Nipponica,* 53(1) (1998), 73–104.

Vaporis, Constantine Nomikos. "Samurai and Merchant in Mid-Tokugawa Japan: Tani Tannai's *Record of Daily Necessities* (1748–1754)." *Harvard Journal of Asiatic Studies,* 60(1) (2000), 105–227.

Vaporis, Constantine Nomikos. "Daimyo Processions: Authority and Theater." *Japan Review,* 17(3) (2005), 3–52.

Vaporis, Constantine Nomikos. *Tour of Duty: Samurai, Military Service in Edo and the Culture of Early Modern Japan*. Honolulu: University of Hawai'i Press, 2008.

Weinberg, David R. *Kuniyoshi: The Faithful Samurai*. Leiden: Hotei Publishing, 2000.

Wert, Michael. *Meiji Restoration Losers: Memory and Tokugawa Supporters in Modern Japan*. Cambridge, MA: Harvard University Press, 2013.

Wilson, William Scott. *Ideals of the Samurai: Writings of Japanese Warriors*. Santa Clarita, CA: Ohara, 1982.

Wilson, William Scott. *The Lone Samurai: The Life of Miyamoto Musashi*. Tokyo: Kodansha International, 2004.

Yamakawa, Kikue. *Women of the Mito Domain: Recollections of Samurai Family Life*. Translated by K. Wildman Nakai. Tokyo: University of Tokyo Press, 1992.

Yamamura, Kozo. *A Study of Samurai Income and Entrepreneurship: Quantitative Analyses of Economic and Social Aspects of the Samurai in Tokugawa and Meiji, Japan*. Cambridge, MA: Harvard University Press, 1974.

Yamamura, Kozo. "Samurai Income and Demographic Change: The Genealogies of Tokugawa Bannermen." In Susan B. Hanley and Arthur P. World, eds., *Family and Population in East Asian History*, 62–80. Stanford, CA: Stanford University Press, 1985.

Yates, Charles L. *Saigô Takamori: The Man Behind the Myth*. London; New York: Kegan Paul International, 1995.

Yukichi, Fukuzawa. *The Autobiography of Fukuzawa Yukichi*. Tokyo: Hokuseidô, 1966.

Yumoto, John M. *The Samurai Sword: A Handbook*. Rutland, VT: Charles E. Tuttle Co., 1996.

Yûzan Daidôji. *The Code of the Samurai*. Rutland, VT: Charles E. Tuttle Co., 1995.

SELECTED WEBSITES

Bakumatsu and Meiji Old Photo Archives (Nagasaki University): http://oldphoto.lb.nagasaki-u.ac.jp

Banners and Flags: http://www.sengokudaimyo.com/miscellany/flags.html

Japan. Images of a People (Smithsonian Institution): http://www.smithsonianedu cation.org/educators/lesson_plans/japan_images_people/index.html

National Museum of Japanese History: http://www.rekihaku.ac.jp

Samurai Archives Japanese History Page: http://www.samurai-archives.com

(The) Samurai Collection. The Ann & Gabriel Barbier-Mueller Museum: http:// samuraicollection.org/mac/index_web.html

(The) Siege of Osaka Castle: http://ngm.nationalgeographic.com/ngm/0312/feature5 /zoomify/main.html

Smith, Henry, ed., *Learning from Shogun: Japanese History and Western Fantasy*: http://www.columbia.edu/~hds2/learning

"Tokugawa Japan." From "Asia Topics . . . an on-line resource for Asian history and culture": http://www.columbia.edu/itc/eacp/asiasite/topics/index.html?topic =Tokugawa+mediatype=Video+subtopic=Intro

Visualizing Cultures (Massachusetts Institute of Technology): http://ocw.mit.edu /ans7870/21f/21f.027/home/index.html

Index

Page numbers in **boldface** indicate the location of main entries; *italics* indicate photos; and followed by *t* indicate tables.

About the Author

Constantine Nomikos Vaporis teaches Japanese and East Asian history at the University of Maryland, Baltimore County. He has received numerous fellowships for research in Japanese history including two Fulbright Scholar's Awards and an NEH Fellowship for College Teachers. He is the author of *Breaking Barriers: Travel and the State in Early Modern Japan; Tour of Duty: Samurai, Military Service in Edo and the Culture of Early Modern Japan; Nihonjin to sankin kôtai (The Japanese and Alternate Attendance)*; and *Voices of Early Modern Japan: Contemporary Accounts of Daily Life during the Age of the Shoguns* (published by ABC-CLIO), which won the Association for Asian Studies' 2013 Franklin R. Buchanan Prize for educational materials. He was awarded the 2013–2016 UMBC Presidential Research Professorship and was twice selected for the ASIANetwork Speakers Bureau (2016–2020). He acted as a historical consultant for the 2012 National Geographic exhibition "Samurai: The Warrior Transformed" and is currently at work on a collection of biographies of samurai entitled *Sword and Brush: Portraits of Samurai Life during the Tokugawa Period*.

CPSIA information can be obtained
at www.ICGtesting.com
Printed in the USA
LVHW061432200222
711015LV00031B/48